METHODS OF BIBLICAL INTERPRETATION

Foreword by
Douglas A. Knight

METHODS OF BIBLICAL INTERPRETATION

Foreword by
Douglas A. Knight

Excerpted from the
DICTIONARY OF BIBLICAL INTERPRETATION

ABINGDON PRESS
Nashville

METHODS OF BIBLICAL INTERPRETATION
Copyright © 2004 by Abingdon Press.

Excerpted from the *Dictionary of Biblical Interpretation*,
edited by John H. Hayes, Abingdon Press, 1999.

This book is printed on acid-free paper

ISBN 0-687-037069

Cataloging-in-Publication Data is available from the Library of Congress.

Scripture quotations, unless otherwise indicated, are from the New Revised Standard Version Bible, copyright © 1989 by the Division of Christian Education of the National Council of the Churches of Christ in the United States of America.

The Hebraica(R) and Graeca(R) fonts used to print this work are available from Linguist's Software, Inc., PO Box 580, Edmonds, WA 98020-0580
tel (206) 775-1130.

04 05 06 07 08 09 10 11 12 13 — 10 9 8 7 6 5 4 3 2 1

MANUFACTURED IN THE UNITED STATES OF AMERICA

CONTENTS

**Literary and Structuralist/Postmodernist
Approaches Methods**

Theological Approaches

Social Science Methods

Contextual Approaches

Liberation or Ideological Approaches

FOREWORD

For biblical scholars in the early part of the twenty-first century it is difficult to imagine a time when methodology did not command a significant part of the academic curriculum and discourse. Virtually all specialists trained since the end of the 1960s and early 1970s have cut their teeth on questions of how and why they work as they do. I offer this observation as one who completed his studies precisely at that early juncture, and I remember vividly a colloquium in which an elder scholar at the time, one whose name is still known internationally as an original and influential interpreter, puzzled publicly over why a certain book had been written detailing the methods of exegesis. A colleague responded with a kind answer: "Not all of us can approach the text with the level of intuition with which you do." Now we would say that no one can or should rely on her or his own intuition, but it has taken us several decades of discussion to reach this near consensus.

Of course, we must also take care not to be so chauvinistic as to think that only we in the present age can produce careful, deliberative methods. It takes little more than a cursory examination of the work of the early Jewish sages to disabuse oneself of such a notion. For several centuries during the first millennium CE devout individuals devoted their lives to the arduous tasks of copying texts, developing a variety of means to ensure textual accuracy, translating the text, commenting on it, and interpreting it according to accepted exegetical methods. Some of their painstaking work has scarcely been replicated until the introduction of computer technology. Jewish and Christian commentators of the medieval period demonstrated a level of insight that stems from a discerning engagement with the text—and for some, such as Maimonides, from a command of the classical Greek and Arabic tradition as well. These early scholars set a high watermark of achievement for later interpreters to reach.

Despite the common criticisms leveled at modernity, we need also to remember that generations of scholars from the Renaissance until the mid-twentieth century conducted their work with sensitivity to their methods and assumptions. Many of the foundational methods of investigation were developed during this period: textual criticism and grammatology during and even before the Renaissance, philology and lexicography in that period as well, source criticism in the eighteenth century, archaeology in the nineteenth century, religion history in the late nineteenth century, form criticism in the early twentieth century, tradition and redaction criticism by the mid-twentieth century. The list could be expanded and subdivided. Their innovators were perceptive critics, even visionaries, who were dissatisfied with the research options they inherited, and they tried to imagine other means of approaching the subject at hand and identifying new subjects worthy of investigation. Martin Noth, himself the co-creator of tradition criticism and the originator of numerous novel ideas, made the point repeatedly that raising appropriate questions is more important than offering answers. (*History of Pentateuchal Traditions,* 1981, v, 4, 16) Can there be a better invitation to engage in methodological inquiry?

Since *ca.* 1970 there has been a veritable blossoming of innovative methods as well as publications devoted to studying them. Prior to 1970 very few exegetical handbooks appeared; more common were histories of research on specific texts, as well as occasional controversies—some quite heated—over specific issues, such as the historiographical value of archaeological evidence. But from the beginning of the 1970s the situation began to change dramatically as different approaches and perspectives emerged as players in the world of biblical interpretation. Many of them were a direct offshoot of critical theory: feminist criticism, critical race theory, ideological criticism. Others followed more of a liberationist direction: liberation theologies, postcolonial criticism. Still others aimed to acknowledge and understand the diverse contexts in which the critics were located: Asian, Hispanic, African, Euro-American, womanist, mujerista. Social-scientific methods were resuscitated after having lain largely dormant since the early part of the twentieth century. Similarly, new attention fell on critical approaches that attended to literary styles, literary genres, rhetorical devices, reader responses. Distinctive directions appeared also in theological interpretations, such as canonical criticism and inner-biblical exegesis. Many of these overlap in terms of their goals, working methods, or philosophical underpinnings. Together, the approaches that originated or found new life since the 1970s total over half of the pages of this book, as would be expected.

It is not that the earlier, more traditional methods have receded as a result. Philological, text-critical, historical-critical, and comparativist analyses continue to appear in considerable number, though generally they have been affected by the insights and agendas of the more novel approaches. The venerable task of history-writing provides an excellent example of how business-as-usual can no longer be accepted by most critics. A historical analysis must now go well beyond the traditional focus on leaders and events and instead needs to encompass the larger social world of the commoners and the powerless. Moreover, one has become justifiably cautious in the evaluation of "evidence," which often turns out to be not as easy to interpret as first impressions may suggest. Histories of Israel, early Judaism, and early Christianity now tend to be, at one and the same time, both more inclusive and more judicious, and they are subjected to heavy criticism when they are not.

Methodology, in other words, has now become an accepted end in itself—and rightly so. There was once a time, closer to the turning point at the beginning of the 1970s, when it was derisively said that those who cannot do well in studying a text will study method. Now, it is commonly acknowledged that, without close attention to methodological steps and presuppositions, one is in danger of operating in an arbitrary and limited manner, and the analytical results are correspondingly questionable. While courses on exegetical and historiographical methods were seldom seen prior to 1970, now they are *de rigueur* in most graduate programs in biblical studies.

Where do we go from here? The development of new approaches and methods is likely to continue, just as the current procedures will be adjusted in light of new circumstances. Postmodernism and deconstruction have highlighted considerations that could scarcely have been anticipated previously, and they will likely continue to affect the discipline before they give way to other hermeneutical and philosophical directions. The biblical literature and the history and society of ancient Israel, Judaism, and

Christianity will never be exhausted in terms of the scrutiny to which they can be subjected—not because of some special quality adhering to them but because of the limitless angles of vision possible for any set of human experiences and expressions.

The present volume represents a splendid culling of methodological articles from what has now become a standard two-volume set devoted to the discipline of biblical studies, *Dictionary of Biblical Interpretation*, edited by John H. Hayes (Nashville: Abingdon, 1999). In it some four hundred authors from many countries collaborated to delineate the scholars, movements, texts, methods, and issues that have steered the course of biblical studies. The current book assembles for ready access the articles in the set devoted to methods in biblical interpretation, and several others are added to complete the picture. Each aims to describe the subject at hand, sketch its history and place in biblical studies, and provide a bibliography for further reference. They are grouped for easy use in classrooms and for occasional consulting as needed. With such a resource students and scholars will find it easier to conduct their work attuned to the range of analytical options and equipped to develop directions for future research.

Douglas A. Knight
Vanderbilt University
December 2003

PUBLISHER'S FOREWORD

This volume collects the articles on exegetical methodology that originally appeared in the *Dictionary of Biblical Interpretation* (ed. J. Hayes, 1999) and is intended as a text for seminary and university classes in exegetical method. It is also suitable for introductory level courses on biblical interpretation and for graduate students preparing for exams. These articles are especially informative on the history of exegesis. The essays provide an overview of the history of development of a given exegetical method and an in-depth summary of both the method and the philosophical issues inherent within it.

The emphasis throughout has been on the questions and issues posed by critical scholarship. Therefore, discussions of pre-Reformation interpretation have in most cases been substantially shortened or eliminated altogether. Discussion of early Christian and medieval exegesis have been retained regarding text criticism and the development of the canon. Several recent methods (postcolonial, cultural studies, postmodern, gay/lesbian, etc.) are so recent that an adequate historical overview of the development of the method remains in the future. Therefore a sketch of their development is not included.

With the major exception of substantially editing the information on early and medieval church interpretation, the essays have not been altered except to correct misprints, correct and update the bibliographies, make minor grammatical corrections, and to adapt the abbreviations and other style matters to the *SBL Handbook of Style*. With one exception, the original phrase "Old Testament" has been consistently changed to "Hebrew Bible" throughout. Given the purpose of the article by T. Stylianopoulos, "Old Testament," was retained throughout the article "Orthodox Biblical Interpretation." Also, J. C. de Moor's original article, "Ugarit and the Bible," has been substantially abridged, renamed "Ugaritic and Bible Translation," and appended to R. G. Bratcher's article, "Translation."

In addition to the original essays, there are five newly commissioned articles: R. DeMaris, "Archaeology and New Testament Interpretation;" A. Hunt, "Historiography of the Hebrew Bible;" S. Porter, "Linguistics and Biblical Interpretation;" J. Fitzgerald, "Lexicography Theory and Biblical Interpretation;" and L. Welborn, "Euro-American Biblical Interpretation." We thank these writers for their willingness to participate at very short notice.

ABBREVIATIONS

General

abr.	abridged	HB	Hebrew Bible
approx.	approximately	Heb.	Hebrew
Aram.	Aramaic	HT	Hebrew Translation
art(s).	article(s)	i.e.	*id est*, that is
aug.	augmented	ibid.	*ibidem*, in the same place
b.	born	ill.	illustration
B.C.E.	Before the Common Era	inc.	incomplete
bib.	biblical	into.	introduction
bk(s).	book(s)	J	Jahwist or Yahwist source (of the Pentateuch)
C.E.	Common Era		
c.	circa	Lat.	Latin
cent(s).	century(ies)	lit.	literally
cf.	compare	LT	Latin Translation
chap(s).	chapter(s)	LXX	Septuagint
comb.	combined	MS(S)	manuscript(s)
contr.	contributor	MT	Masoretic Text
corr.	corrected	NT	New Testament
D	Deuteronomist source (of the Pentateuch)	OG	Old Greek
		OL	Old Latin
d.	died	OT	Old Testament
dept.	department	P	Priestly source (of the Pentateuch)
dir.	director		
diss.	dissertation	par.	paragraph
Dtr	Deuteronomistic (history; writer)	pl.	plural
E	Elohist source (of the Pentateuch)	posth.	posthumous
ed(s).	editor(s)	pt(s).	part(s)
e.g.	*exempli gratia*, for example	pub.	published
Eng.	English	repr.	reprint
enl.	enlarged	repub.	republished
esp.	especially	rev. ed.	revised edition
est.	established	RGS	*Religionsgeschichtliche Schule*
et al.	*et alii*, and others	sec(s).	section(s)
etc.	*et cetera*, and the rest	supp.	supplement
ET	English Translation	tr.	translator/translation
frg(s).	fragment(s)	trans.	transcribed
Ger.	German	Vg.	Vulgate
Gr.	Greek	v(v).	verse(s)
GT	German Translation	vol(s).	volume(s)

Biblical Translations

ASV	American Standard Version
CEV	Contemporary English Version
KJV	King James Version
NEB	New English Bible
NIV	New International Version
NJB	New Jerusalem Bible
NRSV	New Revised Standard Version
REB	Revised English Bible
RSV	Revised Standard Version
TEV	Today's English Version (Good News Bible)

Books of the Bible
Hebrew Bible

Gen	Genesis	Song (Cant)	Song of Songs (Song of Solomon or Canticles)
Exod	Exodus		
Lev	Leviticus	Isa	Isaiah
Num	Numbers	Jer	Jeremiah
Deut	Deuteronomy	Lam	Lamentations
Josh	Joshua	Ezek	Ezekiel
Judg	Judges	Dan	Daniel
Ruth	Ruth	Hos	Hosea
1–2 Sam	1–2 Samuel	Joel	Joel
1–2 Kgdms	1–2 Kingdoms (LXX)	Amos	Amos
1–2 Kgs	1–2 Kings	Obad	Obadiah
3–4 Kgdms	3–4 Kingdoms (LXX)	Jonah	Jonah
1–2 Chr	1–2 Chronicles	Mic	Micah
Ezra	Ezra	Nah	Nahum
Neh	Nehemiah	Hab	Habakkuk
Esth	Esther	Zeph	Zephaniah
Job	Job	Hag	Haggai
Ps/Pss	Psalms	Zech	Zechariah
Prov	Proverbs	Mal	Malachi
Eccl (or Qoh)	Ecclesiastes (or Qoheleth)		

New Testament

Matt	Matthew	1–2 Thess	1–2 Thessalonians
Mark	Mark	1–2 Tim	1–2 Timothy
Luke	Luke	Titus	Titus
John	John	Phlm	Philemon
Acts	Acts	Heb	Hebrews
Rom	Romans	Jas	James
1–2 Cor	1–2 Corinthians	1–2 Pet	1–2 Peter
Gal	Galatians	1–2–3 John	1–2–3 John
Eph	Ephesians	Jude	Jude
Phil	Philippians	Rev	Revelation
Col	Colossians		

Apocrypha and Septuagint

Bar	Baruch	Jdt	Judith
Add Dan	Additions to Daniel	1–2 Macc	1–2 Maccabees
Pr Azar	Prayer of Azariah	3–4 Macc	3–4 Maccabees
Bel	Bel and the Dragon	Pr Man	Prayer of Manasseh
Sg Three	Song of the Three Young Men	Ps 151	Psalm 151
Sus	Susanna	Sir	Sirach/Ecclesiasticus
1–2 Esd	1–2 Esdras	Tob	Tobit
Add Esth	Additions to Esther	Wis	Wisdom of Solomon
Ep Jer	Epistle of Jeremiah		

Periodicals, Reference Works, and Serials
(in alphabetical order, by abbr.)

ABD	*Anchor Bible Dictionary*
ABRL	Anchor Bible Reference Library
ACW	Ancient Christian Writers, 1946-
AES	*Archives européenes de sociologie*
AGJU	Arbeiten zur Geschichte des antiken Judentums und des Urchristentums
AJT	*Asian Journal of Theology*
AnBib	Analecta biblica
ANF	*Ante-Nicene Fathers*
ANRW	*Aufstieg und Niedergang der römischen Welt*
ArBib	Aramaic Bible
ASNU	Acta seminarii neotestamentici upsaliensis
ATANT	Abhandlungen zur Theologie des Alten und Neuen Testaments
ATR	*Australasian Theological Review*
BA	*Biblical Archaeologist*
BASOR	*Bulletin of the American Schools for Oriental Research*
BBB	*Bulletin de bibliographie biblique*
BBB	Bonner biblische Beiträge
BBET	Beiträge zur biblischen Exegese und Theologie
BEATAJ	Beiträge zur Erforschung des Alten Testaments und des antiken Judentum
BETL	Bibliotheca ephemeridum theologicarum lovaniensium
BEvT	Beiträge zur evangelischen Theologie
BFCT	Beiträge zur Förderung chrislicher Theologie
BHS	*Biblica hebraica stuttgartensia*
BHT	Beiträge zur historischen Theologie
Bib	*Biblica*
BiBh	*Bible Bhashyam*
BibInt	*Biblical Interpretation*
Bijdr	*Bijdragen: Tijdschrift voor filosofie theologie*
BiSe	The Biblical Seminar
BIS	Biblical Interpretation Series
BJRL	*Bulletin of the John Rylands University Library of Manchester*
BJS	Brown Judaic Studies
BK	*Bibel und Kirche*
BKAT	Biblischer Kommentar, Altes Testament. Edited by M. Noth and H. W. Wolff
BO	*Bibliotheca orientalis*

BPC	*Biblical Perspectives on Current Issues*
BSac	*Bibliotheca sacra*
BSNA	Biblical Scholarship in North America
BTB	*Biblical Theology Bulletin*
BTZ	*Berliner Theologische Zeitschrift*
BZAW	Beihefte zur Zeitschrift für die alttestamentliche Wissenschaft
BZNW	Beihefte zur Zeitschrift für die neutestamentliche Wissenschaft
CBQ	*Catholic Biblical Quarterly*
CBQMS	Catholic Biblical Quarterly—Monograph Series
CHB	P. R. Ackroyd et al. (eds.), *Cambridge History of the Bible* (3 vols., 1985-87)
Ching Feng	*Ching Feng*
ChrCent	*Christian Century*
ChW	*Cristliche Welt*
ConBOT	Coniectanea biblica: Old Testament Series
ConJ	*Concordia Journal*
ConNT	Coniectanea neotestamentica
CTP	Cadernos de teologia e pastoral
CTM	*Concordia Theological Monthly*
CWS	Classics of Western Spirituality. New York, 1978-
DB	*Dictionnaire de la Bible.* Edited by F. Vigouroux. 5 vols. 1895-1912
DBSup	*Dictionnaire de la Bible: Supplément.* Edited by L. Pirot and A. Robert. Paris, 1907-1953
DMA	J. R. Strayer (ed.), *Dictionary of the Middle Ages* (13 vols. 1982-89)
EAJJ	*East Asia Journal of Theology*
EB	Echter Bibel
EBib	*Etudes bibliques*
EncBrit	*Encyclopedia Brittanica*
EncJud	*Encyclopaedia Judaica*
EncRel	M. Eliade (ed.), *The Encyclopedia of Religion* (16 vols. 1987)
EstBib	*Estudios bíblicos*
EMMÖ	Erlanger Monographien aus Mission und Ökumene
EstTeo	*Estudios teológicos*
ETL	*Ephemerides theologicae lovanieses*
EvErz	*Der evangelischer Erzieher*
EvT	*Evangelische Theologie*
Exp Tim	*Expository Times*
FAT	Forshungen zum Alten Testament
FBBS	Facet Books, Biblical Series
FRLANT	Forschungen zur Religion und Literatur des Alten und Neuen Testaments
GBS	Guides to Biblical Scholarship
GOTR	*Greek Orthodox Theological Review*
GRLH	Garland Reference Library of the Humanities
HBT	*Horizons in Biblical Theology*
HRWG	*Handbuch religionswissenschaftlicher Grundbegriffe*
HSM	Harvard Semitic Monographs
HTR	*Harvard Theological Review*
HUCA	*Hebrew Union College Annual*
IB	*Interpreter's Bible*
ISBL	*Indiana Studies of Biblical Literature*

IDB	*The Interpreter's Dictionary of the Bible.* Edited by G. A. Buttrick. 4 vols. Nashville, 1962
IDBSup	*Interpreter's Dictionary of the Bible: Supplementary Volume.* Edited by K. Crim. Nashville, 1976
Int	*Interpretation*
IRT	Issues in Religion and Theology
IRM	*International Review of Missions*
ISBL	Indiana Studies in Biblical Literature
ITC	International Theological Commentary
IThS	Innsbrücker Theologische Studien
JAAR	*Journal of the American Academy of Religion*
JAF	*Journal of American Folklore*
JANESCU	*Journal of the Ancient Near Eastern Society of Columbia University*
JBL	*Journal of Biblical Literature*
JE	*The Jewish Encyclopedia*
Jeev	*Jeevadhara*
JFSR	*Journal of Feminist Studies in Religion*
JH/LT	*Journal of Hispanic/Latino Theology*
Jian Dao	*Jian Dao*
JITC	*Journal of the Interdenominational Theological Center*
JJS	*Journal of Jewish Studies*
JNSL	*Journal of Northwest Semitic Languages*
JR	*Journal of Religion*
JRT	*Journal of Religious Thought*
JSJ	*Journal for the Study of Judaism in the Persian, Hellenistic, and Roman Periods*
JSNTSup	Journal for the Study of the New Testament: Supplement Series
JSOT	*Journal for the Study of the Old Testament*
JSOTSup	Journal for the Study of the Old Testament. Supplement Series
JSS	*Journal of Semitic Studies*
JTC	*Journal for Theology and the Church*
JTL	*Journal für theologische Literatur*
JTS	*Journal of Theological Studies*
JTSA	*Journal of Theology for Southern Africa*
KD	*Kerygma und Dogma*
LEC	Library of Early Christianity
LTK	*Lexicon für Theologie und Kirche*
MDB	*Mercer Dictionary of the Bible*
MTZ	*Münchener theologische Zeitschrift*
NBf	*New Blackfrairs*
NCB	New Century Bible
NCE	*New Catholic Encyclopedia*
NDIEC	*New Documents Illustrating Early Christianity*
NIB	New Interpreter's Bible
NJBC	*The New Jerome Bible Commentary.* Edited by R. E. Brown et al. Englewood Cliffs, 1990
NKZ	*Neue kirchliche Zeitschrift*
NPNF	*Nicene and Post-Nicene Fathers*
NovT	*Novum Testamentum*

ABBREVIATIONS

NovTSup	Novum Testamentum Supplements
NovTSup	Supplements to Novum Testamentum
NRTh	*La nouvelle revue théologique*
NTAbh	Neutestamentliche Abhandlungen
NTAbhNF	Neutestamentliche Abhandlungen Neue Forschung
NTOA	Novum Testamentum et Orbis Antiquus
NTS	*New Testament Studies*
NTTS	New Testament Tools and Studies
NZM	*Neue Zeitschrift für Missionswissenschaft*
OBO	Orbis biblicus et orientalis
OBT	Overtures to Biblical Theology
OLZ	*Orientalistische Literaturzeitung*
OTL	Old Testament Library
OTS	Old Testament Studies
PAAJR	*Proceedings of the American Academy of Jewish Research*
PEQ	*Palestine Exploration Quarterly*
PerTeol	*Perspectiva teológica*
Proof	*Prooftexts: A Journal of Jewish Literary History*
PRSt	*Perspectives in Religious Studies*
PW	Pauly, A. F. *Paulys Realencyclopädie der classischen Altertumswissenschaft.* New Edition G. Wissowa. 49 vols. Munich, 1980.
QD	Quaestiones disputatae
RB	*Revue biblique*
RCB	*Revista de cultura bíblica*
REB	*Revista eclesiástica brasileira*
RelLife	*Religion in Life*
RelSoc	*Religion and Society*
RevistB	*Revista bíblica*
RGG	*Religion in Geschichte und Gegenwart*
RHPR	*Revue d'historie et de philosophie religieuses*
RMT	Readings in Moral Theology
RelSRev	*Religious Studies Review*
Scr	*Scripture*
SAC	Studies in Antiquity and Christianity
ScEs	*Science et esprit*
ScrHier	Scripta hierosolymitana
SBLDS	Society of Biblical Literature Dissertation Series
SBLBMI	Society of Biblical Literature The Bible and its Modern Interpreters
SBLMS	Society of Biblical Literature Monograph Series
SBLSBS	*Society of Biblical Literature Sources for Biblical Study*
SBLSP	*Society of Biblical Literature Seminar Papers*
SC	Sources chrétiennes. Paris: Cerf, 1943-
SEAJT	*South-east Asia Journal of Theology*
Semeia	*Semeia*
SemSup	Semeia Supplements
SemeiaSt	Semeia Studies
SFSHJ	South Florida Studies in the History of Judaism
SJCA	Studies in Judaism and Christianity in Antiquity
SJLA	Studies in Judaism in Late Antiquity

SJT	*Scottish Journal of Theology*
SNTSMS	Society for New Testament Studies Monograph Series
Sobornost	*Sobornost*
SOTI	Studies in Old Testament Interpretation
SPB	Studia postbiblica
SubBib	*Subsidia biblica*
SVTQ	*St. Vladimir's Theological Quarterly*
SWBA	Social World of Biblical Antiquity
TB	Theologische Bücherei: Neudrucke und Beritche aus dem 20. Jahrhundert
ThBer	*Theologische Berichte*
TBl	*Theologische Blätter*
TBT	*The Bible Today*
TDNT	*Theological Dictionary of the New Testament*
TEH	Theologische Existenz heute
Text	*Textus*
ThSt	Theologische Studiën
TJ	*Trinity Journal*
TLZ	*Theologische Literaturzeitung*
TRE	*Theologische Reakenzyklopädie.* Edited by G. Krause and G. Müller. Berlin, 1977—*TRuNF*
TRu	*Theologische Rundschau*
TSAJ	Texte und Studien zum antiken Judentum
TSK	*Theologische Studien und Kritiken*
TUGAL	Texte und Untersuchungen zur Geschichte der altchristlichen Literatur
UBL	Ugaritisch-biblische Literatur
UCOP	University of Cambridge. Oriental Publications
VF	*Verkündigung und Forschung*
Vid	*Vidyajyoti*
VT	*Vetus Testamentum*
VTSup	Supplements to Vetus Testamentum
WMANT	Wissenschaftliche Monographien zum Alten und Neuen
WUNT	Wissenschaftliche Untersuchungen zum Neuen Testament Testament
WiWei	*Wissenschaft und Weisheit*
YNER	Yale Near Eastern Researches
ZAW	*Zeitschrift für die alttestamentliche Wissenschaft*
ZNW	*Zeitschrift für die neutestamentliche Wissenschaft*
ZRGG	*Zeitschrift für Religions- und Geistesgeschichte*
ZS	*Zeitschrift für Semetistik und verwandte Gebiete*
ZTK	*Zeitschrift für Theologie und Kirche*
ZWT	*(NF?) Zeitschrift für wissenschaftliche Theologie*

CONTRIBUTORS

Andrew K.M. Adam
Seabury Western Theological Seminary
Evanston, Illinois

Kurt Aland (deceased)
Institut für Neutestamentliche
 Textforschung
Westfällische Wilhelms-Universität
Münster, Germany

John R. Bartlett
Dublin, Ireland

Timothy K. Beal
Case Western Reserve University
Cleveland, Ohio

Klaus Berger
Wissenschaftlich-Theologisches
 Seminar
Ruprecht-Karls-Universität Heidelberg
Heidelberg (Altstadt), Germany

Robert F. Berkey
Mt. Holyoke College
South Hadley, Massachusetts

Mark Edward Biddle
Baptist Theological Seminary
Richmond, Virginia

Hendrikus Boers
Emeritus
Candler School of Theology
Emory University
Atlanta, Georgia

Robert G. Bratcher
Chapel Hill, North Carolina

Martin J. Buss
Emory College
Emory University
Atlanta, Georgia

John G. Cook
La Grange College
La Grange, Georgia

Richard DeMaris
Valparaiso University
Valparaiso, Indiana

John R. Donahue
St. Marys Seminary and University
Baltimore, Maryland

Musa W. Shomanah Dube
University of Botswana
Gaborone, Botswana

Cain Hope Felder
School of Divinity
Howard University
Washington, DC

John T. Fitzgerald
University Of Miami
Coral Gables, Florida

Reginald C. Fuller
Emeritus
Virginia Theological Seminary
Richmond, Virginia

Robert Gnuse
Loyola University New Orleans
New Orleans, Louisiana

Moshe Goshen-Gottstein (deceased)
Hebrew University
Jerusalem, Israel

John H. Hayes
Candler School of Theology
Emory University
Atlanta, Georgia

Alice Hunt
The Divinity School
Vanderbilt University
Nashville, Tennessee

A. M. Isasi-Díaz
Drew University
Madison, New Jersey

David Jobling
University of Saskatchewan
St. Andrew's College
Saskatoon, Saskatchewan
Canada

K.A. Keefer
Baytown, Texas

David E. Klemm
University of Iowa
Iowa City, Iowa

Jeffrey Kah-Jin Kuan
Pacific School of Religion
Graduate Theological Union
Berkeley, California

Tod Linafelt
Georgetown University
Washington, DC

Clarice J. Martin
Colgate University
Hamilton, New York

Harvey K. McArthur
Emeritus
Hartford Seminary
Hartford, Connecticut

Cameron S. McKenzie
Providence College
Otterburne, Manitoba
Canada

Edgar V. McKnight
Emeritus
Furman University
Greenville, South Carolina

Gregory Mobley
Andover Newton Theological School
Newton Centre, Massachusetts

Johannes C. de Moor
Emeritus
Theological University Kam
The Netherlands

Gail R. O'Day
Candler School of Theology
Emory University
Atlanta, Georgia

Ben C. Ollenburger
Associated Mennonite Biblical
    Seminary
Elkhart, Indiana

Grant R. Osborne
Trinity Evangelical Divinity School
Deerfield, Illinois

Todd C. Penner
Austin College
Sherman, Texas

Vicki C Phillips
West Virginia Wesleyan College
Buckhannon, West Virginia

J.R. Porter
Emeritus
University of Exeter
Exeter, England

Stanley Porter
McMaster Divinity College
Hamilton, Ontario
Canada

Mark Allan Powell
Trinity Lutheran Seminary
Columbus, Ohio

John F. Priest (deceased)
Florida State University
Tallahassee, Florida

Ilona N. Rashkow
State University of New York
   at Stony Brook
Stony Brook, New York

Robert D. Richardson
Middletown, Connecticut

Wayne G. Rollins
Hartford Seminary
West Hartford, Connecticut

Wolfgang M.W. Roth
Evanston, Illinois

John Sandys-Wunsch
University Of Victoria
Victoria, British Columbia
Canada

Thomas Schmeller
Techical University of Dresden
Institut für Katholische Theologie
Dresden, Germany

Fernando F. Segovia
The Divinity School
Vanderbilt University
Nashville, Tennessee

Gerald T. Sheppard
Emmanuel College of Victoria
   University
Toronto, Ontario
Canada

Abraham Smith
Perkins School Of Theology
Southern Methodist University
Dallas, Texas

Naomi Steinberg
De Paul University
Chicago, Illinois

Ken Stone
Chicago Theological Seminary
Chicago, Illinois

Theodore Stylianopoulos
Holy Cross Greek Orthodox School of
   Theology
Brookline, Massachusetts

R.S. Sugirtharajah
The University of Birmingham
Birmingham, England

Neal H. Walls,
The Divinity School
Wake Forest University
Winston-Salem, North Carolina

Duane F. Watson
School Of Theology
Malone College
Canton, Ohio

CONTRIBUTORS

Laurence L. Welborn
United Theological Seminary
Dayton, Ohio

Gail A. Yee
Episcopal Divinity School
Cambridge, Massachusetts

Mark A. Zier
Campion College of San Francisco
San Francisco, California

ARCHAEOLOGY AND HISTORIOGRAPHY

Archaeology and the Hebrew Bible

1. *Introduction.* Where the term *archaeology* was once understood in a broad sense as referring to the study of the past in general, it is now commonly taken to describe the activity of those who excavate ancient sites. The best definition is perhaps that of the American archaeologist R. Braidwood: "The study of things men [and women] made and did in order that their whole way of life may be understood." The professional archaeologist, using a wide range of techniques, systematically studies the material remains of the past and thus contributes to the general historical task along with other scholars who study literary, inscriptional, artistic, or other recorded evidence. Archaeological evidence from the ancient states of Israel and Judah and from the ancient writings enshrined in our modern Bible are perhaps the two most important sources for the history of the people of ancient Israel and of the early Christian church; but evidence, both archaeological and literary, from the ancient surrounding nations—Egypt (Egyptology and Biblical Studies*§), Syria, Babylonia, Assyria (Assyriology and Biblical Studies§), and the Greco-Roman world—must not be ignored. Correct assessment of the relative value of evidence from these different sources is the concern of the historian. The study of artifactual and literary remains is, in theory, indivisible. Their separation in academic practice has led to much misunderstanding; the literary scholar has not always understood the limitations of the archaeological evidence, and the archaeologist has not always understood the complexities of the literary evidence. The relationship between the biblical student and the archaeologist has been further complicated by the fact that the two do not always share the same historical aims (let alone theological presuppositions).

2. *The Beginnings of Archaeology.* Archaeology as we know it as a scientific discipline did not begin until the nineteenth century. For Palestinian archaeology, the most important scholar to explore Palestine was the American E. Robinson§ professor of biblical literature at Union Theological College, New York. With E. Smith, a Protestant missionary and fluent Arabist, he traveled the length and breadth of Palestine in 1838–39 and in 1852 in order to locate places mentioned in the Bible. He based many of his identifications on the modern Arabic place names, which, he argued, preserved the Semitic names from biblical times. His results were published in *Biblical Researches in Palestine* (1841, 1856[2]). A. Alt§ later commented that, as the identifications of the cities were uncertain, "in Robinson's footnotes are forever buried the errors of many generations" (1939). Robinson had his limitations—he did not recognize that the tells that dotted the Palestinian plains were not natural hillocks but the remains of city mounds—and he was occasionally wrong, but his work is the foundation of all biblical toponymy and remains an essential reference work for the biblical scholar and archaeologist.

By 1850 the initial European exploration of Palestine and Transjordan had been achieved; there remained the accurate surveying and excavation of important biblical sites. An important step was taken with the foundation in 1865 of the Palestine Exploration Fund§, whose aim was the scientific investigation of "the Archaeology, Geography, Geology and Natural History of Palestine." Although at first heavily supported and subscribed to by church leaders, the fund kept to its scientific aims and flourishes still, especially through its journal, *Palestine Exploration Quarterly.* In France, Germany, North America, Israel, and elsewhere, similar societies appeared. The French École Biblique was founded in Jerusalem in 1890 and its journal, *Revue Biblique,* in 1892. The German Deutscher Verein zür Erforschung Palästinas§ was founded in 1877, with its *Zeitschrift des deutschen Palästina-Vereins.* The American Schools of Oriental Research in Jerusalem was founded in 1900, followed shortly by its *Bulletin of the*

American Societies of Oriental Research; in Israel, the Israel Exploration Society (formerly the Jewish Palestine Exploration Society) has produced the *Israel Exploration Journal* (1951).

The first excavation in Palestine was F. de Saulcy's investigation of the "Tombs of the Kings" in 1863, which turned out to be the family tomb of Queen Helena of Adiabene, a first-century convert to Judaism; however, the excavation of this (and of any) Jewish tomb gave some offense to Jews in Jerusalem. Then in 1867–68, C. Warren[§] investigated the topography of ancient Jerusalem; he dug shafts and tunnels to explore the foundations of the Herodian platform of the Haram area, and he too met some opposition on religious grounds. (Sensitivity to the feelings of the present has not always been the first thought of those who explore the past, but it remains important.) Warren was the first to excavate at Jericho (1868), both at Tell es-Sultan and at the site on the Wadi Qelt later identified as the Hasmonean and Herodian palaces.

3. *Egypt and Mesopotamia.* A major contribution to biblical studies in the nineteenth century, both at the scholarly and at the popular level, was made by the growth of archaeological activity in Egypt and Mesopotamia. These activities cannot be reviewed in full here, but scholarly study of Egypt really began with Napoleon's expedition in 1799 and the resulting *Description de l'Égypte.* This led to Champollion's deciphering of the Egyptian hieroglyphs, to the explorations of Lepsius, to the preservation of antiquities by men like Mariette, and to the excavations of E. Naville and W. F. Petrie[§]. Egypt was important for its own sake, but for many it was also important as the scene of the biblical book of Exodus. Much scholarly time has been given to identifying the "store cities," Pithom and Rameses, of Exod 1:11 and to dating the exodus and identifying the pharaoh of the exodus. The discovery of the archive of correspondence from Canaanite vassal kings in Palestine to the Egyptian pharaoh in the mid-fourteenth century B.C.E. (the Amarna letters), with their reference to the military activity in Palestine of the *Habiru* (who sounded suspiciously like the Hebrews) influenced scholarly debate on the date of the exodus from the 1890s to the 1960s, by which time it was generally accepted that neither the equation of Hebrew with Habiru nor the nature of the exodus story was as simple as previously thought.

In Mesopotamia the identification of Assyrian and Babylonian sites by explorers and excavators like C. Rich, E. Botta, and A. Layard, and the deciphering of their scripts and inscriptions by scholars like E. Hincks, H. Rawlinson, and G. Smith[§] (who discovered a tablet giving an account of a flood remarkably similar to the account in Genesis 6–9), stirred even greater popular enthusiasm. In the twentieth century, interest was maintained by L. Woolley's claim (1929) to have discovered evidence of the biblical flood at Ur; by the archival finds from the second millennium B.C.E. at Mari, Nuzi (1925–31), and elsewhere; by H. Winckler's[§] discovery (1911–13) of the Hittites' capital city at Boghaz Koy in north-central Turkey (see Hittitology and Biblical Studies[§]); and by the discovery (1929) of an archive of tablets in cuneiform script and of a Northwest Semitic language (Ugarit and the Bible[§] [see Translation*[§]]) at Ras Shamra on the Syrian coast. The discovery in 1974 of a huge archive of third-millennium texts from Tell Mardikh (ancient Ebla) in Syria raised new speculations about the authenticity of the biblical patriarchal age; but once the alleged reference to Sodom and Gomorrah in one of the texts was proved wrong, public excitement waned. Such discoveries raised both public and scholarly interest in biblical history, but they illuminated the Near Eastern background to the Bible rather than the Bible itself and are now the concern primarily of specialists in these fields.

4. *Stratigraphy and Pottery.* A new era in Palestinian archaeology began with Petrie's work at Tell el-Hesi in 1890. From his examination of this tell he discovered that tells were artificial, not natural, mounds, formed by the accumulated strata of building debris over long periods of time; and that each visible stratum of deposits contained its own distinctive types of pottery. Petrie produced a classified typology of the pottery taken from the different levels exposed on

the mound. This gave a relative dating for the sequence of pottery that could then be used as an aid to dating similar levels elsewhere; the discovery of Egyptian inscriptions or royal scarabs in a stratified context made it possible to link the scheme with the accepted Egyptian chronology and so produced a basic chronology for Palestinian material. The cross-linkage of stratified pottery with Egyptian and Assyrian inscriptional evidence remains vital to the establishment of the Chronology[§] of biblical history to this day. Petrie, however, went on to correlate the strata excavated at Tell el-Hesi with the biblical evidence for the history of Lachish. This was a dangerous procedure, liable to distort his interpretation of the history of the site, for subsequent research has shown that Tell el-Hesi was not Lachish (Doermann 1987, 132-34). Serious misinterpretation of the archaeological evidence resulted in later years from the mistaken identification (by F. Frank, followed by N. Glueck[§]) of Tell el-Kheleifeh with the Ezion-geber founded by Solomon (1 Kgs 9:26) and from the simplistic association of the destruction of the Late Bronze Age cities of western Palestine with the biblical stories of the Israelite conquest of Canaan. The direct association of biblical texts and archaeological evidence has always tempted scholars and needs very careful handling.

Petrie, however, had broken new ground, and his new techniques were influential. The trench method of excavation, with careful observation of stratigraphy and pottery sequences, had come to stay. His successors in the first three decades of the twentieth century applied his methods with greater or lesser skill but on the grand scale. R. Macalister at Gezer (1906–9) paid too little attention to stratigraphy and architecture, while G. Reisner and C. Fisher at Samaria (1908–10) were much more precise. Fisher, P. Guy, and G. Loud at Megiddo (1925–39) attempted to excavate the whole vast city layer by layer but found it too large even for a well-funded enterprise. On a much smaller scale, Glueck took the same approach at Tell el-Kheleifeh (1938–40), with the result that virtually nothing is left from which successors might check his results.

W. F. Albright[§] at Tell Beit Mirsim (1926–32), following the so-called Reisner-Fisher method, approached excavation by means of the locus—a small, easily defined area like a room, a wall, or some other architectural structure. Related structures producing similar pottery were seen as belonging to a common stratum; indeed, for Albright prior knowledge of the pottery typology was all-important and determinative for interpretation of the site's history. (The problem with this approach is that a previously determined pottery typology may determine one's view of the stratification of a site, rather than vice versa. The stratum may become an artificial division rather than an observed one.) A consequence of this emphasis was that the interrelationships of the strata and structures were inadequately observed or recorded. Albright's publications show ground plans rather than stratified sections (Moorey 1981, 26-28). However, Albright greatly refined the Petrie-Bliss pottery chronology, constructing a new and generally accepted ceramic index for Palestine. His polymathic control of historical and linguistic as well as archaeological data established him as the leading interpreter of biblical history and archaeology in his generation. He valued equally the evidence of both biblical text and excavated artifacts and thus produced a synthesis that influenced a whole generation of American scholars.

5. *Bible and Spade.* Inevitably, however, as the twentieth century progressed it became more difficult for scholars to hold together the different tasks of biblical and archaeological research and interpretation. In the late nineteenth century many scholars had seen in archaeological discoveries a corrective to the hypotheses of the more radical biblical scholars like J. Wellhausen[§]; the discovery in Moab of the Mesha Stele (which mentions Israel's wars with Mesha of Moab); the discovery in Egypt of the Amarna letters (which mentioned Habiru active in Palestine in the reigns of Amenophis III and IV) and of the Merneptah Stele (which mentioned Merneptah's defeat of a people called Israel in Palestine); and the discovery at Susa of the code of Hammurabi of Babylon (which contained close parallels to laws found in the Pentateuch) were

all taken as supporting the veracity of the biblical story. S. Driver[§] pointed out that the illustration of the biblical narrative was not the same thing as the confirmation of events described in the Bible (Moorey 1991, 44). Such German scholars as Alt and his pupil M. Noth[§] were well versed in the topography, geography, and archaeology of the land but were even better versed in analysis of the biblical text and wrote from that perspective. Noth, for example, saw archaeological discovery as illuminating the background to the biblical traditions rather than the traditions themselves, whose historical development required careful analysis. This approach differed widely from that of Albright and his pupils in America, who generally had a greater trust in the reliability of the outline of the biblical tradition and used their archaeological findings more positively to support the historical outline presented in the Bible (particularly in the cases of the patriarchal history and the Israelite conquest of Canaan). In Britain, with rare exceptions, biblical scholars and archaeologists kept to their separate trades. J. Crowfoot, J. Garstang[§], J. Starkey, R. Hamilton, and C. Johns were primarily archaeologists, though concerned with biblical history; K. Kenyon[§] studied modern history, assisted Crowfoot at Samaria, and became a protégé of M. Wheeler and a highly professional archaeologist who viewed biblical history from that perspective.

Kenyon developed what became known as the Wheeler-Kenyon technique, using the trench method but refining it by meticulously observing, recording, and checking the stratigraphy by preserving the balk and drawing its vertical section as a record of what has been dug. (Her techniques were adopted and adapted by many American archaeologists—including J. Callaway, who studied under her—but they were not immediately accepted by Israeli archaeologists, many of whom preferred methods that allowed for complete rather than partial excavation of a site and the exposure of architecture on a large scale.) Kenyon's excavation of Jericho (1952–59) by careful observation of stratigraphy corrected Garstang's dating of his so-called double wall from the Late Bronze Age to the Early Bronze Age and denied the existence of any but the smallest settlement at Jericho in the Late Bronze Age, thus undermining an influential view of the dating of the exodus and conquest of Canaan. More important in many ways, Kenyon revealed at Jericho flourishing Middle Bronze and Early Bronze cities and a history of the Neolithic period extending back to the tenth millennium B.C.E. In another major excavation (1961–67) at Jerusalem, she continued the century-old exploration of the topography and history of the city; this work continued in the 1970s and 1980s with dramatic success by the Israeli archaeologists N. Avigad, Y. Shiloh, B. Mazar[§], and others. Kenyon was in no way a biblical scholar and in excavating had no biblical axe to grind. She was concerned to present what the archaeological evidence told her and took the biblical evidence mostly at face value, without critical analysis—if it fit, well and good. Israeli scholars, understandably, have tended to give greater credence to biblical traditions. "Quite naturally, every opportunity is taken to relate archaeological evidence to the biblical text" (Mazar 1988, 127). In this, as also in their approach to pottery analysis and stratification, they have been closer to the Albright tradition than to the British or German scholarly tradition. In particular, Israeli scholars (notably J. Aharoni) have contributed notably and for obvious reasons to our knowledge of the geography, topography, and toponymy of Israel. Major excavations have been those by Y. Yadin[§] at Masada and Hazor, by Mazar and Shiloh at Jerusalem, by Netzer at Jericho, and by Biran at Tell Dan, to mention only a few.

Kenyon was independent of the Bible, yet not indifferent to it, and in her historical presuppositions was deeply influenced by its story. In many ways she belongs to the end of an era of biblical archaeology; her historical approach reveals the same limitations in scope as does that of her predecessors. For a century the Bible had influenced the choice of sites for excavation and the historical and cultural interests of the excavators. Concern to establish dates and to verify the biblical presentation of history led to the search for city walls and palaces, temples and their cult vessels, inscriptions and coins, and evidence of destruction or cultural change at the end of the Late Bronze Age. This data was promptly related to the biblical account of the Israelite conquest of Canaan without further ado. This was not necessarily from motives of biblical fundamentalism (although this element was sometimes present) but rather from an uncritical acceptance of the familiar outline of the biblical story. In the twenty-first century, biblical scholarship has also moved on, and archaeologists have begun to learn from biblical scholars that the historical interpretation of biblical narratives is no simple matter and must be treated critically. Archaeologists are also under pressure from the explosion of information made possible by the development of new techniques and from new critiques of the Albright-Kenyon emphasis on the importance of pottery typology; e.g., H. Franken, in an important and undervalued book, *In Search of the Jericho Potters* (1974), argued that study of the techniques of manufacture might yield more evidence for the development of pottery than would the study of the changing shapes (the shape, after all, depended upon the technique used to create it).

6. *New Concerns.* Archaeology has also discovered other interests apart from the illustration of the political history to be found in biblical narratives. Social and anthropological interests, in fact, have been part of the archaeological agenda throughout its history; thus G. Dalman, for example, director of the German Institute in Jerusalem (1902–14), studied daily life in rural Palestine and produced seven volumes of studies entitled *Arbeit und Sitte im Palastina (Work and Customs in Palestine,* 1928–42). Present archaeological concern is with understanding the settlement patterns and population distribution in ancient times, the ancient use of land and methods of agriculture, flora and fauna, hydrology, ancient technologies, and structures of ancient societies. Along with the excavation of a particular site goes the detailed survey of the surrounding land so that the site can be seen in a wider context; interest is no longer limited primarily to the biblical period but is extended to all periods from Paleolithic times to the present. The number of regional studies is growing rapidly; one might note the Shechem area survey (E. Campbell 1968); work in the Negev by R. Cohen and W. Dever (1972, 1979); R. Gophna's survey of the central coastal plain (1977); R. Ibach's survey of the Hesban region (1976–78); M. Kochavi's survey of Judea, Samaria, and the Golan (1967–68); the work of E. Meyers and others in Galilee and the Golan (1978); and others. Work of this nature—e.g., I. Finkelstein's survey of Late Bronze/Iron Age sites in the hill country of Israel—has had an effect on the interpretation of the biblical narratives of Israel's settlement in Canaan. The surveys of Transjordan, from those of Glueck in the 1930s to those of J. Miller, B. MacDonald, S. Mittmann, S. Hart, W. Jobling, and others in the 1970s and 1980s, have brought new dimensions and added depth to our picture, drawn hitherto mainly from biblical sources, of the history and culture of the Iron Age kingdoms of the Ammonites, the Moabites, and the Edomites. The modern archaeologist has also learned to look for answers to questions about ancient populations and their political, economic, cultural, and religious organization and activities by beginning from observation of contemporary society as well as by drawing inferences from observed patterns of ancient settlements. The dangers of reading backward from the present are obvious; nevertheless, the questions raised are pertinent. Some recent historians have gone so far as to draw their picture of premonarchic and early monarchic Israel from archaeological evidence alone, putting to one side the late Deuteronomistic[‡§] reconstruction of Israel's early history. The interests of classical historiography have been replaced by the concerns of archaeology, anthropology, and the social sciences (Social-scientific Criticism*[§]). Not surprisingly, debates about method fill the archaeological journals.

7. *Archaeology and Biblical Studies.* One major debate concerns the value of archaeology for biblical studies. Clearly, archaeology has thrown light on Israel's material culture—buildings, architecture, city planning, city defenses, burial customs, religious cult, temples, synagogues, *miqvoth,* water supplies, clothing and jewelry, writing, trading, agriculture, domestic life, and

so on. This evidence enables us to set Israel firmly in the wider context of the culture of the ancient Near East and to understand Israel as part of the wider world. On the other hand, few archaeological finds bear directly on the biblical narrative. The pool at el-Jib discovered by J. Pritchard may be the pool beside Gibeon of 2 Sam 2:13. The Siloam tunnel in Jerusalem with its inscription speaks eloquently of Hezekiah's preparation for an Assyrian siege in 701 B.C.E. (although a Hellenistic date for this tunnel has recently been proposed). The tomb inscription of one Shebna in the village of Silwan across the Kedron Valley from Jerusalem may be from the tomb of the man criticized in Isa 22:16. The famous Moabite stone was erected in honor of King Mesha of Moab (2 Kings 3), but although it witnesses to Mesha's existence, it also raises questions for the historian of ancient Israel and Moab. From Assyria we have pictorial records of such events as the payment of tribute by King Jehu in 841 B.C.E. and the capture of Lachish by Sennacherib in 701 B.C.E.; and from Babylon, records relating to the imprisonment of King Jehoiachin of Judah and his sons. Most of these fortuitously refer to people known to us from biblical records; and they at least confirm that the Bible's historical records speak of real people and real events, even if they do not confirm the biblical reports in every detail.

Many interpreters, however, have tried to use archaeology to prove the "truth" of the Bible. The problem here is that archaeology, while it might provide evidence for the site of Solomon's temple, has nothing to say about the validity of such ideas as the kingdom of God or the meaning of the poem in Isaiah 53. Archaeological research has often offered more evidence than was desired, at least in some quarters. The Bible, for example, denies firmly that YHWH has a female consort; yet recent evidence from Kuntillet 'Ajrud has suggested to many scholars that, at least in one place, a female consort of YHWH, Asherah, was worshiped.

A major debate has focused around the term *biblical archaeology.* Albright approved the term, at least in a geographical sense: "Biblical archaeology covers all lands mentioned in the Bible." It was for him a wider term than "Palestinian archaeology"; it was archaeology that had any bearing on biblical studies (Albright 1966, 1). G. E. Wright, one of his pupils, held a similar view; he identified biblical archaeology as "a special 'armchair' variety of general archaeology which studies the discoveries of excavators and gleans from them every fact which throws a direct, indirect, or even diffused light upon the Bible." Its central and absorbing interest is the understanding and exposition of the Scriptures. It is interested in floors, foundations and city walls; but also in epigraphic discoveries and in every indication of what people did with their minds as well as what they did with their hands" (Wright 1957, 7).

Dever objected strongly to the term because it suggests apologetic attempts to use archaeology to prove the Bible true. He preferred the descriptive regional designation "Syro-Palestinian archaeology." Biblical archaeology, he argued, did not describe what he and his colleagues did. They were professional archaeologists who happened to be exercising their skills in one part of the world rather than in another and to be using the same skills as all archaeologists everywhere. Archaeology exists as a discipline independently of the Bible, alongside other disciplines, like anthropology, philology, and philosophy. Dever reflected the fact that archaeology had established itself as a separate, independent academic discipline with its own scholarly agenda; it should no longer be regarded simply as the handmaid of history.

This leaves us with the question of how archaeology and biblical studies should relate. The answer must be that the reconstruction of all aspects of biblical history is an interdisciplinary affair in which linguists, philologists, paleographers, textual critics (Textual Criticism[§]), literary historians, archaeologists, and others all share. The archaeologist is no autonomous superbeing; the archaeologist needs the help of other specialists—architects, radio-carbon dating technologists, paleobotanists, chemists, epigraphists, etc. Archaeology is a discipline that, like all other academic disciplines, thrives only in the company of others. Biblical archaeology, insofar as it exists, refers to archaeology that is relevant to the field of biblical studies. In turn, the biblical scholar needs the expertise of the professional archaeologist to illuminate the biblical record. Difficulties and misunderstandings occur when an archaeologist chooses to interpret an excavated biblical site by uncritical use of the biblical text or when, conversely, a biblical scholar reconstructs history with the help of equally uncritical use of the archaeological evidence. The history of biblical interpretation contains many examples of both errors. It is to be hoped that in the future students of the text and students of the soil will develop mutual respect for one another's disciplines.

Bibliography: **Y. Aharoni,** *The Land of the Bible: From the Prehistoric Beginnings to the End of the First Temple Period* (1979[2]); *The Archaeology of the Land of Israel* (1982). **W. F. Albright,** *Archaeology and the Religion of Israel* (1942); *The Archaeology of Palestine* (1949 and rev. eds.); "The OT and the Archaeology of Palestine" and "The OT and the Archaeology of the Ancient East," *The OT and Modern Study: A Generation of Discovery and Research* (ed. H. H. Rowley, 1951) 1-47; *New Horizons in Biblical Research* (1966); *The Archaeology of Palestine and the Bible* (1973, 1974). **A. Alt,** "Edward Robinson and the Historical Geography of Palestine," *JBL 58* (1939) 373-79. **N. Avigad,** *Discovering Jerusalem* (1984). **J. Aviram** (ed.), *Biblical Archaeology Today: Proceedings of the International Congress of Biblical Archaeology, Jerusalem, April 1984* (1985). **J. R. Bartlett,** *Jericho* (CBW, 1982); *The Bible: Faith and Evidence, A Critical Enquiry into the Nature of Biblical History* (1990). **Y. Ben-Arieh,** *The Rediscovery of the Holy Land in the Nineteenth Century* (1979). **P. Bienkowski** (ed.), *Early Edom and Moab: The Beginning of the Iron Age in Southern Jordan* (1992). **J. A. Blakely,** "F. J. Bliss: Father of Palestinian Archaeology," *BA 56* (1993) 110-15. **F. J. Bliss,** *The Development of Palestine Exploration* (1906). **J. H. Charlesworth and W. P. Weaver,** *What Has Archaeology to Do with Faith?* (1992). **R. B. Coote,** *Early Israel: A New Horizon* (1990). **R. B. Coote and K. W. Whitelam,** *The Emergence of Early Israel in Historical Perspective* (1987). **F. M. Cross,** "W. F. Albright's View of Biblical Archaeology and Its Methodology," *BA 36* (1973) 2-5. **G. Daniel,** *A Hundred and Fifty Years of Archaeology* (1975). **W. J. Dever,** "Impact of the 'New Archaeology,'" *Benchmarks in Time and Culture* (ed. J. F. Drinkard et al., 1988) 337-52; *Recent Archaeological Discoveries and Biblical Research* (1989). **R. W. Doermann,** "Archaeology and Biblical Interpretation: Tell el-Hesi," *Archaeology and Biblical Interpretation* (ed. L. G. Perdue et al., 1987) 129-55. **J. F. Drinkard** et al. (eds.), *Benchmarks in Time and Culture: An Introduction to Biblical Archaeology Dedicated to J. A. Callaway* (1988). **J. Finegan,** *The Archaeology of the NT* (2 vols. 1969, 1981). **I. Finkelstein,** *The Archaeology of the Israelite Settlement* (1988); *Living on the Fringe: The Archaeology and History of the Negev, Sinai, and Neighbouring Regions in the Bronze and Iron Ages* (1995). **H. J. Franken,** "The Problem of Identification in Biblical Archaeology," *PEQ 108* (1976) 3-11; "Archaeology of Palestine: Problems and Task," *The World of the Bible* (ed. A. S. Woude, 1986) 50-62. **H. J. Franken and C. A. Franken-Bettershill,** *A Primer of OT Archaeology* (1973). **H. J. Franken and J. Kalsbeek,** *In Search of the Jericho Potters: Ceramics from the Iron Age and from the Neolithicum* (1974). **W. H. C. Frend,** *An Archaeology of Early Christianity: A History* (1996). **V. Fritz,** *An Introduction to Biblical Archaeology* (1994). **L. T. Geraty and L. G. Herr,** *The Archaeology of Jordan and Other Studies: Presented to S. H. Horn* (1986). **C. J. de Geus,** "The Development of Palestinian Archaeology and Its Significance for Biblical Studies," *The World of the Bible* (1986) 63-74. **N. Glueck,** *The Other Side of the Jordan* (1940, 1970[2]). **C. P. Grant,** *The Syrian Desert* (1937). **H. V. Hilprecht,** *Explorations in Bible Lands During the Nineteenth Century* (1903). **D. C. Hopkins** (ed.), "Celebrating and Examining W. F. Albright," *BA 56* (1993). **T. G. H. James** (ed.), *Excavating in Egypt: The Egypt Exploration Society 1882–1982* (1982). **K. M. Kenyon,** *Archaeology in the Holy Land* (1971); *The Bible and Recent Archaeology* (rev. by P. R. S. Moorey, 1987). **P. J. King,**

American Archaeology in the Mideast: A History of the ASOR (1983). **O. S. LaBianca,** "Sociocultural Anthropology and Syro-Palestinian Archaeology," *Benchmarks in Time and Culture* (ed. J. F. Drinkard et al., 1988) 369-87. **R. A. S. Macalister,** *A Century of Excavation in Palestine* (1925). **B. MacDonald,** *The Wadi el Has? Archaeological Survey, 1979–83, West-central Jordan* (1988). **A. Mazar,** "Israeli Archaeologists," *Benchmarks in Time and Culture* (ed. J. F. Drinkard et al., 1988) 109-28; *Archaeology and the Land of the Bible, 10,000–586 BCE* (1990). **J. M. Miller** (ed.), *Archaeological Survey of the Kerak Plateau* (1991). **P. R. S. Moorey,** *Excavation in Palestine* (1981); *A Century of Biblical Archaeology* (1991). **J. Murphy O'Connor,** *St. Paul's Corinth: Texts and Archaeology* (1983). **M. Noth,** *The OT World* (1940, 19644; ET 1966); "Der Beitrag der Archaologie zur Geschichte Israels" (VTSup 7, 1960) 26-87. **L. G. Perdue** et al., *Archaeology and Biblical Interpretation: Essays in Memory of D. G. Rose* (1987). **G. L. Peterman,** "Geographic Information Systems: Archaeology's Latest Tool," *BA 55* (1992) 162-67. **G. D. Pratico,** *N. Glueck's 1938–40 Excavations at Tell el-Kheleifeh: A Reappraisal* (1993). **E. Robinson,** *Biblical Researches in Palestine, Mount Sinai, and Arabia Petraea in 1838* (1841); *Biblical Researches in Palestine and the Adjacent Regions: A Journal of Travel in the Years 1838 and 1852* (1856). **J. A. Sanders** (ed.), *Near Eastern Archaeology in the Twentieth Century: Essays in Honor of N. Glueck* (1970). **J. A. Sauer,** "Transjordan in the Bronze and Iron Ages: A Critique of Glueck's Synthesis," *BASOR 263* (1986) 1-26. **N. Shepherd,** *The Zealous Intruders: The Western Rediscovery of Palestine* (1987). **N. A. Silbermann,** *Digging for God and Country: Exploration, Archaeology, and the Secret Struggle for the Holy Land 1799–1917* (1982). **D. W. Thomas** (ed.), *Archaeology and OT Study: Jubilee Volume of the Society for OT Study, 1917–67* (1967). **R. de Vaux,** *Archaeology and the Dead Sea Scrolls* (1973); "On Right and Wrong Uses of Archaeology," *Near Eastern Archaeology in the Twentieth Century* (ed. J. A. Sanders, 1970) 64-82. **C. M. Watson,** *Fifty Years of Work in the Holy Land* (1915). **J. Wilkinson,** *Jerusalem Pilgrims Before the Crusades* (1977); *Jerusalem as Jesus Knew It: Archaeology as Evidence* (1978). **G. E. Wright,** *Biblical Archaeology* (1957). "Biblical Archaeology Today," *New Directions in Biblical Archaeology* (ed. D. N. Freedman and J. C. Greenfield, 1971) 167-86; "What Archaeology Can and Cannot Do," *BA 34* (1971) 70-76.

J. R. BARTLETT

ARCHAEOLOGY AND HISTORIOGRAPHY

Archaeology and New Testament Interpretation

1. *Introduction*. American biblical scholars and the general public alike associate biblical archaeology with the ancient Near East of the first and second millennium B.C.E. Of the many current Bible dictionaries and encyclopedias with articles on biblical archaeology or archaeology and the Bible, some offer a history of excavation in Israel and Jordan, others offer a chronology of the ancient Near East dating back to Paleolithic times, but none provides adequate introduction to the extensive archaeological record of the world portrayed in the pages of the New Testament. *The Anchor Bible Dictionary*'s article, William Dever's fine essay on the state of biblical archaeology and its engagement with archaeological theory, says nothing about the Roman period in or outside Palestine, and the dictionary has no companion piece on the New Testament period (1992). These observations reveal much about the standing of archaeology in New Testament studies: in contrast to Hebrew Bible scholarship, its use of archaeology and the material record it has generated is in an embryonic stage.

The reasons why Hebrew Bible scholars turn to the relevant material record more readily than their New Testament counterparts are many. Eric Meyers suggests that what he calls New Testament archaeology has been a victim of the preoccupation with Old Testament biblical archaeology (1987, 21) (Archaeology and the Hebrew Bible*, Archaeology and Biblical Studies§). P. R. S. Moorey, in his important history of biblical archaeology, criticizes New Testament scholarship itself, noting its exclusively textual focus, wariness about nonliterary data, and suspicion of classical archaeology (1991, 21, 48; cf. Reed 2000, 1–3). For whatever reason, there has been no broad movement in the field to utilize the full record produced by archaeology or to engage the discipline itself, even though New Testament scholars are well aware of archaeology's importance to the study of the Dead Sea Scrolls§ and the recovery of papyri, such as the Jesus*§ sayings unearthed at Oxyrhychus (Gnostic Interpretation§).

Two factors may best account for the different status of archaeology in the two major domains of biblical studies. First, unlike their Hebrew Bible counterparts who have access to an identifiably Israelite material culture, New Testament scholars have nothing comparable, for a distinctively Christian material culture did not emerge until the close of the second century C.E. (Snyder 1985, 2). As a consequence, the New Testament scholar's use of archaeology will necessarily be circumstantial. Second, while many Hebrew Bible scholars of the twentieth century busied themselves excavating sites relevant to their textual study, New Testament scholars generally did not. In most cases, sites connected with the New Testament, particularly those in the Aegean basin, were (and still are) in the hands of archaeologists whose disciplinary training and interests did not coincide with those of biblical scholars. These two factors understandably inhibited interaction between archaeology and New Testament studies: the material record was perceived as only tangentially relevant to the task of interpreting texts; lack of contact and experience with excavations has meant that New Testament scholars are generally not equipped to incorporate archaeology in their work, even if they saw its relevance.

The situation has now changed dramatically, but only very recently. A mere decade ago, P. R. S. Moorey was not overstating the case when he claimed, "It is widely acknowledged that New Testament scholars have paid, and largely continue to pay, relatively little attention to archaeology" (1991, 170). Studies that combined archaeology and the New Testament were little more than topographical surveys that employed the material record rather uncritically (Finegan 1969; 1981). More critical studies existed, but they barely tapped the archaeological record. For example, Wayne Meeks and Robert Wilken's *Jews and Christians in Antioch* (1978) did not differ fundamentally from similar studies based solely on literary sources (Brown and Meier 1983). Now, disciplinary shifts both in the field of archaeology and in New Testament studies have altered conditions profoundly, setting the stage for rapport between them.

2. *Theory Matters: Reaching Common Ground.* Archaeology is a more diverse and critically reflective field than it was fifty years ago. An empirical outlook dominated archaeology for much of the twentieth century, promoting scientific principle, standardized excavation techniques, and systematic classification and seriation of finds, especially ceramics. These developments enabled archaeologists to date the phases of habitation revealed by stratigraphic excavation with great precision. As the century progressed, new technologies increased the amount, quality, and kinds of data that could be collected and the types of analysis that could be done. At the same time, intellectual ferment in the discipline fostered debate about the purpose and goals of archaeology. What came to be called new (or processual) archaeology, distinguished by its anthropological orientation and integrative approach, moved beyond artifactual study to testing hypotheses about the cultures and processes that generated the artifacts, making full use of the explosive growth in the material record. As the century closed, debate continued, giving rise to an array of approaches, including ethnoarchaeology, cognitive archaeology, experimental archaeology, and the archaeology of gender (Preucel 1991, 1-29; Preucel and Hodder 1996; Renfrew and Bahn 1996; Hodder 1999).

Continuing attention to the interpretive process (postprocessual archaeology) has made archaeologists even more aware of how theory-laden data collection and analysis are, and, at the same time, how such analysis must be expanded to consider not simply the functional significance of a find but also its broader cultural import. Construction of a Roman road, for instance, had architectural, military, and commercial significance. Yet it also said something about how Romans shaped the environment and created a distinctive landscape. Moreover, if built in a province, the road constituted an element in the process of Romanization and expressed cultural dominance and control. Empirical and quantitative investigation remains a central task of archaeology, but considering the symbolic value of an artifact is now part of archaeological discourse as well (Johnson 1999; Schloen 2001, 7-48).

Drawing inferences about human thought and action—beliefs, ethics, rites—from the material record, once discouraged, now enjoys respectability, especially in the disciplinary branch called cognitive archaeology. Pitfalls in this arena are many, as wonderfully spoofed by David Macaulay (1979). Nevertheless, archaeologists are increasingly unwilling to separate the material from the immaterial world and thus are developing lines of inquiry that bring questions about religious disposition and practice to the study of cultic sites and finds (Renfrew 1985, 1-26). The wider focus of contemporary archaeology, its attention to social systems, cultural change, and even to the ideology implied by the material record, bodes well for New Testament scholars. For they stand to benefit from any enterprise that sheds more light on the social make-up and religious climate of the ancient world.

As with archaeology, New Testament studies has gone through profound reorientation in the last few decades. One major shift has been the introduction of sociohistorical and Social-Scientific*§ interpretation to a field previously dominated by literary and historical approaches. Underpinning this development is the assumption that proper interpretation of New Testament documents depends on contextualizing them as fully as possible. Hence, scholars have turned to constructing the social world of the first century and the community life of Christians in that world as the best way of providing a full context for textual interpretation (Horsley 1994). Such scholarship has relied heavily upon this point on the sizable literary record the Greeks and Romans left behind, but that hardly exhausts all that can be known about Greco-Roman social life. As the endeavor to read texts in richer, more refined contexts continues, tapping the expansive and expanding material record of the ancient Mediterranean becomes imperative. For the archaeological record, while it cannot readily verify or disconfirm the historical accuracy of the biblical text, can certainly help scholars situate it.

3. *Using the Material Record.* Now that New Testament scholars have begun to see the relevance of the ancient Mediterranean's material record for their work, they must next prepare themselves for using that record carefully and responsibly. Basic familiarity with both theoretical and technical aspects of archaeology is prerequisite for those intending to use archaeological data. Few have the opportunity to participate in a dig (which is perhaps the best way to learn about archaeology), but all can benefit from the trailblazing work of Hebrew Bible scholars and archaeologists of the Near East. Articles on archaeological theory—often with its implication for biblical research—have appeared over the last quarter century in *Near Eastern Archaeology* (*Biblical Archaeologist* until 1997), *Bulletin of the American Schools of Oriental Research*, and *Biblical Archaeology Review*. Also worth consulting are book-length studies, both by multiple authors (e.g., Perdue, Toombs, and Johnson 1987) and individuals (e.g., Dever 1990). Such publications underscore the importance of having some grasp of the theories that guide the work of archaeologists, both past and present.

Also instructive is the way classical archaeology is responding to the contemporary developments in archaeology described above. In articles written twelve years apart, Stephen Dyson succinctly described the processual and postprocessual movements and their ramifications for archaeologists of the ancient Mediterranean (1981; 1993). In the meantime, books adeptly combining both theory and the material record have appeared in the field (e.g., Alcock 1993; Morris 1992). Such studies offer good examples of how to keep one's eyes on both theory and the material record. A few voices within New Testament studies have articulated how important this balancing act is, but more attention to interpretive models is urgently needed (Sawicki 2000; Oakman 2001, 109-116).

The technical complexity and multidisciplinary nature of archaeological fieldwork is nothing less than overwhelming, but those who understand what happens in the field will make better sense of the results reported in print. Comprehensive manuals and handbooks on the subject abound (e.g., Joukowsky 1980), as well as series that treat subdisciplines and categories of data, such as the up-to-date Cambridge Manuals in Archaeology (e.g., Orton, Tyers, and Vince 1993). Of special importance to New Testament scholars will be a thorough introduction to Greek and Latin epigraphy, for most will begin their archaeological sojourn with this category of data. A. G. Woodhead's *The Study of Greek Inscriptions* (1981) and Lawrence Keppie's *Understanding Roman Inscriptions* (1991) are standard entrees to the field. Also noteworthy is *Epigraphic Evidence*, edited by John Bodel (2001), which alerts readers to the dangers of taking inscriptions at face value and instructs them how to move from epigraphic data to historical evidence.

4. *Archaeologically-Informed New Testament Studies Today.* What durable form the relationship between archaeology and New Testament studies will take remains to be seen; it is too soon to contemplate a school of archaeological criticism within the field or to predict what lasting impact archaeology will have on existing interpretive approaches. To illustrate where the field is at the moment vis-à-vis archaeology, scholarship in three areas deserves mention:

a. Detailed or comparative studies of one type or several related types of archaeological data are not new, but in recent years they have taken a new direction and become more sophisticated. Frederick Danker's exhaustive study of benefaction in the Greek and Latin epigraphic record, published in 1982, had a purely philological goal and treated inscriptions simply as texts. More recent studies have moved beyond inscriptions, given greater consideration to the context of the archaeological data, and paid more attention to early Roman social life. Carolyn Osiek and David Balch have examined domestic architecture across the Roman world—Ephesus, Palestine, Ostia, Pompeii, and Herculaneum—in order to describe what Roman domestic life was like and, in turn, to characterize the material surroundings of early Christian house churches (Osiek and Balch

1997, 5-35; Osiek 2002, 83-103). Byron McCane has drawn from both the anthropological study of death and mortuary ritual and the archaeological record for graves and tombs in ancient Palestine to discuss gospel passages on death and the dead, including Jesus' burial (2003).

b. Classical archaeologists control most sites of interest in the Aegean basin, and cooperative efforts between the two fields have developed slowly. Nevertheless, some headway has been made here and there. Thanks to the efforts of Helmut Koester and his students at Harvard University (Schmuch 1983), New Testament scholars are becoming more in touch with the archaeological record of the region. A case in point is Holland Hendrix's study of civic honors at Thessalonica (1984). The collection of archaeological data he assembled is now proving useful in the interpretation of the Thessalonian correspondence (Hendrix 1991; Harrison 2002). Koester has also facilitated exchange among archaeologists, historians of religion, and New Testament scholars (1995). Individual archaeologists also deserve acknowledgment for promoting interdisciplinary exchange. For example, Timothy Gregory, director of The Ohio State University Excavations at Isthmia, has fostered the archaeologically based study of Corinthian religion. Research in this area should prove useful to New Testament scholars (Rothaus 2000; cf. DeMaris 2002b).

c. Cooperation between archaeologists of ancient Palestine and New Testament scholars has been greater, in part because the latter have involved themselves in excavations there, especially in northern Israel. Also, archaeologists began alerting biblical scholars to the relevance of early Roman Palestine's material record some time ago (Meyers and Strange 1981), which helps account for the current surge in scholarship (Levine 1992; Edwards and McCollough 1997; Meyers 1999; Reed 2000; Sawicki 2000; Crossan and Reed 2001). The goal of much of it has been to describe the social realities in the Galilee of Jesus' day by correlating the material and literary record. Some of this scholarship comes from archaeologically trained New Testament scholars, some from collaboration between archaeologists and textual scholars. In either case, these are the best examples to date of how to coordinate the two fields.

These pioneering efforts are not without their flaws; many are not fully grounded in archaeological or social-scientific theory. Yet, as a whole they mark a clear advance over earlier studies. Also, they evince the realization on the part of New Testament scholars that textual study should not be done in isolation from the archaeological record of the ancient Mediterranean (Horsley 1996, viii-ix) and that dialogue with archaeologists is necessary (Horsley 1995). Along with that realization should come an end to New Testament scholarship that treats the material record as ancillary to the ancient literary record (DeMaris 2002a).

Bibliography: S. E. Alcock, *Graecia Capta: The Landscapes of Roman Greece* (1993). **J. Bodel** (ed.), *Epigraphic Evidence: Ancient History from Inscriptions* (Approaching the Ancient World, 2001). **R. E. Brown and J. P. Meier,** *Antioch and Rome: New Testament Cradles of Catholic Christianity* (1983). **J. D. Crossan and J. L. Reed,** *Excavating Jesus: Beneath the Stones, Behind the Texts* (2001). **F. W. Danker,** *Benefactor: Epigraphic Study of a Graeco-Roman and New Testament Semantic Field* (1982). **R. E. DeMaris,** "Cults and the Imperial Cult in Early Roman Corinth: Literary Versus Material Record," *Zwischen den Reichen: Neues Testament und Römische Herrschaft* (ed. M. Labahn and J. Zangenberg, Texte und Arbeiten zum neutestamentlichen Zeitalter 36, 2002a) 73-91; review of *Corinth: The First City of Greece: An Urban History of Late Antique Cult and Religion* (by R. M. Rothaus) *JBL* 121 (2002b) 769-773. **W. G. Dever,** *Recent Archaeological Discoveries and Biblical Research* (1990); "Archaeology, Syro-Palestinian and Biblical," *ABD* (1992) 1:354-367. **S. L. Dyson,** "A Classical Archaeologist's Response to the 'New Archaeology'," *BASOR* 242 (1981) 7-13; "From New to New Age Archaeology: Archaeological Theory and Classical Archaeology—A 1990s Perspective," *AJA* 97 (1993) 195-206. **D. R. Edwards and T. McCollough** (eds.), *Archaeology and the Galilee: Texts and Contexts in the Graeco-Roman and Byzantine Periods* (South

Florida Studies in the History of Judaism, 1997). **J. Finegan,** *The Archeology of the New Testament: The Life of Jesus and the Beginning of the Early Church* (1969); *The Archeology of the New Testament: The Mediterranean World of the Early Christian Apostles* (1981). **J. R. Harrison,** "Paul and the Imperial Gospel at Thessaloniki," *JSNT* 25 (2002) 71-96. **H. L. Hendrix,** "Thessalonicans Honor Romans," (Th.D. diss., Harvard University, 1984); "Archaeology and Eschatology at Thessalonica," *The Future of Early Christianity: Essays in Honor of Helmut Koester* (ed. Birger A. Pearson, 1991) 107-118. **I. Hodder,** *The Archaeological Process: An Introduction* (1999). **R. A. Horsley,** "Innovation in Search of Reorientation: New Testament Studies Rediscovering Its Subject Matter," *JAAR* 62 (1994) 1127-1166; "Archaeology and the Villages of Upper Galilee: A Dialogue with Archaeologists," *BASOR* 297 (1995) 5-16; *Archaeology, History, and Society in Galilee: The Social Context of Jesus and the Rabbis* (1996). **M. Johnson,** *Archaeological Theory: An Introduction* (1999). **M. Joukowksy,** *A Complete Manual of Field Archaeology: Tools and Techniques of Field Work for Archaeologists* (1980). **L. Keppie,** *Understanding Roman Inscriptions* (1991). **H. Koester** (ed.), *Ephesos Metropolis of Asia: An Interdisciplinary Approach to Its Archaeology, Religion, and Culture* (HTS 41, 1995). **L. I. Levine** (ed.), *The Galilee in Late Antiquity* (1992). **B. R. McCane,** *Roll Back the Stone: Death and Burial in the World of Jesus* (2003). **D. Macaulay,** *Motel of the Mysteries* (1979). **W. A. Meeks and R. L. Wilken,** *Jews and Christians in Antioch in the First Four Centuries of the Common Era* (SBLSBS 13, 1978). **E. M. Meyers,** "Judaic Studies and Archaeology: The Legacy of Avi-Yonah." *ErIsr* 19 (1987) 21*-27*; (ed.), *Galilee through the Centuries: Confluence of Cultures* (Duke Judaic Studies Series 1, 1999). **E. M. Meyers and J. F. Strange,** *Archaeology, the Rabbis, and Early Christianity* (1981). **P. R. S. Moorey,** *A Century of Biblical Archaeology* (1991). **I. Morris,** *Death-Ritual and Social Structure in Classical Antiquity* (Key Themes in Ancient History, 1992). **D. E. Oakman,** "Models and Archaeology in the Social Interpretation of Jesus," *Social Scientific Models for Interpreting the Bible: Essays by the Context Group in Honor of Bruce J. Malina* (ed. J. J. Pilch, Biblical Interpretation Series 53, 2001) 102-131. **C. Orton, P. Tyers, and A. Vince,** *Pottery in Archaeology* (Cambridge Manuals in Archaeology, 1993). **C. Osiek,** "Archaeological and Architectural Issues and the Question of Demographic and Urban Forms," *Handbook of Early Christianity: Social Science Approaches* (ed. A. J. Blasi, J. Duhaime, and P.-A. Turcotte, 2002) 83-103. **C. Osiek and D. L. Balch,** *Families in the New Testament World: Households and House Churches* (The Family, Religion, and Culture, 1997). **L. G. Perdue, L. E. Toombs, and G. L. Johnson** (eds.), *Archaeology and Biblical Interpretation: Essays in Memory of D. Glenn Rose* (1987). **R. W. Preucel** (ed.), *Processual and Postprocessual Archaeologies* (Center for Archaeological Investigations, Occasional Paper 10, 1991). **R. W. Preucel and I. Hodder** (eds.), *Contemporary Archaeology in Theory* (1996). **J. L. Reed,** *Archaeology and the Galilean Jesus: A Re-examination of the Evidence* (2000). **C. Renfrew,** *The Archaeology of Cult: The Sanctuary at Phylakopi* (British School of Archaeology at Athens, Supplementary Vol. 18, 1985). **C. Renfrew and P. Bahn,** *Archaeology: Theories, Methods, and Practice* (1996²). **R. M. Rothaus,** *Corinth: The First City of Greece: An Urban History of Late Antique Cult and Religion* (Religions in the Graeco-Roman World 139, 2000). **M. Sawicki,** *Crossing Galilee: Architectures of Contact in the Occupied Land of Jesus* (2000). **D. Schloen,** *The House of the Father as Fact and Symbol: Patrimonialism in Ugarit and the Ancient Near East* (Studies in Archaeology and History of the Levant 2, 2001). **E. Schmuch,** "Exploring the Mediterranean Background of Early Christianity," *BA* 46 (1983) 43-48. **G. F. Snyder,** *Ante Pacem: Archaeological Evidence of Church Life before Constantine* (1985). **A. G. Woodhead,** *The Study of Greek Inscriptions* (2d ed., 1981).

R. E. DeMaris

ARCHAEOLOGY AND HISTORIOGRAPHY

Hebrew Bible Historiography and Biblical Interpretation

Discussions over historiography have continually played a significant if not central role in biblical interpretation. Defined as the task of every historian, the practice of writing history, the meanings produced by working histories, and as the history, theories, and principles of historical writing. History is always already built upon tradition, scholarship, and context. While some facets of biblical interpretation appear, at first glance, to be immune to issues of historiography, careful scrutiny reveals a necessary relationship between historiography and every aspect of biblical interpretation. The interwoven nature of this relationship can be seen in a survey of highlights in biblical studies research.

Early historiographers such as Alexander Polyhistor, Nicolaus of Damascus, Justus of Tiberias, and Josephus§, arranged historical events according to the order and presumed historicity of the biblical books, synchronizing them with known world events. For example, even as Josephus wrote to expound upon Judaism for a non-Jewish world, his history covering biblical periods was predominantly a paraphrase of the biblical material, a history that was then placed into the broader context of Josephus' world. While he reworked some portions to coincide with his own worldview, he maintained order and events. Later Christian writers, like Eusebius and Augustine, presumed and followed the same historical scheme. Use of biblical material did not become a historiographic issue until much later.

During the late nineteenth century, A. Kuenen§ and S. Curtiss§ presented contrasting views on historiography in relation to the Hebrew Bible. Kuenen emphasized the non-unique character of the religion of ancient Israel. He established as fundamental two historiographic issues: the appropriate use of source materials for dating and the explicit clarification of operating assumptions. In particular, he acknowledged his own historiographic dependence on the biblical material while, at the same time, stressing the necessity of testing the source material whenever possible.

S. Curtiss engaged Kuenen, particularly in Pentateuchal criticism. His concern was for what he saw as an increasing irreverence toward the biblical material that gave rise to a questioning of biblical authority. He criticized Kuenen for his reliance on science, particularly as it related to Kuenen's confidence that the religion of Israel developed naturally. During this same period, the work of first K. H. Graf§ and then J. Wellhausen§ were to have an indelible impact on historiography and biblical interpretation.

In the assessment of many, the work of J. Wellhausen made the most significant impact on historiography of ancient Israel in the late nineteenth century. Scholars today both assume and continue to respond to the conclusions of his work. Wellhausen, who systematized, schematized, and synthesized to produce a reconstruction of the history of ancient Israel in his *Prolegomena*, was clearly influenced by contemporary conclusions of literary studies, offering a synthesizing culmination of source-critical work. Although deviating on certain points, scholarly consensus still retains the general conceptualization as seen in the JEDP sequence (particularly his dating of P), his notion of cultic centralization, his generally negative view of postexilic life, his *Tendenzkritik*, his confidence that biblical material serves as a historical source even whenas it does not give a direct historical account, his tripartite division of the history of the priesthood, and his notion about covenant.

Wellhausen's work laid a foundation for much of subsequent work in biblical interpretation including form criticism, discourse analysis, narratology, structuralism, feminist interpretation, liberation analysis, ideological criticism, social-scientific studies, and folklore studies. Certainly Wellhausen's work continues to inform many of these methodologies, especially as seen in his central premise that the biblical texts serve as historical sources for the period in which they were written. One of Wellhausen's own underlying principles assists in examining his actual impact on those who use the product of Wellhausen's work. Wellhausen saw the identification of the biblical writer's presuppositions as critical in both literary analysis and historical reconstruction. Using his principle, we can see Wellhausen in almost every facet of biblical interpretation today:. Even the segments of biblical criticism that purport to be at the opposite polarity from historical criticism make historical assumptions.

The historiographical trajectory launched by J. Wellhausen, although productive for many aspects of biblical and historical studies, allows the focuses of historiography to remain on questions of historical reliability, but neglects issues relating to the theory and philosophy of history, thus limiting the kinds of history that may be produced.

The last half of the twentieth century has presented new avenues for discussion. The 1950s and 1960s foregrounded emphasized analysis and interpretation of biblical material in light of its ancient Near Eastern context and provided the forum for a classic historiographic discussion as seen in the contrast between A. Alt and M. Noth's emphasis on history of traditions and William F. Albright's qualified substantiation of the historicity of biblical material. Fundamentally, the methodological issue at hand was the appropriate starting point for writing a history of ancient Israel.

On the heels of these discussions, scholarship saw movement in several areas. Some of Albright's students accentuated the role of archaeology with both D. N. Freedman and G. Mendenhall[§] stressing the need to correlate factual evidence found in archaeology with biblical events. Later Freedman would advocate a role for philology in ascertaining the historical nature for texts and Mendenhall would advance the role of sociological methodology in developing histories.

Scholars began examining historiography in light of specific traditions, focusing attention on historiographic appropriation of source material and raising questions in particular about the patriarchal traditions and moving biblical interpretation to a different level. Soon afterward, scholarly interests and the advent of archaeology as a discipline distinct from biblical studies (forcefully and convincingly averred by another student of Albright, W. Dever) introduced the possibility of asking similar historiographic questions about biblical material traditionally labeled as historical literature (Joshua through Chronicles.) Questions of interest included issues about settlement history, an acceptable starting point for writing history, emergence of the monarchy and acceptable dating for Ezra and Nehemiah.

Issues raised in contemporary historiographic discussions can be seen most clearly in the engagements (or lack thereof) between N. P. Lemche (and sometimes associated with him, T. Thompson, P. Davies, G. Garbini, K. Whitelam, and J. VanSeters) and the traditionalist W. Dever (and sometimes associated with him, F. M. Cross and I. Provan). Lemche, having written prolifically, precisely, and often polemically about biblical historiography, acknowledges the vast contributions of previous critical scholarship to our knowledge of the history of ancient Israel while criticizing traditional, consensus-bound scholarship for presuming for ancient Israel a unilateral uniqueness bound by a common language, geography, and nationality as expressed in biblical narrative. Particularly in his *The Israelites in History and Tradition,* he calls for a foregrounding of historiographical presuppositions that, along with a critical mass of available evidence and analysis, makes new, productive, and meaningful history a possibility. The identification and use of source material remains critical for Lemche. While criticizing earlier scholarship for its appropriation of the central theme of salvation history in biblical interpretation, Lemche selects his own predominant ideology, ethnic identity. Lemche has much to offer the scholarly discussion. He raises pertinent and often helpful questions about the socio-historical context of biblical material. He calls scholars to recognize and name their tasks and methodology as historians. He recognizes operating and underlying assumptions within biblical scholarship. He tries to understand how and why biblical scholarship has tended to use the biblical material as a primary source for history and he encourages writers of history, to be deliberate in designation and use of source material. He takes issue with an assumption of ancient Israel as unilaterally unique, even as he suggests a unilateral desire on the part of the biblical authors to present an ethnic identity. He challenges his readers to evaluate whether and how it is possible to see historical Israel as it was.

W. Dever has also written prolifically about historiography and his work is no less filled with polemics. Enmeshed in recent debates over historicity, he frequently labels his academic opponents as minimalists. Still Dever, sometimes labeled as a maximalist, has at times served as a minimalist in his own right. In 1985, writing about "Syro-Palestinian and Biblical Archaeology" for *The Hebrew Bible and Its Modern Interpreters*, Dever called for an understanding of biblical archaeology as its own unique chapter of American biblical studies. He recognized archaeology related to ancient Israel as an autonomous discipline developing from the decreasing influence of colonialism, the increasing commonalities in archaeological field methods, the necessity of cooperative efforts in the areas of fundraising and recruitment of workers, and the juxtaposition of expense and intellectual sophistication for the field of study. He chastised biblical scholarship for engaging in a debate that was clearly passé. In the methodology and theory of this work, Dever presented himself as a minimalist.

Much later, in 1997, Dever historiographically analyzes the limitations of philological and theological approaches and acknowledges the values inherent in new histories of ancient Israel as found in the works of Soggin, Lemche, Miller and Hayes, and Garbini. Israelite historiography, he says, is in crisis. Instead of focusing on facts, historians must ask meaningful questions of data; these questions should include: What is history? What are the goals of history? How do we distinguish between primary and secondary sources? What are the criteria for verifying facts? What is the appropriate balance between objectivity and relativity? What kind of history do we want? He rightly asserts that biblical texts can and do provide a history of ideas. He calls on an interdisciplinary archeology to write a techno-environmental and socioeconomic history of ancient Israel.

In his most recent work, *What Did the Biblical Writers Know and When Did They Know It? What Archaeology Can Tell Us about the Reality of Ancient Israel*, Dever makes what appears on the face to be an 180° change of direction from his previous "minimalist" methodological and theoretical approach. He re-presents a "maximalist" outcome while maintaining as much as possible of his core approach. For Dever, the Hebrew Bible is clearly edited in its present form and cannot be viewed as history in a modern sense but is nonetheless filled with much history, available to the discriminating eye and obscured only by postmodern revisionists who are set on deconstruction. Dever agrees with his opponents that the biblical material is largely propaganda before proceeding to accuse them of jumping to the conclusions that there is no *real* ancient Israel. Dever acknowledges and stresses the difference between "fact" and "data". He defends the importance of context. For Dever, and for his opponents, all historians create meaning (histories) from possibilities and probabilities that can never be certainties. Subjectivity should be reduced and cannot be eliminated. The Hebrew Bible is "propaganda," a social construct. Dever is careful to remind readers that this cannot render the biblical material irrelevant.

Methodologically Dever again agrees with his opponents: the opportunity for creating effective and meaningful history comes not from discovery of new material but from an appropriate and effective system in asking historical questions; histories of ancient Israel must be based on the possibilities and limitations of texts as source; archaeology should provide a primary source for writing histories. For Dever, all evidence falls under the rubric of artifact – all evidence is therefore "encoded messages," waiting on meaningful interpretation.

Finally, Dever basically, if not fundamentally, agrees with his opponents in his conclusions about what remains when the dust of the current polemical controversy settles. We have, at the most, historical kernels available from pre-monarchical periods. We know little of a united monarchy, except that Dever says the biblical texts have a "ring of truth." For example, demographic changes occurred in the central highlands during Iron I. Historians should take an anthropological view of Saul and David as "chiefs." While Dever represents a "maximalist" position, his theoretical and methodological approach bears remarkable similarity to those often cast as his opponents, differing primarily in notions about the possibility of objectivity and in stance on Solomon.

Other important, though less polemical, contemporary historiographers include Israel Finkelstein, Baruch Halpern, and V. Phillips Long, all of whom raise the prominence of methodology in conjunction with theory and practice of history.

Although debates are heated and standing histories in stark contrast, there is considerable agreement on numerous tenets of methodology as well as a recognition that the historiography providing context for every method of biblical interpretation (implicitly and explicitly) has moved to a broader venue and increasingly seeks to encompass theory, philosophy, and practice of the larger field of history.

Probably as a consequence of these heated debates, history and historiography has not been in the forefront of biblical studies and interpretation over the last ten years. Nevertheless, biblical interpreters, whether or not they acknowledge it, use history, if for nothing else then, to provide context. Only since the turn of the twenty-first century have we seen a reappearance of histories.

Bibliography: W. F. Albright. *From the Stone Age to Christianity: Monotheism and the Historical Process: Second Edition with a New Introduction* (1957). **A. Al**t, *Essays on Old Testament History and Religion* (1967). **J. Bright,** *A History of Israel* (1959). **S. I. Curtiss**, *The Levitical Priests: A Contribution to the Criticism of the Pentateuch* (1877). **W. G. Dever**, *What Did the Biblical Writers Know, and When Did They Know It? What Archaeology Can Tell Us About the Reality of Ancient Israel* (2001); "Philology, Theology, and Archaeology: What Kind of History Do We Want, and What Is Possible," in *The Archaeology of Israel: Constructing the Past, Interpreting the Present*, (ed. N. A. Silberman and D. Small, 1997) 290-310; "The Death of a Discipline," (1995) 50-55, 70; "Syro-Palestinian and Biblical Archaeology," *The Hebrew Bible and Its Modern Interpreters*, (ed. D. A. Knight and G. M. Tucker, 1985) 31-74. **I. Finkelstein**, "The Archaeology of the United Monarchy: An Alternative View." *Levant* 27 (1996) 181-191. **I. Finkelstein**, and N. A. Silberman, *The Bible Unearthed: Archaeology's New Vision of Ancient Israel and the Origin of Its Sacred Texts* (2001). **D. N. Freedman**, "Archaeology and the Future of Biblical Studies 1. The Biblical Languages," *The Bible in Modern Scholarship* (1965) 294-312; "The Real Story of the Ebla Tablets – Ebla and the Cities of the Plain," *Biblical Archaeologist* 41 (1978): 143-64 **B. Halpern**, *The First Historians: The Hebrew Bible and History* (1988). **A. Kuenen**, *The Religion of Israel to the Fall of the Jewish State*, 2 vols. (ET, 1874-5); **N. P. Lemche**, *The Israelites in History and Tradition* (Library of Ancient Israel, Ed. D. A. Knight, 1998). **P. V. Long**, "The Future of Israel's Past: Personal Reflections," *Israel's Past in Present Research: Essays on Ancient Israelite Historiography* (ed. V. Philips Long, 1999) 580-92; (ed.), *Israel's Past in Present Research: Essays on Ancient Israelite Historiography* (Sources for Biblical and Theological Study, ed. D. W. Baker, 1999). **G. E. Mendenhall**, "The Hebrew Conquest of Palestine," *BA* 25 (1961) 66-87; *The Tenth Generation* (1973). **M. Noth**, *Geschichte Israels* (1954[2]; ET 1960); **J. Wellhausen**, *Geschichte Israels* (1878); *Prolegomena to the History of Ancient Israel* (1885).

TEXT CRITICISM, LANGUAGES, AND LINGUISTICS

Hebrew Bible Textual Criticism

Textual criticism of the Hebrew Bible can be divided into two types: (a) Literary Criticism*[§], or content criticism, and Redaction Criticism*[§] and (b) Textual Criticism*[§] of the New Testament. The main difference between the two types of textual criticism is that the text of the Hebrew Bible is generally much more remote from the event described, which in terms of textual criticism means that there were many more occasions for the text to become corrupted. Moreover, the story may be even more complicated since there may have been additional stages at which the text could have changed or suffered damage. We do not have any evidence for intermediary stages, however; therefore, all such stages are pure speculation.

This kind of introductory remark to our survey may seem somewhat unorthodox since, in the past, textual critics used to operate on the tacit assumption that a written text had always existed and that the critic could work with changes of forms and letters (as was assumed in the monograph by Friedrich Delitzch[§] on *Die Lese-und Schreibfehler im AT* 1920). To be sure, at the beginning of this century, scholars mainly held that there had been interchanges between the square letters of the type used since the Second Temple period generally and tended to ignore the fact that there could have been interchanges of letters in the paleo-Hebrew script, which, by that time, had almost disappeared. On the other hand, changes could also have arisen out of mishearings, or else copyists did not always work directly from written sources, since one may have read the text aloud and another have written it down. These considerations, however, do not acknowledge earlier stages of oral tradition.

As in any other area of scholarship, one should always ask what the philosophy is on which textual criticism is based. It is based on the assumption that our procedure enables us to find the primary text (Urtext), if we are lucky, or at least get near it. If the biblical text brings us, indeed, the message of God, that message should be retrievable in its original clarity. While in former times the textual picture suffered from theological prejudices, since the time of L. Valla[§] (fifteenth cent. sacred literature was judged in the same way as profane literature. In other words, special consideration because of the nature of a sacred text would today be unacceptable.

The beginnings of the history of textual (or lower) criticism as a discipline of biblical studies almost coincide with the changes in European thinking in postmedieval times, i.e., the period of Renaissance humanism. At that time the former theological certainties began to disintegrate, and their unique position inside the church became shaky. Part of the humanist revolution was that two additional major classical languages broadened the horizon—Greek and Hebrew. Within a few years, around 1500, clergy started using the original Hebrew text of the Bible as well as the Greek of the Septuagint[§], apart from the Latin of the Vulgate[§]. As soon as the three textual forms were available, the issue of correctness came up. The first scholar who remarked on the differences of texts was a Carmelite monk in Italy, Baptista Spagnuoli (Beato Mantovano), in his treatise *Epistola de causa diversitatis inter interpretes sacrae scripturae* (1476). The main question that emerged later was that, if the Vulgate indeed reflected the *hebraica veritas,* how was it that the Hebrew text transmitted by Jews was different? And how much could a Christian rely on the rabbis and their exegesis if these differed from those of the church? To what extent could these variants be attributed to different Hermeneutics*[§]? To be sure, in the sixteenth century, clergy hardly argued in terms of differences in hermeneutics. In general, the attitude was that Jews were suspect of having changed the text of the Bible so as to expunge any reference to Christ. Nobody cared at all in how many cases such a possibility could exist.

No sooner had this problem been solved than the church split between believers in Roman Catholic doctrine and the Vulgate and those who followed one of the Protestant denominations and the Jewish Canon[§]. Also, humanists became aware of the way the commonly used Latin had lost the elegance of classical diction and the hitherto neglected vernaculars had become respectable for transmission of the biblical message. It is no coincidence that editions of the classical biblical text were published at roughly the same time the first Bible translations (see Translation*[§]) into European languages started to appear. However, for biblical studies there was one positive aspect: The church cared only minimally about the so-called Old Testament and the character of its text. The major clashes between denominations concerned issues of cult and church custom; the question of how the mass should be celebrated was much more important than issues of the Bible text. For the church, it was the practical side that was generally of interest.

In the upheavals of the early days of the Reformation, another issue developed that had pronounced theological overtones. Protestants (each faction in its own way) refused on principle to acknowledge the superior position of what had been taken throughout the Middle Ages as *hebraica veritas,* as rendered into Latin by Jerome[§] in the fourth century (based on the hermeneutics of his Jewish teachers) which itself had undergone textual developments inside the Western church. That attitude remained significant in the subsequent conflict between Protestants and the Roman Catholic Counter-Reformation. However, it seemed impossible to assume that the message of God was beset by ambiguities, and, for centuries, textual criticism stood under the influence of inner-Christian disputes, in which the Jews played no role. Each faction mobilized evidence from Jewish sources but, due to the Jews' inferior status, only pseudonyms of Jews were allowed to appear as evidence in the ecclesiastical court.

This state of affairs continued from the sixteenth to the nineteenth centuries, when historic positivism became a major feature of European thinking. Scholars needed a model of historical development, and an idea such as "original text" was as necessary as "original language." After all, once there must have been one original text, and it was the task of the textual critic to retrieve it.

Modern textual criticism was based on the assumption that scholars had forged the necessary tools to find their way out of the labyrinth of conflicting textual traditions back to the original text from which all later textual forms could be explained satisfactorily. The foundation for all later critical work was laid in the seventeenth century by J. Morin[§] (a French Oratorian priest) with his *Exercitationes biblicae de Hebraei Graecique textus sinceritate* (1633), in which he maintained the superiority of the Septuagint and the inferiority of the MT, which he claimed had been tampered with by the Jews. Basically, this argument renewed the age-old polemic of the church. Whereas Protestants had accepted the Hebrew Bible as a secure basis, Morin claimed that the Septuagint had been taken *ex purissimis hebraeorum fontibus.* It is important that the Roman Catholic Morin praised the Septuagint so highly, and, on that basis, the Vulgate was reaffirmed in circles of the Counter-Reformation. To be sure, in the seventeenth century nobody bothered with the later Greek translations and how the available Greek text had been influenced by them. The work of Morin was not simply a new stage in the growth of textual criticism, however, but rather a mixture of critical attitude and old-time misconceptions.

Although Morin was aware of the textual differences between the Samaritan text of the Pentateuch and other texts, it is not quite clear how he viewed the position of that text. In any case, in his *Exercitationes ecclestasticae in utrumque Samaritanorum Pentateucho* (1631) he hardly dealt with text-critical issues, including only a paragraph regarding agreements between the texts of Jews and of Samaritans (1631, 230). Morin remains for many modern scholars the founder of modern textual criticism, whereas for others he is the embodiment of Roman Catholic prejudice against the MT. Because of this ambiguous position, some modern scholars prefer to view L. Cappel[§] as the real founder of modern textual criticism. In contrast to the Oratorian Morin, Cappel belonged to the French branch of the Calvinist church. Whereas Morin started off with a prejudice against the Jewish text that had become the basis of Calvinist orthodoxy, Cappel felt impelled to find out how the original text of the Bible could best be reconstructed from whatever texts were at his disposal. Cappel composed his *Critica sacra* a few decades after attacking the position of the master Hebraist of the Reformed Church, J. Buxtorf[§]. The starting point for this notorious feud was the Cappel's claim that the dominant Reformed orthodoxy had given the Hebrew vowel signs the same authority as the letters, an issue that had occupied Christian scholars since they had first encountered the phenomenon that Hebrew vowel signs are not part of normal orthography. In fact, around 1500—more than a century before Buxtorf—the most important Hebrew grammarian, E. Levita[§], had argued against the early existence of vowel signs. However, he had directed his remarks to his Jewish coreligionists, even though he was driven to the discussion by the then new guard of Christian Hebraists. Buxtorf, in his time the leading Hebraist of the Swiss Reformed Church, maintained that if vowel signs are not part of the authoritative Hebrew text, one cannot take the Hebrew vowels as authoritative. Later stages of the events that had started with the publication of the attack by Cappel—*Arcanum punctationis revelatum* (1624; subtitled *de punctorum vocalium et accentuum hebraeorum vera et germana antiquitate),* which was published anonymously though T. Erpenius as intermediary and only later under his name—are outside the limits of this survey. Since Morin and Cappel flourished almost at the same time, it makes no sense to debate whose contribution was more significant for the development of textual criticism. Suffice it to say that, although today textual criticism is often judged to be secondary in position, it was the initial step toward biblical criticism in general. Whatever the philosophical trimmings, the undermining of the Authority of the Bible*[§] began with the undermining of the integrity of its text.

A word is in order on the development of different theories with regard to different parts of the Bible. In the early stages, scholars of the Torah text were not quite aware that the division into three traditions—Hebrew, Samaritan, and Greek—only fit the Pentateuch. Actually, all three texts were different manifestations of the Old Palestinian text tradition; nobody paid attention to what a text of Babylonian provenance might have looked like.

In the seventeenth century the facts of the movement of Jewish groups during the time of the second temple were as yet not quite clear, and although the story of the Babylonian exile and the involvement of Ezra in guarding the Torah was general knowledge, the details of the movement of Jewish communities from Babylonia to Palestine were not all clear. The picture painted by Morin was not only tainted by theological prejudice but also did not pay attention to the facts of history. For this reason, the division into those three textual traditions has never been discounted until modern times.

Even in the eighteenth century, scholars still tried to determine the correct facts regarding the Hebrew text. The most representative step was that taken by B. Kennicott[§] who, in the 1770s, announced a major collation of all Hebrew manuscripts then available in European public libraries, which became the basis for his *Vetus Testamentum cum variis lectionibus* (1776-80). Kennicott believed that, since each printed Hebrew Bible claimed that it offered the correct MT, the authoritative text could only be identified by checking all manuscripts. A few years later, G. de Rossi[§] prepared another printing of collations on the basis of manuscripts and editions, *Variae lectiones Veteris Testamenti* (1784-88), followed by his notes *Scholia critica in v.t. libros* (1798). Both undertakings started off with the enthusiastic assertion that, through this collation, the correct Hebrew Bible text could be determined, yet both ended in a whimper. The reason was simple: in European libraries only rather late Hebrew Bible manuscripts were extant. Thus this great enterprise had an inbuilt flaw. The text was too uniform and no conclusions could be drawn from it. Of course, no one could realize this in the eighteenth century; the reasons only became obvious once real textual differences emerged from the Qumran scrolls Dead Sea

Scrolls§, which were over a thousand years older than the run-of-the-mill medieval manuscripts used in the collations of Kennicott and de Rossi.

Yet there was an additional fallacy that marred the work of Kennicott. Hebrew Masoretic codices are characterized by the exactitude of Masoretic notation, chiefly marks of vowels and accents. Those notations were treated rather cavalierly by Christian Hebraists. The reason for this attitude is, at present, of no importance, but the fact is that both Kennicott and de Rossi did not include notes on differences in vocalization. Such notations entered textual criticism only in the editions of S. Baer (1869-1895) and C. Ginsburg§ (1908), although only Ginsburg's edition was intended for the textual critic.

As intimated before, when the Qumran scrolls became known textual critics were at a loss at how to fit the new facts into the existing framework. Up to that time, the differing theories of P. de Lagarde§ and P. Kahle§—neither of whom had ever dealt with the raw facts of the MT—provided the framework into which textual criticism was fitted. Only the Qumran scrolls finally showed that, up to the end of the Second Temple period, there was a much larger variety of textual facts than had been assumed previously. Some texts were almost identical with what was later to become the MT, some were nearer to the prototype of the Septuagint, and still others preserved similarities with the Samaritan Torah. This diversity persisted roughly until the middle of the second century C.E.—the very time that had long been assumed to be the date of the final fixation of the Torah text, which needed stabilization so as to offer a secure basis for rabbinic halakic Midrash§.

Moreover, we must not forget that the destruction of the second temple seemed a far from auspicious time for the survival of Judaism. The textual tradition, which had suffered badly in the time of the Hasmonean wars, seemed now to be in danger of becoming completely destablilized. Thus, both external and internal reasons brought about the final effort for stabilization of the Bible text.

At this juncture, one must deal with the issue of changes in the Greek text. What is commonly known as the Septuagint referred originally only to the Greek text of the Pentateuch, the only part of the Bible whose exact text and interpretation were decisive for the strict observance of the letter of the law. Since the days of Ezra, the reading of the law had become incumbent on all adult men, but the Jews of Egypt were unable to fulfill that duty because they did not understand Hebrew. The so-called OG (Old Greek) text represented the form in which the Hebrew Pentateuch was known, at least in Egypt, around 300 B.C.E., although we have not even one piece of written evidence from that time. Due to the subsequent development of the Hebrew text, the OG had become obsolete by the second century C.E., and a more up-to-date Greek text was needed. Thus, the later Greek texts emerged, connected to the scholars Aquila,§ Symmachus§, and Theodotion§.

The question remains open as to whether these actually were separate new renderings (as assumed in the nineteenth cent.) or, rather, secondary revisions of the OG text. For this reason, one must always remember that all biblical textual criticism must be based on previous analysis by Septuagint textual criticism. In fact, the state of extant Greek manuscripts is such that there is great difficulty in reconstructing the OG text, since the manuscripts mostly contain some textual mixture. Perhaps the model of Archaeology*§ will be helpful. Just as the archaeologist has to uncover layer after layer, so also must the textual critic. And just as the archaeologist cannot be sure of the outcome, neither can the texual critic. Over the decades, previously unknown stages have been uncovered; the formerly assumed textual model has largely broken down. This is not to say that the current picture of textual development is absolutely without basis, but one has to be aware of the fact that textual history never stands still.

Since, in modern scholarship, the rules of textual criticism of sacred texts are not different from that of profane literature, the various reasons for the types of development should not be confused. Obviously, there were different reasons that finally necessitated the crystallization of one stable text acceptable to all. Thus, in discussions among the rabbis on what the text means, there was no dispute regarding the facts used by each of them.

The issue of canonization is intimately connected to the issue of the text and, in the history of modern biblical studies, has probably played a more important role than the issue of textual criticism. The stabilization of the text meant that one first had to decide which books properly belong to the recognized Jewish canon and which do not. Are such books as Ecclesiasticus§ (Ben Sira), Enoch§, or Jubilees§ included? The manner in which quotes from Ecclesiasticus are introduced in Talmudic contexts goes a long way to show that their status was in doubt. As it happened, such writings were finally excluded from the Jewish canon, a judgment taken over after the Reformation by Protestants. The most prominent document prepared by one of the outstanding early representatives of German reform was the treatise by A. von Karlstadt§ *De canonicis scripturis libellus* (1520), which was the first product of Canonical Criticism*§ and precedes all other critical statements. Much of what later became part of higher and lower criticism can already be found here.

It is no coincidence that the so-called Council of Yamnia, in the days of R. Akiba§ (135 C.E.) served as the decisive point for both the end of the canonization process and the final stabilization of the text. Long the position of modern scholars, this was in the end affirmed by the evidence of textual history, as it emerged from the Qumran scrolls. Again, it is no coincidence that the revisions of the Greek text—whether they were actual revisions or more correct new translations—lead us back to roughly the same date.

Much of what can be said about this early state of textual history fits what one can find in older literature, but much has undergone dramatic changes. The old lines between the disputants had to be redrawn; thus today the dispute between Lagarde, Kahle, and their followers only has historic importance.

Regarding other versions, the Septuagint and its derivatives served as Bible only for the Eastern church. In the West, a Latin derivative known as *Vetus Latina,* which was superseded in the fourth century C.E. by the Latin revision (Vulgate§) connected to the name of Jerome, served first. Since Jerome worked out his translation with the help of Jewish teachers in the area of Bethlehem, this version served as a proper substitute for the Hebrew Bible and was known throughout the Middle Ages as *hebraica veritas;* however, it was only with the humanist revival in Renaissance times that scholars were able to peruse the different texts side by side. Theological, not philological, differences between the texts used by the church and by the synagogue had caused long polemics throughout the ages, with Jews at the receiving end, since their social status was inferior.

Modern textual criticism deals not only with differences among the MT, the Septuagint, and the Vulgate, but also with Bible versions in other languages finalized much later, such as the Targumim§, the Peshitta§, and even the Arabic Tafsir (Arabic commentaries on the Hebrew Scriptures). This last version is of special interest since Rav Saadia's§ Tafsir dates roughly to the same time as that of the Masorah text arranged by A. Ben Asher§. In other words, it was prepared roughly at the same time as the Aleppo Codex, the earliest codex of the complete Masoretic Tiberian text, and thus can serve as corroborating or corrective evidence.

This leads us directly to this codex, which is being used as the basic text of the Hebrew University Bible and is at present available in facsimile form to every scholar. The textual critic has to be able not only to handle all primary Bible versions and deal with their history but also to deal with the intricacies of the masoretic system. Moreover, he or she should also be able to evaluate the biblical quotations that abound in the entire rabbinic literature. To be sure, in the common evaluation of various types of biblical criticism, textual criticism—not dealing with the major issues of authorship, source, history, and literature—is still thought of as "lower criticism" in contrast to other areas, which together are thought of as "higher criticism." But in spite of this terminology, textual criticism stands very much at center stage next to the inquiry into the nature of the biblical canon and its history.

Textual criticism has been at the center of exegetical endeavor for a long time, consequently its sub-areas have expanded to such an extent that, at present, there exists hardly a modern general introduction to the Bible that can still deal properly with all of them. Whereas previously most introductions included a discussion of textual criticism, today various specialized introductory treatises deal with the details. In the exegetical tradition up to the twentieth century, almost every commentary dealing with a given part of the text started off with a textual discussion leading to the interpretation of the text (of course, they were not always of the same quality). This was the system of the major commentary series in Protestant Germany and in Anglican England and often also in Roman Catholic France and Italy.

It was quite an innovation when, in 1906, R. Kittel[§] published the first edition of his *Biblia Hebraica,* which did not focus on exegesis at all but on the text. As an aid for the average student of theology, Kittel's edition did not even pretend to deal exclusively with textual facts, but mixed textual corrections based on old versions with conjectural emendation so much that the usual type of student (untrained in the exactness of textual criticism) had a difficult time differentiating between textual facts and hypothetical fiction. This basic attitude has hardly changed in later editions up to the latest *Biblia Hebraica Stuttgartensia* (1997). This mixture of textual facts and hypothetical emendations has been avoided in the latest attempt to prepare a proper text-critical edition, the *Hebrew University Bible,* which began publication in Jerusalem in 1965, with the complete volume of the book of Isaiah appearing in 1995 and that of Jeremiah in 1997. Only the future will show which type of edition will ultimately best serve biblical scholarship.

Bibliography: J. Barr, *Comparative Philology and the Text of the OT* (1968); *The Variable Spellings of the HB* (Schweich Lectures 1986, 1989). **D. Barthélemy,** "Les Tiqquné, Sopherim et la critique textuelle d l'Ancien Testament," VTSup 9 (1963) 285-304; *Etudes d'histoire du texte de l'AT* (OBO 21, 1978); (ed.) *Critique textuelle de l'Ancien Testament* (OBO 50, 1-2, 1982-86). **M. B. Cohen,** *The System of Accentuation in the HB* (1969); "Massoretic Accents as a Biblical Commentary," *JANESCU 4* (1972) 2-11. **F. M. Cross,** *The Ancient Library of Qumran and Modern Biblical Studies* (1958, 1982). **F. M. Cross and S. Talmon** (eds.), *Qumran and the History of the Biblical Text* (1975). **Delitzch, Friedrich,** *Die Lese—und Schreibfehler im Alten Testament: nebst den dem Schrifttexte einverleibten Randnoten klassifiziert: ein Hilfsbuch für Lexikon und Grammatik, Exegese, und Lektüre* (1920). **R. le Díaut,** *Introduction a la littérature targumique* (1966). **A. Diez-Macho,** *Ms. Neophyti I, Targum Palestinense* (6 vols. 1968-81); *El Targum: Introducción a las Traducciones Aramaicas de la Biblia* (1972). **A. Dothan,** "The Relative Chronology of Hebrew Vocalizaton," *PAAJR 48* (1981). **M. Goshen-Gottstein,** "Prolegomena to a Critical Edition of the Peshitta" ScrHier 8 (1960) 26-48; *Text and Language in Bible and Qumran* (1960); "The Rise of the Tiberian Bible Text," *Biblical and Other Studies* (ed. A. Altmann, 1963) 79-122; "Theory and Practice of Textual Criticism," *Text 3* (1963) 130-58; "Introduction," *The Book of Isaiah: Sample Edition with Introduction* (1965); "Hebrew Biblical Manuscripts," *Bib* 48 (1967) 243-90; "Introduction," *Biblia Rabbinica* (repr. 1972); *The Bible in the Syropalestinian Version 1* (1973); "Peshitta and Its Manuscripts," *BO 37* (1980) 13-1; "Biblical Exegesis and Textual Criticism," *Mélanges Dominique Barthélemy* (OBO 38, 1981) 91-107; "Textual Criticism of the OT: Rise, Decline, Rebirth," *JBL 102* (1983) 365-99; "The Book of Samuel-Hebrew and Greek," *Text 14* (1988) 147-61; (ed.), *The Book of Isaiah* (HUB, 1995). **M. Greenberg,** "The Use of the Ancient Versions in Interpreting the HB," VTSup 29 (1978) 131-48. **S. Jellicoe,** *The*

Septuagint and Modern Study (1968). **P. Kahle,** *The Cairo Geniza* (1947, 1959²); *Der hebräische Bibeltext seit Franz Delitzsch* (1961). **M. L. Klein,** *The Fragment-Targums of the Pentateuch According to Their Extant Sources* (2 vols. AnBib 76, 1980); *Genizah Manuscripts of Palestinian Targum to the Pentateuch* (1986). **R. W. Klein,** *Textual Criticism of the OT: The Septuagint After Qumran* (1974). **S. Z. Leiman,** *The Canonization of Hebrew Scripture: The Talmudic and Midrashic Evidence* (1974); (ed.), *Canon and Masorah of the HB* (1978). **E. Levine,** *Aramaic Versions of the Bible* (BZAW 174, 1988). **P. K. McCarter,** *Textual Criticism: Recovering the Text of the HB* (GBS, 1986). **G. Marquis,** "The Text-critical Relevance of the Three in the Book of Jeremiah: An Examination of the Critical Apparatus of the Hebrew Uinversity Bible Project Edition," *Origen's Hexapla and Fragments* (ed. A. Salvesen, TSAJ, 1997) 241-59. **M. J. Mulder** (ed.), *Miqra* (CRINT 2, 1, 1988). **M. J. Mulder and P. B. Dirksen** (eds.), *The Peshitta* (1988). **H. Orlinsky,** "The Origin of the Ketibh-Qere System," VTSup 7 (1960) 184-92. **F. Perez Castro** (ed.), *El Codice de la Cairo* (1979-). **J. S. Penkower,** "Jacob ben Hayyim and the Rise of the Biblia Rabbinica" (diss., Hebrew University, 1982). **C. Rabin, S. Talmon, and E. Tov** (eds.), *The Book of Jeremiah* (HUB, 1997). **B. J. Roberts,** *The OT Text and Versions: The Hebrew Text in Transmission and the History of the Ancient Versions* (1951). **J. A. Sanders,** "Hermeneutics of Text Criticism," *Text 18* (1995) 1-26. **P. W. Skehan,** "The Qumran Manuscripts and Textual Criticism," VTSup 4 (1957) 148-60. **S. Talmon,** "The OT Text," *CHB 1* (1970) 159-99. **E. Tov,** "A Modern Outlook Based on the Qumran Scrolls," *HUCA 53* (1982) 11-27; "The Text of the OT," *The World of the Bible* (ed. A. A. van der Woude, 1986) 156-90; "Die griechischen Bibelübersetzungen," *ANRW 2.20 1* (1989) 121-89; *The Greek Minor Prophets Scroll from Nahal Hever* (DJD 8, 1990); *The Text-critical Use of the Septuagint in Biblical Research* (2nd enl. ed. 1997). **E. C. Ulrich,** *The Qumran Text of Samuel and Josephus* (HSM 19, 1978); "Horizons of OT Textual Research at the Thirtieth Anniversary of Qumran Cave 4," *CBQ 46* (1984) 613-36. **I. Yeivin,** *Introduction to the Tiberian Masorah* (ed. J. Revell, 1980). **A. van der Koij,** *Die alten Textzeugen des Jesajabuches: Ein Beitrag zur Textgeschichte des Alten Testaments* (OBO 35, 1981). **E. Würthwein,** *Der Text des Alten Testaments: Eine Einführung in die Biblia Hebraica* (1952, 1988⁵; ET of 1974⁴ in 1979).

M. GOSHEN-GOTTSTEIN

TEXT CRITICISM, LANGUAGES, AND LINGUISTICS

New Testament Textual Criticism

Since the preserved writings of the New Testament are all written in Greek, New Testament textual criticism remains within the framework of the rules and methods worked out by classical philologists over the course of many generations. Nevertheless, New Testament textual criticism finds itself in a special situation compared with classical philology. Complete copies of texts in classical Greek literature can only be dated back to the ninth century C.E. Numerous fragments from the preceding centuries exist; however, the quality of these fragments is often questionable, making reconstruction of complete copies a very difficult task. In the case of the New Testament we have a continuous manuscript tradition, from its beginnings to the invention of printing. Three papyri are preserved from the second century (one of them, P^{52}, located in Manchester, containing John 18 from the first half of the second century, not long after the writing of the Gospel of John). Around 200 C.E., an extensive transmission of papyrus writings began. Up to the third and fourth centuries there are more than fifty preserved examples, and a total of 115 up to the eighth century. Named after those who purchased them, the most important of these are the Chester Beatty papyri—P^{45}, P^{46}, P^{47}, and P^{97}—known since the 1930s (currently in Dublin); and the Bodmer papyri—P^{66}, P^{72}, P^{73}, P^{74}, and P^{75}—known since the 1950s (currently in Cologny near Geneva). Supplementing one another, they preserve almost a complete text of the New Testament: P^{45} (third cent.) preserves large parts of the Gospels and Acts; P^{46} (c. 200) contains large parts of the letters of Paul[†§]; P^{47} (end of the third cent.) consists of Revelation 9-17; P^{66} (c. 200) retains John 1-14 still in the original book block (the rest of the gospel is preserved in fragmentary form); P^{72} (third and fourth cents.) holds 1-2 Peter and Jude; and P^{75} (beginning of the third cent.) accommodates large portions of Luke and John (up to 15:10 with few gaps).

Alongside the papyri are the so-called majuscules from the fourth century on (only five are known from the previous period) or uncials, so named because they are written in capital letters, in contrast to the minuscules (small letters) that began to appear in the ninth century. Parchment was the writing material for both majuscules and minuscules until paper came to be used in the ninth century. The latest majuscules derive from the eleventh century; afterward, the field is dominated by minuscules. There are more than 300 majuscules and c. 2,860 minuscules, along with 115 papyri, which is c. 3,270 manuscripts of texts. To these has to be added the group of c. 2,400 lectionaries—that is, liturgical readings—in which the New Testament writings do not appear in consecutive order but, rather, in pericopes divided up for church services. Thus far that makes c. 5,670 manuscripts of the New Testament, with more being discovered each year.

The extraordinary number of manuscripts is significant and points up another difference between New Testament textual criticism and classical philology: there is simply an oppressive surplus of material for the former. In addition to the Greek manuscripts, there are ancient translations (Translations of the New Testament; e.g., the Latin, the Syriac, the Coptic) that originated at the close of the second century, and the innumerable New Testament citations in the church fathers. The sheer breadth of the material presents one of the greatest and most difficult problems for New Testament textual criticism.

The same can be said about the differences among the manuscripts themselves. The manuscripts of texts were copied countless times from one another over the course of many centuries (the losses from normal wear and tear, persecution, war, fire, and other causes must be estimated as considerable). They were, at first, copied totally independently. However, from the time of Constantine on, a period when the church had won its freedom (and governmental support), the bishops were able to guide the freely growing text in a certain direction. They could choose a model text for the official scriptoria (centers for writing) they had set up, and this text served as the basis for the copies of the New Testament.

From the sixth century on, the expanding imperial Byzantine church tried to establish a uniform New Testament text. There are, for example, ornamented parchment manuscripts from the sixth century (the so-called Purple uncials N 022, O 023, φ 043, whose parchment pages are dyed purple, with the text written in silver and gold ink, as well as the Codex Rossanensis Σ 042) accompanied by numerous miniatures. Producing a normal parchment manuscript (for which many goats or sheep died) was expensive and could only have been commissioned and paid for by high church or governmental offices that undoubtedly intended it for important occasions and churches. Since all of them present the so-called *Koine*, imperial Byzantine New Testament majority text, it is clear that the text of the official church was moving in this direction; however, in spite of official support, the text was certainly not smooth. From the beginning the copiers tenaciously tried to preserve what they found in their New Testament *Vorlagen,* or source manuscripts. The medieval Byzantine church's attempt (the continuation in the ninth and twelfth cents. of a process started in the sixth cent.) to create a uniform New Testament text resulted in the overwhelming number of preserved New Testament manuscripts (more than 2,000 come from the ninth cent. and later) containing the standard Byzantine text. Still, elements of the older text, deriving from the earliest days of the church, were preserved even in these manuscripts. The older text is witnessed to by several hundred manuscripts, even if these have often fallen under the influence of the Byzantine text.

Nonetheless, one can assume that the manuscripts that emerged and were used in the fourteenth and fifteenth centuries preserved the Byzantine text. The misfortune for the history of the New Testament text lay in the fact that, in his first critical edition of the New Testament (1516), Erasmus[§] used only a few manuscripts (probably five), which he found in the library of Basel. In its five editions and numerous other reprintings, Erasmus's edition and method were directly determinative for the subsequent period. They also had an indirect effect because every edition in the sixteenth and seventeenth centuries (Colinaeus 1534; Stephanus 1546, 1550, 1551; Beza 1565-1611; Elzevier 1624-78) was based on late medieval minuscules, although their editors had access to (or even owned) old majuscule manuscripts (Beza owned D 05 and D 06!). Along with the works of Erasmus and the Complutensian Polyglot[§] (1514, pub. 1522), these editions were based on a growing number of minuscules predominantly found in their editors' environs. In the apparatus to his 1675 edition, the Oxford bishop J. Fell[§] named more than one hundred minuscules and noted readings from the ancient translations. The text of this period was called the Textus Receptus, according to the effective publicity slogan of Elzevier's second edition in 1633, which allowed the users to presume that they had before them a text accepted by everyone *(textum ab omnibus receptum),* in which nothing was changed or spoiled.

J. Bengel[§] initiated modern New Testament textual criticism as such, and, in 1725, proposed the plan for his 1734 edition. In it, the Textus Receptus served as a critical basis (he switched from one Vorlage to another), and the Codex Alexandrinus was used for the text of Revelation. The notes, which divided the readings into five categories, were decisive: three of the five categories are to be preferred to the Textus Receptus or are equally justified. An extensive commentary accompanied his decisions. Although Bengel's edition was greatly surpassed by that of J. Wettstein[§] (1751-52) in inclusiveness and penetration of the material, it continued to be influential. Bengel advanced for the first time the detailed genealogical penetration of the manuscript tradition. His overall structure was further developed by J. Semler[§] and especially by J. J. Griesbach[§], who had already distinguished the Western, Alexandrian, and Byzantine textual forms, thereby laying out the fundamental lines of the discussion still current.

The decisive turning point occurred when a classical philologist from Berlin, K. Lachmann[§], who in 1830 supported the abandonment of the late Textus Receptus, argued for a return to the fourth-century text, which at that time was the oldest form that could be reconstructed. He thus he pioneered the way for establishing the original text of the New Testament, which since then has been at the forefront of the text-critical debate. The most important textual critics of the nineteenth century were C. von Tischendorf[§], B. F. Westcott[§], and F. Hort[§]. Without Tischendorf's *Editio octava critica maior* (1869-72), it is impossible even today to work text-critically. He offered in this work all the materials (and dependably, which is not the rule in many editions) that were known in his day, including about sixty majuscules, twenty-one of which he had discovered on his journeys in search of manuscripts. The most significant of these is Codex Sinaiticus ℵ 01), whose discovery was the sensation of the century, and which, to a large extent, influenced the text presented by Tischendorf. The latter had little and only belated access to Codex Vaticanus (B 03), which had just become known to the public. With Westcott and Hort, whose *New Testament in the Original Greek* appeared in 1881, it was a different story; for them Codex Vaticanus played a decisive role.

With these two editions (as well as that of S. Tregelles 1857-72, which took a backseat to Tischendorf's because of their contemporaneity), the age of the Textus Receptus came to a close, at least in scholarly circles. It became the least valuable textual form, as had been the judgment of Bengel and Griesbach. One would think that the battle had been decided after 200 years of controversy, but the Textus Receptus was firmly anchored in the consciousness of the Anglican Church and in English-speaking areas, where it remained the official text until 1880. Even the British and Foreign Bible Society took it as the basis for their editions until 1904, when they began to use the Nestle text (see below), which had been published six years earlier. Up to that time the English Bible circulated only in the KJV. In 1881 this "authorized version" was followed by the "revised version," which ran parallel to the text of Westcott-Hort. Thus even the layperson could clearly recognize the changing situation. J. Burgon's campaign in the 1870s and 1880s against Westcott-Hort and in favor of the Byzantine text found corresponding support. It was unsuccessful, however, because textual critics were acutely aware of the secondary character of the Byzantine text: its linguistic and stylistic adjustments (which may seem insignificant to us but which were extraordinarily meaningful in the first millennium); formulations influenced by the church, with inclusions of edifying additions; etc.

In the modern period, Burgon's views are experiencing a resurgence, especially in the United States. His polemical writings are being reprinted and repeated in recent publications. Moreover, a new edition of the majority text has been presented (Z. Hodges and A. Farstad 1982), with a justification that violates all philological and historical knowledge. The proponents of this text, as had earlier generations, base their arguments on the great number of manuscripts coming from every ecclesiastical province (the bulk of them come from the ninth century and later). The main argument (which impressed many people)— that this text was the "text of the church"—is easily countered by asking, "Which church?" The answer is, of course, the Byzantine church of the Middle Ages, which is merely a historical phenomenon for us; it has no binding influence. For the textual critic, only the earliest text can serve this authoritative function. (K. Aland 1987).

The Westcott-Hort edition exerted an extraordinary influence on textual criticism late into the twentieth century, and rightly so, for the wisdom of its theoretical expositions (especially in the accompanying volume written by Hort, but even in the appendix to vol. 1 with its discussion of selected passages) is remarkable. Still, from a current perspective questions remain. Westcott and Hort explained that their edition reflects the New Testament "in the original Greek," but in fact they present only the fourth-century text (a goal announced by Lachmann fifty years earlier). Their manuscript witnesses do not go beyond that date. In order to reconstruct the text of the earlier period, they laboriously appealed to the OL and to the Old Syriac traditions, their chief support being Codex Bezae Cantabrigiensis (D 05). They believed that "the text of D presents a truer image of the form in which the Gospels and Acts were most widely read in the third and probably a great part of the second century than any other extant Greek manuscript" (1881, 149). This claim is now inaccurate, since none of the papyri, original witnesses from the second and third centuries, confirm this assumption (only two or three of them, dating from the second half of the third cent., should be considered as representing the early stages of D).

To the textual forms assumed since the time of Bengel and Griesbach—the Syrian, the Constantinopalitan (Byzantine), the Alexandrian, and the Western texts—Westcott and Hort added the so-called neutral text, represented by Codex Vaticanus (B), which correspondingly played a decisive role in their edition. However, there is no "neutral" text. Without doubt, Codex Vaticanus B presents the most important majuscule manuscript of the New Testament (this position is strengthened even more since P75 pushes its text for Luke and John back at least to the beginning of the third century or perhaps even farther). However, the theory of a neutral text is obviated by the fact that the letters of Paul illustrate a different textual character in Codex Vaticanus than do the remaining writings in the codex.

In the twentieth century the situation changed completely. For the first time, textual criticism could deal with the New Testament text "in the original Greek," specifically with the Chester Beatty and Bodmer papyri. Moreover, for the first time, the complete Greek tradition became available to textual critics. Both circumstances changed the situation fundamentally.

The publication of Eberhard Nestle's *Novum Testamentum Graece* (1898) at the Württemberg Bibelanstalt introduced twentieth-century textual criticism. This New Testament provides nothing more than an average text principle from Tischendorf's and Westcott-Hort's editions. Where divergences were involved, the edition of R. Weymouth was initially used as a standard; from 1901 on, B. Weiss's[§] edition served this purpose for deciding what belonged in the text and what belonged in the apparatus. This edition's text was not, strictly speaking, a scholarly work. Nevertheless, it acquired a decisive significance because it summarized text-critical work in the nineteenth century and because the majority principle had eliminated the unique readings of ℵ 01 (Tischendorf) and B (Westcott-Hort). This edition has dominated the New Testament scene, especially since 1904, when it was appropriated by the British Bible Society, and since Erwin Nestle supplemented it from the thirteenth printing in 1927 on with an increasingly improved text-critical apparatus. In comparison, the contemporary pocket editions of H. Vogels (1922, 1955[4]); A. Merk (1933, 1984[10]; repeated in a Greek-Italian ed., 1990); J. Bover (1943, 1968[5]); and J. O' Callaghan (1977, 1988[2]) played only a limited role because, as a rule, they allocated too much space to the Byzantine text (dependent on H. von Soden). The following editions are also worth mentioning: (1) A. Souter's first edition appeared in 1910, the second in 1947, with both being reprinted numerous times. Its significance lies in its critical apparatus, not in its text, which accommodates the Textus Receptus to the 1881 RV. (2) R. Tasker attempted to establish the Greek text underlying the NEB (1964). (3) In 1981 G. Nolli presented an edition (proceeding from Merk) that is inadequate in every respect.

Von Soden's critical text (1902-13) is currently the only completed attempt to establish a "great edition" comparable to those of the nineteenth century. Its goal was announced in the title: *The Writings of the New Testament in Their Oldest Attainable Textual Form Based on the History of the Text.*" The decisive weakness of von Soden's work is also addressed in this title. He proposed the scheme of three text types: K (Koine text, Byzantine text), H (Hesychian text, Egyptian text), and I (Jerusalem text). Where two of these three types preserve the same text, we have the archetype still used by Origen[§]. In other words, we have the original text, assuming it had not been corrupted by the influence of Tatian[§] (the Gospels) or Marcion[§] (Paul). Even in this case there are considerable doubts. The decisive weakness of von Soden's theory is his assumption of a Jerusalem text, to which he subordinated everything that did not fit elsewhere. Overlooking the fact that Jerusalem was not a great textual center and considering the facts of ecclesiastical history, some decisive consequences arise from von Soden's proposal. If K should emerge as a witness of equal value, and if two text types are sufficient to establish the Urtext, then the combination of the secondary textual form (K) with an empirically nonexistent one (I) must lead to a text that cannot be understood as the Urtext. Nevertheless, von Soden's edition has remained significant because its critical apparatus provides the most complete collection of variants, even though its complicated designations for manuscripts and its arrangement make it difficult to use. Unfortunately, it evidences many inadmissible printing errors. The volumes of this edition represent a gold mine that has not yet been fully exploited, although many sensational text-critical discoveries have been culled from it.

S. Legg's editions of Mark (1935) and Matthew (1940) were planned as competitors to the great editions of the nineteenth century, although Legg did not present a critical text, instead using the text of Westcott-Hort. The editions were so severely criticized that the publisher did not accept Legg's already finished manuscript of Luke. In its place an American-British "International Greek New Testament Project" was initiated, which, after forty years of work, presented a two-volume edition of Luke (1984-87) and later an edition of John (vol. 1, The Papyri, 1995). This work's significance lies in its inclusive apparatus, which, nevertheless, is not easy to use. The Textus Receptus was chosen as its text base; thus it must be used as a mirror image, so to speak, if one desires to reconstruct the original text. The Textus Receptus was not selected on its own merits but (long before an attempt was made to revive it) was chosen in order to keep the apparatus briefer by not listing the Byzantine manuscripts.

In comparison to the nineteenth century, changes have occurred with reference to the New Testament text. Nestle's text (through its twenty-fifth ed.), with its mechanical origin and its basis in the understanding and information of the nineteenth century, has increasingly come to be viewed in a critical light. The Württemberg Bibelanstalt (with the express approval of Erwin Nestle) commissioned K. Aland to review the existing text critically in light of new discoveries. He was already involved in this task when the American Bible Society came up with a plan to create its own edition of the New Testament for its 150th anniversary in 1966. The result was the *Greek New Testament* (1993[4], more commonly known as UBS[4]) and the Nestle-Aland *Novum Testamentum Graece* (1993[27], known as NA[27]), both edited by B. Aland, K. Aland, J. Karavidopoulos, C. Martini, and B. Metzger). Both editions have the same text; even the punctuation is identical. They differ in their critical apparatus and their goals. The UBS[4] is intended for translators. Its critical apparatus preserves two or three variants per page, which are especially important in translating; and the beginning of each apparatus item is marked by capital letters (A, B, C, D) in order to indicate the evaluation of evidence for the text. NA[27] is directed toward students and theologians; therefore, it offers many more variants in its apparatus (up to twenty or more per page). According to an agreement between the Vatican and the United Bible Societies, both editions are to be used as the basis for every translation into different languages or revisions.

Undoubtedly, the text as presented in UBS[4] and NA[27] represents a great advance over the nineteenth-century text. The new papyri were used in establishing it; other manuscript discoveries and connections made between them in the twentieth century, the new editions of the ancient translations, and the works of the church fathers were also used. Yet the "new Tischendorf" (an edition with a new text and all the evidence in the critical apparatus deriving from the Greek manuscripts, along with the ancient translations and the church fathers, all of which is necessary for the establishment of the Urtext and of major dates in textual history), which was discussed from the beginning of the twentieth century, did not come to fruition until the end of the century.

After a long time of preparation (special eds.: *Das Neue Testament auf Papyrus* 1986, 1989, 1994; *Das Neue Testament in syrischer überlieferung* 1986, 1991, 1995; special studies: *Text und Textwert der griechischen Handschriften des Neuen Testaments,* K. Aland et al. 1987, 1991, 1993, 1998), in 1997 the Institute for New Testament Studies in Münster published the first fascicle of the *Novum Testamentum Graecum: Editio Critica Maior* (ECM) vol. 4, *The Catholic Epistles,* installment 1, "The Epistle of James," edited by B. Aland, K. Aland, G. Mink, and K. Wachtel. The Acts of the Apostles will follow the Catholic Epistles as vol. 2. The ECM offers the full range of textual source materials that is of great significance for first-millennium C.E. New Testament text history, including the Greek manuscripts, quotations up to the seventh- and eighth-century Christian writers, and early renderings of the Greek (i.e., Latin, Coptic, Syriac). The ECM, therefore, presents all variant readings that emerged during the first millennium C.E. and thus allows for the possibility of New Testament research in the area of textual criticism as well as in transmission history.

For the first time in the history of New Testament textual study, the selection of Greek manuscripts has been based on an assessment of all preserved manuscript materials. In order to determine the textual value of various manuscripts, more than 1,200 test passages were studied to reveal the distinct characteristics of each manuscript. As a result, the vast majority of manuscripts appeared to be of the Byzantine type; only about 500 manuscripts contain larger portions of the ancient text and are, therefore, of special significance for establishing the original New Testament text. Those manuscripts selected through this procedure will be registered in the ECM together with their variants. The large number of Byzantine manuscripts, which are to a great extent identical, will be represented by a relatively small selection. The complete representation of textual material will not only create a new base for the constitution of the text but will also invite further insights into the history of the New Testament. Consequently, the text of the New Testament as we have it today (NA[27], UBS[4]) will be further supported, its base having become much more solid than before.

With each new installment of the ECM will appear supplementary material that will contain a great deal of information expanding the critical apparatus itself: the location of patristic quotations, details as to the readings of the ancient translations, and information about the lacunae of each given manuscript. In addition, each volume of the ECM will be accompanied by supplementary studies in which, among other things, the entire scope of the material will be assessed in a text-critical commentary. All manuscript material will be critically evaluated and further transmission-historical research will be proposed.

The text of the NA[27] and UBS[4] New Testament, as it appears to be supported by the ECM (at least in the epistle of James), profited from the decisive transformation that the twentieth century brought to textual criticism, in particular as a result of access to the early papyri but also (even if only partially) because it is now possible to penetrate the entire body of Greek manuscripts. Because of the publications of the institute at Münster, it is possible for anyone to gain access to the materials for the Catholic Epistles, the letters of Paul, Acts, and the Synoptic[§] Gospels. By using these publications, each manuscript can be compared with the others. Thus a new phase of text-critical work has begun—assuming that the experts will take advantage of the currently available possibilities. Thousands of New Testament manuscripts have not yet been studied with respect to their textual character and value. Until the late twentieth century, every judgment made about the placement of manuscripts into families, groups, etc. rested only on the manuscripts that by accident came into the hands of those who discovered them. That type of analysis is now in the past. The volumes in *Text und Textwert der griechischen Handschriften des Neuen Testaments* (K. Aland et al.) are fully neutral and consciously limited to a presentation of the evidence (see also the list of manuscripts in K. Aland and B. Aland 1989[2]).

Without reference to the previously established or hypothesized groupings, the manuscripts can be placed into five categories. Category 1 includes manuscripts of special quality, which should always be considered when establishing the original text. Category 2 consists of manuscripts of special quality, which are distinguished from the manuscripts of Category 1 by foreign influence (especially the Byzantine text), but which are important for the establishment of the original text. Category 3 includes manuscripts with an independent text, often significant for the establishment of the original text but especially for textual history. Category 4 consists of manuscripts of the D text. Category 5 includes manuscripts with a purely or predominantly Byzantine text. Readings are assigned to Categories 1-2, which have been adopted from manuscripts with an "ancient" text into manuscripts with the Byzantine text (i.e., the Byzantine text at these places has preserved the original text). This position does not deny the previous results of scholarly investigation (except for von Soden's Jerusalem text) or even question them, but makes possible a method of controlling and supplementing them while exhausting the whole material. Thus a path would be open for the systematic classification of all the evidence.

It can be said that only the Byzantine and D text-types are absolutely certain, but no longer should one refer to a "Western" text. The Egyptian papyri from the second half of the third century reveal that the D text developed in stages, and D 05 from the fifth century or its precursor presents only the conclusion of a continuing process of development. The same is true for the Byzantine text and its early manifestation, the *Koine,* which is not Lucian's[§] creation *ex nihilo.* This text also grew in stages, for it is clear that tendencies characteristic of the Byzantine text could be found in the church at an early period.

The following distinctions may be made for manuscripts preserving an Egyptian text that have heretofore had diverse designations: the Alexandrian text (e.g., P^{75} and B 03) and the Egyptian text (for manuscripts whose text came from Alexandria but especially for those infiltrated by the Byzantine text). As long as the so-called Caesarean text has not been studied extensively, and as long as it has not been discovered widely in the writings of Origen and Eusebius of Caesarea,[§] its existence remains doubtful. Its character might be demonstrated in light of the entire body of existing manuscripts.

The general fundamentals and principles of New Testament textual criticism can perhaps be summarized as follows: (1) Only one reading can be original, no matter how many variants may exist for a passage. (2) A reading is most probably original if it easily explains the emergence of the other readings (the genealogical principle). It can only be original if the external and internal criteria are in optimal agreement. (3) Textual criticism must always begin with the findings in regard to manuscript transmission. Only then can internal criteria (the context of a passage, the style and vocabulary, the theological ideas of the author, etc.) be considered, for they alone cannot substantiate a text-critical decision. (4) The weight of a text-critical decision depends on the Greek tradition, whereas transmission in the versions and in the church fathers in general only has a controlling and supplemental function. (5) Manuscripts should be weighed not counted, with the specific peculiarities of each manuscript being taken into account. No single manuscript or group of manuscripts should be followed mechanically, even if certain combinations of witnesses deserve to be trusted more than others at the outset. Instead, text-critical decisions must be made on a case-by-case basis (the local principle). (6) Variants may not be dealt with in isolation; the context of the tradition must always be considered. (7) The *lectio difficilior is the lectio potior*—"the harder reading is the preferred reading." Nevertheless, this principle may not be applied mechanically. The old maxim *lectio brevior lectio potior*—"the shorter reading is the preferred reading"—is correct in many cases, but likewise should not be used rigidly. This principle loses its force when the text of certain witnesses does not fit into the framework of the normal rules of textual transmission but, instead, constantly deviates from them because of a redactor's willful abbreviations and expansions (e.g., D 05). (8) These rules may not be applied in isolation, only in the proper combination. Experience is the best teacher in New Testament textual criticism. Anyone who has completely collated a single manuscript (preferably more)—whether an early papyrus, an important majuscule, or a minuscule—will acquire a point of view different from the person who only makes spot investigations.

Additional studies of the history of the ancient church are urgently needed. Many text-critical judgments of the past can be explained as arising from a neglect of this premise (the dating of the emergence and development of the lectionaries is typical). The textual history of the New Testament did not happen in a vacuum but, rather, within the history of the church.

Bibliography: B. **Aland** and A. **Juckel,** *Das Neue Testament in syrischer überlieferung* (ANTT 7, 14, 1991; 23, 1986, 1995). **B. Aland and J. Delobel** (eds.), *New Testament Textual Criticism and Church History: A Discussion of Methods* (CBET 7, 1994). **K. Aland,** "The Text of the Church?" *Trinity Journal 8 NS* (1987) 131-44. **K. Aland et al.,** *Studien zur überlieferung des Neuen Testaments und seines Textes* (ANTT 2, 1967); (ed., with others), *Die alten übersetzungen des Neuen Testaments, die Kirchenväterzitate und Lektionare* (ANTT 5, 1972); *Repertorium der griechischen christlichen Papyri, vol., 1, Biblische Papyri* (PTS 18, 1976); *Kurzgefasste Liste der griechischen Handschriften des Neuen Testaments* (ANTT 1, 1994²). **K. Aland and B. Aland,** *The Text of the NT: An Introduction to the Critical Editions and to the Theory and Practice of Modern Textual Criticism* (1989²). **K. Aland** et al., *Text und Textwert der griechischen Handschriften des Neuen Testaments* (ANTT 9-11, 16-19, 20-21, 26-27, 1987, 1991, 1993, 1998). **D. A. Black,** *NT Textual Criticism: A Concise Guide* (1994). **E. C. Colwell,** *Studies in Methodology in Textual Criticism of the NT* (NTTS 9, 1969). **E. von Dobschütz,** *Eberhard Nestle's Einführung in das Griechische Neue Testament* (1923). **J. K. Elliott,** *A Survey of the Manuscripts Used in Editions of the Greek NT* (NovTSup 57, 1987); *A Bibliography of Greek NT Manuscripts* (SNTSMS 62, 1989); (ed.), *The Principles and Practice of NT Textual Criticism: Collected Essays of G. D. Kilpatrick* (BETL 96, 1990); *Essays and Studies in NT Textual Criticism* (Estudios de Filogog¡a Neotestamentaria 3, 1992). **K. Elliott and I. Moir,** *Manuscripts and the Text of the NT* (1995). **C. R. Gregory,** *Textkritik des Neuen Testamentes* (3 vols. 1900-1909, repr. 1976). **Z. Hodges and A. Farstad** (eds.), *The Greek NT According to the Majority Text* (1982). Institut für neuestestamentliche Textforschung. *Das Neue Testament auf Papyrus* (ANTT 6, 12, 22, 1986, 1989, 1994). **F. G. Kenyon,** *Handbook to the Textual Criticism of the NT* (1912); *The Text of the Greek Bible* (1937). **B. M. Metzger,** *The Early Versions of the NT: Their Origin, Transmission, and Limitations* (1977); *New Testament Studies: Philological, Versional, and Patristic* (NTTS 10, 1980); *The Text of the NT: Its Transmission, Corruption, and Restoration* (1992). **F. H. A. Scrivener,** *A Plain Introduction to the Criticism of the NT* (2 vols. 1894). **H. A. Sturz,** *The Byzantine Texttype and NT Textual Criticism* (1984). **L. Vaganay and C.-B. Amphoux,** *An Introduction to NT Textual Criticism* (1991²). **B. F. Westcott and F. J. A. Hort,** *NT in the Original Greek* (1881).

K. ALAND (rev. B. KOSTER)

TEXT CRITICISM, LANGUAGES AND LINGUISTICS

Linguistics and Biblical Interpretation

1. *Introduction.* Interpreting the Bible rightly involves a significant linguistic component, since the texts of the Hebrew Bible and New Testament are transmitted to us solely in the form of ancient written texts. Therefore, Hebrew Bible and New Testament studies—regardless of whatever else they may be—are textually based disciplines. More particularly, they are written in two (or three) ancient languages for which there are now no native speakers as interpreters but only our reconstructed knowledge on the basis of these and related written texts. However, exegetes have widely and thoroughly studied these biblical texts for so long using the conventions of classical and related philology, that many interpreters today believe that the insights to be gained from study of the language of these now familiar texts are minimal. Classical philology, with its appreciation and assessment of texts from the standpoint of their artistic and literary merit, raises a different set of questions than those the linguists of the last one hundred years have come to ask.

Modern linguistics cannot be described as a single approach with one set of assumptions. Nevertheless, it reflects a different orientation to language than does classical philology (Porter 1989*b*). Several of the most commonly held assumptions are that it is empirically based and explicit (a feature greatly enhanced by the development of corpus linguistics, in which entire corpora of texts are studied); systematic in its method and concerned with the structure of language; synchronic over diachronic in its analysis; and descriptive, rather than prescriptive, in nature. As a result, modern linguistics does not focus upon the history of a language to determine its usage and is not concerned with etymologizing to determine the meanings of words (although linguistic transparency can be important). It is not concerned simply with the best authors and most beautiful texts (as is classical philology), is not simply traditional grammar with its Latin based categories applied to any and all languages, and is not incumbent upon one's ability to translate to be able to understand.

Realizing the benefits of utilizing modern linguistics in biblical interpretation requires a conscious effort. Nevertheless, there are at least two hindrances for the linguistic study of ancient Hebrew, Aramaic, and Greek. One is the fact that, until recently, many of the standard critical tools for study of these languages methodologically, if not chronologically, pre-dated the development of modern linguistics. Thus the study of these ancient languages is hindered by the lack of availability of modern resources (Porter and Reed 1992; notable exceptions are Merwe 1999; Porter 1992). A second hindrance is that much of the work of modern linguistics is based on modern languages, especially English. As a result, linguists have not, in a number of instances, applied the results of their modern discoveries to the ancient biblical texts, but have left that task to exegetes. This has clearly retarded the pace of development. Nevertheless, a number of important recent advances merit attention, including several introductory volumes (see D. Black 1988; Cotterell and Turner 1992; Croom 2003), as well as more intensive work in at least three broad areas.

2. *Advances in Linguistic Interpretation of the Bible.* Modern linguistics has been applied to biblical studies in various ways. Three categories of these advances can be conveniently surveyed to give insight into the recent work. I will briefly define each category and then select one example for more detailed presentation and discussion.

a. Morphology, Syntax, and Related Areas. Morphology is concerned with the smallest units of meaningful structure in a language. Syntax is concerned with the arrangement of elements at the level of the clause or sentence. Traditional study of language has been concerned with isolating particular units within the language, often confined to units no larger than the word or sentence, and tracing the history of their development (e.g. the development of the dative case in Greek, or the history of the prefixed or suffixed form in Hebrew). Insights from modern linguistics into morphology and syntax have increased the knowledge of biblical Greek and Hebrew even at this basic level of exploration. Recent suggestive work related to morphology and syntax include, among others, the morphology of the tense-systems in Hebrew and Greek, the Greek case system (Louw 1966; Wong 1997) and case-frame analysis (Danove 2001), conjunctions and transition markers (S. Black 2002; Holmstrand 1997), and Hebrew and Greek sentence structure and word order (Andersen 1974; Miller 1999; Shimasaki 2002; Porter 1993).

Verb structure is one of the areas that has shown the most significant research and gain in insight. The major question for researchers has been whether the verbal forms are more concerned with the time of an action or the kind of action. Traditionally, verbal forms were understood as being tense forms, as having strict temporal values (past, present, future, and various subtle combinations thereof). In Hebrew studies, Ewald (1881) and S. R. Driver (1892) revised this framework, arguing that the two major Hebrew verbal stems refer to the kind of action as either complete or incomplete. A similar progression took place in discussion of the Greek tense-forms, with the strictly temporal view giving way at the beginning of the twentieth century to the concept of *Aktionsart* ("kind of action"), which attempted to characterize the objective nature of the verbal action. In the middle of the twentieth century (and especially in discussion since the mid 1980s), more and more scholars began to see that *Aktionsart* had not gone far enough to recognize that Greek tense-forms were concerned with expressing, not the time of the event, but the author's perspective in characterizing it, by selecting a particular tense-form. In both Hebrew and Greek studies there has been some resistance to these theories, but most recent work has reinforced some form of aspectual theory for tense structure, and there continues to be refinement and further definition of what the verbal aspects mean in relation to each other and their contexts of use (e.g. for Greek Porter 1989*a*, from which this summary comes; Fanning 1990; McKay 1994; Porter 1996; for the Septuagint, Evans 2001; for Hebrew, Niccacci 1990).

The implications of this shift in perspective can be briefly summarized. One implication is a shift from seeing the tense-forms as indicating the time of an action to indicating how the speaker or writer conceives the action. Once this is established, one is able to analyze the meaningful relations between the actions or events being depicted on the basis of the verbal aspect being conveyed. A further implication is that the tense-forms are used to structure a larger unit of language and not simply to indicate a single sentence's time of occurrence (see below on text-linguistics and discourse analysis).

b. Semantics and Lexicography. Ever since James Barr's seminal *Semantics* (1961), a number of scholars have been aware of what linguists already knew—that words cannot be equated with concepts. Nevertheless, it has been very difficult for biblical scholars to rid themselves of these preconceptions, since theological presuppositions have often dictated the conclusions that some scholars have wanted to see. Traditional lexicography often relied upon etymologizing as an aid to establishing the theological significance of words, and then the entire theological framework was read into a single occasion of the word's use. This often led to numerous generalizations about not only language, but how either the Hebrew or Greek mind worked. Recent developments in lexicography (Lexicography*§, Lexicography Theory*) have the potential to free biblical scholars from these unhelpful remnants of the biblical theology movement (Porter 1996). Furthermore, these developments in lexicography have gone hand in hand with developments in semantic theory (Louw 1982; Silva 1983), that is, how it is that words mean and mean in relation to each other.

Modern biblical lexicography, especially New Testament lexicography, has been substantially helped by the development of semantic field theory. This theory recognizes that the vocabulary of any language is not ordered alphabetically as is the standard lexicon. Instead, a language's vocabulary is organized into semantic fields or domains. Semantic field theorists note that words are used, not in isolation, but within specific contexts, and that the words are used by speakers and writers to divide the world of experience, feelings, and events into the various realms that words delimit. The major difficulties with semantic field theory are establishing the fields and then quantifying the relationships of the words within them. A major step forward in lexicography of all sorts has been the United Bible Society's semantic domain lexicon (Louw and Nida 1988; cf. Nida and Louw 1992). This lexicon attempts to classify the entire vocabulary of the New Testament—treating this as a dialect of Greek—into semantic domains. Within these domains, the various lexical items are listed and glossed. This lexicon has been criticized for failing to encompass a wider scope of ancient Greek than simply the Greek of the New Testament, and for failing to include syntactical information. It also tends to categorize all words at the same level, rather than realizing that they have hyponymic relations (hierarchical relations, such as "flower" being higher in a hierarchy with "tulip" and "rose" beneath). The attempt to quantify meanings has been aided by the Spanish New Testament Greek lexicon project, which attempts to provide a schematized semantic framework for each word in the lexicon (Mateos and Pelaez 2000–). To my knowledge, no lexicon like this has been developed for biblical Hebrew.

There are at least two implications for the development of modern lexicographical tools for biblical studies: First, biblical languages are freed from the theological strictures that enveloped them in the past, so that every word was thought to be a theological cipher. Second, it is now recognized how words work in a language, both in terms of referring to entities in the world, and, perhaps more importantly, in terms of how they mean in relation to each other, that is, their specific contextual sense.

c. Text-Linguistics or Discourse Analysis. One of the shortcomings of much traditional language study is that it has confined itself to the word or to the sentence as the basic unit of analysis. The result has been an emphasis upon word studies, sentence diagramming and the like. Recent developments in modern linguistics have forced scholars to recognize that language is simply not used in this way, and that study of it, no matter how much attention it pays to individual parts of the language (and there is no denying that they are important), must always pay attention to the larger linguistic and contextual frameworks in which language is used. Text-linguistics (or discourse analysis) is a broad term that encompasses a number of methods that have been developed in order to study entire discourses. (European scholarship has tended to call this discipline text-linguistics, in some ways the better term, while English language scholarship has tended toward discourse analysis.)

There are a number of discourse analysis models that scholars utilize in New Testament studies today (Porter 1995; cf. D. Black 1992; Porter and Reed 1999): methods developed by the Summer Institute of Linguistics with its Bible translation work (e.g. Levinsohn 1992); a model from South Africa that emphasizes the colon as the unit of analysis and the logical relations among them (e.g. Louw 1987); a European model that attempts to combine semantics, pragmatics, communications theory and rhetoric into a single linguistic model (e.g., Olsson 1974; Johanson 1987; Hartman 1997); and the English-Australian model that draws upon the work of systemic-functional linguistics and applies it in a more formally based way to ancient Greek (e.g., Reed 1997; Martín-Asensio 2000). In Hebrew Bible studies, several different models of discourse analysis have also been utilized, many of them overlapping with forms of the ones mentioned above (Longacre 1989; Dawson 1994; Bodine 1995).

What distinguishes these models of discourse analysis is the attempt to find a means of discussing an entire discourse. As a result, interpreters bring much of the work of modern linguistic investigation—morphology, syntax, semantics, and pragmatics—into play, and also pay attention to larger categories of thought, such as the context of the entire work and the entire cultural context in which the text originates (Porter 1992). A fully-fledged discourse analysis is not only concerned with the smallest units within the language, but is also concerned for how these smaller units comprise ever more complex and larger units. Exegetes often turn this model on its head, so that an analyst works from the largest linguistic unit down to its constituent individual units. Researchers concerned with discourse analysis, therefore, draw upon all of the available linguistic tools in order to analyze their texts. Biblical discourse analysts have been concerned with at least three major areas of research (Guthrie 1994; Reed 1997): discourse boundaries, cohesion and coherence, and prominence. Discourse boundaries are the means by which the boundaries of a discourse, and of the individual units within a discourse, are established. A number of different features can be used, often in conjunction with each other, to indicate these boundaries. These include connecting words, shifts in person or tense-form, or lexicographical shifts. Cohesion is concerned with the means by which a text holds together. The task of discourse analysis is to discover what features are used to establish a text's cohesion. Elements of cohesion can include various lexical items, and the use of lexical items within the same domains. It can also include various morphological features that link elements, such as person endings or tense-forms. There are also a variety of connecting words, phrases or larger elements that can be used to establish cohesion. Larger patterns of usage can also be used to establish cohesion. Many discourse analysts are also concerned with the coherence of a text. If cohesion is concerned with the structural elements by which a text is held together, coherence is concerned with the ideational level, the level at which the ideas communicated make sense. The informational structure of a discourse is often important for establishing coherence. Once it has been established that one has a discourse unit to analyze and that one can establish both its cohesion and its coherence, the discourse analyst will often wish to analyze how it is that certain ideas, persons, or events are made to stand out against others in the discourse—i.e., prominence (Booth 1996; Martín-Asensio 2000; Heimerdinger 1999; Shimasaki 2002). The ways that prominence is established vary, and often include a variety of elements. These can often include use of more heavily marked tense-forms, shifts in word order and syntax that focus particular elements, and the use of redundant structures to draw attention to themselves. As one may well imagine, in the analysis of even a relatively small discourse, there is an abundance of data to consider, which must be carefully sifted for useful results.

The benefits of discourse analysis include the fact that the kinds of information that are gained from other areas of linguistic investigation, such as syntactical data, etc., are utilized in a broader and more inclusive framework. One of the hallmarks of modern linguistic analysis is that elements of a language are not used in isolation, but are seen within in their larger contexts. Discourse analysis argues that the appropriate context is the discourse. With this larger context established, the interpretation of the individual elements can then take place. Recently, corpus linguistics has argued further that another context for consideration is the largest possible corpus of texts available in that language, and as a result efforts are being made to establish such corpora for comparative linguistic analysis (O'Donnell 1999).

3. *Conclusions.* Modern linguistics is not a simple panacea for heretofore unsolved difficult exegetical questions. Neither should exegetes view modern linguistics as an optional add-on after they have exhausted traditional exegetical methods. Modern linguistics simply reflects the developments that have taken place in the analysis of language over the last one hundred years. In the same way that other social sciences have developed and been brought to bear in biblical studies, in the way that new historical data and frameworks have been incorporated in exegesis, and in the way that various theological positions have developed and been utilized, so modern linguistics must become a fundamental part of biblical study. The promise of linguistics is not necessarily that new insights are to be gained (although many new ones have already been

realized), or that it will overthrow all traditional opinions (although a number of unfounded traditional opinions have been called into question), but that it will provide the proper interpretive foundation for a discipline such as biblical studies that begins with a set of ancient written texts.

Bibliography: F. I. Andersen, *The Sentence in Biblical Hebrew* (Janua linguarum. Series practica 231, 1974). **J. Barr,** *The Semantics of Biblical Language* (1961). **D. A. Black,** *Linguistics for Students of New Testament Greek: A Survey of Basic Concepts and Applications* (1988). **D. A. Black with K. Barnwell and S. Levinsohn** (eds.), *Linguistics and New Testament Interpretation: Essays on Discourse Analysis* (1992). **S. L. Black,** *Sentence Conjunctions in the Gospel of Matthew* (JSNTSup 216, Studies in New Testament Greek 9, 2002). **W. R. Bodine** (ed.), *Discourse Analysis of Biblical Literature: What it is and What it Offers* (SemeiaSt, 1995). **S. Booth,** *Selected Peak Marking Features in the Gospel of John* (1996). **P. Cotterell and M. Turner,** *Linguistics and Biblical Interpretation* (1989). **P. L. Danove,** *Linguistics and Exegesis in the Gospel of Mark: Applications of a Case Frame Analysis and Lexicon* (JSNTSup 218, Studies in New Testament Greek 10, 2001). **D. A. Dawson,** *Text-Linguistics and Biblical Hebrew* (JSOTSup 177, 1994). **R. J. Decker,** *Temporal Deixis of the Greek Verb in the Gospel of Mark with Reference to Verbal Aspect* (Studies in Biblical Greek 10, 2001). **S. R. Driver,** *A Treatise on the Use of the Tenses in Hebrew* (1892³; repr. Biblical Resource Series, 1998). **T. V. Evans,** *Verbal Syntax in the Greek Pentateuch: Natural Greek Usage and Hebrew Interference* (2001). **H. Ewald,** *Syntax of the Hebrew Language of the Old Testament* (trans. J. Kennedy; 1881). **B. M. Fanning,** *Verbal Aspect in New Testament Greek* (Oxford theological monographs, 1990). **S. Groom,** *Linguistic Analysis of Biblical Hebrew* (2003). **G. H. Guthrie,** *The Structure of Hebrews: A Text-Linguistic Analysis* (NovTSup 73, 1994). **L. Hartman,** *Text-Centered New Testament Studies: Text-Theoretical Essays on Early Jewish and Early Christian Literature* (ed. D. Hellholm, WUNT 102, 1997). **J.-M. Heimerdinger,** *Topic, Focus and Foreground in Ancient Hebrew Narratives* (JSOTSup 295, 1999). **J. Holmstrand,** *Markers and Meaning in Paul: An Analysis of 1 Thessalonians, Philippians and Galatians* (ConBNT 28, 1997). **B. C. Johanson,** *To All the Brethren: A Text-Linguistic and Rhetorical Approach to 1 Thessalonians* (ConBNT 16, 1987). **S. H. Levinsohn,** *Discourse Features of New Testament Greek* (1992, 2000²). **R. E. Longacre,** *Joseph: A Story of Divine Providence* (1989). **J. P. Louw,** 'Linguistic Theory and the Greek Case System," *Acta Classica* 9 (1966) 73-88; *Semantics of New Testament Greek* (SemeiaSt, 1982); *A Semantic Discourse Analysis of Romans* (2 vols. 1987). **J. P. Louw and E.A. Nida,** *Greek–English Lexicon of the New Testament Based on Semantic Domains* (2 vols. 1988). **K. L. McKay,** *A New Syntax of the Verb in New Testament Greek: An Aspectual Approach* (Studies in Biblical Greek 5, 1994). **G. Martín-Asensio,** *Transitivity-Based Foregrounding in the Acts of the Apostles: A Functional-Grammatical Approach to the Lukan Perspective* (JSNTSup 202, Studies in New Testament Greek 8, 2000). **J. Mateos and J. Pelaez,** *Diccionario Griego–Español del Nuevo Testamento* (2 vols. 2000–). **C. H. J. van der Merwe** et al., *A Biblical Hebrew Reference Grammar* (Biblical languages: Hebrew Series 3, 1999). **C. L. Miller** (ed.), *The Verbless Clause in Biblical Hebrew: Linguistic Approaches* (Linguistic studies in ancient West Semitic 1, 1999). **A. Niccacci,** *The Syntax of the Verb in Classical Hebrew Prose* (trans. W. G. E. Watson, JSOTSup 86, 1990). **E. A. Nida and J. P. Louw,** *Lexical Semantics of the Greek New Testament* (SBLRBS 25, 1992). **M. B. O'Donnell,** "The Use of Annotated Corpora for New Testament Discourse Analysis: A Survey of Current Practice and Future Prospects," *Discourse Analysis and the New Testament: Approaches and Results* (ed. S. E. Porter and J. T. Reed, JSNTSup 170, Studies in New Testament Greek 4, 1999) 71-117. **B. Olsson,** *Structure and Meaning in the Fourth Gospel: A Text-Linguistic Analysis of John 1:1-11 and 4:1-42* (ConBNT 6,1974). **S. E. Porter,** *Verbal Aspect in the Greek of the New Testament, with Reference to Tense and*

Mood (Studies in Biblical Greek 1, 1989*a*); "Studying Ancient Languages from a Modern Linguistic Perspective: Esssential Terms and Terminology," *Filología Neotestamentaria* 2 (1989*b*) 147-72; *Idioms of the Greek New Testament* (Biblical languages: Greek Series 2, 1992); "Word Order and Clause Structure in New Testament Greek: An Unexplored Area of Greek Linguistics Using Philippians as a Test Case," *Filología Neotestamentaria* 6 (1993) 177-205; "Discourse Analysis and New Testament Studies: An Introductory Survey," *Discourse Analysis and Other Topics in Biblical Greek* (ed. S. E. Porter and D. A. Carson, JSNTSup 113, 1995) 14-35; *Studies in the Greek New Testament: Theory and Practice* (Studies in Biblical Greek 6, 1996). **S. E. Porter and J. T. Reed,** "Greek Grammar since BDF: A Retrospective and Prospective Analysis," *Filología Neotestamentaria* 4 (1991) 143-64. **S. E. Porter and J. T. Reed** (ed.), *Discourse Analysis and the New Testament: Approaches and Results* (JSNTSup 170, Studies in New Testament Greek 4, 1999). **J. T. Reed,** *A Discourse Analysis of Philippians: Method and Rhetoric in the Debate over Literary Integrity* (JSNTSup 136, 1997). **K. Shimasaki,** *Focus Structure in Biblical Hebrew: A Study of Word Order and Information Structure* (2002). **M. Silva,** *Biblical Words and their Meaning: An Introduction to Lexical Semantics* (1983). **S. Wong,** *A Classification of Semantic Case-Relations in the Pauline Epistles* (Studies in Biblical Greek 9, 1997).

S. E. PORTER

TEXT CRITICISM, LANGUAGES, AND LINGUISTICS

Lexicography: Hebrew Bible

1. *Hebrew and Aramaic Lexicons.* Saadia[§] compiled the first Hebrew lexicon of the Bible in Arabic early in the tenth century, but it was not comprehensive. Menaham ben Saruk produced the first complete lexical treatment of the words in the Hebrew Bible, the *Mahberet,* in Spain in 960 (ed. H. Filipowski 1854). His pupil, Judah ben David Hayyuj, determined the future shape of Hebrew lexicographyby arguing that all Hebrew word roots were triconsonantal. These three-letter roots, however, could be modified when conjugated with a weak letter or elided or assimilated to a letter with a dagesh. J. Ibn JanAh, an early eleventh-century grammarian, followed Hayyuj's perspectives in his lexicon (Arabic version, ed. A. Neubauer 1875 [HT W. Bacher 1896]), which marked a high point in medieval Jewish lexicography and remained influential into the nineteenth century.

In 1479, D. Kimhi[§] produced the most widely used lexicon in the medieval period. J. Reuchlin[§], the first major Christian Hebraist, produced *De rudimentis hebraicis* in 1506, which had enormous influence and eclipsed Pellicanus's *De modo legendi et intelligendi Hebraeum* (1504), the first Hebrew grammar written by a Christian.

The Complutensian Polyglot[§], printed in 1517 but not published until 1522, contained in vol. 6 a vocabulary of Hebrew Bible Hebrew and Chaldee (= Aramaic) prepared by A. Zamorensis. Subsequently the production of Hebrew lexicons became rather common, the most important being those of S. Münster[§] (1530), S. Pagninus[§] (1536), E. Hutter (1586), J. Buxtorf[§] the elder (1607), V. Schindler (1612; a pentaglotton that included Syriac, rabbinic Hebrew, and Arabic material), E. Leigh (1639; English rather than Latin), J. Hottinger (1661), J. Cocceius[§] (1669), and E. Castell[§] (1669). Of these, Schindler, Hottinger, and Castell drew upon comparative Semitics. The latter's *Heptaglotton,* published as an auxiliary volume to the London Polyglot, contained lexical material for Hebrew, Aramaic, Syriac, Samaritan, Ethiopic (Ethiopian Biblical Interpretation[§]), Arabic, and Persian.

Hebrew lexicography reached a new peak in the early nineteenth century. J. Ben-Ze'eb's *Ozar ha-Shorashim* ("Treasury of Roots") appeared in 1807 (1816[2], 1839-44[3], 1862-64[4]). Pride of place, however, belongs to the work of H. Gesenius[§], whose *Hebräisch-deutsches Handwärterbuch über die Schriften des Alten Testaments* (2 vols.) first appeared in 1810-12. A shorter version was published in 1815 (ET 1824) and was expanded in subsequent editions (1823[2], 1828[3], 1834[4]). In addition, Gesenius produced *a Thesaurus philologicus-criticus linguae Hebraeae et Chaldaeae Veteris Testamenti* (1829-58; completed after his death by A. Rödiger). His *Lexicon manuale Hebraicum et Chaldaicum in Veteris Testamenti libros* (1833). The latter is still in print in English as *Hebrew and English Lexicon of the Old Testament* (E. Robinson, trans.; F. Brown, S. R. Driver, and C. A. Briggs, eds., 1959). *The Hebrew and English Lexicon* (= BDB) edited by F. Brown[§], S. Driver[§], and C. Briggs[§] (1907, corrected ed. 1953, with reprints coded to J. Strong's concordance) was based on Robinson's 1836 translation of Gesenius, "edited with constant reference to the Thesaurus of Gesenius as completed by E. Rödiger, and with authorized use of the latest German editions of Gesenius's *Handwörterbuch über das Alte Testament.*" The first fascicles of BDB were published in 1891, so only limited consideration could be taken of the various editions of Gesenius published at the time under the editorship of Buhl (1895[12], 1899[13], 1905[14]). Like most Hebrew lexicons of the period, BDB classifies words according to their presumed roots or stems rather than alphabetically. However, BDB was the first to isolate and publish Hebrew Bible Aramaic words in a separate section, a practice followed by Buhl from 1895. A German lexicon similar in orientation to BDB is E. König's *Hebräisches und aramäisches Wörterbuch zum Alten Testament* (1910, 1936[7]).

Unlike most lexicons, the *Hebräisches Wörterbuch zum Alten Testament* ßzum Alten Testament by C. Siegfried and B. Stade[§] (1893) excludes references to other Semitic languages and forgoes most etymological considerations and hypotheses about primary meanings. Instead, vocabulary and idioms are the primary focus.

A new Hebrew lexicon appeared in 1953, *Lexicon in Veteris Testamenti libros* (= KB), under the editorship of L. Koehler and W. Baumgartner[§], with both German and English renderings. The *Supplementum ad Lexicon in Veteris Testamenti libros* was published in 1958, and this, together with the original lexicon, was called the second edition. The lexicon draws upon all recent Semitic study, including the Ugaritic texts (Ugarit and the Bible[§] [see Translation*]) and is organized alphabetically. The third edition of KB, *Hebräisches und aramäischen Lexikon zum Alten Testament,* begun under the editorship of Baumgartner, has now been published and translated into English as *Hebrew and Aramaic Lexicon of the Old Testament* (4 vols. 1994-98). W. Holladay published *A Concise Hebrew and Aramaic Lexicon of the Old Testament* in 1971, based on the lexicon of Koehler-Baumgartner and utilizing the material of their first and second editions and the third edition through the letter samek.

A number of other Hebrew/Aramaic lexicons should be noted. F. Zorell's *Lexicon hebraicum et aramaicum Veteris Testamenti* (1940-54, incomplete), in Latin, contains only the Hebrew portion but includes the vocabulary of the Hebrew text of Ecclesiasticus (Sirach). E. Vogt's *Lexicon linguae aramaicae Veteris Testamenti documentis antiquis illustratum* (1971) contains what was planned as the Aramaic portion of Zorell. It illustrates biblical Aramaic with nonbiblical texts and draws extensively on secondary literature. *A Student's Hebrew and Aramaic Dictionary of the OT* (1971 [ET 1973]) has been edited by G. Fohrer. *The Analytical Hebrew and Chaldae Lexicon* was published by S. Davidson[§] as a parsing guide (1848, frequent reprints). B. Einspahr (1976) and M. A. Robinson (1981) have published indexes to BDB.

Several Hebrew Bible lexicons are in the process of publication or have been published since the mid 1980s. The eighteenth edition of Gesenius's *Hebräisches und aramäisches Handwärterbuch über des Alte Testament* is being edited by H. Donner and R. Meyer (1987–). D. Clines is editing *The Dictionary of Classical Hebrew* (1990–), which is being published under the auspices of the British Society for Old Testament Study. In addition to including all ancient Hebrew texts (the Bible, Sirach, Dead Sea Scrolls, etc.) to c. 200 C.E., the *DCH* will incorporate some basic features of modern linguistics and is intended as a replacement for BDB. A new Hebrew-French lexicon (ed. P. Reymond) and a Hebrew-English lexicon (ed. J. Roberts) are in preparation (see *Zeitschrift für Althebraistik* 3 1990, 73-89), while the *Diccionario Biblico Hebreo-Español* has been published under the general editorship of L. Alonso Schökel (1994).

The Academy of the Hebrew Language in Jerusalem is preparing a historical dictionary of the Hebrew language "based on a computer-stored lexical archive of (at least) twenty-five million quotations from thousands of literary and non-literary sources of all periods of the Hebrew language covering almost 3,000 years of recorded history." The work will be based on Hebrew roots; thus far, only a one hundred-page specimen of a single root (*'rb*) has been published.

2. *Lexicons of the Septuagint.* Influenced by the Pasor's New Testament lexicon (see below), Z. Rosenback produced the first lexicon for the Septuagint, *Moses omniscuis sive omniscientia Mosaica . . .* , which appeared in 1633. Rosenback organized the words thematically rather than alphabetically. In seventy-two sections he brought together the terms according to related fields, e.g., words relating to time, parts of the body, etc. The major standard lexicon on the Greek Hebrew Bible remains the work of J. Schleusner, *Novus thesaurus philologico-criticus, sive lexicon in LXX et reliquos interpretes Graecos ac scriptores apocryphos Veteris Testamenti* (3 vols. 1820-21), based on the work of J. Biel (3 vols. 1779). A Greek-English Lexicon of the

Septuagint is currently being published under the general editorship of J. Lust. T. Muraoka has published a lexicon to the Greek text of the twelve prophets (1993).

3. *Other Hebrew/Aramaic Lexicons*. A number of lexicons not directly concerned with biblical Hebrew and Aramaic are often of service to Hebrew Bible scholars. E. Ben-Yehuda's *Millôn hallᴀ sôn ha'ibrît hayyusᴀ nᴀ h wuhahadᴀ s ᴀsh: Thesaurus totius hebraitatis et veteris et recentioris* (1908–; repr. 8 vols. 1960) is a lexicon of both ancient and modern Hebrew. Although written in Hebrew, the basic meanings of words are also given in English, French, and German.

Over the centuries, both Jews and Christians have produced numerous lexicons of postbiblical Hebrew/Aramaic. The following works are noteworthy: G. Dalman[§], *Aramaisch-neuhebräisches Handwörterbuch zu Targum, Talmud und Midrasch* (1897, 1938[3], repr. 1967); M. Astrow[§], *A Dictionary of the Targumim, the Talmud Babli and Yerushalmi, and the Midrashic Literature* (1886-1900; frequent reprints); and J. Levy, *Chaldäisches Wörterbuch über die Targummim und einen grossen Teil des rabbinischen Schrifttums* (1867-68, 1881[3]) and *Neuhebräisches und chaldäisches Worterbuch über die Talmudim und Midraschim* (4 vols. 1876-89, with supplement, *Nachträge und Berichtigungen* (1924).

4. *Word Books, Encyclopedias, and Theological Dictionaries*. These often overlap with some of the functions of a lexicon, and a number provide valuable word studies. A detailed multivolume encyclopedia of the Hebrew Bible, written primarily by Israeli scholars, is *'Ensîqlôpedah miqrᴀ 'ît: Thesaurus rerum biblicarum alphabetico ordine digestus* (ed. S. Sukenik, 1950-). More theological in nature are E. Jenni and C. Westermann's[§] *Theologisches Handwörterbuch zum Alten Testament* (2 vols. 1971-76 [ET *Theological Lexicon of the OT;* 3 vols. tr. M. Biddle, 1997]); R. Harris, G. Archer, Jr., and B. Waltke's (eds.) *Theological Wordbook of the OT* (2 vols. 1980); and J. Botterweck and H. Ringgren's (eds.), *Theologisches Wörterbuch zum Alten Testament* (1970– [ET *Theological Dictionary of the OT* 1977–]). The latter work parallels G. Kittel's[§] *Theological Dictionary of the New Testament* and provides surveys of ancient Near Eastern lexical materials relevant to Hebrew words as well as a discussion of biblical materials.

Bibliography: W. Bacher, "Dictionaries, Hebrew," *JE* 4 (1903) 579-85. **F. W. Danker,** *Multipurpose Tools for Bible Study* (1970[3]) 97-114. **G. Delling,** "Das erste griechisch-lateinische Worterbuch zum Neuen Testament," *NovT 18* (1976) 213-40. **J. A. Fitzmyer,** *An Introductory Bibliography for the Study of Scripture* (SubBib 3, 19812) 48-56. **G. Friedrich,** "Pre-History of the Theological Dictionary of the NT," *TDNT 10* (1976) 613-61. **J. E. Gates,** *An Analysis of Lexicographic Resources Used by American Scholars Today* (SBLDS 8, 1972). **H. Hirschfeld,** *Literary History of Hebrew Grammarians and Lexicographers* (1926). **R. A. Kraft** (ed.), *Septuagintal Lexicography* (1972). **J. A. L. Lee,** *A Lexical Study of the Septuagint Version of the Pentateuch* (1983). **J. Lust,** "J. F. Schleusner and the Lexicon of the Septuagint," *ZAW 102* (1990) 256-62. **E. Mangenot,** "Dictionnaires de la bible," *DB 2* (1899) 1419-22. **R. Merkin, Z. Busharia, and E. Meir,** "The Historical Dictionary of the Hebrew Language," *Literary and Linguistic Computing 4* (1989) 271-73. **C. Mitchell,** "The Use of Lexicons and Word Studies in Exegesis," *ConJ 11* (1985) 128-33. **B. Pick,** "The Study of the Hebrew Language Among Jews and Christians," *BSac 41* (1884) 450-77; *BSac 42* (1885) 470-95. **H. Schlosser,** "Die erste Grammatik des neutestamentlichen Griechisch und das erste Septuagints-Wörterbuch," *Neutestamentliche Studien G. Heinrici* (1914) 252-60. **J. Schmid,** "Bibellexika," *LTK 2* (1958) 367-70. **S. Segert and T. Sabar,** "Hebrew and Aramaic Lexicography," *Wörterbücher: Ein internationales Handbuch zur Lexikographie* (3 vols. ed. F. J. Hausmann, 1989-91) 2:424-38. **M. Steinschneider,** *Bibliographisches Handbuch über die theoretische und praktische Literatur für hebräische Sprachkunde* (1859).

J. H. Hayes

Lexicography: New Testament

1. *The Sixteenth Century.* The first person to compile a separate glossary of New Testament Greek words was J. Lithocomus (= J. Steenhouwer), who, like the editors of the Complutensian Polyglot, included words drawn from the Septuagint*§ (1552). The *Antwerp Polyglot* printed by C. Plantin (1572), on the other hand, contained a lexicon that purported to cover the New Testament as well as all Greek authors. It was not until 1614, exactly one hundred years after the printing of the Complutensian Polyglot, that the first glossary devoted exclusively to the New Testament was published. The compiler, E. Lubin, provided brief definitions of words but no references to passages where they occur.

G. Pasor produced the first substantive New Testament dictionary, the *Lexicon Graeco-Latinum* (1619), to have true scientific merit, being arranged according to word roots. The simple form of the verb was usually listed first, then all the words sharing the same stem. For the words he covered, Pasor gave the basic meaning (as well as any special meanings or uses), provided biblical references (sometimes with citations of the Greek text accompanied by a Latin translation), discussed some of the more important exegetical questions, gave grammatical information (e.g., the gender and genitive ending of nouns), listed the tense forms of verbs, provided the Hebrew equivalents for words occurring in the Septuagint, and frequently suggested the Hebrew or Aramaic word from which he thought a Greek word derived. Unfortunately, some of his derivations were rather fanciful; for example, he attempted to derive the Greek word for "head" *(kephale)* from the Hebrew verb "to double" *(kΛpal),* because the head has two eyes, two ears, and two nostrils. Despite its limitations, the *Lexicon* was enormously successful and was reprinted or revised for more than 150 years. Pasor personally revised and expanded it three times (1621[2], 1626[3], 1632[4]) and appended to it a work on etymology *(Etyma nominum propriorum* 1622). A register of Greek words listed in alphabetical order was included in the *Lexicon* so that the group to which an individual word belonged could be easily determined. The value and utility of the work was also enhanced by an index of Latin words that referred to the pages where the Greek equivalents were discussed. In addition to the *Lexicon,* Pasor also produced two popular abridgments: a medium-sized *Manuale* (1624) and a miniature *Syllabus* (1632). For both of these smaller lexicons Pasor presented the individual Greek words in simple alphabetical sequence.

2. *New Testament Lexicography in the Seventeenth to Nineteenth Centuries.* Of the Greek-Latin lexicons published in the two centuries following Pasor's pioneering efforts, the more important were those of Ludovicus Lucius (Ludwig Lutz) 1640; C. Stock 1725; J. Schöttgen 1746; J. Schleusner 1792; C. Wahl 1822; K. Bretschneider 1824; and C. Wilke§ 1841. J. Fischerrevised Stock's lexicon (1752) and Pasor's *Manuale* (1755) and judiciously assessed the strengths and weaknesses of other lexicons in his *Prolusiones de vitiis lexicorum NT* (1791), a work that greatly influenced subsequent New Testament lexicography. E. Leigh published the first Greek-English lexicon (1639). It was followed by the lexicons of J. Parkhurst (1769) and E. Robinson§, who translated Wahl's work into English (1825) and produced his own dictionary in 1836 (rev. ed., 1850).

In the latter half of the nineteenth century, C. Grimm provided the best Greek-Latin lexicon which, using the second edition of Wilke's 1851 lexicon as his basis, produced a vastly improved dictionary that was virtually a new work (1868). Among its many merits was the inclusion of textual readings found in the critical Greek New Testament editions of J. J. Griesbach§, K. Lachmann§, and C. Tiscendorf§. The second edition (1879) was translated into English and further improved by J. Thayer (1886; corrected ed., 1889), whose work served as the standard Greek-English lexicon until the second half of the twentieth century and is still often reprinted, sometimes with various enhancements (1981).

3. *Twentieth-century New Testament Lexicons*. At the turn of the twentieth century, A. Deissmann§ called attention to the importance of papyri, inscriptions, and colloquial Hellenistic Greek for New Testament lexicography. Although Deissmann never completed the lexicon on which he labored for many years, his emphasis was reflected in many early twentieth-century works on the grammar and vocabulary of the New Testament. F. Zorell (1911, 1961³), H. Ebeling (1913, 1929³), and A. Souter (1916) were among the first to use the papyri in a lexicon. The major contributors in this area were J. Moulton and G. Milligan, who ably illustrated the vocabulary of the New Testament from both the papyri and other nonliterary sources (1930).

Of the lexicons produced in this century, the most important have been those associated with the name of W. Bauer§, whose first effort appeared in 1928 as the fully revised second edition of E. Preuschen's 1910 Greek-German lexicon. The third edition of this dictionary (Bauer's second) appeared in 1937, the fourth in 1952, and the fifth in 1958 (corrected ed., 1963). Bauer shared Deissmann's conviction that the New Testament represents, in general, the *Koine* of the Greco-Roman period; to demonstrate this he cited (especially in the 4th and 5th editions) a wealth of materials from secular Greek literature. At the same time, he argued that the Septuagint outweighed all other influences on early Christian literature and frequently cited it as well as other representatives of Hellenistic Judaism.

Bauer's fourth edition was translated into English, with adaptations and additions by W. Arndt and F. Gingrich (1957 = BAG). The fifth edition was similarly translated and significantly augmented by Gingrich and F. Danker (1979 = BAGD). A sixth edition of Bauer's lexicon, edited by K. Aland§, B. Aland, and V. Reichmann, was published in 1988 and, despite its considerable shortcomings (R. Borger 1989; G. Strecker 1991), is now the standard Greek-German New Testament lexicon (= BAAR). Based on the Greek text common to the twenty-sixth edition of the *Novum Testamentum Graece* (1979) and the third edition of the United Bible Societies' *Greek New Testament* (1975; corrected ed., 1983), the sixth edition contains approximately 250 new articles not found in previous editions. Most of these stem from the increased citation of words from the apostolic fathers, the second-century apologists, the early New Testament Apocrypha†§, and other early Christian documents. Elegantly printed, it contains about a third more material than the fifth German edition and includes word-frequency statistics as well as many new references to textual variants, the intertestamental Pseudepigrapha†§, and Hellenistic Jewish texts.

Danker published a revision of BAGD in 2000 (= BGAD which incorporated the contributions of BAAR and also contained an emphasis on definition of words, greater attention to semantic field, and the placement of terms within their various cultural contexts. Such features (as well as greater attention to inscriptions and the papyri) make the BGAD more useful for addressing contemporary sociological and anthropological concerns. The BGAD is now the standard Greek-English lexicon of the New Testament.

Finally, in contrast to the standard alphabetical listing of words found in Bauer and in most lexicons, J. Louw and E. Nida produced a Greek-English New Testament lexicon (1988) in which the vocabulary of the New Testament is analyzed according to ninety-three semantic domains, which are frequently further divided into subdomains. All words that have closely related meanings are grouped together (e.g., eighty-three different words are treated in five related groups as part of the semantic domain "know"). This lexicon, which contains full descriptive definitions based on distinctive meanings of particular terms, constitutes a valuable supplement to traditional New Testament lexicons.

4. *Theological Dictionaries of the New Testament*. Although its initial articles are already more than sixty years old, the German theological dictionary edited by G. Kittel§ and G. Friedrich (= TWNT 1932-1979) and translated into English by G. Bromiley (= TDNT 1964-76; abridged ed., 1985) remains the standard against which all others are measured. Its precur-

sors include works by M. Flacius Illyricus[§] (1567), W. Teller (1772), F. Oetinger (1776), and especially H. Cremer (1866, 1902[9]), whose biblical-theological dictionary was translated into English by D. Simon and W. Urwick (1872, 1892[4], repr. 1954) and underwent a thorough revision by his student J. Kögel (10th German ed., 1915, 1923[11]). The most important work since the completion of TWNT/TDNT is the *Theologisches Begriffslexikon zum NT* (1967-71), edited by L. Coenen, E. Beyreuther, and H. Bietenhard. It has been translated into English, with additions and revisions, under the editorship of C. Brown and is entitled *The New International Dictionary of New Testament Theology* (1975-78).

Some preliminary discussions have been held about producing a new theological dictionary as a replacement for TWNT/TDNT. Such a replacement is highly desirable for a variety of reasons, many having to do with the deficiencies of TWNT/TDNT: Its articles are not only dated but are also uneven in both quality and length, the philological assumptions that underlie many of the earlier (and some of the later) articles are outmoded and problematic (J. Barr 1961), the dictionary is the product of German Protestant theological scholarship of the mid-twentieth century and does not adequately represent the interests and perspectives of other traditions and continents, and many of the articles represent an overreaction to the excesses of the *Religionsgeschichtliche Schule**[§] and operate with a bias against the relevance of Hellenistic texts and in favor of the pertinence of Jewish materials. Therefore, there is a pressing need for a new theological dictionary that will draw on the results of modern scholarship, be philologically sound, reflect an awareness of and an appreciation for the diverse theological concerns of the contemporary world, and exhibit balance in the use of Jewish and non-Jewish materials. Such a dictionary will necessarily be a collaborative effort and will take decades to produce, but efforts could profitably begin by securing the philological base of the endeavor through an extensive study of the semantic range of early Christian vocabulary.

5. *Other Lexicons and Lexical Aids.* In addition to the works mentioned in the preceding sections, the following lexicons, lexical aids, and publications are pertinent to the study of the Greek New Testament and other early Christian literature: J. Alsop's indexes to both BAG (1964) and BAGD (1981); G. Abbott-Smith's manual lexicon (1921, 1937), often useful as a supplement to Bauer's lexicons; C. Spicq's three-volume *Notes de lexicographie néo-testamentaire* (1978-82), also available in an English translation by J. Ernest under the title *Theological Lexicon of the NT* (= TLNT 1994), which contains numerous important references to the papyri and inscriptions; and H. Balz and G. Schneider, *Exegetisches Wörterbuch zum Neuen Testament* (1978-83), also available in English as *Exegetical Dictionary of the NT* (1990-93), which often contains valuable comments on New Testament terminology. Another useful resource is *New Documents Illustrating Early Christianity,* an informative series of papyrological and epigraphic studies. The first five volumes were edited by G. Horsley (1981-89) and the more recent ones by S. Llewelyn in collaboration with R. Kearsley (1992-). Horsley's volumes in the series were produced as a step toward the "New MM Project," an important endeavor (funded mainly by the Australian Research Council) that aims to produce a replacement volume for the now severely outdated one done by Moulton and Milligan in 1930. The chief investigators are Horsley and J. Lee, who are currently engaged in electronic searching (via the CD-ROM PHI 6) for documentary parallels to the New Testament, systematic new lexical analysis of the words in the New Testament, and preparation of interim entries for publication. Some of their preliminary results will be exhibited in a forthcoming article entitled "A New Lexicon of Epigraphic and Papyrus Parallels to the New Testament Vocabulary: Some Interim Entries." Other helpful texts include: G. Lampe, *A Patristic Greek Lexicon* (1961-68), which is often useful for NT exegesis as well as the study of patristic literature; and, for the Syriac New Testament, G. Kiraz, *Lexical Tools to the Syriac New Testament* (1994).

Works designed especially for those with only a basic knowledge of Greek include the following: S. Kubo, *A Reader's Greek-English Lexicon of the New Testament and a Beginner's Guide for the Translation of New Testament Greek* (1975), useful for more rapid reading of the Greek New Testament; analytical Greek lexicons, which provide a grammatical analysis of every inflection of every word occurring in the Greek New Testament and include H. Moulton's 1977 revision of a work from 1852, now entitled *The Analytical Greek Lexicon Revised*; W. Perschbacher, *The New Analytical Greek Lexicon* (1990); W. Mounce, *The Analytical Lexicon to the Greek New Testament* (1993); parsing information and grammatical analysis is provided by A. Robertson, *Word Pictures in the New Testament* (1930-33); N. Han, *A Parsing Guide to the Greek New Testament* (1971); F. Rienecker and C. Rogers Jr., *A Linguistic Key to the New Testament* (1980); P. Guillemette, *The Greek New Testament Analyzed* (1986); M. Zerwick and M. Grosvenor, *A Grammatical Analysis of the Greek New Testament* (1996[5]); some electronic programs like those produced by the Gramcord Institute; J. Greenlee, *A New Testament Greek Morpheme Lexicon* (1983), which displays the words in BAGD according to their component parts; the word studies of M. Vincent (1887), W. Vine (1900), K. Wuest (1940-55; 3 vol. ed. 1973), W. Barclay (1964) and N. Turner (1980), which provide basic information but should be used with an awareness of their limitations; and R. Trench, *Synonyms of the NT* (1880[9], repr., 1980; rev. ed. by J. Hughes and C. Hughes 1989).

Of the lexicons and lexical aids not concerned specifically with the vocabulary of early Christianity, the more important are as follows: H. Liddell and R. Scott, *A Greek-English Lexicon* (rev. H. Jones, with the assistance of R. McKenzie; 1940[9], LSJ or LSJM); the 1968 supplement edited by E. Barber has now been replaced with a new, extensively revised and expanded supplement, produced under the editorship of P. Glare and the assistance of A. Thompson (1996), that contains more than 20,000 entries and incorporates Linear B forms as well as words and forms from the papyri and inscriptions; R. Renehan, *Greek Lexicographical Notes* (1975 and 1982), two volumes that supplement LSJ; F. Preisigke and E. Kiessling, *Wörterbuch der griechischen Papyrusurkunden* (1925–), with its supplement (1969–); E. Sophocles, *Greek Lexicon of the Roman and Byzantine Periods* (1870; corrected ed., 1887; repr. 1983); the Latin dictionaries of C. Lewis and C. Short (1879), A. Souter (1949), and Glare (1982); and, for unusual verbal forms, G. Traut's *Lexikon über die Formen der griechischen Verba* (1867; repr., 1968), and N. Marione and F. Guala's *Complete Handbook of Greek Verbs* (1961).

Bibliography: J. Barr, *The Semantics of Biblical Language* (1961). **R. Borger,** "Zum Stande der neutestamentlichen Lexicographie," *Göttingische Gelehrte Anzeigen* 241 (1989) 103-46. **L. Cohn,** "Griechische Lexikographie," *Handbuch für klassischen Altertumswissenschaft* (1910[4]) 2/1:679-730. **F. W. Danker,** *A Century of Greco-Roman Philology* (1988) 43-55; *Multipurpose Tools for Bible Study: Revised and Expanded Edition* (1993) 109-47. **A. Deissmann,** *Light from the Ancient East: The NT Illustrated by Recently Discovered Texts of the Graeco-Roman World* (1927) 401-9. **G. Delling,** "Das erste griechisch-lateinische Wörterbuch zum Neuen Testament," *NovT* 18 (1976) 213-40; "G. Pasor als Lexikograph," *NovT* 22 (1980) 184-92. **G. Friedrich,** "Das bisher noch fehlende Begriffslexikon zum Neuen Testament," *NTS 19* (1972-73) 127-52; "Pre-History of the Theological Dictionary of the NT," *TDNT* 10 (1976) 613-61. R. E. Gaebel, "The Greek Word-Lists to Virgil and Cicero," *BJRL* 52 (1969-70) 284-325. **F. W. Gingrich,** "NT Lexicography and the Future," *JR* 25 (1945) 179-82; "Lexicons: II. Lexicons of the Greek NT," *Twentieth Century Encyclopedia of Religious Knowledge* (ed. L. Loetscher, 1955) 2:657-59. **C. L. W. Grimm,** "Kritisch-geschichtliche Uebersicht der neutestamentlichen Verballexika seit der Reformation," *TSK* 48 (1875) 479-515. **C. J. Hemer,** "Towards a New Moulton and Milligan," *NovT* 24 (1982) 97-123. **G. Horsley,** "The Greek Documentary Evidence and NT Lexical Study: Some Soundings," *NDIEC* 5 (1989) 67-93.

J. Kramer, *Glossaria bilinguia in papyris et membranis reperta* (1983). **J. A. L. Lee,** *A History of New Testament Lexicography* (2003). **E. Mangenot,** "Dictionnaires de la Bible," *DB* 2 (1899) 1419-22. **M. Naoumides,** "The Fragments of Greek Lexicography in the Papyri," *Classical Studies Presented to B. E. Perry* (1969) 181-202. **R. A. Pack,** *The Greek and Latin Literary Texts from Greco-Roman Egypt* (1965²). **O. A. Piper,** "NT Lexicography: An Unfinished Task," *Festschrift to Honor F. W. Gingrich* (1972) 177-204. **R. Reitzenstein,** *Geschichte der griechischen Etymologika* (1897). **H. and B. Riesenfeld,** *Repertorium lexicographicum Graecum: A Catalogue of Indexes and Dictionaries to Greek Authors* (1954). **R. Seider,** *Paläographie der lateinischen Papyri, vol. 2.2, Literarische Papyri: Juristische und Christliche Texte* (1981). **G. Strecker,** "W. Bauers Wörterbuch zum Neuen Testament in neuer Auflage," *TLZ 116* (1991) 81-92. **J. Tolkiehn,** "Lexikographie," *PW* 12 (1925) 2432-82. **K. Wachtel and K. Witte,** *Das Neue Testament auf Papyrus, vol. 2, Die paulinischen Briefe, Teil 2, Gal, Eph, Phil, Kol, 1 u. 2 Thess, 1 u. 2 Tim, Tit, Phlm, Hebr* (1994) LXVII-XC. **A. Wouters,** *The Chester Beatty Codex Ac. 1499: A Graeco-Latin Lexicon on the Pauline Epistles and a Greek Grammar* (1988).

J. T. FITZGERALD, JR.

TEXT CRITICISM, LANGUAGES, AND LINGUISTICS

Lexicography Theory and Biblical Interpretation

As the preceding history of New Testament lexicography (Lexicons: New Testament*§) reveals, biblical scholars have rarely, if ever, started from scratch when producing their own lexicons but have typically drawn upon the work of their predecessors. This quite understandable practice means that the current standard New Testament lexicon, F. W. Danker's *A Greek-English Lexicon of the New Testament and Other Early Christian Literature* (2000 = BDAG), is hardly an original or independent work. While bearing the unmistakable imprint of Danker's exegetical judgments and lexical expertise, it also marks the culmination of many centuries of biblical lexicography. That is, while Danker has based his new lexicon explicitly on the German and English versions of Walter Bauer's famous dictionary, the latter was itself heavily indebted to the labors of his predecessors and part of an ongoing lexicographical tradition.

The practice of building upon and refining the work of previous lexicographers has had both beneficial and baneful consequences. Positively, it has ensured that the keen insights and felicitous formulations of others have been preserved, and it has resulted in a rich repository of references to various ancient texts in which biblical terms also occur. Negatively, it has functioned to ensure the retention of far too many errors and faulty judgments by previous lexicographers. In his recent history of New Testament lexicography, J. A. L. Lee (2003) has emphasized the deleterious results of relying too confidently upon the "assured results" of the lexicographical tradition, and supports his claim by producing case studies of a dozen words that thus far have not been satisfactorily treated and require renewed attention in light of his discussion: *agapētos*, *akroatērion*, *anatassō*, *gynaikarion*, *dexiolabos*, *dianuō*, *eidea*, *hexis*, *kratos*, *oikonomia*, *plēn*, and *synagō*. As his analysis shows, the inadequate or flawed treatment of these terms is not an isolated occurrence but symptomatic of a larger problem. It would be easy to add to the list, as the recent discussion of *aparchē* by D. E. Aune shows (2003). In short, we should be grateful for the labors of generations of lexicographers but also recognize both the limitations of their achievements and the enormous tasks still unaccomplished.

From the beginnings of lexicography, both biblical and nonbiblical, the gloss has reigned supreme, so that the history of lexicography is largely one of glossography. The practice of glossing foreign words is reflected in the New Testament itself, where, for instance, two Semitic reverential appellations for sages are transliterated into Greek as *rabbi* and *rabbouni* and both are glossed with the single Greek word *didaskale* (John 1:38; 20:16). As these examples already demonstrate, glosses are not always literal renderings of foreign words. The Hebrew *rab* means "great" (adjective) or "chief" (noun), but rather than translating the terms literally with either "O great one" or "my master," the Gospel of John renders them functionally with "teacher." If modern Americans were to follow John's procedure, they would render the address "Your Honor" by its functional equivalent "Judge," since it is judges who are addressed as "Your Honor" in American courts of law.

In recent years, the practice of using glosses to render Greek and Hebrew terms has come under attack, with many lexicographers now preferring the semantic domains approach (Linguistics and Biblical Interpretation*) pioneered in New Testament studies by Louw and Nida (1988). Lee, for example, unabashedly supports this method, which uses definitions of terms rather than glosses. Both he and G. H. R. Horsley are using this method as they prepare their *A Greek-English Lexicon of the New Testament with Documentary Parallels*, which is intended to update and replace the classic work of Moulton and Milligan (1930). The influence of this new approach can be seen in Danker's new lexicon. Whereas both BAG (1957) and BAGD (1979) employ glosses, BDAG uses extended definitions (printed in bold roman typeface), formal equivalents or glosses (printed in bold italics), and translation equivalents (printed in normal italic type). As a result, the semantic content of early Christian terms is generally conveyed with much greater clarity than in BAG and BAGD, but Danker has rightly been criticized not only for failing consistently to follow this scheme for the entire lexicon but also for his treatment of certain entries (Fitzgerald, Roberts, Malherbe, Klauck, and Attridge 2002). It seems certain that future biblical lexicographers will make a much greater use of definitions, but it remains to be seen whether most will combine this approach with the traditional one of glosses or endeavor to use definitions exclusively.

Many of the issues in modern biblical lexicography are, in fact, unresolved problems. Chief among these is the fact that New Testament lexicons are built upon an incredibly small database of comparative evidence of how biblical words are used in other ancient sources. In the past, this evidence was slowly accumulated as scholars read through various texts and noted uses of words that were comparable to what one finds in early Christian literature. In this way, most of the important occurrences in literary and philosophical texts were incorporated into New Testament lexicons. But with the discovery and publication of papyri, inscriptions, and other ancient materials during the last century and a half, there are now literally thousands of texts that have yet to be examined by biblical lexicographers. With the advent of the *Thesaurus Linguae Graecae* and the possibility of doing electronic searches for the relevant vocabulary, a major issue now confronting lexicographers is how to systematically do this and make the results available. It is utterly beyond the ability of any single scholar to do this kind of research. In the future, various teams of biblical lexicographers will need to work collaboratively, and they must begin to make their results available in different media. Quite likely there always will be a need for printed editions of lexicons, but for research purposes, the New Testament lexicon of the future needs to be a vast repository of information that is available electronically. Yet it remains unclear how such an enormous undertaking can be concretely organized and adequately funded (Lee 2003, 177-90).

Ironically, among the neglected sources of the Greco-Roman world are the ancient lexicographers, such as Hesychius of Alexandria (fifth century C.E.). The latter, for example, glosses the noun *katallagē* with *philia*, reflecting the widespread ancient idea that "reconciliation" involves the reestablishment of "friendship" between two "enemies" or hostile parties. There is no hint at all of this in BDAG's treatment of the term *katallagē*, though it is faintly reflected in the definition offered for the verb *katallassō* as "the exchange of hostility for a friendly relationship" (2000, 521). Yet the theological implications of this meaning are enormous, for implicit within God's reconciliation of the world is the depiction of God as the believer's "friend" (Fitzgerald 2001). This points to another problem in biblical lexicography— a tendency to treat words simply as individual entities rather than as part of their larger linguistic linkage groups. That is, certain terms and ideas were closely linked both linguistically and culturally in the ancient world, and they were transmitted from one generation to another as a unit, not as isolated entities. For example, the traditional antonym of "friendship" was "enmity," so that it is not surprising that John immediately turns from the theme of friendship with Jesus (15:12-17) to its axiomatic corollary, the world's enmity (15:18-25). To be truly useful to users, biblical lexicons must not simply provide the semantic content of terms but also indicate the linguistic linkage groups to which they belong.

The famous Derveni papyrus merits discussion as a conspicuous example of a newly discovered text not yet exploited by New Testament lexicographers. This papyrus, which was written ca. 350 B.C.E., was discovered in 1962 not far from ancient Thessalonica. The papyrus is possibly a copy of a prose work by Diagoras of Melos (late fifth century B.C.E), the alleged "atheist" whom the Athenians sentenced to death for mocking the Eleusinian mysteries (Janko 1997, 2001). As R. Janko points out, "in the fields of Greek religion, the sophistic movement, early philosophy, and the origins of literary criticism, it is unquestionably the most important textual discovery of the 20th century" (2002, 1). The author of the papyrus puts forth the revolutionary thesis that all the Greek deities, such as Zeus, Kronos, Fate, Aphrodite, and Rhea, "are all one and the same God" (see esp. col. XXI.5-7; XXII.7-11) and argues that "to take rituals and sacred texts literally, rather than interpret them allegorically . . . , is to risk losing one's faith" (Janko 2002, 3). Orpheus, he says, "did not want to tell them unbelievable riddles, but important things in riddles. In fact, he is speaking allegorically from his very first word right through to his last" (col. VII.5-8, trans. Janko). So important is this text that Janko argues that it "will completely transform our understanding of the religious crisis of the time, the Greek equivalent of the Reformation and Counter-Reformation" (2002, 3). Among the theological words found in both the papyrus and BDAG are the following: *Hadēs, daimōn, euchē, theos, thusia [thusiē], hieros, magos, manteuomai, hymnos*, and *hyperetes*.

The importance of the papyrus extends far beyond the simple matter of overlapping vocabulary. For instance, the close link between ignorance and lack of belief that is found in 1 Tim 1:13 ("I had acted ignorantly [*agnoōn*] in unbelief [*apistia*]") appears also in the Derveni papyrus, where they are in fact equated (col. V.10: "Disbelief [*apistie* = *apistia*] and ignorance [*amathie* = *amathia*] are the same thing" [trans. Janko]). In addition, certain key terms are used here in the same way as they are in the New Testament; for instance, the papyrus uses the verb *hagneuo* of moral rather than ritual purity (VII.11), just as early Christians used the noun *hagneia* of moral purity. Again, BDAG (590) correctly notes that the verb *lego* ("I say") is sometimes used in the sense of "proclaim as teaching." The Derveni papyrus offers support for this claim when the author notes, "'to say' (*legein*) and 'to teach' (*didaskein*) can have the same sense" (col. X.3).

Another problem in New Testament lexicography is that in certain cases the comparative texts cited have little or nothing to do with the biblical text. For example, the Greek word *amathes* ("ignorant") occurs only once in the New Testament, at 2 Pet 3:16. BDAG (2000, 49) correctly notes that it is used "of incompetent interpreters," but the key text to which it refers readers is Plutarch, *Mor.* 25c, where we are told that the Stoics hold that "the ignorant man is completely wrong in all things." The problem is that this assertion has nothing specifically to do with the interpretation of texts but rather belongs to the standard Stoic contrast between the vicious fool and the virtuous sage, "who is right about everything." Furthermore, Plutarch himself rejects this Stoic thesis both in general and as a hermeneutical principle, arguing instead that interpreters need to recognize that virtue and vice are commingled in poetic texts. Instead of citing this occurrence of the word in Plutarch, it would have been much more useful for BDAG to have referred readers to passages where those with competing interpretations of the same text are called ignorant, even if the specific word *amathes* does not occur. For instance, the author of the Derveni papyrus refers both derisively and repeatedly to non-allegorical interpreters as those who "do not understand" (*ou ginoskontes*: col. IX.2; XII.5; XVIII.14; XXIII.5; XXVI.8; see also XX.2). Inasmuch as such people are identical to those who refuse to learn (*ou manthanousin*), they are in a state of ignorance (*amathie*: col. V.9-10) and thus "quite mistaken" (*exhamartanousi*) in their interpretations (col. XII.4-5). Allegorists such as himself, by contrast, are counted among "those who correctly comprehend" (*tois orthos ginoskousin*: col. XXIII.2) because they have deciphered the difficult riddles found in the texts of Orpheus (col. VII.4-5). Such references are much more relevant to the situation of the pseudonymous author of 2 Pet, who denounces those with alternative interpretations of Paul's letters, which, like Orpheus's texts, contain passages that are difficult to understand (3:16).

A final problem is that, in certain cases, some of the information provided by New Testament lexicons is simply wrong. In many of these instances, the New Testament lexicographer has relied on inaccurate or misleading information in other lexicons. For example, BDAG (2000,

943) claims that *stergō* is "seldom used for sexual expression" and thus defines the word in non-sexual terms as "to have a benevolent interest in or concern for" (with "love, feel affection for" given as the Greek verb's formal English equivalents). This definition fits well those instances in which the verb is used to describe the mutual affection of parents and children, but it is misleading to the extent that it implies that the word does not include the affection that is part of sexual intimacy. That the word is used of the love of husband and wife already suggests that sexual expression is implicit when this relationship is in view, and the two instances of the verb in early Christian literature cited by BDAG both deal with the love of the wife for her husband (*1 Clem.* 1.3; Pol. *Phil.* 4.2). In the latter instance, moreover, Polycarp contrasts the love (*stergousas*) that the wife is to have for her husband with the *chaste* love (*agapōsas*) that she is have for all others (loving them "in all chastity"). BDAG's treatment of the term is highly influenced by the claim of LSJ (1639) that *stergō* is "seldom of sexual love." Whatever the merits of this claim for the Classical period, it is certainly not true for the Hellenistic period, where the verb is often used of both heterosexual and homosexual erotic affection (Sider 1997, 144, with numerous examples). In Philodemus' amatory epigrams, for instance, the philosopher-poet (first century B.C.E.) praises the sexual charms of a woman by the name of Philainion in these words: "Small and dark is Philainion, but with hair curlier than celery and skin tenderer than down; and with a voice sexier than Aphrodite's she offers her all, often forgetting to set a price. May I love (*stergoimi*) such a Philainion until, golden Aphrodite, I find another, more perfect one" (*Epigram* 17, trans. Sider 1997, 122).

Implicit in the preceding histories of biblical lexicography are various presuppositions with which different lexicographers have worked and a host of theoretical issues and practical problems that they have confronted. These have ranged from diverse assumptions about the nature of the biblical languages to differing judgments about the importance of providing etymologies for biblical words and of including vocabulary from texts that are not part of the Hebrew Bible (such as Sirach) or of the New Testament (such as the Apostolic Fathers). Although scholars of both Testaments share certain challenges and opportunities (e.g., how best to incorporate ideas derived from modern linguistic theory), they also must deal with issues, problems, and needs that are particular to their own discipline and to the texts with which they work.

For example, whereas New Testament scholars and students have in F. W. Danker's *A Greek-English Lexicon of the New Testament and Other Early Christian Literature* (= BDAG; an indispensable one-volume lexicon that was published in 2000) the standard one-volume Hebrew-English lexicon remains BDB. The first fascicles of the latter were published in 1891, with the entire lexicon initially appearing in 1907. Therefore, portions of BDB are already more than one hundred years old and this will soon be the case for the lexicon as a whole. As these facts suggest, BDB reflects the scholarship of the late nineteenth century and contains no references to the many Semitic texts (such as the Dead Sea Scrolls) discovered since its publication. But BDB is, in fact, even more dated, based as it is on the 1836 English translation of H. Gesenius' lexicon. Consequently, there is a pressing need for a new one-volume English lexicon of the Hebrew and Aramaic vocabulary that occurs in the Bible and in texts relevant to biblical study.

As far as multi-volume lexicons are concerned, the situation is reversed. Whereas there is no multi-volume equivalent of BDAG available for students of the New Testament, there are two such lexicons for Hebrew Bible scholars. These are *The Hebrew and Aramaic Lexicon of the Old Testament* (= HALOT), which is the English translation (1994-2000) of the work by L. Koehler and W. Baumgartner, and *The Dictionary of Classical Hebrew* (= DCH), which is being edited by D. Clines (1993–). Both lexicons capitalize on advances made in Semitic linguistics and take into account the readings of the Dead Sea Scrolls, yet they are quite different in terms of conception and content. *DCH* makes an extensive use of both semantic and syntagmatic analyses, indicating, for example, what nouns are used as the objects of particular verbs. Although such an analysis can be extremely helpful when dealing with a specific author or texts from the same time period, it is less helpful and often misleading when dealing with a language that develops over time and undergoes a number of changes. Because *DCH* presupposes that Hebrew is a synchronic rather than a diachronic language, it has rightly been criticized as fundamentally flawed in this respect (Vaughn 2002). *HALOT*, by contrast, treats Hebrew as a diachronic language and consistently relates Hebrew lexemes to their Semitic cognates. As a result, it is perhaps most helpful with regard to words that occur infrequently, especially the numerous *hapax legomena* (i.e., words that occur only once), which pose a special problem for lexicographers of the Hebrew Bible. In addition, this five-volume work is now conveniently available on CD-ROM (2001) and in an unabridged two-volume study edition (2001).

Just as Gesenius's lexicon has exercised an enormous influence on Hebrew lexicography (Miller 1927), the lexicons produced by earlier generations of New Testament scholars have left their mark on subsequent works. Indeed, as the preceding history of New Testament lexicography reveals, biblical scholars have rarely, if ever, started from scratch when producing their own lexicons but have typically drawn upon the work of their predecessors. This quite understandable practice means that BDAG, the current standard New Testament lexicon, is hardly an original or independent work. While bearing the unmistakable imprint of Danker's exegetical judgments and lexical expertise, it also marks the culmination of many centuries of biblical lexicography. That is, while Danker has based his new lexicon explicitly on the German and English versions of W. Bauer's famous dictionary, the latter was itself heavily indebted to the labors of his predecessors and part of an ongoing lexicographical tradition.

In conclusion, biblical lexicography is an ongoing tradition, with any given lexicon such as BDAG a cumulative product. Like most things inherited from earlier generations, it contains much of value but also things that need to be discarded and redone. To do so with industry and insight is the task of lexicographers in the new millennium.

Bibliography: D. E. Aune, "Distinct Lexical Meanings of *aparche* in Hellenism, Judaism, and Early Christianity," *Early Christianity and Classical Culture* (ed. J. T. Fitzgerald, T. H. Olbricht, and L. M. White, 2003) 103-29. **J. T. Fitzgerald**, "Paul and Paradigm Shifts: Reconciliation and Its Linkage Group," *Paul Beyond the Judaism/Hellenism Divide* (ed. T. Engberg-Pedersen, 2001) 241-62, 316-25. **J. Fitzgerald, T. Roberts, A. J. Malherbe, H. -J. Klauck, and H. W. Attridge**, review of F. W. Danker (ed.), *A Greek-English Lexicon of the New Testament and Other Early Christian Literature*, Third Edition (BDAG), *RBL* (2002) 33-59. **R. Janko**, "The Physicist as Hierophant: Aristophanes, Socrates and the Authorship of the Derveni Papyrus," *ZPE* 118 (1997) 61-94; "The Derveni Papyrus (Diagoras of Melos, *Apopyrgizontes logoi*?): A New Translation," *CP* 96 (2001) 1-32; "The Derveni Papyrus: An Interim Text," *ZPE* 141 (2002) 1-62. **J. A. L. Lee**, *A History of New Testament Lexicography* (2003). **E. F. Miller**, *The Influence of Gesenius on Hebrew Lexicography* (1927). **D. Sider**, *The Epigrams of Philodemos* (1997). **A. G. Vaughn**, review of vol. 4 of L. Koehler and W. Baumgartner (eds.), *The Hebrew and Aramaic Lexicon of the Old Testament*, *RBL* (2002) 138-40.

J. T. FITZGERALD

TEXT CRITICISM, LANGUAGES, AND LINGUISTICS

Translation

Translation is both the science and the art that attempts to represent, with the least possible distortion, the meaning and the impact of a text in a language different from the one in which it was originally written. For Bible translation, this process involves not only ancient languages vastly different from most modern languages, but also (and more importantly) ancient cultures that have little in common with modern cultures.

The King James translators (1611) expressed the matter eloquently: "Translation it is that openeth the window to let in the light; that breaketh the shell, that we may eat the kernel; that putteth aside the curtain, that we may look into the most Holy place; that removeth the cover of the well, that we may come by the water."

A translation aims at an impossible goal—namely, to make it possible for the readers of the translated text to understand it in the same way that the readers of the original understood their text. Not only that: The translator also wants the readers of the translation to react to it as did the readers of the original. It is obvious that this cannot be done. E. Goodspeed§ expressed it well in the preface of his translation of the New Testament (1923): "It has been truly said that any translation of a masterpiece must be a failure." The tractate *Kiddushin 49a* of the Babylonian Talmud*§ succinctly states the translator's dilemma: "He lies, who renders a verse as it is, with strict literalness; he blasphemes, who makes additions." And the grandson of Ben Sira, translating his grandfather's book, Ecclesiasticus†§, from Hebrew to Greek, begged the reader's indulgence: "You are invited therefore to read it with goodwill and attention, and to be indulgent in cases where, despite our diligence in translating, we may seem to have rendered some phrases imperfectly. For what was originally expressed in Hebrew does not have exactly the same sense when translated into another language. Not only this book, but even the Law itself, the Prophets, and the rest of the books differ not a little when read in the original."

A translator wants, above everything else, to be faithful to the meaning and impact of the original text, vowing to translate the text, the whole text, and nothing but the text. How is this vow kept? What are the contemporary issues involved in keeping this vow?

1. *The Task of Translation.* The Bible translator's task is threefold: to determine the form of the original text, to ascertain the meaning of the original text, and to transfer the meaning to the target language in such a way that the readers of the translation understand it as did the readers of the original.

a. The biblical text. There is general agreement on the form of the biblical text. For Jewish and Christian translators, the BHS (1990) is widely regarded as the best available edition of the standard Hebrew text, the MT. This does not mean that the MT will be slavishly followed at all times. In a book like 1 Samuel, for example, modern translations, largely on the basis of the Qumran texts (see Dead Sea Scrolls§), freely depart from the MT. One recent count showed that while the NIV departs from the MT only fifteen times, the NAB departs 230 times. In between come the GNB (fifty-one times), the NRSV (110 times), and the NEB (160 times). The NRSV's inclusion at the end of 1 Samuel 10 of a fairly long passage from a Qumran manuscript is an example of such a departure.

The MT copyists often placed in the margin a reading that they thought should replace the text. The marginal reading was called *qere* ("to be read"); the text, *kethiv* ("it is written"). There are around 1,300 such marginal notes. In addition, there is what is called the *qere perpetuum*— that is, the marginal "the Lord" to be read instead of the text's YHWH, the holy name of God, a total of 6,283 times. Traditionally, Bible translations, including the NRSV and the NIV, have preferred the *kethiv*, usually in the form of small capital letters (the LORD). But the ASV, the various editions of the Jerusalem Bible (French, English, Spanish, Portuguese), and a number of Bibles in Portuguese, Spanish, and other languages all use a form of the tetragrammaton: Jehovah, Yahweh, Jav, or Iahwe. It seems certain that future translations will continue to differ on this translation.

Translators also differ in their handling of the *tiqqune sopherim* (the corrections of the scribes), passages in which scribes deliberately changed texts that seemed offensive to God (traditionally there were eighteen such passages). In Gen 18:22, for example, the text read: "Yahweh continued to stand before Abraham"; this was changed to "Abraham continued to stand before Yahweh." Psalm 106:20 was changed from "they exchanged the glory of God" to "they exchanged their glory"; and in Job 32:3, the change was made from "they declared God to be wrong" to "they declared Job to be wrong."

The Greek Orthodox Church still prefers the Septuagint§ for the Hebrew Bible and the Greek Textus Receptus for the New Testament. The Syriac churches hold to the Syriac Peshitta§ (fifth century C.E.) as their Bible.

For the New Testament, the vast majority of translators use the United Bible Societies' *Greek New Testament* (1993⁴), whose text is the same as that of the Nestle-Aland *Greek New Testament* (1993²⁷). But there are many passages in which important witnesses to the text vary; in such passages the UBS text provides variant readings and rates them according to the degree of probability that the preferred variant is correct. The rating varies from A (the text is certain) to D (the committee had great difficulty deciding which text is original). In such instances (especially in passages that are rated C and D) a translator may prefer a variant reading. In John 7:8 did Jesus say to his brothers, "I am not [*ouk*] going to this festival" or "I am not yet [*oupo*] going to this festival"?

b. The meaning of the text. There is widespread consensus on the meaning of the greater part of the biblical text. Differences of opinion will always exist as to the intent and meaning of a given passage—what else explains the appearance, almost yearly it seems, of a new set of commentaries and additional biblical Dictionaries and Encyclopedias§? But agreement does prevail about the surface meaning of the greater part of the text, as a comparison of any number of modern translations will show. Some passages, however, are not easily exegeted. What does the first verse of the Bible mean? Most translations will say it means: "In the beginning God created the heavens and the earth." Other translations, however, such as the NRSV and the NJV (the Tanakh), take it to mean "when God began to create the heavens and the earth."

c. Translating the text. This is the translator's most daunting task. At first sight it might appear to be very simple indeed. All the translator has to do is to ascertain the meaning of the biblical text and then express that meaning in the target language in such a way that the readers will understand the text in the same way that the readers of the original did. To take one of the simplest passages in the Greek New Testament, the opening words of the Gospel of John, "In the beginning was the Word." Will today's English-speaking reader understand "the Word" in the same way as did the original readers of the Greek *ho logos*? Most likely not. And how can a modern businesswoman in Melbourne, London, or New York, truly comprehend Ps 23:1, "The LORD is my shepherd"?

R. Knox expressed it thus: "A translation is a good one in proportion as you can forget, while reading it, that it is a translation at all" (1949, 94). And the English man of letters H. Belloc defined translation as "the resurrection of an alien thing in a native body; not the dressing up of it in native clothes, but the giving to it of native flesh and blood."

Semantic differences are difficult to solve. Languages work in a variety of ways, and a translator has to be aware of the differences between the biblical languages and the target language. Rhetorical questions, however, are a fairly simple problem to overcome. The question, "Did I not choose you, the twelve?" (John 6:70), if translated literally in many languages, will mean that Jesus in fact did not choose the twelve. In such cases, the translation must express the meaning with a statement, "I chose you, the twelve."

Figures of speech must be handled with care. Many biblical figures of speech are part of current language for native speakers of English—"a hard heart," "an evil eye," "Abraham's bosom," "the salt of the earth"—but the biblical meaning of these figures is quite different from the meaning assigned them in current English. The widely used NIV still conserves the figure "the horn of salvation" (2 Sam 22:3; Ps 18:2; Luke 1:69) as well as "He will . . . exalt the horn of his anointed" (1 Sam 2:10). Does the reader of this translation have a clear notion of what the writer is talking about? And what does the reader of the NRSV make of the statement that the distance between the Mount of Olives and Jerusalem was "a sabbath day's journey" (Acts 1:12)?

Cultural equivalents have to be provided in languages where biblical cultural items are unknown. In Isa 1:18 God promises the people that their sins "will be like snow...will be like wool." In areas of the world where snow is unknown, a cultural equivalent must be found. In some cultures it will be the egret's feather. In other places where sheep have only brown or black wool, the biblical "wool" must be replaced with its cultural equivalent in that regional language. Hope is spoken of as "an anchor of the soul" in Heb 6:18-19; in one translation in a landlocked region of Africa, it became "the picketing-peg of the soul," inasmuch as in that culture a picketing-peg does for animals what an anchor does for a ship.

Connotative equivalents must also be dealt with. In Matt 5:45 Jesus praises the indiscriminate goodness of God, who sends rain to all, the just and the unjust alike. In the rain jungles of the Amazon region, rain is not a blessing—it is a curse. Jesus' statement in John 6:35, "I am the bread of life" could not be translated literally in the Chol language of Mexico. Bread is known and there is a word for it; but it is a delicacy, to be served only on special occasions. The corn cake *waj* in that culture is the equivalent of "bread" in the biblical culture; so in Chol Jesus says, "I am the *waj* that sustains life."

Many languages have a precise system of honorifics—that is, different ways of addressing people depending on their relation to the speaker, whether equal, inferior, or superior. Does Pilate address Jesus as an equal? Does Jesus address Nicodemus as an equal? Do the disciples treat Jesus as an equal? The relation between siblings must be respected: One brother, for example, is always referred to as older or younger than the other. Who was older: Simon or Andrew? James or John? Many languages make a difference between the inclusive and exclusive use of the first plural pronouns "we," "us," and "our." These are formal distinctions, and in dialogue the translator must determine whether the person being addressed is included. For example, in Mark 4:38 the disciples say to Jesus, "Teacher, do you not care that we are perishing?" Is Jesus included in that "we"? Was he also in danger of drowning? A language like English need not bother to answer the question; but in languages where such distinctions are mandatory, the translator must say, "Do you not care that we, your disciples, are perishing?" or "Do you not care that all of us are perishing?" Some languages are very precise in certain activities. John 19:17 states that Jesus went out "carrying his cross." How did he carry it? In his arms? On his shoulder? On his head? On his back? The translation must say specifically how Jesus carried his cross. An unusual instance arose in the Akha language in northern Myanmar (Burma) when the translators came to Heb 11:37, "They were sawn in two." "Which way?" they asked. "Lengthwise or across?"

2. *Current Trends.* Increasingly sensitive to the readers' reaction to the biblical text, translators are more and more willing to translate in such a way as not to offend potential readers. Usually this willingness falls under the rubric of reader sensitivity.

a. Inclusive language. Traditional English language translations (e.g., KJV, RSV) have translated inclusive Greek and Hebrew words using gender-specific English words (the inclusive *anthropoi* was often translated "men"). Inclusive language translations strive to be as gender inclusive as the original text (see B. Metzger's statement in "To the Reader" in the NRSV). To do this one can shift from the singular "his" to the plural "their"; use "people," "humans," or "humankind" instead of "man" or "men"; or shift from the third person to the second person.

Some words in both Hebrew and Greek—such as "man," "sons," and "brothers"— are often obviously inclusive; they do not, in a given context, restrict themselves to male human beings. Current translations appropriately and rightly use inclusive words (e.g., "humankind" instead of "man" in Gen 1:27 and 5:1). In his letters, Paul[†§] often addressed his readers as *adelphoi*, traditionally translated as "brothers." It is evident that Paul is addressing all his readers, women and men alike. Faithfulness in translation demands that *adelphoi* be translated "brothers and sisters," as the NRSV does consistently.

This practice is well established (e.g., TEV 1992[21]), so it came as a great surprise to the publisher when many users of the NIV raised strong objections to the International Bible Society's plan to distribute in the United States the same gender-inclusive edition it had been distributing in Great Britain (see esp. *Christianity Today*, Oct. 27, 1997). The protests were so vehement that the society dropped its plans and recalled all copies of the gender-inclusive edition still extant.

On the opposite end of the spectrum, one published translation (*The Inclusive New Testament* 1994) has gone so far as to obscure or even obliterate the sexual identity of biblical characters. Instead of "the Son of God" it has "God's Own." In the place of "Father" (used of God), it reads "Abba God." Whether this is the wave of the future remains to be seen.

b. Anti-Semitism in the New Testament. This is a particularly sensitive matter, and translators have wrestled with it for a number of years. The third edition of the TEV New Testament (1976) tried to translate the frequently occurring *hoi Ioudaioi*—"the Jews"—in the Gospel of John in such a way as not to imply that all the Jewish people (especially the citizens of Jerusalem) were fierce enemies of Jesus and his followers (see *The Bible Translator 26* October 1975, 401-9). The CEV (1995) has done much the same, but goes even further in some instances (see its handling of Luke 21:12; Acts 6:9; 19:14). Such scholars as H. Kee and J. Sanders[§] posit that the Gospels and Acts, written decades after the events they are reporting, retrojected into the events that took place in the thirties of the first century the conditions that prevailed at the time these books were written, particularly the deep animosity between the Jewish community and the Christian community. They propose that somehow translators dismantle this unhistorical framework so that the accounts accurately reflect the current situations and not those that developed decades later. How this can be done remains to be seen, but certainly the debate will continue.

c. Reader Sensitivity. Besides anti-Semitism and androcentric language, both of which are deeply offensive to many readers, the translation of Isa 7:14 is a particular instance of how the readers' reaction can affect the translation. Current Jewish and Christian scholarship is practically unanimous that in this passage the Hebrew *ha-almah* means "the young woman [is pregnant]." In Matt 1:23 the passage is quoted as it appears in the Septuagint: "The virgin [*he parthenos*] will become pregnant." In light of this, the NIV, among others, translates the verse "The virgin will be with child and will give birth to a son."

3. The Future of Bible Translation. R. Miller published a scholarly compilation of all extant Gospel texts in modern translation in 1995. At present, there is still no similar edition for the Hebrew Bible. Other than that, it would seem that, for language communities that have a large number of Bible readers, different kinds of translations are called for: a traditional translation appropriate for church and liturgical usage; a common-language translation especially suitable for people with a limited amount of formal education, for children, and for people who speak and read the language as a second language; and perhaps a literary translation using the full range of the language in matters of vocabulary and style, such as the NEB (and, to a lesser degree, the REB).

Bibliography: R. A. Bullard, "Texts/Manuscripts/Versions," *MDB* (ed. W. E. Mills, 1990) 890-96. **R. A. Knox,** *On Englishing the Bible* (1949). **B. M. Newman,** *Creating and Crafting the CEV* (1996). **E. A. Nida,** "Theories of Translation," *ABD* 6:512-15; "Translations: Theory and Practice," *The Oxford Companion to the Bible* (ed. B. M. Metzger and M. D. Coogan, 1993) 750-52. **H. M. Orlinsky and R. G. Bratcher,** *A History of Bible Translation and the North American Contribution* (1991). **J. H. P. Reumann,** *The Romance of Bible Scripts and Scholars: Chapters in the History of Bible Transmission and Translation* (1965). **W. M. Smalley,** *Translation as Mission* (1991). **P. G. Stine** (ed.), *Bible Translation and the Spread of the Church: The Last 200 Years* (Studies in Christian Mission 2, 1990).

R. G. BRATCHER

UGARITIC AND BIBLE TRANSLATION

Ugarit is the name of a city buried in the Ras Shamra tell on the Syrian coast. Ugarit was the capital of a kingdom of the same name that flourished in the Bronze Age, especially between 1400-1190 B.C.E. French archaeologists have been excavating Ugarit since 1928. Among the spectacular finds were not only tablets written in the syllabic Babylonian cuneiform script but also tablets with a hitherto unknown cuneiform script, which, when deciphered, turned out to be a Semitic alphabet. Scholars then realized that these Canaanite texts would have an enormous impact on biblical studies, a realization confirmed by ongoing research. It is fitting to start this short survey with a serious warning to the nonspecialist. Ugaritic is still a very difficult language that is only partially understood, and scholars differ widely regarding the interpretation of texts. Consequently, it is often hard to decide whether or not a parallel to some passage in the Bible has been claimed legitimately. One should always consult several different translations.

Apparently, Ugaritic belongs to the same family of Northwest Semitic or "Canaanite" languages as Hebrew. Being somewhat older and representing a northern branch of that family, Ugaritic has helped grammarians gain insight into the development of the Hebrew language. In its long history, certain grammatical phenomena became outdated and were no longer understood by later generations (as with the so-called enclitic *mêm,* which was often erroneously read as a plural ending or as a personal suffix). Its frequent use in Ugaritic has helped scholars discover a number of convincing examples of this kind of misunderstanding. Rare forms like ' s for normal y s (2 Sam 14:19; Mic 6:10; mss Prov 18:24), masculine infinitives of three *waw/yod* verbs (Gen 18:18; 26:28; 48:11), and rare functions of the verb like the narrative *yiqtol* and the optative perfect all found a reasonable explanation on the basis of Ugaritic.

In many other respects, however, standard Ugaritic is quite different from standard Hebrew. The causative stem of the verb, for example, is not the Hiphil, but a Shaphil, as in Akkadian. The relative particle *d* is closer to Arabic and Aramaic than to Hebrew. However, in both cases, rare examples of the same morphemes do occur in Hebrew. Other grammatical phenomena that are quite common in Hebrew—*matres lectionis,* the article, the consecutive perfect—start to appear only in nonliterary Ugaritic texts.

From a lexical point of view, biblical Hebrew has always presented the exegete with formidable difficulties. The total number of different words in the spoken language of ancient Israel may be estimated at 24,000. Only 8,000 of them eventually found their way into the CANON, and about one-third of these are words occurring only once. As a result, the meaning of words and expressions found only rarely in the Hebrew Bible was often forgotten, and, in such cases, even the earliest translations are guesswork. Ugaritic has proved to be extremely helpful in solving such puzzles.

The verb צ *t'* in Isa 41:10 for example, which the Septuagint*§ translates "to wander," actually means "to be afraid" and is attested with this meaning in Ugarit. In Ps 89:20, *'zr* should not be rendered "help" (as in the Septuagint) but "hero," since it is clearly related to the Ugaritic *ǵzr*. The apparently corrupted Hebrew text of Prov 26:23 could be restored with the help of Ugaritic: *ksp sygym*, "like silver of dross," should be read *kspsgm*, "like glaze" (the same Ugaritic word may also denote a vessel, like our "glass" or "delft blue"). In 2 Kgs 4:42, the unintelligible *bṣqlnw* appears to be a corruption of *bṣqlnm*, "bulging fresh ears of grain," as found in Ugaritic (confusion of -*nw* and -*m* is a fairly common error in Hebrew manuscripts).

When used with caution, linguistic parallels from Ugaritic can clarify many obscure words and grammatical constructions in Hebrew. Thus the translator can more clearly and easily render the ancient biblical text into an intelligible, useful contemporary translation.

Bibliography: **Y. Avishur,** *Stylistic Studies of Word-pairs in Biblical and Ancient Semitic Literatures* (AOAT 210, 1984); *Studies in Hebrew and Ugaritic Psalms* (1989; ET 1994).
G. J. Brooke et al. (eds.), *Ugarit and the Bible* (UBL 11, 1994). **P. C. Craigie,** *Ugarit and the OT* (1983). **A. Curtis,** *Ugarit (Ras Shamra)* (1985). **M. Dahood,** *Ugaritic-Hebrew Philology* (BibOr 17, 1965, 1989[2]). **L. R. Fisher and S. Rummel** (eds.), *Ras Shamra Parallels* (AnOr 49-51, 3 vols. 1972-81). **J. Gray,** *The Legacy of Canaan: The Ras Shamra Texts and Their Relevance to the OT* (VTSup 5, 1957, 1965[2]). **W. J. Jobling,** "Canaan, Ugarit, and the OT" (diss. University of Sydney, 1974). **A. S. Kapelrud,** *The Ras Shamra Discoveries and the OT* (1965). **S. E. Loewenstamm,** *Comparative Studies in Biblical and Ancient Oriental Literature* (AOAT 204, 1980). **P. van der Lugt and J. C. de Moor,** "The Spectre of Pan-Ugaritism," BO 31 (1974) 3-26. **D. Sivan,** *A Grammar of the Ugaritic Language* (HO 28, 1997). **S. Talmon,** "Emendation of biblical texts on the basis of Ugaritic parallels," ScrHeir 31 (1986) 279-300. **G. D. Young** (ed.), *Ugarit in Retrospect: Fifty Years of Ugarit and Ugaritic* (1981).

J. C. DE MOOR

Septuagint

Palestinian dissatisfaction with the adequacy of parts of the LXX's Translation*§ of the Hebrew Bible eventually led to revisions and/or new translations in the first centuries of the Christian era, as seen in some Greek biblical texts from Qumran. Further changes occurred as the early church gradually separated from its Jewish roots. When the Christian church emerged from its Jewish background after 70 C.E. and became a Gentile institution, it quite naturally adopted the LXX as its Bible. Its use of the LXX as Canon§ formed, in turn, its basis for discussion and argument with the Jews; this made Jewish dissatisfaction with the LXX even more intense, with the result that new attempts at rendering the Bible into Greek were made during the second century. The most Jewish of these was that of Aquila§ (Aq), a disciple of R. Akiba, whose exegetical rules he attempted to apply in his translation. The result was a brilliant but bizarre piece of work that only someone thoroughly familiar with the Hebrew text could possibly understand. Symmachus§ (Sym) also rendered the Hebrew text carefully into Greek, but for him the demands of the target language were paramount; thus his translation, though on the whole rendering the sense of the original, is not literalistic. Jerome§ extensively used Sym in his Vulgate*§ translation of the Hebrew Bible. A translation designated as Theodotion§ (Th) is a Palestinian revision of the LXX text, parts of which must be much earlier than the second century since this text is sometimes cited in the New Testament, particularly in Revelation. In fact, for Daniel it is the Th text rather than that of the LXX that was adopted by the Christian church.

By the third century arguments between Christians and Jews had reached such intensity that Origen§ undertook the task of writing the Hexapla, a massive scholarly attempt to present all the evidence available to him whereby Christian scholars could assess the "correctness" of the LXX translation. As its name implies, it consisted in the main of six columns (occasionally more, as in the psalter). The first column presented the Hebrew text of Origen's day in Hebrew script; the second, in a Greek transcription. The purpose of this second column is not clear and is much debated by modern scholars. The third column was devoted to the text of Aq as the most literalistic rendering of the Hebrew; the fourth was that of Sym; the fifth, of the LXX text; and the last, of Th, although for Psalms the text used for the sixth column has been identified as that of Quinta. (Readings from Quinta, Sexta, and Septima, revisions of unknown origin, are occasionally cited in the fathers or in manuscripts.)

It is the fifth column that had an impact on the later LXX text. Since the work was arranged in columns, only one or at most two Hebrew words could appear on a line, and the corresponding words in the translations would be placed on the same line. When the word order of the LXX did not correspond to that of the Hebrew, Origen was compelled to adapt it (i.e., the word order was "corrected"). More seriously, the text of the LXX was sometimes longer than that of the Hebrew, sometimes shorter. When the LXX contained text without an equivalent in the Hebrew, Origen marked the onset with an obelus and its end with a metobelus; when the LXX had nothing to correspond to the Hebrew, he borrowed from one of the other three, preferably from Th, using an asterisk to show its onset and a metobelus for its end (see Origen *Comm. in Mt.* 15:14). These signs are known as Aristarchian signs because they were presumably first used (although with a different meaning) by Aristarchus of Alexandria in the late third century B.C.E. for his edition of Homer.

Unfortunately the Hexapla, except for fragments, did not survive the Muslim onslaught of Syria in the seventh century, and its size precluded its being copied in full. Parts of it, however, were copied; a fragmentary codex found by Mercati in the Ambrosiana in Milan—containing in palimpsest columns two to six of the Hexapla of parts of Psalms 17, 23-31, 34-35, 45, 48 and 88—has been published. The fifth column could be copied more easily alone and, according to Eusebius[§] (*Vita Const.* 4.35ff.), fifty copies were prepared by him and Pamphilus on orders from Emperor Constantine. Later copyists of this text were not as careful as these fathers presumably had been and, not understanding what the Aristarchian signs meant, often omitted them or placed them incorrectly, thereby creating textual chaos rather than the well-ordered scholarly aid intended by Origen.

According to Jerome (*Preface to the Books of Chronicles*). Eusebius and Pamphilus promulgated this text throughout the Palestinian provinces, whereas Alexandria and Egypt lauded Hesychius as the author of their LXX; and the text of Lucian[§] the Martyr was approved from Constantinople to Antioch. In fact, Jerome maintained that the entire world was at odds by reason of this threefold variety (*trifaria varietate*).

Of these three recensions the Origenian, or Hexaplaric, is the best defined. The Lucianic recension is usually attributed to the Lucian who suffered martyrdom in 311/312. Commonly thought to be somewhat more Atticistic than the old LXX, its text is longer and contains numerous doublets; its identification has been severely questioned for certain parts of the Hebrew Bible. This recension is usually identified by its use in the works of Chrysostom[§] and Theodoret[§]. The third recension is most problematic. It is not even clear who Hesychius was, although Eusebius speaks of him as a martyr-bishop, an identification by no means certain. Nothing is known of his recension, although J. Grabe's identification of the text of Codex B (Vaticanus) as Hesychian has received some scattered support. A critical edition of the text of Cyril of Alexandria[§] might shed some light, though even this is quite uncertain.

Meanwhile, as Christianity spread, the Bible could no longer serve universally as canon for the faithful in its Greek dress. Already, in the second century the LXX was being translated into Latin as a North African vulgate form of the Scriptures. This OL text underwent constant revision, particularly when it spread to the European continent, since most well-educated speakers of Latin were also acquainted with Greek. Latin writers like Augustine[§] often "corrected" their OL texts, with the result that one can quite properly speak of OL versions. In Egypt, the LXX was being rendered into Coptic dialects by the early third century. Of these the Bohairic is still used in the modern Coptic Church, whereas the Sahidic (from upper Egypt) is substantially extant in fragmentary manuscripts. At least parts of the Hebrew Bible were also rendered into Achmimic and Fayyumic, but these have almost completely disappeared.

During the fourth century the Hebrew Bible was also translated into Ethiopic (Ethiopian Biblical Interpretation[§]), probably by Frumentius of Tyre. This text underwent at least two revisions, both represented in manuscripts that require careful evaluation for use in LXX studies. For Armenian[§], translated under the inspiration of Mesrop, the textual evidence is much more of one piece in spite of the large number of manuscripts extant. Based on Greek manuscript(s) from Constantinople, much of the text is a good witness to the Hexaplaric recension and, for some books, to the Lucianic/Byzantine tradition. The best Hexaplaric evidence among the versions is the Syrohexaplar (Syh), translated during the second decade of the seventh century under the supervision of Paul, bishop of Tella. Much of the Hebrew Bible is extant, and for many books it is the best extant source for the Hexaplaric signs as well. Other late versions of less importance for LXX studies are Arabic, Georgian, Gothic, and Slavonic.

Since the LXX and its versions constituted the canonical text for a large part of the Christian church up to modern times (i.e., the sixteenth cent.), commentaries, questiones, and homilies on books of the Hebrew Bible are all part of LXX studies in theory; in practice, patristic evidence is largely limited to textual rather than to exegetical collations and, for practical reasons, to the early centuries. One form of LXX studies needing separate mention is the evolution of *catena* texts. *Catena* manuscripts contain not only the biblical text as *lemata* but also large numbers of *catenae*, or extracts from the fathers. Since many of the *catenae* come from works no longer extant, they constitute a valuable source of information, containing both homiletical/exegetical comments and textual notes that often give lexical information as well as non-LXX readings (especially from Aq, Sym, and Th).

Modern LXX studies may be said to begin with the Renaissance rediscovery of Hebrew as the original language of most of the Hebrew Bible. The appearance of J. Reuchlin's[§] *De Rudimentis Linguae Hebraicae* in 1506 meant that Christian scholars could now compare the LXX with the "original" Hebrew text and, in turn, use the Greek for both understanding, and at times correcting, the Hebrew. It is no exaggeration to state that, with the appearance of Reuchlin's work, Hebrew Bible Textual Criticism*[§], in the modern sense of the term, was born. Evidence for this new trend in biblical scholarship came with the appearance of the *Complutensian Polyglot*[§] (Hebrew Bible in 4 vols.), printed in 1514-17 but issued in 1520-22 under the sponsorship of Jiménez Decisneros.[§] This Polyglot contained the Hebrew, the Vulgate, and the LXX as well as *Tg. Onqelos* for the Pentateuch. According to the preface, a large number of manuscripts were used (mainly Spanish), including some on loan from the Vatican Library. Unfortunately, the LXX text is not always trustworthy since corrections based on the Hebrew text rather than on Greek manuscripts do occur.

Appearing at approximately the same time (1518-19) was the Aldine edition. The editor, A. Asolanus, used manuscripts from the Bibl. Marciana in Venice for his edition, and its text is free of emendations. The finest edition of the LXX was, however, the Sixtine edition, appearing in Rome in 1587 under the editorship of A. Carafa. The text was primarily based on Codex B, an excellent fourth-century uncial, supplemented by a number of cursives not only from the Vatican Library but also from other Italian libraries. Notes with readings from the fathers as well as readings from Aq, Sym, and Th were also provided by P. Morinus at the end of individual chapters and in supplements by F. Nobilius. The Sixtina became extremely popular and was reprinted repeatedly, including such a well-known edition as the London (or Walton) Polyglot of 1655-57 and those by L. Bos (1709), Holmes-Parsons (1798-1827), and C. von Tischendorf[§] (1850). An early edition of the LXX that ought not to be overlooked is that of J. Grabe (1707-20) based on Codex A (Alexandrinus), a fifth-century uncial housed in the British Museum. Grabe's edition contains a number of corrections or emendations still accepted by most modern scholars as correct.

Early works in which the LXX is used extensively that are worth reading even today include A. Masius[§], *Josuae imperatoris historia illustrata atque explicata* (1574); J. Drusius[§], *Veterum interpretum graecorum in totum VT fragmenta* (1622) and the earlier pamphlet *In Psalmos Davidis veterum interpretum quae extant fragmenta* (1581), both extensive collections of Hexaplaric materials; L. Cappel[§], *Critica sacra* (1651; see Critici Sacri[§]); I. Voss, *De LXX interpretibus* (1661-63); J. Morin[§], *Exercitationum biblicarum de hebraei graecique textus sinceritate* (1669); and J. Carpzov[§], *Critica sacra VT* (1728).

The year 1705 marked a turning point in the perception of LXX origins. Prior to the publication of H. Hody's[§] essay *Contra historiam LXX interpretum Aristeas nomine inscriptam in his De bibliorum textibus originalibus*, few questioned the historicity of the Letter of Aristeas[§]; afterward, few accepted it as anything but a legendary apology for the LXX. The letter attributes the origin of the LXX Pentateuch to Ptolemy Philadelphus's (285-247 B.C.E.) desire to have the Hebrew Torah rendered into Greek for his library at Alexandria. Accordingly, he sent a delegation to the high priest in Jerusalem, who acceded to his request for a good copy of the Torah as well as for seventy-two translators (six from each tribe). On their arrival at Alexandria, the translators were feted and interrogated by the king, then taken to the island of Pharos, where they finished their task in seventy-two days. The result was first read to the Jewish community in Alexandria and then presented to the king, who ordered it deposited in the library. Hody demonstrated conclusively that the story is pure fiction. The only item that might be deemed factual is that the letter originated in third-century B.C.E. Alexandria.

The nineteenth century was propaedeutic to modern LXX studies; it saw the publication of numerous tools useful for detailed LXX research. The old (1820) Lexicon*[§] by G. Biel[§] and E. Mutzenbecher (1779-80), was superseded by that of J. Schleusner (1820). A first Concordance[§] had already appeared in 1607 (K. Kircher), to be replaced by that of A. Trommius (1718), and finally by that of E. Hatch[§] and H. Redpath[§] (1892-1906). Collections of Hexaplaric materials were made by B. de Montfaucon (*Originis Hexaplorum quae supersunt* 1713) and, in 1875, F. Field published a new collection with the same name, based on, but enlarging, the earlier collections of Nobilius, Drusius, and Montfaucon. The century also saw the publication of editions and/or facsimiles of most of the uncial texts, as well as the discovery of Codex Sinaiticus by Tischendorf at Mt. Sinai.

Modern approaches to LXX studies largely center around two scholars of the nineteenth century: Z. Frankel and P. de Lagarde[§]. The first set forth his principles in his *Vorstudien zu der Septuaginta* (1841) and, ten years later, illustrated them for the Pentateuch in his *Über den Einfluss der palästinischen Exegese auf die alexandrinische Hermeneutik*. Frankel maintained that each book of the LXX had to be examined individually as a reflection of the context in which it was created. The work of each translator had to be studied in order to understand his attitudes, prejudices, and understanding. The translation technique, as well as the translator's cultural milieu, needed to be understood before any decisions on glosses, secondary readings, emendations, etc., could be made.

The second was P. de Lagarde, whose approach was a textual one. Beginning with Jerome's *trifaria varietas*, the three recensions of the LXX prevailing in the fourth-century Christian church, he attempted to identify the manuscript and the fathers representing each recension. Once each recension was identified and all the recensional elements removed, he believed, the prerecensional (i.e., original) LXX would emerge as the critical text. In 1883, he prematurely published the first part of what he regarded to be the Lucianic recension as *Librorum VT canon: Pars prior graece*.

This approach presupposes that the entire Greek Hebrew Bible manuscript tradition is a lineal descendant of a single *Urseptuaginta* that can be recovered by stripping it of all secondary elements. In order to accomplish this task, all relevant materials had to be assembled, all manuscripts had to be collated, the fathers read and their readings gathered, all the versions first restored to their autographa as much as possible and then collated to the Greek. Lagarde was never able to realize this gigantic project even for one book of the Hebrew Bible, and it was left for later generations to bring to fruition in the Göttingen Septuagint.

Meanwhile, in Great Britain, this programmatic vision was being realized in a compromised fashion. H. Swete[§] was preparing a manual edition of the LXX (1887-94), consisting of a reproduction of the text of Codex B (with only gross errors removed) and, where B was lacking, the text of the next oldest manuscript. Then, for the large Cambridge LXX, a selection of well-chosen representative manuscripts, a number of Greek and Latin fathers, and the principal versions were all collated to the text of Codex B; the readings were presented without further classifications in an apparatus. A further apparatus with Hexaplaric readings also appeared at the bottom of each page, while the appropriate text of B (or its substitute) appeared at the top of each page, as in the case of the manual edition. The first editors were A. Brooke, N. McLean, and subsequently H. Thackeray. The first fascicle appeared in 1906 and the last (3, pt. 1) in 1940, with no further fascicles envisioned.

The death of Lagarde in 1891 did not end interest in the recovery of the original or at least of the oldest recoverable LXX text. Lagarde's student O. Rahlfs[§] continued the work of his mentor, and in 1908 a proposal by R. Smend[§] and J. Wellhausen[§] of the Göttingen Academy of Sciences led to the establishment of the LXX *Unternehmen* for the express purpose of preparing the way for the eventual publication of critical editions. Rahlfs was appointed the first Leiter of the Unternehem, a position he occupied until his death in 1935. He personally prepared an editio minor for the Gottingen Septuagint in *Psalmi cum Odis* (1931).

The Lagardian program, however, was not universally accepted. In 1925 F. Wutz revived an old theory first proposed by O. Tychsen (1734-1815), that the LXX was a translation based on a Hebrew text in Greek transcription (1925, 1937). By clever manipulation of different transcription systems, he recovered what he believed to be an original text that was often at variance with the MT. Since the Greek alphabet badly reproduces the phonemes of Hebrew, Wutz reconstructed hypothetical Urtexte that no one but he could accept. Although his theory was initially greeted with some enthusiasm, its bizarre results soon lost all support; in his last major work, a Joban commentary, it was no longer applied.

Much more serious a challenge to the Lagardian program was that posed by P. Kahle[§]. First proposed in 1915 (TSK 85, 399-439) and reiterated and expanded in various publications throughout his life, his theory directly contradicted Lagarde's reconstruction of the textual history of the LXX. Kahle maintained that the LXX text, as adopted by the Christian church, evolved out of a plethora of translations or Targumim*[§] that existed in the first century C.E. To Kahle, a single standard text could only be an end product, and the isolation of the strands in the trifaria varietas does not bring one closer to the original text of the Greek. Kahle used the analogy of *Tg. Onqelos* and *Tg. Jonathan*, where, he maintained, the stilted and literal renderings into Aramaic betray revision from earlier Targumim now largely lost. Kahle was a learned man, a fascinating speaker and writer, and many scholars fell under his spell, but his reconstructions were largely theoretical and based on extremely slender evidence easily admitting other and more plausible interpretations. Since his death, his theories have been largely abandoned, and no serious LXX scholar today consistently follows his lead.

Meanwhile, serious work on the grammar of LXX literature was stimulated by A. Deissmann's[§] identification of biblical Greek (which naturally includes LXX and New Testament Greek) as *koinē*, or ordinary Hellenistic Greek. LXX grammars were published by R. Helbing (1907), Thackeray (1909), and Hlubovskyj (1927). A number of detailed grammatical studies were made by M. Johannessohn; see also Helbing, *Die Kasussyntax der Verba bei der LXX* (1928) and J. Psichari (1908, 161-208). Modern grammatical studies focusing on specific syntactic problems are especially centered in Helsinki around I. Soisalon-Soininen and his students.

The establishment of critical texts of LXX books has now been made much more difficult by the appearance of Barthélemy's book on Aquila's predecessors (1963). The Murabbaat Scroll of the Greek Minor Prophets shows a text with a number of recensional characteristics, the most obvious of which is the rendering of the Hebrew particle (*wĕ) gam* by the Greek *kaige* (now popularly, but unfortunately, called the *kaigē* recension). Barthélemy noted that these characteristics reflect the influence of the Palestinian rabbinate "in a time when a scrupulous literalism was flourishing." He then extended his study to translations and/or recensions that showed similar characteristics, finding these particularly in portions of 2 Samuel and 1-2 Kings and, in varying degrees of correspondence, in Lamentations, Canticles, Ruth, Judges, and Nehemiah (as well as in Th and Quinta).

What Barthélemy demonstrated clearly is that Palestinian exegesis of the first and second centuries C.E. exerted an enormous influence on the Greek Hebrew Bible in a variety of ways: by translations; by thoroughgoing revisions of existing texts; by occasional or sporadic intrusions into the text; and even, at times, by substituting new translations for existing ones, as in the case of Daniel. The impact of Palestinian rules of exegesis on the Greek tradition was a gradually evolving one that eventually found its high point in the work of Aquila, which won the day in the case of Ecclesiastes. It constituted a reassertion of dominance by Palestinian Jewry over the Egyptian Diaspora, an assertion that has immeasurably complicated the task of recovering the earliest possible text. One thing is clear: No single designation for the *kaige* group (the neutral term used by Barthélemy) is adequate; it is neither a recension nor a translation, although either may fit into this category.

What is also clear from this study is that one must reassess some of the more facile identifications of earlier times. The textual history of the books of the LXX cannot be solely based on Jerome's trifaria; it begins much earlier and is much more complex than Lagarde could have imagined over a century ago.

The current situation with respect to LXX studies shows a great deal of activity. Septuagint dissertations are appearing in various centers (Oxford, Helsinki, Harvard, Notre Dame, Philadelphia, Toronto, to mention but a few). Some work on critical editions of the versions is being carried on, though it is limited. The Vetus Latina Institut at Beuron continues its work on the OL with renewed vigor, with B. Fischer's *Genesis* (1951), W. Thiele's *Sapientia Salomonis* (1977) and *Sirach Ecclesiasticus* (1987), and R. Gryson's *Esaias* (1987). A number of other books have been assigned to various scholars; the introduction of one, *Gregorius Eliberritanus: Epithalamium sive explanatio in Canticis Canticorum* by E. Schulz-Flügel, has also been published. For Armenian, the editions of Deuteronomy (C. Cox 1979) and of Genesis (A. Zeytounian) have appeared. M. Peters has edited some of the volumes of the Bohairic Pentateuch (1983), P. Nagel is working on an edition of the Sahidic Hebrew Bible, and M. Goshen-Gottstein published the remains of the Syropalestinian version of the Pentateuch and the Prophets.

The International Organization for Septuagint and Cognate Studies (IOSCS) was founded in 1968, and its annual Bulletin has provided a focus for information on activity and bibliography. It has also led to interest in the application of computer technology to Hebrew Bible textual criticism in general, and to LXX problems in particular. It has embarked on an ambitious long-term project of translating the LXX into English—the New English Translation of the Septuagint (NETS)—for which a translators' manual has been issued as well as a model rendering of the Greek psalter (both by A. Pietersma). Most, if not all, of the books have been assigned to various translators.

Meanwhile, critical editions of the books of the LXX as the *sine qua non* for basic LXX studies continue to appear in the Göttingen Septuaginta series. The following major editions have been published: W. Keppler, *Maccabaeorum book 1* (original ed. 1936); R. Hanhart, *Maccabaeorum book 2* (1959) and *3* (1960), *Esther* (1966), *Esdrae I* (1974), *Judith* (1979), *Tobit* (1983), and *Esdrae II* (1993); J. Ziegler, *Isaias* (1939), *Duodecim Prophetae* (1943), *Ezechiel* (1952), *Susanna, Daniel, Bel et Draco* (1954), *Jeremias, Baruch, Threni, Epistula Jeremiae* (1957), *Sapientia Salomonis* (1962), *Sapientia Jesu Filii Sirach* (1965), and *Iob* (1982); and J. W. Wevers, *Genesis* (1974), D*euteronomium* (1977), *Numeri* (1982), *Leviticus* (1986), and *Exodus* (1991). The following are actively in preparation: *Ruth* (U. Quast), *Iosue* (U. Quast), *Daniel* (revision of LXX; O. Munich), *Regnorum I et II* (1 and 2 Samuel; A. Aejemlaeus) and *Paralipomenon I et II* (R. Hanhart).

Bibliography: D. Barthelémy. *Les devanciers d'Aquila* (VTSup 10; 1963). **S. P. Brock, C. T. Fritsch, and S. Jellicoe,** *A Classified Bibliography of the Septuagint* (1973), up to 1972. **C. Dogniez,** *Bibliography of the Septuagint/Bibliographie de la Septante 1970-93* (from 1972). **R. Helbing,** *Die Kasussyntax der Verba bei der LXX* (1928). **J. Psichari,** *REJ 55* (1908) 161-208. **F. Wutz,** BWANT, 2nd ser., 9 (1925); *Systematische Wege von der Septuaginta zum hebr. Urtext* (1937).

For up-to-date lists of recent literature, see the various issues of the IOSCS Bulletin.

J. W. WEVERS

TEXT CRITICISM, LANGUAGES, AND LINGUISTICS

Vulgate

The history of the Latin Bible is surely one of the most complex histories of any Western text. Indeed, it is at least as much a history of the interaction of the intellectual currents carried forward by the dominant personalities and authorities of Christian history as it is of any one text type. Even the history of Jerome's[§] work, commonly described as the "Vulgate," is complicated by the fact that Jerome did not edit the entire Bible. Some books were revised only slightly, others underwent multiple revisions, and still others he left entirely untouched in the OL. Beyond that, the contributions of Cassiodorus[§], Isidore[§], the Irish, the Anglo-Saxons of Northumbria, Theodulf, Alcuin[§], and the anonymous stationers who compiled the Paris text in the twelfth and thirteenth centuries, together with their "correctors," do not exist in independent exemplars but, rather, almost invariably in mixed text types in which many characteristics and readings are shared. This state of affairs is in no small measure due to the fact that the physical transmission of the text rarely took the form of a complete copy from a single-volume exemplar (pandect). Generally speaking, any given copy of the Bible would consist of a collection of codices, each containing a subset of the biblical Canon[§] (Pentateuch, Gospels, Prophets, etc.). The quality and provenance of any one of these collections could conceivably be (and sometimes was) as heterogeneous as the textual tradition as a whole. Moreover, the project of the church in the first few centuries following Constantine was governed, not primarily by the canons of Textual Criticism*[§], but rather by the needs of preachers and missionaries, who would choose the version of the text best suited to moral exhortation and the teaching of the faith.

1. *The Starting Point: Jerome.* Jerome, who served as secretary to Pope Damasus from 382 to 385 C.E., was charged by him with the revision of the Gospels. Prior to Jerome there had been no consistent version of the OL text, and yet the OL had become enshrined in the liturgical use of the church. Consequently, his revision, which followed the most ancient Greek manuscripts available to him, was limited to correcting only those passages that departed from the meaning of the original Greek. Jerome may have extended this revision to the balance of the New Testament, although there is evidence that suggests an anonymous reviser for this part of the Bible. Jerome also prepared at this time a revision of the OL psalter, corrected against its source, the Septuagint*[§]. Although this first revision of Psalms appears now to be lost, the Roman psalter, so-called by virtue of its popularity throughout Italy and with the papacy until modern times, is likely to be very close to Jerome's work. Following the death of Damasus in 384 C.E., Jerome settled in Palestine where he undertook a revision of the OL Translation*[§] of the Hebrew Bible with the aid of Origen's[§] Hexapla. His most influential work of this period was his second revision of the psalter, called the Gallican (probably through the influence of Gregory of Tours and the significant number of manuscripts of it that derive from southern Gaul). No doubt local liturgical custom later influenced Alcuin, who chose this version for his edition. Jerome occasionally corrected the Latin against the Hebrew and added Origen's diacritical marks to note what was present in the Greek but not in the Hebrew and to note what had been added from the Hebrew in Theodotion's[§] version. In this stage of his work he also prepared revisions of Job, Chronicles, Ecclesiastes, the Song of Songs, and probably the rest of the Hebrew Bible as well. But his studies, particularly of the Hebrew language (in which he had become proficient) led him ultimately to undertake a new translation from the *Hebraica veritas*, the Hebrew text from Genesis to Chronicles, including the Aramaic portions of Ezra and Daniel. Of the Apocrypha, he translated the Greek portions of Daniel and Esther as well as the Aramaic versions of Tobit and Judith. The deuterocanonical books—Wisdom, Sirach, the first two books of the Maccabees and Baruch—he left in their

OL versions. This, then, is the version of the Latin Bible that came to be called the Vulgate in the sixteenth century.

2. *Diffusion of Jerome's Text*. The *editio vulgata*, or conventional edition, of the Bible of Jerome's day was the OL version of the text, and it was only in the seventh century that Jerome's text began to dominate. Over the course of the next four hundred years, Jerome's version (especially in its better witnesses) spread from Italy and southern Gaul, refracted though liturgical use and through the authority of local versions (especially in Spain). We are fortunate that Cassiodorus[§] described the nature of the Bibles he had with him at his monastery at Vivarium: a working copy of the OL text in nine volumes; the Codex grandior (brought to Northumbria by Ceolfrid at the beginning of the eighth century), containing Jerome's earlier hexaplaric revision of the Hebrew Bible, his revision of the Gospels, and the balance of the New Testament in the OL; and a smaller one-volume Bible containing the Vulgate text throughout. It would seem that Cassiodorus restricted his editorial work to external features of the text and did not attempt a critical analysis of manuscript witnesses or textual traditions in the modern sense. His goal was to produce manuscripts of the sacred text that conformed to the most ancient and reliable witnesses, punctuated throughout by cola and commata (lines of text formed of a single clause from nine to sixteen syllables and lines of text containing a single clause that does not exceed eight syllables, respectively), provided with chapter headings, and modified orthographically only rather modestly. The canons of the Latin language rarely if ever entered into the emendation of the text, and throughout the Middle Ages these guidelines dominated all attempts at improving the biblical text. Although Vivarium was destroyed not long after Cassiodorus's death, his library had an enduring influence through the cartloads of books that were sent from Vivarium to the Lateran palace in Rome.

The dissemination of the Vulgate text, however, had begun long before Cassiodorus. Even in Jerome's lifetime, scribes had come from Spain with the specific task of copying his work. The development of the early Spanish text is sometimes linked to Peregrinus, about whom little is known. The version of the text associated with his name shows the typical signs of additional material from the OL grafted into Jerome's Vulgate, together with prefaces intended for Jerome's hexaplaric revision of other books. For his own part, the scholar and encyclopedist Isidore, bishop of Seville, produced an edition of the text much closer to Jerome's original and followed more closely the canonical order of the Hebrew. But over the course of the seventh century, there inevitably arose a conflated "Peregrinus-Isidore" text type that dominated the Iberian peninsula and had some impact beyond it.

Spanish traditions found their way north of the Pyrenees perhaps most significantly in the person of Theodulf. Born and educated in northern Spain, he fled north from the Moors, taking his library with him. Late in the eighth century, Charlemagne appointed him to the see at Orleans. The textual version associated with Theodulf follows Isidore's canon and exhibits prefatory material taken from Isidore and Peregrinus but follows essentially an Italian text type. Theodulf adopted Jerome's Hebrew psalter, and his work evidences corrections directly from the Hebrew. Unfortunately, his efforts to provide a rudimentary apparatus in the form of marginal notations of variant readings inevitably led in later manuscripts to the introduction of the variants into the text itself.

The influences that converged on Carolingian efforts to revise the biblical text came not only, or even principally, from Spain but, rather, from Italy by way of the north. Here again Hieronymean traditions jostled with the OL. Irish monks, whose presence was ubiquitous throughout Europe, often brought with them a mixed text, although a purer form of Jerome's text can be found in the Book of Armagh and in the Book of Durrow (both Gospel books). It is not impossible that the latter was produced at Iona, whence Irish monks established Lindisfarne, whose Gospels bear a close affinity to the Codex Amiatinus produced by Ceolfrid at Jarrow before 716 and modeled after, though not copied directly from, Cassiodorus' Codex grandior. The Northumbrian traditions, represented in the Codex Amiatinus, together with Irish traditions, had spread to Europe by mid-century, as witnessed in the Codex Fuldensis, a missionary Bible left at Fulda by the Anglo-Saxon Boniface.

Augustine of Canterbury had brought from Rome a mixed text type, which, by the time of Alcuin, had reached Northumbria and, together with the version represented by the Codex Amiatinus and the Lindisfarne Gospels, became the basis of the text he used at Tours. Alcuin, who had received his education at York and had taken charge of Charlemagne's palace school at Aachen, was abbot of St. Martin's at Tours from 796 until his death in 804; it was there that he produced a corrected text of the Bible and published it in a sumptuous presentation copy that Charlemagne had commissioned to present to the pope in 800. As with Cassiodorus, Alcuin's editorial goals were conservative, limited to punctuation, grammar, and orthography. But it was not strictly the quality of the text of Alcuin's Bible—rather poor at the beginning of the ninth century but improved over the decades—so much as the external circumstances surrounding its production that gave it prominence throughout the empire. Although not officially sponsored by the crown, by the end of the ninth century it had become the norm.

Up to this time, practical and sometimes pastoral concerns governed the correction of the textual tradition. But from Carolingian times down to the Renaissance, there was an increasing tendency to emend the text to harmonize it with the fathers. Already in the ninth century, and especially in the twelfth and thirteenth, the development of the Vulgate text was influenced by the growing authority of patristic authors, both in their use of Scripture and in their articulation of doctrine. With the ascendence of the *Glossa Ordinaria*[§] (a "study edition" that included the text of the Vulgate and sections of commentary taken from the church fathers) in the first half of the twelfth century and the appearance of the *Sentences* (1155-58) of Peter Lombard[§], the patristic witness that they marshaled made an impact on the copying of the Vulgate in subtle ways, especially as the stationers of Paris (who were largely responsible for the diffusion of the Paris text) were not governed by any particular form of the text. This is especially obvious in the case of the Gloss, where discrepancies between the reading of the biblical display text and the patristic usage in the marginal commentary would stand side by side on the same page. There were occasional attempts to purge the Vulgate text of accretions, especially among the early Cistercians. S. Harding and N. Majacoria represent this movement, but their efforts run counter to the general trend.

3. *Corrections and Revisions of the Vulgate Text.* The plethora of alternative readings, especially as found in the fathers, led to the publication of *correctoria* in the thirteenth century by both Dominicans and Franciscans, which generally suggested alternative Latin translations from the original languages and occasionally proposed variants from authoritative Latin manuscripts. This led to confusion that some scholars, like R. Bacon[§], complained was worse than the problem the correctors sought to remedy. This intensified interest in the biblical text also led to the production of such aids for study as Concordances[§] (the first of which was produced at the Dominican convent of St. Jacques in Paris under the direction of Hugh of St. Cher[§]) and standardized chapter divisions (c. 1225), which go back to S. Langton[§].

Under the stimulus of the philological advances of the fifteenth century, the impulse to correct the Vulgate text against the Hebrew and Greek intensified. But as confessional lines hardened in the sixteenth century, this approach became untenable for the Roman Catholic Church. And with the decree of Trent that only the Vulgate was to be used in public reading, disputations, and sermons (1546), the efforts of several scholars to produce new translations from the original languages were circumscribed. The attempts to produce a corrected, scholarly edition of the Vulgate also met with considerable resistance. Between 1528 and 1540, R. Estienne produced under royal privilege (but with the opprobrium of many Paris theologians) three editions based increasingly on manuscript witnesses. (In a later edition in 1555 he introduced the verse divisions still in use.) The official revision of the Vulgate was finally undertaken by the Dominican Henten at Louvain based on Estienne's 1540 edition and was published at Antwerp in 1547. A revision of this Louvain Bible by A. Montanus was published in 1574. But it was only at the instigation of Sixtus V that yet another edition was prepared, this time at Rome, to be published at the Vatican in 1590 together with the papal injunction that no other edition was to be used. Yet its errors were sufficiently numerous that, shortly after Sixtus's death, the copies of the 1590 edition were recalled and a corrected edition was prepared under the impetus of R. Bellarmine[§] and published in 1592, under the name of Sixtus but in the pontificate of Clement VIII. Until the late nineteenth century this Sixto-Clementine edition was the only edition of the Vulgate in official public use.

4. *Critical Editions and New Translations.* With the advent of new photographic technologies and the stimulus they gave to other arenas of textual research, not to mention the unending attempts over the centuries to produce new and improved Latin translations of the Bible, Pope Pius X established a commission in 1907 to produce a critical edition of the Vulgate. The first fascicle appeared in 1926 under the direction of H. Quentin; and the last, only in 1995. Concomitantly in 1969 there appeared from the Württembergische Bibelanstalt a new version (now in its third ed.) under the direction of Weber, B. Fischer, and J. Gribomont, together with an ecumenical team of scholars; a version that was, rather than simply the Clementine text with variants, an edition based on a substantial number of witnesses and closely paralleling the critical edition.

While this work on the Vulgate was proceeding, new Latin translations of various parts of the Bible began to be authorized and put into circulation, with the aim of emending obscurities and barbarisms. This development culminated in the promulgation in 1969 of a *Biblia vulgata nova* under the direction of Cardinal Bea. Completed in 1977, this new Latin version should not be confused with the critical edition of the Vulgate. The twentieth century has also seen the undertaking of a critical edition of the OL Bible, the *Vetus Latina*, is now underway and is, in many ways, a much more difficult task, since it does not owe its origin to a single author, as does much of the Vulgate. Publications associated with the *Vetus Latina* began to appear in 1949 under the editorship of B. Fischer and will continue well into this century.

Editions

Biblia Sacra iuxta vulgatam versionem ad codicum fidem, cura et studio monachorum Abbatiae pontificiae Sancti Hieronymi in Urbe O.S.B. edita 1-18 (1926-95).

Vetus Latina (1949-).

Biblia vulgata nova (1969-77).

Biblia Sacra iuxta vulgatam versionem (ed. B. Fischer, 1983).

Bibliography: S. Berger, *Histoire de la Vulgate pendant les premiers siècles du moyen age* (1893). **F. J. Crehan,** "The Bible in the Roman Catholic Church from Trent to the Present Day," *CHB* 3 (1963). **B. Fischer,** *Lateinische Bibelhandschriften im Frühen Mittelalter* (1985). **B. Hall,** "Biblical Scholarship: Editions and Commentaries," *CHB* 3 (1963). **R. Loewe,** "The Medieval History of the Latin Vulgate," *CHB* 2 (1969). **B. M. Peebles,** "Bible IV.13: Latin Versions," *NCE* 2 (1965). **E. F. Rice,** *Saint Jerome in the Renaissance* (1985). **E. F. Sutcliffe,** "Jerome," *CHB* 2 (1969).

For further bibliography see especially the articles in *CHB* and *NCE*.

M. A. ZIER

Midrash

The Hebrew term *midrash* (from *drš*, "to seek out, investigate, inquire of") refers to (1) the particular mode of scriptural interpretation practiced by the rabbis of the land of Israel and Babylonia in late antiquity, (2) any individual rabbinic interpretation ("a midrash"), and (3) the corpus of edited literature composed of rabbinic scriptural interpretations.

1. *Midrashic Hermeneutics.* As a mode of scriptural interpretation, midrash is characterized by its dense overreading of the biblical text. Every lexical element is deemed to bear syntactic meaning. Meaning also is generated associatively through the juxtaposition of superficially similar textual elements (i.e., words, phrases, verses) from throughout Scripture that are construed as indicating substantive similarities and interrelationships among their discrete contexts (intertextual reading; Intertextuality*§). Underlying these hermeneutical techniques (Hermeneutics*§) is the conviction that the scriptural text in all its details constitutes the revealed word of God. Hence, every textual element is significant and conveys a meaning (frequently multiple meanings) intended by the divine Author; there are no redundancies. Moreover, Scripture is treated as a kind of oracle requiring interpretation; many of the techniques employed by the rabbis are common to ancient dream interpretation, oracle interpretation, and divination (S. Lieberman 1950). Thus the act of interpretation is deemed to be an encounter with the revealed mind of God.

A midrash is simultaneously exegesis and eisegesis: the rabbinic value system and worldview are read into the text, but the textual details themselves associatively generate or trigger the reading. In this manner, the ongoing religious significance of the biblical text is salvaged for its latter-day rabbinic interpreters.

2. *Types of Midrash.* The rabbis distinguish between legal (*midrash halakah*) and nonlegal (*midrash haggadah* or *aggadah*) midrash. Legal midrash extends and specifies the laws of the Torah, primarily through the hermeneutical techniques of inclusion, exclusion, and analogy. Rhetorically, it seeks to justify and find normative significance in the precise wording of Scripture (Harris 1994). The so-called *Baraita of Rabbi Ishmael* (prefaced to *Sipra*, on which see below) enumerates thirteen hermeneutical techniques for legal exegesis of Scripture. Some of the material in the legal midrashic compilations, however, is a series of *post facto* exercises artificially pegging to Scripture rabbinic rulings found in apodictic form in the Mishnah and Tosefta. (Many of these rulings, in fact, are derived from Scripture, but through logical extension of biblical law rather than through overreading of isolated lexical elements in the biblical text; J. Neusner 1977, 63-71.)

Nonlegal midrash exhibits greater interpretive license. Its methods are primarily associative and figurative, while its purposes are didactic and hortatory. For the rabbis, the biblical narratives in their minutest textual details became a series of timeless paradigms displaying the underlying values and beliefs of rabbinic culture; the primacy and salvific value of Torah study (already engaged in by the patriarchs); the ubiquity of God's providence, ultimately rewarding the righteous and punishing the wicked measure for measure; the persistence of God's love and concern for the divinely chosen people, notwithstanding the destruction of the temple and Israel's current subjugation to pagan (subsequently, Christian) Rome; and the trustworthiness of Israel's hope for ultimate vindication and redemption in the messianic future. Nonlegal midrashic hermeneutical techniques include the filling out of ellipses in the biblical text (some of them manufactured by the midrashists); concretization and historical application of abstract texts, particularly in poetic passages; juxtaposing and mutually interpreting discrete verses (intertextual readings); and wordplays. The rabbis (and rabbinic redactors) allowed the validity of multiple nonlegal interpretations of any verse. As long as basic tenets of the rabbinic world-view and ethos were not violated, a lesson derived by an authorized interpreter was deemed to have been intended by the divine Author.

3. *Midrashic Literature.* The corpus of midrashic literature was created in the land of Israel between the third and ninth centuries C.E. (additional midrashic materials are found in the Talmuds of Palestine and Babylonia). This literature displays a variety of styles and editorial strategies. The earliest documents, the so-called Tannaitic, or halakic midrashim dating from the third or fourth century C.E., contain both legal and nonlegal exegesis and take the form of verse-by-verse commentaries, often supplemented by expansive rhetorical constructions, on entire biblical books. These are: *Mekhilta de-Rabbi Ishmael* (on Exodus, beginning with chap. 12), *Mekhilta de-Rabbi Simeon bar Yohai* (on Exodus; fragmentarily preserved), *Sipra* (on Leviticus), *Sipre* (on Numbers, beginning with 5:1, and Deuteronomy), and *Sipre Zuta* (on Numbers; fragmentarily preserved). The next documents, from the fourth through sixth centuries, contain only nonlegal exegesis and are linguistically and stylistically akin to the Talmud*§ of Palestine. These are: *Bereshit Rabbah* (on Genesis), *Eikha Rabbah* (on Lamentations), *Wayiqra Rabbah* (a series of literary homilies on selected verses from Leviticus), and *Pesiqta de-Rab Kahana* (a series of literary homilies on the synagogue lections for the holidays and special sabbaths of the liturgical year). These documents characteristically make use of a literary-rhetorical structure called a *petihta*, which is an extended form of intertextual reading. A third group of documents, from the sixth through ninth centuries, is genuinely homiletical. These texts rework nonlegal materials from the earlier documents. They are characterized by the use of halakic *petihta*, which homiletically connect well-known Mishnaic rulings with the scriptural verse to be expounded. These are: *Midrash Tanhuma* (on the entire Pentateuch), *Debarim Rabbah* (on Deuteronomy), *Pesiqta Rabbati* (on synagogue lections for the holidays and special sabbaths), and the second parts of *Shemot Rabbah* (on Exodus) and *Bemidbar Rabbah* (on Numbers). Later works include midrashic compilations on Song of Songs, Ruth, Esther, Ecclesiastes, Psalms, and Proverbs (H. Strack and G. Stemberger 1991).

Bibliography: P. S. Alexander, "Midrash," *A Dictionary of Biblical Interpretation* (ed. R. J. Coggins and J. L. Houldin, 1990) 452-59. **D. Boyarin,** *Intertextuality and the Reading of Midrash* (1990). **M. Fishbane,** *The Garments of Torah* (1989). **S. Fraade,** *From Tradition to Commentary: Torah and Its Interpretation in the Midrash Sifre to Deuteronomy* (1991). **J. Harris,** *How Do We Know This? Midrash and the Fragmentation of Modern Judaism* (1995). **I. Heinemann,** *Darkhei ha'aggadah* (1954²). **M. D. Herr,** "Midrash," *EncJud* (1972) 11:1507-14; "Midreshei Halakhah," *EncJud* 11:1522-23. **L. Jacobs,** "Hermeneutics," *EncJud* (1972) 8:366-72. **J. L. Kugel,** "Two Introductions to Midrash," *Proof* 3 (1983) 131-55. **J. L. Kugel and R. A. Greer,** *Early Biblical Interpretation* (LEC 3, 1986). **S. Lieberman,** "Rabbinic Interpretation of Scripture," *Hellenism in Jewish Palestine* (1950) 66-82. **J. Neusner,** *A History of the Mishnaic Law of Purities. XXII. The Mishnaic System of Uncleanness* (SJLA 6, 1977); *Judaism and Scripture* (1986); *What Is Midrash?* (GBS, 1987); *Introduction to Rabbinic Literature* (ABRL 8, 1994). **G. G. Porton,** "Defining Midrash," *The Study of Ancient Judaism* (ed. J. Neusner, 1981) 1:55-92; "Midrash," *ABD* (1992) 4:818-22. **D. Stern,** "Midrash," *Contemporary Jewish Religious Thought* (ed. A. A. Cohen and P. Mendes-Flohr, 1987) 613-20; "Midrash and Indeterminacy," *Critical Inquiry* 15 (1988) 132-61; *Parables in Midrash: Narrative and Exegesis in Rabbinic Literature* (1991). **H. L. Strack and G. Stemberger,** *Introduction to the Talmud and Midrash* (1982⁷; ET 1991). **L. Zunz and H. Albeck,** *Haderashot beyisrael* (1954²).

R. S. SARASON

EARLY JEWISH APPROACHES

Targumim

Targumim is the plural (and Hebraized) form of the Aramaic noun *targum*, which means simply "translation." As a result of the Diaspora and Persian domination, Aramaic became the *lingua franca* of Judaism; and scriptural rendering into that language became convenient and, for many Jews, increasingly necessary. The actual shape of Targumim between the Persian and Herodian periods, however, is a matter of conjecture. Such written documents as are presently attested cannot be dated until after the destruction of the temple in 70 C.E., and the vast majority of extant manuscripts are much later than that.

Aramaic renderings of Leviticus and Job have been discovered among the Dead Sea Scrolls§ (in caves 4 and 11), but they do not present those paraphrastic explanations, composed for the purpose of worship in synagogues, that are part of the classical Targumim (J. Fitzmyer 1979, 167-75). According to a *haggadah* contained in *b. Šabb.* 115a, Gamaliel ordered a written Aramaic version of Job buried within a construction of the temple during the period of its Herodian extension. Whether, as has been conjectured, that document may be identified with the *Targum of Job*, the story may provide confirmation of the rabbinic ethos of the early period, according to which Targumim were to be promulgated in synagogues orally from memory, not from written scrolls (cf. *m. Meg.* 4:4-10, with *b. Meg.* 23b-25b, and D. Barthélemy 1963, 151-52).

Equally, the story about Gamaliel indicates that the rabbis were familiar with precisely those materials they formally proscribed. They actively sought to regulate how Scripture was translated (Translation*§), as in the case of Lev 18:21. *M. Meg.* 4:9 states that this verse should not be related to intercourse with Gentiles, a proscription *Pseudo-Jonathan* (described below) violates. The rabbis even sought to prevent the rendering of certain passages, like the reference to Reuben's taking his father's concubine (see *Meg.* 4:10 and Gen 35:22; and for a discussion of both examples of the apparent contradiction of the Mishnah by the Targumim, see M. McNamara 1966, 46-51). However great their efforts may have been, other forces seem to have been greater: All extant Targumim to the Pentateuch (Pentateuchal Criticism‡§) render the offending verse, although *Targum Neofiti* I (also characterized below) does so in a truncated fashion, perhaps out of a partial deference to the Mishnaic prescription.

Sipre (Deuteronomy 161) describes Targum as a discipline between Bible and Mishnah, and many of the existing versions uphold this conclusion. The rabbis granted that Targumim were to be used in synagogal meetings but insisted they should be oral, and they developed guidance for their formulation. On the other hand, they referred appreciatively to the written Targum to the Pentateuch (known as *Onqelos*) as "our Targum" (e.g., *b. Qidd.* 49a) and so conspire in the abrogation of their own halakhah. If nothing else is clear in targumic study, the pluralism of early and rabbinic Judaism at least becomes apparent beyond any reasonable contradiction.

The rabbis refer to Targumim as already being produced by Ezra and describe the author of the *Targum of the Prophets* as taught by Haggai, Zechariah, and Malachi (*b. Meg.* 3a). The first claim is evidently anachronistic, since no extant Targum dates from the period of Ezra, but it does suggest that the perception of the antiquity of the Targumim influenced their reception as authoritative (or at least as quotable). The second claim is patently anachronistic, since the author of the *Targum of the Prophets* is said in the same haggadah to have been Jonathan ben Uzziel, a first-century rabbi. The haggadah may be referring, with its apparently inept Chronology§, to the quasi-prophetic authority of the work, which sometimes offers considerable expansions of its Hebrew *Vorlage* among other substantive deviations. Whatever their directly historical value, such haggadoth serve to illustrate the rabbinic understanding that the practice of explaining Scripture in synagogue is warranted by Scripture itself, as in the case of Ezra (cf. Neh 8:8, cited in *Meg.* 3a), and that targumic authority was not merely a function of rabbinic authority but was, in some sense, prior to it. It is notable that in the present haggadah, after Jonathan translates the Prophets, a divine voice says, "Who has revealed my secrets to the sons of men?" The Targumim appear to have carried considerable weight even as they skirted the boundaries of what it is prudent to say in the name of Scripture. They might be partially tamed, but neither complete domestication nor suppression appears to have been practicable.

1. *Targumim to the Pentateuch.* The Targum called *Onqelos* after its putative author appears best to represent the rabbinic ideal for the practice of the *meturgeman* (Aram. "interpreter"). Its most obvious feature is its relatively faithful representation of the Hebrew text of the Pentateuch once allowance is made for the usual, paraphrastic efforts of all Targumim to speak of God and divine revelation with due reverence. It was once argued that *Targum Onqelos* did not emerge as an authoritative Targum in Palestine until as late as 1000 C.E. (M. Black 1978, 18), but the discovery of Aramaic documents at Qumran, Naḥal Ḥever, Murabbaat, and elsewhere (Fitzmyer 1979, 57-84) has brought about a revolution in the study of Aramaic dialects. The idiom of *Onqelos* now appears much more primitive than was once supposed, and it has been suggested that the Targum is as early as the second century. There was clearly a concerted effort by rabbis at that time to standardize translations according to the emerging Hebrew text, as is shown in revisions of the Septuagint*§ (Aquila, Theodotion, and the fragments of the Minor Prophets found at Murabba'at; Barthélemy 1963, 163-270). On the other hand, that was also a period in which the orality of Targumim was insisted upon; a dating of *Onqelos* in the third century has therefore seemed more plausible to many scholars. Such a dating would also accord with the considerable interest displayed in targumic matters by rabbis of that period (B. Grossfeld 1971, 841-44).

The Targum known as *Neofiti I,* named after the library in the Vatican where it was discovered (miscataloged), presents a very different profile (Díez Macho 1968-79, 6.1:19-20). Although it corresponds in a formal way to its Hebrew *Vorlage, Neofiti I* paraphrases and offers considerable expansions, often of a haggadic nature. It is written in a dialect of Aramaic known as Palestinian, comparable to the language reflected in the Palestinian (or Jerusalem) Talmud*§. Once dated as early as the second century B.C.E., the newer understanding of dialects would place it in the third century C.E., contemporaneous with *Onqelos* but produced nearer Tiberias than Babylon. In it, the figure of Cain denies the resurrection, judgment, and divine justice over all (Gen 4:8) in a manner reminiscent of the rabbinic perception of heterodoxy (J. Bassler 1986, 56-64). Such considerations support the later dating of the document, which, in any case (like *Onqelos*), is not attested textually until well after the Talmudic period.

Targum Pseudo-Jonathan is the last of the complete Targums to the Pentateuch. Its mention in Gen 21:21 of Muhammed's wife and daughter (under the names Adesha and Fatima; see R. LeDéaut 1978, 211) provides a rather obvious date after which the document as a whole could have been written. (It owes its curious name to the belief that an abbreviation for "Jerusalem" [its proper name] was misunderstood for "Jonathan," the supposed author of the *Targum of the Prophets.* But the name Jonathan has been used since the document became known in the medieval period, and so the designation has lived on, albeit in its amended form.) Also to be associated with *Pseudo-Jonathan* and of somewhat later periods (between the seventh and the eleventh centuries) are the fragments from the Cairo Geniza (M. Klein 1986). Last, the *Fragmentary Targum* is not a fragmentary version of an original whole, but a collection of occasional alternatives cited during the Middle Ages and of the same expansionistic nature of *Neofiti I, Pseudo-Jonathan,* and the fragments from the Cairo Geniza (Klein 1980, 1:12-42). These Targumim are so closely related to one another that their relationship sometimes appears synoptic, and in view of their common traits (both linguistic and substantive) they are styled "Palestinian Targumim."

2. *Targumim to the Prophets*. The Prophets, both former and latter, are ascribed to Jonathan ben Uzziel, the disciple of the elder Hillel§. Linguistically, that attribution is not impossible, since Jonathan has close affinities with *Onqelos*. But in addition to the caution expressed in respect to dating the latter Targum, certain factors demand an even greater skepticism. As has long been recognized (see Z. Frankel 1872,13-16), certain dialectical features of *Tg. Jonathan* (in contrast to *Onqelos*) present an affinity with *Pseudo-Jonathan*. Moreover, although the Former Prophets in *Jonathan* sometimes approximate to *Onqelos* in a formal correspondence to the Hebrew text, there is also a greater freedom in offering explanatory additions. In the case of the Latter Prophets, *Jonathan* is unevenly paraphrastic and expansionistic. This uneven development is such that each Targum within *Jonathan* must be dated separately according to its exegetical and thematic interests as these can be correlated with rabbinic literature (B. Chilton 1982). The Talmud ascribes targumic activity to the fourth-century sage Joseph bar Ḥiyya, the fourth-century-century sage of Pumbeditha, a plausible time period for the collection as a whole. The Codex Reuchlinianus to Jonathan (and a newly identified manuscript in the Bibliotheque Nationale; Chilton 1997) represents expansionistic versions from the medieval period that serve a function analogous to that of the *Fragmentary Targum* to the Pentateuch.

3. *Targumim to the Writings*. The Targumim on the Writings are even less coherent than Jonathan. In the case of Psalms, they appear more midrashic (Midrash*§) than targumic, and Proverbs is widely held to have been retroverted from the Syriac of the Peshitta§ (M. Goshen-Gottstein 1983, xix). Contemporary study of these documents may well alter scholarly assessment, but they appear to reflect the late, almost esoteric, vogue for targumic production as represented in the *Fragmentary Targum* and in Codex Reuchlinianus. Ironically, the genre of Targum, which had initially been designed for general consumption and was influenced by folk usage of Scripture, became the appropriate milieu of academic play for the simple reason that Aramaic had been supplanted by Arabic and survived as an academic tongue.

4. *Use in Biblical Interpretation*. Once the purposes, dates, and exegetical tendencies of the Targumim are appreciated, their usefulness in biblical interpretation becomes evident. In the first place, there is no question of any extant Targum providing immediate access to a more primitive Hebrew Bible text than we would otherwise know. Because most of them do not undertake the direct representation of a Hebrew *Vorlage*, immediate retroversion from Aramaic to Hebrew by textual critics is less likely to provide a primitive text than an artifact of modern erudition. Nonetheless, once the characteristics of a Targum are known, it may be of use in assessing the Hebrew text presupposed by it. In any case, every Targum does directly represent some community's understanding of Scripture. The nature of a particular Targum is cognate to its function for reading in synagogue, reflection in rabbinic discussion, esoteric speculation, or some combination of the three. To that extent Targumim are useful sources of the history of scriptural interpretation within Judaism. Indeed, their relatively straightforward format as translations of familiar texts makes them more accessible to most non-expert readers than are the midrashim, Talmud, and Mishnah. A project to publish all extant Targumim in English is now nearly completed and may promote a more general understanding of and sympathy for the place of Scripture in early and rabbinic Judaism.

In recent years, increasing attention has focused on the Targumim from the perspective of understanding the New Testament (McNamara 1966, 1972). Although the thesis of a coherent pre-Christian version of the Bible in Aramaic available in the Palestinian witnesses has been put to rest, the fact remains that certain readings from extant Targumim are strikingly similar to passages in the New Testament. Examples from Jesus'*§ sayings include Luke 6:36 (which is comparable to *Tg. Ps.-J.* Lev 22:28) and Mark 4:11-12 (which appears to reflect an understanding of Isa 6:9-10 such as *Jonathan* preserves; Chilton 1984, 44, 90-98). Even an elementary knowledge of targumic development precludes any argument that Jesus and/or his followers had actual access to the documents we can read today. On the other hand, it is even more difficult to sustain the argument that the *meturgemanim* (Aram., "interpreter") simply appropriated Christian teaching. Rather, it would appear that the Targumim took shape over so long a period that they sporadically preserve early Jewish materials from the first century. Sometimes they are of a proverbial nature and may have been unattached to any Targum originally, as may be the case in *Tg. Ps.-J.* Lev 22:28. But on other occasions, as in Mark 4:11-12, the New Testament accords with targumic readings as a rendering of the Hebrew Bible. In such instances, it is all but impossible to resist the argument that Jonathan at least partially reflects the appropriation of Scripture in the first century, whatever else it may do.

Among the latest developments in the study of the Targumim, two may be singled out (Chilton 1986, 1-14). The first is that, in rendering the Scripture into Aramaic, the *meturgemanim* gave voice to the theology of their day; here is open reference to the messiah, the kingdom of God, the Holy Spirit, Prophecy†‡§, the covenant, the temple, and other central concepts of interest equally to scholars of Judaism and of early Christianity. The second, related development is that attention is now being given to the fact that the Targumim present their theologies as construals of the meaning of Scripture. They give us direct access to the manner in which Scripture was appropriated, transformed, and conveyed to others in a way that might prove to be of vital significance in appreciating how the Hebrew Bible and the New Testament were understood by the many communities that used them.

Bibliography: D. Barthélemy, *Les devanciers d'Aquila: Premiere publication intégrale du texte des fragments du Dodé,caprophéton trouvés dans le désert de Juda. . . .* (VTSup 10, 1963). **J. M. Bassler,** "Cain and Abel in the Palestinian Targums: A Brief Note on an Old Controversy," *JSJ* 17 (1986) 56-64. **M. Black,** "Aramaic Studies and the Language of Jesus," *In Memoriam P. Kahle* (BZAW 103, 1978) 17-28. **B. D. Chilton,** *The Glory of Israel: The Theology and Provenience of the Isaiah Targum* (JSOTSup 23, 1982); *A Galilean Rabbi and His Bible: Jesus' Use of the Interpreted Scripture of His Time* (1984); *Targumic Approaches to the Gospels: Essays in the Mutual Definition of Judaism and Christianity* (1986); *The Isaiah Targum* (ArBib, 1987); "'HEBR. 75' in the Bibliothéque Nationale," *Targum Studies* (1997). **E. G. Clarke** et al., *Targum Pseudo-Jonathan of the Pentateuch: Text and Concordance* (1984). **A. Díez Macho**, *Neophyti 1: Targum Palestinense MS de la Biblioteca Vaticana* (6 vols. 1968-79). **J. W. Etheridge,** *The Targums of Onqelos and Jonathan ben Uzziel on the Pentateuch with the Fragments of the Jerusalem Targum from the Chaldee* (1862, repr. 1968). **J. A. Fitzmyer,** "The First-century Targum of Job from Qumran Cave XI," *A Wandering Aramean: Collected Aramaic Essays* (SBLMS 25, 1979) 161-82; "The Phases of the Aramaic Language," ibid., 57-84. **Z. Frankel,** *Zu den Targum der Propheten* (1872). **M. Goshen-Gottstein,** *Fragments of Lost Targumim, pt. 1* (1983). **B. Grossfeld,** "Bible. Translations. Ancient Versions. Aramaic: The Targumim," *EncJud* 4 (1971) 842-51. **D. Harrington and A** J. Saldarini, *Targum Jonathan of the Former Prophets* (ArBib, 1987). **C. T. R. Hayward,** *The Targum of Jeremiah* (ArBib, 1987). **M. L. Klein,** "Nine Fragments of Palestinian Targum to the Pentateuch from the Cairo Geniza (Additions to MS A)," *HUCA* 50 (1979) 149-64; *The Fragment-Targums of the Pentateuch According to Their Extant Sources* (2 vols. AnBib 76, 1980); *Geniza Manuscripts of Palestinian Targum to the Pentateuch* (1986). **R. LeDéaut,** *Targum du Pentateuque: Traduction des deux recensions palestiniennes complètes avec introduction, parallèles, notes et index* (SC, 1978), a continuing series. **S. H. Levey,** *The Targum of Ezekiel* (ArBib, 1987). **M. McNamara,** *The NT and the Palestinian Targum to the Pentateuch* (AnBib 27, 1966); *Targum and Testament, Aramaic Paraphrases of the HB: A Light on the NT* (1972). **A. Sperber,** *The Bible in Aramaic Based on Old Manuscripts and Printed Texts* (5 vols. 1959-73).

B. Chilton

EARLY JEWISH APPROACHES

Talmud

As conventionally understood, the Talmud consists of the Mishnah (compiled ca. 220 C.E.) and the Talmud proper (also called the Gemara), consisting of the Palestinian Talmud (compiled ca. 400 C.E.) and the Babylonian Talmud (compiled ca. 500 C.E.). For the study of biblical interpretation in the Talmudic period (the first five centuries in Palestine and Babylon), however, the works known as the midrashim (see Midrash*§), containing much material from the same period, must be referred to, since there are no basic differences between Talmud and midrashim in the matter of interpretation. This article, consequently, considers biblical interpretation in the whole of the Talmudic literature.

1. *Canonization and Authorship.* The biblical books are divided into three sections—(a) the Torah (the Pentateuch; Pentateuchal Criticism‡§); (b) the Neviim (the Prophets); and (c) the Ketuvim (the Hagiographa)—hence the name Tanakh for the Hebrew Bible as a whole. The Torah, as the very word of God to Moses, is the most sacred of the biblical books. The Neviim, or the Prophets (Prophecy and Prophets, Hebrew Bible‡§), conceived of as the product of the intense form of divine inspiration*§ known by prophetic vision, is next in degree of sanctity. The Hagiographa, conceived of as the product of a lower degree of inspiration (that of *ruah ha-kodesh*, "the Holy Spirit"), is the least sacred of the three divisions of Scripture. Thus, if a scroll of the Torah has been sold, the money may not be used to purchase a book of the Prophets or of the Hagiographa, for that would result in a diminuation of sanctity (m. Meg. 3:1).

The term used to denote that a book is sacred and belongs in the Canon§ (though this term is Christian and occurs nowhere in the Talmudic literature) is that it "contaminates the hands"— that is, the hands have to be ritually cleansed after having touched the book. The reason for this curious rule is, evidently, that a taboo was placed on a sacred book in order to prevent it being treated in an over-familiar manner. Long before the Talmudic period, the Torah and the Prophets had been accepted as sacred writ ("the Law and the Prophets"), but there were debates among the rabbis about the sanctity of some of the books in the third division, notably Song of Songs and Ecclesiastes (*m. Yad.* 3:5 and 4:5-6). It was eventually decided, however, that all the books of the Ketuvim do contaminate the hands.

The *locus classicus* for the order and authorship of the biblical books is in *b. B. Bat.* 14b-15a, where the order of the prophetic books is given as Joshua, Judges, Samuel, Kings, Jeremiah, Ezekiel, Isaiah, and The Twelve. The order of the Hagiographa is Ruth, Psalms, Job, Proverbs, Ecclesiastes, Song of Songs, Lamentations, Daniel, Esther, Ezra, and Chronicles. This makes a total of nineteen books (with the Twelve counted as a single book). With the addition of the five books of the Torah, this makes a total of twenty-four sacred books, a number that appears frequently in the literature in this context.

The passage continues with a statement regarding the authorship of the books: "Moses wrote his book, the Pentateuch, the portion of Balaam (Numbers 23 and 24) and Job. Samuel wrote his book, Judges and Ruth. David wrote the book of Psalms using the work of ten elders, namely, Adam, Melchizedek, Abraham, Moses, Heman, Yeduthan, Asaph, and the three sons of Korah. Jeremiah wrote his book, the book of Kings, and Lamentations. Hezekiah and his associates wrote Isaiah, Proverbs, Song of Songs, and Ecclesiastes. The men of the Great Synagogue (the Postexilic teachers wrote Ezekiel, the Twelve, Daniel, and Esther. Ezra wrote his book and the genealogies to his own." This second-century source is supplemented in the same passage by editorial material probably dating from the late fifth century C.E., which notes that the second-century source also states: "Joshua wrote his book and the last eight verses of the Torah" (Deut 34:5-11, dealing with Moses' death). It points out that R. Simeon (second cent.) disagreed and held that Moses wrote the last eight verses as well, but "with tears in his eyes" at the thought of his demise, and further states that the opinion that Moses wrote the book of Job is a minority opinion, with others holding that the book was compiled by a much later author whose identity is hard to determine. This is followed by a midrash on Job in which a view is recorded that Job is not a historical person at all and that the book is a work of inspired fiction.

That Moses wrote the Pentateuch at the dictation of God is taken for granted thoughout the Talmudic literature. It must be appreciated that even the heretics in Talmudic times believed that Moses was the author of the Pentateuch, although they maintained that he made it up. The issue was not that of the Mosaic authorship; that was accepted by all, unbelievers as well as believers. The real, dogmatic question was whether the "Torah is from Heaven" (*Sanh.* 99a), whether it was Moses' own work, or whether Moses acted simply as a scribe taking down the divine dictation. In a similar vein in another passage (*t. Yad.* 2:14, ed. M. Zuckermandel 1882, 683; and *b. Meg.* 7a), there is a debate on whether Ecclesiastes contaminates the hands. Those who held that it does believed that it was compiled by Solomon under the influence of the Holy Spirit. Those who held it does not were of the opinion that the work was not compiled under the influence of the Holy Spirit but is purely "the wisdom of Solomon." Both accepted without question that Solomon was the author of the book (although it was not actually written down by him). The dogmatic, doctrinal element in the Talmudic discussions regarding the authorship of the biblical books has to do with the question of inspiration, not with the very different question of who actually compiled the books and who recorded them in writing.

The statement that Moses wrote the pentateuchal portion of Balaam seems odd since this is part of Moses' book in any event. The parallel passage in the Palestinian Talmud (*Sota* 5:6, 20a) puts it rather more clearly: "Moses wrote the five books of the Torah then he wrote the book of Balak and Balaam and then he wrote the book of Job." That the portion of Balaam is described as a separate book is no doubt because it is an account of the oracles of a prophet other than Moses, even though recorded by Moses in "his" book. All six books belong to the divinely dictated book of the Torah, unlike the book of Job, which, even on the opinion that it was compiled by Moses, possesses no more than the lesser degree of sanctity possessed by the Ketuvim. On the manner in which the Pentateuch was written, there was a debate (*Git.* 60a) between the early third-century teachers, R. Johanan and Resh Lakish, one holding that each part of the Torah was "given" (i.e., dictated by God to Moses for him to record in writing at the time the events actually took place); the other holding that it was all dictated and written down toward the end of the forty-year journey through the wilderness.

The ten elders said to have contributed to the book of Psalms are either the persons mentioned in the superscriptions to certain psalms or those whose identity is arrived at by the application of the midrashic process. Thus Adam is "found" in Ps 139:16, "Your eyes beheld my unformed substance," referring to the clay from which Adam was formed. Melchizedek appears in Ps 110:4, read as "according to the order of Melchizedek." To Moses is attributed Psalm 90 because of the superscription "A Prayer of Moses the man of God." As for Abraham, the Talmudic editors point to the midrashic identification of Ethan the Ezrahite with the patriarch Abraham in the superscription to Psalm 89. Heman appears in the superscription to Psalm 88; Jeduthan to Psalms 39, 62, and 77; Asaph to Psalms 50 and 73-83; the three sons of Korah to Psalms 42, 44, 48, 85, 87, and 88. That there are three sons of Korah is based on their identification with the three sons of Korah in the book of Exodus (6:24). The artificiality of all this and of a good deal of midrashic interpretation generally is startling until one realizes that it is intentionally homiletical. The statement about the ten elders on whose work David drew in his composition of the psalms is not intended as an established tradition or a real historical reconstruction. The aim is, rather, to discover in the book instances of the sacred number ten. The *Midrash to Psalms* (on Ps 1:6; ed. S. Buber 1891, 9) observes, "Just as the Psalms bear the names of ten authors, so do they bear the names of ten kinds of song."

Although it is acknowledged that the book of Psalms is of a composite nature, all the elders who are said to have contributed to the book lived before David. Throughout the Talmudic literature the possibility is accepted unquestioningly that there can be a prophetic telling of the future in detail. Thus David is held to be the author of Psalm 137, foretelling not only the destruction of the first temple but also of the second (*Git.* 57b). The statement in one source (*Midr. Eccl. Rab.* 1:17)—that Ezra is one of the ten elders—is due in all probability to a scribal error (perhaps a confusion with Ethan the Ezrahite who, in fact, is not mentioned in the list of the ten given in this Midrash).

Throughout the talmudic literature, Proverbs, Ecclesiastes, and the Song of Songs are the words of Solomon— he was the author of the inspired words, although the books were not recorded in writing by him, but by Hezekiah and his associates. This is obviously based on the title of Proverbs 25: "These are the other proverbs of Solomon that the officials of King Hezekiah of Judah copied."

. 2. *Halakic Interpretation.* Halakhah is that branch of teaching dealing with the law in all its ramifications. Haggadah consists of the nonlegal side: preachments, theology, ethics, history, Folklore*§, science, medicine, and so forth. Talmudic-midrashic interpretation of the Bible is twofold: (a) halakic, the drawing out of rules and regulations from biblical texts, mainly from the Pentateuch and (b) haggadic, the use of the Bible to convey more general ideas and teachings on the conduct of life. The halakic interpretation predominates. It is more hard and fast, far more categorical than is the fluid haggadic interpretation, which is more poetry than prose, often a reading into the text rather than real exegesis.

Halakic exegesis proceeds by the application of hermeneutical principles (Hermeneutics*§) known as *middot*, "measures." Seven of these are attributed to Hillel*§ in the first century B.C.E. (*Sipra*, Introduction 1:7), and these were extended to thirteen by R. Ishmael§ in the second century C.E. (*Sipra*, Introduction 1-6). Behind these principles is the idea that all parts of the Pentateuch—the written Torah (in contradistinction to the oral Torah, the traditional interpretation of the former)—form a unified whole, so that it is possible to draw out its fullest implications by careful examination of each word and by comparing what is said in one portion with what is said in another.

Of R. Ishmael's thirteen principles, the ones chiefly employed throughout the talmudic literature are *kal va-ḥomer, gezerah shavah*, and *kelal u-ferat*. The *kal va-ḥomer* ("from the light to the severe") is the argument from the minor to the major, and it is used by the rabbis in the Bible itself (*Midr. Gen. Rab.* 92:7, referring to Gen 44:8; Exod 6:12; Deut 31:27; 1 Sam 23:3; Jer 12:5; Ezek 15:5). For example, Deut 21:23 states that the corpse of a criminal executed by the court must not be left on the gibbet overnight, which R. Meir (second cent.) took to mean that God is distressed at the criminal's death. Hence this teacher argued, "If God is troubled at the shedding of blood of the ungodly, how much more (*kal va-ḥomer*) at the blood of the righteous" (m. Sanh. 6:5). This is a halakic use of the argument: "If priests, who are not disqualified from serving in the temple by reason of age, are disqualified by reason of bodily defects (Lev 21:16-23), then Levites who are disqualified by reason of age (Num 8:24-26) are certainly disqualified by reason of bodily defects" (Ḥul. 24a).

The *gezerah shavah* ("similar expression") means that, if the same or a similar word occurs in two separate passages, then any elaboration found in one of the passages can be applied to the other. For example, the word *běmô' ădô* ("in its appointed time") is used both in connection with the perpetual offering (Num 18:2) and with regard to the paschal lamb (Num 9:2). Of the former it is stated explicitly that it has to be offered even on the sabbath, when work is forbidden; and this demonstrates that the term *běmô' ădô* denotes "even on the sabbath," yielding the rule that if the day when the paschal lamb is to be offered falls on the sabbath, it must be offered on that day (*Pesah* 66a).

Kelal u-ferat ("general and particular") denotes that, if a law is first stated in general terms and then specific instances are given, the law embraces only those instances. "You shall bring an offering of the livestock, even of the herd and flock" (Lev 1:2). Even though the term "livestock" might have included nondomesticated cattle, these are excluded by the particular instances that follow the general rule, only "from the herd and the flock" (*Sipra*, Introduction). *Perat u-kelal* ("particular and general"), on the other hand, means that, where a specific instance is followed by a general statement, it is all-inclusive (e.g., "when someone delivers to another a donkey, ox, sheep, or any other animal . . ." Exod 22:10). Here, the general statement "or any other animal" follows the statement of the particulars, so that beasts other than those specified are also included (*Sipra*, Introduction).

A combination of the above two principles is *kelal u-ferat u-kelal* ("general, particular, general"). Here the rule is: You may derive other things than those specified but only if they resemble those specified. "Spend the money for whatever you wish [general]—oxen, sheep, wine, strong drink [particular], or whatever you desire [general]" (Deut 14:26). Things other than those specified may be purchased, but only if they are items of foods and drink like those specified, garments being excluded (*Sipra*, Introduction).

Frequently, new laws are derived by logical extension of the laws stated. For example, the law that a man is responsible for damage done by the pit he has left uncovered (Exod 21:33-34) is extended to include his responsibility for harm done by a stone he has placed where it can do damage; or the law that a man is responsible for damage done by a fire that spreads from his field (Exod 22:6) is extended to damage done by an object that fell from his roof (*B. Qam.* 2b-5b). The prohibition of placing a stumbling block in front of a blind man (Lev 19:14) is extended to one who gives another bad advice (*Sipra* to the verse); to giving wine to a Nazirite (*Pesa* 22b), and to hitting a grownup son who might be tempted to retaliate (*Moed Qa*17a).

The method of deriving laws through the type of biblical exegesis mentioned above is known as a *derashah* or a midrash (both from the root *darash*, "to search, to inquire"). A major problem, much discussed by modern scholars, is which came first: the halakhah, the particular law, or the midrash or derashah on which it is said to be based (H. Albeck 1959; I. Heinemann 1976; D. Weiss-Halivni 1986)? Did the rabbis really derive the law from their close examination of Scripture, or did the law develop independently, the *derashah* being no more than an attempt to find scriptural support for what had been developed? In many instances, it is obvious that the law came first. For instance, one of the plants to be used in worship during the Feast of Tabernacles (Lev 23:40) is described as the fruit of "majestic trees," (*hadar*), a Hebrew word of uncertain meaning. The Talmud (*Sukk.* 35a) gives a number of extremely far-fetched attempts at proving, by the application of midrashic method, that it is the etrog, the citron, that is specified. Yet there was a tradition that it is the citron long before any of these attempts at proving it were made. On the other hand, the *derashah* does seem to be the actual source of the law in the many instances where debates on what the law is depend on the different ways of understanding the scriptural verse.

3. *Haggadic Interpretation.* The main feature to be noted of haggadic interpretation of Scripture is the effort to apply the texts to the contemporary scene. Like preachers everywhere, the rabbis used the Bible to convey what they believed the people they were addressing needed to hear in the particular circumstances in which they found themselves. Eisegesis, rather than exegesis, is at work in haggadic interpretation. Ideas are often read into a text with not the slightest suggestion that this is what the text really means. Maimonides[§] (Guide 3.43.573) saw this feature when he referred to the talmudic interpretation (*Ketub.* 5a) of the verse: "And you shall have a peg (*yātēd*) upon your weapon (*'ăzēnekā*)" (Deut 23:14; the wordplay is lost in

English). The comment reads the word *'ăzĕnekā* as if it were *'oznĕkā* ("your ear"). The "peg" is further taken to be the peg-shaped finger, yielding the thought "If a man hears an unworthy matter let him plug his ears with his fingers." Maimonides, followed by the majority of modern scholars, saw this type of Midrash as poetic fancy, "a witty conceit by which to instill some noble, moral quality."

Yet, in addition to this ubiquitous poetic element, the Talmudic haggadah allows itself great freedom in the belief that Scripture, in its richness as the word of God, can have levels of meaning other than the plain surface meaning. In the school of R. Ishmael it was taught (Sanh. 34a): "'Is not my word like fire?' says the Lord, and like a hammer that breaks a rock in pieces?' (Jer 23:29). Just as the rock is split into many splinters, so also one biblical verse may convey many teachings." In this midrash, the word of the Lord is identified with the text of Scripture, and this leads to its extension to the students of the Torah who peruse God's word. "Rava said, 'If a young scholar flies into a rage it is because the Torah inflames him, as it is said: "Is not my word like as a fire?" says the Lord'" (*Ta'an.* 4a). Similarly, the verse "Ho, everyone who thirsts, come to the waters" (Isa 55:1) is interpreted to teach that, just as water flows from a higher to a lower level, so also the words of Torah only endure in one who is meek (*Ta'an.* 7a). And once the verse in Isaiah has been interpreted to identify water with the Torah, the midrashic authors allowed themselves homiletical license to interpret every water reference in Scripture as applying to the Torah, even if this takes a verse entirely out of context. "And they went three days in the wilderness and found no water" (Exod 15:22) is interpreted to mean that when the people go for three days without hearing the reading of the Torah in the synagogue, they become exhausted (*B. Qam.* 82a). Again, since the verse says, "The waters wear away the stones" (Job 14:19), and since "water" refers to the Torah, the thought emerges that the way to overcome the stony heart is to engage in the study of the Torah (*Qidd.* 30b).

By the talmudic period, the doctrine of the hereafter, on which the Bible is comparatively silent, had become so thoroughly developed and accepted in rabbinic Judaism that it was natural for the rabbis to read it into the biblical verses. The verse "You make darkness, and it is night; when all the animals of the forest come creeping out" (Ps 104:20) is made to refer to this world of darkness, where the wicked pursue their nefarious schemes. A following verse (v. 23): "People go out to their work and to their labor until the evening" is made to refer to the righteous, who are given the reward of eternal bliss after their life on earth has come to its close (*B. Meṣ* 83b).

From these examples quoted, and they could easily be multiplied many times, it can be seen that the haggadic teachers treated the biblical verses piecemeal, as it were; using the texts in isolation in a consciously fanciful way to suit their purposes. In this, although each haggadist had his own individual application of the ideas, certain key concepts are used by all of them—(e.g., "water is Torah"). Thus, everywhere in the literature the divine name *Elohim* is made to refer to God's judgment, while the Tetragrammaton, YHWH, is made to refer to God's mercy. For example, the change from Elohim in the first chapter of Genesis to YHWH in the second is explained (*Gen. Rab.* 12:15) on the basis of the idea that God created the world in his quality of judgment but then added the quality of mercy that the world might endure. Everywhere, too, "wisdom" in the book of Proverbs refers to "the wisdom of the Torah," and the Song of Songs is seen as a dialogue between God and the community of Israel.

Religious polemics is also a prominent feature of haggadah. For instance, while the plural form is used in the verse "Let us make humankind in our image" (Gen 1:26), the next verse, "so God created mankind in his image," is in the singular in order to refute any dualistic notions (*Sanh.* 38b). A dualist, quoting the verse "For lo, the one who forms the mountains, creates the wind" (Amos 4:13), said to R. Judah the Prince, "He who created the mountains did not create the wind." "Fool," replied the rabbi, "look to the end of the verse: 'The Lord of Hosts is His name'" (Hul. 87a). The third-century Palestinian teacher, R. Abbahu, evidently preaching against both dualistic philosophies and Christian doctrine, quoted the verse "I am the first, I am the last, and beside Me there is no God" (Isa 44:6) and commented: "I am the first, for I have no father; I am the last, for I have no son; and beside Me there is no God, for I have no brother" (Exod. Rab. 29:5). In all this there is, without doubt, a background of actual debates between the rabbis and those they considered to be engaging in heretical interpretation of Scripture.

Bibliography: **H. Albeck,** *Mevo la-Mishnah* (1959) 3-62. **S. Buber** (ed.), *Midrash Psalms* (1891). **H. Danby** (tr.), *The Mishnah* (1933). **I. Epstein** (ed. and tr.), *The Babylonian Talmud* (1948). **M. Friedmann** (ed.), *Sifre* (1864). **D. W. Halivni,** *Peshat and Derash: Plain and Applied Meaning in Rabbinic Exegesis* (1990). **I. Heinemann,** *Darkhe ha-Agadah* (1976). **J. Heinemann,** *Aggadot ve-toledotehen* (1974). **I. Jacobs,** *The Midrashic Process* (1995). **L. Jacobs,** "Hermeneutics," *EncJud 8* (1971) 366-72. **N. Krochmal,** *Moreh nevukhey ha-zeman in Kitve Rabi Nahman Krochmal: Arukhim `al yede Shimòn Ravidovitz* (ed. S. Ravidovitsh, 1961) 189-256. **Krotoschin** (ed.), *The Palestinian Talmud* (1866). **S. Lieberman,** *Hellenism in Jewish Palestine: Studies in the Literary Transmission, Beliefs, and Manners of Palestine in the First Century* (1950) 47-82. **R. Loewe,** "The 'Plain' Meaning of Scripture in Early Jewish Exegesis," *Papers of the Institute of Jewish Studies, London* (ed. J. G. Weiss, 1964) 140-85. **Maimonides,** *The Guide of the Perplexed* (tr. S. Pines, 1963). **G. F. Moore,** *Judaism in the First Centuries of the Christian Era: The Age of Tannaim* (1958) 161-78, 235-50. **J. Roth,** "Talmud, Exegesis and Study of," *DMA 11* (1988) 583-87. **J. Schachter,** *The Students' Guide Through the Talmud by Z. H. Chajes* (1952). **H. L. Strack,** *Introduction to the Talmud and Midrash* (1982[8]; ET 1996[2]). **Vilna** (ed.), *Midrash Rabbah* (1911); (ed.), *The Babylonian Talmud* (1922). **I. H. Weiss** (ed.), *Sifra* (1863). **D. Weiss-Halivni,** *Midrash, Mishnah, and Gemara: The Jewish Predilection for Justified Law* (1986). **M. S. Zuckermandel** (ed.), *Tosefta* (1882).

L. JACOBS

FOLKLORE, RELIGION, AND MYTH

Folklore in Hebrew Bible Interpretation

1. *Defining Folklore*. The single term *folklore* refers to the primary material, the lore, and the formal task of studying these materials. While there is no standard definition of folklore, most definitions emphasize the concepts of oral and traditional, contrasting oral with written and traditional with novel. Such a discipline has much to offer biblical interpreters, since much of the Bible has roots in oral performance. Furthermore, parts of the Bible appear to represent traditions that were handed down over generations before appearing in written form.

The concept of tradition requires additional comment. One aspect of the term "traditional" is "communal" authorship. In cases where lore has been handed down and shaped by many persons in a culture over time, the concept of an individual creative author is insignificant. Such a chain of tradition has so many links that, in the end, the material reveals more about the ethos of the group than it does about any individual. As a discipline, folklore emphasizes the relationship between lore and the group that produced and bore it.

A common assumption about the term traditional is that it means "old." Folklore can, but need not, be as old as the hills, since folklore continues to be created. By definition, all communication in a group into which writing has not been introduced is folklore. Yet even among literate groups folklore persists as an alternative, often informal, mode of communication. This latter type of folklore, observed in such genres as greetings, gossip, jokes, and urban legends, is traditional in that it draws on a standard repertoire of conventions; at the same time, variations on these conventions are coined every day. Ancient Israel was a culture in transition from primary orality to some degree of literacy in which oral and written styles coexisted and overlapped. This means that one cannot assume that a given passage with a high degree of orality (a subjective assessment) is earlier than a parallel treatment with a high degree of literary features.

The hallmark of folklore is patterned repetition. Because oral communication is ephemeral, its composers repeat themselves on multiple levels to make their points, relying on conventions mutually intelligible to performer and audience (W. Ong 1982, 31). This holds true for the Bible; words, phrases, and ideas are repeated or, better, "seconded" (J. Kugel 1981). Typical episodes ("traditional episodes" in D. Irvin 1978, 9-13; "type-scenes" in R. Alter 1981, 47-62, though he considers them as a literary rather than an oral-traditional phenomenon), and stock characters—like the hero (R. Hendel 1987, 133-165), the trickster (S. Niditch 1987), the wise woman, the strange woman (C. Camp 1985), and the wild man (G. Mobley 1997)—are used. On the thematic level, such key themes as creation or exodus are repeated and reinterpreted in new contexts (Niditch 1985; D. Ben-Amos 1992, 823). One of the most basic levels of patterning in folklore is that of rhythmic speech, although there is no consensus among biblical scholars regarding the metrical quality of ancient Hebrew verse (see M. O'Connor 1980; J. Kugel 1981).

Despite its reliance on the formulaic, there is originality in folklore in the choice and arrangement of traditional materials and in the way that each performance is a unique interaction between composer and audience. Furthermore, these redundant patterns are more than mere repetition; conventions are commonly subverted in contrasting, surprising ways.

2. *The Relevance of Folklore to the Hebrew Bible*. Folklore, as a discipline that observes, describes, and analyzes repetitive patterns in traditional discourse, has implications for Hebrew Bible study. First, many parts of the Bible have roots in oral performance. Examples include oracles delivered by prophets (Prophecy and Prophets, Hebrew Bible[‡§]), victory songs chanted by musicians, psalms offered by worshipers, proverbs uttered by teachers, and teachings

spoken by priests. Second, "folkloristic" motifs can be detected throughout the Bible's prose and poetic sections (Poetry, Hebrew Bible[‡§]) and can be compared with folkloric material outside the Bible.

Third, folklore provides tools for reconstructing the oral traditions of Israel (Ben-Amos 1992, 819). Through analogy with extrabiblical folklore, light is shed on Israelite popular traditions alluded to in the Bible but not given full treatment: e.g., the story of the primeval battle between God and the dragon of chaos. This is important both for understanding the social world out of which the Bible emerged and for giving fuller shape to material the Bible preserves incidentally. Folklore, then, provides tools for digging out Israelite popular traditions submerged in the Bible.

At the same time, the limits of folklore must be recognized. Contemporary folklore research is based on fieldwork with living informants and on the collection of many variants of a given type of story, song, or proverbial saying. Biblical researchers do not have access to native informants; however, in some cases it is possible that traditions preserved in late Second Temple, rabbinic, early Christian, and even medieval literature preserve lore stemming from the biblical period (Ben-Amos 1992, 819-20). It is clear that Second Temple and rabbinic texts contain details and elaborations of oriental mythological themes that preserve oral traditions from the First Temple period. This is particularly evident in the creation stories and their recurring themes.

In certain cases the Bible itself preserves variants of a given type of traditional tale, like the three stories in Genesis in which a patriarch pretends his wife is his sister (Gen 12:10-20; 20:1-18; 26:6-11). For the most part, the paucity of extant native variants inevitably leads biblical folklorists to other cultural fields in search of parallel material, thus risking "parallelomania" (Sandmel 1962; see below regarding J. Frazer). The comparative method is fundamental to folklore research but must be used with care (S. Talmon 1993).

The very application of methods designed for use with oral tradition to a literary corpus may seem inappropriate. This, however, is not just a problem for biblical folklore specialists; all research into the folklore of past cultures must rely on texts. How does one isolate oral tradition in written text? Many schemes, like Olrik's laws, purport to offer trait lists of oral tradition (A. Olrik 1965; more recently, see Ong 1982, 36-57). Often these observations about the characteristics of oral narrative are based on a certain cultural corpus—in Olrik's case European folktales—and cannot be assumed to be universal. Furthermore, much of the data Olrik considered was written material with putative oral roots, like the Bible. This does not mean that there are not recognizable differences between oral and written discourse. Nevertheless, there is no sure methodological filter capable of empirically isolating the oral residue in written materials.

Then why even use the methods of folklore in biblical study? Because the Bible, although literature, is a certain kind of literature: traditional literature (Niditch 1987, xiii-xiv). Reliance on literary methods, largely devised for the interpretation of contemporary prose and poetic forms, has its own potential for distorting material rooted in oral performance or composed in the oral style and shaped by many tradents rather than by a single author. The tools of folklore must be utilized along with the tools of Literary*§ analysis in order to adequately account for the Bible's oral and written qualities.

3. *The Use of Folklore in Biblical Studies.* The collection of folklore materials—e.g., myths, legends, and tales—and their juxtaposition with similar biblical materials has had a dramatic effect. This comparative task has underscored the similarities between ancient Israel and other cultures, serving as an antidote to dogmatic tendencies that overemphasize the uniqueness of the Bible. At the same time, the comparative task illuminates what is distinctive and unique about the Bible by exposing how the lore is integrated into this specific cultural context (Niditch 1993, 11).

84

The pioneer in comparative folklore was H. Gunkel§, who initially sought to expose Israelite popular tradition through comparisons with ancient Near Eastern myths deciphered from cuneiform (1895). Eventually, he expanded his analyses to the larger world of folktales drawn from ancient and contemporary sources (1917). In the three editions of his Genesis commentary, Gunkel systematically described and traced the development of the basic genres (*Gattungen*) in Israelite oral tradition. According to him, these conventional forms developed from brief poetic units, each functioning in a different performance arena, or "setting in life" (*Sitz im Leben*). A class of storytellers wove these into larger, coherent narratives that later became the basis for the literary sources already detected by J. Wellhausen§ and others.

Gunkel's assumptions about the character of oral tradition were shaped by the anthropology of his day. He imagined that oral traditions were, by definition, brief, poetic, and reflective of a kind of childlike mentality. On the one hand, his emphasis on oral tradition provided a foil to theories about the development of biblical literature that emphasized the documentary quality of formative biblical traditions. The multiform quality of biblical material may be evidence of the variation characteristic of oral tradition rather than of the existence of distinct literary documents secondarily spliced together by later editors. On the other hand, Gunkel's insistence that the oral repertoire consisted of brief isolated units facilitated an atomization of biblical materials akin to that produced by the subsequent excesses of some source critics. Subsequent research into oral tradition has made clear that traditional materials can be quite extensive and complex (A. Lord 1960).

Nevertheless, Gunkel's work with folklore remains valuable. Although he was not alone in this, his analysis of biblical texts in light of Near Eastern myth took biblical studies across a threshold from which it has never returned. His basic method of adducing parallels from myth and folklore as a means of highlighting the popular motifs embedded in biblical narratives is sound, although this exercise in itself is a half-measure that must be accompanied by a thoroughgoing analysis of how a given motif functions in its host culture. Gunkel, however, did not neglect what we now call the ethnographic task. His Form Criticism*§ of Genesis and the psalms can be seen as early attempts to observe and describe Israel's own traditional forms.

Frazer's *Folk-lore* (1918), appearing in the same period, arranged colorful stories and obscure customs from the Bible alongside a wide-ranging collection of textual artifacts—legends, myths, and travelers' accounts of the "savage" races—in an attempt, in the fashion of a Victorian museum, to illustrate the stages of humanity's social evolution. Beyond his outdated assumptions about the "primitive" nature of the ancients, the mere adducing of anecdotal and impressionistic parallels with no attention to geographic and chronological settings (Chronology, Hebrew Bible§) often obscures what is distinctive about the original subject. Despite its lack of discrimination, Frazer's compendium has been used as a "quarry" of suggested parallels (J. Rogerson 1978, 73).

In the vein of catalogues of lore, T. Gaster's (1969) revision of Frazer is a better quarry to mine. Although he intended to revise Frazer, his work advanced far beyond Frazer's because, as a Semiticist, Gaster was able to see in texts patterns related to Israel and its neighboring cultures. This kind of work, which adduces parallels from folklore and mythology*§ in selected passages throughout the Bible, is out of step with recent ethnographic approaches that attempt to detect native genres and elements rather than universal ones. Nevertheless, Gaster's work remains the best single comparative reference for biblical folklore. Even with its occasional forced parallel, the overall impact dramatically shows that the Bible cannot be adequately interpreted in isolation from comparative folklore and myth.

Beyond the confines of biblical scholarship, the major reference works for cross-cultural folklore analysis are A. Aarne and S. Thompson's *Types of the Folktale* (1964) and S. Thompson's *Motif-Index of Folk Literature* (1955-58). Aarne and Thompson are part of the

Historical-Geographic school, whose approach is to assemble all the variants of a type or feature of a tale. By tracing each variant, the movements of folklore through time and place become exposed. However, given the paucity of extant variants and the myriad complications of dating biblical materials and detecting their original provenance, it is virtually impossible to genetically trace the family tree of biblical folklore. These indexes, however, are useful in a more general way. They have provided folklorists with a common analytic language and, despite their largely European scope, have sketched a reliable portrait of the shape of common tales and their constituent parts. The *Motif-Index* is of more direct help to biblical scholars than *Types of the Folktale* because the Bible contains few (if any) intact folktales (perhaps Jotham's fable of the trees in Judg 9:8-15) but abounds in folkloristic motifs. Gaster provides a cross-reference to Thompson's *Motif-Index*.

There are comparative approaches that focus on the form of materials rather than their content. Loosely described as types of Structuralism*§, these involve a secondary translation of linguistic materials into abstract codes that reveal the form, or structure, underneath the surface details. The two most influential forms of structuralism in folklore have been those of C. Lévi-Strauss (1968) and V. Propp (1958). Eschewing surface details of content, Lévi-Strauss isolated elements in Native American myths that expressed binary oppositions representative of "the primary conflicts of human existence" (W. Doty 1986, 200). Myths function to resolve these dilemmas by introducing third, anomalous terms that mediate the conflict. Lévi-Strauss's work has not been influential among biblical folklorists beyond the level of drawing attention to these binary oppositions (Leach 1969; critique by Rogerson 1974, 109-12,124).

More influential has been the work of Propp, whose study of Russian fairy tales was written in 1928 but not widely known in Europe and the United States until the early 1960s. Propp charted the linear sequence of events ("functions") in these fairy tales, all of which, according to him, contain a limited number of functions that occur in an unvarying order, although every possible function is not present in each tale. Propp's abstract scheme of traditional plot sequence demonstrates how the fairy tales worked out problems of human development, beginning with the hero leaving home, then confronting various dangers, and ultimately marrying. Some biblical scholars have closely followed Propp's scheme, employing his terms for these plot functions (J. Sasson 1989); others have used his work as a model for examining on a synchronic level the sequence of actions in biblical narratives (H. Jason 1979; D. Patte 1980; R. Culley 1976a, 69-115).

Since the 1960s, folklorists have paid increasing attention to ethnic studies, the analysis of materials within specific cultural contexts, eschewing Cross-Cultural*§ analytic concepts of genre in favor of native terms. Closely aligned with this is an emphasis on performance context. Ben-Amos observes that the imposition of European categories—like folktale, myth, or legend—on biblical materials is anachronistic (1976, 217). He charts a promising new direction for biblical folklorists that begins with an analysis of the Hebrew Bible's own terms for poetic (e.g., *sîr, mizmôr, qînâ, dĕbar YHWH, ḥāzôn, maśśā*), prose (*ma'ăśĕh, niplā'ôt*), and conversational (*māsāl, hîdâ*) genres and suggests performance contexts for each (1992, 823-26). The contemporary emphasis on performance continues and updates Gunkel's attempt to define the life settings of oral traditions in Genesis and the psalms.

Other scholars have used comparative material and various modern folklore theories to refine the picture of Israel's ethnic repertoire. These range from studies of traditional formulas in the psalms (Culley 1967), to the genre of proverbs (C. Fontaine 1982), to the shape of the Israelite heroic biography (R. Hendel 1987), and to the ethos of Israelite folklore as seen in its attraction to the theme of the underdog (Niditch 1987).

4. *From Oral Tradition to Oral Register*. The most important work in oral tradition has been that of A. Lord. Based on fieldwork with south Slavic folk singers, Lord suggests that oral epic

86

is composed by persons immersed in all the conventions of a tradition: formulaic phrases, larger motifs, and even larger typical narrative patterns. In each performance, the composer extemporaneously creates a unique version of the song, although the constituent elements of the performance are traditional.

This oral-formulaic theory has been employed by biblical scholars to understand the conventional language with its myriad variations in the Hebrew Bible (Culley 1976b). Most of this work has been done in poetic genres, although some has been done with prose genres (Culley 1976a; D. Gunn 1974). Biblical scholars have been slow to extend this theory beyond poetic genres. Part of this hesitancy, perhaps, lies in too great a reliance on the metrical element in Lord's theory, which was formulated on the basis of a genre with a high degree of metrical organization. It is as if one based a general theory of oral tradition on the performances of square-dance callers. There are countless other oral modes without the rhythm of poetry and the accompaniment of music. Other of Lord's general principles—the immersion in a traditional repertoire, the variations produced by the creative arrangement of these conventions in performance—need not be tied to the metrical principle. Charting their course from contemporary specialists in oral tradition (J. Foley 1992), biblical folklorists need to advance more readily into nonpoetic genres.

A recent development in oral tradition is the emergence of the concept of "register" (see Foley, 287-89; Niditch 1996). In vocal music, the term refers to a portion of the entire range of a voice. A person can sing in different registers, articulating from the chest or from the head, as in falsetto. The concept of an oral register recognizes a variety of speech styles available to speakers depending on the social situation. For instance, in informal settings one uses one voice; in formal settings, another. Each register has its own repertoire of conventions. This concept bridges the great divide between oral and written modes of communication, both of which are available simultaneously to speakers and cultures.

What are the implications of this for biblical study? From the beginnings with Gunkel, biblical scholars, laboring under the contradiction of analyzing the written with tools designed for the oral, have struggled to isolate the oral substratum in written texts. The concept of "register" fundamentally recognizes transitional modes between these falsely drawn oppositions. In the Bible, for instance, most of the prose narratives in the primary history (Genesis-Kings), draw on the oral register whether their origins are in oral tradition or in written documents. The biblical authors had heard more stories than they had read; and, even when they wrote, their materials reflect the kinds of traditional characterizations, formulaic language, and patterned repetition of oral tradition, of folklore. Furthermore, many of the written portions of the Bible in Jewish tradition, often referred to as *Miqra'* ("Proclamation"), were formulated for the express purpose of public reading.

This does not mean that it is all folklore; nor does it mean that all parts and genres of the Bible draw equally from the oral register. It does mean that the tools of folklore, alongside those of literary criticism, can and must be applied to the kind of writings contained in the Bible, which emerged from a culture in gradual transition from primary orality to some degree of popular literacy (A. Demsky 1988, 15-20). Folklore analysis, then, has implications for biblical writings beyond those with clear performance contexts and beyond those genres (e.g., myths, legends, and folktales) commonly thought of as "folkloristic."

Bibliography: A. Aarne and **S. Thompson,** *The Types of the Folktale: A Classification and Bibliography* (1964). **R. Alter,** *The Art of Biblical Narrative* (1981). **D. Ben-Amos** (ed.), "Analytical Categories and Ethnic Genres," *Folklore Genres* (1976) 215-42; "Folklore in the Ancient Near East," *ABD* (1992) 2:818-28. **C. Camp,** *Wisdom and the Feminine in the Book of Proverbs* (Bible and Literature 11, 1985). **R. C. Culley**, *Oral Formulaic Language in the*

Biblical Psalms (1967); *Studies in the Structure of Hebrew Narrative* (Semeia Sup., 1976*a*); (ed.), "Oral Tradition and the OT: Some Recent Discussion," *Semeia* 5 (1976*b*) 1-33; "Exploring New Directions," *The HB and Its Modern Interpreters* (ed. D. Knight and G. Tucker, 1985) 167-200. **A. Demsky,** "Writing in Ancient Israel and Early Judaism: The Biblical Period," *Mikra* (ed. J. Mulder, 1988) 1-38. **W. Doty,** *Mythography: The Study of Myths and Rituals* (1986). **J. M. Foley,** "Word-Power, Performance, and Tradition," *JAF 105* (1992) 275-301. **C. Fontaine,** *Traditional Sayings in the OT* (1982). **J. G. Frazer,** *Folk-lore in the OT* (1918). **T. H. Gaster,** *Myth, Legend, and Custom in the OT* (1969). **H. Gunkel,** *Schöpfung und Chaos in Urzeit und Endzeit* (1895); *Das Märchen im Alten Testament* (1917, 1921; ET *The Folktale in the OT* 1987). **D. Gunn,** "Narrative Patterns and Oral Tradition in Judges and Samuel," *VT* 24 (1974) 286-317. **R. Hendel,** *The Epic of the Patriarch* (HSM 42, 1987). **D. Irvin,** *Mytharion: The Comparison of Tales from the OT and the Ancient Near East* (AOAT 32, 1978). **H. Jason,** "The Story of David and Goliath: A Folk Epic?" *Bib* 60 (1979) 36-70. **P. Kirkpatrick,** *The OT and Folklore Study* (JSOTSup 62, 1988). **D. Knight,** *Rediscovering the Traditions of Israel* (SBLDS 9, 1975). **J. Kugel,** *The Idea of Biblical Poetry: Parallelism and Its History* (1981). **C. Lévi-Strauss,** "The Structural Study of Myth," *Myth: A Symposium* (ed. T. Sebeok, 1968) 81-106. **E. Leach,** *Genesis as Myth and Other Essays* (1969). **A. Lord,** *The Singer of Tales* (1960). **G. Mobley,** "The Wild Man in the Bible and Ancient Near East," *JBL* 116 (1997) 217-33. **S. Niditch,** *Chaos to Cosmos: Studies in Biblical Patterns of Creation* (SPSHS 6, 1985); *Underdogs and Tricksters* (New Voices in Biblical Studies, 1987); (ed.), *Text and Tradition: The HB and Folklore* (SemeiaSt, 1990); *Folklore and the HB* (Guide to Biblical Scholarship OT Series, 1993); *Oral Word and Written Word: Ancient Israelite Literature* (1996). **M. O'Connor,** *Hebrew Verse Structure* (1980). **A. Olrik,** "Epic Laws of Folk Narrative," *The Study of Folklore* (ed. A. Dundes, 1965) 129-41. **W. J. Ong,** *Orality and Literacy: The Technologizing of the Word* (1982). **D. Patte** (ed.), "Genesis 2 and 3: Kaleidoscope Structural Readings," *Semeia 18* (1980) 1-164. **V. Propp,** *The Morphology of the Folktale* (1928; ET tr. L. Scott, Bibliographical and Special Series of the American Folklore Society 9, 1958). **J. W. Rogerson,** *Myth in OT Interpretation* (BZAW 134, 1974); *Anthropology and the OT* (Growing Points in Theology, 1978). **Samuel Sandmel,** "Parallelomania." *JBL* 81 (1962) 1-13. **J. M. Sasson,** *Ruth* (1989). **S. Talmon,** "The Comparative Method in Biblical Interpretation: Principles and Problems," *Congress Volume* (ed. W. Zimmerli et al., 1977) 320-56. **S. Thompson,** *Motif-Index of Folk Literature* (1932-36; rev. and enl. ed., 6 vols. 1955-58).

G. MOBLEY

FOLKLORE, RELIGION, AND MYTH

Myth and Ritual School

This expression is used primarily to designate the group of scholars who contributed to the two symposia *Myth and Ritual* (1933) and *The Labyrinth* (1935), under the editorship of S. Hooke[§]. It should be noted that Hooke always denied that a clearly defined school had ever existed; and certainly the original authors, who included W. Oesterley[§], T. Robinson[§], and E. James, did not always speak with one voice. In some respects, their general outlook derived from the anthropological approach of J. Frazer[§], especially his functional view of myth (Mythology and Biblical Studies*[§]), but they differed from him in their understanding of myth as essentially the spoken part of ritual and in their questioning of his purely comparative method. Hooke noted that the roots of the approach lay in the so-called diffusionist movement associated with the British scholars G. E. Smith and W. Perry (Hooke 1958, 1).

Most significantly, the scholars in question postulated the existence of a general myth-and-ritual pattern common to the ancient Near East, which found its fullest expression in a great annual new year celebration fundamental for the community's welfare during the ensuing year. As seen most clearly in the Babylonian new year (or *akitu*) festival, this celebration had five basic components, which also lay behind many other rites: a dramatic representation of the death and resurrection of the god, a recitation of the creation myth, a ritual combat in which the deity overcomes his enemies, the sacred marriage, and finally a great procession culminating in the god's enthronement. Further, the Myth and Ritual group claimed that a similar and equally significant celebration existed in ancient Israel and was represented by the autumnal complex of celebrations centering on the Feast of Ingathering, or Booths, which was to be understood as a new year festival.

Ancient Near Eastern archaeological discoveries (Archaeology and Biblical Studies*[§]) played a major part in this reconstruction, and later discoveries, notably the Ugaritic (Ugarit and the Bible[§] [see Translation*]), were held to confirm it. As far as Hebrew Bible studies are concerned, the work of the Myth and Ritual school marked a revolution of abiding significance. Up to that time modern scholarship had tended to find the distinctive religion of Israel in the great prophets (Prophecy and Prophets, Hebrew Bible[‡§]), who were anti-cultic and proclaimed a spiritual faith opposed to that represented by the priesthood. By contrast, it could now be seen how central a part the cult played in the nation's religion and that full weight had to be given to this aspect in any assessment of ancient Israelite society.

Another new development in Hebrew Bible scholarship largely initiated by the Myth and Ritual writers was the understanding of the religious role of the king. In Hooke's reconstruction of the new year festival, the king took the leading part, even to the extent of representing the deity in the ritual. Hitherto, largely as a result of the concentration on the prophets, the Israelite monarchy had generally been viewed in a negative light, with the king depicted as a secular figure. But in a seminal essay in *The Labyrinth* (and more fully in a subsequent study), A. Johnson[§] (1955), one of the younger Myth and Ritual scholars, argued that the king was the chief actor in the great Israelite annual celebration, undergoing a symbolic "death" and "resurrection" in the ritual. Johnson drew his evidence largely from the psalms, building on the work of H. Gunkel[§], who had recognized that a number of psalms originally referred, not to a future "messiah," but to the actual Davidic monarch. However, Johnson found indications of the king's cultic role in a much wider range of psalm material, and in this he has been followed by many subsequent writers. It is, perhaps, this Myth and Ritual view of Israel's monarchy that has been most widely acknowledged, as shown by the contents of the final Myth and Ritual collection, *Myth, Ritual, and Kingship* (1958).

The theories of the school have provoked intense discussion and criticism. Near Eastern specialists have claimed that their postulate of a universal pattern was too theoretical and overlooked fundamental differences between the religious systems of Mesopotamia and Egypt. While these differences are important—and the Myth and Ritual scholars were more aware of them than has often been recognized—the demonstration by these scholars of a basic similarity in the religious structure of the whole area over two millennia has not been seriously shaken. Certain of the more imaginative suggestions of some, though not all, of the Myth and Ritual scholars—YHWH being a dying and rising god, the existence in Israel of the sacred marriage, or the Davidic king as being in a real sense "divine"—have not found wide support among English-speaking authorities. On the other hand, considerable attention has been devoted to the traditions connected with Mount Zion and to the Canaanite elements they incorporated from the pre-Israelite Jebusite sanctuary. As a result, It has become increasingly recognized that there was a festival of the enthronement of YHWH on the occasion of the autumn celebrations, characterized by a great procession with the ark as the symbol of the divine presence (although its precise significance is still a matter of debate). Theories of a fusion between YHWH and *El Elyon*, the old Canaanite deity of Jerusalem, have emphasized Israel's God as Creator and the source of fertility, aspects prominent in the outlook of the Myth and Ritual school.

The ideas of the Myth and Ritual authors have been influential, not only in Great Britain, but also in other countries (e.g. H. J. Kraus's *Worship in Israel,* 1954, reflects the new developments they inaugurated). But they have had their main effect above all in Scandinavia, where a group of scholars centered at the University of Uppsala enthusiastically embraced them. Indeed, to some degree, the views of the Myth and Ritual school were anticipated by the Norwegian scholar S. Mowinckel[§], who, in the second volume of his *Psalmenstudien* (1922), interpreted a number of psalms as the liturgy for a festival of Yahweh's enthronement in connection with the autumnal new year festival. But it was the Swedish scholar I. Engnell[§] who gave the most unqualified support to the general Myth and Ritual thesis and pressed it in directions with which its original proponents might not fully have concurred.

Four aspects of Engnell's studies (1943) merit particular mention. First, a central point to his whole outlook is the basic Myth and Ritual concept of a common ancient Near Eastern religious pattern centered on the new year celebration, of which Israel's religion could only be understood as a variant. Second, he stressed the fundamental importance of the king in the pattern, including ancient Israelite kingship. He did not hesitate to call the king "divine," the earthly embodiment of the deity and the source of blessing and fertility for society through the enactment of the god's death and resurrection and the sacred marriage. Other Scandinavian scholars, notably G. Widengren (1955), have more systematically developed this understanding of the Hebrew Bible monarchy. Third, in a long series of articles in the biblical encyclopedia *Svenskt Bibliskt Upplagsverk,*thirteen of which have been translated into English, Engnell applied his theories to the exegesis of the Hebrew Bible to illustrate how the myth-and-ritual pattern provides the correct understanding for many biblical narratives and concepts like Passover and exodus (of which J. Pederson[§] had already given a cultic interpretation in 1940), or Messiah and Son of Man. In the case of the last two concepts and for understanding Second Isaiah's Suffering Servant, the sacral monarch was the determinative factor. These insights were further worked out in an important study by the Danish scholar A. Bentzen[§]. Fourth, in his investigation of prophetism, Engnell strongly attacked the common assumption that the great prophets were divorced from the cult. Some of them, like Amos, were actual cultic officials; some of the prophetic books were temple liturgies, or at least close reflections of them; and much in all of them reproduced the themes and language of Israelite worship. Again, other more detailed studies have carried forward this approach, e.g., those by A. Haldar in Sweden (1945) and Johnson in England (1944). Engnell has been the clearest follower of the methods of the Myth and Ritual school and the decisive influence on the younger scholars who may be said to constitute the Uppsala school. Not even in Scandinavia have his more extreme views always won acceptance, but the basic approach of the Myth and Ritual school has been very marked on biblical scholarship there as well as in other countries, including Germany, where the general consensus has often appeared hostile to it.

Bibliography: G. W. Anderson, "Some Aspects of the Uppsala School of OT Study," *HTR* 43 (1950) 239-56. **A. Bentzen,** *King and Messiah* (1948; ET 1955). **I. Engnell,** *Studies in Divine Kingship in the Ancient Near East* (1943, 1967²); "The Ebed Yahweh Songs and the Suffering Messiah in 'Deutero-Isaiah,'" *BJRL* 21 (1948) 54-93; "Methodological Aspects of OT Study," VTSup (1960) 13-30; *A Rigid Scrutiny* (1969); *Critical Essays on the OT* (1970). **A. Haldar,** *Associations of Cult Prophets Among the Ancient Semites* (1945). **S. H. Hooke** (ed.), *Myth and Ritual: Essays on the Myth and Ritual of the Hebrews in Relation to the Culture Pattern of the Ancient East* (1933); *The Labyrinth: Further Studies in the Relation Between Myth and Ritual in the Ancient World* (1935); *Myth, Ritual, and Kingship: Essays on the Theory and Practice of Kingship in the Ancient Near East and in Israel* (1958). **A. R. Johnson,** The Cultic Prophet in Ancient Israel (1944, 1962²); *Sacral Kingship in Ancient Israel* (1955, 1967²). **H. J. Kraus,** *Worship in Israel: A Cultic History of the OT* (1954; ET 1966). **S. Mowinckel,** *Psalmenstudien,* vol. 2 (1922); *He That Cometh* (1951; ET 1956); *The Psalms in Israel's Worship,* vol. 1 (1951; ET 1962) chaps. 3 and 4. **J. Pedersen,** "The Crossing of the Reed Sea and the Paschal Legend," *Israel: Its Life and Culture iii-iv* (1940) 728-37. **J. R. Porter,** "Two Presidents of the Folklore Society: S. H. Hooke and E. O. James," *Folklore* 88 (1977) 131-45. **G. Widengren,** *Sakrales Königtum im Alten Testament und im Judentum* (1955).

J. R. PORTER

FOLKLORE, RELIGION, AND MYTH

Mythology and Biblical Studies (to 1800)

"Of all the phenomena of human culture, myth and religion are the most refractory to a merely logical analysis" (Cassirer 1944, 72). This thought may help to explain differences in terminology and approaches to myth over the years.

The fourth-century Christian writer Origen's allegorical interpretation of mythical biblical materials set the tone that dominated biblical interpretation until the Renaissance and Reformation. By the medieval period, allegorical interpretation had developed into a complex fourfold interpretive schema: Every Scripture text possessed a literal, allegorical, moral, and anagogical meaning.

With the coming of the Renaissance and the Enlightenment, implicit faith began to give way to the inquiry of reason; as made evident by the quote: "Man is the measure of all things." Human standards as to what is reasonable took the place of an unquestioning acceptance of dogmatic tradition. The Bible was now coming to be viewed as one piece of literature among many others to which the same principles of interpretation applied; the clear signs of human fallibility in its composition involved a reassessment of its supernatural features, especially divine manifestations and miracles. Thus, for B. Spinoza§, miracles were impossible since Nature was immutable, being itself God's will; as a result, the account of a miracle could be seen as a myth that expressed humanity's ignorance of natural causes (1670, chap. 7). On the other hand, the Reformation had brought with it an even more rigid view of the infallible Bible in its literal sense, and thus the struggle over interpretation was to continue.

The Deists (Deism§) brought matters to a head. By ridiculing the biblical narrative as nothing but a collection of fables and by assuming a developed level of culture on the part of the authors, the Deists accused the biblical authors of deceit and imposture. It was R. Lowth§ who indicated the general lines of a reply by analyzing Hebrew Poetry‡§ as any other literature, considering it aesthetically without special reference to its truth (Lowth 1753). He held that religious poetry, especially Hebrew, was the highest point of all poetry and was able to instill in the human soul principles of morality (Feldman and Richardson 1972, 144-50). Though he held that image-full poetry was the earliest form of human expression, he distinguished between poetry derived from nature (like the earliest human speech) and poetry as conscious art. J. G. Herder§, in some ways not unlike Lowth, was the poet rather than the critic, concerning himself with the poetry and spirit of ancient literatures and traditions and urging the need to "live" them in order to understand them and their world. Original traditions were, he thought, poetical. Later, he opined that orally transmitted primitive sagas originated before developed poetical structures. Herder had a deep love of the Hebrew Bible, although he was reluctant to commit himself as to its historical content (1782-83; 1967; Suphan ed., 11, 324). He regarded Genesis 1-3 as saga with a historical basis, although he considered Adam's naming the animals as something like fable. The tradition as a whole—myth, saga, and fable—expressed truths about the nature of the human species and its existence in the world (Feldman and Richardson 1962, 224-40).

It was left to J. G. Eichhorn§ to work out clear principles for the interpretation of the biblical narratives. In his *Urgeschichte: Ein Versuch* (1779) he rejected the idea, once shared by Herder and still widely held today, that primitive people lived in a golden age and possessed fully developed faculties. The first age, he maintained, was rather the age of the childhood of humankind, in which faculties were undeveloped, sources for gathering knowledge limited, and experience restricted. It could, however, be regarded as a happy state, at least initially, for primitive people knew no other. They were ignorant of the cause of events and hence ascribed to the direct action of God many things modern persons would attribute to secondary causes. Genesis 2-3 relates the true history of how our first parents desired perpetual youth. Seeing the snake eating the fruit, they did likewise. Their own thoughts were attributed to a talking snake; there is nothing to suggest a devil was tempting them. They were driven out of the garden by thunder and lightning, and when they tried to return, they were always prevented. God speaking was probably thunder, which was known as the voice of Yahweh. Believing as he did in the Mosaic authorship of the Pentateuch (Pentateuchal Criticism[‡§]), Eichhorn asked whether Moses could have purposefully inserted a mythological memoir into his first book without any guarantee that it would be interpreted correctly. He concluded that, at this stage, the story was basically factual, transmitted (and of course embellished) along the way, from the earliest times.

The idea of the childhood of humankind and its association with myth was developed by C. Heyne, Eichhorn's former professor of classical studies (Feldman and Richardson, 215-23). We are indebted to him for bringing order to the study of myth and especially for his distinction between the original myth, the stuff of ancient tradition, and the later poetical form, which was usually the result of a long period of development. Thus, without resorting to allegory, a knowledge of which was out of the question in the earliest times, it was now possible to find an explanation for the unacceptable features of the biblical narrative considered to be history. These features should be seen, not as a conscious deception by the authors of the later poetical production, but as an artless and unsophisticated account in oral tradition. Myth is not fiction, but its contents are varied. Heyne distinguished three types of myth: (1) historical myth—about real persons or events, but with mythological additions; (2) philosophical myth—about ethical problems (e.g., evil in the world) and natural phenomena (e.g., creation accounts); and (3) poetical myth—artistic combinations of earlier myths, with the addition of new stories and poetic embellishments. Thus, myth, not poetry, was the earliest stage of human thought and expression. Homer and Hesiod did not make up their stories; they gave them poetic shape.

In 1788, Eichhorn (*ABBL*, 1:984) asked: Need one be surprised if the Semitic nations, like the Greeks, also had their myths? Advances in science and historical research had shown that, in Genesis 2-3, the historical link could no longer be defended. The narrative now seemed to him to be a philosophical myth about the loss of the happy days of primitive innocence. As intellect and experience developed people began to desire more than they had ("the grass next door is greener"). Envy awoke, unrest followed, and contentment had left. They desired the "food of the gods." Soon these experiences, expressed in *Bildersprache*, or metaphorical language, took the form of a saga. As Heyne had shown, primitive humans, unaccustomed to abstract thought, saw and expressed only the material and the individual. Unable to "stand back" from events and lacking the capacity to compare them with other experiences, they tended to "blow up" extraordinary events to more than life size, consequently transforming them into supernatural manifestations. But myths are not fables (fictitious stories that impart a moral); they are, rather, the oldest history and philosophy, passing on the events and experiences of primitive humanity in the sense modes of the thought and speech of those early times (Eichhorn 1790-93, 2:260).

By 1790, Eichhorn was collaborating with a former student, J. P. Gabler[§] (then professor at Altdorf), who brought out a new edition of the *Urgeschichte* (3 vols. 1790-93) comprising "an exact and complete historical-critical review of the different modes of interpretation." Gabler criticized equally the traditional approach, especially allegory, which so often read back Christian doctrine into the text, and the Deists, who ignored historical development. In historical myth, events were described, not as a modern person would do, but as the primitive authors conceived them to have happened. Moreover, the mere presence of an event in an account did not define the myth as historical. The event might be included to illustrate an idea, which would then make it a philosophical myth like the fall of humanity and the Tower of Babel. As historical myth developed through time, the names of great men became more prominent in them; but, at the same time, recollection faded and the actual facts became cloudier. Stories became attached to the names, however, and often etymological meanings in keeping with the role of the person were added. Although fables might, at this later stage, be added to the myth, this would not justify describing the myth as fable. On the other hand, should one regard as unhistorical only those parts that must necessarily be unhistorical? Or should one not, rather, in a myth that is clearly philosophical, interpret the details in harmony with the leading idea? Should one not, rather, regard Adam (man) and Eve (woman) as being just as etymological as Prometheus and Pandora?

Gabler's vigorous advocacy of mythological interpretation aroused immediate opposition on the part of traditionalists, who thought that the literal interpretation should not be questioned (even though they never suggested that Greek myths should be taken literally), and Deists, who could not accept the literal meaning. But Eichhorn and Gabler were not arguing about the literal truth of Scripture; they were concerned with the accusation of dishonesty leveled against the biblical authors. The "childhood of mankind" (G. Lessing) applied to all of them. Eichhorn could not envisage a unique Hebrew relationship with the deity. The special character of the Hebrew writings could consist only in their relatively exalted nature by comparison with other records from the same period of primitive culture. Nor would Eichhorn and Gabler allow a mixed exposition of the contested chapters—part literal-historical, part allegorical-typological. Principles had to be applied consistently. Gabler held that some form of revelation was necessary if the human species was to progress from passion to reason, but this appeared to resemble truths of natural religion rather than the distinctive Hebrew tradition.

The interpretation of many episodes as mythological now spread, not only throughout the Hebrew Bible (e.g., Balaam and his donkey, Elijah in his fiery chariot) but also into the New Testament (e.g., the temptation of Jesus*§, in which the story of his withdrawal into the desert had been embellished with mythological detail to express inner decisions). The supposed lack of time for myth to develop in the New Testament was countered by the response that it was not the few years of Christ's public ministry that were crucial, but the age-old Jewish tradition, much of which had already been classed as myth (miracles, divine appearances, diabolical possession, angels, devils, sickness caused by malign influences). One now spoke less about "primitive humans" and more of the "oriental mind" that lay behind these ideas and expressions.

In his *Hebräische Mythologie* (1802), G. Bauer§ produced a comprehensive survey of the findings of the mythology school that satisfied Gabler's desire for a *Mythologia Sacra*. But where Eichhorn and Gabler would have recognized myth in the New Testament, Bauer suggested that Jesus was merely accommodating the current views and tradition: e.g., "I watched Satan fall from heaven like a flash of lightning" (Luke 10:18); "their angels continually see the face of my Father in heaven" (Matt 18:10); "Be silent, and come out of him" (to the unclean spirit, Mark 1:25). This concession Bauer would not extend to the disciples, however. Unlike Eichhorn and Gabler, Bauer was preoccupied with distinguishing history from myth. He proposed other criteria for identifying myth: (1) events connected with world origins, which no one witnessed; (2) events attributed directly to the action of God or to heavenly beings; (3) actions and speech where only thought took place (e.g., the temptation of Jesus, Jacob and the angel); and (4) events that could never have occurred in the course of nature. In general, he included all unverifiable assertions, considering verifiability to be essential. One must ask not only whether something could have happened but also how it could be known. Thus the whole of Genesis and parts of the other books of Moses and of Joshua-Judges were mythical. Elohim were originally gods, but as Yahweh came to be recognized as the only God, they became angels ("Where the Hebrews speak of an angel appearing, there, Homer sees a god.") Bauer further noted that similar events produced similar myths: Noah's and Deucalion's floods; the stories of Samson and of Hercules. Bauer classified a number of New Testament events as myth (e.g., Christ's birth, the angel of the agony), but then went on, illogically it seems, to give "natural" explanations of some details (e.g., a phosphorous light at Christ's birth, a dove flying past at the baptism) where there was no evidence at all. On the whole, however, Bauer's concern for fact made him prefer historical to philosophical myth, even though in doing so he limited the range of meaning. The stage was thus set for even more radical understandings of the Bible as myth.

Bibliography: T. **Bowman**, *Hebrew Thought Compared with Greek* (Library of History and Doctrine, 1960). E. **Cassirer**, *An Essay on Man* (1944). J. G. **Eichhorn**, *Allgemeine bibliothek der biblischen Litteratur* (10 vols. 1787-1801); "Urgeschichte" (1790-93) 2:260. F. W. **Farrar**, *History of Interpretation: Eight Lectures Preached Before the University of Oxford* (1886). B. **Feldman and** R. **Richardson**, *The Rise of Modern Mythology, 1680-1860* (1962). R. C. **Fuller**, *Alexander Geddes, 1737-1802: A Pioneer of Biblical Criticism* (HTIBS 3, 1984). J. P. **Gabler** (ed.), *J. G. Eichhorn's "Urgeschichte," mit Einleitung und Anmerkungen* (1790-93). C. **Hartlich and** W. **Sachs**, *Der Ursprung des Mythosbegriffes in der modernen Bibelwissenschaft* (SSEA, 1952). J. G. **Herder**, *Vom Geist der hebräischen Poesie* (1782-83); *Werke* (Suphan ed.). N. **Lohfink**, *The Christian Meaning of the OT* (1969). R. **Lowth**, *De Sacra Poesi Hebraeorum* (1753). J. **Rogerson**, *Myth in OT Interpretation* (BZAW 134, 1974). E. S. **Shaffer**, *"Kubla Khan" and the Fall of Jerusalem: The Mythological School in Biblical Criticism and Secular Literature, 1770-1880* (1975). **Spinoza**, *Theologico-Political Treatise* (1670) chap. 7.

R. C. FULLER

FOLKLORE, RELIGION, AND MYTH

Mythology and Biblical Studies (1800-1980)

Questions about the nature and function of myth in both the Hebrew Bible and the New Testament were significant in nineteenth-and twentieth-century biblical studies. The critical enterprises of such major biblical critics as D. F. Strauss[§] and R. Bultmann[§] have important roots in the closing decades of the eighteenth century. From the time of J. G. Eichhorn[§], it was necessary for serious scholars to come to terms with the problem of myth in the Bible (Mythology and Biblical Studies [to 1800]*[§]). Eichhorn's *Einleitung in das Alte Testament* (1780-82) treats the Hebrew Scriptures "not merely as the vehicle of a revelation, but as in form Oriental books, to be interpreted in accordance with the habits of mind of Semitic peoples" (T. Cheyne 1893, 14). Eichhorn found a good deal of myth and legend in the books of the Hebrew Bible and brought to the serious and systematic study of biblical texts certain ideas about myth that had been discussed in English and French Deism[§] for a hundred years (Mythology and Biblical Studies [to 1800]*[§]). He also drew on R. Lowth's[§] *De Sacra Poesi Hebraeorum* (1753), a work translated into German and annotated by J. D. Michaelis[§]. Lowth, an Englishman, regarded the Hebrew Bible as the incomparably sublime poetry[‡§] of a deeply religious people. His work was read in Germany by both Eichhorn and his friend J. G. Herder[§], whose *Vom Geist der Ebraischen Poesie* (1782-83 [ET 1833]) extends Lowth's position. For Herder, the Bible is the primitive poetry of the ancient Hebrews. To be understood it must be looked at through the eyes of its creators and accepted as the local, national utterance of a given people at a given time in a given place. He believed that the Bible contains myths that embody deeply important truths. Indeed, Herder was "the first important expression of the romantic affirmation of myth as creative primal wisdom and sublime spiritual power, of myth as vitally true" (Feldman and Richardson 1972, 224). Against this new affirmation of myth as the necessary formal expression of primitive spiritual life may be set the negative view of myth often associated with the Enlightenment and with such figures as F. Diderot, J. D'Alembert, Voltaire[§], P. Holbach, and T. Paine[§], for whom myth was simply primitive superstition, unworthy and erroneous, something that would vanish when exposed to the light of reason. Eichhorn's detailed and unimpassioned analysis of biblical texts as a diverse collection of legends, oral traditions, earlier books or documents, and fabulous stories may be seen as the beginning of a modern "objective" or "detached" criticism of myth, avoiding as it does the strident denunciations of Voltaire or Paine and the enthusiastic, passionate assent and acceptance of Herder.

The modern biblical study of myth begins, then, at a time when there were in circulation two diametrically opposed evaluations of myth. One group, usually, if not quite fairly, labeled "Enlightenment" thinkers, generally regarded myths as erroneous prescientific, savage thought marked by superstition and credulity and of no serious modern interest or value. The other group, often thought of as Romantic or pre-Romantic, affirmed myth as high truth expressed symbolically by a primitive people at a primitive time. In understanding various modern biblical scholars' approaches to myth, it is necessary to understand not only their conception of myth but also their underlying evaluation of myth and mythological habits of mind.

Despite his tone of "objectivity," Eichhorn shared the negative view of myth. In the Hebrew Bible, for example, he found myth and miracle everywhere, but he did not find them valuable or significant, and he uniformly sought to recover the "naturalistic" or historical phenomena that lie behind them. From this point of view, "the appointment of Moses to be the leader of the Israelites was nothing more than the long cherished project of the patriot to emancipate his people, which when presented before his mind with more than usual vividness in his dreams, was believed by him to be a divine inspiration. The flame and smoke which ascended from Mount

Sinai at the giving of the law was merely a fire which Moses kindled in order to make a deeper impression upon the imagination of the people, together with an accidental thunderstorm that arose at that particular moment. The shining of his countenance was the natural effect of being overheated; but it was supposed to be a divine manifestation, not only by the people, but by Moses himself, he being ignorant of the true cause" (Strauss 1835, 48). Eichhorn interpreted myth as a process that starts with a nucleus of historical fact; thus any given myth can be reduced to its historical core or kernel. Eichhorn was, then, in Strauss's phrase, a Christian Euhemerus.

In his *Einleitung in das Neue Testament* (1804-27) Eichhorn argued that the Gospels were also full of supernatural myths, for which he again supplied natural explanations (1804-27). He also maintained that the canonical Gospels (Canon of the Bible[§]) were not original or eyewitness accounts but rested instead on various translations and versions of a primary Aramaic gospel. Eichhorn's work was influential. In Germany, J. P. Gabler[§], the young Schelling, J. Semler[§], and G. Bauer[§] carried on his ideas. In England, the Regius Professor of Hebrew, H. Lloyd, was interested but could not get church or university patronage for a translation of Eichhorn's *Introduction to the Old Testament*. In the United States, A. Norton's *Evidences of the Genuineness of the Gospels* (1837-44) was essentially intended as a refutation of Eichhorn.

Among Eichhorn's immediate followers, H. Paulus (also a Christian Euhemerist) sought for naturalistic—that is, nonsupernatural—explanations for everything in the New Testament in his *Commentar ueber das Neue Testament* (1800). G. Bauer produced a more sophisticated taxonomy of myths, starting from the position of C. Heyne (Feldman and Richardson 1972, 215-23) that the earliest records of all people are necessarily myths. In his 1802 volume, Bauer provided various ways to identify a myth (Mythology and Biblical Studies[§] [to 1800]*[§]). A narrative is a myth "first, when it proceeds from an age in which no written records existed, but in which facts were transmitted through the medium of oral tradition alone; secondly, when it presents an historical account of events which are either absolutely or relatively beyond the reach of experience, such as occurrences connected with the spiritual world, and incidents to which, from the nature of the circumstances, no one could have been witness; or thirdly, when it deals in the marvelous and is couched in symbolic language" (Strauss 1835, 52). In 1817, W. de Wette[§] published his *Lehrbuch der historiche-kristischen Einleitung in die Kanonische und Apocryphischen Bücher des Alten Testaments*, the fifth edition (1840) of which was translated into English and nearly doubled in size with annotations by the American T. Parker[§] in 1843. De Wette followed Bauer in paying especially close attention to the process by which a legend becomes a myth. "But in the popular legend, there came an idealo-poetic element, and mingled itself with the real historical elements. By this means the tradition was gradually transformed into the miraculous and the ideal. The popular songs conduced chiefly to bring about this end; for they, in the bold lyric flights of imagination, represented what was surprising and wonderful in a supernatural light, and a people credulous of miracles easily misunderstood the account. Thus the miracle in Josh 10:13*b* arose from the lyric hyperbola of [vv. 12-13*a*]" (Parker 1843, 2:38-29).

This effort to discriminate between historical fact or event, on the one hand, and various kinds of myth, on the other hand, was extended and applied to New Testament studies most famously—indeed, notoriously—by Strauss in his *Das Leben Jesu*, a book that was said to have made the year 1835 as memorable in theology as 1848 was in politics, and for the same reason. Concentrating on the Gospels, Strauss found myth everywhere, and he distinguished several kinds: "We distinguish by the name evangelical mythus a narrative relating directly or indirectly to Jesus, which may be considered not as the expression of a fact, but as the product of an idea of his earliest followers." (Strauss, like other German writers of the time, tried to formalize a terminology for myth studies in which *mythus* meant a single mythological narrative, with *mythi* for the plural.) He divided evangelical myths into two kinds, pure and historical. The pure mythus is one "constituting the substance of the narrative" and arising either from "the Messianic ideas and expectations existing according to their several forms in the Jewish mind before Jesus" or from "that peculiar impression which was left by the personal character, actions and fate of Jesus" (1835, 86). The historical mythus is "an accidental adjunct to the actual history," having for its basis a "definite individual fact which has been seized upon by religious enthusiasm, and twined around with mythical conceptions culled from the idea of the Christ." Strauss gave as examples of the latter "a saying of Jesus such as that concerning 'fishers of men' or the barren fig tree, which now appear in the Gospels transmuted into marvelous histories" (1835, 87), applying these concepts so rigorously to the gospel narratives that almost nothing of the historical Jesus*[§] remained unchallenged. His conclusion was bleak: "The results of this inquiry which we have now brought to a close, have apparently annihilated the greatest and most valuable part of that which the Christian has been wont to believe concerning his saviour Jesus, have uprooted all the animating motives which he has gathered from his faith, and withered all his consolations." He then asserted that it remains "to re-establish dogmatically that which has been destroyed critically" (1835, 757).

Strauss tried to do this by claiming that the true meaning of Christ is not as an individual, or a god-man, but as the human race itself; and he was able to conclude, "by faith in this Christ, especially in his death and resurrection, man is justified before God; that is, by the kindling within him of the idea of Humanity, the individual man participates in the divinely human life of the species" (1835, 780). Strauss's work was widely read and reviewed. In the United States, T. Parker published a seventy-page review of it in *The Christian Examiner* (1840). In England, Strauss was answered by *Voices of the Church in Reply to Dr. D. F. Strauss* (1845), and the novelist G. Eliot translated Strauss's work in 1846. Strauss was widely attacked in Germany, and he ultimately published another *Life of Jesus for the German People* in 1864 with a somewhat less sweeping conclusion. It has been repeatedly pointed out that he failed to preface his work with a critical discussion of the sources; that is, he failed to evaluate the historical status of each of the gospel narratives, let alone sift their relationship to each other. Thus, much of the seeming cogency of Strauss's mythological hypothesis was undercut when, as early as 1838, C. WEISSE put forward the hypothesis that the earliest gospel is that of Mark, with Matthew and Luke derived from it. At almost the same time, L. Feuerbach's *The Essence of Christianity* (1841) carried Strauss's argument one step further, denying the existence of an abstract divine being and turning theology "completely and finally into anthropology" (K. Barth 1947 [ET 1972], 534).

From this point forward, the study of myth in the Bible is increasingly complicated because it is often carried on as part of the enterprise of anthropology or one of the newly rising fields of history of religion, comparative religions, or folklore*[§]. The philological school, typified by F. Müller's "Comparative Mythology" (1909), explained myth as a "disease of language" and saw in myths only linguistically distorted accounts of such natural events as the coming of the dawn. The fullest application of this theory to the Bible is I. Goldziher's *Mythology Among the Hebrews and Its Historical Development* (1877). An opponent of Müller's, A. Lang[§], took up E. Tyler's animist theories about the origin of myth (1871) and found widespread evidence that the earliest religions were, against all previous opinion, both monotheistic and strongly ethical. This view, in which primitive myth establishes primitive monotheism, put forward in Lang's *Myth, Ritual, and Religion* (1887) and *The Making of Religion* (1909[3]), was taken up and extended to biblical studies by W. Schmidt in *Der Ursprung der Gottesidee* (1926[2]). The so-called ritual school of mythological interpretation viewed all myth as founded solely in primitive ritual. J. Harrison's *Themis* (1912) is the major early work here, while S. Hooke's[§] *Myth, Ritual, and Kingship* (1958) is a late development. J. Fraze[§] linked biblical stories to folklore traditions in *Folklore in the Old Testament* (1918), a view revised and revived by T. Gaster[§] in

Myth, Legend, and Custom in the Old Testament (1969). Lang and Schmidt's claims for primitive monotheism had the effect of renewing the positive emphasis on myth as important early religious truth. This is also the effect of those modern writers who may loosely be called the phenomenological school, including E. Cassirer (1946), G. van der Leeuw (1967), M. Eliade, and P. Ricoeur[§]. Van der Leeuw begins with L. Levy-Bruhl's (1922) idea that primitive thought as expressed in myth is "prelogical." Instead of criticizing the primitive mentality as nonscientific, however, van der Leeuw sees it as a valid, worthy mental process in its own right. So does Eliade, who gives the following definition: "Myth narrates a sacred history; it relates an event that took place in primordial time, the fabled time of the beginnings. . . . Myth, then, is always an account of a 'creation'; it relates how something was produced, began to be . . . the myth is regarded as a sacred story and hence a 'true history' because it always deals with realities" (1964, 5-6). Building upon earlier work of Eliade, Riceour's *La Symbolique du Mal* (1950) undertakes a detailed study of the Hebrew Bible to show how myths are an attempt to explain the basic human experiences of defilement, guilt, and sin in the presence of the divine. Somewhat analogous are the structuralists' (Structuralism and Deconstruction*[§]) fragmentary findings that stress the importance of myth as a given in a culture, as something that expresses itself through the human, not as something the human can manipulate at will. C. Levi-Strauss's method, as illustrated in "The Structural Study of Myth" (1958), has been taken up by E. Leach in *Genesis as Myth* (1969) and "The Legitimacy of Solomon" (1966), and by M. Douglas in "The Abominations of Leviticus" (1966).

In biblical studies, the later nineteenth century saw an increasingly sophisticated source criticism and a general consensus that was anti-Strauss and interested in expanding, not contracting, the historical Jesus and the historical Moses. This revived historicism reached a peak with J. Wellhausen's[§] *Prolegomena to the History of Israel* (1885), in which the Pentateuch (see Pentateuchal Criticism[‡§]) is seen to consist of three strata of law and three strata of tradition coming down to us through four main sources and confirming an essentially historical outline of a story of Moses.

Building on Wellhausen was the work of H. Gunkel[§], generally regarded as the founder of modern biblical Form Criticism*[§]. Gunkel's *Schöpfung und Chaos* (1895), showed how Babylonian myths about the fight between the creator god and the god of chaos provided a pattern for the authors of Genesis to describe the eschatological victory of God over the chaotic forces of evil. Since this book, numerous scholars have pursued the Mesopotamian underpinnings and antecedents of parts of the Bible (B. Childs 1960; F. M. Cross 1973; T. Jacobson 1976; H. Gese 1970; F. McCurley 1983).

Gunkel's celebrated taxonomy of legend or saga, the starting point for much modern form criticism, is the introduction to his 1901 commentary on Genesis. He claimed that Genesis is largely made up of *sage* (sometimes translated "legend," sometimes "saga"), which he divided into two broad classes: primitive sagas "of the origin of the world and of the progenitors of the human race" and patriarchal sagas, "legends of the patriarchs of Israel" (1901, 13). It is principally the primitive legends that have a "mythical" character and may be "faded myths." But in general, Gunkel applied a very narrow and specific definition of myth and held that there are no myths in Genesis because monotheism is hostile to myths. Following H. Ewald (1843) and, ultimately, the brothers Grimm, Gunkel defined a myth as a story of the gods. Taken literally, then, no story of just one god qualifies as a myth. There must be two gods in a story for it to be a myth (1901, 15). For this reason Gunkel used the terms *legend* or *saga* to describe the basic constituent unit of Genesis. When he classified the sagas according to Literary*[§] form (rather than content) into historical, etiological, ethnological, etymological, ceremonial, and mixed forms, it should be noted that most of what he calls legends or sagas would have been called myths using the older and larger concept of myth that was in use from Eichhorn through

Strauss. If Gunkel's definition of myth is accepted, then modern form criticism can be seen as diverging from myth studies because its material is non-mythic. If one uses a wider conception of myth, then form criticism is a modern extension and sophistication of nineteenth-century myth criticism.

In his 1892 work in New Testament studies, J. Weiss[§] demonstrated that the kingdom of God of which Jesus spoke was eschatological, not historical, and that Jesus understood it to stand outside our time and our earth, being one of the four "last things." In 1901, W. Wrede[§] called the historical value of Mark into question. These two developments had the effect of seriously weakening the historical consensus about the life of Jesus. The historical base seemed less sure, the mythological conception stronger.

Just as Wrede's work set the stage for Bultmann's *History of the Synoptic Tradition*, so also Weiss's argument set the stage for Bultmann's demythologizing project first put forward in an essay on "New Testament and Mythology" in *Offenbarung und Heilsgeschehen* (1941) and restated in a series of lectures in 1951 published as *Jesus Christ and Mythology* (1958). Bultmann began with Weiss's work, pointing out that the "hope of Jesus and of the early Christian community was not fulfilled. The same world still exists and history continues. The course of history has refuted mythology" (1958, 14). More broadly, he said, "The whole conception of the world which is pre-supposed in the preaching of Jesus as in the New Testament generally is mythological; i.e., the conception of the world as being structured in three stories, heaven, earth and hell; the conception of the intervention of supernatural powers in the course of events; and the conception of miracles" (1958, 15).

Bultmann abandoned the narrow, technical definition of myth found in Gunkel and his followers and revived and reapplied a much older and broader conception of myth that has strong affinities with the Enlightenment view (R. Johnson 1974). Bultmann, indeed, defined the world of the New Testament as "mythological because it is different from the conception of the world which has been formed and developed by science since its inception in ancient Greece and which has been accepted by all modern men" (1958, 15). He sounded very much like Eichhorn or Strauss when he said, "Modern men take it for granted that the course of nature and of history, like their own inner life and their practical life, is nowhere interrupted by the intervention of supernatural powers" (1958, 16).

For Bultmann, the question was whether Jesus' preaching of the kingdom of God has any meaning or importance for modern human beings. Like critics in the Eichhorn tradition, he regarded mythology as a step away from the truth, not (as with Herder and his successors) a step toward truth. Bultmann thought myth preserves and presents the particular world of a particular people at a particular time. Since the true meaning of Jesus' message is not local but universal, not historical but existential, we must "abandon the mythological conceptions precisely because we want to retain their deeper meaning." Thus Bultmann sought to strip away mythological elements to leave an existential *kerygma*, the true Christian preaching that is "a proclamation addressed not to the theoretical reason, but to the hearer as a self" (1958, 36). He contended that the essence of Christianity is in this *kerygma*, understood existentially, and that, as a result, we can dispense with the worldview of the Scriptures, which is "mythological and is therefore unacceptable to modern man whose thinking has been shaped by science and is therefore no longer mythological."

This line of argument has a simplicity and clarity about it reminiscent of the Enlightenment and Eichhorn and Strauss. Like those critics before him, Bultmann has been elaborately and repeatedly answered. The problem with his view is essentially one of limits. How far can it be carried, and what will be the result? As one of Bultmann's most careful commentators puts it, "Just how irrelevant can the factual content of the gospel become without its ceasing to be a gospel?" (J. McQuarrie 1960, 20).

Bibliography: K. Barth, *Protestant Thought in the Nineteenth Century* (1947; ET 1972).
G. L. Bauer, *Hebräische Mythologie des alten und neuen Testaments mit Parallelen aus der Mythologie anderer Völker, vornehmlich der Griechen und Römer* (1802). **J. R. Beard,** *Voices of the Church in Reply to Dr. D. F. Strauss* (1945). **R. Bultmann,** "NT and Mythology," *Offenbarung und Heilsgeschehen* (1941); *Jesus Christ and Mythology* (1958). **E. Cassirer,** *Language and Myth* (1946). **T. K. Cheyne,** *Founders of OT Criticism: Biographical, Descriptive, and Critical Studies* (1893). **B. Childs,** *Myth and Reality in the OT* (SBT 27, 1960). **F. M. Cross,** *Canaanite Myth and Hebrew Epic: Essays in the History of the Religion of Israel* (1973). **W. M. L. de Wette,** *A Critical and Historical Introduction to the Canonical Scriptures of the OT* (1817, 1840[5]; ET 1843). **M. Douglas,** "The Abominations of Leviticus," *In Purity and Danger: An Analysis of the Concepts of Pollution and Taboo* (1966). **J. G. Eichhorn,** *Einleitung in das Alte Testament* (1780-82); *Einleitung in das Neue Testament* (1804-27). **M. Eliade,** *Myth and Reality* (World Perspectives 31, 1964). **H. Ewald,** *Geschichte des Volkes Israel bis Christus* (1843). **B. Feldman and R. Richardson,** *The Rise of Modern Mythology, 1660-1860* (1972). **L. Feuerbach,** *The Essence of Christianity* (1841). **J. Frazer,** *Folk-Lore in the OT* (1918). **T. Gaster,** *Myth, Legend, and Custom in the OT: A Comparative Study with Chapters from Sir J. G. Frazier's Folklore in the OT* (1969). **H. Gese,** *Die Religionen Altsyriens, Altarabiens, und der Mandäer* (1970). **I. Goldziher,** *Mythology Among the Hebrews and Its Historical Development* (1876; ET 1877). **J. Grimm,** *Teutonic Mythology* (4 vols. 1819-37; ET 1966). **H. Gunkel,** *Schöpfung und Chaos in Urzeit und Endzeit: Eine Religionsgeschichtliche Untersuchung uber Gen 1 und Ap Joh 12* (1895); *The Legends of Genesis* (1901). **J. E. Harrison,** *Themis: A Study of the Social Origins of Greek Religion* (SSEA, 1912). **C. Hartlich and W. Sachs,** *Der Ursprung des Mythosbegriffes in der modernen Bibelwissenschaft* (SSEA, 1952). **J. G. Herder,** *The Spirit of Hebrew Poetry* (2 vols. 1782-83; ET 1833). **S. H. Hooke** (ed.), *Myth, Ritual, and Kingship* (1958). **T. Jacobsen,** *The Treasures of Darkness: A History of Mesopotamian Religion* (1976). **R. Johnson,** *The Origins of Demythologizing: Philosophy and Historiography in the Theology of R. Bultmann* (1974). **A. Lang,** *Myth, Ritual, and Religion* (1887); *The Making of Religion* (1909[3]). **E. R. Leach,** *Genesis as Myth and Other Essays* (Cape Editions 39, 1969); "The Legitimacy of Solomon," *AES 7* (1966) 58-101. **G. van der Leeuw,** *Religion in Essence and Manifestation* (1967). **L. Levy-Bruhl,** *Primitive Mentality* (1922; ET 1923). **C. Levi-Strauss,** "The Structural Study of Myth," *Myth: A Symposium* (ed. T. A. Sebeok, 1958) 50-66. **R. Lowth,** *The Sacred Poetry of the Hebrews* (1787). **F. R. McCurley,** *Ancient Myths and Biblical Faith: Scriptural Transformations* (1983). **J. MacQuarrie,** *The Scope of Demythologizing: Bultmann and His Critics* (1960). **F. M. Müller,** *Comparative Mythology: An Essay* (1909). **A. Norton,** *Evidences of the Genuineness of the Gospels* (3 vols. 1837-44). **H. Paulus,** *Commentar ueber das Neue Testament* (1800). **P. Riceour,** "La Symbolique du Mal," *Philosophie de la Volunte, pt. 2, sec. 2,* "Finitude et culpabilit" (1950). **J. W. Rogerson,** *Myth in OT Interpretation* (BZAW 134, 1974). **E. S. Schaffer,** *"Kubla Khan" and the Fall of Jerusalem: The Mythological School in Biblical Criticism and Secular Literature* (1975). **W. Schmidt,** *Der Ursprung des Gottesidee: Eine historische-kritische und positive Studie* (1926-55). **A. Schweitzer,** *The Quest of the Historical Jesus: A Critical Study of Its Progress from Reimarus to Wrede* (1906; ET 1910). **D. F. Strauss,** *Das Leben Jesu: Kritisch bearbeitet* (1835; ET 1846); *A New Life of Jesus* (1865). **E. B. Tyler,** *Primitive Culture* (1871). **J. de Vries,** *The Study of Religion: A Historical Approach* (1967). **J. Weiss,** *Jesus' Proclamation of the Kingdom of God* (1892; ET 1971). **C. H. Weisse,** *Die evangelische Geschichte kritisch und philosophisch bearbeitet* (1838). **J. Wellhausen,** *Prolegomena to the History of Israel* (1878; ET 1885). **W. Wrede,** *The Messianic Secret* (1901; ET 1971).

R. D. RICHARDSON, JR.

FOLKLORE, RELIGION, AND MYTH

Mythology and Biblical Studies (1980 to present)

The monographs of B. Lincoln (1999) and W. Doniger (1998) and W. Doty's introductory text (second ed., 2000) reflect scholarly analysis of myth at the end of the twentieth and the beginning of the twenty-first centuries. One of the most influential and methodologically rigorous voices in myth studies has been R. Segal, whose 1980 article remains an excellent survey of methodological approaches to the study of myth (see also Segal 1999; A. Dundes 1984). T. Sienkewicz's 1997 annotated bibliography is valuable for the state of the field at the end of the twentieth century. G. Natt surveys the use of the terms "symbol" and "myth" in nineteenth- and twentieth-century biblical hermeneutics (2000). R. Walsh surveys the use of myth in biblical interpretation and its applicability in a postmodern world (2001).

Since J. Rogerson'§ *Myth and Old Testament Interpretation* (1974), the most programmatic discussions of myth and the Hebrew Bible have been written by R. Oden (1987, 1992a, 1992b), B. Batto (1992), M. Smith (1994), and N. Wyatt (1996). Oden's articles in the *Anchor Bible Dictionary* and a long chapter in his 1987 book offer a conscientiously methodological perspective for biblical scholars. Smith's article is also very helpful in surveying the issues of the identity of myth and the practice of "myth-making" in ancient Israel.

Significant book-length studies of myth and Hebrew Bible interpretation include works by F. McCurley (1983) and especially Batto, who attempts to demonstrate how "myth permeates virtually every level of the biblical tradition from the earliest to the latest" and that myth is "one of the chief mediums by which biblical writers did their theologizing" (1992, 1). Wyatt similarly calls for the recognition of "the pervasive mythological element in the Hebrew Bible" in his provocative book (1996, 423). He contrasts a mythological reading of the Hebrew Bible with the historicist perspective of much contemporary Hebrew Bible scholarship in his study's final chapter, "The Problem of a Biblical Mythology," in which he also explicitly addresses the nature of myth. B. Anderson (1994) revisits the issue of creation and mythopoeic dimensions of biblical faith from a theological perspective, and J. Levenson (1988) similarly uses mythological themes to address the theological issues of theodicy and divine omnipotence in the Hebrew Bible. The collected essays of H. P. Müller (1991) should be noted for both exegetical and theological topics. G. Garbini has recently discussed the relationship between history and myth in the Hebrew Bible (2003).

The majority of work from biblical scholars interested in myth is devoted to the relationship between ancient Near Eastern myth and the Hebrew Bible rather than to methodological or theological reflection. Taking a history-of-religion perspective (*Religionschichtliche Schule**§) on the religion of ancient Israel, these studies usually trace the influence of Akkadian and Ugaritic myths (Ugarit and the Bible§ [see Translation*]) on the Hebrew Bible (e.g., J. Bailey 1987; W. Lambert 1988; D. Bodi 1991; Smith 1990). The most prolific source of such studies has been F. M. CROSS, who has directed studies on mythological topics by E. Mullen (1980), H. Wallace (1985), R. Hendel (1987), W. Propp (1987), P. Day (1988), C. L. Seow (1989), and H. Page (1996). Mullen surveys the mythological image of the divine council in Canaanite and Israelite texts, while other authors analyze specific biblical texts. Page explores the mythological traditions found in Isaiah 14 and Ezekiel 28. R. Shipp has recently reinvestigated the mythological background of Isa 14:4b-21 (2002).

Much of the discussion of myth and the Bible has naturally centered on Genesis 1-11, with commentaries (C. Westermann 1974 [ET 1984]), text studies (Wallace), and comparative perspectives (Dundes 1988). The relation of these narratives to other ancient Near Eastern cosmogonies and anthropogonies has received much attention (R. Hess and D. Tsumura 1994;

Batto). R. Clifford has written an important book (1994) and edited another with J. Collins (1992) on this topic. Mythological elements in the psalms have also received consideration (e.g., C. Petersen 1982). The most influential of the various studies of Yahweh's conflict with primordial forces is the work by J. Day (1985; see also C. Kloos 1986). N. Forsyth (1987) traces this theme into early Christian literature.

Other sections of the Hebrew Bible have also been considered by scholars interested in myth. Oden calls for the recognition of myth in Genesis beyond chapter 11. The focus of Wyatt's previously mentioned book is on Canaanite and Israelite mythological traditions of kingship (see also T. Mettinger 1987). The discussion concerning the imagery and mythological allusions in Daniel 7 is summarized by J. Collins in his Daniel commentary (1993) and in his 1993 article, and G. Fuchs (1993) discusses mythological elements in Job. Structuralism*§ is now a common literary tool of biblical exegesis, but few practitioners consider the mythological quality of the biblical texts. The rarer application of structuralist methods to biblical texts categorized by the authors as myth can be seen in E. Leach and D. Aycock (1983), as well as in the more recent book on Genesis by S. Kunin (1995).

Many studies of ancient Near Eastern deities have been produced since 1980. T. Frymer-Kensky (1992) traces the transformation of goddess traditions into the Hebrew Bible (see also U. Winter 1986), and the goddess Asherah has received special attention as a possible consort of Yahweh in recent monographs. These and other studies are referenced in the *Dictionary of Deities and Demons in the Bible* (1995). John Day studies in detail the relationship between Yahweh and the various Canaanite gods and goddesses (El, Baal, Asherah, Astarte, Anat, astral deities, and underworld deities) and discusses how Yahwistic monotheism developed from Canaanite polytheism (2000). Less work has been done on myth in Second Temple Jewish literature. An important exception to this tendency is the work of H. Kvanvig (1988), which explores the Mesopotamian background of both the Enoch figure and the Son of Man traditions (cf. M. Barker's more daring speculations 1992).

In comparison to Hebrew Bible studies, current New Testament research has exhibited little interest in mythological influences on the New Testament or the role of myth in biblical Theology*§. The debate over R. Bultmann'§ demythologizing program has largely subsided (B. Jaspert 1991) and the word "myth" has become increasingly conflicted as scholars turn to discussions of narrative, metaphor, and ideology (Ideological Criticism*§) rather than mythology. B. Mack (1988) describes the Gospel of Mark as a "myth" since it functions as a social group's foundational document, but New Testament studies generally avoided using the term in reference to the Gospels (cf. Dundes 1990). Recently, New Testament scholars have shown a renewed, if muted, interest in myth. P. Klumbies uses the concept of myth to study the Markan Passion Narrative (2001) and R. Girard uses comparative analysis of myths of violence and his theory of "mimetic desire" to interpret Jesus' crucifixion (2001). New Testament scholars have largely neglected the use of myth in Revelation since J. Court's 1979 book, but attention from A. Y. Collins (1981), J. van Henten (1994), and J. Roloff (1993) should be noted. The relevance of myth to eschatology and biblical theology is most fully addressed by T. Schmidt (1996). Finally, the importance of the essays in volumes edited by H. Schmid (1988) and K. Kertelge (1990) should be recognized for their attention to exegetical and theological topics in the New Testament.

Bibliography: B. W. Anderson, *From Creation to New Creation: OT Perspectives* (OBT, 1994). **J. Bailey,** "Initiation and the Primal Woman in Gilgamesh and Genesis 2-3," *JBL 89* (1987) 137-50. **M. Barker,** *The Great Angel: A Study of Israel's Second God* (1992). **B. F. Batto,** *Slaying the Dragon: Mythmaking in the Biblical Tradition* (1992). **D. Bodi,** *The Book of Ezekiel and the Poem of Erra* (OBO 104, 1991). **R. J. Clifford,** *Creation Accounts in the Ancient Near*

East and in the Bible (CBQMS 26, 1994). **R. J. Clifford and J. J. Collins** (eds.), *Creation in the Biblical Traditions* (CBQMS 24, 1992). **A. Y. Collins,** "Myth and History in the Book of Revelation," *Traditions in Transformation: Turning Points in Biblical Faith* (ed. B. Halpern and J. Levenson, 1981) 337-403. **J. J. Collins,** *Daniel: A Commentary on the Book of Daniel* (Hermeneia, 1993); "Stirring up the Great Sea: The Religio-historical Background of Daniel 7," *The Book of Daniel in the Light of New Findings* (ed. A. S. van der Woude, BETL 106, 1993) 121-36. **J. Court,** *Myth and History in the Book of Revelation* (1979). **J. Day,** *God's Conflict with the Dragon and the Sea: Echoes of a Canaanite Myth in the OT* (UCOP 35, 1985); *Yahweh and the Gods and Goddesses of Canaan.* (JSOTSup 265; 2000). **P. L. Day,** *An Adversary in Heaven: Śaṭan in the HB* (HSM 43, 1988). **W. Doniger.** *The Implied Spider: Politics and Theology in Myth* (1998).**W. G. Doty,** *Mythography: The Study of Myths and Rituals* (1986, 2000). **A. Dundes** (ed.), *Sacred Narrative: Readings in the Theory of Myth* (1984); (ed.), *The Flood Myth* (1988); "The Hero Pattern and the Life of Jesus," *In Quest of the Hero* (ed. R. A. Segal, 1990) 179-223. **N. Forsyth,** *The Old Enemy: Satan and the Combat Myth* (1987). **T. Frymer-Kensky,** *In the Wake of the Goddesses: Women, Culture, and the Biblical Transformation of Pagan Myth* (1992). **G. Fuchs,** *Mythos und Hiobdichtung: Aufnahme und Umdeutung altorientalischer Vorstellungen* (1993). **G. Garbini,** *Myth and History in the Bible* (JSOTSup 362, 2003). **R. Girard,** *I See Satan Fall like Lightning* (2001). **R. Hendel,** "Of Demigods and the Deluge: Toward an Interpretation of Genesis 6:1-4," *JBL 106* (1987) 13-26; *The Epic of the Patriarch: The Jacob Cycle and the Narrative Traditions of Canaan and Israel* (HSM 42, 1987). **J. W. van Henten,** "Dragon Myth and Imperial Ideology in Rev 12-13," *SBLSP* (1994) 496-515. **R. S. Hess** and **D. T. Tsumura** (eds.), *I Studied Inscriptions from Before the Flood: Ancient Near Eastern, Literary, and Linguistic Approaches to Genesis 1-11* (Sources for Biblical and Theological Study 4, 1994). **T. Holtz,** "Mythos. IV. Neutestamentlich," *TRE 23* (1994) 644-50. **B. Jaspert** (ed.), *Bibel und Mythos: Fünfzig Jahre nach R. Bultmanns Entmythologisierungsprogramm* (1991). **K. Kertelge** (ed.), *Metaphorik und Mythos im Neuen Testament* (QD 126, 1990). **C. Kloos,** *YHWH's Combat with the Sea: A Canaanite Tradition in the Religion of Ancient Israel* (1986). **Paul-Gerhard Klumbies,** *Der Mythos bei Markus* (BZNW 108, 2001). **S. D. Kunin,** *The Logic of Incest: A Structuralist Analysis of Hebrew Mythology* (JSOTSup 185, 1995). **H. Kvanvig,** *Roots of Apocalyptic: The Mesopotamian Background of the Enoch Figure and of the Son of Man* (WMANT 61, 1988). **G. Lambert,** "OT Mythology in Its Ancient Near Eastern Context," VTSup 40 (1988) 126-43. **E. Leach and D. Aycock,** *Structuralist Interpretations of Biblical Myth* (1983). **J. D. Levenson,** *Creation and the Persistence of Evil: The Jewish Drama of Divine Omnipotence* (1988). **B. Lincoln,** *Theorizing Myth: Narrative, Ideology, and Scholarship* (1999). **F. R. McCurley,** *Ancient Myths and Biblical Faith: Scriptural Transformations* (1983). **B. L. Mack,** *A Myth of Innocence: Mark and Christian Origins* (1988). **T. N. D. Mettinger,** *King and Messiah* (ConBOT 8, 1987). **R. H. Moye,** "In the Beginning: Myth and History in Genesis and Exodus," *JBL* 109 (1990) 577-98. **E. T. Mullen, Jr.,** *The Divine Council in Canaanite and Early Hebrew Literature* (HSM 24, 1980). **H.-P. Müller,** *Mythos-Kerygma-Wahrheit: Gesammelte Aufsätze zum AT in seiner Umwelt und zur biblischen Theologie* (BZAW 200, 1991). **G. Natt,** *Symbol und Mythos: zwei Denkbegriffe qur Bibelhermeneutick des 19. und 20. Jahrhunderts* (2000). **R. A. Oden, Jr.,** *The Bible Without Theology: The Theological Tradition and Alternatives to It* (1987); "Mythology," *ABD* (1992*a*) 4:946-56; "Myth in the OT," *ABD* (1992*b*) 4:956-60. **H. R. Page, Jr.,** *The Myth of Cosmic Rebellion: A Study of Its Reflexes in Ugaritic und Biblical Literature* (VTSup 65, 1996). **C. Petersen,** *Mythos im Alten Testament: Bestimmung des Mythosbegriffs und Untersuchung der Mythis den Elemente den Psalmen* (BZAW 157, 1982). **W. H. Propp,** *Water in the Wilderness: A Biblical Motif and Its Mythological Background* (HSM 40, 1987). **J. Roloff,** "Myth in the Revelation of John," *The Revelation of John* (1993) 142-45. **H. H. Schmid** (ed.), *Mythos und Rationalität* (1988).

T. Schmidt, *Das Ende der Zeit: Mythos und Metaphorik als Fundamente einer Hermeneutik biblischer Eschatologie* (BBB 109, 1996). **W. H. Schmidt,** "Mythos. III. Alttestamentlich," *TRE* 23 (1994) 624-44. **R. A. Segal,** "In Defense of Mythology: The History of Modern Theories of Myth," *Annals of Scholarship 1* (1980) 3-49; (ed.), *Theories of Myth: From Ancient Israel and Greece to Freud, Jung, Campbell, and Lévi-Strauss* (6 vols. 1996); (ed.), *Theorizing About Myth.* (1999). **C. L. Seow,** *Myth, Drama, and the Politics of David's Dance* (HSM 44, 1989). **R. M. Shipp,** *Of Dead Kings and Dirges: Myth and Meaning in Isaiah 14:4b-21* (Academica Biblica 11, 2002). **T. Sienkewicz,** *Theories of Myth: An Annotated Bibliography* (1997). **M. S. Smith,** *The Early History of God: Yahweh and the Other Deities in Ancient Israel* (1990); "Mythology and Myth-making in Ugaritic and Israelite Literatures," *Ugarit and the Bible* (ed. G. J. Brooke et al., UBL 11, 1994) 293-341. **K. van der Toorn** et al. (eds.), *Dictionary of Deities and Demons in the Bible* (1995). **H. Wallace,** *The Eden Narrative* (HSM 32, 1985). **Richd G. Walsh,** *Mapping Myths of Biblical Interpretation* (Playing the Texts 4, 2001). **C. Westermann,** *Genesis 1-11: A Commentary* (BKAT 1, 1974-82; ET 1984). **U. Winter,** *Frau und Göttin: Exegetische und ikonographische Studien zum weiblichen Gottesbild im alten Israel und in dessen Umwelt* (OBO 53, 1986). **N. Wyatt,** *Myths of Power: A Study of Royal Myth and Ideology in Ugaritic and Biblical Tradition* (UBL 13, 1996).

N. H. WALLS

Religionsgeschichtliche Schule

This designation (RGS) originally denoted a group of scholars in Göttingen, also referred to as *die kleine Göttinger Fakultät* (none of whom were full professors at the time), who found themselves unified in the interpretation of the origins of Christianity as a religious-historical movement of Hellenistic Christianity. K. A. A. L. Eichhorn[§], as first among equals, H. Gunkel[§], W. Wrede[§], and W. Bousset[§] could be considered the founders of the school. Other members of the original generation included J. Weiss[§], E. Troeltsch[§], W. Heitmüller[§], and P. Wernle. Important collaborators from outside biblical studies and theology included R. Reitzenstein[§] and P. Wendland from the area of classical philology. To a second generation belonged, among others, H. Gressmann, M. Dibelius[§], R. Bultmann[§], and S. Mowinckel[§].

It should be noted that some members of this second generation were open to other influences that caused them to move in significant ways from the original intentions of the RGS. Bultmann's comment in the introduction to the fifth edition of Bousset's *Kyrios Christos* expresses this movement: "A word should be said about the intention of the [RGS] to present the religion of primitive Christianity and to use the New Testament as a source for this. Today we can ask whether this intention can do justice to the New Testament, and whether we are not rather to turn back again to the old question about the theology of the New Testament" (1913, VI [ET 1970, 9]). With that statement, Bultmann abandoned a key assumption of the RGS: namely, that primitive Christianity could be interpreted adequately, not as a theology, but, rather, as a religion that developed in a "world which was certainly not made up solely of writers and books" (Gunkel 1899, 588).

The RGS was not primarily concerned with nonbiblical religions or with first-century Judaism, but with Christianity. The concern with other religions arose only secondarily, as a means to a better historical understanding of Christianity. Likewise, investigations of early Christian history could not remain within the limits of the New Testament Canon[§], as Wrede argued (1897 [ET 1973]). Wrede outlined programmatically the task for a so-called New Testament Theology*[§]: the description of the history of primitive Christianity as a developing religion. He set the temporal limit for such a history before the time of the apologists, who mark a turning point in Christianity. Bousset went even further, including the apologists as well as Irenaeus[§] in his "history of the belief in Christ" (1913 [ET 1970]).

The RGS scholars focused on Christianity as a developing religion of Hellenistic antiquity, a religion they understood to have been influenced primarily by Hellenistic Judaism and only secondarily by pagan Hellenistic religions. In that regard, it would be better to translate the name of the movement as the "history-of-religion school" in the singular, in contrast to the distinctively different concerns of the discipline known as "history of religions." Central to the RGS was the understanding of New Testament faith as an inner-historical phenomenon, based on the conviction that the New Testament documents were rarely the original products of their final authors but mostly resulted from long, complex developments. In considering the RGS, the issue is less that the school made use of nonbiblical materials to interpret the Bible than it is how the school did so. What made the RGS come to look at its task in this particular way?

With the publication in 1895 of Gunkel's *Schöpfung und Chaos and Bousset's Der Antichrist*, the characteristic RGS interpretive method made its first public appearance, following such antecedents as Bousset's *Jesu Predigt* (1892). J. Wellhausen's[§] (1899) largely negative reaction to *Schöpfung und Chaos* provided Gunkel with the opportunity to defend the *religionsgeschichtliche* method at some of its most crucial points. Wellhausen rejected Gunkel's tracing of large parts of Jewish Apocalypticism*[§] back to Babylonian origins, but his main objection was that Gunkel's, attached so much weight to the question of origins. According to Wellhausen, the task of the interpreter is not to uncover the origins of apocalyptic statements, but to determine the meanings the author expressed through them. The origins, Wellhausen observed, are of purely antiquarian interest; yet Gunkel had set his Tradition*§-Historical approach in opposition to a contemporary-historical (*zeitgeschichtliche*) method in such a way that the one excluded the other.

In his reply, Gunkel drew attention to many places in *Schöpfung und Chaos* where he discussed the particular meanings the apocalyptic materials received in later Jewish and also Christian understanding; but he maintained that such interpretations do not exhaust their meanings (1899). He pointed out how much of the apocalyptic material Wellhausen discarded without further ado as "fantastic chaff," with the result that his interpretation in terms of contemporary events remained hanging in the air. The search for the origins of the meanings of certain features of a text is not out of antiquarian interest but out of recognition that a purely contemporary-historical interpretation fails to clarify a text at so many points. Moreover, the issue is not errors in tradition-historical details—Gunkel admitted that he may have erred frequently—but the procedure itself, which demands that justice be sought for every detail of a text in its own terms.

The key to the problem is that, although Wellhausen admitted that there is material in the apocalypses "that is not absorbed into the conception of a writer . . . and frequently leaves our interpretation with an unintelligible residue" (1899, 233), he did not recognize that the biblical writers themselves were participants in the history of that material and remain unintelligible if some of that history is excluded from the interpretation. As Gunkel stated, "In [his declarations that the origins of such materials have at the most an antiquarian interest] Wellhausen falls into conflict with fundamental principles which are everywhere recognised in historical science, and which are conceded and followed in other fields by Wellhausen himself. The cardinal principle of historical study is this: that we are unable to comprehend a person, a period, or a thought dissociated from its antecedents, but that we can speak of a real living understanding only when we have the antecedent history" (ET 1903, 404).

A widespread misunderstanding of the RGS is that it was biased in favor of a pagan Hellenistic interpretation of primitive Christianity. What may have contributed to this misunderstanding is that one of the school's best-known works, Bousset's *Kyrios Christos*, traces "the history of the belief in Christ from the beginnings to Irenaeus" largely within the framework of the New Testament's pagan Hellenistic environment. In that same work Bousset nevertheless expressed greater appreciation for the Palestinian Christian community than for the later Greek-speaking churches. "Thus the [Palestinian] community embellished and decorated the life portrait of its master. But by doing so it accomplished more: It preserved a good bit of the authentic and original life. It preserved for us the beauty and wisdom of his parables in their crystalline form—a Greek community would no longer have been able to do so" (1913, 74 [ET 1970, 116]). One merely needs to look at Bousset's list of publications to verify how much more he had been involved in research concerning the Jewish origins of Christianity than with work on the influence of the pagan Hellenistic religions in its further development, beginning with *Jesu Predigt* (1892), continuing with *Der Antichrist* (1895) and *Die Religion des Judentums im neutestamentlichen Zeitalter* (1903), and five years before his death, *Jüdisch-Christlicher Schulbetrieb in Alexandrien und Rom* (1915).

This concern with the Jewish thought of New Testament times does not make things easier for a traditional understanding of the origins of Christianity, however. The effect is indeed far more devastating: Christianity was not merely influenced in its further development by Hellenistic religions; it derived from them in the form of Judaism as a Hellenistic religion (in the broader sense of the term). It is noteworthy that in *Jesu Predigt* Bousset tried to negate the decisive influence of Judaism on Jesus*§, in contrast to the famous work of a fellow member of the school, J. Weiss's *Die Predigt Jesu vom Reiche Gottes* (published earlier in the same year). Weiss interpreted the concept "the kingdom of God" in Jesus' preaching as a product of Jewish apocalypticism. Bousset's negative reaction shows clearly that the interpretation of primitive Christianity within the framework of Hellenistic Judaism and pagan religions was not a point of departure for the school.

A. Ritschl's[§] influence was one of the most crucial factors in the RGS's development. He drew to Göttingen those scholars who subsequently constituted its membership. From him they learned to understand Christianity historically; but it was against his particular understanding of history that they found themselves united as a group, subsequently as a school.

Ritschl was one of the rare scholars who followed J. P. Gabler's[§] call for a separate biblical Theology[*§] as preparation for a dogmatic theology. The second volume of his D*ie christliche Lehre von der Rechtfertigung und Versöhnung* (1870-74), the only volume not translated into English, is a biblical—more specifically, a New Testament—theology, which prepared for the systematic presentation of his own thought in the third volume. His treatment of the New Testament materials is at the same time appealing and unsatisfactory. His insistence that the New Testament writings are to be understood religiously, not doctrinally, is appealing; but this approach is overshadowed by a lack of sensitivity for the historical setting of the New Testament, notwithstanding his claim to offer a historical interpretation. The frustration of the young scholars who had come to Göttingen to study under him becomes understandable when one notes these opposing features of his work: on the one hand, there is the charm of an undogmatic interpretation; on the other, the disappointment in a lack of historical sensitivity.

In their rejection of Ritschl, the young scholars were influenced by P. de Lagarde[§] and encouraged by Eichhorn. Their rejection was not complete, however; Ritschl's theological system remained an important influence in their understanding of the Christian faith. Weiss made this clear in *Die Predigt Jesus vom Reiche Gottes*, the work in which he broke historically with Ritschl's conception of the kingdom of God. In the preface he pointed out that even though the kingdom of God, in Ritschl's thought, had nothing in common with the same expression in Jesus' preaching, he nevertheless remained convinced that Ritschl's system of thought—especially his conception of the kingdom of God—remained most appropriate for a vital contemporary Christianity. Even though they may not have offered such an explicit comment, the understanding of Christianity found in other members of the RGS was not basically different from that of Ritschl, including his emphasis on Christianity as fundamentally a religion of ethical values. So, for example, Bousset wrote concerning the Palestinian community: "It bowed down before the stark heroism of [the] ethical demands [of Jesus] which were rooted in an equally daring faith in God" (*Kyrios Christos*, 74 [ET, 116]).

Secure in their Ritschilian religious convictions, the members of the RGS were unfettered by the concern for a historical confirmation of their faith. So, for example, the truth of Christianity was established for Bousset already in the first two chapters of *Kyrios Christos*. In the rest of the book he made it relevant in changing historical circumstances. Thus he was not the least put off by what may seem strange ideas. He wrote of the Palestinian community: "Only by using the figure of the heavenly Son of Man, the Lord and Judge of the world, to back up the gospel of Jesus...did the community make the picture of Jesus of Nazareth influential. An age which did not live solely on the simply ethical and simply religious, but on all sorts of more or less fantastic eschatological expectations . . . needed just such a picture of Jesus as the first disciples of Jesus had created, and accepted the Eternal proclaimed in it, in the colorful wrappings of temporal clothing" (*Kyrios Christos* (1913), 75 [ET, 117-18]).

For the RGS, the truth of Christianity was dependent neither on its historical manifestation nor on the biblical religion and, strictly speaking, not even on Jesus' message. The result was that the members of the RGS were very relaxed about what they found in history and about historical details; it was the larger picture that counted. This attitude was well illustrated by Gunkel in a remark concerning fundamental differences between himself and Bousset on the interpretation of Revelation 12, particularly on its religious background (Babylonian according to Gunkel, Egyptian and subsequently Iranian according to Bousset). Gunkel argued that such differences may be set aside in favor of the one fundamental point "that this chapter is based on mythical traditions. . . . Whether the myths were originally Babylonian or Egyptian is secondary; subsequent generations may break their heads on that" (1903, 55).

The difference between the RGS and its opponents may best be illustrated with regard to Bousset's wavering on the interpretation of *maranatha*. He gave one explanation in *Kyrios Christos* (1913), that it originated in the bilingual area of Antioch, Damascus, and Tarsus; another in *Jesus der Herr* (1916), that it was an oath directed to God; and then returned to the former explanation in the second edition of *Kyrios Christos* (1921²), never wavering in his conviction that it could not have originated in Palestinian Christianity. This was identified as the Achilles heel of his understanding of the development of the cult of Christ the Lord by A. Rawlinson§ (*The New Testament Doctrine of the Christ* 1926), a critique endorsed by O. Cullmann§ (*Die Christologie des Neuen Testaments* 1957, 219-20 [ET, 213-14]). Nothing can reveal more clearly the difference between the RGS and its critics than this controversy. For Bousset, all that was at stake was the best possible historical interpretation. If someone would have been able to make historically plausible a cult of Christ in the temple in Jerusalem, it could only have contributed to the clarification of the historical picture of the development of the cult of Christ the Lord. Nothing was at stake theologically for him, and future generations could continue to struggle with the details. For Rawlinson and Cullmann, however, the historical explanation carried considerable theological weight.

At the same time it must be said that this historical openness sometimes came at the cost of religious sensitivity. Troeltsch formulated the issue well: "Every act of religious devotion considers itself within its own realm fundamentally and self-evidently as absolute, and each universal religion does the same for every possible sphere" (1912, 110 [ET 1971, 132]). Gunkel may have been right when he claimed that "the insatiable hunger of the human heart after God and the ineradicable search after Truth . . . come from one and the same Divine source" (1926-27, 535), but not when he concluded that they "can therefore never contradict each other" (1926-27, 535). Troeltsch's statement contradicts Gunkel's assertion that "We are not entitled to select from the course of history some isolated facts or some entire periods and declare that these and these alone are of God and supernatural" (1926-27, 535-36). Whatever else may be said about Gunkel's claim, most scholars would agree that religious conviction elevates precisely some relative historical fact to absoluteness by taking it as more than history, by understanding it as myth.

In arguments with opponents, the RGS had an advantage religiously in not being bound in principle to a purely historical framework. Because its conceptions did not depend on historical proof, it remained open to a course leading to the mythological formulation (Mythology and Biblical Studies*§) of religious truth as a radicalizing of history. By contrast, interpretations that depend on historical verification must remain within the bounds of the historical.

An important element of the RGS was its conviction that the final purpose of biblical interpretation is the meaning it has for the individual modern believer. This conviction was expressed in extensive lectures by members of the RGS, lectures of a more popular nature offered in local congregations. It was also expressed by the founding of a series of generally accessible interpretations of Christianity for educated laypersons, the *Religionsgeschichtliche Volksbücher für die deutsche christlicher Gegenwart*, inaugurated with Bousset's *Jesus* (1904), and by publication of *Die Religion in Geschichte und Gegenwart* (1909-13, 1927-32², 1957-62³) as counterpart to the more academically oriented *Realencyklopädie für protestantische Theologie und Kirche*.

The RGS's program of biblical interpretation never came to a conclusion; it was interrupted by the rise of dialectical theology, to which even such an eminent second-generation member as Bultmann was attracted. The misfortune of this for biblical scholarship is not that the answers of the RGS have been lost—to the contrary, they have been refined by sympathizers and opponents alike. The misfortune is rather that their questions have been forgotten without having been fully addressed.

Bibliography: H. Boers, *What is NT Theology? The Rise of Criticism and the Problem of a Theology of the NT* (GBS, 1979) 39-66. **W. Bousset,** *Jesu Predigt in ihrem Gegensatz zum Judentum: Ein religionsgeschichtlicher Vergleich* (1892); *Der Antichrist in der überlieferung des Judentums, des Neuen Testaments, und der alten Kirche* (1895); *Die Religion des Judentums im neutestamentlichen Zeitalter* (1903); *Jesus* (Religionsgeschichtliche Volksbücher für die deutsche christlicher Gegenwart, 1904); *Kyrios Christos: Geschichte des Christusglaubens von den Anfangen des Christentums bis Irenaeus* (1913; ET 1970); *Jüdisch-Christlicher Schulbetrieb in Alexandrien und Rom: Literarische Untersuchungen zu Philo und Clemens von Alexandria, Justin, und Irenaus* (1915); *Jesus der Herr: Nachtrage und Auseinandersetzungen zu "Kyrios Christos"* (1916). **Bultmann, R.** "Introductory Word," *W. Bousset Kyrios Christos: Geschichte des Christusglaubens von den Anfangen des Christentums bis Irenaeus* (1913[5]; ET 1970) 7–9. **C. Colpe,** *Die religionsgeschichtliche Schule: Darstellung und Kritik ihres Bildes vom gnostischen Erlösermythus* (FRLANT 78, 1961). **O. Eissfeldt,** "Religionsgeschichtliche Schule," *RGG*[2] 4 (1930) 1898-905. **H. Gressmann,** *A. Eichhorn und die Religionsgeschichtliche Schule* (1914). **H. Gunkel,** *Schöpfung und Chaos in Urzeit und Endzeit: Eine religionsgeschichtliche Untersuchung über Gen 1 und Ap Joh 12* (1895); "Aus Wellhausen's neuesten apokalyptischen Forschungen," *ZWT* NF 7 (1899) 581-611; "The Religio-Historical Interpretation of the NT," *The Monist* 13 (1903) 398-455; *Zum religionsgeschichtlichen Verständnis des Neuen Testaments* (FRLANT 2, 1903); "The 'Historical Movement' in the Study in Religion," *Exp Tim* 38 (1926-27) 532-36. **J. Hempel,** "Religionsgeschichtliche Schule," *RGG*[3] 5 (1961) 991-94. **G. W. Ittel,** *Urchristentum und Fremdreligionen im Urteil der religionsgeschichtliche Schule* (1956); "Die Hauptgedanken der 'religionsgeschichtliche Schule,'" *ZRGG* 10 (1958) 61-78. **W. Klatt,** *H. Gunkel: Zu seiner "Theologie der Religionsgeschichte" und zur Entstehung der formgeschichtlichen Methode* (FRLANT 100, 1969). **W. Kümmel,** *Das Neue Testament: Geschichte der Erforschung seiner Probleme* (1958) 259-414 (ET 1972) 206-324. **G. Lüdemann,** "Die Religionsgeschichtliche Schule," *Theologie in Göttingen: Eine Vorlesungsreihe* (ed. B. Moeller, Göttinger Universitätsschriften A/1, 1987) 325-61. **G. Lüdemann** and **M. Schröder,** *Die Religionsgeschichtliche Schule in Göttingen: Eine Dokumentation* (1987). **R. Morgan,** "Introduction: The Nature of NT Theology," *The Nature of NT Theology: The Contributions of W. Wrede and A. Schlatter* (SBT 2nd. ser. 25, 1973) 2-26. **R. Morgan** with J. Barton, *Biblical Interpretation* (Oxford Bible Series, 1988) 93-110. **H. Paulsen,** "Traditionsgeschichte und religionsgeschichtliche Schule," *ZTK* 75 (1958) 22-55. **H. Räisänen,** *Beyond NT Theology: A Story and a Programme* (1990) 13-31. **K. Rudolph,** "Religionsgeschichtliche Schule," *EncRel* 12 (1987) 293-96. **E. Troeltsch,** *Die Absolutheit des Christentums und die Religionsgeschichte* (1912; ET *The Absoluteness of Christianity and the History of Religions* 1971); "Die 'kleine Göttinger Fakultät' von 1890," *ChW* 18 (1920) 281-83. **J. Weiss,** *Die Predigt Jesu vom Reiche Gottes* (1892; ET 1971). **J. Wellhausen,** "Zur apokalyptischen Literatur," *Skizzen und Vorarbeiten* (1899, repr. 1985) 215-49. **W. Wrede,** *Über Aufgabe und Methode der sogenannten neutestamentlichen Theologie* (1897; ET 1973).

H. BOERS

Hebrew Bible Form Criticism

The term *form criticism* designates, not just one procedure, but several different ones that deal in one manner or another with patterns usually thought of as dynamic and oriented toward a function. The variations reflect, in part, divergent conceptions of form. Procedures designated thus include (1) the study of kinds of speech (genre analysis, *Gattungsforschung*), which has been carried out throughout the history of biblical interpretation; (2) the tracing of the history of a type of speech (genre history, *Gattungsgeschichte* or *Formengeschichte*), of which there are only a relatively few examples, two of them provided by H. Gunkel[§]; (3) the reconstruction of the history of a tradition on the basis of formal considerations, largely in the belief that the simplest forms are early (history on the basis of form, often *Formgeschichte*), attempted to some extent by Gunkel and even more by many of his followers; and (4) the examination of the structure of a particular text (form-oriented criticism), as executed by W. Richter (*Formkritik*) and (with attention to genres) by many ancient and modern exegetes, including recent contributors to the series *The Forms of Old Testament Literature*.

Classical Greek theory distinguished between rhetorical and poetic genres, although it did not draw an altogether sharp line between them, and discussed levels of style in terms of phenomena belonging to both. Insofar as one follows this distinction, Rhetorical*[§] and poetic (or Literary*[§]) study become subdivisions of formal analysis. One can also contrast a portrayal of general patterns (theory, including attention to genres) with the examination of the structure of a specific text; the former plays a greater or lesser role in the various operations that go under the name form criticism.

Genres were described by Gunkel in 1924 as involving characteristic thoughts and feelings, typical lexical and syntactic features ("form" in a narrow sense), and a traditional connection with human (especially social) life (*Sitz im Leben*). It thus became characteristic of work inspired by Gunkel to give attention to all three of these aspects, which are comparable to the semantic, syntactic, and pragmatic dimensions of linguistics.

During the sixteenth century, Erasmus[§], T. Cajetan[§], Luther, P. Melanchthon[§], Zwingli, Calvin[§], J. Bullinger[§], T. Cranmer[§], and others made stylistic and classificatory comments. The Lutheran M. Flacius Illyricus[§] presented a thorough analysis of biblical patterns. Although he sought to be less humanistic than Melanchthon, he was deeply influenced by Aristotle. He believed that genres, determined especially by content, but also by style, each have a special impact on life, so that a consideration of them clarifies the aim of biblical literature. Biblical genres, as he described them, form a rich set of structures, including both divine address and speech directed toward God. Thereafter, often in association with Aristotelian ideas, classifications of biblical materials continued to appear, as in treatments by C. Lapide[§] (1625), A. Francke[§] (1693), and J. Turretin.

Three major tendencies moving away from a consideration of general forms marked the period from the sixteenth to the eighteenth centuries: (1) a strong interest in factual history, (2) increased attention to differences between the styles of individual authors, and (3) removal of content from rhetorical analysis. The last of these reflected, in part, skepticism about coherence in reality, e.g., about the question of an appropriateness of forms of expression in relation to thought.

Another tendency related to these was the placing of a dividing line between biblical forms and those of classical or other non-Christian traditions. It showed itself in directions that state that one should not combine in the same poem contents derived from both of these sources and in analyses that suggest that sacred rhetoric has special rules. One of the factors contributing to this differentiation was a sharpened contrast between faith and reason characteristic of particularism; another was a sense for the variety of traditions, which is an integral part of that outlook. A third, more special one was an avoidance of ornate forms in middle-class public speaking, causing the style of biblical speech, like that of the prophets, to seem out of the ordinary. R. Lowth[§] in 1753 effectively addressed these and related issues in what is probably still the finest overall study of biblical poetry (Mythology and Biblical Interpretation [to 1800]*[§]; Mythology and Biblical Interpretation [1800-1980]*[§]; Poetry, Hebrew Bible[‡§]). He solved the problem of style by characterizing prophecy (together with parallelism, which had previously been considered a rhetorical feature) as poetic. In regard to differences in poetic standards, he argued that the biblical forms were more basic and less special or artificial than the Greco-Roman. In its careful treatment of biblical structures together with their purposes, this work represents, in important ways, the culmination of a classical approach, while showing sensitivity to the newer movement toward a historical outlook.

M. Mendelssohn[§] (in a January 1757 letter to G. Lessing) pointed in this new direction by rejecting the idea of separate classes in literature. Nevertheless, he recognized three kinds of poetry—song, elegy, and ode (the last kind, reflective)—in the psalms. J. G. Herder[§], who interacted with him, provided sensitively drawn pictures of biblical literature in *The Spirit of Hebrew Poetry* (1782-83) and other studies. He continued to employ classifications but did so quite loosely and sometimes in an unusual manner; for instance, he classed the psalms according to their complexity (1787). A sign of the change in outlook is that J. G. Eichhorn[§] (1780-83) viewed genres as external forms (*Einkleidung,* "clothing").

W. de Wette rejected Mendelssohn's typology since de Wette believed that Hebrew poetry is "formless and special." Radicalizing an older view that each genre requires a special Hermeneutics*[§], he said that "every writing requires its own hermeneutic" (1807, 25). He ordered the psalms by "content," however; the resulting classification was very similar to the one later set forth within a different theoretical framework by Gunkel. Somewhat like de Wette, F. Bleek[§] (in his 1860 introduction) regarded older psalms as personal in character and later ones as imitations.

One consequence of the emerging historical orientation was a sequencing of genres according to their antiquity. Thus myth was treated as the oldest form of expression by the classicist C. Heyne near the end of the eighteenth century and, following him, by Eichhorn, J. P. Gabler[§], G. Bauer[§], and J. Jahn (who was Catholic). This perspective modified the one according to which revelation took place during an original period, now envisioning progress (at least intellectually) beyond that time.

The liberal critical approach, nevertheless, far from dominated all publications. Conservative works or those oriented toward a general public continued to present Literary*[§] and full-scale rhetorical analyses, usually with extensive typologies. They included analyses by A. Gügler, J. Wenrich, C. Plantier, G. Gilfillan, I. Taylor, C. Ehrt, T. Nöldeke (1869), J. Fürst, and D. Cassel. The majority of these authors (the last two of whom were Jewish) were not specifically biblical scholars. In a partial contrast, specialists in the field attended more closely to external forms not directly related to content, like meter.

As particularism reached a high point during the nineteenth century, its problematic side also became apparent. Intellectually, it threatened all rationality. Socially, it created a free-for-all in which the strong defeated the weak. Some thinkers, notably Nietzsche, largely affirmed these consequences. Many, however, found them intellectually and ethically unacceptable and resurrected a partial interest in commonness, which supported an integrative role in society for the socioeconomic lower class.

The new social orientation was important to a "school" that pursued a *Religionsgeschichtliche**[§] approach, meaning by *religion* a general category of human experience. For the

114

content of its investigation, this school gave close attention to the social structures that embody popular life. Its members, including Gunkel (who politically held some sympathy for socialism), made efforts in lectures and writings to propagate the results of their investigations to a broad audience.

Sensitive to the social dimension, Gunkel reversed the position of the psalms held by de Wette and Bleek; he regarded standardized features not as secondary developments but as temporally primary generic patterns that are adapted in individual psalms. For other traditions, Gunkel also envisioned highly predictable structures that closely relate to recurring events in the life of a group where they have their "seat in life" (*Sitz im Leben*). Still, Gunkel was ambivalent about individuality. He appreciated the "living" character of patterned popular, largely oral, culture; but he valued, at least equally, the individualized personal expressions available in the written documents (e.g., in his commentary on Psalms 1926).

Gunkel's interest in generality reached far beyond the Israelite or even the Near Eastern sphere. By frequently citing evidence from all parts of the world, he made clear that he was concerned with human structures and not merely with isolated and accidental phenomena. This general orientation was not shared by all of the many scholars inspired by him; it was, however, well represented by H. Jahnow[§] in her study of the dirge (1923).

Gunkel considered linguistic form to be an easily recognizable feature, but he listed content first among the determiners of a generic structure. Accordingly, he could take over de Wette's content-oriented classification of psalms. Thus, the word *form* in the term form criticism, as it was applied by other scholars to his procedure, refers, not primarily to external phenomena, but to a structure or pattern. Crucial for Gunkel was the connection of genres with life; that interest gave his work a sociological cast (Sociology and Hebrew Bible Studies*[§]). Mood, a psychological category (Psychology and Biblical Studies*[§]), was also significant for him and was placed next to thought as a part of content.

Gunkel's generic and structural orientation fits in well with the revolt against individualism and historicism widely current in the culture. For him as for others, however, the question was not one of choosing between the different visions but one of finding appropriate ways to combine them. In regard to the historical dimension, he made the debatable assumption that the early stage of genres as well as of particular texts exhibited simple and pure forms, while later ones combined those into complex structures.

Quite a few scholars took this historical view very seriously and attempted to reconstruct on its basis a prehistory for a text, often thought to be oral. Many, especially in New Testament studies, focused exclusively on small units. Somewhat differently, G. von Rad[§] argued that the ritual "credo" of Deut 26:4-9 formed one of the two basic structures out of which the Hexateuch as a whole emerged (1938). (More holistically, G. Mendenhall derived the structure of the Pentateuch and many other features of biblical literature from Hittite and other treaty forms [1954].) Gradually, however, it became clear that the assumption that early forms are simple or pure is largely unfounded. Thus the enterprise of writing history on the basis of formal consideration (form criticism in the third sense above) came under a cloud; the procedure used (formal analysis) was not well matched to this aim (history).

A significant consequence of a concern with genres was the realization that many of them were complementary to one another, operating simultaneously in the service of varied human needs. Indeed, it became apparent that, although biblical literature was given its shape over a period of perhaps one thousand years (much of it after the first fall of Jerusalem) the genres exhibited in it were virtually all co-present in the culture even before the exile. Although few scholars denied that genres changed to some extent over the centuries, there was a widespread willingness to acknowledge that many biblical psalms, proverbs, ritual laws, etc., were preexilic in a form at least closely approximating that in which they now appear. Similarly, in structural-functional sociology and anthropology, a largely synchronic view could displace a primarily diachronic one.

The shift in perspective was far from universal, of course. The historian A. Alt[§] (1934) viewed the several kinds of Israelite law as competing structures derived from different traditions. With a widened knowledge of ancient culture and a more functional view, H. Cazelles argued that they represent complementary genres with a range comparable to that of both Hittite and modern laws and instructions (1946).

When structural and historical perspectives, each with its own procedure, were combined systematically, a history of a genre or of a group of related genres resulted. Gunkel furnished such histories for Prophecy[†‡§] (1917) and psalms (1933, with J. Begrich). The same topics were treated again, with at least some attention to history, by S. Mowinckel[§] (psalms 1951 [ET 1962]); C. Westermann (psalms 1954 [ET 1981], judgmental prophecy 1960 [ET 1967], words of salvation 1987); and J. N. Aletti and J. Trublet (psalms 1983). P. Hanson, among others, traced the emergence of apocalyptic forms (1975; Apocalypticism*[§]). Partial histories of the genres of wisdom included one by H. Schmid (1966). A. Rof examined prophetic stories from a developmental perspective (1982 [ET 1988]); S. Niditch, symbolic visions (1983); J. Van Seters, historiography (1983); and D. Damrosch, narrative forms more generally (1987).

A step partially diverging from Gunkel was to envision a genre, not as a structure lying behind and utilized in a text, but as the dynamic pattern of the text seen as an actually or potentially general one. It was possible to follow this line only if a genre was permitted to have a considerable amount of variability, for clearly the individual texts that are examples of the genre are not completely stereotyped.

Thus, Mowinckel considered most of the biblical psalms as being cultic, i.e., used on organized ritual occasions (1916). In this, he was followed (at least partially) by many others. H. G. Reventlow took the cultic approach perhaps farther than anyone else, especially by viewing Jeremiah's confessions largely in nonpersonal terms. In most cultures, to be sure, the line between organized ritual and other expressions of religion is very fluid, if it can be drawn at all. Perhaps to some extent aware of that (his father was an important Africanist), Westermann rejected a specifically cultic view and related the psalms to the basic operations of praise and lament (1954). W. Brueggemann reformulated their patterns in sociopsychological terms (orientation, disorientation, and new orientation, 1984).

Westermann's analysis of genres grouped its features into substructures—within a lament there are first-person, second-person (often God-directed), and third-person (enemy, etc.) elements. This kind of patterning resembles that characteristic of Structuralism*[§]. P. Beauchamp, a representative of that movement, provided a view of the systematic interweaving and contrasting of elements of this sort as they occur in different genres, so that a system of genres becomes visible (1971). Somewhat similarly, the cult-oriented tradition represented by Mowinckel stood close to the work of what can loosely be called the Myth and Ritual School*[§], which emphasized, as its name implies, both structure and type of context. Structuralism and a "patternism" appearing within the myth and ritual school represent, of course, anti-particularist perspectives.

One line of endeavor has related the structures of biblical literature to linguistics. W. Richter (1971), who moved in this direction, distinguished between form and genre. In his view, form represents the organization of a particular text; he treated separately its "external" syntactic-stylistic and "inner" meaning aspects. A genre, according to Richter, is to be identified on the basis of the external features of texts. Unlike most twentieth-century linguistic theorists, he held that one should operate inductively, proceeding from the particular to the general. His was thus a thoroughly particularist viewpoint, which, as noted, typically separates the external from the internal. K. Koch (1974) also sought to relate genre criticism to linguistics. He referred to a version of the latter known as "text linguistics" or "discourse analysis," which, as is not well known, has absorbed insights from biblical studies. C. Hardmeier (1978) provided a detailed reformulation of form criticism in terms of a theory of linguistic action. He had been reinforced by linguistics in the view that verbal features are not strictly correlated with content or situation. A reflective analysis of biblical genres within the framework of a general communication theory that explores the human meaning of the literary structures was furnished by a group of scholars in a work edited by F. Deist and W. Vorster (1986).

The works just mentioned entered increasingly into the realm of theoretical discussions of language that, especially since about 1920, had focused on the variety of speech "functions" (expressed especially by the first, second, or third person, according to K. Bühler), language "games" (constituting "forms of life," L. Wittgenstein), or speech "acts" (performances, J. Austin). A theological wing of this discussion had begun, also about 1920, with a distinction between personal ("I" and "you") and impersonal speech. Following this tradition, a number of biblical scholars and theologians emphasized the personal thrust of much of biblical speech. Thus, A. Heschel[§] showed the directedness of divine speech toward humanity (1936 [ET 1962]); W. Zimmerli[§] discussed divine self-presentations (1963); and C. Westermann argued that many biblical expressions are not assertion but direct address (1984, 202). It was also noted that psalms are often directed toward God. A number of theologies of the Hebrew Bible (including von Rad's, with his focus on *Heilsgeschichte* 1957 [ET 1962]) were based largely on attempts to identify, in the text, generic patterns like those outlined above. Rather than focus on particular ideas or directives, the theologian focused on generic forms and structures to understand how these forms functioned in the faith community.

A recognition of different types of speech with divergent functions allowed those who believe in the divine verbal inspiration of the Bible to distinguish between biblical truth and historical or scientific accuracy. Such an orientation has been discussed intensively by Roman Catholics since the turn of the twentieth century (M. J. Lagrange 1896), resurrecting and extending medieval and earlier reflections. It was given official approval by the encyclical *Divino afflante Spiritu* (1943), which encouraged the study of genres. Similar considerations have moved a number of traditional Protestants to reject a highly literal (or, better, historicist) interpretation of biblical narratives, although not many of them have gone so far as C. Pinnock (1984). Analyses along these lines should not be understood as being primarily negative, for their main interest is in apprehending on the basis of literary types the purposes of the texts (e.g., W. Kaiser 1981, 95), in a manner not unlike that of earlier exegesis.

Interpreters who are more questioning of biblical Authority*[§], including non-theologians, also found in literary analysis a way to reveal the character and significance of the Bible and to do so in relation to a broad public. C. Briggs[§], who presented an overview of the literary forms (types and styles) of the Bible with the aim that "the ordinary reader can enjoy it" without being a professional (1883, 216), believed that a new critical period was dawning, for which literature rather than history would be the central focus (1899, 247). This judgment proved to be largely correct. Not only biblical specialists but others provided an extensive and notable succession of literary, often generic, studies. Representing a variety of religious orientations, they included M. Arnold[§], W. R. Harper[§], R. Moulton[§], C. Kent, J. Gardiner, H. Fowler, L. Wild, J. Muilenburg[§], A. Culler, M. Buber[§], F. Rosenzweig, E. Goodspeed[§], S. Freehof, Z. Adar, E. Good, J. Ackerman, and L. Ryken. Many of them were deeply involved in social issues, including women's rights. A number of the studies did not concentrate on providing technical information for the academic specialist and consequently have been partially forgotten in academia. Repeatedly, however, they raised profound theoretical issues about the relation of the content and manner of biblical expression to human life.

Twentieth-century applications of rhetorical criticism included a number of analyses based on a narrow conception of rhetoric, with a focus primarily on external form as it had been advocated by members of the particularist tradition since the fifteenth century. Other studies partially revived a more comprehensive classical approach, attending closely to content. Interaction with Folklore*§ studies has been fruitful and was important, for example, to people like Gunkel. An analysis that can serve as a model for form criticism was furnished by C. Fontaine (1982); she integrates a folklore perspective informed by Gunkel's approach in attending simultaneously to content and use without following his more questionable assumptions.

The acquisition of a posthistorical perspective—one that includes, but is not limited to, historical criticism—has not been an easy one for biblical scholarship. Older ways of thinking have repeatedly been resurrected without much change and added to the historical, even though they are not strictly compatible. Specifically, Gunkel and many others following him relied in good part on Aristotelian essentialism—the notion that there is only one correct typology for objects. In doing so, they failed to take part in an intellectual development that in a certain way both synthesizes and transcends the previous approaches. Most important, for a point of view often called relationism (closely connected with pragmatism, following C. Peirce) both particularity and generality are fundamental, playing roles in real relations; an object is not separated from a subject (M. Buss 1999). Characteristic of this view is an acceptance of probability connections (partial indeterminacy) and of a variety of orders (with relativity to a standpoint). Within this outlook, form can be treated as a complex of relations.

A number of attempts have been made to reformulate the form-critical task along such lines. A probabilistic multidimensional approach was applied by M. Buss to Hosea (1969). In a theoretical article, R. Knierim opposes a "monolithic conception of genre" (1973, 467), as, in fact, some scholars did before him. G. Fohrer, in his Old Testament introduction (1965 [ET 1968, 28]), rejects the equating of a life setting with an "institution"; other scholars followed suit by arguing for a loose connection between texts and situations insofar as these are externally describable. The question then arises whether particularism should prevail after all—or perhaps skeptical relativism. One can answer in the negative by pointing to a rationale that places phenomena at least partially into intrinsic relations (as opposed to those, including J. Barton, who see genres only as conventions [1984, 32]). An exploration of such relations requires the continued and expanded investigation of psychological and sociological, as well as logical, questions.

Around 1970, a group of scholars gathered to produce an overview of the forms of Hebrew Bible literature. G. Tucker (1971) presented a model for their procedure based in good part on the joint discussions. It is notable that the procedure discusses particular texts in the light of applicable genres and that it provides an outline ("structure") and identifies a context ("setting") and thrust ("intention") for each unit, both large and small. This procedure implies a basically synchronic understanding of the task of form criticism. It may also reflect some skepticism about the feasibility of describing separately the many genres of biblical literature; nevertheless, an essentialist tendency appears in the series in that its form of presentation typically implies that a text's structure and especially its genre are correctly identifiable in only one way. A consequence of this text-centered, synchronic, and partially Aristotelian approach is that the analysis resembles medieval, especially scholastic, exegesis—a fact that is largely to its credit. It does not simply represent a return to earlier exegesis, however, for a critical-historical perspective shines through at various points.

A basic issue remains current, mentioned when R. Murphy, a member of the group just discussed, calls the psalms a "school of prayer" (1983, 113). Do biblical forms constitute models for the expressions and beliefs of all time? Insofar as forms are not just particular they potentially apply to the present, but are there not divergences between past and present that require changes in speech and behavior? In answer, one can say that a relational analysis, with a recognition of the roles of forms in their contexts, provides a basis for an application of the principle of analogy, which joins sameness with difference.

Bibliography: J. N. **Aletti** and J. **Trublet**, *Approche poétique et théologique des psaumes: analyses et méthodes* (1983). L. **Alonso Schökel**, *Estudios de poética hebrea* (1963); *The Inspired Word* (1966; ET 1967). A. **Alt**, *Die Ursprünge des israelitischen Rechts* (1934). I. **Baldermann**, *Einführung in die Bibel* (1988). H. **Barth** and O. **Steck**, *Exegese des Alten Testaments* (1978[8]). J. **Barton**, *Reading the OT: Method in Biblical Study* (1974, rev. 1996). P. **Beauchamp**, "L'analyse structurale et l'exégèse biblique" *Congress Volume: Uppsala, 1971* (VTSup 22, 1971) 113-28. W. **Brueggemann**, *The Message of the Psalms: A Theological Commentary* (1984). C. **Briggs**, *Biblical Study* (1883); *General Introduction to the Study of Holy Scripture* (1899). M. J. **Buss**, *The Prophetic Word of Hosea: A Morphological Study* (1969); *Biblical Form Criticism in Its Context* (JSOTSup 274, 1999). H. H. **Cazelles**, *Études sur le code de l'alliance* (1946). D. **Damrosch**, *The Narrative Covenant: Transformations of Genre in the Growth of Biblical Literature* (1987). J. **Daniélou**, "Les genres littéraires d'après les Pères de l'Église," *Los generos literarios de la Sagrada Escritura* (Congreso de Ciencias Eclesiásticas, 1957) 275-83. F. E. **Deist** and W. S. **Vorster** (eds.), *Words from Afar* (1986). W. **de Wette**, *Beiträge* 2 (1807) 25. J. G. **Eichhorn**, *Introduction to the Study of the OT* (1780-83; ET 1888). G. **Fohrer**, *Introduction to the OT* (1965; ET 1968). C. **Fontaine**, *Traditional Sayings in the OT* (Bible and Literature Series 5, 1982). A. **Francke**, *Manductio ad lectionem Scripturae Sacrae* (1693). H. **Gunkel**, *Die Propheten* (1917); "Der Micha-Schluss," *ZS* 2 (1924) 145-78 (ET *What Remains of the OT and Other Essays* 1928) 115-49; *Die Psalmen* (HZAT 24, 1926). H. **Gunkel** (with J. Begrich), *Einleitung in die Psalmen: Die Gattungen der religiosen Lyrik Israels* (GHAT 2, 1933). H. **Hahn**, *OT in Modern Research* (1954). P. **Hanson**, *The Dawn of Apocalyptic* (1975). C. **Hardmeier**, *Texttheorie und biblische Exegese* (1978). W. R. **Harper** (ed.), *The Biblical World 1* (1893) 243-47. J. H. **Hayes** (ed.), *OT Form Criticism* (1974). J. G. **Herder**, *The Spirit of Hebrew Poetry* (1782-83; ET 1833). A. **Heschel**, *The Prophets* (1936; ET 1962). H. **Jahnow**, *Das Hebräische Leichenlied im Rahmen der Völkerdichtung* (BZAW 36, 1923). W. **Kaiser, Jr.**, *Toward an Exegetical Theology* (1981). R. **Knierim**, "OT Form Criticism Reconsidered," *Int 27* (1973) 435-68. K. **Koch**, *Was ist Formgeschichte?* (1974[3]; ET of 2nd ed. *The Growth of the Biblical Tradition* 1969). M. J. **Lagrange**, "L'inspiration et les exigences de la critique," *RB* (1896) 496-518. C. A. **Lapide**, *Duodecim minores prophetas* (1625). G. E. **Mendenhall**, "Ancient Oriental and Biblical Law," *BA 17* (1954) 24-46; "Covenant Forms in Israelite Tradition," ibid., 49-76. S. **Mowinckel**, *The Psalms in Israel's Worship* (1951; ET 1962). H.-P. **Müller**, "Formgeschichte/Formenkritik, I. Altes Testament," *TRE 11* (1983) 271-85. R. **Murphy**, *Wisdom Literature and Psalms* (IBT, 1983). S. **Niditch**, *The Symbolic Vision in Biblical Tradition* (HSM 30, 1983). T. **Nöldeke**, *Untersuchungen zur Kritik des Alten Testaments* (1869). G. **Osborne**, "Genre Criticism-Sensus Literalis," *TJ 4, 2* (1983) 1-27. C. **Pinnock**, *The Scripture Principle* (1984). G. **von Rad**, *The Problem of the Hexateuch and Other Essays* (1938; ET 1966); *OT Theology* (1957; ET 1962). W. **Richter**, *Exegese als Literaturwissenschaft* (1971). A. **Robert**, "Littéraires (genres)," *DBSup* 5 (1957) 405-21. R. B. **Robinson**, *Roman Catholic Exegesis Since "Divino Afflante Spiritu"* (1988). A **Rof**, *The Prophetic Stories: The Narratives About the Prophets in the HB, Their Literary Types and History* (1982; ET 1988). H. H. **Schmid**, *Wesen und Geschichte der Weisheit: Eine Untersuchung zur altorientalischen und israelitischen Weisheitsliteratur* (1966). G. M. **Tucker**, *Form Criticism of the OT* (Guides to Biblical Scholarship, 1971). J. **Van Seters**, *In Search of History: Historiography in the Ancient World and Origins of Biblical History* (1983). C. **Westermann**, *Praise and Lament In the Psalms* (1954; ET 1981); *Basic Forms of Prophetic Speech* (BBET 31, 1960; ET 1967); *The Parables of Jesus in the Light of the OT* (1984; ET 1990). W. **Zimmerli**, *I Am Yahweh* (1963; ET 1982).

M. J. BUSS

SOURCE, FORM, AND REDACTION CRITICISM

New Testament Form Criticism

1. *Definition.* Form criticism (in German, usually *Form-* or *Gattungsgeschichte*) is understood in both a broad and a narrow sense.

a. The broader and older meaning. New Testament form criticism relates above all to the transmission of the Gospels, less so of the Epistles. Its goal is the reconstruction of the oral stages of tradition lying behind the fixed written products accessible to us now. This procedure is called form criticism because, in the initial attempt to solve the Synoptic[†§] question, it came to be oriented toward the pure forms of oral transmission. It was assumed that only in the course of the traditions' further transmission and reduction to written form, with subsequent editorial changes, were they robbed of their purity. With the reconstruction of the presumed pure form of a text, one theoretically had access to its oldest form, a situation that often tempted scholars to take this reconstruction to be the words of Jesus*[§] himself (*ipsissima vox*).

The standard assumptions in this undertaking were hypotheses drawn from biblical Folklore*[§] studies, according to which a basic entity in the course of time becomes increasingly enriched (like an onion covered with layers of skin) and is linked with other entities. The question of form in older form criticism thus stood in the service of the question of the pre-Easter "historical" Jesus. Wherever this mode of inquiry was employed outside the Gospels, it focused on the fragments of songs and confessional formulas that had been part of the early presentation of the *kerygma* (this was particularly the case, on the heels of H. Conzelmann, with K. Wengst). Here, too, interest was directed completely to the "fragments of the very oldest" transmission stages (even if, in this case, only to those of the immediately post-Easter period). Accordingly, form criticism became the embodiment of critical-methodical New Testament research in general, since "critical" was employed precisely in the sense of a separation of the older, genuine material from the younger, subsequent accretions.

b. The more recent, narrower meaning. More recent form criticism is oriented toward modern Literary*[§] criticism (linguistics) and to questions concerning textual types and genres. This cooperation between exegesis and linguistics is heralded by such scholars as R. A. de Beaugrande and W. Dressler (*Introduction to Text Linguistics* 1981) and H. Kalverkämper (*Orientierung zur Textlinguistik* 1981). The point of departure for the classification of forms and genres is no longer the larger classical genres (epic, drama, lyric poetry). Text classification is now determined on the basis of those dominant elements (and thus not simply the ones prevailing overall) that lie fairly close to the textual surface or that betray the composition of a text by means of connective or organizational signals. Thus, characteristics of linguistic form in the narrower sense of the term determine the subdivisions into textual types and genres. Accordingly, it has been discovered by de Beaugrande-Dressler that for descriptive texts, attributes and description of conditions are important; for narrative texts, the portrayal of temporal sequence according to the model of cause, ground, purpose, and possibility is important; and for argumentative texts, conflict (opposition), value judgments, and the statement of reasons are important. Using these beginnings as a point of departure, K. Berger employed the tripartite division of ancient rhetoric into *symbuleutic* (admonishing), *epidictic* (descriptive), and *dikanic* (judgmental) textual types and attempted to transfer into this framework the various results of previous form and genre research (including Hebrew Bible research). Given this orientation toward rhetoric, the intended effect on the reader is particularly important for the determination of genre. This intended effect stands in close relationship to the means of forming and molding the textual surface, hence the question of origin (and prehistory) of the material contained in a text is not what stands in the foreground, but, rather, the problem of its function. By function we mean the persuasive power of a text for the addressee, its actual effect, and the contextual connection to certain situations in primitive Christian history.

Discussions in the last decades of the twentieth century uncovered at least some problems within the older model of form criticism. The most important are the postulate that the pure form stood at the beginning of a development (since even the reverse is easily possible and documented; namely, that, through the editorial process, oral variety is reduced to its basic framework); the optimism concerning the unbroken continuity between the oral and written forms of a text; and the deprecation of the present written text (which in form criticism led particularly to a neglect of the literature of the Epistles). The frequently extreme and somewhat subjective employment of literary criticism for the purpose of separating sources has also become questionable since literary criticism is often precipitously engaged whenever the interpreter, simply because of the influence of modern logic and world views, insists on questioning the unity of a text.

2. *Form Criticism and "Situation in Life"* (*Sitz im Leben*). New Testament research took over the concept of the "situation in life" from Hebrew Bible scholars, most notably H. Gunkel[§]. This concept refers to the institutionally recurring recitation of certain texts in the life of a community. The problem in older form criticism was that, almost exclusively, such life situations could only be imagined as cultic occasions (precisely in the sense of a recitation of holy texts). This left, as Christian cultic occasions, only baptism, Eucharist, and sermon; texts in question were accordingly assigned to one of these three. Thus, for example, 1 Peter was understood as the rendering of a baptismal service rather than as a letter addressed to the exiles of the Dispersion (1 Pet 1:1). The less that was known about the religious services of the early Christians, the greater the attempt to fill out that knowledge with the postulated life situations in a kind of circular logic. One can say, therefore, that, aside from the questionable literary-critical delimitation of the song and confessional fragments, this mode of inquiry has not proved reliable.

More recent form criticism, on the other hand, inquires much more comprehensively into the function of a genre in "typical situations of early Christian history," a procedure that includes rather than excludes situations within religious services. It can be demonstrated, for example, that certain genres of miracle stories served to resolve problems within early Christian communities that had to do with the topic of "full authority" (e.g., deprecation of the Jewish purity commandments) or that Parables[†§] served as argumentative vehicles to suggest or encourage certain behavior (e.g., the acceptance of those who joined the community at a later period, Matt 20:1-16). Thus, one can conclude that a text was read anew and with different intentions in different phases of the history of early Christianity.

3. *The Relationship Between Oral Character and Written Character.* Older form criticism developed out of a religiously motivated and almost complete veneration of the oral character of materials in tandem with a strong resistance to any kind of "literature." This holds true, in spite of different points of departure, for J. Herder[§] as well as for F. Overbeck[§]. Herder concluded that only an oral character is appropriate for the gospel, since written character is an attribute of "law." Therefore, his efforts, like those of later form criticism, are already directed toward the reconstruction of the oral, original gospel. For Overbeck, the early Christian tradition is anything but literature. This verdict influenced scholars right up to M. Dibelius[§], who was unable to attribute any of the more rigidly defined or literary forms to early Christianity with its intense eschatological expectations. Overbeck arrived at his thesis of Christianity as a proto-literature essentially on the basis of his hypothesis of the world-negating, eschatological character of the earliest Christian faith. Consequently, form criticism also became the arena in which the systematic problem of the relationship between church and world was treated.

More recent form criticism, on the other hand, no longer possesses the optimism to assume, apart from isolated sayings and formulas, that one can reconstruct the form of that initial oral character at all. Instead, its substitute is the offer to paraphrase or circumscribe the content of the older stages of tradition much more broadly and cautiously by listing motifs. (For example, the tradition lying behind Mark 14:1-10, Luke 7:36-50, and John 12:1-9 cannot be described as an original or proto-text but rather almost certainly in the sense of a "motif field": When Jesus sits at the table and is anointed by a woman, the other participants at the meal are incensed. Jesus concludes the scene according to the form of the *chria* with a brief word justifying the woman's objectionable behavior.) Only in individual instances do concretely identifiable words belong to this common corpus of tradition.

This means, however, that the written text in question has gained in value in comparison to every oral preliminary stage. On the one hand, the possibility of reconstructing that oral stage has been reduced since the criteria that J. Jeremias[§] and E. Käsemann[§] proposed in the 1950s and 1960s have disappeared, namely, the identifying characteristics of later, communal constructions: allegorization, traceable roots in Judaism or in typical interests of the Christian community, and additions or accretions to the purer forms. On the other hand, ideological prejudices against written forms and literary characteristics have been at least partly, if not yet completely, overcome. Thus it is no longer assumed unconditionally that eschatological expectation precludes expressing oneself in forms also common to literature. The immediate manifestation of this change of perspective was the discussion concerning the nature of a "gospel."

4. *Form-critical Discussion of the Genre "Gospel."* For Overbeck, the Gospels belong to proto-literature because "alongside the book itself there is no room for the life of the author" (1962, 90). Dibelius and R. Bultmann[§] integrated this concept of "unliterary lesser literature" from Overbeck. For Dibelius, the substantive contrast between gospel and world has consequences in the realm of form criticism. The history of primitive Christian forms is the history of an increasing secularization and, simultaneously, a paganization. The struggle between gospel and world is directly manifested in the history of forms ("form history" *Formgeschichte*), for the pure and simple forms of the initial Christian preaching still stand completely under the auspices of near eschatological expectation. Dibelius's concept, however, stands or falls with the historically related question of whether anything like genuinely Christian or pagan forms exist at all. Hence, in the end, this project proves to be, in a certain sense, apologetic, since it attempts to demonstrate both formally and substantively the particularity and uniqueness of the gospel.

Bultmann's hypothetical assumption of the existence of a complete genre similarly originates from systematic premises. For the genre "aretalogy"—allegedly presupposed by the Gospels—there exists not one single independent example from antiquity in the sense of the listing of the miraculous deeds of a human hero (Berger 1982, 1218-31). In the subsequent exegetical scholarship influenced by Bultmann, this genre is needed not only for reconstructing the (hypothetical) *semeia* (sign) source in the Gospel of John but also to support the assumption of pre-Markan miracle story collections. This systematic agenda suggests that these genres became orthodox Christian only after being linked with the theology of the cross, because the cross criticizes naive faith in miracles. According to Bultmann, only in this way could the unique genre "gospel" originate at all. Bultmann asserts that this genre is unique (and not, e.g., to be confused with the genre "biography") because the miraculous intervention of God in the world is suspended by reference to the cross. As with Dibelius, the basic position here is apologetic and concentrated around the concept of gospel. Dibelius's eschatological expectation (and delay of the Parousia) corresponds to Bultmann's theology of the cross; both are also well-known parts of the moveable scenery of theological discussion in subsequent German scholarship.

In more recent form criticism, the discussion centers intensively on the relationship between gospel and the biography of antiquity. A. Dihle (1983) has categorically denied any connection between Christian gospel and ancient biography, whereas the connection was, in principle, not excluded in Anglo-Saxon research (C. Talbert 1977, R. Tannehill 1981) and was affirmed by Berger (1984). In this view, the Gospels are more strongly bound to a mythologically oriented type of biography (it must be pointed out that the genre biography does not exist; one should speak rather of variously organized arrangements of biographical material). *The Lives of the Ten Speakers,* by Plutarch, is an example of such (in part, weakly structured) collections.

5. *Form-critical Research of Epistolary Literature.* A. Deissmann's[§] old differentiation between the more literary epistles (Hebrews in the New Testament) and the private letter of antiquity, to which the Pauline letters (Paul[†§]) stood particularly close, was based on social-romantic premises similar to those underlying the older form criticism of the Gospels. The alleged folkloric-popular elements of the Pauline letters, their artlessness—allegations based on the papyrus letters found in Egypt—corresponded all too precisely to the thesis of the Gospels as proto-literature. This thesis was an attempt to keep early Christianity far from the world of literature. This form-critically established path (in the older sense of "form-critical," with the sociological implications related to the "folk" in the early communities) proved untraversable. Paul's acquaintance with the rules of ancient rhetoric has been amply demonstrated (see F. Siegert 1984; M. Bünker 1984; the works of A. J. Malherbe; and J. Schoon-Janssen 1990).

If one not only views the New Testament letters as the repositories of fixed fragments (from hymns and confessions; see Wengst 1972) but also takes their literary form as an object of form criticism, then the works of Bultmann (1910) and H. Thyen (1955) appear to be genuine contributions to the form criticism of letters, similarly the investigations of S. Stowers (1981) and T. Schmeller (1987) concerning the diatribe. It is not just a matter of style, but a case of the relationship between the oral and written characters and precisely of the contributions to the form of specific sections. Furthermore, the form of the "diatribe" has a specific function that concerns pastoral care and presupposes a certain hierarchy of authority between the sender and the recipient. Research, especially in the United States, has contributed a series of works concerning New Testament epistolary formulas dealing with the epistolary thanksgiving and the self-recommendation as well as the genre of the epistolary recommendation. Concerning the epistolary prescript and postscript, the work of S. Schnider and W. Stender (1987) should be mentioned (also Berger 1974; and D. Lührmann 1980, who has compared the analogies of "household codes" to the ancient *oikonomikos*). The so-called hymns in the epistolary literature might have analogies in the ancient *enkomion*. From this perspective it is possible to explain affinities to the biographical elements within the Gospels through form criticism. For future research it would be of particular importance to identify additional typically epistolary forms in comparison with other letters of antiquity in order to describe and evaluate them for theological statements.

6. *Future Tasks of Form Criticism.*

a. Relationship of Christian forms to Jewish and Greco-Roman literature. From a history-of-religion perspective, the relationship between gospel and biography should be determined on the basis of the entire range of biographical material from antiquity. Similarly, as has already been done with the pronouncement stories, the historical-critical comparative material concerning individual genres should be made available and discussed in a comprehensive fashion. Of prime importance is an ordering of the New Testament material within the literature of early Judaism and the first three Christian centuries. The question of the reception and utilization of Hellenistic forms by the early rabbinate is also important.

b. Relationship to tradition criticism. The separation of form criticism and the history of textual transmission (tradition criticism) must be taken seriously. Instead of the relatively fruitless and endless discussion of the Synoptic[†§] and Johannine[†§] questions using source hypotheses, it would be preferable to see a discussion that reckons not only with fixed sources but also with a common oral tradition, thus freeing the way for a history of theology (also with regard to a relationship with the epistolary literature of the New Testament).

c. Methodological issues. Clarification is needed concerning such basic methodological questions as the relationship between form and *Sitz im Leben* (understood in the more comprehensive sense) and between form and content. Clarification is also needed concerning the structure of Christian worship services in the first century C.E. The individual stations of primitive Christian daily life are still unknown. Concerning the methodological clarification of TRADITION History*§, the phenomenon of semantic fields will have to be investigated more intensively, both theoretically and practically. Also, the methodological questions of the origin and delimitation of genres needs to be discussed (e.g., are miracle stories a genre?).

d. Ideology. The ideological background of the history of form criticism needs to be investigated critically as well. This includes the critical relativization of the importance of the Easter faith for traditional form criticism. Scholars also need to examine whether the pronounced inclination of Protestant theology against the aesthetic examination of forms and against rhetoric (which is considered demagogic and worldly) does not mirror the phenomenon already discernible in the church fathers that whoever makes the most sovereign and comprehensive use of rhetoric in preaching is considered theoretically least worthy of trust.

7. Theological-Substantive Meaning of Form Criticism. In older form criticism this question had multiple theological implications: Scholars focused on determining the oldest material concerning Jesus, thereby presupposing a contrast between Jesus and the Christian community and between Jesus and Judaism. Apologetically, the uniqueness of primitive Christian literature was to be demonstrated as lying as far as possible from literature as such and closer to the "lower classes" and, in general, as "simple" or "naive." Apologetic agendas of the older *religionsgeschichtliche schule**§ were also perpetuated. Form criticism was only partly critical since the notion persisted that one did have access to (at least hypothetically) reliable material concerning Jesus as well as to early confessions as witnesses to the earliest orthodoxy.

Such apologetic agendas are missing within recent form criticism, as are the questionable attempts to separate Jesus from Judaism and from everything connected with "church," including the attempts to turn such distinctions within texts into form-critical arguments. Rather, form criticism has come to be concerned with determining the substantive value of the individual forms and genres: What is substantively being indicated by the fact that a certain genre is employed at all (e.g., biographical genres for portraying Jesus)? Or what does it mean when early Christianity takes up the genre tradition of household codes (or of the *oikonomikos*, etc.)? In other words, what substantive statement is made concerning the whole of a text by the genre itself? Form criticism not only enormously facilitates history-of-religion comparisons (by at least comparing analogous entities) but also draws attention to the substantive and rhetorical implications of the form in question. The reception of more recent form criticism is admittedly influenced by the traditional prejudice against rhetoric by Kantian-influenced theology (see Kant§).

Bibliography: P. Benoit, "Reflexions sur la 'Formgeschichtliche Methode,'" *RB* 53 (1956) 481-512. **K. Berger,** *ZNW* 65 (1974) 190-231; *Exegese des Neuen Testaments* (UTB 658, 1977, 1991³); "Hellenistische Gattungen im Neuen Testament," *ANRW* II 25.2 (1982) 1218-31; *Formgeschichte des Neuen Testaments* (1984); *Einführung in die Formgeschichte* (UTB 1444, 1987); "Form und Gattungsgeschichte," *HRWG* 2 (1990) 430-45; *Studien und Texte zur Formgeschichte* (TANZ 7, 1992). **G. Bornkamm,** "Evangelien, formgeschichtlich," *RGG³* 2 (1958) 749-53; "Formen und Gattungen," *RGG³* 2 (1958) 999-1005. **R. Bultmann,** *The History of the Synoptic Tradition* (1921, 1979; ET 1963, 1968); *Der Stil der paulinischen Predigt und die kynisch-stoische Diatribe* (FRLANT 13, 1910). **M. Bünker,** *Briefformular und rhetorische Disposition im 1. Korintherbrief* (1984). **A. Deissmann,** *Light from the Ancient East* (1910, 1923⁴; ET 1910, 1926³). **M. Dibelius,** *From Tradition to Gospel* (1919, 1971⁶; ET 1934); "Zur

Formgeschichte der Evangelien," *TRu* NF 1 (1929) 185-216. **A. Dihle,** "Die Evangelien und die biographische Tradition der Antike," *ZTK* 80 (1983) 33-49. **W. G. Doty,** "The Discipline and Literature of NT Form Criticism," *ATR* 51 (1969) 257-321. **E. Fascher,** *Die formgeschichtliche Methode* (BZNW 2, 1924). **B. Gerhardsson,** *Memory and Manuscript: Oral and Written Transmission in Rabbinic Judaism and Early Christianity* (ASNU 22, 1961, 1964²). **F. C. Grant,** *The Gospels: Their Origin and Their Growth* (1957). **K. Grobel,** *Formgeschichte und synoptische Quellenanalyse* (FRLANT 53, 1937). **E. Güttgemanns,** *Candid Questions Concerning Gospel Form Criticism* (BEvT 54, 1971; ET 1979). **G. Iber,** "Zur Formgeschichte der Evangelien," *TRu* NF 24 (1957-58) 283-338. **A. Jolles,** *Einfach Formen: Legende, Sage, Mythe, Rätsel, Spruch, Kasus, Memorabile, Märchen, Witz* (1930, 1958²). **E. Kamlah,** *Die Form der katalogischen Paränese im NT* (WUNT 7, 1964). **H. Köster,** "Form-geschichte/ Formenkritik II: Neues Testament," *TRE* 11 (1983) 286-99. **G. Lohfink,** *The Bible: Now I Get It! A Form Criticism Handbook* (1973, 1974; ET 1979). **D. Lührmann,** *NTS* 27 (1980) 63-97. **E. V. McKnight,** *What Is Form Criticism?* (Guides to Biblical Scholarship, 1969). **G. W. E. Nickelsburg,** "The Genre and Function of the Marcan Passion Narrative," *HTR 73* (1980) 153-84. **E. Norden,** *Agnostos Theos: Untersuchungen zur Formgeschichte religiöser Rede* (1913, 1956⁴). **F. Overbeck,** *über die Anfänge der patristischen Literatur* (1882, repr. 1970); *Overbeckiana; Übersicht über den Franz-Overveck-Nachlass der Universitätsbibliothek Basel.* (ed. Martin Tetz, et al. 2 vols. 1962). **H. Riesenfeld,** *The Gospel Tradition and Its Beginnings: A Study in the Limits of "Formgeschichte"* (1957). **J. M. Robinson and H. Koester,** *Trajectories Through Early Christianity* (1971). **T. Schmeller,** *Paulus und die "Diatribe": Eine vergleichende Stilinterpretation* (1987). **W. Schmithals,** "Kritik der Formkritik," *ZTK* 77 (1980) 149-85. **S. Schnider and W. Stender,** *Studien zum neutestamentlichen Briefformular* (1987). **J. Schoon-Janssen,** *Umstrittene Apologien in Paulusbriefen* (1990). **F. Siegert,** *Argumentation bei Paulus* (1985). **S. Stowers,** *The Diatribe and Paul's Letter to the Romans* (1981). **P. Stuhlmacher** (ed.), *Das Evangelium und die Evangelien* (WUNT 28, 1983, 1991). **C. H. Talbert,** *What Is a Gospel? The Genre of the Canonical Gospels* (1977). **R. C. Tannehill** (ed.), *Pronouncement Stories* (Semeia 20, 1981). **G. Theissen,** *Urchristliche Wundergeschichten* (SNT 8, 1974). **H. Thyen,** *Der Stil der jüdisch-hellenistischen Homilie* (FRLANT 65, 1955). **K. Wengst,** *Christologische Formeln und Lieder des Urchristentums* (1972, 1973²). **A. N. Wilder,** *The Language of the Gospel: Early Christian Rhetoric* (1964). **W. Wrede,** *The Messianic Secret* (1901; ET 1971).

K. Berger

SOURCE, FORM, AND REDACTION CRITICISM

Tradition History

This method of analysis is known by several names, including the tradition-history method and tradition-historical criticism, all of which are English translations of German terms: *Traditionsgeschichtliche Studien* and *Überlieferungsgeschichtliche Studien*. In New Testament scholarship, the preferred term is Redaction Criticism*[§], especially in reference to the critical evaluation of the Gospels. This diversity in nomenclature parallels the even greater range in approaches exhibited by individual scholars in their evaluation of particular texts. Thus one must make a very broad definition of the method to encompass the range of exegetical studies available.

In general terms, those using the method seek to reconstruct hypothetically the evolution of a biblical text, set of texts, or theme and the ways this text or theme may have communicated different messages to its ancient audience over the years. The scholar hypothesizes this evolutionary trajectory through both oral and written stages of development. In addition, the method is used to study how a text relates to its greater literary context in our present Canon[§]. The scholar wishes to rediscover how cycles of texts grew into even larger cycles in the process of oral and written transmission. Once these stages of development have been discerned, creative suggestions can be made concerning the social and religious needs of the audiences addressed by the evolving text at each significant stage of growth. This provides the modern reader with deeper insight into the overall meaning of that biblical text.

1. *History*. The tradition-historical method grew out of the form-critical method (see Form Criticism*[§]) in the 1930s and 1940s. The form-critical method had arisen in 1900-1930 through the work of H. Gunkel[§] (1895, 1901), H. Gressmann[§] (1913), H. Klostermann[§], A. Alt[§] (1953-59), and others who sought to reconstruct the theoretical oral prehistory and original oral form of a literary biblical text. The later tradition-historical critics, many of whom were already form critics, extended their evaluation to include all the hypothetical stages of development for a biblical text, from its original oral form to the final written canonical text.

The first serious tradition-history scholarship was contributed by G. von Rad[§] and M. Noth[§]. Von Rad's seminal work (1938 [ET 1966]) suggested that the Pentateuch evolved out of short oral creeds and that the Yahwistic historian was the first to combine the Sinai traditions with the accounts of the wilderness wanderings and conquest. Von Rad also articulated a significant Old Testament Theology*[§] based on tradition-historical reconstruction. Noth (1948 [ET 1972]) advanced the theory that great cycles of oral tradition (patriarchs, exodus, wilderness, Sinai, and entrance into arable land) and some shorter cycles evolved into the pentateuchal sources (Yahwist, Elohist, and priestly source) and that the Deuteronomistic History‡[§] was composed by one creative author, not out of pentateuchal sources, but out of diverse and fragmentary traditions (1943 [ET 1981]).

Scandinavian scholars (referred to loosely as the Uppsala school) contributed greatly to the development of this method. In contrast to their German counterparts, many Scandinavians rejected Literary*[§] or source criticism, maintaining that the development of biblical traditions occurred primarily in the oral stage before their precipitation into writing during the Babylonian exile and, hence, that the method was concerned only with oral tradition. H. S. Nyberg[§] may have begun this movement with a study of oral tradition in Hosea (1935). Significant scholars included I. Engnell[§] (1960, 1969), who wrote numerous essays in critical methodology; and S. Mowinckel[§] (1946), who moderated between Scandinavian emphasis on oral tradition and German source criticism. Other Scandinavian contributions include the work of I. Hylander on 1 Samuel (1932); H. Birkeland[§] on the prophets (1938); A. Haldar on the prophets (1945);

E. Nielsen on oral tradition and the Ten Commandments (1950, 1965); G. Ahlström[§] on Psalm 89 (1959); R. Carlson on 2 Samuel (1964); and M. Saebø on Second Zechariah (1969).

More recent practitioners have combined the German and Scandinavian approaches by surveying the development of a text, set of texts, or theme through both oral and written stages. Significant works have included those of H. Gese on Ezekiel 40-48 (1958); W. Richter on Judges 3-9 (1964); K. Koch on methodology (1967 [ET 1969]); R. Rendtorf on the pentateuchal sources (1977 [ET 1990]); M. Fishbane on Innerbiblical*[§] exegesis (1985); and C. Dohmen on the prohibition against images (1987). R. Gnuse (1996) has even used the method to analyze texts in the writings of Josephus[§]. D. Knight has provided an excellent history of the tradition-historical method (1975); W. Rast has generated a text on the method (1972); and further collections of essays outlining the method's history (Jeppesen and Otzen 1984) and probing its wider implications (Knight 1977) have appeared.

The comparable discipline in New Testament studies is Redaction Criticism* [§], which seeks to trace the evolution of oral tradition from the Jesus*[§] sayings down to their final literary form as written gospels. R. Bultmann[§] (1931 [ET 1963]) was a pioneer in this regard. Scholars who have analyzed the theological assumptions of gospel authors in their use of the Jesus tradition include G. Bornkamm[§] (1960 [ET 1963]); W. Marxsen (1956 [ET 1969]); H. Conzelmann (1953 [ET 1960]); J. L. Martyn (1968); and W. Kelber (1983). Emphasizing the creative work of the final author, New Testament scholars pay more attention to the final stage of transmission, since the New Testament oral tradition is much shorter than that of Hebrew Bible texts. Hence New Testament scholars use the term *redaction*, which refers more directly to that final stage, whereas Hebrew Bible scholars prefer a term like *tradition history*. A fine introduction to the New Testament method was provided by N. Perrin (1969).

Criticism of tradition history has emerged among Hebrew Bible scholars. J. Van Seters (1975, 1992, 1994), T. Thompson (1987), and R. Whybray (1987) have questioned whether an extensive oral tradition really lies behind biblical narratives and, if so, whether it can be reconstructed out of the final literary text. They and other critics suggest a process of literary creation during the Babylonian exile and thereafter out of little or no prior traditions. In the future, scholarly discussion may rage concerning the actual viability of tradition history as an exegetical method.

2. *Steps in the Method.* In studying a text, set of texts, or theme, the tradition-historical critic will have a particular agenda for the analysis, which will vary depending upon the text's genre—e.g., narrative, legal text, prophetic oracle, psalm, wisdom saying, novella, etc. Certain texts lend themselves to a full tradition-historical scrutiny, especially if they appear to have a long evolutionary prehistory, as might be the case with narrative passages. In assessing a particular passage, the critical scholar might envision five stages of development worthy of consideration and, depending on the text, might focus intensely on one or more of these stages.

The first area of consideration would be ancient Near Eastern or Hellenistic parallels to the biblical passage(s). The critic considers comparable texts that may have influenced biblical authors in the oral or written formation of the biblical text. Even if these comparable texts were not directly available to the biblical authors, they may have been part of a familiar genre. Biblical authors used well-established formulas and stereotypic language to communicate with their audience, sometimes employing analogous language and literary genres to communicate similar ideas and sometimes evoking imagery used by their foreign contemporaries in order to critique or reject ideas advanced by those contemporaries. Examples of the former include prophetic oracles, which adapted the messenger formula of ancient Near Eastern diplomatic correspondence: "Thus says the king," became "Thus says the Lord." Examples of the latter are the biblical accounts of creation and the flood in Genesis 1–3 and 6–9, which reworked the Babylonian and Egyptian mythic accounts (Egyptology[§]).

Critics must be cautious, however, when searching for parallel ancient Near Eastern and classical texts, lest they engage in "parallel-mania"—that is, finding ancient texts that bear only a superficial resemblance to biblical texts. The parallel texts must share significant modes of expression, format, and purpose with the biblical passage in order to be helpful in comparative analysis. Furthermore, in the subjective opinion of the critical scholar, the parallel text or a similar genre must have been reasonably accessible to the biblical author either directly from the foreign culture or through the mediation of other biblical texts. Too often, modern scholars have dredged up inappropriate parallel texts from the ancient world and obtained skewed results from their analysis of biblical passages.

The second area of consideration is the possible oral prehistory of the biblical text being studied. Not every biblical passage passed through a significant oral stage of transmission, but scholars generally assume that pentateuchal and deuteronomistic narratives as well as prophetic oracles and some psalms had an oral prehistory. Careful scrutiny of our present literary text may discern some of the stages of this developmental process, including the original form, message, and social setting. Thus the tradition-historical critic seeks to answer several questions: (a) What was the original extent of the oral form in contrast to the present written text? What lines have been added secondarily in the later oral and written transmission? (b) What was the shape of the original oral form? Is there a discernible outline or pattern? Does this pattern conform to a genre that would have been recognized by its audience, e.g., epic, hero-tale, legend, myth, chronicle, fable, song, etc. (as in the narratives) or lament, parable, lawsuit, disputation, salvation oracle, taunt, etc. (as in prophetic oracles)? The form communicated as much to the ancient audience as the actual content. (c) What was the original message, and how might it be different from the messages communicated in later oral and written stages? (d) Who spoke the original oral form (priests, Levites, bards, prophets, etc.), and why did this form originate with them? (e) To whom was the oral form addressed, and what were the needs to which this form spoke? This analysis is form criticism, which early form critics used exclusively in analyzing texts (especially psalms). For tradition-historical critics, form criticism is only one stage in the process of exegesis.

The third area of investigation is envisioning how the biblical text might have grown into its present literary context. How did the passage become connected with other texts, and how did that process evolve through various stages? The critic is interested not only in the transformation of meaning experienced by that passage as other texts are connected to it but also in how the passage fits into the greater cycle of texts in terms of meaning. Early literary or source critics assumed that this amalgamation of texts occurred in written or literary fashion; but since the rise of form and tradition-historical criticisms, scholars assume that these early collections, or cycles, arose in oral form.

Once the oral narrative became part of a larger cycle, it functioned in a larger theological tradition with overarching themes that united a number of texts. The individual narrative was subordinate to the themes of the greater cycle, and whoever crafted the larger oral or written corpus often changed some of the language in the shorter forms to conform to these greater themes. The scholar seeks to observe how the original form now relates to passages around it and to discover which of those passages might have been woven together in a separate oral or written cycle at some point of transmission. Diverse texts are associated with one another on the basis of common vocabulary, themes, and theological ideas; they are distinguished from other passages that might have belonged to a separate cycle of traditions because the latter are duplicate accounts of those in the first cycle or because the latter share their own common language. Once this distinct larger cycle of texts has been isolated, the critic seeks to articulate its distinct characteristic theology or ideology (Ideological Criticism*§).

At this stage the tradition-historical critic engages in what traditionally has been called source or literary criticism. In Pentateuchal‡§ studies, this would be the point where scholars evaluate texts as being part of the Yahwist, Elohist, or priestly tradition. In the Deuteronomistic History[‡§] scholars delineate cycles, such as the rise of David (1 Samuel 16–2 Samuel 8), the succession narrative (2 Samuel 9–20; 1 Kings 1–2), or the court history of Solomon (1 Kings 3–11). In legal corpora one would isolate the book of the covenant (Exodus 21–23), the holiness code (Leviticus 17–26), or the deuteronomic laws (Deuteronomy 12–26). In the prophetic tradition (Prophecy and Prophets, Hebrew Bible[‡§]) one would isolate early editions of each prophet's oracles, which contain the core of the prophet's original oracles and early additions by disciples.

The fourth area of evaluation is reflection on how the great cycle of narratives was connected to an even larger segment of literature. At this point the biblical texts most likely precipitated into written form. The tradition-historical critic asks how the original form and its larger cycle now fit into a much larger entity—the Deuteronomistic History (c. 620-550 B.C.E.); the priestly edited version of the pentateuchal narratives (c. 550-400 B.C.E.); the final written form of a prophetic book like Isaiah (with Proto-, Deutero-, and Trito-Isaiah brought together); or even the prophetic corpus as a whole. Again, the critic inquires subjectively as to how the even greater context affects the original passage and how that passage adds to the message of the greater corpus.

At this stage the scholar is interested in an editorial process, observing additions to the text that appear literary in origin and may be from scribal hands. These additions, as well as the way sources are woven together, reflect sophisticated theological assumptions; and clever literary style and intellectual depth is observable in the allusions, foreshadowings, genealogies, thematic speeches, editorial comments, and other literary links that unite large sections of literature. Early source critics often denigrated these later editorial additions but, in the past two generations, scholars have come to respect these final editors as perhaps the most theologically profound contributors to the process.

At this point, the tradition-historical critic has engaged in Redaction Criticism*[§]: the study of the literary and editorial process that created the final text. In New Testament scholarship redaction criticism is done on the Gospels when critical scholars inquire how the gospel writers theologically formulated the literary text of each gospel.

The final area of scholarly reflection is one in which tradition-historical critics too often have been remiss: consideration of how the individual text fits into the message of the entire biblical canon and into biblical theology as a whole. This analysis would consider how the original text(s) under consideration might have been used and reinterpreted by the later biblical tradition, e.g., by books in the Kethubim (Writings) generated during the postexilic era or by writings in the New Testament. This innerbiblical exegesis has been developed recently by such scholars as Fishbane (1985).

This level of reflection has been called Canonical Criticism*[§] by scholars who have advocated it in the last generation, including B. Childs[§] (1970, 1974) and J. Sanders[§] (1972, 1984). Although sometimes considered a methodology separate from the other critical methods described above, it actually is the final and theologically culminating stage of the tradition-historical method. At this point, the biblical exegete attempts to discern the ultimate religious message of the biblical text for people today.

In retrospect, tradition history or the tradition-historical method evaluates the theoretical evolution of a biblical passage and, in so doing, absorbs the techniques of several other methods. In seeking to understand the message of a text at each stage of its evolution, tradition history demonstrates the dynamic growth of the biblical tradition as each generation reinterprets and develops its past traditions.

3. *Representative Exegesis.* Given the complexity of the tradition history method as outlined above, it may be helpful to consider a text for analysis using the method. In analyzing 1 Samuel 3—the theophany of Yahweh to Samuel at Shiloh (Gnuse 1984)—the five stages of evaluation

would be as follows: (a) A review of ancient Near Eastern literature would focus on comparable prophetic narratives and dream reports. Mesopotamian sources offer many suggestive parallels, especially nighttime prophetic dream reports received in shrines at Mari (c. 1800 B.C.E.). Even more relevant are dream reports from Egypt and Mesopotamia that fall into patterns of "auditory message dreams" and "visual symbolic dreams." Comparison with 1 Samuel 3 demonstrates striking similarities with auditory message dreams.

(b) Form-critical evaluation of 1 Sam 3:1-21 leads to a sense that the original form of the text was vv. 1-18. In the plot development of the narrative are sensitive literary devices, including the artistic contrast of innocent young Samuel and the old priest Eli, who had failed to control his evil sons, and the threefold call of Samuel by Yahweh designed to heighten the suspense of an impending theophany in an age when the "word of the Lord" was rare. At this point, the scholar observes form-critical similarities between this text and other biblical prophetic call narratives (Moses, Exod 3; Gideon, Judg 6; Saul, 1 Sam 9; Jeremiah, Jer 1; and Ezekiel, Ezek 1–2), as well as the auditory message dreams of Assyria (Assyriology and Biblical Studies*[§]) and Chaldean Babylon (c. 700-550 B.C.E.). The account appears crafted to conform to both formats.

(c) The scholar then observes how 1 Sam 3 fits into the greater Samuel idyll in 1 Samuel 1–3, which, as a whole, contrasts the young prophet with the evil priests. This cycle shares themes with the larger cycle in the Pentateuch called the Elohist, which likewise has auditory message dreams in the patriarchal accounts, a positive attitude toward prophets, and a distrust of priests (Exod 32–33, the golden calf incident). How the Samuel idyll is connected to the Elohist tradition is highly debated, however.

(d) The critical scholar expands the observation of how 1 Samuel 3 fits into its greater context by observing further redaction. First Sam 1–3 became part of the narrative cycle concerning the rise of the monarchy in 1 Sam 1–15, wherein old narratives sympathetic to the monarchy (1 Sam 9:1-10:16; 11; 13–14) appear woven together with later (perhaps deuteronomistic) texts critical of kingship (1 Sam 7–8; 10:17-27; 12; 15). The Samuel idyll reinforces a pejorative perception of Saul and kingship by stressing the sufficiency of Samuel as Israel's leader and the general superiority of prophets over kings. This editorial work appears to come from Deuteronomistic Historians. The same editors then connected 1 Sam 1–15 with other major sections of literature to create the books of 1–2 Sam, wherein the decline of Saul before David is justified and David becomes a standard by which to evaluate other kings in the history of 1–2 Kings. First Sam 3 plays a pivotal role in preparing for the unfolding of later history and for stressing the prophetic word as an ultimate Authority*[§].

(e) On a canonical level, the critic may observe how the Deuteronomistic History fits into the greater biblical theological message of the Hebrew Bible, especially in regard to such themes as covenant, obedience, divine revelation, and prophetic calling. First Sam 3 contributes to all these themes. Canonical criticism also draws the tradition-historical critic into reflection on how 1 Sam 3 foreshadows Jesus in the infancy narratives of Matt 1–2 (where auditory message dreams occur again) and Luke 1–2. The prophet Samuel foreshadows the prophetic ministry of Jesus, who also opposed corrupt priests. Hence, 1 Sam 3 ultimately unites with other texts that proclaim the nature of the prophetic calling that all Jews and Christians seek to heed.

4. *Theological Significance.* The importance of the tradition-history method is found not only in its ability to attempt a reconstruction of the oral and literary evolution of biblical texts. Above all, the method implies that the biblical text is not a static repository of absolute truths revealed by God but the record of a dynamic process of human and divine interaction over many generations, in which sacred texts were received and reinterpreted by subsequent generations. It may imply that the tradition-making process is part of revelation itself (Knight 1977). It further implies that sacred texts may contain several levels of meaning, as those meanings have been

imparted by successive generations of transmitters—the sacred texts are polyvalent, capable of multiple interpretations, even today. Consequently, the critical scholar may suggest creatively that a wealth of meaning lies beneath a surface reading of the text, on which the modern reader may draw for use in contemporary theology, pedagogy, preaching, and piety.

Critics have assailed the tradition-history method for being too historicistic (i.e., for attempting to reconstruct the history of Israel from the subjective analysis of literary texts). Much of this criticism is deserved, for too often biblical scholars have attempted to reconstruct history on the basis of too little evidence. The history of Israel may be reconstructed only through a subtle interplay of archaeological data (Archaeology and Biblical Studies*§), critical analysis of literary texts, and the application of appropriate Social-Scientific*§ and anthropological models. In actuality, the tradition-historical method and the other methods (source, form, redaction, etc.) are not historical in the sense that a historian would recognize. Rather, they seek to trace ideational and religious development in a sacred text and to perceive its growth in relationship to other texts in the canon.

In general, the tradition-history method should be seen as primarily a subjective and creative art, not an empirical, scientific method. It is scientific only in that it rigorously analyzes a text by setting aside theological and denominational beliefs and the assumptions of modern interpreters and temporarily suspends the meaning imparted by the rest of the biblical tradition. The interpreter tries to be rigorously objective. Also, it may be scientific in that occasionally historical, archaeological, and social-scientific data can be used to facilitate understanding the biblical passage under scrutiny. Yet, ultimately, the reconstruction of the previous evolutionary development of a literary text is a subjective and hypothetical task. This is evidenced by the multitude of diverse interpretations rendered by scholars on any given biblical text. However, even in the face of such interpretive uncertainty, we should not disparage the method. Its purpose is neither to ascertain ultimate truth nor to determine the perfect reconstruction of a process that can no longer be empirically observed. Rather, the method is suggestive and creative, offering possibilities for understanding latent meanings in the biblical text. The scholar offers new possibilities for understanding texts to the theologian, the preacher, the student of the Bible, and the person of faith in order to enhance their insight and appreciation of the biblical text.

Bibliography: G. **Ahlström,** *Psalm 89: Eine Liturgie aus dem Ritual des leidenden Königs* (1959). A. **Alt,** *Kleine Schriften zur Geschichte des Volkes Israel* (3 vols. 1953-59). H. **Birkeland,** *Zum hebräischen Traditionswesen* (1938). R. **Bultmann,** *History of the Synoptic Tradition* (1931; ET 1963). G. **Bornkamm, G. Barth, H. J. Held,** *Tradition and Interpretation in Matthew* (1960; ET 1963). R. A. **Carlson,** *David, the Chosen King: A Traditio-historical Approach to the Second Book of Samuel* (1964). B. **Childs,** *Biblical Theology in Crisis* (1970); *Exodus* (OTL, 1974). G. **Coats,** "Tradition Criticism, OT," *IDBSup* 9 (1976) 12-14. H. **Conzelmann,** *The Theology of St. Luke* (1953; ET 1960). C. **Dohmen,** *Das Bilderverbot: Seine Entstehung und seine Entwicklung im Alten Testament* (BBB 62, rev. ed., 1987). I. **Engnell,** "Methodological Aspects of OT Study," VTSup 7 (1960) 13-30; *A Rigid Scrutiny: Critical Essays on the OT* (1969). C. A. **Evans and J. A. Sanders** (eds.), *Early Christian Interpretation of the Scriptures of Israel: Investigations and Proposals* (JSNTSup 148, 1977); *The Function of Scripture in Early Jewish and Christian Tradition* (JSOTSup 154, 1998). M. **Fishbane,** *Biblical Interpretation in Ancient Israel* (1985). H. **Gese,** *Der Verfassungsentwurf des Ezechiel (Kap. 40-48) traditionsgeschichtlich untersucht* (BHT 25, 1958). R. **Gnuse,** *The Dream Theophany of Samuel: Its Structure in Relation to Ancient Near Eastern Dreams and Its Theological Significance* (1984); *Dreams and Dream Reports in the Writings of Josepus* (AGJU 36, 1996). H. **Gressmann,** *Mose und seine Zeit* (1913). H. **Gunkel,** *Schöpfung und Chaos in Urzeit und*

Endzeit (1895); *Genesis* (1901, 1910³; ET 1997). **A. Haldar,** *Associations of Cult Prophets Among the Ancient Semites* (1945). **I. Hylander,** *Der literarische Samuel-Saul-Komplex (I. Sam 1-15) traditionsgeschichtlich untersucht* (1932). **K. Jeppesen and B. Otzen,** *The Productions of Time: Tradition History in OT Scholarship* (1984). **W. H. Kelber,** *The Oral and the Written Gospel: The Hermeneutics of Speaking and Writing in the Synoptic Tradition* (1983). **D. Knight,** *Rediscovering the Traditions of Israel* (SBLDS 9, rev. ed., 1975); (ed.), *Tradition and Theology in the OT* (1977); "Tradition History," *ABD* (1992) 6:633-38. **K. Koch,** *The Growth of the Biblical Tradition: The Form-critical Method* (1967; ET 1969). **J. L. Martyn,** *History and Theology in the Fourth Gospel* (1968, 1979²). **W. Marxsen,** *Mark, the Evangelist: Studies on the Redaction History of the Gospel* (1956; ET 1969). **S. Mowinckel,** *Prophecy and Tradition* (1946). **E. Nielsen,** *Oral Tradition* (1950; ET SBT 11, 1954); *The Ten Commandments in New Perspective* (1965; ET SBT 2nd ser. 7, 1968). **M. Noth,** *The Deuteronomistic History* (1943; ET JSOTSup 15, 1981); *A History of the Pentateuchal Traditions* (1948.; ET 1972). **H. S. Nyberg,** *Studien zum Hoseabuch* (1935). **N. Perrin,** *What Is Redaction Criticism?* (GBS, 1969). **G. von Rad,** "The Form-critical Problem of the Hexateuch," *The Problem of the Hexateuch and Other Essays* (1938; ET 1966) 1-78; *OT Theology* (2 vols. 1957, 1960; ET 1962, 1965). **W. Rast,** *Tradition History and the OT* (1972). **R. Rendtorff,** *The Problem of the Process of Transmission in the Pentateuch* (BZAW 147, 1977; ET JSOTSup 89, 1990). **W. Richter,** *Die Bearbeitungen des "Retterbuches" in der deuteronomischen Epoche* (BBB 21, 1964). **M. Saebø,** *Sacharja 9-14* (1969). **J. A. Sanders,** *Torah and Canon* (1972); *Canon and Community: A Guide to Canonical Criticism* (GBS, 1984). **T. Thompson,** *The Origin Tradition of Ancient Israel* (JSOTSup 55, 1987). **J. Van Seters,** *Abraham in History and Tradition* (1975); *Prologue to History: The Yahwist as Historian in Genesis* (1992); *The Life of Moses: The Yahwist as Historian in Exodus-Numbers* (1994). **R. N. Whybray,** *The Making of the Pentateuch* (JSOTSup 53, 1987).

R. GNUSE

SOURCE, FORM, AND REDACTION CRITICISM

Hebrew Bible Redaction Criticism

Redaction criticism analyzes the techniques by which a redactor (or redactors) assembled, shaped, and supplemented preexistent materials to form a new work, seeking insight into the literary dynamics of the product. While Literary*[§] criticism focuses on documentary sources and Form Criticism*[§] on oral genres, redaction criticism concentrates on the formation of the final text. Recognizing that a redactor may have had any number of written and oral sources, redaction criticism examines the redactor's creative role.

Although the term was coined only recently by an New Testament scholar (Marxsen 1954), redaction criticism has significant antecedents in Hebrew Bible studies, reaching back at least to the observations of the medieval rabbinic scholars Rashi[§] and A. Ibn Ezra[§] (eleventh and twelfth centuries, respectively) concerning late editorial activity in the Torah. A. Masius[§] (1574) distinguished between the apparently older materials in the book of Joshua and the younger materials that frame them. He described a process of "compilation" and "redaction" by which Ezra combined these older "annals" and "diaries." A century later, the Mennonite scholar A. van Dale (1696, 685-88) hypothesized that the narrative and legal portions of the Torah were authored by Ezra and Moses, respectively, and that Ezra incorporated the Mosaic material into the narrative framework.

Methodologies and programs of inquiry in Hebrew Bible studies have generally been developed and sharpened first with regard to the Pentateuch. Classical Pentateuchal Criticism[‡§] pursued earlier insights concerning the composite nature of the Torah and sought to identify and characterize these components. For the most part, eighteenth- and nineteenth-century pentateuchal critics hoped that critical tools would enable them to strip accretions from the text, identify the ancient documentary witnesses to Israel's early history, and thus gain a historically reliable vantage point. Consequently, they did not credit the redactor(s) responsible for shaping the Pentateuch with any creative role. One notable exception, H. Hupfeld[§] (1853), prefigured the viewpoint of redaction criticism. Although his identification of three documentary sources for Genesis paralleled the emerging source-critical consensus in many respects, he also argued that these documents were not compiled in a purely mechanical fashion. Instead, they were skillfully harmonized according to a well-conceived plan in the service of an independent theological program.

Pentateuchal studies did not focus significantly on the assessment of the final shape of the Torah, however, until the middle of the twentieth century. Several calls went out in the 1920s and 1930s for a true history of Hebrew Bible literature that would overcome the deficits of source criticism's fragmentation of the text by attending to the constructive process of selection, arrangement, and supplementation that produced complete literary works (e.g., W. Staerk 1924; O. Eissfeldt 1927, 1928; J. Hempel 1930-34; and H. Hertzberg 1936).

The first extensive attempts at a new approach were made by G. von Rad[§] (1938) and M. Noth[§] (1948). Both sought to understand how the authors of the final source documents shaped the traditions at their disposal. Von Rad was first to note that neither source analysis nor form analysis had accounted for the organic structure and overall unity of the final form of the source documents. In order to examine these questions, he employed Tradition*[§] criticism, an extension of the form-critical interest, to include the history of the combination of discrete traditions into lengthier blocks of material. He then noted the widespread occurrence of "brief historical creeds" throughout the Pentateuch and beyond, which he regarded as the simplest and most ancient forms of Israel's cultic confession of salvation history. Positing that this simplicity reflects a phase in the history of the cult when the various traditions concerning Israel's beginnings had not yet been systematically interrelated, he concluded that the Yahwist must be seen as a creative author/theologian who combined these originally distinct themes into a continuous history.

Although differing with von Rad on several details, Noth's 1948 study of the Pentateuch agreed that the authors of the source documents engaged in creative theological reflection. Indeed, theological creativity continued, in his view, in the combination of the source documents into the finished Pentateuch: "The juxtaposition of the two creation stories can be considered most readily as theologically significant. . . . These stories, by mutually supplementing one another, reach a new unity" (1948, 251).

In attempting to correct further the static viewpoint of the documentary hypothesis, a number of scholars have sought to address the question of the formation of the tradition from fresh redactional perspectives. F. Winnett[§] (1965) and J. Van Seters (1975) argued that the components of the Pentateuch may be described more accurately as redactional layers rather than as documentary sources, emphasizing the dynamic process of growth behind the final form. Similarly, H. Schmid (1976) argued that the so-called J material in the Pentateuch is not unified to the degree that might be expected of a single author but that it represents a layer of materials related to the deuteronomistic movement (Deuteronomistic History[‡§], Pentateuchal Criticism[‡§]). R. Rendtorff (1976) argued that a number of tradition complexes (i.e., Gen 1-11) with separate histories were combined by a Dtr redactor into the present Pentateuch. This line of inquiry has been continued by others (E. Blum 1984 and G. Rendsburg 1988).

With regard to the prophets (Prophecy and Prophets, Hebrew Bible*[§]), S. Mowinckel[§] suggested as early as 1913 (similarly in 1933 and more systematically in 1946) a redactional model for understanding the formation of the prophetic corpus. He rejected Scandinavian tradition criticism, which regarded prophetic books as the product of verbatim oral transmission of prophetic preaching, so that the documents virtually represented the *ipsissima verba* of the prophets. Rather, he envisioned a dynamic process of growth throughout a long period of oral transmission of prophetical sayings; the accretion of tradition complexes; and, finally, the production of the extant prophetic books. Mowinckel's dynamic model of selection, reinterpretation, and redaction also questioned the "authentic/inauthentic" categories of earlier source analyses of the prophets. Like source criticism of the Pentateuch, such analyses had primarily sought to identify later glosses and insertions in order to reconstruct a pristine original. In place of this interest in originality, redaction critics after Mowinckel came to regard the prophetic books as testimony to a living tradition that continually actualizes the prophetic message (W. Zimmerli 1979; J. Jeremias 1983; and M. Biddle 1990).

Redactional studies of the prophets have continued to struggle with models of prophetic activity and with the formation of prophetic books. Representative studies include H. W. Wolff's[§] commentary on the book of Amos (1969), which posited a long process of growth, reception, reinterpretation, and actualization of the Amos tradition lasting into the postexilic period. The phenomenon of the Isaiah scroll is perhaps the most incontrovertible evidence of the capacity of prophetic traditions to generate new statements; consequently, it has lent itself to a number of redactional studies. O. Kaiser[§] (1963, 1973) subjected the book of Isaiah to a stringent redactional examination, rejecting any attempt to identify genuine texts in favor of a model of redactional composition by an Isaianic school. J. Vermeylen (1977-78) identified successive redactions of the book of Isaiah, revealing the continuing interest of later eras in appropriating the message of the prophet. Several other scholars have pursued the question of prophetic books as archives of living traditions (e.g., P. E. Bonnard 1972; E. Sehmsdorf 1972, 517-76; B. Renaud 1977; R. Carroll 1981, 1986; W. Brueggemann 1984, 89-107; and J. Vermeylen 1989).

Such analyses of prophetic books have occasioned questions and criticism regarding the historical connections of later reinterpretation to the prophetic message. In response to J. Garscha

(1974), G. Fohrer§ (1975, 396) raised the objection, for example, that the approaches that regard virtually an entire prophetic book as a redactional product are tantamount to assurances of inauthenticity. Some scholars have addressed this issue by questioning the fidelity of prophetic tradition to prophetic message. In an examination of the prose sermon material in the book of Jeremiah, material noted for its affinities with deuteronomisticism, E. Nicholson (1970) has emphasized, for example, the fact that the authors of this material were motivated to actualize faithfully the message of the prophet. The redactional process, the reapplication and restatement of the message given impetus by the prophet, ought not be considered a pious fiction, therefore, but a genuine expression of the prophetic message. From a different perspective, JEREMIAS suggested, in his Hosea commentary, that the very existence of certain prophetic books might best be attributed to the reception of the prophetic message by a first generation of tradents and redactors. If the prophets saw themselves as God's messengers in a specific context, interest in preserving this message in a more universally applicable form best explains the collection of the prophet's oracles. In Jeremias's view, then, no "authentic" form of certain prophetic books (in the sense in which source critics would have used the term) may have ever existed.

The historical books of the Hebrew Bible have also been a focus of redaction-critical studies. As von Rad did with respect to the Yahwist, Noth portrayed the Deuteronomistic Historian as an author/redactor who did not simply compile sources but who creatively selected and arranged materials and freely composed supplementary sections of the history. Although his characterization of the process as a creative endeavor and not simply as mechanical compilation has been widely accepted, Noth's suggestion that the Deuteronomistic History‡§ is the work of one author/redactor has essentially been abandoned. A number of redaction critics have seen stylistic and, more significantly, Ideological*§ and theological tensions as evidence for two or more redactions of the work (see von Rad; Wolff; R. Nelson 1981; E. Jenni; A. Radjawane; M. Rose; and R. E. Friedman 1981). Issues include (1) whether the Deuteronomistic History is, as Noth argued, basically pessimistic with regard to a future for Israel after the fall of Jerusalem, or whether there are texts (from the hand of a later Deuteronomist) that suggest the possibility of restoration, as von Rad, Wolff, and others suggest, and (2) whether the books of Deuteronomy, Joshua, and Judges (in particular) ever existed apart from the Deuteronomistic History as a whole, so that differing assessments of the monarchy in different sections of the history, for example, may be attributed to the sources instead of to multiple redactions.

Many other portions of the Hebrew Bible have been subjected to redactional analyses. The books of Chronicles theoretically offer a unique opportunity for redaction criticism in that the major documentary source of the chronicler, the Deuteronomistic History, is also available to the modern critic, so that the chronicler's selection, arrangement, and correction may be assessed more transparently. There are, however, vexing questions regarding the text of 1—2 Sam and 1—2 Kgs available to the chronicler (Lemke 1965, 349-63) and the degree to which additions to the chronicler's history may be identified (W. Rudolph 1955; J. Botterweck 1956, 12-31). Redaction-critical studies have also been fruitfully undertaken for the book of Esther, extant in three clearly distinct editions (D. Clines 1984), Proverbs, Psalms, and Job.

Several issues face redaction criticism at this juncture. First, there is some disagreement among practitioners as to the proper scope of the method and the precise definition of the central term. R. Knierim (1985) has identified three basic approaches. One distinguishes between redactor and author in an approach resembling the classical distinction between original and secondary materials; another terms the penultimate operation "composition" and reserves "redaction" for the ultimate editorial procedure; and a third considers the entire history of a written text as successive phases of redaction. This disunity reflects more than terminological imprecision; it corresponds to various models of the process of literary fixation. No clear boundaries among redaction, composition, and tradition have been established; any solution must incorporate an awareness that the literary history of many Hebrew Bible texts seems to have been a truly fluid phenomenon. How does the reworking of documents differ from the reworking of oral traditions at the moment of literary fixation? Which stage of the process should be considered the basis for evaluating later additions/alterations/redactions? Is a text immune to the continued influence of the circle that produced and preserved it?

Second, recent advocates of newer methods informed by linguistics and literary theory have questioned the fruitfulness of diachronic investigation altogether. Reasserting the canonical priority of the final form, they have attempted to expose the ideology and subjectivity of any reading of a text. It remains to be seen whether redaction critics will champion the method's potential to combine diachronic and synchronic concerns. After all, redaction criticism was initiated in response to a perceived need to appreciate the text, not simply as a repository of older sources but also as a finished product. To deny the historical processes that produced the final text, however, is to force symphonic voices into unison.

A related third issue concerns how the questions of Authority*[§], authenticity, and individual readings of texts are to be resolved. Newer methods often shift the locus of meaning even beyond the final form of the text to the reader (Reader-response Criticism*[§]). Can the perspective of redaction criticism provide a means for appreciating the authority of tradition? The process of reception, reinterpretation, and actualization may not only provide a model for hermeneutical method (Hermeneutics*[§]), but may also establish directions for contemporary interpretation. Redactors and tradents stood within received traditions. They did not offer replacements; they preserved, reinterpreted, and actualized traditions that were authoritative for them. Similarly, modern interpreters may reapply and actualize; but the basis for this activity remains the received tradition, including interpretive and intertextual movements (Intertextuality*[§]) contained within it.

Bibliography: G. W. **Anderson** (ed.), *Tradition and Interpretation: Essays by Members of the Society for OT Study* (1979). U. **Becker,** *Richterzeit und Königtum: Redaktionsgeschichtliche Studien zum Richterbuch* (BZAW 192, 1990). M. **Biddle,** *A Redaction History of Jeremiah 2:1-4:2* (ATANT 47, 1990); *Polyphony and Symphony in Prophetic Literature: Rereading Jeremiah 7-20* (SOTI 2, 1996). E. **Blum,** *Die Komposition der Vätergeschichte* (WMANT 57, 1984); *Studien zur Komposition des Pentateuch* (BZAW 189, 1990). P. E. **Bonnard,** *Le Second Isaïe* (EB, 1972). J. **Botterweck,** "Zur Eigenart der chronistischen David-geschichte," *FS Viktor Christian* (1956) 12-31. W. **Brueggemann,** "Unity and Dynamic in the Isaiah Tradition," *JSOT* 29 (1984) 89-107. R. **Carroll,** *From Chaos to Covenant* (1981); *Jeremiah: A Commentary* (OTL, 1986). D. **Clines,** *The Esther Scroll* (JSOTSup 30, 1984). O. **Eissfeldt,** "Die kleinste literarische Einheit in den Erzählungsbüchern des AT," *TBl* 6 (1927) 333-37; *OT Essays* (ed. D. C. Simpson, 1927) 85-93; "Text-, Stil-, und Literarkritik in den Samuelisbüchern," *OLZ* 31 (1928) 801-12. G. **Fohrer**[§] "Bücgherschau" *ZAW* 87 (1975) 396. M. **Fox,** *The Redaction of the Books of Esther: On Reading Composite Texts* (SBLMS 40, 1991). R. E. **Friedman,** *The Exile and Biblical Narrative: The Formation of the Deuteronomistic and Priestly Works* (HSM 22, 1981). J. **Garscha,** *Studien zum Ezechielbuch* (1974). J. H. **Hayes,** *An Introduction to OT Study* (1979). J. **Hempel,** *Die althebräische Literatur und ihr hellenistisch-jüdisches Nachleben* (Handbuch der Literaturwissenschaft 21, 1930-34). H. W. **Hertzberg,** "Die Nachgeschichte alttestamentlicher Texte innerhalb des Alten Testaments," *BZAW* 66 (1936) 110-13. H. **Hupfeld,** *Die Quellen der Genesis und die Art ihrer Zusammensetzung* (1853). J. **Jeremias,** *Der Prophet Hosea* (ATD 24, 1, 1983). O. **Kaiser,** *Isaiah 1-12* (1963, 1983[5]; ET, OTL 1983); *Isaiah 13-39* (1973; OTL 1974). R. **Knierim,** "Criticism of Literary Features: Form, Tradition, and Redaction," *The HB and Its Modern Interpreters* (1985; ed. D. A. Knight and G. M. Tucker) 123-66. K. **Koch,** *The Growth of the Biblical Tradition: The Form-critical Method* (1967; ET

1969). **H.-J. Kraus,** *Geschichte der historisch-kritischen Erforschung des Alten Testamewnts* (1982³). **W. Lemke,** "The Synoptic Problem in the Chronicler's History," *HTR* (1965) 349-63. **S. McKenzie,** *The Trouble with Kings: The Composition of the Book of Kings in the Deuteronomistic History* (VTSup 42, 1991). **W. Marxsen,** *Der Evangelist Markus: Studien zur Redaktionsgeschichte des Evangeliums* (FRLANT NS 49, 1954). **A. Masius,** *Josuae imperatoris historia illustrata atque explicata* (1574). **S. Mowinckel,** *Zur Komposition des Buches Jeremiah* (1913); *Die Komposition des Jesajabuches* (AcOr 11, 1933); *Prophecy and Tradition: The Prophetic Book in the Light of the Study of the Growth and History of the Tradition* (1946). **R. D. Nelson,** *The Double Redaction of the Deuteronomistic History* (JSOTSup 18, 1981). **E. Nicholson,** *Preaching to the Exiles: A Study of the Prose Tradition in the Book of Jeremiah* (1970). **J. Nogalski,** *Literary Precursors to the Book of the Twelve* (BZAW 217, 1993); *Redactional Processes in the Book of the Twelve* (BZAW 218, 1993). **M. Noth,** *Überlieferungsgeschichtliche Studien* (1943; ET *The Deuteronomistic History* [JSOTSup 15, 1981] and *The Chronicler's History* [JSOTSup 50, 1987]); *A History of Pentateuchal Traditions* (1948; ET 1972). **A. van Dale,** *Dissertationes de Origine ac Progressu Idolatriae et superstitionum* (1696) 685-88. **G. von Rad,** *The Problem of the Hexateuch and Other Essays* (1938; ET 1966). **B. Renaud,** *La formation du livre de Michee: Tradition et actualisation* (1977). **G. Rendsburg,** *The Redaction of Genesis* (1988). **R. Rendtorff,** *The Problem of the Process of Transmission in the Pentateuch* (1976; ET JSOTSup 89, 1990). **W. Rudolph,** *Chronikbücher* (HAT 1955). **H. H. Schmid,** *Der sogenannte Jahwist: Beobachtungen und Fragen zur Pentateuchforschung* (1976). **E. Sehmsdorf,** "Studien zur Redaktionsgeschichte von Jes 56-66" *ZAW* 84 (1972) 517-76. **W. Staerk,** "Zur alttestamentlichen Literarkritik," *ZAW* 42 (1924) 34-74. **O. H. Steck,** *Gottesknecht und Zion: Gesammelte Aufsatze zu Deuterojesaja* (FAT 4, 1992). **W. Thiel,** *Die deuteronomistische Redaktion von Jeremia 1-25* (WMANT 41, 1973). **R. Thompson,** *Moses and the Law in a Century of Criticism since Graf* (VTSup 19, 1970). **J. Van Seters,** *Abraham in History and Tradition* (1975). **J. Vermeylen,** *Du prophète Isaïe à l'Apocalyptique* (2 vols. EB, 1977-78). **J. Vermeylen** (ed.), *Le livre d'Isaïe* (BETL 81, 1989). **P. Weimar,** *Untersuchungen zur Redaktionsgeschichte des Pentateuch* (BZAW 122, 1971). **J. Wharton,** "Redaction Criticism, OT," *IDBSup* (1976) 729-32. **F. V. Winnett,** "Re-Examining the Foundations," *JBL* 84 (1965) 1-19. **H. W. Wolff,** *Joel und Amos* (1969; ET Hermeneia, 1977); "The Kerygma of the Deuteronomic Historical Work," *The Vitality of OT Traditions* (ed., W. Brueggemann and H. W. Wolff, 1975) 83-100 = *ZAW* 73 (1961) 171-86. **W. Zimmerli,** *Ezekiel: A Commentary on the Prophet Ezekiel* (1979; ET Hermeneia, 2 vols. 1979-83).

M. E. BIDDLE

SOURCE, FORM, AND TRADITION CRITICISM

New Testament Redaction Criticism

As a literary and historical method associated mainly with gospel research, redaction criticism is "concerned with the theological motivation of an author as revealed in the collection, arrangement, editing, and modification of traditional material and in the composition of new material or the creation of new forms within the traditions of early Christianity" (Perrin 1969, 1). The method has evolved to comprise distinct operations: collection of the editorial alterations of a tradition; attention to the literary context of every pericope, its immediate context as well as its location in the structure of a given gospel; comparison of this context to that in other gospels; attempts to define verses or whole pericopes that were "composed" (i.e., written by the final author/redactor); and synthesis of these results with suggestions about the theological purpose of a given pericope or of the gospel as a whole. Although admitting that much of the gospel material may reflect the historical situation of JESUS ministry as well as other situations in the early church (e.g., the delay of the Parousia), redaction critics are primarily interested in the final shape of the material. Along with analysis of the text to uncover the literary activity of the final editors, redaction critics postulate theological reasons for this activity and suggest a community context for this theology (the *Sitz-im-Leben* of the gospel).

1. *Origin of the Method.* From the 1920s until the mid-1950s, gospel research was dominated by Form Criticism*§, the attempt to define the literary forms and shape of the traditions that were incorporated into the Synoptic*§ Gospels, as well to suggest a social context (*Sitz-im-Leben*) for the origin and development of traditional material. The evangelists were seen primarily as collectors who arranged material with minimal editorial changes. Although R. Bultmann*§ (1921) spoke of the editing (*Redaktion*) and composition of traditional material and of the theological character of the Gospels, this theology was that of the tradition rather than a creative contribution of the evangelists.

The term *Redaktionsgeschichte* (lit., "history of the editing") was first coined by W. Marxsen in a review of H. Conzelmann's *Die Mitte der Zeit* in *Monatsschrift für Pastoraltheologie 6* (1954). Conzelmann's work, along with Marxsen's studies and the essays of G. Bornkamm§, G. Barth, and H. J. Held (1960) are seminal works that initially defined the method and determined the shape of future research. In contrast to form criticism's interest in the pregospel tradition, these authors studied the alterations and arrangement of traditional material by the evangelists. Along with concern for the editing of traditional material, special attention was given to the arrangement or composition of material in a given gospel, often called composition criticism. The term composition, however, became ambiguous, designating the arrangement of blocks of material as well as the writing of new material. As the method has evolved, redaction criticism has become an umbrella concept involving all the activities mentioned in PERRIN's definition.

2. *Precursors of the Method.* Study of the Gospels with concern for the theology of the final redaction and as an entree to the life of a community behind a specific gospel, rather than as sources for the quest for the historical Jesus*§, has antecedents prior to the 1950s. In the nineteenth century, F. C. Baur§ sought the "tendency" of each gospel and situated it within his developmental schema of early church history (*Tendenzkritik*). According to Baur, Mark was the latest of the Synoptic Gospels and represented a synthesis of the Jewish Matthew with Gentile Luke. While neither Baur's late dating of the Gospels (mid-second cent.) nor his theory of synoptic relationships has prevailed, the desire to correlate the theology of the Gospels with social, historical, and theological developments within early Christianity remains normative.

Three figures stand out in the early twentieth century. Against the background of the Markan hypothesis (i.e., Mark as a primitive gospel that provides the best access to the Jesus of history), F. Wrede[§] (1901) argued that the "Messianic secret" in Mark (i.e., places where Jesus enjoins silence about his mighty works or divine status, e.g., 1:34, 44; 3:12; 5:43; 7:36; 8:26; 9:9) was not historical, but a Markan theological construct. Mark, according to Wrede, like the Gospel of John, belongs to the history of Christian dogma. In two insightful volumes (1903, 1905), J. Wellhausen[§] anticipated both form and redaction criticism, arguing that the sources of the Gospels were oral traditions that circulated in small units and that the combining of such material was the work of an author "with literary ambitions" (1905, 3). Although often overlooked in the history of redaction criticism, B. Bacon[§], best known for his theory of the five-book structure of Matthew (1930), is a seminal figure. Under the strong influence of Baur, Bacon constructed an elaborate theory of sources for the Gospels and correlated these with other streams (e.g., Pauline and Petrine) in the development of early Christianity. He described his method as aetiological—i.e., "the effort retrospectively to account for and justify existing practice and beliefs" as reflected in the gospel narratives (1910, 56). For Bacon, the pregospel tradition consisted of "loosely connected anecdotes strung together for the purpose of explaining or defending beliefs and practices of the contemporary church" (see R. Harrisville 1976, 11).

These early attempts to take the gospel writers seriously as theologians concerned with problems of their communities were overshadowed by the rise of form criticism, by the ongoing quest for the historical Jesus, and by the rise of dialectical theology. However, such scholars as E. Lohmeyer[§] (1936) and R. H. Lightfoot[§] (1934, 1938) continued to argue that, on the basis of its topical and geographical references, the Gospel of Mark embodied theological perspectives distinctive from the traditions received.

3. *The Flowering of Redaction Criticism.* In the mid-sixties, when redaction criticism took hold, Perrin, one of its chief practitioners and chroniclers, described it as a "lusty infant" (1966, 298). It soon developed into the dominant method of gospel research, with multiple contributions, and took on distinct emphases in different settings. German scholarship stressed the difference between tradition and redaction and the need to write a careful history of the tradition. At the Pontifical Biblical Institute in Rome, important studies appeared (Q. Quesnell 1969; W. Thompsom 1970) focusing less on the distinction between tradition and redaction and more on the literary style and composition of a given gospel. In North America, early redaction-critical studies worked with the tradition/redaction model, but the method soon developed into full-scale LITERARY criticism (understood, not as source criticism, but as the application to biblical material of a wide variety of methods used by secular literary critics).

The Synoptic Gospels became the major area for application of the method, yielding fruitful understandings of their distinctive theologies and communities. The synoptic evangelists were called theologians as readily as an earlier generation had so named PAUL and John. Each Gospel has a distinctive Christology; important elements of the tradition (e.g., Jesus' proclamation of the kingdom and his summons to discipleship) are interpreted differently in each. Redaction criticism underscored the pluralism among and within the different communities that received the Gospels and, on the basis of evidence in the text, sketched out conflicts faced by them (R. Brown 1979; T. Weeden 1971).

a. Redaction criticism of Q. Various attempts have been made to distinguish levels in the composition of Q—that collection of material, mostly sayings, shared by Matthew and Luke but not found in Mark—and to describe the groups or community that preserved and adapted it (see J. Kloppenborg 1984; F. Neirynck 1982). Although no consensus exists on the precise content or evolution of the traditions contained in Q, collections of wisdom sayings traceable to the historical Jesus are generally thought to have been supplemented by apocalyptic (Apocalypticism*[§]) and prophetic (Prophecy and Prophets‡[§]) material. G. Theissen (1978) traced much of the

Q material to the "Jesus movement," itinerant preachers who lived the radical lifestyle commended in many Q sayings (e.g., Luke 10:5-12). Such material was then supplemented by apocalyptic material in which the community expressed its hope of vindication by the returning Son of Man. By incorporating this material into their gospels, Matthew and Luke simultaneously preserved and reinterpreted the radical prophetic strain within early Christianity.

b. Redaction Criticism of the Gospel of John. The Fourth Gospel also provided fertile ground for redaction criticism. Bultmann (1941 [ET 1971]) proposed that the evangelist incorporated and edited a "signs source" (behind the miracles of chaps. 1-12); "revelatory discourses," characterized by their poetic structure and GNOSTIC motifs (the core of which are found in such chapters as John 10, 15, and 17); and a "passion source" (John 18-20). The content and structure of the canonical gospel is due to an "ecclesiastical redactor" who also added John 21 and select verses throughout (e.g., John 5:28-29; 6:51c-58). Although Bultmann's suggestions have rarely been accepted *in toto*, most subsequent studies are strongly influenced by them. R. Fortna (1979) and W. Nicol (1972) attempted further description of the signs source and its relation to the final text. W. Langbrandtner (1977) postulated an early gnostic "foundation gospel" (*Grundschrift*) that was expanded by the redaction. There then emerged a "nearly hopeless disarray of proposals for what the tradition [behind the gospel] was and how the evangelist employed it" (Kysar 1983, 315). Subsequent research attempted to trace the history of the Johannine[†§] community without giving an exact description of sources and traditions. J. L. Martyn[§] (1968) argued that John produced a "two-level" drama in which much of the controversial material (e.g., John 9:1-40) reflects the separation of the community from Judaism toward the end of the first century. Brown pursued the same approach with an elaborate developmental schema of the Johannine community from its inception through the letters of John.

4. *Assessing Redaction Criticism.* Although dominant and fruitful, the method is attended with problems. When there is no clear document (as in the case of Q or the Johannine signs source) or no clear source for a given document (e.g., for Mark, according to the generally accepted two source theory, or for John), the separation of tradition from redaction is always problematic, as is the designation of a particular passage or literary technique as typical of the final redactor. R. Pesch, the author of a seminal work distinguishing tradition and redaction (1968), later criticized such attempts as arbitrary (1976, 102) and proposed a radical composition criticism according to which virtually everything in Mark is tradition, with the theological creativity of the evangelist discernible only in the arrangement (1976, 1977). Likewise, ascribing a theological intention to an editor on the basis of literary phenomena is disputed and can be easily intertwined with the theological perspective of the interpreter.

From its origin, redaction criticism was a counter to the fragmentation of a text into traditional units to the detriment of a holistic look at the individual gospels. It provided a way for both the specialist and lay readers to engage the text at hand. Although still an important method in New Testament study, other methods have developed from redaction criticism and taken on lives of their own. Concern for the text as a literary unit has spawned full-scale Literary*[§] criticism, which embraces virtually every movement within secular literary criticism from the New Criticism to deconstructionism (Structuralism and Deconstruction*[§]). The other major transformation of redaction criticism has been in the direction of social analysis of New Testament documents, a natural outgrowth of interest in the community behind the given gospel. Like its literary counterpart, it brought biblical scholarship into dialogue with other secular disciplines (sociology, cultural anthropology).

Redaction criticism continues to be enhanced by other emerging concerns of New Testament studies. In assessing the difference between tradition and redaction, more attention must be given to the manner in which ancient writers take over preexisting traditions. Such ancient historians as Thucydides and Josephus[§] extensively rewrote their sources and traditions in their own style. In the absence of clear sources, it is problematic whether the paring off of editorial accretions (as is still customary in much German redaction criticism) can ever disclose a "tradition." Renewed interest in the literary forms of antiquity (e.g., the *chreia*) and in ancient rhetoric will more accurately disclose the literary activity and social location of a given author. The diverse communities behind the Gospels will be better understood in light of the expansion of knowledge about the diversity within first-century Judaism both in Palestine and in the Diaspora.

Bibliography: J. Ashton, *Studying John: Approaches to the Fourth Gospel* (1994). **B. W. Bacon**, *The Beginnings of the Gospel Story* (1909); "The Purpose of Mark's Gospel," *JBL 29* (1910) 41-60; *Is Mark a Roman Gospel?* (1919); *Studies in Matthew* (1930). **C. K. Barrett**, *Luke the Historian in Recent Study* (1961). **G. Bornkamm**, G. Barth, and H. J. Held, *Tradition and Interpretation in Matthew* (1960; ET 1963). **J. Becker**, "Aus der Literatur zum Johannesevangelium (1978-80)," *TRu 47* (1982) 279-301, 305-47; "Das Evangelium in Streit der Methoden (1980-84)," *TRu 51* (1986) 1-78. **F. Bovon**, *Luke the Theologian: Thirty-three Years of Research (1950-83)* (1978; rev. ET 1987). **R. E. Brown**, *The Community of the Beloved Disciple* (1979). **R. Bultmann**, *Die Geschichte der synoptischen Tradition* (1921, 1931[2]; ET 1931[2] 1963); Evangelium des Johannes (1941; ET 1971). **H. Conzelmann**, "Literaturbericht zu den Synoptischen Evangelien," *TRu 37* (1972) 220-72; 43 (1978) 3-51, 321-27.; Die Mitte der Zeit (1954; ET *The Theology of St. Luke* 1960). **N. A. Dahl**, "Wellhausen on the NT," *Semeia* 25 (1982) 89-110. **J. R. Donahue**, "Redaction Criticism? Has the Hauptstrasse Become a Sackgasse?" *The New Literary Criticism and the NT* (ed. E. S. Malbon and E. McKnight, 1994) 27-57. **J. Dewey**, "Recent Studies on Mark," *RelSRev 17* (1991) 12-16. **J. Fitzmyer**, *The Gospel According to Luke I-IX* (AB 28, 1981) 1-283. **R. Fortna**, "Redaction Criticism, NT," *IDBSup* (1962) 733-34; The Gospel of Signs: A Reconstruction of the Narrative Source Underlying the Fourth Gospel (1979). **D. Harrington**, "Matthean Studies Since J. Rohde," *Light of All Nations: Essays on the Church in NT Research* (1982) 375-88; "A Map of Books on Mark (1975-84)," *BTB 15* (1985) 12-16. **R. A. Harrisville**, *B. W. Bacon: Pioneer in American Biblical Criticism* (1976). **S. Kealy**, *Mark's Gospel: A History of Its Interpretation from the Beginning Until 1979* (1982). **J. Kloppenborg**, "Tradition and Redaction in the Synoptic Sayings Source," *CBQ 46* (1984) 34-62. **R. Kysar**, *The Fourth Evangelist and His Gospel: An Examination of Contemporary Scholarship* (1975); "The Gospel of John in Current Research," *RelSRev 9* (1983) 314-23. **W. Langbrandtner**, *Weltferner God oder Gott der Liebe: Der Ketzerstreit in der johanneischen Kirche* (1977). **R. H. Lightfoot**, *History and Interpretation in the Gospels* (1934); *Locality and Doctrine in the Gospels* (1938). **A. Lindemann**, "Literaturbericht zu den Synoptischen Evangelien, 1978-83," *TRu 49* (1984) 223-76; "Literaturbericht zu den Synoptischen Evangelien, 1984-91," *TRu 59* (1994) 41-100, 113-85. **E. Lohmeyer**, *Galiläa und Jerusalem* (1936). **J. L. Martyn**, *History and Theology in the Fourth Gospel* (1968). **W. Marxsen**, *Monatsschrift für Pastoraltheologie 6* (1954) 254; *Mark the Evangelist: Studies on the Redaction History of the Gospel* (1956; ET 1969). **J. L. Mays** (ed.), *Interpreting the Gospels* (1981). **F. Neirynck**, "Recent Developments in the Study of Q and Q Bibliography," *Logia: Les Paroles de Jesus-The Sayings of Jesus* (Memorial J. Coppens, ed. J. Delobel, BETL 59, 1982) 29-75, 561-86; "Q Bibliography: Additional List," *ETL 62* (1986) 157-65. **W. Nicol**, *The Semeia in the Fourth Gospel: Tradition and Redaction* (1972). **N. Perrin**, "The Wredestrasse Becomes the Hauptstrasse," *JR 46* (1966) 296-300; *What Is Redaction Criticism?* (1969). **R. Pesch**, *Naherwartungen: Tradition und Redaktion in Mark 13* (1968); *Markusevangelium* (HTKNT 2.1.2., 2 vols. 1976-1977). **Q. Quesnell**, *The Mind of Mark: Interpretation and Method Through the Exegesis of Mark 6:52* (1969). **V. Robbins**, "Text and Context in Recent Studies of the Gospel of Mark," *RelSRev 17* (1991) 16-23.

J. Rohde, *Rediscovering the Teaching of the Evangelists* (1968). **W. Schmithals,** "Redaktionsgeschichte," *TRE 10* (1982) 609-26. **G. Sloyan,** *What Are They Saying About John?* (1991). **S. Smalley,** "Redaction Criticism," *NT Interpretation* (ed. I. H. Marshall, 1977) 181-95. **D. M. Smith,** "Johannine Studies," *The NT and Its Modern Interpreters* (ed. E. J. Epp and G. W. MacRae, 1989) 271-76. **G. Stanton,** "The Origin and Purpose of Matthean Scholarship from 1945-80," *ANRW II.25.3* (1984) 1889-1951. **G. Theissen,** *Sociology of Early Palestinian Christianity* (1978). **W. Thompson,** *Matthew's Advice to a Divided Community* (1970). **H. Thyen,** "Aus der Literatur zum Johannesevangelium," *TRu 39* (1974) 295-355; *42* (1977) 211-70; *43* (1978) 328-59; *44* (1979) 97-134. **T. Weeden,** *Mark: Traditions in Conflict* (1971). **J. Wellhausen,** *Das Evangelium Marci* (1903); *Einleitung in die drei ersten Evangelien* (1905). **W. Wrede,** *The Messianic Secret* (1901; ET, 1971). **H. Zimmermann,** *Neutestamentliche Methodenlehre* (1978).

J. R. DONAHUE

LITERARY AND STRUCTURALIST/
POSTMODERNIST APPROACHES METHODS

Hermeneutics

The term "hermeneutics" derives from the Greek *hermeneuein*, which carries the senses of expression (uttering a thought or intention), explication (interpreting an utterance), and translation (mediating meanings from one language to another). Hermeneutics denotes the theoretical and methodological process of understanding meanings in signs and symbols, whether written or spoken. Hermeneutics has vital importance for the task of interpreting the Bible because it is the discipline through which people reflect on the concepts, principles, and rules that are universally necessary for understanding and interpreting any meanings whatsoever. Biblical interpretation must be intelligible as a particular form of interpretation in general.

Hermeneutics as an explicit theoretical construction did not appear until the seventeenth century, when the Latin word *hermeneutica* was first used in this sense (although various authors had scattered insights into interpretive processes in antiquity).

Modern hermeneutics is distinguished by three important characteristics. First, it begins with universal theories of interpretation that were developed independently of any received tradition of interpreting a particular body of texts, such as the Bible, classical literature, or civil laws. Second, it is linked to the emergence of philosophical critique as a power to dislodge the being of whatever appears as self-evidently given, including any objects considered to be sacred in themselves (e.g., the Bible, clergy, and eucharistic bread and wine). Third, it is conscious that objects of interpretation are always situated in complex historical contexts; various strata of presuppositions, beliefs, and interests both shape and are reflected in texts from the past.

F. Schleiermacher[§] is frequently credited with having founded modern hermeneutics. Prior to Schleiermacher, however, several other scholars wrote normative and technical theories of interpretation, including J. Dannhauer, J. Chladenius, and G. Meier. Schleiermacher did not publish a major work on hermeneutics; he left behind only his handwritten lecture notes on the subject (amply supplemented by student notes) and two addresses to the Berlin Academy of the Sciences from 1829. Nonetheless, the quantity of material and the quality of thought in these manuscripts, coupled with Schleiermacher's enormous influence on subsequent theories, secure his central place in the history of hermeneutics.

Schleiermacher was a systematic thinker *par excellence*. In his 1819 notes on hermeneutics, as well as in his 1822 lectures on dialectic, he related hermeneutics both to dialectic and to rhetoric. He viewed the three as fundamental and interrelated philosophical arts (*Kunstlehren*) and held living dialogue to be the natural home and empirical starting point of each. Everything he said about interpretation was intended to illuminate the everyday processes by which people do, in fact, come to know others. The problem of understanding texts from the distant past always derives from the primary hermeneutical problem of understanding others. Most simply put, Schleiermacher claimed that hermeneutics is the art of understanding, rhetoric the art of speaking, and dialectic the art of thinking. Hermeneutics and rhetoric are, therefore, simply the reverse sides of each other. In any conversation with another person, one is either uttering words or listening to words uttered by the other. Hermeneutics and rhetoric primarily have to do with language in actual use. However, insofar as language is the exterior of thinking and thinking is the interior of language they both have an intrinsic reference to dialectic.

Dialectic is dependent on hermeneutics and rhetoric, according to Schleiermacher, because dialectic is both produced and understood through the principles and rules of rhetoric and hermeneutics, respectively. But hermeneutics and rhetoric are in the nature of the case subordinate to dialectic. Hermeneutics without dialectic is interpretive free association lacking ground in the author's thought; rhetoric without dialectic is unscrupulous persuasion for personal ends without regard to truth. Interest in dialectic arises whenever there is concern for truth in understanding or speaking; dialectic, thus, is the measure of both hermeneutics and rhetoric. More properly put, hermeneutics is thinking about the principle and rules for true understanding of the meaning of judgments articulated in particular linguistic signs. Rhetoric is thinking about the principle and rules for truthful and effective presentation of judgments in new discourse. Dialectic is thinking about the principle and rules of relating the forms of thinking with the material of being in true judgments.

Schleiermacher reversed the inherited tendency in hermeneutics to assume that understanding occurs on its own accord, so that hermeneutics assists in avoiding misunderstanding. He proposed instead that misunderstanding, rather than understanding, naturally takes place and that hermeneutics makes us aware of the scope and depth of our misunderstanding. To understand well is an infinite interactive task for finite humans, who always find themselves in the middle of an ongoing conversation without the means to elevate themselves above their limited perspectives. Schleiermacher believed that interpretation is a never-ending process that always inadequately approximates the ultimately unattainable truth of things.

Schleiermacher distinguished two kinds of interpretation: grammatical and technical/psychological. He further specified two methods of interpretation: comparative and divinatory. Methodical interpretation uses both methods in both kinds of interpretation. Comparison is the objective-analytic method of distinguishing the material element of discourse from the formal element in order to find the right concepts for understanding particular meanings. Divination, by contrast, is the subjective-intuitive method of directly apprehending individuals as living combinations of formal and material elements, universal concepts, and particular meanings.

Grammatical interpretation is the art of finding the precise sense of a given statement from its language; it requires knowledge of the languages common to the author and the original audience. Grammatical interpretation uses the comparative method to determine the objective meaning of each word, sentence, and paragraph accessible to any competent user of the language; it uses the divinatory method to apprehend the subjective meaning of the text for the original audience. Technical/psychological interpretation is the art of finding the theme of the work grasped as its unity, i.e., the dynamic motive and leading thought that impels the author; it requires knowledge of the different ways humans think. Technical/psychological interpretation uses the comparative method to focus on the text as a work of art, concentrating on the author's distinctive style and means of composition within the established genre; it uses the divinatory method to understand the text as a creative event in the author's life. The aim of interpretive activity is to produce at least partial agreement among the results of these four possibilities. Schleiermacher stated quite clearly that the "true" meaning of a text is no more to be found through grammatical interpretation than through technical/pyschological interpretation, no more through the comparative method than through the divinatory method. The genre of the text determines, in part, what proportion of skills one brings to it. For example, maps require less psychological than grammatical skill; personal letters require more psychological than grammatical skill. Schleiermacher advised everyone to identify personal hermeneutical strengths and weaknesses and to work on the weaknesses to help transform misunderstanding into understanding.

Following Schleiermacher, a new development had an impact on modern hermeneutics. Schleiermacher was fully aware that texts from the past are written from their own conceptual, linguistic, and social contexts. He was less attentive, however, to the fact that modern interpreters likewise understand these texts from their own historically situated presuppositions, beliefs, and interests. The problem of historicism thereby arises: If modern interpretations of historical texts are themselves historical, then how is historical knowledge possible?

W. Dilthey[§] is notable for directly addressing the problem of historicism. A philosopher who concentrated his efforts on providing an epistemological foundation for the human sciences, he attempted to conceive a critique of historical reason that would secure theoretical justification for the human sciences with the same rigor that I. Kant's[§] critique of pure reason had done for the natural sciences. In his later writings (1900 and following), Dilthey sought this basis in hermeneutics, which he called the methodology of the interpretation of written records. In his famous essay "The Development of Hermeneutics" (1900), he focused on three ideas connected to hermeneutics so conceived. First, whereas the natural sciences study outer appearances through the senses, the human sciences study expressions of the "inner reality [*Erlebnis*] directly experienced in all its complexity." This inner reality is the immediate experience of a whole human being, which always includes a movement of reflexive self-awareness. In other words, when persons see or hear something in the world to which they feel an inner response, they are also immediately aware of themselves as seeing, hearing, and feeling something. In Dilthey's conception, the phenomenon of self-consciousness grows directly out of the experiences of life. According to his famous distinction, the natural sciences explain outer appearances with reference to causal laws; but the human sciences understand states of inner psychological reality by means of the initially diverse and strange words and gestures that express these states of self-awareness.

Second, the human sciences are possible because understanding is a universal rule-governed activity that reaches from linguistic expressions back to the inner reality that gives rise to them. Dilthey maintained that verbal expressions refer to historically conditioned systems of cultural meaning and to states of inner experience. The art of understanding explores both references and coordinates them into meaningful wholes. Historical understanding involves empathetically transposing oneself into the inner experiences of other human beings by means of and within their proper worlds of cultural and linguistic meanings.

Third, understanding of others is possible because of two central conditions of human life: First, no matter how different people may be, they share a common human nature as historical and meaning-conferring beings; therefore, nothing human is altogether alien to another human being. Second, everywhere and at all times, people express their thoughts and experiences in structured, translatable languages that enable interpreters to reconstruct cultural settings radically different from their own.

Modern hermeneutics underwent a profound transformation through the thought of philosopher M. Heidegger. In his early lectures leading up to the publication of *Being and Time* in 1927, Heidegger revised the concept of hermeneutics inherited from Schleiermacher and Dilthey, rejecting the view of hermeneutics as a distinctive art or method of understanding whose explication can ground the human sciences. Rather than framing hermeneutics within epistemology, he referred it to fundamental ontological inquiry. Heidegger no longer considered understanding primarily to be a particular mode of knowing but, rather, a basic element of the human mode of being, *Dasein*. *Dasein* is the being whose structure is care, for it is characterized by concern for itself—concern about what it means to be the one it is. In its care-structure, *Dasein* exhibits a preunderstanding of the meaning of its own being as well as the meaning of being at all. It is thus the opening or clearing in the whole of being, where the meaning of being is manifest for interpretation. In *Being and Time*, Heidegger constructed a hermeneutics of facticity in which he interpreted the basic elements of *Dasein's* care-structure in order to make explicit its preunderstanding of the meaning of being. He held that the goal of hermeneutics is philosophical self-understanding, conceived as a way of combating a pervasive forgetfulness of what it means to be human.

According to Heidegger, the essence of *Dasein* lies in its existence, in that its being differs fundamentally from that of a thing bearing properties. *Dasein* is a "who," not a "what"; its being is always one of possibilities rather than fixed actualities. *Dasein* is its possibilities to be, in that it is always deciding who it is in its everyday understanding of itself in the world. Moreover, *Dasein* is, in each case, "mine." Each person, as *Dasein,* is his or her own existence and must make the individual choice to be so. Because *Dasein* is, in each case, essentially its own possibility to be itself, it can either gain itself authentically by accepting responsibility for its own choices or lose itself inauthentically by allowing popular opinion or unexamined traditions to determine its choices.

In *Being and Time*, Heidegger analyzed the basic elements of *Dasein's* being as care. The first of these structural elements is *Befindlichkeit* (mood or state of mind). *Dasein* always finds itself "there," thrown into the world, delivered over to its being, not knowing from whence it comes or where it is going. Through its fundamental moods, especially that of anxiety, *Dasein* is disclosed to itself as thrown and is opened to the question of the meaning of its own being and of being anything at all. The second and equally original element is *Verstehen* (understanding). *Dasein* orients itself within the situation of its "thrownness" by projecting possibilities for things to be; in perceiving something, one thinks of it "as" something and thereby understands a possibility of its being. For example, one sees a stone and thinks of it as a tool for pounding or as a beautiful object for one's shelf. By projecting possibilities for the being of worldly things, *Dasein* also projects an understanding of its own being as the one for whose sake it understands. In its capacity to understand, *Dasein* reveals its capacity to transcend its given situations in the world. A third element is *Rede* (discourse). *Dasein's* capacity for language is similarly rooted in its care-structure in that mood and understanding come to light in language.

Interpretation, another basic structural element of *Dasein*, is the working out of the possibilities projected in understanding. In interpreting something that is already understood, *Dasein* makes explicit the content of what was projected. Understanding so interpreted is never merely a matter of perceiving or conceiving, but is an activity of figuring or imagining the possible relations between perceiving and conceiving. Understanding is a social practice of seeing what possibilities for thought and action a situation calls for. There is no presuppositionless understanding or naked perception of uninterpreted objects. *Dasein* is always making sense of what it has already understood by projecting onto it *Dasein's* own interests.

Heidegger's concept of *Dasein* and his ontological redirection of hermeneutics were immensely influential for subsequent thinkers. For example, R. Bultmann[§], the New Testament scholar and theologian, made direct use of Heidegger in interpreting the meaning of faith as a possible mode of human being. Christian faith, according to Bultmann, is a decision the self as *Dasein* makes to entrust itself to the grace of God that breaks into the world through the *kerygma* of the New Testament. Basically, *Dasein* can understand itself either inauthetically, as having to secure its own existence in the world (unfaith) or authentically, as trusting in an invisible and liberating power that comes to the self from outside in the word of the gospel (faith).

The enormous amount of attention given to hermeneutics since 1960 is in large degree due to the publication of *Truth and Method* in that year by the Heidelberg philosopher, H. G. Gadamer. Whereas Heidegger largely ignored the methodological concerns of Schleiermacher and Dilthey, Gadamer's magnum opus returned to the question of legitimating the human sciences by articulating the method proper to them. Gadamer revisited that issue on the grounds of Heidegger's early work on the hermeneutics of existence as well as Heidegger's later thinking about language in relation to being. Gadamer questioned the demand that the human sciences produce in hermeneutics a method appropriate to their objects of study in order to justify themselves as sciences. He argued that the modern dogma—that method is the privileged path to truth—in fact instantiates a basic attitude of alienation from the objects of humanistic inquiry. This methodically imposed alienation covers up a more primordial belongingness to human meanings where the truth appropriate to the human sciences in fact appears. *Truth and*

Method is a historical and systematic analysis of how methodologism obscures the essential dimension of participation in the human experiences of truth manifested in art, history, and language. Gadamer's philosophical hermeneutics extend and deepen Heidegger's insights into the role of preunderstanding in all three spheres.

The first part of *Truth and Method* is dedicated to aesthetic experience. Gadamer discovered an experience of truth in art that precedes and is obscured by the application of aesthetic methods of analysis. In experiencing a work of art, one undergoes something similar to the experience of play in games. The participants in both are drawn into an event with its own subjectivity and life. Releasing oneself to the structured movement of play, one can say both "I play the game" and "the game plays itself through me." In playing a game, a higher subjectivity than that of the players manifests itself. So too with art: We experience truth in art when the work draws us into its play of meaning and allows us to see something previously hidden about the everyday world in which we live.

The second part of *Truth and Method* focuses on historical consciousness. Both Schleiermacher and Dilthey, among others, were aware of the difficulties of achieving historical knowledge that does not rewrite the past in the modern historian's image. Their tendency was to work out interpretive methods that would reduce, as much as possible, the intruding influences of the historian, and thereby to allow the voices of history to speak without distortion. Gadamer acknowledged that it is not possible to impose a method that will eliminate subjective interference with the historical objects as they are in themselves. His concept of *wirkungsgeschichtliches Bewusstsein* (consciousness that is open to the effects of history) shows that it is an illusion to think that historians can elevate themselves above the stream of historical effects. For example, someone who writes a history of the French Revolution cannot rise above the ongoing effects of the event; the historian belongs to that historical stream and participates in those effects. Any understanding of the historical world is itself historical. According to Gadamer, historians are better advised to recognize how their deeply rooted prejudices (preunderstandings, prejudgments) are historically shaped and historically effective. By entering a back-and-forth movement of question and answer, which includes allowing the voices of the past to pose questions to the historians, they can come to understand, in a self-critical way, the truth of historical existence. The historian belongs to the effects of history in a much more profound way than history belongs to the historian as a neutral object of study.

In the third section of *Truth and Method*, Gadamer universalized the hermeneutical experience of belongingness to language. Language is not a separate sphere alongside art and history; it is the medium of our entire experience of the world. All understanding happens as an event within language or, indeed, as an event of language. Understanding occurs in the back-and-forth movement of genuine dialogue, and what is understood is being. Language allows being to show itself, and being shows itself only in language. Language, however, is not the prison of understanding; it is the universal medium of the self's dialogical openness to the other. Gadamer's hermeneutics is an eloquent testimony to the finitude of all human interpretations and to the infinity of meaning in which we participate as linguistic beings. For Gadamer, we always understand more than we can say.

Gadamer's hermeneutics have had a widespread influence on biblical interpretation, especially through G. Ebeling and his followers. Ebeling emphasized that the New Testament writers were highly aware of how understanding the gospel message can result in the gift of faith mediated through "word event." For both Ebeling and Gadamer, understanding a text from the past and applying its meaning to our present circumstances occur together and not as two separate events.

The French philosopher P. Ricoeur[§] has been a major contributor to modern hermeneutical inquiry. Ricoeur works on the basis of the key insights into philosophical hermeneutics proposed by Heidegger and Gadamer: Human being is distinguished as a mode of being through understanding; the intentional object of the activity of understanding is being; and language is the universal medium through which humans understand being. At one level, Ricoeur has been a key figure in mediating German philosophical hermeneutics to the much broader domains of Anglo-American analytic philosophy and cross-disciplinary methodological discussions. His highly complex philosophical program is nonetheless quite different from those of Heidegger and Gadamer. Ricoeur criticizes Heidegger's sudden reversal of hermeneutics from an essentially epistemological concern into an ontological one. He is interested in the meaning of human finite being and in the meaning of being itself, but he does not want to short-circuit the legitimate hermeneutical interest in understanding and interpreting as modes of thinking that intend knowing. He places ontology at the end, not the beginning, of his program. Moroever, Ricoeur criticizes Gadamer's apparent dichotomy between inquiry into truth in the human sciences and method. He wants to recover Schleiermacher's methodological interest in articulating the principles, concepts, and rules of interpreting written texts truthfully. Ricoeur does not want to eschew method in favor of truth but to place method in service of truth.

Ricoeur's program began with the two-volume *Philosophy of the Will*. The second volume has two independently published parts: *Fallible Man*, a phenomenological reflection on the essential structures of finite thinking, willing, and feeling; and *The Symbolism of Evil*, a hermeneutical study of human testimony of evil-doing in Greek myths and tragedies and in biblical texts. *Fallible Man* reveals the essential rift or split that runs through thinking, willing, and feeling; this rift constitutes the possibility of evil and presents a limit-point for philosophical reflection. The *Symbolism of Evil* follows the irrationality of the fall into the language of confession and posits hermeneutics as the methodology appropriate for the study of symbolic language. Subsequently, Ricoeur has written a series of studies in philosophical hermeneutics, including works on the functions of language (both literal and figurative), the nature and interpretation of texts, the conflicts among different kinds of interpretations, the relation between the temporality of human existence and the narrative form of texts, and the interpretation of human action and character on the basis of its text-like nature. He has also written hermeneutical reflections on various New Testament texts, including the Parables of Jesus[†§] and the Gospel of Mark[†§].

Bibliography: J. Bleicher, *Contemporary Hermeneutics: Hermeneutics as Method, Philosophy, and Critique* (1980). **W. Dilthey,** *Der Aufbau der Geschichtlichen Welt in den Geisteswissenschaften* (1958). **M. Ermarth,** *W. Dilthey: The Critique of Historical Reason* (1978). **H.-G. Gadamer,** *Truth and Method* (1960, 1975[4]; ET 1975, 1989[2]); *Philosophical Hermeneutics* (ed. and tr. D. E. Linge, 1976). **J. Grondin,** *Introduction to Philosophical Hermeneutics* (1994); *Sources of Hermeneutics* (1995). **M. Heidegger,** *Being and Time* (1927; ET tr. J. Macquarrie and E. Robinson, 1962; ET tr. J. Stambaugh, 1996); *Ontologie (Hermeneutik der Faktizität)* (1988; ed. K. Bröcker-Oltmans). **W. Jeanrond,** *Theological Hermeneutics: Development and Significance* (1991). **D. Klemm,** *The Hermeneutical Theory of P. Ricoeur: A Constructive Analysis* (1983). **D. Klemm** (ed.), *Hermeneutical Inquiry* (AAR.SR 43-44, 2 vols. 1986). **D. Klemm and W. Schweiker** (eds.), *Meanings in Texts and Actions: Questioning P. Ricoeur* (SRC, 1993). **R. Makkreel,** *Dilthey: Philosopher of the Human Studies* (1975, 1992). **K. Müller-Vollmar** (ed.), *The Hermeneutics Reader* (1985). **O. Pöggeler,** *M. Heidegger's Path of Thinking* (Contemporary Studies in Philosophy and Human Sciences, 1987). **P. Ricoeur,** *Fallible Man* (1950; ET 1965); *Philosophy of the Will* vol. 1, *Freedom and Nature* (1950; ET 1966); vol. 2, *Finitude and Guilt* (1960; ET 1965); *Conflict of Interpretations: Essays in Hermeneutics* (ed. D. Ihde, 1974); *Interpretation Theory* (1976); *Essays on Biblical Interpretation* (ed. L. Mudge, 1980); *Time and Narrative* (3 vols. 1984,

1985, 1988); *Oneself as Another* (1992). **F. D. E. Schleiermacher**, *Hermeneutics: The Handwritten Manuscripts* (ed. H. Kimmerle, tr. J. Duke and J. Forstman, 1977); *Hermeneutik und Kritik* (ed. M. Frank, 1977). **J. Van Den Hengel**, *The Home of Meaning: The Hermeneutics of the Subject of P. Ricoeur* (1982). **G. Warnke**, *Gadamer: Hermeneutics, Tradition, and Reason* (1987). **J. Weinsheimer**, *Gadamer's Hermeneutics: A Reading of Truth and Method* (1985); *Philosophical Hermeneutics and Literary Theory* (1991).

D. E. KLEMM

LITERARY AND STRUCTURALIST/
POSTMODERNIST APPROACHES METHODS

Intertextuality

As a self-conscious literary-critical approach, intertextuality emerged in the late 1960s and early 1970s and has significantly informed the practice of criticism and contemporary understandings of literary history in North America and Europe. The root concerns of this approach are not new: the role of tradition in literature, the relationship of newly created literary works to the classics of a given "canon," and the role of literary and cultural systems of meaning in literary composition. Intertextual methods, however, offer alternatives to the stringent evolutionary and historically determined models with which these concerns have been conventionally addressed. Beginning in the late 1970s and early 1980s, biblical scholars have increasingly used the methods of intertextual studies to interpret biblical texts.

The progenitor of contemporary intertextual studies was T. S. Eliot's 1919 essay, "Tradition and the Individual Talent." Eliot wrote this essay against the backdrop of Romantic theories of poetic inspiration and the genius of the poet, which claimed that the poet's originality is an expression of personality. Eliot challenged these conventional assumptions about genius and inspiration by reclaiming the centrality of literary tradition. His central thesis was that no poet or artist receives complete meaning in isolation, but must be set "among the dead," saying, "we shall often find that not only the best, but the most individual parts of his work may be those in which the dead poets, his ancestors, assert their immortality most vigorously" (1950, 4).

Eliot replaced the evolutionary model of influence with a model of literary interrelationships. The poet incorporates the traditions of the past into a work so that it transforms past and present. Poetry is "a living whole of all the poetry written"; "what happens when a new work of art is created is something that happens simultaneously to all the works of art which preceded it" (1950, 49-50). Eliot conceived of literature as a "system of coequal, copresent texts" that hold "literature as history and literature as system" in balance (Morgan 1989, 242).

Eliot's most lasting contribution to intertextual studies is this emphasis on literature as a system of interrelated texts. Subsequent work in intertextuality is developing his observations in two distinct, but not wholly unrelated, directions. The first stream of intertextuality focuses on literary interrelationships and patterns of literary borrowing within literature proper. The second stream broadens the understanding of "text" to include a variety of linguistic phenomena and thus studies the interrelationship of text and culture.

Scholars employ a wide variety of methodologies to study intertextual relations in literary texts. For example, H. Bloom (1973, 1975) draws on theories from modern philosophy and Freudian Psychology*§ to identify and explain the dynamics and motivations of literary borrowing. Although Bloom attempts to distance himself from what he perceives as the classical and Christianizing tendency of Eliot, his study of "intra-poetic relationships" shares with Eliot similar conceptualizations of influence and the interaction of past and present in literary composition. Bloom maintains that every reading of a text is a misreading. A new poet creates a personal space by misreading the poetic precursors. Bloom describes this misreading in terms of a Freudian struggle between fathers and sons. His psychological orientation leads him to focus on authorial intention, a focus other intertextual studies often try to avoid.

A second methodology can be seen in the work of J. Hollander (1981), which belongs to the more general category of Rhetorical Criticism*§. He identifies allusions to and echoes of earlier poets in the work of their successors, and studies the way those textual echoes create new meanings. "Echo" is understood as a rhetorical trope that establishes links between texts chronologically removed from one another. Hollander's work proceeds by close readings of individual poetic texts and by design is more suggestive of intertextual possibilities than it is methodologically precise. Under the general category of rhetorical approaches to intertextuality, one can also place studies that investigate the way various rhetorical figures are used (e.g., citation), the effects produced by literary borrowing, and the reader's experience of literary borrowing.

A third methodology used to study intertextuality within literature proper is SEMIOTICS. Unlike semiotic studies that focus more broadly on text and culture (see below), the semiotic studies of M. Riffaterre (1978) and G. Genette (1982), for example, focus on the act of reading specific literary texts. Both assume that intertextuality is operative in all literature, and their studies attempt to identify what the reader must do in order to recognize and follow the inter-textual signals in any given text. Riffaterre provides close readings of texts "to show how each literary text guides the reader toward its own intertexts" (Morgan 1989, 262). Genette offers a taxonomy of intertextual signs and relations to enable the reader to follow the dynamics of intertextuality. (For a thorough discussion of Riffaterre and Genette, see Morgan, 262-71.)

When the definition of intertextuality broadens to include relationships between text and culture, structuralist (Structuralism and Deconstruction*§) and semiotic methods move to the fore-front. Semiotics speaks of "text" differently from rhetorical and more traditional literary critics. "Text" includes any system of signs, not simply a literary text. In this broader understanding of text, all communication is seen as inherently "intertextual"—which is to say that any act of communication always occurs in the context of other signs. The semiotic approach to text and culture splits into two divergent philosophical camps. One approach, modeled on the linguistic theory of R. Jacobson and embodied in the structural anthropology of C. Lévi-Strauss, believes that one can identify the structures and basic elements that account for and explain the signify-ing practice of a "text." This approach operates with linguistic models and metaphors, but it shares a basic presupposition about the stability of texts and communication with the methods discussed above. The second semiotic approach to text and culture is critical of any sense of the stability of language and literature and uses semiotic models to point toward the increasing ambiguity and instability of communication. The key figures in this second approach are M. Bakhtin, R. Barthes, J. Kristeva, J. Culler, and J. Derrida. With these literary critics, intertextu-ality becomes part of a broader deconstructionalist reading of literature (see Morgan 1989, 256-61, 272-74).

In biblical studies, the narrower use of intertextuality—that is, patterns of literary borrowing among literary texts proper and textual relationships between specific literary corpora—is most prevalent. Intertextuality in the broader sense has been absorbed into general deconstructionist biblical interpretation.

Intertextual biblical interpretation attempts to address the interaction between traditions and texts without recourse to answers of strict historical construction. It attempts to hold together literature as history and literature as system without dissolving the tension between these two understandings of literature. Historical criticism tends to explain the presence of an earlier tra-dition or text with the formula, "the use of . . . . " or "the influence of . . . on. . . . " This under-standing of textual interrelationships dominated studies of the relationship between the Hebrew and Christian canons until the second half of the twentieth century (C. H. Dodd 1952; B. Lindars 1961; D. Carson and H. Williamson 1988). This approach is grounded in an exclu-sively diachronic understanding of texts and an evolutionary model of influence. Its focus is primarily apologetic, and consequently its concerns revolve around authorial intention.

The work of M. Fishbane (1985, 1986) provides a compelling alternative to an evolutionary and apologetic model of textual interrelations. Fishbane makes explicit connections between his work and the categories proposed by Eliot (Fishbane 1986, 34-36), but his concern is not theo-retical. He defines intertextual relations in terms of inner-biblical interpretation and exegesis within the Hebrew Canon§, focusing on the textual-exegetical dimensions of the Jewish imagination and suggesting that it is the essence of biblical texts to be reinterpreted by successive generations. He brings together the imaginative and social dimensions of Jewish exegesis and transforms a strictly evolutionary model of influence into a model grounded in the ongoing and unending life of literary traditions. Like Eliot, Fishbane holds together literature as history and literature as system in a way that reflects the richness and complexity of inner-biblical interpretation. He also clearly articulates the difference between Tradition History*[§] and inner-biblical exegesis. Tradition history moves backward from written sources to oral traditions. Inner-biblical exegesis starts with a received text and moves forward to subsequent interpretations based on it (Fishbane 1985, 7-13).

Fishbane excludes the gospel writers and Paul[†§] from the category of inner-biblical interpretation, maintaining that the christological dimension of their work stresses fulfillment and supersession rather than the reanimation of tradition (1985, 10). Yet because these writers were schooled in the same textual-exegetical imagination as the Jewish interpreters, the exegetical and interpretive methods that Fishbane indentifies within the Hebrew canon do seem to illuminate the play of traditions within the Christian canon (O'Day 1990). His assessment of the handling of Hebrew traditions by the gospel writers and Paul actually provides a telling critique of those interpreters cited above who reduce the relationship between the Hebrew and the Christian canons to prophecy/fulfillment and apologetic motives. Forcing scholars of the Christian canon to reassess their working exegetical assumptions, he restores a balance to scholarly understanding of the interplay of traditions.

Other biblical scholars have studied intertextual relations with more explicit reference to contemporary Literary Theory*[§], employing a wide variety of methodologies. S. Handelman (1982) grounds her study of the Moses tradition in biblical and rabbinic writings in the psycho-rhetorical categories of H. Bloom. R. Hays (1989) employs the rhetorical categories of J. Hollander to study "echoes of scripture" in Paul. D. Boyarin (1990) uses M. Riffaterre's semiotic categories in his reading of Midrash*[§]. These studies provide alternatives to the traditional evolu-tionary models of intertextual influence. Intertextual studies provide a bridge between strictly diachronic and strictly synchronic approaches to biblical texts, challenging traditional notions of influence and causality while at the same time affirming that every biblical text must be read as part of a larger literary context.

Bibliography: M. Bakhtin, *Problems of Dostoevsky's Poetics* (1973). **H. Bloom,** *The Anxiety of Influences* (1973); *The Map of Misreading* (1975). **D. Boyarin,** *Intertextuality and the Reading of Midrash* (1990). **D. A. Carson and H. G. M. Williamson** (eds.), *It is Written: Scripture Citing Scripture. Essays in Honor of Barnabas Lindars* (1988). **J. Culler,** *The Pursuit of Signs: Semiotics, Literature, Deconstruction* (1981). **C. H. Dodd,** *According to the Scriptures: the Substructure of NT Theology* (1952). **S. Draisma** (ed.), *Intertextuality in Biblical Writings: Essays in Honour of Bas van Iersel* (1989). **T. S. Eliot,** *Selected Essays 1917-1932* (1950). **M. Fishbane,** *Biblical Interpretation in Ancient Israel* (1985); "Inner Biblical Exegesis: Types and Strategies of Interpretation in Ancient Israel," *Midrash and Literature* (ed. G. H. Hartmann and S. Budick, 1986) 19-37. **G. Genette,** *Palimpsestes: La Literature au second degre* (1982). **S. Handelman,** *The Slayers of Moses: The Emergence of Rabbinic Interpretation in Modern Literary Theory* (1982). **R. Hays,** *Echoes of Scripture in the Letters of Paul* (1989). **J. Hollander,** *The Figure of Echo: A Mode of Allusion in Milton and After* (1981). **B. Lindars,** *NT Apologetic* (1961). **T. Morgan,** "The Space of Intertextuality," *Intertextuality and Contemporary American Fiction* (ed. P. O'Donnell and R. C. Davis, 1989) 239-79. **G. O'Day,** "Jeremiah 9:22-23 and 1 Corinthians 1:26-31: A Study in Intertextuality," *JBL 109* (1990) 259-67. **M. Riffaterre,** *Semiotics of Poetry* (1978).

G. R. O'DAY

LITERARY AND STRUCTURALIST/
POSTMODERNIST APPROACHES METHODS
Literary Theory, Literary Criticism, and the Bible

1. *Introduction.* The state of relations between literary theory, literary criticism, and biblical studies toward the end of the twentieth century may be aptly characterized by a title word from one of J. Derrida's earliest essays: dissemination. That is, the various approaches and theoretical discourses of the present scene often spill over into each other, overlapping and diffusing, and frustrate any strictly genealogical tracing of movements. Indeed, the notion of large-scale movements of biblical studies (e.g., Form Criticism*§, the Myth and Ritual School*§, etc.) has, in many ways, been replaced by smaller pockets of activity, no doubt reflecting the dissemination of academic biblical training itself beyond the confines of a few dominant divinity school related institutions. What follows, therefore, is not a comprehensive glossary or exhaustive presentation of some unified "new literary criticism" of the Bible, which would be entirely fictional anyway, even if that presentation were narrowed to focus on any one particular "movement." Rather, the purpose is to open up, albeit only slightly, several key places, or topoi, of convergence in order to provide an overall sense of how literary theory and literary criticism have found their way into conversations with biblical studies (and sometimes vice-versa) and to encourage reflection on the immensity of challenges and possibilities introduced by these developments. (For a fuller engagement of issues concerning relations between recent literary theory and biblical criticism, see The Bible and Culture Collective 1995, which involves the work of both New Testament and Hebrew Bible critics, and S. Moore 1989, 1992, 1994 on New Testament criticism; for more traditional literary approaches, see R. Alter and F. Kermode 1987; D. Gunn 1987; Gunn and D. Fewell 1993; W. Kort 1988.)

Although this essay focuses on literary theory and the Bible, beginning in the 1960s and moving through the last three decades of the twentieth century, it is important to note that the Bible has been read in various ways that can be broadly defined as "literary." Indeed, until very recently scholarship focused on source criticism, and text history (in the wake of J. Wellhausen's "documentary hypothesis") was commonly called biblical "literary criticism." Also notable, and moving in very different directions, has been the well-known "Bible as literature" movement, which has roots at least as far back as the eighteenth-century scholar R. Lowth§ and which gained momentum during the first half of the twentieth century (see D. Norton 1993 and D. L. Jeffrey 1992). Although these and other earlier approaches are based on literary theory— insofar as they begin with certain assumptions about textuality, writing, and interpretation— only recently has explicit theoretical discourse or self-critical awareness of these assumptions been exposed by their critics.

Although the line is permeable, it is important to maintain some distinction between theory and method (see T. Beal 1992, 27-39). Literary theory is not literary-critical method and, in many cases, it cannot be easily translated into one. Methodology is inherently practical, aimed at developing a clear approach to and a way through a particular text or set of texts (Gr. *meta* + *hodos* = "with way" or "with road"). Such aims are not always shared by literary-theoretical discourses, especially in critical theory, which is associated with a kind of intransigent negativity, a "thinking the limits" of any particular construal of reality, textuality, literary history, meaning, etc. This kind of theoretical discourse stands in contrast to more constructive theories, which aim to develop a system of representation for understanding relations between authors, texts, and readers, among other things, and which therefore often lead to the development of an appropriate methodology. In neither critical theory nor more constructive theory, however, is there any single self-evident method to which a particular theory must be attached. Not all literary theory is practical in a methodological sense, a fact that has often been overlooked by biblical scholars. As a result, some theoretical discourses, especially those falling under the name "poststructuralism," often have been either negatively evaluated as confusing and unhelpful or forced into a practical approach aimed at saving biblical studies from its own current (perpetual?) identity crisis and/or at answering every critical question about some text or texts once and for all. Although we will be discussing both literary-critical methods and literary theory as they have pertained to biblical study, we will mostly defer from asserting any particular understanding of the relationship between the two, especially with regard to how particular theoretical discourses should or should not translate into particular literary-critical methodologies. Bibliographical references along the way will offer examples of how relations have been negotiated by particular biblical scholars. (For a more direct introduction to these relations, see S. McKenzie and S. Haynes 1993, esp. pt. 3, and A. Adam 1995.)

2. *J. Muilenburg's Rhetorical Criticism.* While contemporary literary methodological approaches to the Bible did not originate with Muilenburg[§], he offers a convenient starting point for a survey. Muilenburg was enormously influential as a writer and teacher, and his approach—which he called Rhetorical Criticism*[§]—produces the type of reading most commonly associated with recent literary criticism. The approach is set out most clearly in his 1968 Society of Biblical Literature[§] presidential address, "Form Criticism and Beyond" (published in 1969), although one can see it in practice in his writings from the mid-1950s on. Muilenburg argued that, while Form Criticism*[§] as a methodology is certainly crucial and must not be abandoned, there is a need for a focus on the rhetorical intentionality of biblical texts in their present literary form. Modeling the approach on poetic texts in the Hebrew Bible (Poetry, Hebrew Bible[‡§]), he suggested that the critic pay close attention to rhetorical markers (like shifts in speaker and the repetition of key words), which he believed give clues to the intentionality of the text itself.

Muilenburg's approach had clear affinities with formalism or, as it came to be known in the United States, "New Criticism" (see also the "rise of English" cultural movement in Great Britain during the first half of the 20th century, discussed in T. Eagleton 1983, 17-53). One of the basic theoretical points of New Criticism is that the meaning and intentionality of a text can be found through a close analysis of the text itself, without extensive research into questions of social, historical, and literary contexts. For example, one need not have knowledge of the psychological state or social circumstance of a poet or knowledge of cognate poetic texts from Ugarit[§] (see Translation*) in order to understand a poem. The poem, as a self-contained object of study, is all that is needed. Such an approach has often found greater appeal in biblical studies than in English literature studies because research into contexts of influence (political, cultural, environmental, literary, etc.) for biblical literature has been based largely on conjectures and hypotheses built from very limited and ever-changing bodies of data. In this regard, rhetorical criticism and other literary approaches have served as escape routes for many scholars and students in biblical studies who have been frustrated with the historical-critical hegemony that has characterized the field until the end of the twentieth century.

Muilenburg's influence on biblical criticism extended beyond his publications. Among his students were W. Brueggemann, E. Good, P. Trible, and F. Buechner—each of whom has taken Muilenburg's rhetorical criticism in new directions and influenced a new generation of graduate students and biblical scholars.

3. *Structuralism and Beyond.* Even as Muilenburg gave his SBL address in 1968, there were other conversations in the academy pertaining to literary theory and the Bible. By this time, for example, structuralist readings of biblical texts had begun to be produced, although mostly from outside the field of biblical studies and mostly by those interested in structural anthropology rather than structural linguistics (e.g., studies on family and genealogy in Genesis; Russian

160

formalism and folklore studies earlier in the twentieth century were also important precursive movements). In other intellectual circles, especially in continental Europe, literary-theoretical discourse was on the verge of a massive revolution due to major developments in Marxism, Feminist*§ theory, psychoanalysis (Psychoanalytic Interpretation*§), and linguistics. In 1967, for example, three major works appeared in French by the philosopher J. Derrida, the most well-known theorist of poststructuralism. Indeed, Derrida gave his first address in English at Johns Hopkins University in 1966, two years before Muilenburg's SBL address. Although these developments made no initial splash in biblical studies, the seismic reverberations from their entry into academic space has been felt among biblicists with greater intensity every year since. Some background in structural linguistics, which remains an important field in biblical studies, will provide a helpful entry into these other important literary-theoretical developments of the 1960s and 1970s.

Structuralism*§ (both within and without biblical studies) constitutes a diverse body of scholarship. The accessibility of the literature is hindered by its often arcane, thickly coded language. What characterizes all structural readings, however, is their debt to F. de Saussure's programmatic treatment of the sign (see below) in his posthumously published *Course in General Linguistics* (1959). Writing just after the turn of the century, Saussure set the grammar for much of twentieth-century scholarship in a variety of fields, including linguistics, psychoanalysis, philosophy, anthropology, and literary theory.

Saussure's fundamental insight was that the relationship between the signifier and the signified is arbitrary. To put it more simply, any word can be chosen to stand for any thing or concept: e.g., a "signified" is the thing we call a "tree" and the "signifier" is the four letters t-r-e-e, there being no necessary relationship between the letters and the object. What is important, then, is not the actual sound of the words or the marks on a page when it is written but, rather, the network of interrelationships in the particular linguistic system of which the word is a part. Structuralist research (in whatever field) is concerned, not with why a particular signifier is connected with a particular signified, but with how that signifier functions within the structure of a given system. This type of research became known as synchronic (concern for the workings of a single system) as opposed to diachronic (concern for the significance of language elements before, after, and outside the system through the history of language change and through study of cognate languages). Thus, structuralists search not so much for the meaning of a text as for the structures and patterns that make meaning possible. They aim to identify the "deep structures" that function like grammars to govern and determine meaning on the surface of the text and that tend to take the form of codes based on binary oppositions like inside/outside, margin/center, male/female, positive/negative, immanent/transcendent, life/death, etc. (Many structuralists have gone so far as to argue that human thought itself, and perhaps the human unconscious, is ordered by such a binary oppositional code.) Structural critics often rely on charts and diagrams that attempt to delineate the way different pieces of the text fit with one another.

Structuralist biblical criticism seeks to identify organizing codes within the deep structure of the text. The particular surface content of a narrative or poem is less important than whatever irreducible codes or structures one can locate beneath it. For example, a structuralist reading of the creation story in Genesis 1 identifies a number of binary oppositions reflected in the concern for division—light/dark, water/land, human/divine—culminating in the division between life and death. A similar analysis might then be made of Job's opening curse in Job 3; thus one might begin to see deeper connections between the two texts. M. Douglas's (1966) analysis of the dietary laws in Leviticus is one of the best examples of structuralist biblical criticism at work. She shows how the internal structuring principle of boundary maintenance (i.e., realms of water, land, and air) might be understood to establish a code for determining whether a particular creature is clean or unclean. Unclean animals are those perceived as anomalous insofar as they possess characteristics that cross over (literally, trans-gress) between two or more realms (e.g., a bird with wings that cannot fly, a sea creature with legs instead of fins, etc.). In New Testament studies, one finds prime examples of detailed structuralist readings in the work of D. Patte (1976). Structuralist exegesis experienced a flourish of popularity in the late 1970s and early 1980s (see, e.g., several of the early issues of *Semeia*) but now has few practitioners who would see themselves, strictly speaking, as structuralists.

While appropriating much of structuralism's language and many of its basic insights, the movement now known as poststructuralism nevertheless challenged some of the presuppositions of structuralist criticism. For example, while accepting Saussure's notion of the arbitrary nature of the sign, poststructuralist thought extends this insight so that meaning is not just a product of the structural relationships between signifiers but is rather endlessly deferred in the chain of signification. A signifier has meaning only in relation to another signifier, but this other signifier cannot serve as an anchor for meaning since it, too, is in relation to other signifiers. (To continue the example above, t-r-e-e refers to a plant with branches, leaves, and a trunk, but each of the words in the definition also refers to other words, ad infinitum.) Rather than a closed system of referral that one can master and work within, there is an open network of deferral over which mastery must remain elusive. Poststructuralism recognizes that structures of meaning are almost never complete and sufficient unto themselves. Instead, they tend to be incomplete and overlapping in nature, thus making their negotiation by the interpreter necessarily tentative.

Many scholars argue that structuralism anticipates its own beyond, its own "post-." Articulation of this point of view was perhaps best provided by Derrida but also by many others writing in the same intellectual circles and at roughly the same time, especially the so-called French feminists, the three most well-known of whom are J. Kristeva, L. Irigaray, and H. Cixous. None of these writers should be considered peripheral to the phenomenon of poststructuralism typically associated with Derrida. It is worth noting in this regard that Intertextuality*§, which has emerged as key in poststructuralist discourse, was first developed by Kristeva (see Beal 1992). In fact, structuralism's apprehension of its own post-, which is especially clear in its identification of binary codes involving sexual identity and sexual politics, is best exemplified in the writings of such scholars. As Kristeva (1993) suggests, structural (or semiotic) analysis is important for identifying the "systematic constraints" within a given piece of discourse, but one should not stop there; rather, one should then look for what "falls outside" the constraints of that system as well as for the system's rupture points (1986, 26-27). In this sense one might see S. de Beauvoir's classic analysis *The Second Sex* (1952)— which was highly influential on Kristeva, Irigaray, Cixous, and others— as an early structural analysis of how, in politics as in literature, "woman" has been constructed as man's "other" within a system of binary oppositional codes for sexual identity: self/not-self, subject/object, possession/lack (of a penis), transcendent/immanent, etc. This system, then, forms a Western patriarchal structure. The poststructuralist move made by Kristeva, Irigaray, Cixous, and others is to begin reading closely (even exegetically) for the problematic weak spots, slippages, and indeterminacies within this system that suggest its nonessential character (not biological, not ontological, etc.) and, therefore, its susceptibility to breakdown. The example is also important in showing that poststructuralism is by no means politically innocuous in relation to feminism, as many critics have falsely alleged.

Kristeva and Irigaray are informed by the linguistical approaches of Derrida and Saussure but are grounded in the psychoanalytical approach of J. Lacan, with his concept of language as the symbolic realm and as the realm of the Father (see J. Lacan 1977 and The Bible and Culture Collective 1995). Kristeva and Irigaray's critique of psychoanalytic discourse, which focuses on the ways language and the symbolic realm are structured around male sexual identity (implied in much of Beauvoir's analysis as well), is likewise best understood as poststructuralist (see esp. the opening essay in Irigaray 1985; in relation to biblical literature, see I. Rashkow 1993 and The Bible and Culture Collective 1995, 187-224). Although not explicitly engaged with recent literary theory, Trible's powerful and highly influential *God and the Rhetoric of Sexuality* (1978) may be best understood as a brilliant convergence of Muilenburgian rhetorical-critical exegesis with a concern for details within biblical literature that fall outside (and even work to subvert) the literature's overall "patriarchal stamp." This, in turn, attests to the force and continued life of rhetorical criticism, which, primarily by its close attention to the details (including the cracks and rupture points) of texts, can often call into question conclusions reached by cursory readings across the broader contours of biblical writings.

The most widely recognized name in poststructuralism is Derrida, who was also the first to use the word "deconstruction" (which, to his surprise, quickly gained a life and momentum of its own outside his writings). As noted above, three major publications of Derrida's came out in 1967 (ET *Speech and Phenomena* 1973, *Of Grammatology* 1977, and *Writing and Difference* 1978). While Derrida was by no means solely responsible for the development of poststructuralist thought, much of its basic orientation can be found in these three books, which should perhaps be supplemented by *Dissemination* (1972 [ET 1981]). It is striking that these classic texts of Derrida are primarily exegetical and are close engagements with philosophical and/or literary texts; so close, in fact, that one begins to see how the dominant structuring principles of the texts begin to expose their own problematics and even backfire. It is through attention to details—and refusal to overlook the ambiguities, tensions, puns, afterthoughts, etc., therein—that one is able to challenge the structuralist assumptions about the synchronic unity of systemic wholes.

Poststructuralist engagements of biblical texts began to appear only late in the twentieth century. A particularly lucid account of Derrida's theoretical approach is combined with a creative reading of Leviticus 10 in E. Greenstein's "Deconstruction and Biblical Narrative" (1985; Beal and T. Linafelt 1996 revisit the same text in connection with Derrida's *Cinders* 1979 [ET 1991]). Three issues of the journal *Semeia* have been devoted to Derrida and poststructuralism, edited by R. Detweiler (1982), G. Phillips (1990; see esp. Phillips's opening article), and D. Jobling and Moore (1992; see esp. Jobling's article, "Deconstruction and Political Analysis of Biblical Texts," 95-127). Very little book-length work by Hebrew Bible scholars has yet appeared. Especially noteworthy are those by M. Bal (1987, 1988a, 1988b), Jobling (1986), and Fewell and Gunn (1993). For interesting new theological directions in dialogue with poststructuralist theory, see also D. Blumenthal (1993), H. Eilberg-Schwartz (1994), and Linafelt (1996). Commentaries by P. Miscall (1993) and Good (1990) also make significant forays into poststructuralist writing. With respect to the New Testament, S. Moore has been most successful at putting poststructuralist writing into conversation with biblical criticism.

Especially with regard to Hebrew Bible studies, it is interesting to note the convergences between rabbinic traditions of Midrash§ and literary-theoretical discourse. S. Handelman (1982) makes a strong case that much of contemporary literary theory evidences an "emergence" of midrashic exegetical practices from the rabbinic period. In fact, many major figures in literary theory at the end of the twentieth century had Jewish backgrounds, and many of them have been explicitly concerned with questions of Jewish identity generally and biblical literature specifically (e.g., Derrida and Cixous). This connection is explored further in the collection of articles edited by G. Hartman and S. Budick (1986) and with a much tighter focus in D. Boyarin's (1990a) book on the relation between Midrash and poststructuralist theories of intertextuality.

4. *Other Directions.* E. Auerbach§ contrasted the art of biblical literature with the art of Homer by the following list of characteristics: "certain parts brought into high relief, others left obscure, abruptness, suggestive influence of the unexpressed, 'background' quality, multiplicity

of meanings and the need for interpretation, universal-historical claims, development of the concept of historically becoming, and preoccupation with the problematic" (1953, 23). One quickly recognizes that several characteristics—that which is left obscure, abruptness, influence of the unexpressed, background quality, multiplicity of meanings, and the need for interpretation—would be shared by engagements of biblical literature broadly understood as "poststructuralist." The emphasis on "things brought into high relief" and the idea that biblical narrative makes "universal-historical claims" (by which Auerbach referred to "its claim to absolute authority" as it seeks to "overcome our reality") have most often been shared by Narrative Criticism*[§]. When these characteristics are emphasized, the interpretation of the others in Auerbach's list often takes on very different significances, turning the scholar's attention away from what falls outside the constraints, as Kristeva put it, and toward the way these details that seem (on the surface) to be points of indeterminacy, gaps, and so forth might actually be part of the narrative's strategy to "claim" its authority over the reader (i.e., to constrain the reader from reading it wrongly).

Although generally narrative criticism covers a wide variety of approaches (nearly anything focused on the literary qualities and peculiarities of biblical narrative), here we refer to that brand of criticism that often draws its influence from early mid-twentieth-century works by Auerbach and N. Frye (1957, 1971) and from later works by H. Frei (1974) and A. Wilder (1991). Adherents of this approach read biblical narrative as artfully constructed, realistic historical fiction. To a great extent, narrative criticism came to prominence because of growing uneasiness with a prevalent historicism that tended to dissect the text. In contrast, narrative criticism focuses synchronically on the text and understands the biblical narrative as a construction of a "narrative world" to which the reader is subjected. In Hebrew Bible studies one may point to the narrative poetics of M. Sternberg (1985) and Alter (1981) as examples. Gunn helped to pioneer narrative criticism in his analysis of the stories of David and Saul in the books of Samuel and Kings; but, like many biblical scholars interested in relations between biblical literature and literary theory, he has since moved in directions more attuned to the questions and issues of poststructuralism. Fewell and Gunn (1991) offer a much-needed critique of Sternberg's approach (see Sternberg's counterattack 1992 and D. Boyarin's comparative analysis 1990).

In New Testament studies, this type of approach has proliferated, especially in readings of the Gospels and Acts. New Testament narrative critics have relied heavily on W. Booth's *The Rhetoric of Fiction* (1961) and S. Chatman's *Story and Discourse* (1978). Both authors investigate the way in which author and reader relate to each other, using the categories of real author/real reader, implied author/implied reader, and narrator/narratee. For instance, in *The Adventures of Huckleberry Finn*, Mark Twain is the real author, Huck is the narrator, and a third person who does not consider Huck completely reliable is the implied author. A particular person is the real reader, someone who is with Huck is the narratee, and someone who takes Huck's words with a grain of salt is the implied reader. Booth's delineation of these categories with Chatman's subsequent refinement serves as the background for a vast amount of New Testament scholarship.

Not only does narrative criticism investigate how the text works by asking questions about these narrative levels, it also focuses on such traditional topics as character, plot, and setting. Narrative critics tend to read the Bible as literature and, unlike source or redactional critics, assume that the texts are unified rather than discontinuous. Historical questions, though not ignored, are secondary to questions about the flow and structure of the story. (For a discussion of where narrative criticism has been and suggestions for how it might evolve, see Gunn's article in McKenzie and Haynes 1993.)

Another important and highly productive interdisciplinary literary engagement has been between biblical studies and philosophical Hermeneutics*§. Although the term "hermeneutics" has come to connote interpretation in general, it specifically designates a philosophy of interpretation (nurtured primarily in Germany during the nineteenth century) that gradually gained influence throughout Europe and the Americas during the latter half of the twentieth century. F. Schleiermacher§ is often considered the father of hermeneutics, and other major figures include W. Dilthey§, E. Husserl, M. Heidegger, H. G. Gadamer, and P. Ricoeur§. Each of these scholars explored the dynamics of the hermeneutical circle in which an interpreter with certain experiences and questions approaches a text. The text then addresses the reader and answers those questions, causing the reader to reformulate his or her way of framing those questions. Each time the reader reads the text, this interaction between reader and text occurs, creating a circular dynamism. This approach to and explanation of the mechanics of interpretation usually focuses on the overall meaning of texts rather than on specific details; hermeneuticians are interested in what the text means, not what it says. The most prominent New Testament scholar of the twentieth century, R. Bultmann§, provides one of the best examples of an exegete influenced by philosophical hermeneutics. His project of demythologizing—seeking the meaning of the text underneath the clothing of mythical language (Mythology and Biblical Studies*§)—fits within the larger stream of hermeneutics. Perhaps the most thorough engagement of philosophical hermeneutics in biblical scholarship is that of A. Thiselton (1992; see also D. Bryant 1989).

Somewhat related to both narrative criticism and philosophical hermeneutics is Reader-response Criticism*§. Although using many of the same categories as narrative criticism, Reader-response Criticism, as the name implies, highlights the reader instead of the text. Reader-response has its roots in German reception theory (especially H. Jauss and W. Iser) and in American pragmatism. The leading figure of reader-response criticism in North America is S. Fish, who has most vigorously argued that the reader completely creates the meaning of a text. Few biblical critics have destabilized the independence of the text as much as he. A reader-response critic will strive to show how the reader reacts to a character rather than how that character develops in the story; the reader replaces the text as a primary locus of meaning. Of course, reader-response theorists will disagree on the extent of the reader's shaping influence (Fish 1980). Most biblical scholars who focus on the reader still allow that the text has a certain autonomy, but they maintain that it also needs a reader to fill in the gaps. Some of J. D. Crossan's work on the Parables†§ (1980) uses insights from reader-response theory to show how the reader/hearer helps to create the meaning of parables (Ricoeur 1975). R. Fowler (1991) has both employed reader-response theory and pointed out some of its shortcomings through studies of Mark. Moore provides a helpful introductory discussion of reader-response theory and biblical studies (1989, 71-130; cf. The Bible and Culture Collective 1995, 20-69), while E. Conrad's Reading Isaiah (1991) is an example of reader-response analysis of Hebrew Bible texts. J. Darr (1992) and K. Pfisterer Darr (1994) draw especially from Iser's writings and focus particularly on the intertextual field that the original author(s) would have expected readers to know. The most important contribution of this genre of literary theory has been its focus on the dynamics of reading, which encourages self-critical awareness of assumptions about relations between texts, readers, and "reading communities."

Future possibilities are innumerable and beyond prediction. More than anything, it is hoped that the engagement of literary theory and criticism will enable biblical studies to find its way out of what has often been its own self-made ghetto of extreme disciplinary specialization and into larger academic and intellectual conversations, which have too often both given religious texts a central place and have caricatured them and made simplistic assumptions regarding them.

Bibliography: A. K. M. Adam, *What Is Postmodern Biblical Criticism?* (1995). **R. Alter,** *The Art of Biblical Narrative* (1981). **R. Alter and F. Kermode** (eds.), *The Literary Guide to* *the Bible* (1987). **E. Auerbach,** *Mimesis: The Representation of Reality in Western Literature* (1946, 1959²; ET 1953). **M. Bal,** *Lethal Love: Feminist Literary Readings of Biblical Love Stories* (1987); *Death and Dissymmetry: The Politics of Coherence in the Book of Judges* (1988*a*); *Murder and Difference: Gender, Genre, and Scholarship on Sisera's Death* (1988*b*). **T. K. Beal,** "Glossary" and "Ideology and Intertextuality," *Reading Between Texts: Intertextuality and the HB* (ed. D. N. Fewell, 1992) 21-24, 27-39. **T. K. Beal and T. Linafelt,** "Sifting for Cinders: Strange Fires in Lev 10:1-5," *Semeia 69/70* (1995) 19-32. **S. de Beauvoir,** *The Second Sex* (1949; ET 1952). Bible and Culture Collective, *The Postmodern Bible* (1995). **D. Blumenthal,** *Facing the Abusing God: A Theology of Protest* (1993). **W. Booth,** *The Rhetoric of Fiction* (1961). **D. Boyarin,** *Intertextuality and the Reading of Midrash* (1990*a*); "The Politics of Biblical Narratology: Reading the Bible Like/As a Woman," *Diacritics 20* (1990*b*) 31-42. **W. Brueggemann,** "The 'Baruch Connection': Reflections on Jer 43:1-7," *JBL* (1994) 405-20. **D. Bryant,** *Faith and the Play of Imagination: On the Role of Imagination in Religion* (1989). **S. Chatman,** *Story and Discourse: Narrative Structure in Fiction and Film* (1978). **E. W. Conrad,** *Reading Isaiah* (1991). **J. D. Crossan,** *Cliffs of Fall: Paradox and Polyvalence in the Parables of Jesus* (1980). **J. A. Darr,** *On Character Building: The Reader and the Rhetoric of Characterization in Luke-Acts* (1992). **K. P. Darr,** *Isaiah's Vision and the Family of God* (1994). **J. Derrida,** *Speech and Phenomena* (1967; ET 1973); *Of Grammatology* (1967; ET 1977); *Writing and Difference* (1967; ET 1978); *Dissemination* (1972; ET 1981); *Cinders* (1979; ET 1991). Good, *In Turns of Tempest: A Reading of Job, with a Translation* (1990). **R. Detweiler** (ed.), *Derrida and Biblical Studies* (*Semeia* 23, 1982). **M. Douglas,** *Purity and Danger: An Analysis of Concepts of Pollution and Taboo* (1966). **T. Eagleton,** *Literary Theory: An Introduction* (1983). **H. Eilberg-Schwartz,** *God's Phallus and Other Problems for Men and Monotheism* (1994). **D. N. Fewell and D. M. Gunn,** "Tipping the Balance: Sternberg's Reader and the Rape of Dinah," *JBL 110* (1991) 193-211; *Gender, Power, and Promise: The Subject of the Bible's First Story* (1993). **S. Fish,** *Is There a Text in This Class? The Authority of Interpretive Communities* (1980). **R. Fowler,** *Let the Reader Understand: Reader-response Criticism and the Gospel of Mark* (1991); "Who Is the Reader in Reader-response Criticism?" *Semeia 31* (1985) 31-53. **H. Frei,** *The Eclipse of Biblical Narrative: A Study in Eighteenth and Nineteenth Century Hermeneutics* (1974). **N. Frye,** *Anatomy of Criticism: Four Essays* (1957); *The Criticial Path: An Essay on the Social Context of Literary Criticism* (1971); *The Great Code: The Bible and Literature* (1982). **E. Greenstein,** "Deconstruction and Biblical Narrative," *Proof 9* (1989) 43-71. **D. M. Gunn,** "New Directions in the Study of Biblical Hebrew Narrative," *JSOT 39* (1987) 65-75. **D. M. Gunn and D. N. Fewell,** *Narrative in the HB* (1993). **S. Handelman,** *The Slayers of Moses: The Emergence of Rabbinic Interpretation in Modern Literary Theory* (1982). **G. Hartman and S. Budick** (eds.), *Midrash and Literature* (1986). **L. Irigaray,** *Speculum of the Other Woman* (1974; ET 1985). **D. Jasper** and **S. Prickett** (eds.), *The Bible and Literature: A Reader* (1999). **D. L. Jeffrey,** *The Dictionary of Biblical Tradition in English Literature* (1992). **D. Jobling,** *The Sense of Biblical Narrative: Structural Analysis in the HB* (vols. 1 and 2 1986). **D. Jobling and S. D. Moore** (eds.), *Poststructuralism as Exegesis* (*Semeia* 54, 1992). **W. Kort,** *Story, Text, and Scripture: Literary Interests in Biblical Narrative* (1988). **J. Kristeva,** "The System and the Speaking Subject," *The Kristeva Reader* (ed. T. Moi, 1986) 25-33. **J. Lacan,** *Ecrits: A Selection* (1977). **T. Linafelt,** "The Undecidability of BRK in the Prologue to Job and Beyond," *BibInt 4* (1996) 154-72. **S. L. McKenzie and S. R. Haynes,** *To Each Its Own Meaning: An Introduction to Biblical Criticisms and Their Application* (1993). **P. Miscall,** *Isaiah* (1993). **S. D. Moore,** *Literary Criticism and the Gospels* (1989); *Mark and Luke in Poststructuralist Perspectives: Jesus Begins to Write* (1992); *Poststructuralism and the NT: Derrida and Foucault at the Foot of the Cross* (1994). **J. Muilenburg,** "Form Criticism and Beyond," *JBL 88* (1969) 1-18.

D. Norton, *A History of the Bible as Literature* (2 vols. 1993). **D. Patte,** *What Is Structural Exegesis?* (1976). **G. A. Phillips** (ed.), *Poststructural Criticism and the Bible: Text/History/ Discourse* (*Semeia* 51, 1990). **I. N. Rashkow,** *The Phallacy of Genesis: A Feminist-Psychoanalytic Approach* (1993). **P. Ricoeur,** "Biblical Hermeneutics," *Semeia* 4 (1975) 29-148. **F. de Saussure,** *Course in General Linguistics* (ed. C. Bally, A. Sechehaye, and A. Reidlinger, 1959). **M. Sternberg,** *The Poetics of Biblical Narrative: Ideological Literature and the Drama of Reading* (1985); "Biblical Poetics and Sexual Politics," *JBL* 111 (1992) 463-88. **A Thiselton,** *New Horizons in Hermeneutics: The Theory and Practice of Transforming Biblical Reading* (1992). **A. N. Wilder,** *The Bible and the Literary Critic* (1991).

T. K. BEAL, K. A. KEEFER, AND T. LINAFELT

LITERARY AND STRUCTURALIST/
POSTMODERNIST APPROACHES METHODS

Narrative Criticism

Narrative criticism focuses on stories in biblical literature and attempts to read these stories with insights drawn from the secular field of modern Literary*§ criticism. The method is eclectic, drawing from such related fields as Structuralism*§ and Rhetorical Criticism*§, with the goal of determining the effects the stories are expected to have on their audiences.

Narrative critics grant that biblical stories may function referentially as records of significant history but insist that they also function poetically to fire the imagination, provoke repentance, inspire worship, and so forth. An oft-cited metaphor suggests that historical criticism treats biblical narratives as windows that enable readers to learn something about another time and place, while narrative criticism treats these same texts as mirrors that invite audience participation in the creation of meaning. For the narrative critic, texts shape the way readers understand themselves and their present circumstances.

Narrative criticism is also viewed as compatible with Reader-response Criticism*§, although it is distinct from this discipline as well. Typically, reader-response methods focus on ways in which interpretation of a text may be shaped to fit the interests or circumstances of diverse readers. Without denying these interpretative possibilities, narrative criticism attempts to determine how various signals within a text guide readers in deciding what the text means. In practice, the two approaches often appear to be in conflict, but the distinction is primarily one of degree and emphasis. Only the most extreme reader-response critic would maintain that texts offer no guidance for interpretation, and only the most extreme narrative critic would deny that individual readers make contributions to the interpretative process.

A common paradigm that clarifies these distinctions describes historical criticism as "author-oriented," reader-response criticism as "audience-oriented," and narrative criticism as "text-oriented." The latter orientation is evident in two key constructs of narrative criticism: the "implied author" (or author as known from the text) and the "implied reader" (or audience presupposed by the text).

Narrative criticism seeks to interpret texts with reference to their implied authors rather than with reference to their actual, historical authors. By "implied author," narrative critics mean the perspective from which the work appears to have been written, a perspective that must be reconstructed by readers on the basis of what they find in the narrative. In secular studies, the concept of implied authors was first developed by critics who wished to interpret stories without reference to anything extrinsic to the text itself. They claimed that biographical information concerning the author's agenda or personality should not be imposed on the story. Thus modern readers may know that Jonathan Swift was concerned with the relations of Protestants and Catholics in Ireland, but since this issue is not explicitly addressed in *Gulliver's Travels* the meaning of that work should not be circumscribed by so limited an application. In fact, in literary studies, a "classic" is by definition a work that continues to be meaningful in times and places that were not originally envisioned by the historical author.

The concept of implied authors is significant for interpreting works that have multiple authors or that are anonymous. Even a work that has no real author—such as a tale that developed over a period of time as it was passed down from generation to generation—can be studied according to the perspective of its implied author. Regardless of the process through which a narrative comes into being, it will always evince particular values, beliefs, and perceptions that can be described as representative of its implied author. For biblical narrative critics, then, the identification of various source documents (J, E, D, P) that were eventually woven together to form the book of Genesis is largely irrelevant. Narrative critics are not interested in discerning the historical reliability or theological agenda of source strata that lie behind the text but in determining the effect that the text as it now stands has on readers.

To be more precise, narrative criticism seeks to determine the expected effects of stories on implied readers without taking into account all of the possible effects that they may have on actual readers. The concept of implied readers parallels that of implied authors. Implied readers are those who actualize the potential for meaning in texts, who respond to texts in ways consistent with the expectations ascribed to their implied authors. This approach often defines meaning with less specificity than a historical concern for how a document was intended to affect its original audience. If the original readers of *Gulliver's Travels* were intended to draw lessons from the story regarding a specific crisis, the implied readers are expected to draw lessons appropriate to analogous crises in their own situation, to discern how the story's satirical message concerning the foolishness of war applies to them. Thus narrative criticism is generally more open to polyvalence (plurality of meaning) than is historical criticism, although the idea of implied readers places limits on this concept. An interpretation of Swift's story that failed to regard it as a satire and understood it instead as a literal historical report would lie outside the range of what would be expected for its implied readers.

A common misunderstanding of narrative criticism holds that the discipline somehow privileges the perspective of implied readers such that expected readings are "right" and unexpected readings "wrong." This is not necessarily true. Most narrative critics would grant that texts may legitimately come to affect people in unexpected ways. The reception of *Gulliver's Travels* as an entertaining children's story probably constitutes an unexpected reading, but few critics would want to say children are wrong to enjoy the story at a level other than that on which it was intended to be received. Likewise, many Christians will defend christological interpretations of Hebrew Bible texts as valid unexpected readings. The point in distinguishing expected and unexpected readings is to increase the self-awareness of the interpreter. The concept of implied readers is a heuristic construct that allows critics to limit the subjectivity of their analysis by distinguishing between their own responses to a narrative and those that the text appears to invite. Thus, the textually constructed implied reader may serve a function analogous to that of a control group in a scientific experiment. Readers may compare their own responses to a text with those that seem to be expected of its implied readers and then seek to explain any divergences.

In exploring the expected effects of texts on their implied readers, narrative critics make some assumptions about a normative process of reading. They assume, for instance, that the narrative is to be read sequentially and completely with all of its parts being related to the work as a whole. Thus the expected effects of the biblical story of David and Goliath (1 Sam 17) cannot be determined by considering the passage as an isolated pericope but only by considering the role the passage plays in the entire narrative. Readers may also be assumed to desire consistency and to make connections necessary to resolve apparent tensions within a text in favor of the most consistent interpretation.

A normative process of reading also assumes that readers know certain things. To determine the effects that Matthew's Gospel is expected to have on its readers we must assume that these readers know what a Pharisee is, what a centurion does, how much a denarius is worth, and so forth. On the other hand, the determination of the expected effects of a work is often contingent upon assuming the readers do not know certain things. Readers of Mark's Gospel, for instance, are not expected to have read the Gospel of Matthew, and, therefore, the implied readers of Mark's Gospel do not think of JESUS as one who has been born of a virgin.

In the same vein, narrative criticism interprets stories from the perspective of readers who accept the beliefs and values that undergird those stories. Normative reading involves an implicit contract by which readers agree to accept the dynamics of the story world that are established by the implied author. If a story features talking animals or flying spaceships, readers are expected to suspend their disbelief and to accept that, in this story, that is the way things are. In the story world of the Bible, God speaks audibly from heaven, fantastic miracles are commonplace, and human beings interact freely with spiritual creatures like angels and demons. Narrative criticism is not interested in questioning the accuracy of such reports or in determining what historical occurrences might have inspired the tales. Rather, the expected effects of the stories can only be determined if we adopt the perspective of readers who accept these and other elements of the story as real, or at least real within the world of the story. Since narrative criticism demands that texts be interpreted from the faith perspective their readers are assumed to evince, narrative critics may be required to focus their imagination in the opposite direction of that required for historical critics. Whereas historical critics may be expected to suspend faith commitments temporarily in order to interpret texts from the perspective of objective, disinterested historians, narrative critics may be expected to adopt faith commitments temporarily in order to determine how texts are expected to affect their implied readers.

In practice, narrative criticism is a complex process that calls for attention to numerous literary dynamics. For convenience, narrative critics usually speak of stories as consisting of events, characters, and settings. They also pay a great deal of attention to what is called the "discourse" of a narrative—that is, the rhetoric through which the story is told.

"Events" are simply the incidents or happenings that occur within a story. The order in which a narrative relates events is important because readers are expected to consider each new episode in light of what has gone before. Sometimes narratives report events "out of order," by presenting flashbacks concerning what happened earlier (Mark 6:17-29) or by including predictions or allusions that foreshadow what is still to come (Luke 2:34-35). Likewise, the duration or frequency of an event, as well as the amount of space given to reporting it, or the number of times it is referenced in the narrative may indicate its significance. Narrative critics are particularly interested in discerning links between events, indications that one event caused another to happen or at least made the occurrence of a subsequent event possible or likely. Furthermore, the extent to which events contribute to the development or resolution of conflict may be of utmost importance. Practically all narratives contain elements of conflict that drive the plot and involve the readers in adjudication of opposing tendencies.

"Characters" are the actors in the story, and the manner in which they are presented is especially significant for determining the effect the narrative is expected to have on its readers. Characters may be flat and predictable like the Pharisees in most of our gospel stories, or they may exhibit a wide variety of traits, like Jesus' disciples, who are presented as enlightened in one instance and as lacking insight in another. Characters may remain pretty much the same throughout the narrative, or they may develop and change in response to what transpires as the story progresses. Readers' perceptions concerning characters may be shaped by comments from the narrator; by reports of the characters' own words, deeds, or perceptions; or by reports of the words, deeds, or perceptions of others.

"Settings" are the spatial, temporal, and social locations for events. Readers may respond differently to a story if an event occurs on a mountain or in a boat, on a Sabbath or at a wedding, in private or in a crowd. In the Bible, settings are often fraught with symbolic meaning. The Jordan River, for example, becomes an apt symbol for entrance into the Promised Land.

Attention to a narrative's discourse includes recognition of what is called "point of view." Narratives typically present diverse perspectives concerning what is transpiring in the story, and readers are expected to regard some of these as more reliable than others. In biblical narratives, the point of view of God is normative for truth, and the perspective of the narrators is always reliable. When God declares that Jesus is "my Son, the Beloved" (Luke 3:22) or when the narrator of Luke's Gospel says that Jesus is "full of the Holy Spirit" (Luke 4:1), readers are not expected to wonder whether these things are really so. Similarly, the perspectives of angels, prophets (Prophecy and Prophets‡†§), and Jesus himself are all shown to be reliable in the Gospel of Luke because they always concur with the point of view evinced by God and by the narrator. But when the crowds proclaim that Jesus is a prophet (Luke 7:16) readers may be expected to regard this point of view with some ambiguity, for the crowds also think he is John the Baptist risen from the dead, a point of view that is clearly wrong (Luke 9:7, 19).

   Narrative critics also study the use of such rhetorical devices as symbolism, irony, structural patterns, and Intertextuality*§ (the citation of one text within another). By paying attention to such literary cues, they believe they are able to determine with some accuracy the effects that biblical literature is expected to have on its implied readers.

Bibliography: R. **Alter,** *The Art of Biblical Narrative* (1981). **A. Berlin,** *Poetics and Interpretation of Biblical Narrative* (Bible and Literature Series 9, 1983). **R. W. Funk,** *The Poetics of Biblical Narrative* (Foundations and Facets, 1988). **J. D. Kingsbury** (ed.), *Gospel Interpretation: Narrative-critical and Social-scientific Approaches* (1997). **E. McKnight,** *The Bible and the Reader: An Introduction to Literary Criticism* (1985). **P. D. Miscall,** "Introduction to Narrative Literature," *NIB* (1998) 2:539-52. **S. Moore,** *Literary Criticism and the Gospels: The Theoretical Challenge* (1989). **M. A. Powell,** *What Is Narrative Criticism?* (GBS, NT Series, 1990). **M. A. Powell, C. Gray, and M. Curtis,** *The Bible and Modern Literary Criticism: A Critical Assessment and Annotated Bibliography* (BIRS 22, 1992). **M. Sternberg,** *The Poetics of Biblical Narrative: Ideological Literature and the Drama of Reading* (ISBL, 1985).

M. A. POWELL

LITERARY AND STRUCTURALIST/
POSTMODERNIST APPROACHES METHODS

Postmodern Biblical Interpretation

There is no singular method that can be called "postmodern biblical interpretation," no singular approach, no singular paradigm. Indeed, the impulse to provide a definition for this nonentity introduces a problematic asymmetry in a dictionary that does not also define and delimit "modern biblical interpretation." If, under duress, one were obliged to approximate a definition for postmodern biblical criticism, one would have to characterize it as the practice of resisting and recentering the assumptions and norms of modern biblical interpretation.

For instance, modern biblical interpretation has typically assumed that time is of the essence in biblical criticism. Time marks the biblical text as ancient, foreign, past, and thereby obliges interpreters (marked in time as "modern" or "contemporary") to adopt academically approved methods to bridge the chronological gulf that separates interpreters from their biblical text. Time also marks specific interpretations in a way that favors the most recent efforts at bridging the abyss. The first of these assumptions rests on the premise that the passage of years generates a gap in understanding between past and present that only academic interpreters can address.

This gap, however, does not exist of itself (otherwise, introductory courses would not have to work hard to inculcate historical-critical sensibilities in students); on the contrary, the succession of commentators, interpreters, and communities of worship establishes broad avenues of continuity between past and present. The existence of a chronological "gap" or a continuous "treasury" depends on the assumptions one brings to bear on interpretation, not on a supposedly natural or necessary condition of temporality. The second assumption is persuasive to the extent that one is already committed to its truth, but it rings hollow to interpreters who hold a different repertoire of interpretive assumptions. How would one prove that contemporary interpretations (various as they are) of Genesis 2–3 are truer than earlier efforts or that they mark a clear progress beyond previous interpretations, especially to someone who does not share modern assumptions about progress?

The myth of progress figures among the "metanarratives" of which postmodern interpreters are dubious. Under the banner of progress (whether that progress aims toward the triumph of liberal democracy and the free market, that of the industrial proletariat, or that of the chosen people of God), dominant social groups have ridden roughshod over reticent dissenters. The modern claim that casualties are necessary in the cause of progress, in the name of the greater good that modernity promises, sounds unconvincing to postmodern ears. Modern critics see no reason to attend to indigenous, "primitive," or simply naive interpretive priorities, except as quaint illustrations of inferior hermeneutical understandings (Hermeneutics*§). One could even read the later history of biblical criticism as a struggle for hegemony between the theological metanarratives and the metanarrative of Enlightenment rationality's commitment to scientific inquiry. Representatives of each camp anathematize their opponents as "heretics" or "fundamentalists"; in contrast, the postmodern observer can opt out of such sterile conflicts by noting that the opposing parties derive their legitimation from their respective metanarratives. Rather than living out the dictates of an imperious metanarrative (and excoriating anyone who presumes to live by another metanarrative), the postmodern biblical interpreter may follow a particular line of interpretation because it displays hitherto unnoticed aspects of the biblical text, because it would be useful for one purpose or another, or simply because it is interesting.

A further way that time defines modern biblical criticism is by tempting interpreters to parse the history of interpretation into constituent periods. The "post-" in postmodern sometimes incites scholars to assume that postmodern interpretation has to take place after modern interpretation, consigning modern criticism to a rubble heap of obsolete worldviews much as modernity relegates ancient perspectives to its own closet of intellectual bad dreams. Postmodern biblical interpretation does not surpass, improve, perfect, contravene, or undermine modern biblical interpretation except when modern interpreters claim the exclusive prerogative to determine interpretive legitimacy on their own modern terms. The impulse to regard postmodernity as a period among others, as an innovation that improves the endeavor of biblical interpretation, partakes of the modern attraction to everything novel and the modern inclination to characterize projects as a succession of phases, each refining its predecessors. Likewise, the advent of postmodern criticism need not represent a new, improved stage in the history of biblical interpretation; modernity thrives on novelty and supersession, whereas a postmodern sensibility can coexist with its alternatives. Debates over whether the postmodern era has begun (or is over or will never start) occlude the extent to which a particular body of critics is actually practicing postmodern interpretation and others are comfortably working out premodern interpretations.

Modern biblical critics likewise typically assume that highly trained biblical scholars possess a unique authority for propounding legitimate interpretations. "Don't try this at home," they warn would-be Bible readers, "lest you fall prey to the inevitable pitfalls that await insufficiently trained readers." This interpretive elitism fits the broader modern inclination to define proper fields of expertise by distinguishing them from other fields and limiting the expert's attention to matters pertinent to the proper field. (Even when modern biblical interpreters devise "new" or "interdisciplinary" approaches they deploy these supposed novelties in the interest of familiar modern ends: the quest for sources, the identities of the historical actors, the authors' attitudes, and so on.)

Modern biblical interpretation thus fosters a cult of expertise that demands interpretive authority far out of proportion to plausible justification of that authority; while we may see an overwhelming basis for advanced training in (for instance) brain surgery, the necessity of doctoral training in biblical interpretation is less clear. Although the traditional curriculum for expertise in biblical studies is undeniably helpful, its narrow focus has constricted the discourse of biblical interpretation in noteworthy ways. Perhaps most obviously, modern conventions have restricted the genres of biblical interpretation that critics deem legitimate. "Legitimate" biblical interpretation is exclusively discursive and is limited to very few varieties of discourse (preeminently, the commentary and the monograph). Whereas one might once have promulgated academically respectable interpretation in a sermon, now this relatively conventional genre is vulnerable to the suspicion of theological ideology; more unusual media for biblical interpretation—poetry, sculpture, video, graphical representation—need not even hope for an academic *nihil obstat*. Modern biblical experts simply have not been trained to evaluate such interpretations and consider such efforts at best as "soft" or "unscientific," if they consider them at all.

One further characteristic of modern biblical experts is the adherence to norms—usually unstated—of univocity, objectivity, and universality. Though the number of scholars who adhere publicly to the notion that biblical interpretations can be objective or universally true has probably diminished, there remains a strongly committed core of interpreters who promote the notion that there is one legitimate meaning to each textual unit, that the single legitimate meaning is encoded in the text, and that this meaning remains the same in all circumstances. Modern interpreters' commitment to this goal provides one reason why they so bitterly oppose anything that smacks of the allegorical interpretation by which other interpreters have found many legitimate meanings for each text.

By contrast, postmodern interpreters who have learned their lessons in deconstruction (Structuralism and Deconstruction*§) suspect that any univocity is the product of an interpretive violence that suppresses ambiguity by a will to unity. Such modern assumptions ground the lingering sense that politically active interpreters (say, proponents of lesbian/gay interests) propound interpretations that impose an alien context on the true meaning of the text. Yet postmodern interpreters can comfortably remind their modern colleagues that all interpreters are ideologically entangled (Ideological Criticism*§); the principal difference is that the dominant ideology has the privilege of making a pretense of objectivity. Whenever social groups change, the standards of objectivity change with them. When modern interpreters profess to seek, not an illusory objectivity, but a more attainable approximation thereof, they run the danger of aggravating the very problem they are trying to avoid. With this gesture they congratulate themselves both for avoiding a discredited positivism and for avoiding partisan advocacy.

In sum, modern biblical criticism reflects the tacit knowledge by which generations of critics have progressed from naiveté to the sophistication that enables them to distinguish exegesis (which allegedly "leads out" the meaning from the text) from eisegesis (which "reads in" the meaning an interpreter is already looking for). Postmodern biblical interpretation, on the other hand, flouts the received wisdom of the discipline in the interest of learning those things that modern criticism will not reveal. Postmodern biblical critics operate with a different tacit knowledge. They may know that time is not an absolute horizon for interpretation, that biblical interpretations vary from place to place and time to time without necessarily progressing, or that expertise in interpretation may come from imaginative faculties that have not been certified at the bar of higher education. In all these cases, modern biblical critics typically respond by claiming that if one disregards the modern criteria for interpretation, no criteria at all will remain—the result will be hermeneutical anarchy. Modern critics disregard the fact that criteria are always inescapably immanent to the audiences, institutions, and social formations within which nonmodern interpreters propose their readings.

Postmodern interpreters may enact their freedom from the tyranny of time in any number of ways. They may sit loose to the modern imperative that distinguishes ancient past from hypermodern present, treating Paul†§ as a contemporary to M. Foucault, characterizing the Gospels in terms translucent to today's concerns, or articulating the persistent traces of the past that live on in present aspects of the Bible. In doing so, they do not so much ignore the differences between past and present as they mark those chronological differences as bearing less importance than the lines of continuity they can draw, the urgency of identifying the relevance of a biblical text, or the intriguing conclusions they can weave out of discursive threads from many times.

Postmodern interpreters who have been freed from the tyranny of time and the obligation to ascertain single, universal meanings may find that these related amnesties permit them to understand the history of interpretation differently. Since interpretation involves the task of explaining that which is less well-known in terms that are better-known, postmodern interpreters may view each chapter in the history of interpretation as a species of allegorical interpretation whereby Christians have brought the Bible into engagement with the particular concerns of their cultures. At times, those concerns have involved the legitimacy of early Christianity as a movement (which elicited an emphasis on topological connections between the Hebrew Bible and the New Testament); the resolution of doctrinal disputes (which encouraged allegorical exegeses to enlist the Bible as a witness on behalf of dogmatic concerns); the historical accuracy of the biblical accounts (which stimulated interpretations that identify particular figures and sayings in the Bible with particular figures and interests in the histories of Israel and of the first Christian generation); or the individual's growth toward moral and spiritual integrity (which interpreted the Bible as a sourcebook for legal or ethical reasoning). If the formal quality of interpretation is thus always allegorical, a postmodern interpreter is in a much stronger position to appreciate and learn from earlier interpreters than would be a critic who participates in the modern critics' resolute resistance to and defamation of allegory.

Further, postmodern interpreters may productively disregard the modern norms that restrict interpretation to discursive genres. Although such interpretations might not readily be judged by strictly modern criteria, reviewers could draw on the critical wisdom relative to the genre in question to supply what is lacking in the modern repertoire. A film representation of the Davidic monarchy would not be answerable simply to the customary questions relative to historicity, anachronism, verisimilitude, and scholarly integrity, but would also be answerable for the quality of lighting, staging, direction, acting, and soundtrack. A modern critic might wince at the thought that exquisite casting and a compelling soundtrack could redeem a filmed interpretation that fell short of a perfectly accurate historical interpretation, but a postmodern critic could articulate a judgment that took account of more dimensions than only the historical foundations.

The work of S. Moore stands as a prominent example of postmodern criticism in practice. (No single practitioner of postmodern Hebrew Bible criticism has emerged as prominently as Moore, though M. Bal, T. Beal, J. C. Exum, and T. Linafelt all have made significant contributions.) Moore's interpretations cross the disciplinary divisions that define the limits of critical-biblical inquiry, reverse relations of temporal priority to illuminate the writing of the New Testament authors, and set biblical rhetoric in the frame of various contemporary discourses, from deconstruction to post-Freudian psychoanalysis (Psychoanalytic Interpretation*§) to bodybuilding. His work moves comfortably from the judgments of modern exegetes to quotations from tabloid papers back to the biblical text. In *Mark and Luke in Poststructualist Perspectives: Jesus Begins to Write* (1992), Moore conducts a seminar among the two evangelists, modern biblical scholars, J. Lacan, J. Derrida, Plato, and James Joyce, with cameo appearances by countless other noteworthies. *Poststructuralism and the New Testament* (1994) sketches a Derridean perspective on John and a Foucauldian exploration of the theology of the cross. *God's Gym* (1996) interweaves the biblical discussions of God's body and the body of Christ with bodybuilders' observations on their own field. Although Moore's contributions do little or nothing to advance the cause of modern biblical scholarship—as modern scholars' consternation at his work shows—he has shown the ballroom dancers of the biblical guild that "there's a whole lot of shakin' goin' on" in other venues. Where the modern judges of biblical scholarship may thunder, "There are no new steps!" Moore's extravagant *pasa doble* demonstrates that biblical interpretation cannot be constricted to modernity's mannered rumba.

Biblical scholars will not all adopt a markedly postmodern perspective, nor will most postmodern interpreters restrict their interpretive practice to obviously postmodern efforts. In this sense, postmodernism will not take hold in biblical criticism—at least not in the foreseeable future. More important, however, the field has already registered the impact of postmodern biblical criticism as claims about determinancy, universality, univocity, and legitimacy sound increasingly muted and defensive. As generations of scholars who are accustomed to postmodern sensibilities enter the field of biblical criticism, the field should change from a hegemony of modern authority to a networked, postmodern polyphony of interpreters whose interests and works emphasize different interpretive practices—an appropriately postmodern development.

Bibliography: **A. K. M. Adam,** "The Future of Our Allusions," *SBLSPS* (1992) 5-13; *What Is Postmodern Biblical Criticism?* (1995); "Twisting to Destruction: A Memorandum on the Ethics of Interpretation," *PRSt 23* (1996) 215-22. **G. Aichele,** "On Postmodern Biblical Criticism and Exegesis," *Forum 5, 3* (1985) 31-35. **J. C. Anderson and S. Moore** (eds.), *Mark and Method: New Approaches in Biblical Studies* (1992). **J. C. Anderson and J. Staley** (eds.), *Taking It Personally* (*Semeia* 72, 1995). **J. Arac** (ed.), *Postmodernism and Politics* (1986). **S. Aronowitz,** *Dead Artists, Live Theories, and Other Cultural Problems* (1994). **D. Attridge, G. Bennington, and R. Young** (eds.), *Poststructuralism and the Question of History* (1987). **M. Bal,** *Lethal Love: Feminist Literary Readings of Biblical Love Stories* (1987); *Death and*

Dissymmetry: The Politics of Coherence in the Book of Judges (1988); *Murder and Difference: Gender, Genre, and Scholarship on Sisera's Death* (1988). **Z. Bauman,** *Modernity and Ambivalence* (1991); *Imitations of Postmodernity* (1992); *Postmodern Ethics* (1993). **T. K. Beal,** *The Book of Hiding: Gender, Ethnicity, Annihilation, and Esther* (1997). **T. K. Beal and D. M. Gunn** (eds.), *Reading Bibles, Writing Bodies: Identity and the Book* (1996). **W. Beardslee,** "Poststructuralist Criticism," *To Each Its Own Meaning* (ed. S. McKenzie and S. Haynes, 1993) 221-36. **C. Belsey,** *Critical Practice* (1980). **M. Berman,** *All That Is Solid Melts Into Air: The Experience of Modernity* (1982). The Bible and Culture Collective, *The Postmodern Bible* (1995). **D. Boyarin,** *A Radical Jew: Paul and the Politics of Identity* (1994). **F. Burnett,** "Postmodern Biblical Exegesis: The Eve of Historical Criticism," *Semeia 51* (1990) 51-80. **J. Butler,** *Gender Trouble: Feminism and the Subversion of Identity* (1990). **M. Calinescu,** *Five Faces of Modernity: Modernism, Avant-garde, Decadence, Kitsch, Postmodernism* (1987). **J. Caputo,** *Radical Hermeneutics: Repetition, Deconstruction, and the Hermeneutic Project* (1987). **M. de Certeau,** *The Practice of Everyday Life* (1984); *Heterologies* (1986); *The Writing of History* (1988). **D. J. A. Clines,** *What Does Eve Do to Help? And Other Readerly Questions to the OT* (1990). **S. Critchley,** *The Ethics of Deconstruction: Derrida and Levinas* (1992). **S. Croatto,** *Biblical Hermeneutics: Toward a Theory of Reading as the Production of Meaning* (1987). **G. Deleuze and F. Guattari,** *Anti-Oedipus: Capitalism and Schizophrenia* (1985); *A Thousand Plateaus: Capitalism and Schizophrenia* (1987). **J. Derrida,** *Of Grammatology* (1976); *Writing and Difference* (1978); *Limited Inc* (1988); *A Derrida Reader* (1991); *The Gift of Death* (1995); *Points* (1995). **J. C. Exum,** *Fragmented Women: Feminist Subversions of Biblical Narratives* (1993); "Feminist Criticism," *Judges and Method: New Approaches in Biblical Studies* (1995; ed. G. A. Yee) 65-90. **D. N. Fewell,** "Deconstructive Criticism," *Judges and Method: New Approaches in Biblical Studies* (ed. G. A. Yee, 1995) 119-45. **S. Fish,** *Is There a Text in This Class? The Authority of Interpretive Communities* (1980); *Doing What Comes Naturally: Change, Rhetoric, and the Practice of Theory in Literary and Legal Studies* (1989). **H. Foster** (ed.), *The Anti-Aesthetic: Essays on Postmodern Culture* (1983). **M. Foucault,** *Language, Counter-memory, Practice: Selected Essays and Interviews* (1977); *Discipline and Punish* (1979); *The Foucault Reader* (1984). **S. Fowl,** "Texts Don't Have Ideologies," *Biblical Interpretation* (1995) 15-34. **R. Fowler,** "Postmodern Biblical Criticism," *Forum 5, 3* (1989) 3-30. **N. Fraser,** *Unruly Practices: Power, Discourse, and Gender in Contemporary Social Theory* (1989). **H. L. Gates, Jr.** (ed.), "Race," *Writing, and Difference* (1986). **J. Habermas,** *The Philosophical Discourse of Modernity: Twelve Lectures* (1987). **I. Hassan,** The Postmodern Turn: Essays in Postmodern Theory and Culture (1987). **O. O. Hendricks,** "Guerrilla Exegesis: 'Struggle' as a Scholarly Vocation-A Post-Modern Approach to African-American Biblical Interpretation," *Semeia 72* (1995) 73-90. **L. Hutcheon,** The Politics of Postmodernism (1989). **A. Huyssen,** "Mapping the Postmodern," New German Critique (1984) 5-52. **L. Irigaray,** This Sex Which Is Not One (1985); *Speculum of the Other Woman* (1985); *The Irigaray Reader* (1991); *Sexes and Genealogies* (1993). **F. Jameson,** *Postmodernism or the Cultural Logic of Late Capitalism* (1992). **D. Jobling** (ed.), *Ideological Criticism of Biblical Texts* (Semeia 59, 1993). **D. Jobling and S. Moore** (eds.), *Poststructuralism as Exegesis* (Semeia 54, 1992). **L. E. Keck,** "The Premodern Bible in the Postmodern World," *Int 50* (1996) 130-41. **S. Lovibond,** "Feminism and Postmodernism," *New Left Review* (1989) 5-28. **J.-F. Lyotard,** *The Postmodern Condition* (1984); *The Differend* (1988); *The Inhuman* (1991); *The Postmodern Explained* (1992); *Political Writings* (1993). **E. V. McKnight,** *Postmodern Use of the Bible: The Emergence of Reader-oriented Criticism* (1988). **E. McKnight and E. S. Malbon** (eds.), *The New Literary Criticism and the NT* (1995). **P. de Man,** *Allegories of Reading: Figural Language in Rousseau, Nietzsche, Rilke, and Proust* (1979); *Blindness and Insight: Essays in the Rhetoric of Contemporary Criticism* (1983[2]). **J. P. Martin,** "Towards a Post-critical

Paradigm," *NTS 33* (1987) 370-85. **J. Milbank,** *Theology and Social Theory: Beyond Secular Reason* (1990). **S. Moore,** *Literary Criticism and the Gospels: The Theoretical Challenge* (1989); "Postmodernism and Biblical Studies: A Response to R. Fowler," *Forum 5, 3* (1989) 36-41; *Poststructuralism and the NT: Derrida and Foucault at the Foot of the Cross* (1994); *God's Gym: Divine Male Bodies of the Bible* (1996). **T. Nataoli and L. Hutcheon** (eds.), *A Postmodern Reader* (1993). **C. Norris,** *Deconstruction: Theory and Practice* (1982); *Derrida* (1988); *The Truth About Postmodernism* (1993). **D. Olson,** "Deuteronomy as De-centering Center: Reflections on Postmodernism and the Quest for a Theological Center of the Hebrew Scriptures," *Semeia* 71 (1995) 119-32. **G. Phillips** (ed.), *Text/History/Self in Structural and Poststructural Exegesis* (*Semeia* 51, 1990). **R. Rorty,** *Consequences of Pragmatism: Essays, 1972-80* (1985); *Contingency, Irony, and Solidarity* (1989). **A. Ross** (ed.) *Universal Abandon? The Politics of Postmodernism* (1988). **E. Said,** *The World, the Text, and the Critic* (1983); *Culture and Imperialism* (1993). **I. Salusinszky** (ed.), *Criticism in Society* (1989). **S. Schneiders,** "Does the Bible Have a Postmodern Message?" *Postmodern Theology* (ed. F. B. Burnham, 1989) 56-73. **B. H. Smith,** *Contingencies of Value: Alternative Perspectives for Critical Theory* (1988). **G. Spivak,** In *Other Worlds: Essays in Cultural Politics* (1988). **H. Staten,** "How the Spirit (Almost) Became Flesh: Gospel of John," *Representations* 41 (1993) 34-57. **P. G. P. de Villiers,** "The End of Hermeneutics? On NT Studies and Postmodernism," *Neot* 25 (1991) 145-56. **C. West,** "Nietzsche's Prefiguration of Postmodern American Philosophy," *boundary* 2 (1981) 241-69; "F. Jameson's Marxist Hermeneutics," *boundary* 2 (1982/83) 177-200. **R. Williams,** *The Politics of Modernism: Against the New Conformists* (ed. T. Pinkney, 1996)

A. K. M. ADAM

LITERARY AND STRUCTURALIST/ POSTMODERNIST APPROACHES METHODS

Reader-Response Criticism

This approach views literature in terms of its readers and their values, attitudes, and responses, thus supplementing or displacing approaches to literature that focus on either the universe imitated in the work, the author, the original audience, or the work itself. The nature and role assigned to the reader, however, vary according to the critical theory being used and the explicit or implicit worldview of which the theory is an integral part.

1. *Factors in Reader-Response Criticism.* Developments in the critical theory of S. Fish illustrate reader-response criticism and introduce significant factors in this approach. The background for his work is New Criticism and its argument that only the text is stable, since the intentions of the author are unavailable and the responses of the reader are too variable. As Fish first focused the issue, the source of meaning has to be either the text or the reader; and, since the temporal dimension of reading rather than the spatial form of the text is the essential factor in meaning, he argued in favor of the reader rather than the text.

In his early emphasis on the reader, Fish viewed the variability of readers' responses negatively, as did New Criticism. To maintain a concept of validity, he distinguished two levels of experience in reading—a level shared by all readers regardless of differences in education and culture and a secondary level that could be seen as a reaction (emotional or intellectual) to the experience of the primary level. For Fish, the proper practice of Literary*§ criticism involved the suppression of the subjective and idiosyncratic in favor of the response shared by all readers.

From a later perspective, Fish acknowledged that the argument for a common reading experience required an object (the text) in relation to which readers' experiences could be seen as uniform. He was in reality retaining the most basic of new critical principles—the integrity of the text—in order to claim universality and objectivity for his method. The radical move away from new critical assumptions came when he discerned that literature is a conventional category dependent on subjective perception. This involves the denial of a basic or neutral language unrelated to perception and response. The conclusion is that "it is the reader who 'makes' literature." Fish qualifies this subjectivism by defining the reader as a member of a community that determines the attention given by the reader and the kind of literature made by the reader. "Thus the act of recognizing literature is not constrained by something in the text, nor does it issue from an independent and arbitrary will; rather, it proceeds from a collective decision as to what will count as literature, a decision that will be in force only so long as a community of readers or believers continues to abide by it" (1980, 11).

The later work of Fish redefines the activity of criticism as a matter of persuasion rather than of demonstration. The business of criticism is the determination of the perspective from which reading will proceed. This determination is not one that is made once and for all by some objective standard. The decision must be made and remade "whenever the interests and tacitly understood goals of one interpretive community replace or dislodge the interests and goals of another" (1980, 16).

2. *Theoretical Context of Reader-Response Criticism.* Theoretical considerations enter most obviously when Fish questions the status of the knowledge involved in literature and the nature of the self or the subject in the reading process. A careful look at these considerations indicates that in reader-response criticism we do not have minor revisions of some previous system; in fact, a revolution is taking place. An indirect, but powerful, influence on this revolution is the philosophical questioning of the intrinsic limits of epistemology. The limits of knowledge have

been emphasized in a dramatic fashion in the skeptical deconstruction associated with the name of J. Derrida and the failure to establish some final foundation for knowledge. Skepticism, however, is not the only possible conclusion. G. W. F. Hegel's anti-foundational epistemology, for example, was accompanied by an attempt to justify knowledge in a nonlinear, circular fashion through the relationship of the results obtained to the beginning point. This circular epistemology was expanded to include ontology. Thought is not sovereign; it is dependent on being. And this being against which thought is tested is being revealed in experience.

Reader-response criticism has been directly influenced by fields of study intimately related to both epistemology and textual interpretation: Hermeneutics*§, Structuralism*§ and poststructuralism, and phenomenology. Long before the advent of reader-response criticism, hermeneutics transformed the question of interpretation into the question of knowledge (How do we know?) and the question of being (What is the mode of being of that being who only exists through understanding?).

R. Bultmann and the New Hermeneutic used the relationship between being, language, and humankind postulated by M. Heidegger. But the theological framework and the lack of an appropriate concept of language caused the New Hermeneutic to stagnate. Some forms of reader-response criticism, however, move back to Heidegger's idea that the understanding of a text does not simply involve the discovery of an inner meaning contained in the text; to understand a text is to unfold the possibility of being that is indicated by that text.

The structural tradition has also become important for reader-response criticism. French literary structuralism became popular in the 1960s and 1970s, with its emphasis on order and necessity rather than on human choice and freedom—factors emphasized by the existentialism that was its background. In poststructural developments associated with Derrida, order is replaced with a radical disordering. The structural linguistics of Saussure, then, was used for both French structuralism's positivism and poststructuralism's emphasis on the differential nature of meaning and the continual deferring of any final meaning.

The opposition between French structuralism and poststructuralism or deconstruction was actually mediated in the application of structuralism to literary study prior to French structuralism. By the late 1920s, Russian formalism as a whole had integrated the structural view of a work with history and with the individual. The structural view of the literary work as an organized whole influenced the way culture and the individual were related to the literary work by such scholars as J. Tynjanov and J. Mukarovsky. Tynjanov viewed literature as a system standing in correlation with other systems that define literature. Literature in general, and also specific works of literature, are therefore influenced by changes in culture. The individual was first seen by Tynjanov and Mukarovsky as defined by culture, but Mukarovsky eventually shifted attention from impersonal cultural codes to human beings as the subject and ultimate source of aesthetic interaction. The individual is then seen as the crucial aspect of aesthetic interaction; no longer an irrelevant individual superimposing private associations on a social meaning, the reader is an active force indispensable to meaning from the beginning.

The phenomenological tradition conceives of the literary work of art in such a way as to emphasize the role of the reader. In the phenomenological approach of R. Ingarden, the work of art is distinguished from the work as an aesthetic object that is constituted or concretized through the intentional act of reading. The complexity of a literary work and its apprehension are such that the reader cannot give himself or herself equally to all the components of the total apprehension. Only a few of the many experienced and interwoven acts become central, while the rest are only co-experienced. This means that there is constant change with regard to which component acts are central at any particular moment. The same literary work is apprehended, then, in a variety of changing aspects.

3. *Varieties of Reader-Response Criticism.* The pluralism of contemporary reader-response theory results from the lack of domination of any one worldview and critical theory. The various methodologies depend on views taken of language, self, world, text, and meaning and the relationships between all of these and other factors. Moreover, no one tradition is "pure," for wave after wave of influence has swept over literary criticism, and criticism has responded in different ways.

a. The autonomous reader. Although the concept of an autonomous reader determining the meaning of an autonomous text has been severely relativized, this conventional critical approach has not been completely displaced. "Postmodern" approaches (including radical reader-response approaches) are still dependent on the "modern" critical model.

b. The implied reader. The concept of implied reader does not really move away from the text and the author as the source of meaning. W. Booth speaks of implied authors and readers as rhetorical devices of the actual author that are to be discerned by the reader on the basis of such elements as the explicit commentary of the narrator, the kind of tale being told by the author, the meanings that can be extracted, and the moral and emotional content of the characters' actions. The goal of a real reader is to become the implied reader and to find the implied author.

c. Reader-reception criticism. The history of readers' reception is the concern of H. Jauss (1982). This approach attempts to situate a literary work within the cultural context of its production and then to explore the shifting relations between this context and the changing contexts of historical readers. The work of Jauss is an attempt to rehabilitate literary history in the tradition of Mukarovsky, and Jauss is credited with making the reader a central factor in the study of literature in West Germany.

d. Aesthetic-response criticism. W. Iser (1978), a colleague of Jauss at the University of Constance, has emphasized the process by which a reader actualizes a text. Iser's work falls within the hermeneutical tradition but more directly within the phenomenological tradition of Ingarden. Iser is not concerned with Jauss's goal of formulating "a theory of the aesthetics of reception" arising from the history of the readers' judgments, but with the formulation of "a theory of aesthetic response" that "has its roots in the text" (1978, x). Iser makes the "gaps" and their completion by the reader a central factor in literary communication. A text is seen as a system of processes whereby language is broken up and reconstituted. This process is marked by gaps that must be completed and blanks that must be filled in. Communication begins when the reader fills in the blanks and bridges the gaps.

e. Psychological approaches. Psychological approaches to the reader emphasize the stages of development of individual readers or (as in the case of N. Holland 1973) the role played by the "psychological set" of readers. In an early period Holland saw the literary text as providing readers with a fantasy that they introjected and experienced as their own, supplying their own associations to it. In a later period he acknowledged the limitations of viewing the literary text as an embodiment of the psychological process and moved to a description of the interdynamics of the reading experience on the basis of the four principles of expectation, defense, fantasy, and transformation.

f. Radical views of reader-response. Radical reader-response approaches see the result of reading, not in terms of interpretation or the specification of meaning, but in terms of an effect on the reader. This is visualized in different ways. J. Culler (1982), for example, suggests that the process of reading shows the reader the problems of his condition as maker and reader of signs and that this is the meaning of a work. Iser views the process of reading as the coming together of text and imagination in an experience of continual modification closely akin to our experience in life. Because of the nature of the process, the reality of the experience of reading illuminates the basic pattern of real experiences. G. Poulet (1977) emphasizes the achievement of self-transcendence. In reading, the object of the reader's thought is the thought of another; yet it is the reader who is the subject in the act of reading. The subject exists in the work. In reading, there is a movement beyond the objective elements of a work, with the purpose (or at least result) of elevating criticism "to the apprehension of a subjectivity without objectivity."

Radical reader-oriented approaches are foreign to the experience of historically oriented biblical critics because of different views of the use of language and of the nature of biblical literature. It is difficult to overcome this strangeness because conventional views of language and life reinforce one another. Both are governed by the Enlightenment model in which subject and object—humankind and nature—are distinct, with the subject—humankind—dominating. Language is a tool of reference used by humans, and the truth of the reference is validated by the human subject through establishment of correspondence between the statement and that to which it refers. In radical reader-response criticism, the subject-object dichotomy is dissolved, the subject even becoming the object in the process of reading. This may be a return to an earlier view of language, in which humankind and nature were not separated but were united by a common power. In this view, language can affect nature. In reader-response criticism, of course, language is seen as affecting the reader rather than nature.

R. Fowler suggests that "in arguing for a temporal model of reading, rather than a spatial one, we are actually returning to an understanding of language that has affinities with the language of oral culture." Different modes of consciousness are involved. The spatial written word "constitutes a literate/visual mode of consciousness," while the temporal spoken word "constitutes an oral/aural mode" (1985, 20). This may not be the only or the best way to reimage the use of biblical language, but it supports the view that the nature and function of biblical language and literature must be reconsidered before reader-response criticism can have its fullest effect.

Bibliography: **A. Bach,** *Women, Seduction, and Betrayal in Biblical Narrative* (1997). The Bible and Culture Collective, "Reader-response Criticism," *The Postmodern Bible* (1995) 20-69. **S. Brown,** "Reader Response: Demythologizing the Text," *NTS* 34 (1988) 232-37. **E. Cheney,** *She Can Read: Feminist Reading Strategies for Biblical Narrative* (1996). **D. J. A. Clines,** *Interested Parties: The Ideology of Writers and Readers of the HB* (GCT 1, 1995). **J. D. Culler,** *On Deconstruction: Theory and Criticism after Structuralism* (1982). **J. A. Darr,** *On Character Building: The Reader and the Rhetoric of Characterization in Luke-Acts* (1992). **R. Detweiler** (ed.), "Reader Response Approaches to Biblical and Secular Texts," *Semeia 31* (1985). **J. C. Exum,** *Plotted, Shot, and Painted: Cultural Representations of Biblical Women* (JSOTSup 215, 1996). **J. Fetterley,** *The Resisting Reader: A Feminist Approach to American Fiction* (1978). **S. Fish,** *Is There a Text in This Class? The Authority of Interpretive Communities* (1980). **R. W. Fowler,** "Who Is the 'Reader' in Reader Response Criticism?" *Semeia 31* (1985) 5-23; *Let the Reader Understand: Reader Response Criticism and the Gospel of Mark* (1991). **E. Freund,** *The Return of the Reader: Reader-response Criticism* (1987). **P. Harner,** *Relation Analysis of the Fourth Gospel: A Study in Reader-response Criticism* (1993). **N. N. Holland,** *Poems and Persons: An Introduction to the Psychoanalysis of Literature* (1973). **W. Iser,** *The Act of Reading: A Theory of Aesthetic Response* (1978). **H. R. Jauss,** *Towards an Aesthetic of Reception* (1982). **J. G. Lodge,** *Romans 9-11: A Reader-response Analysis* (1996). **E. V. McKnight,** *The Bible and the Reader: An Introduction to Literary Criticism* (1985); *Post-modern Use of the Bible: The Emergence of Reader-oriented Criticism* (1988); "Reader-response Criticism," *To Each Its Own Meaning: An Introduction to Biblical Criticisms and Their Application* (ed. S. L. McKenzie and S. R. Haynes, 1993) 197-220. **S. D. Moore,** *Literary Criticism and the Gospels: The Theoretical Challenge* (1989); *Let the Reader Understand: Reader Response Criticism and the Gospel of Mark* (1991).

G. Poulet, *Entre Moi et Moi: Esai critiques sur la conscience* (1977). **T. Rockmore,** *Hegel's Circular Epistemology* (1986). **E. Struthers Malbon and E. V. Knight** (eds.), *The New Literary Criticism and the NT* (1994). **J. P. Tompkins** (ed.), *Reader-response Criticism: From Formalism to Post-structuralism* (1980). **R. C. Webber,** *Reader Response Analysis of the Epistle of James* (1996).

E. V. McKnight

LITERARY AND STRUCTURALIST/
POSTMODERNIST APPROACHES METHODS

Hebrew Bible Rhetorical Criticism

1. *Rhetorical Competence in the Hebrew Scriptures.* "One who knows how to speak. . . . "
Rhetorical competence is one of the qualities that commends the young David to Saul's court,
and several speeches put into the mouth of Jesse's son bear out the judgment (1 Sam 16:18; cf.
1 Sam 17:45-47; 24:8-15; 25:21-22; 2 Sam 1:19-27). Not surprisingly, Hebrew Bible narrative
literature offers many examples of persuasive speechmaking: Judah's pleading with Joseph not
to keep Benjamin as hostage (Gen 44:18-34); Moses' sermon-like conclusion of his farewell
discourse, setting before Israel the choice between life and death (Deuteronomy 29—30);
Samuel's sobering lecture on "the ways of the king . . . over you" (1 Sam 8:10-18); Abigail's
honed words restraining David from rash action (1 Sam 25:23-31); Nathan's surprise-charged
parable of the ewe lamb (2 Sam 12:1-6); not to mention the alluring argumentations through
which two royal counselors compete for Absalom's ear (2 Sam 16:15—17:14). Also, narrative
epilogues to the fall of the kingdoms of Israel and Judah (2 Kgs 17:7-23; Jer 44:1-14) as well
as the story of Jerusalem's rescue from Sennacherib's siege (Isa 36—37) show persuasive pens
at work, as do Abijah's self-assured sermon addressed to his wayward Israelite opponents
(2 Chr 13:4-12) and the narrative of Ruth, the model of a biblical short story. Vivid and varied
vocabulary, appealing style, pronounced point of view, functional character portrayal, and unity
as well as variation in design characterize these examples of biblical eloquence, which, like that
of Homer or of the ancient Egyptian sages (M. Fox 1983), is "preconceptual" (G. Kennedy
1980, 120).

Rhetorical competence is made the subject of reflection in Proverbs: "The mind of the wise
makes their speech judicious, and adds persuasiveness to their lips" (Prov 16:23). Various
aspects of the art of speaking well are noted in Proverbs: the need to listen with care and to react
at the right time (15:23; 18:13); the necessity to ponder an issue in depth and to respond dis-
passionately (17:27*b*); the urging to be brief and to the point (17:27*a*); and the importance of
fitting words and persuasive arguments (16:21). In short, "death and life are in the power of the
tongue," and "a gentle tongue is a tree of life" (18:21*a*; 15:4*a*).

However, in the story of Moses' call, his lack of rhetorical competence is the retarding, yet
essential, element. He responds to the divine call to speak on God's behalf with the statement
that he had "never been eloquent [but was] slow of speech and slow of tongue." However, he
finds himself overruled by the divine affirmation that God will teach him what to say (Exod
4:10-12). The revelation he then proceeds to convey is thus a divine rhetoric that is not mediated to its human addressees through any human rhetorical competence. It is this antithesis that
eventually set Jewish and Christian canonical writings, as divine revelation, apart from human
eloquence. Holy writ is, by definition, not subject to standards of rhetorical competence.

2. *Classical Rhetorical Criticism and Biblical Interpretation.* This embedded tension
accounts for the nearly complete absence of formally conceptualized Greek and Roman rhetorical criticism from biblical interpretation until the last decades of the twentieth century. In the
Middle Ages and until the Enlightenment, teachers and homilists in synagogue and church carried out biblical interpretation within institutionally defined parameters and in support of then-
prevalent conceptualizations of the religious heritage. This state of affairs changed, especially
in Western Christianity, with the Renaissance and the Enlightenment. From the mid-eighteenth
century onward exegetes were increasingly unwilling to see themselves as suppliers of proof
texts to dogmaticians and began to embark on exegesis as an interpretive enterprise in its
own right. In the course of the two centuries since then, various critical methods of Literary*§

analysis and synthesis practiced in the disciplines of the humanities were adopted and, as needed, adapted to meet institutional limitations. Occasionally, however, rhetorical considerations were explicitly made part of interpretive approaches. Thus, C. Briggs[§] briefly discussed "logical and rhetorical interpretations" as part of interpretation generally (1900, 478); and E. König[§] discussed at length "the nature of the style" in biblical literature, covering many of the traditional topics within a psychologically-defined framework (Psychology and Biblical Studies*[§]). The papal encyclical *Divino Afflante Spiritu*[§] (1942) removed for the Roman Catholic Church the taint of "modernism" from the new methods of interpretation and affirmed their validity for church-related exegesis. The same is now largely true for all but Orthodox Judaism. The range and variety of approaches is considerable and defined by linguistic, sociological (Sociology and Hebrew Bible Studies*[§]), psychological, or philosophical perspectives (see the survey by A. Suelzer and J. Kselman 1990).

3. *The "New" Rhetorical Criticism*. The emergence of Hebrew Bible rhetorical criticism as an identifiable approach is usually based on J. Muilenburg's[§] 1969 paper "Form Criticism and Beyond" (W. Wuellner 1987, 451; Suelzer-Kselman, 1127). The title suggests what his argumentation lays out: Form Criticism*[§], proceeding as it does analytically, needs to be followed by a synthetically oriented examination of "literary composition . . . exhibiting . . . structural patterns . . . discerning the many and various devices by which the predictions are formulated and ordered into a unified whole." This method Muilenburg described as "rhetorical criticism" (1969, 8).

Muilenburg's identification of this step beyond form criticism is, however, problematic in that it introduces as a separate move beyond form criticism the kind of inquiry that H. Gunkel[§], the father of form criticism, considered an integral part of the method. More important, the suggested term "rhetorical criticism" refers to a scholarly discipline practiced since Aristotle, Cicero, Quintilian, and Augustine that may be defined as the study and practice of the art of speaking/writing well.

Ancient rhetorics identify three kinds of speeches: judicial speeches, related to the past and, in its positive formulation, constituted as defense, in its negative form, as accusation; deliberative or political speeches, related to the future either as exhortation or warning; and demonstrative speeches, related to the present either as praise or reproach. The process of composition moves through three stages: The conception of the line of argumentation (*inventio*) is followed by the selection of the fitting style (*elocutio*), then the composition of its structure (*dispositio*). The argument is supported by two kinds of proofs: nontechnical (like documents or oaths) and technical (based on such considerations as probability). Important aspects of the speech are the speaker's stature (*ethos*), the rationality of the speech (*logos*), and the emotional element with which the audience of the speech is addressed (*pathos*). The parts of the speech usually include an introduction (*exordium*); a narration (*narratio*), which may appear throughout the work; positive or negative lines of proof (*confirmatio/confutatio*); and a conclusion (*peroratio*). Based on K. Ziegler (1979), this incomplete survey shows that classical rhetoric deals only with prose; poetry is discussed separately as "poetics."

The terminological difficulty introduced by Muilenburg into Hebrew Bible interpretation is illustrated by the different way in which the 1984 work by Kennedy programmatically defines and practices New Testament Rhetorical Criticism*[§] in terms of the classical system based on Aristotle. Kennedy's brief discussion (1980) notes that although "rhetorical consciousness is entirely foreign to the nature of biblical Judaism," it is nevertheless "fairly obvious that both as a whole and in its various books there are signs of oral, persuasive intent" (1980, 120-21). As far as a definition of Hebrew Bible rhetorical criticism is concerned, the summary of an emerging consensus by C. Black (1989) commends itself: Rhetorical criticism is "the study of the characteristic linguistic and structural features of a particular text in its present form, apart from its generic rootage, social usage, or historical development" (1988–89, 253; similarly M. Kessler 1982, 14).

Given this definition, literary-critical analyses that are not expressly identified as rhetorical criticism are equally of importance, e.g., D. Robertson's discussion of "the Old Testament and the literary critic" (1977) or R. Alter's two books on "the art of biblical narrative and of biblical poetry" (1981, 1985). By the same token, discussions of such topics as "the rhetoric of sexuality" (P. Trible 1978, 1984) also need to be included because they not only combine rhetorical analysis with a specific hermeneutical perspective (Hermeneutics*§) but also illustrate the range and variety of approaches presently being practiced. The latter is documented in an instructive discussion of contemporary "ways of analysing text" in D. Birch's survey of "language, literature and critical practice" (1989).

4. *Perspectives and Representative Publications.* Muilenburg's move to rhetorical criticism was not meant to discard form criticism—on the contrary, it perceived the former as a logical step beyond the latter. However, his commentary on Deutero-Isaiah proceeded synchronically— that is, made the text as it stands the basis of exegesis. As expected, the relation between the diachronic nature of earlier critical approaches and the synchronic character of rhetorical criticism has become a matter of debate. M. Weiss (1967), for instance, considered form criticism "irrelevant to biblical criticism," while others assume continuity between diachronic and synchronic approaches (M. Kessler 1982, 5, 12).

In the practice of rhetorical interpretation the most important decision is made at its inception. What is the extent of the unit to be analyzed? An intentionally conceived and formulated composition is not only structured and plotted but also defined by its beginning and ending. Thus, analysis begins with the definition of the extent of the unit; rhetorical interpretation, at least in its basic sense, is concerned only with integral and complete units that expressly present themselves as such (e.g., the books of Ruth, Amos, or Job). Book chapters or lectionary pericopes are rarely primary units; also, sections of relative conceptual and literary integrity like Genesis 24 or 2 Kings 22–23 are part of larger texts that constitute the primary parameters of rhetorical analysis. This consideration locates exegesis of subunits in a larger interpretive perspective but, by the same token, does not rule it out (note the fruitful exegeses of small text units in the collections edited by J. Jackson and M. Kellers 1974; D. Clines, D. Gunn, and A. Hauser 1982; and D. Patrick and A. Scult 1990).

Rhetorical criticism cannot help but surface the social nature of all discourse. The search for the rhetoric of non-Western culture—and that of the Jewish scriptures is indeed so categorized—reveals, in the words of a recent reviewer, "a significant fact both about rhetoric and about the nature of its Western tradition: the true rhetoric of any age and of any people is to be found deep within what might be called attitudinizing conventions, precepts that condition one's stance toward experience, knowledge, tradition, language, and other people" (T. Sloan and C. Perelman 1974, 802). It comes as no surprise, then, when rhetorical criticism takes readers "away from a traditional message—or content-oriented reading of Scripture—to a reading which generates and strengthens ever-deepening personal, social, and cultural values" and leads its practitioners to "personal or social identification and transformation" (Wuellner 1987, 460-61, with reference to K. Burke's approach).

Representative publications include several monographs that deal with both theory and practice of rhetorical approaches generally: Alter, S. Bar-Efrat (1989), A. Berlin (1983), N. Frye (1957), L. Alonso Schökel (1965), M. Sternberg (1985), and Weiss. Other publications are concerned with certain parts of the Bible: J. Fokkelman (1975, 1981), M. Garsiel (1983), D. Jobling (1978, 1986), and R. Polzin (1980, 1989), with parts of the Law and the Former Prophets; F. Andersen and D. N. FREEDMAN (1980), M. Fox (1980), Y. Gitay (1981), W. Holladay (1976), and J. Lundblom (1975), with the Latter Prophets. Fox (1983) provides an instructive example of (preconceptual) rhetorical competence in ancient Egypt. The collections by Jackson and Kellers and Clines, Gunn, and Hauser, as well as M. Fishbane's book (1979), interpret smaller text units. On the other hand, Trible is an example of rhetorical interpretation from the perspective of Feminist*[§] hermeneutics.

5. *Method in Rhetorical Criticism: An Emerging Consensus?* Three review articles include descriptions of steps to be followed in rhetorical criticism (Kessler 1982, 8-9; Wuellner 1987, 455-58; Black 1989, 254-55). On the basis of these works, five stages are suggested: (a) Determination of the extent of the unit. What are the opening and closing paragraphs, strophes, or sentences? How is the unit they delimit marked by compositional completeness and conceptual integrity? If the unit is a subunit of a larger text, what is its place and function within that macro-structure? In turn, if the unit is extensive and anthological or otherwise composite, what considerations need to qualify rhetorical analysis? (b) Identification of the rhetorical situation. What constellation of persons, circumstances, and events led to the composition of the text? How does the unit as a persuasion-oriented composition relate to the historical, social, and psychological setting of the composer? What options were available to the composer, and what is the creative, inventive element in the unit? (c) Identification of the rhetorical disposition. What encompassing strategy carries the argument? What is the latter, and how do the composer's stature, the perspicuity of the presentation, and the appeal to the expectations of the audience serve it? How is the text structured as a unified whole? (d) Determination of rhetorical technique. What style is used? What supporting proofs and clarifying illustrations are employed? What techniques, such as repetition, type-scenes, and reticence, are used? What is the nature of the imagery, and in what manner are social and historical legacies drawn into the presentation? (e) Review of the analysis. In what manner do the insights gathered in analysis fit into a consistent and substantial understanding of the passage? How does the analysis of the whole unit lead to an understanding that is more than the sum of its individual stages?

Bibliography: L. Alonso Schökel, *The Inspired Word: Scripture in the Light of Language and Literature* (ET 1965). R. Alter, *The Art of Biblical Narrative* (1981); *The Art of Biblical Poetry* (1985). F. I. Andersen and D. N. Freedman, *Hosea: A New Translation with Introduction and Commentary* (1980). Aristotle, *The Rhetoric and the Poetic of Aristotle* (ed. E. P. J. Corbett, 1954, 1988). S. Bar-Efrat, *Narrative Art in the Bible* (JSOTSup 70, Bible and Literature Series 17, 1989). A. Berlin, *Poetics and Interpretation of Biblical Narrative* (Bible and Literature Series 9, 1983). D. Birch, *Language, Literature, and Critical Practice: Ways of Analysing Text* (The Interface Series, 1989). C. C. Black, "Keeping Up with Recent Studies, pt. 16: Rhetorical Criticism and Biblical Interpretation," *ExpTim 100* (1989) 252-58. C. A. Briggs, *General Introduction to the Study of Holy Scripture* (1899). K. Burke, *A Rhetoric of Motives* (1950). D. J. A. Clines, D. M. Gunn, and A. J. Hauser (eds.), *Art and Meaning: Rhetoric in Biblical Literature* (JSOTSup 19, 1982). E. P. J. Corbett, *Classical Rhetoric for the Modern Student* (1965). T. B. Dozeman, "Old Testament Rhetorical Criticism," *ABD* (1992) 5:712-715. R. K. Duke, *The Persuasive Appeal of the Chronicler: A Rhetorical Analysis* (JSOTSup 88, Bible and Literature Series 25, 1990). M. Fishbane, *Text and Texture: Close Readings of Selected Biblical Texts* (1979). J. P. Fokkelman, *Narrative Art in Genesis: Specimens of Stylistic and Structural Analysis* (SSN 17, 1975); *Narrative Art and Poetry in the Books of Samuel: A Full Interpretation Based on Stylistic and Structural Analyses* (SSN 20, 23, 27, 31, 1981). M. V. Fox, "The Rhetoric of Ezekiel's Vision of the Valley of the Bones," *HUCA 51* (1980) 1-15; "Ancient Egyptian Rhetoric," *Rhetorica 1* (1983) 9-22. N. Frye, *Anatomy of Criticism: Four Essays* (1957); *The Great Code: The Bible and Literature* (1982). M. Garsiel, *The First Book of Samuel: A Literary Study of Comparative Structures, Analogies, and Parallels* (1983; ET 1985). Y. Gitay, *Prophecy and Persuasion: A Study of Isaiah 40-48* (FThL

14, 1981). **W. L. Holladay,** *The Architecture of Jeremiah 1-20* (1975). **J. J. Jackson and M. Kessler** (eds.), *Rhetoric Criticism: Essays in Honor of J. Muilenburg* (PThMS 1, 1974). **D. Jobling,** *The Sense of Biblical Narrative 1, 2* (JSOTSup 7, 39, 1978, 1986). **G. A. Kennedy,** *Classical Rhetoric and Its Christian and Secular Tradition from Ancient to Modern Times* (1980); *NT Interpretation Through Rhetorical Criticism* (SR, 1984). **M. Kessler,** "A Methodological Setting for Rhetorical Criticism," *Art and Meaning: Rhetoric in Biblical Literature* (ed. D. J. A. Clines et al., 1982) 1-19. **E. König,** *Stilistik, Rhetorik, Poetik in Bezug auf die biblische Literatur* (1900). **J. R. Lundblom,** *Jeremiah: A Study in Ancient Hebrew Rhetoric* (SBLDS 18, 1975). **R. Meynet,** "Histoire de 'l'analyse rhétorique' en exégèse biblique," *Rhetorica 8* (1990) 291-320. **J. Muilenburg,** "Isaiah 40-66 (Exegesis)," *IB* (1956) 5:422-773; "Form Criticism and Beyond," *JBL 88* (1969) 1-18. **D. Patrick and A. Scult,** *Rhetoric and Biblical Interpretation* (JSOTSup 82, Bible and Literature 26, 1990). **R. Polzin,** *Moses and the Deuteronomist: Deuteronomy, Joshua, Judges* (1980); *Samuel and the Deuteronomist* (1989). **I. Rabinowitz,** "Pre-modern Jewish Study of Rhetoric: An Introductory Bibliography," *Rhetorica 3* (1985) 137-44. **D. Robertson,** *The OT and the Literary Critic* (GBS, 1977). **T. O. Sloan and C. Perelman,** "Rhetoric," *EncBrit* (1974[15] 798-805. **M. Sternberg,** *The Poetics of Biblical Narrative: Ideological Literature and the Drama of Reading* (Indiana Literary Biblical Series, 1985). **A. Suelzer and J. S. Kselman,** "Modern OT Criticism," *NJBC* (1990) 1113-29. **P. Trible**, *God and the Rhetoric of Sexuality* (OBT, 1978); *Texts of Terror* (OBT, 1984). **D. F. Watson and A. J. Hauser,** *Rhetorical Criticism of the Bible* (Biblical Interpretation Series, 1994). **M. Weiss,** *The Bible From Within: The Method of Total Interpretation* (1962; ET 1984). **W. Wuellner,** "Where Is Rhetorical Criticism Taking Us?" *CBQ 49* (1987) 448-63; "Hermeneutics and Rhetorics," *Scr* (Journal of Bible and Theology in Southern Africa S 3, 1989). **K. Ziegler,** "Rhetorik," *Der Kleine Pauly: Lexikon der Antike in fünf Bänden* (ed. K. Ziegler and W. Sontheimer, 1979) 4:1396-414. **M. Zulick,** "The Active Force of Hearing: The Ancient Hebrew Language of Persuasion," *Rhetorica 10* (1992) 367-80.

W. M. W. ROTH

LITERARY AND STRUCTURALIST/ POSTMODERNIST APPROACHES METHODS

New Testament Rhetorical Criticism

1. *Origins and History*. The rhetoric of Paul was of great interest to the Reformers. ERASMUS analyzed 1-2 Corinthians rhetorically in his *Paraphrasis in duas epistolas Pauli ad Corinthios* (1519). Calvin§ gave a rhetorical analysis of Romans in his *Testamenti Epistolas, atque eti in Epistol ad Hebraeos commentaria luculentissima* (1551). Of special note is the work of P. Melanchthon§, whose commentaries on Romans and Galatians use classical conventions of invention, arrangement, and style as well as more contemporary rhetorical conventions (1540). After the Reformation, rhetorical analysis of the New Testament did not cease but was limited until German scholarship of the late eighteenth to early twentieth centuries revitalized the discipline. Very influential was K. Bauer's two-volume study of Paul's use of classical rhetorical techniques, entitled *Rhetoricae Paullinae, vel, Quid oratorium sit in oratione Paulli* (1782). In his *Die neutestamentliche Rhetorik: Ein Seitenstück zur Grammatik des neutestamentlichen Sprachidioms*, the German lexicographer C. Wilke§ analyzed the stylistic features, sentence structure, and argumentation of the New Testament (1843). Other important works were written by F. Blass, E. König§, J. Weiss§, R. Bultmann§, and H. Windisch§.

Despite this important stream of tradition at the turn of the twentieth century, New Testament studies largely became isolated from rhetoric. E. Norden§ (1898) measured the Pauline epistles according to the classical canons of artistic prose style and found them unHellenic. This assessment remained dominant, and its influence was undergirded by the diminishing role of rhetorical instruction in Western school curricula. In New Testament studies, a subsequent trickle of works reduced rhetorical analysis to matters of style, neglecting the more substantial aspects of invention and arrangement.

In the last three decades of the twentieth century, rhetorical criticism of the New Testament was revived, partly due to dissatisfaction with Form*§ and Redaction Criticism*§ and to the renewed interest in rhetoric in the humanities, philosophy, and classics (as seen in the work of C. Perelman and L. Olbrechts-Tyteca 1969). In New Testament studies, A. Wilder (1964) and R. Funk (1966) noted the rhetorical qualities of forms and genres and their relationship to their socio-historical settings. However, the major turning point for reintroducing rhetorical criticism to biblical studies was J. Muilenburg's§ 1968 presidential address to the Society of Biblical Literature§ (1969), in which he urged that biblical studies move beyond form criticism through the use of rhetorical criticism.

This reintroduction came in earnest with the work of H. Betz on Galatians (1975, 1979). He argued that Paul's epistles were composed with classical categories of invention, arrangement, and style in mind and that these could be used as a tool of interpretation. Although Betz has been challenged on several points, he reemphasized interpreting the Pauline Epistles by using Greco-Roman rhetorical and epistolary theory in their complete form. At about the same time, W. Wuellner was bringing Greco-Roman and more modern rhetorical theory to bear on Romans, arguing that the Pauline Epistles should be approached primarily as argumentative and rhetorical (1976). Since these beginnings, hundreds of works have been produced (D. Watson and A. Hauser 1994).

2. *Contemporary Methodologies*. Currently, a wide variety of methodologies are being used in rhetorical criticism of the New Testament. These methodologies are based on Greco-Roman rhetorical conventions, on modern rhetorical theories, or on a mixture of both. Even within these broader categories variety abounds. The field is currently occupied with the refinement of methodology (D. Stamps 1992).

a. Using Greco-Roman Rhetoric. Rhetorical criticism can analyze the New Testament using Jewish and Greco-Roman rhetorical conventions, thereby helping to place the New Testament texts amid their oral and written cultures. It is a historical enterprise standing between ahistorical LITERARY criticism and historical criticism. This approach assumes that the New Testament authors were familiar with rhetoric either from formal education or through interaction with oral and written Hellenistic culture, which was permeated with rhetorical practice, and that the biblical documents are argumentative in nature.

The classicist G. Kennedy (1984, 33-38) was the first scholar to provide a methodology for rhetorical criticism of the Gospels and the Epistles of the New Testament according to Greco-Roman rhetorical conventions. His methodology has five interrelated steps: (1) determine the rhetorical unit; (2) define the rhetorical situation; (3) determine the rhetorical problem or stasis and the species of rhetoric, whether judicial (accusation and defense), deliberative (persuasion and dissuasion), or epideictic (praise and blame); (4) analyze the invention, arrangement, and style ("invention" is argumentation by ethos, pathos, and logos). "Arrangement" is the ordering of the various components, such as the *exordium* (introduction), *narratio* (statement of facts), *probatio* (main body), and *peroratio* (conclusion). "Style" is fitting the language to the needs of invention and includes such things as figures of speech and thought; and (5) evaluate the rhetorical effectiveness of the rhetorical unit in meeting the exigence.

This approach to rhetorical criticism of the New Testament has been very fruitful but has raised several questions: Did rhetorical convention influence the epistolary genre to the extent that these conventions can be used to analyze an epistle? To what extent did Greco-Roman rhetoric influence Jewish culture by the first century C.E.? Can such rhetoric be used to analyze texts from a predominantly Jewish context? What role does Jewish rhetoric play in early Christian rhetoric?

Besides these questions, there are possible pitfalls in using the method, such as the temptation to rigidly apply rhetorical categories to biblical texts. Also, this approach has depended largely on rhetorical theory alone. Such theory is an abstraction from rhetorical practice, so practice reflected in extant letters and speeches composed by orators of Greece and Rome must also be brought to bear in analysis.

b. Using modern rhetoric. Many interpreters consider rhetorical analysis of the New Testament solely using Greco-Roman rhetorical conventions to be too limited and in need of supplementation with modern rhetorical theory (J. Botha 1989, 14-31; L. Thurén 1990, 41-78; Wuellner 1991, 171-85). Ancient rhetoric does not address all theoretical, practical, and philosophical questions posed by speech and, since the New Testament texts are rhetorical, they are capable of being analyzed by the principles of both Greco-Roman and modern rhetoric. Greco-Roman rhetorical theory is primarily interested in the creation of communication as oriented to the speaker, although some consideration of the audience reaction is present; whereas modern rhetoric concentrates on the effect of rhetoric on the speaker and the audience and on the larger social context of communication, which includes speaker and audience. Rhetorical criticism using modern rhetorical theory is a philosophical reconceptualization of Greco-Roman rhetoric, a synchronic approach to argumentation that does not suit purely historical investigation.

Use of the "new rhetoric" represented by Perelman and Olbrechts-Tyteca and others has been prominent. It redefines rhetoric as argumentation with a persuasive intent and focuses on the audience/readers of the rhetoric. The historical and social situation that produced speech and in which it was enacted becomes central. Rhetoric is a liaison between text and social context, assessing the latter through the former.

Wuellner identifies four features of theory and practice using modern rhetoric: (1) "the turn toward argumentation . . . and the designation of arguments as a text-type distinct from narrative and description"; (2) a "focus on the text's rhetorical intentionality or exigency"; (3) "the social, cultural, ideological values imbedded in the argument's premises, topoi, and hierarchies"; and (4) "the rhetorical or stylistic techniques . . . are seen as means to an end, and not as merely formal, decorative features" (1991, 176-77). Also, modern rhetorical analysis of the New Testament often enlists literary criticism, text linguistics, SEMIOTICS, stylistics, READER-RESPONSE CRITICISM, discourse analysis, and/or speech act theory.

3. *Rhetorical Criticism of the Gospels.* Many individual rhetorical features of the Gospels have been studied, but a thorough assessment of the rhetoric of an entire gospel is as yet rare. Although Kennedy's method has been applied to portions of the Gospels, it fails to account for more elaborate argumentative schemes or for overall rhetorical structure. Ancient rhetoric did not have a theory of narrative that discussed plot development and would have aided in Gospel analysis.

The study of the ancient *chreia* has illumined the rhetoric of the Gospels (B. Mack 1987; Mack and V. Robbins 1989). A *chreia* (pl. *chreiai*) is "a saying or action that is expressed concisely, attributed to a character, and regarded as useful for living" (R. Hock and E. O'Neil 1986, 26); e.g., "Diogenes the philosopher, on being asked by someone how he could become famous, responded: 'By worrying as little as possible about fame'" (1986, 85). *Chreiai* were central to oral and written communication and to argumentation in the Greco-Roman world and were the basis of many rhetorical exercises described in the *progymnasmata* (preliminary exercises) used in rhetorical instruction in postsecondary education. These exercises taught students to work out the meaning of the saying or action in the *chreia* using long-established topics, including paraphrase, expansion, condensation, refutation, and confirmation.

Chreiai were used by the rabbis in the time of JESUS and can be found in contemporary literature from a Jewish provenance. The works of Plutarch and Diogenes Laertius show that they were also collected and expanded for use in biographies. As expected by their Jewish provenance and similarities to ancient biography, *chreiai* elaborations are basic literary units of the Gospels and include the words and deeds of Jesus (e.g., Matt 8:18-20), which were transmitted as oral and written *chreiai*. Teachers, preachers, and the Gospel writers elaborated them according to rhetorical conventions to suit their polemical, theological, and literary needs. This is demonstrated by the fact that a *chreia* in one Gospel is elaborated in its parallel account; e.g., Mark 10:13-16 is an elaborated *chreia* that is found in a more condensed form in Matt 19:13-15. The traditional understanding of form criticism that the sayings of Jesus were preserved separately in an oral tradition independent of a narrative context is no longer tenable (Mack 1987, 29-41; Mack and Robbins 1989, chaps. 1-2).

Besides the use of *chreiai* in rhetorical criticism, there are studies showing that portions of the Gospels were written according to rhetorical imitation of texts and narrative paradigms. Alongside rhetorical analysis primarily based on Greco-Roman rhetoric there are also many important studies that use varying degrees of modern rhetorical theory, literary criticism, Narrative Criticism*§, and Sociology*§.

4. *Rhetorical Criticism of the Epistles.* Currently there is great debate about the extent to which Greco-Roman rhetorical theory influenced the epistolary genre in antiquity. Specifically, the debate concerns the relationship between rhetoric and the Epistles of the New Testament, particularly those of Paul (R. Anderson 1996; G. Hansen 1989, chaps. 1-2; Thurén, 57-64). Some interpreters limit rhetoric's influence on New Testament epistles to matters of style and some invention (C. Classen 1993), while others view the epistles of the New Testament as speeches in epistolary form that can be analyzed using Greco-Roman rhetorical theory (K. Berger 1974; Watson 1988). Still others recognize that both rhetorical and epistolary theory affect the epistle to varying degrees or at different levels (Thurén 1990, 58).

Epistolary and rhetorical theories were developed separately in antiquity; however, there are functional parallels between rhetorical and epistolary classifications and arrangement and some shared stylistic features. Regardless of this lack of articulated integration, by the first century rhetoric had exerted a strong influence on epistolary composition (e.g., the epistles of Demosthenes). Rhetorical handbooks may not have addressed letter writing because they were dominated by the concerns of oral delivery in judicial contexts.

To what extent did Paul receive rhetorical training, and did he employ rhetorical conventions in a conscious manner when writing his epistles? Opinions range from studied and conscious, to merely imitating or functionally related, and to unconsciously borrowing from the experience of oratory. Entire Pauline Epistles, or significant portions, have been successfully analyzed according to the conventions of invention, arrangement, and style. Since Paul's Epistles were to be read in the churches, it is logical to assume that they were fashioned like speeches.

Rhetorical criticism of the New Testament Epistles that examines Greco-Roman rhetorical conventions has been used in conjunction with traditional historical-critical methodologies to define more precisely rhetorical strategies and specific types of argumentation as well as more intricate elaboration of arguments and themes, amplification techniques, and much more. The use of modern rhetoric in this analysis has been extremely interdisciplinary, employing discourse analysis, text-linguistics, and Reader-Response Theory*§, to name a few other disciplines.

The future of rhetorical criticism of the New Testament will be interdisciplinary. This future is glimpsed in the development of socio-rhetorical criticism (Robbins 1996), which uses a variety of methodologies to examine the inner texture, intertexture, social and cultural texture, ideological texture, and sacred texture of the New Testament texts.

Bibliography: R. D. Anderson Jr., *Ancient Rhetorical Theory and Paul* (Contributions to Biblical Exegesis and Theology 18, 1996). K. Berger, "Apostelbrief und apostolische Rede: Zum Formular fruhchristlicher Briefe," *ZNW 65* (1974) 190-231. H. D. Betz, "The Literary Composition and Function of Paul's Letter to the Galatians," *NTS 21* (1975) 353-79; *Galatians: A Commentary on Paul's Letter to the Churches in Galatia* (Hermeneia, 1979); "The Problem of Rhetoric and Theology According to the Apostle Paul," *L'apôtre Paul: Personnalité, style et conception du ministère* (ed. A. Vanhoye, BETL 73, 1986) 16-48. C. C. Black, "Rhetorical Criticism and Biblical Interpretation," *Exp Tim 100* (1989) 252-58. J. Botha, "On the 'Reinvention' of Rhetoric," *Scriptura 31* (1989) 14-31. C. J. Classen, "St. Paul's Epistles and Ancient Greek and Roman Rhetoric," *Rhetoric and the NT: Essays from the 1992 Heidelberg Conference* (ed. S. E. Porter and T. H. Olbricht, JSNTSup 90, 1993) 265-91. R. W. Funk, *Language, Hermeneutic, and Word of God* (1966). G. W. Hansen, *Abraham in Galatians: Epistolary and Rhetorical Contexts* (JSNTSup 29, 1989). R. F. Hock and E. N. O'Neil, *The Chreia in Ancient Rhetoric, vol. 1, The Progymnasmata* (Graeco-Roman Religion Series 9, SBLTT 27, 1986). G. A. Kennedy, *NT Interpretation Through Rhetorical Criticism* (1984). J. Lambrecht, "Rhetorical Criticism and the NT," *Bijdr 50* (1989) 239-53. B. L. Mack, *Anecdotes and Arguments: The Chreia in Antiquity and Early Christianity* (Occasional Papers of the Institute for Antiquity and Christianity 10, 1987); *Rhetoric and the NT* (GBS, 1990). B. L. Mack and V. K. Robbins, *Patterns of Persuasion in the Gospels* (Foundations and Facets: Literary Facets, 1989). P. Melanchthon, *Commentarii in epistolam ad Romanos hoc anno MDXL recogniti et locupletati* (1540). J. Muilenburg, "Form Criticism and Beyond," *JBL 88* (1969) 1-18. E. Norden, *Die antike Kunstprosa vom VI. Jahrhundert vor Christus bis in die Zeit der Renaissance* (1898). C. Perelman and L. Olbrechts-Tyteca, *La Nouvelle Rhétorique: Trait, l'argumentation* (1958; ET tr. J. Wilkinson and P. Weaver, *The New Rhetoric: A Treatise on Argumentation,* 1969). V. K. Robbins, *The Tapestry of Early Christian Discourse: Rhetoric, Society, and Ideology* (1996). D. Stamps, "Rhetorical Criticism and the Rhetoric of NT Criticism," *JTL 6* (1992) 268-79. L. Thurén, The Rhetorical Strategy of 1 Peter with Special

Regard to Ambiguous Expressions (1990). **D. F. Watson,** Invention, Arrangement, and Style: Rhetorical Criticism of Jude and 2 Peter (SBLDS 104, 1988). **D. F. Watson and A. J. Hauser,** Rhetorical Criticism of the Bible: A Comprehensive Bibliography With Notes on History and Method (BIS 4, 1994). **A. Wilder,** *The Language of the Gospel: Early Christian Rhetoric* (1964). **W. Wuellner,** "Paul's Rhetoric of Argumentation in Romans: An Alternative to the Donfried-Karris Debate Over Romans," *CBQ* 38 (1976) 330-51; "Where Is Rhetorical Criticism Taking Us?" *CBQ* 49 (1987) 448-63; "Rhetorical Criticism and Its Theory in Culture-critical Perspective: The Narrative Rhetoric of John 11," Text and Interpretation: New Approaches in the Criticism of the NT (NTTS 15, 1991; eds. P. J. Hartin and J. H. Petzer) 171-85.

D. F. WATSON

LITERARY AND STRUCTURALIST/
POSTMODERNIST APPROACHES METHODS

Semiotics

The British philosopher J. Locke[§] was apparently the first modern philosopher to use the word *semeiotik?* for the doctrine of signs and, in particular, for the study of words (1690, 1959, 4.21.4). C. Peirce first brought the term into general use in his work on logic (1932, 2:227). *Semeiotikos* was used by the Greeks to refer to a person skilled in interpreting signs, and medical writers used the term for diagnosis and prognosis. The philosopher Sextus Empiricus (*Adv. Log.* 1.25) wrote of a person who was a "semiotician" and therefore claimed to be able to make inferences from observable signs. "Semiotics" has been adopted by the International Association of Semiotic Studies for the study of any sign system with no necessary dependence on linguistics (U. Eco 1979, 30). Eco (1979, 9-13) notes that the discipline can concern itself with such fields as the communicative behavior of animals, olfactory signs, tactile communication (e.g., a kiss), musical codes, natural and formalized languages, and cultural codes (e.g., etiquette systems).

The Stoics, as described by Sextus (*Adv. Log.* 2.11, 12), made some basic distinctions that remain in use by many semioticians today: "They [the Stoics] say three things correspond to one another: what is signified, what signifies and what is the reality [happening-object or event]. Of these, on the one hand, the signifier is the sound such as 'Dion.' The signified, on the other hand, is the thing itself made known by the sound which [i.e., the thing] we perceive as corresponding to our understanding. But the barbarians do not understand even though they hear the sound. The reality is that which exists outside—e.g., Dion himself."

Peirce spoke of a sign as "something that stands to somebody for something in some respect or capacity" (1932, 2:228). The object is what the sign stands for (Dion himself in the quote above). The interpretant is what the sign creates in the mind of another person (what is "signified" in the example above). A sign stands for an object, not in all respects, but in reference to an idea that Peirce called the "ground" of a sign. A sign cannot describe all the characteristics of an object but has to make a selection of those characteristics. Peirce related the interpretant to human conduct (N. Kretzmann 1967, 395-96).

F. de Saussure, one of the pioneers of modern linguistics, similarly distinguished between signifier (the imprint the sign makes on our senses) and signified. The relation between the two is arbitrary. In other words, a word can mean whatever the users of a language choose it to mean (1928[2], 98-100). De Saussure also distinguished between *langue* (the system of a language) and *parole* (the use of a language in a given situation; 1928[2], 37). A word like "parable" can be investigated on the abstract level of its use in English (*langue*). It can also be investigated as to its use in a particular sentence of the English language as uttered by a person at a specific time (*parole*).

K. Bühler, the German linguist and psychologist, developed a model of language understood as an *organum* ("tool"; cf. Plato *Cratylus,* 388*b*) with which a person communicates something about things to another person (Bühler 1932, 1982[2], 24-25). In his model, Bühler includes the sign, the sender, the receiver, and the realm of objects and relations. The sign is a "symbol" of the objects and relations that it expresses. It is a "symptom" because of its dependence on a sender whose inner state it expresses. It is also a "signal" because of its appeal to the hearer, whose outer and inner behavior it guides (like traffic signals; 1982,[2] 28). Corresponding to the concepts "symbol," "symptom," and "signal," Bühler also uses the equivalent terms "representation," "expression," and "appeal."

The behavioral psychologist C. Morris used a semiotics similar to Bühler's. He defined pragmatics as the study of "the relation of signs to interpreters." Semantics is the study of the "relations of signs to the objects to which the signs are applicable," and syntactics is the study of the "formal relations of signs to one another" (1946, 217-18). Morris gave a behavioral interpretation of the sign process: A sign sets up in an interpreter the disposition to react in a certain kind of way (the interpretant) to a certain kind of object (the signification) under certain conditions (the context). Taking the dance of bees as an example, Morris called the dance itself the sign; the other bees influenced by the dance are interpreters; the disposition of the bees to react in a certain way to the dance is the interpretant; the object (e.g., food or exploring new hive locations) toward which the bees are prepared to react is the signification; and the context is the position of the hive (1964, 2-3; see 1946, 17-18).

The philosopher G. Klaus included four categories in his semiotic model (1973, 47, 56): the objects of mental reflection (things, qualities, relations), linguistic signs, mental images, and people who use and understand signs. The objects are what are referred to by the signs. For example, a word like "angel" can refer to the angel Gabriel (the object). The word angel has a conceptual meaning—what Klaus calls a mental image. He defines syntax as the relation of one sign to another or R(S, ?), where R stands for relation, S stands for sign, and ? stands for other signs. Sigmatics is the relation between signs and the objects of mental reflection or R(S,O), where O stands for objects. Semantics is the relation between signs and mental images or R(S, I), where I is the mental image. Pragmatics is the relation between signs and people R(S,U), where U is the user. Klaus integrated the above categories in another article (1969, 978) in which he defined pragmatics to be a four-place relation between the senders (or receivers) of the sign, the sign itself, its meaning, and its reference. If one abstracts from the sender and the receiver, then semantics is the relation between signs and meanings and sigmatics is the relation between signs and their references. If one abstracts from users and meanings, then syntax is the relationship of signs to each other. D. Hellholm (1980, 23) simplifies the schema by including sigmatics in the discipline of semantics and by replacing O and I with D for *designatum*, or "meaning."

Semiotics has gone in a very different direction in the work of A. Greimas. One of his important contributions is his semiotic square, which he describes as the logical articulation of a semantic category (1982, 308-10). His semiotics concentrates on what has been called semantics above. His square is presented in a simplified form here:

> A   non-A
> not non-A   not A

A and non-A are contraries. A and not A are contradictories, as are non-A and not non-A. As an example Greimas gives this square:

> Being   seeming
> non-seeming   non-being

The examples from biblical scholars that follow will be divided into syntax, semantics, and pragmatics. Hellholm uses the concept of text-syntax (1980, 12, 29, 30) to illuminate the *Visions of Hermas*. One aspect of syntax is anaphora, or pointing back in a text, and *kataphora*, or pointing forward in a text. One of Hellholm's arguments for making a break between the fourth and fifth visions of Hermas uses this aspect of text-syntax. In the *Book of Visions* there are several examples of *kataphora* to following visions (*Vis.* 2.4.2; 3.13.4b), but none of them point to texts beyond Vision 4. Anaphora is also found in the references to the three visions in 3.10.7-3.13.4 and finally in 4.3.6. None of the examples of anaphora point to the other books of Hermas either. In the *Book of Mandates*, on the other hand, there is an example of anaphora to the books of visions (*Vis.* 5.5). There is another similar example in the *Book of Similitudes* 9.1 (these last two examples may be secondary). These examples discussed by Hellholm are an example of syntax— the relation of signs to other signs.

Word studies are a well-known technique in biblical studies. What is more unusual is the use of semiotic categories in such studies. G. Caird (1980, 54), for example, claims that the word *mystērion* used in both Ephesians and Colossians has the identical sense of "secret" and uses that hypothesis to question the arguments against Pauline authorship (Paul*[§]) based on the different uses of the word in each letter. However, the referent of *mystērion* is different in the two letters, and Caird does not consider the possibility that this could be an indication of different authors. In a similar approach, J. Louw (1982, 50) notes that in Revelation *drakōn* means "dragon" and refers to the devil. *Paraklētos* in 1 John 2:1 has the meaning "helper" and the reference Christ.

Scholars can also use semantics to look at larger units of text, as in the investigation of H. Boers. Employing the work of Greimas, Boers uses semiotic squares to analyze John 4. Interpreting John 4:39-42 by means of one of the squares, he states that when the villagers recognized JESUS as a universal savior, they affirmed salvation for all people (1988, 129, 180, 199), whereas their earlier belief in Jesus as Messiah through the woman's testimony did not affirm universal salvation. In Boers's square, the contrary of universal salvation is partisan salvation. His square (slightly simplified) is as follows (1988, 129): S (the subject) stands for the villagers; O (the object) stands for the concept of universal salvation; and non-O stands for the concept of partisan salvation.

S is conjoined with non-O	S is conjoined with O
S is disjoined with O	S is disjoined with non-O

Boers employs these squares to clarify the logical relationships of the values in the text.

Pragmatics (the relation of signs, meaning, and users) surfaces in the work of many scholars in different forms. P. Maartens, in a discussion of Mark 4:24-25, notes that "watch what you hear" is a perlocutionary speech act. A speech act such as a warning (as in Mark 4:24-25) may have an effect on a hearer, and this effect is the perlocution. If a reader actually heeded the warning, the perlocutionary act would be successful. Maartens (1991, 77) writes: "Mark 16:8 confronts the reader with the rule of the resurrected Lord. The real reader concretizes the speech act in a situational frame that encompasses himself. His faith produces hope. The text re-enacts this hope: Even in times of persecution, oppression and suffering, the hope of the implied reader perseveres." This attention to the effect of signs on a reader is an example of pragmatics. In a discussion of irony in John 4, G. O'Day (1986, 95) remarks that "Johannine irony creates the revelation experience for the reader as a result of the imaginative participation in the text which it encourages." Approaches that concentrate on the reader are semiotic in character (cf. G. Stibbe 1990, 418).

Semiotics overlaps with many other fields of research, e.g., work in Intertextuality*[§]. The semiotician J. Kristeva describes a horizontal dimension of a word in which a word concerns both the subject of the writing (or author) and the receiver of the text. At the same time there is a vertical dimension of a word in a text and its orientation to a preceding or contemporary literary corpus. A word (or text) then is a crossing of words (or texts), where one reads at least another word (or text). Kristeva writes, "Every text is constructed as a mosaic of citations, every text is an absorption and transformation of another text." She bases her understanding of intertextuality on this model (1969, 84-85). Elsewhere she defines intertextuality: "The term intertextuality denotes this transposition of one (or several) sign system(s) into another" (quoted in

P. Maartens 1991, 75). Semiotics also overlaps with Structuralism*§. The American-German tradition of semiotics described above concerns itself with syntax, semantics, and pragmatics. The French tradition of semiotics is concerned mainly with issues of semantics, as in the work of the structuralist Greimas. Semiotic methods in biblical studies will stand or fall on their perceived usefulness in illuminating aspects of the text. The exegetical results may not be totally new, but the different questions such methods ask may throw new and exciting light on old questions.

Bibliography: K. Baldinger, *Semantic Theory: Towards a Modern Semantics* (1980). **H. Boers,** *Neither on this Mountain nor in Jerusalem: A Study of John 4* (SBLMS 35, 1988). **K. Bühler,** *Sprachtheorie: Die Darstellungsfunction der Sprache* (1934, 1982). **G. B. Caird,** *The Language and Imagery of the Bible* (1980). **U. Eco,** *A Theory of Semiotics* (1979). **A. J. Greimas and J. Courts,** *Semiotics and Language: An Analytical Dictionary* (Advances in Semiotics, 1982). **D. Hellholm,** *Das Visionenbuch des Hermas als Apokalypse: Formgeschichtliche und texttheoretische Studien zu einer literarischen Gattung* (ConNT 13, 1, 1980). **G. Klaus,** "Semiotik," *Philosophisches Wörterbuch* (ed. G. Klaus and M. Buhr, 1969⁶) 978; *Semiotik und Erkenntnistheorie* (1973). **N. Kretzmann,** "Semantics, History of," *Encyclopedia of Philosophy* 7 (1967) 358-406. **J. Kristeva**, *Semeiotike: Recherches pour une sémanalyse* (1969). **J. Locke,** *An Essay Concerning Human Understanding* (1690; ed. A. C. Fraser, 1959). **J. P. Louw,** *Semantics of NT Greek* (1982). **P. J. Maartens,** " 'Sign' and 'Significance' in the Theory and Practice of Ongoing Literary Critical Interpretation with Reference to Mark 4:24 and 25: A Study of Semiotic Relations in the Text," *Text and Interpretation: New Approaches in the Criticism of the NT* (ed. P. J. Hartin and J. H. Petzer, 1991) 63-79. **C. Morris,** *Signs, Language, and Behavior* (1946); *Signification and Significance: A Study of the Relations of Signs and Values* (1964). **G. R. O'Day,** *Revelation in the Fourth Gospel: Narrative Mode and Theological Claim* (1986). **C. S. Peirce,** *Collected Papers of C. S. Peirce, vol. 2, Elements of Logic* (ed. C. Hartshorne and P. Weiss, 1932). **F. de Saussure,** *Course in General Linguistics* (1928²; ET 1959). **M. W. G. Stibbe,** "Semiotics," *A Dictionary of Biblical Interpretation* (ed. R.J. Coggins and J. L. Houlden, 1990) 618-20.

J. G. COOK

LITERARY AND STRUCTURALIST/
POSTMODERNIST APPROACHES METHODS
Structuralism and Deconstruction

The term *structuralism*, which came into vogue in the 1950s and 1960s, refers properly to a set of techniques for the analysis of literary texts and other human productions, together with the specific theory on which the techniques are based. Construed more broadly, it has become a focusing term (almost a code word) for a wide-ranging theoretical rejection of historicism. A human production is to be analyzed primarily in terms of the rules of its internal organization, not primarily in terms of the process that produced it. As the theoretical debate has developed and as the early structuralist claims have become more muted, other focusing terms have appeared, including *deconstruction*. The latter sometimes indicates a technique for Literary*§ analysis but more often denotes a way of looking at current critical theory, particularly at the debate over structuralism. While it does not reverse structuralism's rejection of historicism, deconstruction suggests the reopening of the question of history in a new framework.

Within biblical studies structuralism has developed in the context of a revolt that began to gain power in the 1960s and continues with increasing vigor against the predominance of historical criticism in biblical studies. Despite the vast accomplishments of historical criticism, it has been widely felt that there are significant dimensions of biblical meaning that historical criticism is unable to illuminate, in particular, literary dimensions. In response, a wide range of literary approaches has been proposed and tried out, many of them simply refinements of age-old sensitivity to the Bible as literature. But some biblical scholars have found in the extra-biblical debate over structuralism and deconstruction a much more radical approach to the literary analysis of texts and to the whole question of meaning in texts, pointing eventually to a rethinking of the whole enterprise of biblical studies.

1. *Extra-biblical Developments. a. Stages of development.* There are three main stages in the development of structuralism that have become significant for biblical studies.

i. Linguistics: F. de Saussure. The first is the linguistics of F. de Saussure. When we hear an English sentence, such as "Yesterday I got into my car and drove to work," we automatically process it as a piece of information about the speaker. What remains almost always unconscious is our processing it as a piece of language, yet this is the precondition of it having any meaning for us. In constructing the sentence, the speaker has used numerous linguistic rules that we also use to decode it; some are very general (e.g. the order of elements in a syntactically well-formed English sentence); others, detailed and subtle (e.g. the verb get must be treated in this case as part of an irreducible combination "get into," hence "enter," rather than "acquire").

Saussure contrasted *parole*, any actual linguistic event (e.g., a spoken sentence), with *langue*, the underlying system of relationships among the elements of a language (the French words are usually retained in English discussion). The system is more basic than the event, but it is an abstraction to which we have access only through the study of utterances the linguistic community deems acceptable. Knowledge of the system is by no means necessary in order to use the language. *Langue* is an abstraction in another sense too. It implies that we can stop language at a moment in time and examine its structure, whereas, in fact, language is in constant flux. This suggests the distinction, of the utmost importance to all of structuralism, between synchronic and diachronic method. Saussure stresses synchronic linguistics, the study of the language at one point in time, at the expense of diachronic, the study of its development over time. One other tenet of his system is of key importance—namely, that the elements of a language do not have intrinsic meaning but, rather, have meaning only as a result of their place in the system, of their relations with other elements. (A classic example is the noncorrespondence of color terms in different languages. What the majority of French-speakers call *bleu* will not exactly correspond to what the majority of English-speakers call blue. The meaning of blue is "what the majority of English-speakers do not regard as better described by some other color term"!)

ii. Generalization of linguistics to other systems: C. Lévi-Strauss. The second stage involves a generalization of these insights to human systems other than natural languages. (A glance at an anthology like that of J. Ehrmann [1970] or M. Lane [1970] will show in how wide a variety of disciplines structural methods have been tried.) The most important figure, indeed the founder of structuralism as a self-conscious method, is Lévi-Strauss. In his anthropological work he has analyzed subsystems (or "codes") of primitive societies as having a quasi-linguistic structure. Examples are dietary or kinship rules (thus permissible versus impermissible marriages in a kinship system are analogous to syntactical versus asyntactical sequences of words). In each case, members of the society have so internalized the system that they can differentiate between acceptable and unacceptable combinations without being consciously aware of the underlying logic. All these codes are ways in which a society organizes reality, and Lévi-Strauss believes in an innate human necessity to organize the world in this way. The message encoded by each subsystem in a given society is ultimately the same (see esp. Lévi-Strauss 1967).

Lévi-Strauss's most extensive and important work has been on myth (for a programmatic statement, see Lévi-Strauss 1963), culminating in a four-volume magnum opus on Amerindian mythology (1970, 1973, 1978, 1981). A primitive society deals with the irresoluble contradictions it experiences in the world through myth (Mythology and Biblical Studies[§]), which creates the illusion of resolution so that the world can be experienced otherwise than as merely incomprehensible. Lévi-Strauss reads a myth as a set of logical operations that bring the terms of experience into relation with one another. The various myths of a culture (and, eventually, all myths) are "transformations" of each other, any change in a single term being correlative with changes in other terms of the system. All these operations, however complex, can be reduced analytically to binary oppositions (life versus death, animal versus vegetable food, etc.), which the myth posits and mediates. For example, the total contradiction between life and death can be displaced into an opposition between this world and a world beyond this one; and various beings can then be introduced who (although they cannot be both alive and dead) can move between one world and the other.

iii. Structural analysis of narrative: A. Greimas. The third stage is the structural analysis of narrative, especially the work of Greimas (1983, 1987, 1988). Narrative is language, and one way of thinking of such analysis is as an extension of Saussurean linguistics beyond the scope of sentences to whole narrative sequences. Greimas has tried to define the most elementary units of narrative and to frame laws governing their acceptable combination. An important precursor in this enterprise was V. Propp (1968), who analyzed about one hundred Russian folktales into their sequential plot elements, or "functions" (e.g., "the hero is pursued," "the villain is exposed"). He defined thirty-one such functions and found that, although a given tale never included all of them, those it did contain proved always to be in the same order. This strongly suggests that the community producing these tales screened them for "syntactical" structure by a process analogous to the construction of sentences in a natural language.

Greimas builds consciously on Propp, but finds Propp's functions too diffuse and repetitive. Many of them are simply logical transformations of one another (e.g., the finding and equipping of the hero has the same logical structure as the hero's combat with the villain) and can be reduced to relatively few binary oppositions and their mediation. Thus Greimas looks for schemata of maximum abstraction and generality as the linguistic rules for all human narrative. The best known of these is his "actantial model" for anything done (or intended) in narrative. A sender transfers an object to a receiver by the agency of a subject whom other agents may help or oppose:

Sender   Object   Receiver

Helper   Subject   Opponent

This scheme can be used to map a whole story, but it can also map units of story action down to the most elementary so that the story can be analyzed as an interlocking set of actantial models.

b. Issues. Because of its large claims, structuralism has, from its inception, brought to the fore a mass of theoretical questions. Many contemporary commentators consider that, having failed to answer such questions, it is already passé. Certainly the early structuralist proposals cannot survive unchanged, but a truer assessment would be that structuralism has been extraordinarily fecund in initiating theoretical debate (literary and other). It retains its vibrancy in this sense, even if fewer researchers now call themselves structuralists. But it is senseless any longer to discuss structuralism in isolation from the larger theoretical field. (For an excellent discussion, see P. Caws 1988.) Four issues, which cannot be cleanly separated from one another, may be highlighted.

i. The relation of structural and historical methods. The most persistent problem has been the relation of structural to historical methods of research. Are the "deep structures" of human productions changeless over time? To the extent that they apparently are not, to what historical variables are they correlative? How can structural and historical methods combine to give a theoretical account of stability and change? What, in this connection, are the historical conditions for the rise of structuralism itself?

ii. The relation of structural methods to literature. To what kinds of literature are structural methods appropriate? Lévi-Strauss confines himself to "primitive" texts (myths) and doubts that his methods are at all applicable to texts generated out of a historical consciousness. Propp worked with folktales, and it was largely with these that Greimas and other narrative structuralists preferred to work at the outset. But what of modern literature? Insofar as early structuralism took it up at all, it was in its most highly stereotyped genres, the detective novel or even the cartoon strip. Is there something about modern literature that resists the application of structural methods? R. Barthes devoted a whole book, the influential *S/Z* (1974), to the analysis of a short story by Balzac (cf. Greimas 1988 on Maupassant). But the most characteristic modern form, the novel, has not been much taken up by structuralists (see, however, G. Genette 1980 on Proust).

iii. The relation of structural analysis to textual laws. A directly related question is how structural analysis of the individual text is related to positing general laws that govern texts. Barthes (already in *S/Z*) moved beyond structuralism into what he called "textualism" to stress the uniqueness of the single text. However, when Greimas devotes a study to a single text, it is with an eye to the potential for generalizing the results. But his effort to formulate elementary laws governing all narrative does not imply that all narrative texts are essentially the same. Rather, it is necessary to think of a hierarchy of structures. The analysis of a text may demonstrate universal structures but also structures specific to the text's culture, its literary genre, etc., as well as structures specific to itself. The text partakes of various "universes of meaning" out of which its own particular universe is created.

iv. Structuralism in relation to the reader. Structuralism has tried to pattern itself on the model of an objective natural science. Its theoretical claim—that any reader using its techniques would discover the same structure—is not the case in practice. One reason is that the text is only a part of the whole process of communication (or "enunciation") in which the reader, in particular, has a role to play (Reader-response Criticism*§). Theory is being developed regarding the reader as an interactive participant in the creation of the structures of meaning that literary analysis discovers (J. Tompkins 1980). Another theoretical development that has forced structuralism out of its objective mode is a growing insistence (in part under the influence of the American philosopher C. Peirce) that it is one part of a pervasive and fluid human need to create systems of signs. Proponents of this development prefer the term SEMIOTICS to *structuralism* (U. Eco 1976).

c. Deconstruction: J. Derrida. The theoretical issues surrounding structuralism must now be pursued in relation to deconstruction (there are valuable surveys in J. Culler 1982; R. Harland 1987; V. Leitch 1983). Derrida, with whom this term is most associated, developed his ideas in a French context dominated by structuralism and directed much of his early critique to the structuralist pioneers Saussure and Lévi-Strauss (1976, 27-73, 101-40). As a philosopher, Derrida takes up nothing less than the whole metaphysical tradition in Western philosophy, which he sees (1978) as the attempt to posit a fixed center (God, human, consciousness, reason, etc.; the comprehensive term for all such systems is logocentric) from which the rest of reality can be reliably organized. But the history of modern thought is simply the story of the forced abandonment of each proposed center (the earth as center in the Copernican revolution, consciousness as center in the Freudian, etc.). Deconstruction attempts a radical decentering by unearthing and subverting the unquestioned assumptions on which the metaphysical tradition is based.

The relationship of this kind of deconstruction to structuralism is a double one. On the one hand, it is by structural analysis that deconstruction most characteristically proceeds. The metaphysical tradition works by positing binary oppositions (some common ones are rational/irrational, clear/obscure, original/imitation, central/peripheral, simple/complex, serious/frivolous) and by systematically affirming the superiority of the first over the second term. The work of deconstruction can be thought of as the careful demonstration of the arbitrariness of these procedures, of the inner contradiction they cannot avoid (e.g., anything affirmed as original can always be shown to be imitative). On the other hand, Derrida sees structuralism as belonging to, even as a culmination of, this same Western metaphysical tradition, creating binary oppositions of its own and affirming the superiority of one term over the other (*langue* over *parole*, synchronic over diachronic). Structuralism becomes yet another logocentric attempt to control reality through a system.

The positive interest shown in the structuralism/deconstruction debate by feminists (FEMINIST INTERPRETATION) and Marxists is extremely significant. Previously, structuralism was seen as outmoded, at least in the North American context. Deconstruction was taking on the very narrow connotation of a method of literary criticism that stresses the limitless plurality, or "undecidability," of meaning in the literary text. From the perspective of political engagement, this approach seemed irrelevant or retrograde. But the implications of the development of structuralism and deconstruction in France, in a highly charged political context, have now been taken more seriously in the United States. It is increasingly understood that the metaphysical tradition's striving for structure and hierarchy has always gone along with accumulating and hierarchizing political power, thus Derrida's deconstruction of metaphysics is also the deconstruction of the structures of real power.

There are many examples of the politicization of the current debate, including the structural Marxism of L. Althusser (ET 1969), with its extension into literary criticism by P. Macherey (1978), or the analysis by M. Foucault (ET 1978) of how power operates in scientific discourse. But the most obvious example is provided by feminism, where there a clear link between the male/female opposition in Western metaphysics (with its endless correlates: rational/irrational, domination/submission, etc.) and the political oppression of women. This philosophical and linguistic creation of the categories of male and female has been much analyzed in French feminism (T. Moi 1985), and recently a flood of feminist literary criticism in North America has taken up related issues (e.g., G. Greene and C. Kahn 1985; more generally on feminism and poststructuralism, C. Weedon 1987).

Among the most interesting examples of the new trend is the work of F. Jameson (1981), who attempts a Marxist analysis of texts from FOLKLORE to the modern novel, informed by the entire structuralism/deconstruction debate, notably by Greimas (see his foreword to Greimas 1987). He insists on the question of the relation of text to history, although not in the sense of facile correspondence between the text and some history independent of the text. Rather, the "world of meaning" in the text (what Jameson calls its "political unconscious") is correlated with the ideology under which it was produced. Specifically, study of the text's inner contradictions can help discern the contradictions inherent in the ideology. But if all texts need, in this sense, to be historicized, so also all history needs to be "textualized," deconstructed, read in terms of the arbitrary relationship of its language to meaning. Jameson both draws structuralism into the service of Ideological*§ analysis and performs an ideological analysis of structuralism itself. (On Marxism and deconstruction, see also M. Ryan 1982.)

2. *Biblical Developments*. The response within biblical studies has been diverse, with theoretical boundaries not always clearly drawn. Only recently have biblical scholars engaged the critical issues raised by deconstruction. Significant developments have usually been first announced in the periodical *Semeia*, founded as a direct result of structuralist interest in the Bible. The range of topics *Semeia* now takes up is a good index of the range of theoretical debate in which biblical structuralism is involved (see also The Bible and Culture Collective 1995 and D. Jobling 1995).

a. *Structural analysis*. The first application of structural analysis to the Bible was an essay by the anthropologist E. Leach (1969) on Genesis 7–23. In it, and elsewhere, Leach follows closely Lévi-Strauss's procedures for myth analysis. Biblical specialists find this essay facile, but another of Leach's analyses—"The Legitimacy of Solomon" (1969, 25-83), based on Lévi-Strauss's work on kinship—is widely conceded to have opened up quite unexpected and important horizons. The main problem is that Leach treats the Bible as a concatenation of quasi-mythic fragments, paying no attention to its character as sequential narrative. (On the impact within biblical studies of Lévi-Strauss's work on kinship, M. Donaldson 1981and T. Prewitt 1990. While not a follower of Lévi-Strauss, M. Douglas also applies structural anthropology to the Bible, e.g., to the Levitical prohibitions [1966].)

b. *Literary and textual issues*. Most biblical structuralists have pursued specifically literary/textual issues. The main inspiration has been Greimas, although many scholars have continued to find Lévi-Strauss's techniques for myth analysis useful in dealing with the deep structural elements that narrative analysis posits. A considerable school of French scholars (notably J. Calloud 1976) has, since the 1960s, pursued a Greimasian approach to biblical texts (for a more idiosyncratic use of Greimas, see Barthes 1988), which has had a decisive impact on biblical structuralism in America through the ongoing work of D. Patte and his associates (1978, 1991).

The first organized work in North America, devoted to the synoptic Parables*§, was issued in *Semeia* 1 and 2. It was the result of a convergence of interest between Patte, in his attempt to establish structuralism within American biblical studies, and a group interested in the literary reading of the parables (especially J. D. Crossan 1995; R. Funk 1982; and D. Via 1967). This early work was rather eclectic, but it provided an important impulse and is still interesting for opening up a variety of structural possibilities. But it is in Patte's own developing work that structuralism has decisively moved beyond a marginal position in biblical studies. In 1978, he and A. Patte proposed a precise method of structural analysis that they claimed anyone could apply to biblical texts with controllable results (1978, 11-38). They defined procedures by which the reader can move from the complex gospel narrative, through the system of simple subnarratives that underlie it and the symbolic system these subnarratives imply, to the text's "semantic universe" or world of meaning. This method underlies D. Patte's books on Paul†§

(1983) and Matthew (1987), in which he sets out to display the structure of the biblical authors' convictions, or faith. This structure constrains the way the author organizes his material, whatever its source (e.g., Matthew's convictions shape what he may take from Mark or Q). In later works (1990*a*, 1990*b*), Patte has considerably refined his method.

Through the 1970s and 1980s, a number of other important contributions emerged from the circle around Patte. E. Malbon's 1986 work on the "geographical code" in Mark demonstrates the continuing vibrancy of Lévi-Strauss's impulse; she shows how the structural organization of spaces (Galilee and Judea, sea and land, inhabited land and desert, etc.) provides a major key to what is going on in this gospel. D. Jobling (1986), working in the Hebrew Bible, pursues a line more loosely adapted from Lévi-Strauss and Greimas. R. Polzin (1980) explores a very different and important direction in applying the methods of the Russian formalists to a part of the Deuteronomistic History‡§. Of particular interest is *Semeia* 18, which offers a large collection of alternative structural exegeses of a single text (Genesis 2–3). In his introduction, Patte takes up the issue of how there can be a variety of valid structural methods.

c. Deconstruction. Biblical scholars, including many structuralists, were initially slow to become involved in the debate over deconstruction. This may be because, in the United States, this debate was largely carried on by specialists in modern literature. This was false to Derrida's initiative, since it is precisely the foundational documents of Western culture that he has taken up (e.g., Plato, but also, on several occasions, biblical texts; Derrida 1982, 1991).

After the breakthrough in *Semeia* 23 (*Derrida and Biblical Studies*), contributions began to appear steadily: Crossan's deconstructive reading of John (1983); G. Phillips's reading of Matthew 13 in the light of Derrida and Foucault (1985); major collections of essays in *Semeia* 51 (*Poststructural Criticism and the Bible*) and 54 (*Poststructuralism as Exegesis*); and, at book length, P. Miscall (1986, on 1 Samuel) and S. Moore (1992, on Mark and Luke; for a survey and critique of contributions, see The Bible and Culture Collective 1995, 119-48). S. Handelman (1982) has probed the historical links between rabbinic biblical interpretation and deconstruction. Phillips (1990*b*) and H. White (1991) have taken a lead in broadening the theoretical framework of biblical structuralism by considering developments in semiotics. All these works demonstrate the possibility and necessity of a fully critical reading of the Bible, a reading that takes current critical debate with full seriousness and intends to make its own contribution to that debate. But such a reading is threatening to traditional views of the Bible, since it starts to unpack the Bible's Authority*§, uniqueness, sacredness, and so on, forcing the question of how the Bible's centrality in Western culture has been implicated in the establishment of the logocentric metaphysical tradition. The Fourth Gospel's programmatic statement that "the Word was God" sounds, from a deconstructionist point of view, like a summary of the whole problem!

Several of the above authors and collections work on the boundary between deconstruction and the political or ideological analysis of texts. An important precursor was the materialist reading of F. Belo (1981). Drawing on both French structuralism (especially Barthes's textualism) and Marxist theory, he has produced an astonishing reading of the Gospel of Mark in which he analyzes how this text unravels the two incompatible systems whereby Judaism understands sin as pollution and as debt (Belo's work is not so much a deconstruction of Mark as a claim that Mark deconstructs the Torah). Contributions include a representative collection of essays in *Semeia* 59 (*Ideological Criticism of Biblical Texts*), R. Boer's (1996) definitive treatment of the relevance (both theoretical and exegetical) of Jameson's work to biblical studies, and the pursuit of related issues of pedagogy by Patte and Phillips (Patte 1995). Feminist writers informed by deconstruction, particularly M. Bal (1987, 1988*a*, 1988*b*), press the issue of the Bible's implication in entrenched structures of oppression (on Bal, Jobling 1991; further on critical feminist reading, J. C. Exum [1995] and D. Fewell [1995], who provide annotated bibliography; and Exum 1993).

3. *Conclusion.* Structuralism and deconstruction, in conjunction with other literary approaches, have played a large role in demonstrating the narrowness and arbitrariness of the previously dominant historical-critical method in biblical studies. They have helped create a climate in which attention to the biblical text in its final form takes precedence over hypothetical reconstruction of its possible earlier forms. They have altered the grounds on which debate over appropriate biblical methodology is conducted. Although they still need greater representation in introductions and commentaries, they have already generated major works of biblical scholarship

Bibliography: L. **Althusser,** *For Marx* (ET 1969). **M. Bal,** *Lethal Love* (1987); *Death and Dissymmetry* (1988a); *Murder and Difference* (1988b). **R. Barthes,** *S/Z* (1974); "The Struggle with the Angel," *The Semiotic Challenge* (1988) 246-60. **F. Belo,** *A Materialist Reading of the Gospel of Mark* (1981). The Bible and Culture Collective, *The Postmodern Bible* (1995). **R. Boer,** *Jameson and Jeroboam* (1996). **P. Caws,** *Structuralism: The Art of the Intelligible* (1988). **J. Colloud,** *Structural Analysis of the Narrative* (SemSup 4, 1976). **J. D. Crossan** (ed.), *The Good Samaritan, Semeia 2* (1974); *The Dark Interval: Towards a Theology of Story* (1975); "It is Written: A Structuralist Analysis of John 6," *Semeia* 26 (1983) 3-22. **J. Culler,** *On Deconstruction* (1982). **J. Derrida,** *Of Grammatology* (1976); "Structure, Sign, and Play in the Discourse of the Human Sciences," *Writing and Difference* (1978) 278-93; "Of an Apocalyptic Tone Recently Adopted in Philosophy," *Semeia* 23 (1982) 63-97; "Des Tours de Babel," *Semeia* 54 (1991) 3-34. **R. Detweiler** (ed.), *Derrida and Biblical Studies* (*Semeia* 23, 1982); *Reader Response Approaches to Biblical and Secular Texts* (*Semeia* 31, 1985). **M. E. Donaldson,** "Kinship Theory in the Patriarchal Narratives: The Case of the Barren Wife," *JAAR 49* (1981) 77-87. **M. Douglas,** *Purity and Danger* (1966). **U. Eco,** *A Theory of Semiotics* (1976). **J. Ehrmann***, Structuralism* (1970). **J. C. Exum,** *Fragmented Women* (1993); "Feminist Criticism," *Judges and Method* (ed. G. A. Yee, 1995) 65-90. **D. N. Fewell,** "Deconstructive Criticism," *Judges and Method* (1995) 119-45. **M. Foucault,** *The History of Sexuality* (ET 1978). **R. Funk** (ed.), *A Structuralist Approach to the Parables, Semeia 1* (1974); *Parables and Presence: Forms of NT Tradition* (1982). **G. Genette,** *Narrative Discourse* (1980). **G. Greene and C. Kahn,** *Making a Difference: Feminist Literary Criticism* (1985). **A. J. Greimas,** *Structural Semantics: An Attempt at a Method* (1983); *On Meaning* (1987); *Maupassant* (1988). **S. A. Handelman,** *The Slayers of Moses* (1982). **R. Harland,** *Superstructuralism: The Philosophy of Structuralism and Post-structuralism* (1987). **F. Jameson,** *The Political Unconscious* (1981). **D. Jobling,** *The Sense of Biblical Narrative: Structural Analysis in the HB* (2 vols. 1986); "M. Bal on Biblical Narrative," *RelSRev 17* (1991) 1-9; "Structuralist Criticism," *Judges and Method* (1995) 91-118. **D. Jobling and T. Pippin** (eds.), *Ideological Criticism of Biblical Texts* (*Semeia* 59, 1992). **M. Lane** (ed.), *Introduction to Structuralism* (1970). **E. Leach,** *Genesis as Myth and Other Essays* (1969). **V. B. Leitch,** *Deconstructive Criticism* (1983). **C. Lévi-Strauss,** "The Structural Study of Myth," *Structural Anthropology* (1963) 206-31; "The Story of Asdiwal," *The Structural Study of Myth and Totemism* (ed. E. Leach, 1967) 1-47; *The Raw and the Cooked* (1970); *From Honey to Ashes* (1973); *The Origin of Table Manners* (1978); *The Naked Man* (1981). **E. S. Malbon,** "'No Need to Have Any One Write'?: A Structuralist Exegesis of 1 Thessaloinans," *Semeia* 26 (1983) 57-84; *Narrative Space and Mythic Meaning in Mark* (1986). **P. D. Miscall,** *1 Samuel: A Literary Reading* (1986). **T. Moi,** *Sexual/Textual Politics* (1985). **S. D. Moore** (ed.), *Post Structuralism as Exegesis* (*Semeia* 54, 1991); *Mark and Luke in Poststructuralist Perspectives* (1992). **D. Patte,** *Genesis 2 and 3: Kaleidoscopic Sctructural Readings* (*Semeia* 18, 1980); "Method for a Structural Exegesis of Didactic Discourses. Analysis of 1 Thessalonians," *Semeia* 26 (1983a) 85-130; *Paul's Faith and the Power of the Gospel* (1983b); *The Gospel According to Matthew*

(1987); *The Religious Dimensions of Biblical Texts* (1990a); *Structural Exegesis for NT Critics* (1990b); *Ethics of Biblical Interpretation* (1995). **D. Patte and A. Patte,** *Structural Exegesis* (1978). **D. Patte and G. A. Phillips,** "A Fundamental Condition for Ethical Accountability in the Teaching of the Bible by White Male Exegetes," *Scriptura 9* (1991) 7-28. **G. A. Phillips,** "History and Text: The Reader in Context in Matthew's Parables Discourse," *Semeia* 31 (1985) 111-38; "'This is a Hard Saying. Who Can Be Listener to It?' Creating a Reader in John 6," *Semeia* 26 (1983) 23-56; (ed.), *Post-Structural Criticism and the Bible: Text/History/Discourse* (*Semeia* 51, 1990a); "Exegesis as Critical Praxis: Reclaiming History and Text from a Postmodern Perspective," *Semeia* 51 (1990b) 7-49. **R. Polzin,** *Moses and the Deuteronomist* (1980). **T. J. Prewitt,** *The Elusive Covenant* (1990). **V. Propp,** *Morphology of the Folktale* (1968). **M. Ryan,** *Marxism and Deconstruction* (1982). **F. de Saussure,** *Course in General Linguistics* (ET 1959). **J. P. Tompkins** (ed.), *Reader-response Criticism* (1980). **D. O. Via,** *The Parables* (1967). **C. Weedon,** *Feminist Practice and Poststructuralist Theory* (1987, 1997²). **H. C. White,** *Narration and Discourse in the Book of Genesis* (1991).

D. JOBLING

THEOLOGICAL APPROACHES

Authority of the Bible

Implicit in any endeavor to interpret the Bible is the interpreter's presuppositions regarding biblical authority. Christians have affirmed the authority of the Bible in church life, but different theologians, denominations, and schools of thought have exhibited great diversity in understanding the nature of this authority. Thus, contemporary interpretative methods reflect and are affected by these underlying presuppositions and diversity.

1. *Recent History of Biblical Authority.*

Modern debates regarding biblical authority have their roots in the rise of biblical criticism in the nineteenth century. The roots of this method lay in seventeenth-century English Deism and the eighteenth-century German Enlightenment (H. G. Reventlow [ET 1985] 1-414). Combined with the philosophical idealism of G. W. F. Hegel and the Romantic theology of F. Schleiermacher, the greater majority of theologians moved from orthodoxy to liberalism. Authority was posited in the human dimension, in the religious experience, or in the intellectual quest for understanding. Inspiration was attributed to the persons who created the Scriptures rather than to the biblical text itself (W. Sanday 1894) and was defined as religious genius. New Testament methods were pioneered by the Tübingen school, and J. Wellhausen outlined the evolution of Hebrew Scriptures.

Critical thought influenced theology greatly, and the late nineteenth century witnessed the rise of liberal theologians like A. von Harnack, A. Ritschl, and E. Troeltsch. Only a few theologians adhered either to confessional movements or to traditional orthodoxy. The most notable examples of the latter position were the Reformed Princeton theologians (A. Alexander, C. Hodge, A. A. Hodge, B. B. Warfield), who combined the scholastic theology of the seventeenth-century Calvinist F. Turretin with the eighteenth-century Scottish commonsense realism of T. Reid (1710–96) as mediated through J. Witherspoon (1723–94) in America (M. Noll 1983). Their view of the Bible as inerrant became the point of dispute in the modernist-fundamentalist debates among twentieth-century Protestants (Rogers and McKim, 235-361).

Although at first only conservative Protestants were threatened by critical thought, the controversy also came to Roman Catholic circles, in which debate over the nature of inspiration arose in the nineteenth century. Advocates of "content inspiration" (Ger., *Realinspiration*; Lat., *res et sententiae*) proposed that only certain portions of Scripture were inspired, while other sections reflected a limited biblical worldview (J. Franzelin; F. Lenormant; C. Pesch; J. Newman 1967). Most proponents of this view were Jesuits, and their position was criticized by Dominican theologians who advocated a more strict "verbal inspiration" (H. Denzinger, M.J. Lagrange). The former position predominated until the encyclical *Providentissimus Deus* (1893) of Leo XIII; then the latter view was ascendant until the modernist controversy (1907–20) cast suspicion upon both positions. Encyclicals like *Pascendi Domenici Gregis* (1907) by Pius X and *Spiritus Paraclitus* (1920) by Benedict XV condemned all views of inspiration that lacked the notion of inerrancy. This trend was reversed, however, when in 1943 Pius XII issued the encyclical *Divino Afflante Spiritu*[§], which accepted critical biblical methods. Roman Catholic biblical scholarship began anew, and the document "Verbum Dei" by Vatican II furthered this impetus (B. Vawter 1972, 70-71, 143-50; J. Burtchaell 1969, 58-163).

Among Protestants in the twentieth century, a wide range of opinions has been presented on biblical authority and inspiration. K. Barth, E. Brunner, and other neo-orthodox theologians proclaimed the Bible as the medium through which the authoritative Word of God might address people. Related biblical studies used the model of salvation history to describe the Bible, and the authority behind the text lay in the events to which it testified (see G. von Rad; G. E. Wright;

J. Bright 1967; O. Cullmann). Existential theology maintained that the text was authoritative when it addressed the situation of the reader or listener (R. Bultmann). Such trends in theology as process thought, theology of hope, liberation theology, feminist theology (Liberation Interpretation*§, Feminist Interpretation*§), various postmodern and deconstructionist theologies (Structuralism and Deconstruction*§), and others have moved in a more liberal direction; but they still attend to the biblical text as a primary theological resource. Concern with the hermeneutical approach to the Bible typifies the quest of these more contemporary theologies.

2. *Models of Biblical Authority.* The following typology may reflect in a general fashion the ways in which biblical authority has been understood.

a. *Inspiration.* The most frequently affirmed model is to declare the Bible authoritative by virtue of its inspiration or authorship by God (2 Tim 3:16; 2 Pet 1:20-21). Since the divine/human relationship in the process of inspiration is not explained by the text, great debate has arisen over its exact nature.

A modern conservative view declares the very words to be inspired or dictated by God (verbal inspiration) and the text to be inspired in all parts (full or plenary inspiration). The text is without error in matters of faith and human knowledge, though inerrancy is sometimes limited only to the original texts or autographs. Early advocates appeared in the age of orthodoxy (Gerhard, Quenstedt, Turretin), but the concept of inerrancy was developed most fully among the nineteenth-century Princeton theologians. For them, Scripture was absolute truth, and texts were treated as propositional revelation for the articulation of theology and morals. Contemporary advocates stress biblical accuracy in matters of science and history and sternly criticize Christians who adhere to a position other than this (R. Pache, T. Engelder, E. Young, F. Schaeffer, J. Packer, J. Montgomery, J. Gerstner, G. Archer). Others who are less dogmatically inclined admit authentic Christian theology can be done without such a strict definition of inerrancy (E. Carnell; C. Henry 1976; D. Fuller; C. Pinnock 1984; J. R. Michaels).

Many evangelicals (Evangelical Biblical Iinterpretation*§) affirm a more flexible definition that views Scripture as inspired and infallible in regard to theology and morals, but not inerrant in matters of history and science. Culturally and historically conditioned literature was produced by human authors through whom God communicated by accommodation. This view appears to reflect the position of Augustine§, Luther§, and Calvin§ more sensitively. Modern proponents have included European Reformed theologians (H. Bavinck; A. Kuyper; G. Berkouwer 1975; J. Orr 1910) and Roman Catholics who advocated verbal inspiration (M. J. Lagrange; A. Bea; G. Lohfink; O. Loretz 1964 [ET 1968]; D. Harrington; J. Scullion 1970). Contemporary evangelical Protestants defending this view, however, often find themselves on the defensive in denominational controversies (D. Beegle 1973; S. Davis 1977; R. Alley 1970; D. Hubbard; P. Jewett; Rogers; McKim; see R. Johnston 1979, 15-47).

Some theologians perceive only the ideas or content to be inspired, considering the words to be the product of people culturally conditioned. The word of God, mixed with erring human words, speaks authoritatively because it arises from theological, intellectual, and deep experiential dimensions (J. Semler, W. R. Smith, Franzelin, Newman). J. H. Newman§, for example, said that Scripture has authority in matters of faith, but the rest of the text, the *obiter dicta* (or incidental remarks), is not binding and could contain error (1967, 102-53).

Inspiration might be associated with the experience of the biblical spokespersons but not the writings, since the writings were produced by different people. Inspiration may refer to the divine/human encounter or to the religious genius of a sensitive individual, to the communion of a person with the divine force either externally or internally. This genius has authority today when it exhibits the power to create a religious community and relive the experiences of the original prophets (Prophecy and Prophets‡†§). Levels of inspiration exist according to the degree of divine truth expressed. This notion was born under the impulse of Romanticism, and was followed by later German idealists and by the confessional Erlangen School (see J. G. Herder, J. J. Griesbach). More recent articulation was offered by W. Sanday (1894), H. Fosdick, and especially C. H. Dodd (1929, 27-28, 264-70).

The modern scholarly perception that the biblical text was the result of a long process—oral tradition, precipitation into writing, written redaction, and finally canonization—has led to a view of inspiration attributing the *charism* to the entire community of faith that produced Scripture. Roman Catholics like P. Benoit (1965), K. Rahner (1961), D. McCarthy, and especially J. McKenzie, have defined this as "social inspiration." Their more organic view understands the relation of Scripture and tradition, although the discussion about inspired community may lead to theological rationales for ecclesiastical authority (Rahner). Protestants like J. Barr use similar imagery, but the emphasis lies on individuals within the community who participated in the developmental process of creating Scripture. Since such individuals often stand in tension with their religious communities (Job, Paul), the *charism* (or inspiration) should not be attributed to the entire community (McKenzie 1962).

b. *Salvation history.* Late twentieth-century biblical theologians viewed the Bible as the record of salvific events initiated by God for the chosen people, a record of divine irruptions into human history (exodus of Israel, resurrection of Jesus) whereby God delivered, constituted, and preserved the holy people. The community of faith was created by those events and looks to them for self-understanding. Traditions develop around those primal events, and theological interpretation turns to them as the norm for faith. The Bible's authority is derived from the events to which it testifies (von Rad; Wright 1952, 11-128; Cullman; Bright; P. Minear).

Several scholars have been reluctant to point to the events as the source of authority since events are inascertainable things, and all we have are interpretations of the events. An event is meaningless until interpreted by faith within the religious community, be it Israel or the ancient church. Von Rad and Bultmann considered Scripture to be faith interpretations of events with little or no historicity. Not only is the original history unrecoverable, it is unimportant, since the interpretations alone have meaning and authority for us.

W. Pannenberg (ET 1968, 90-152), J. Moltmann (ET 1967, 15-238), T. Rendtorff, U. Wilckens, and others moved the locus of authority from the text to the arena of history itself, turning to the present social and historical realities as the sources for theology. God does more than offer revelation in history; rather, history is revelation, the continuing arena of divine self-disclosure. Thus history becomes the primary category in theologizing rather than mere reports of divine events.

c. *Existentialism.* Existential models move the locus of authority from the text or the category of history to the individual who hears and responds to the word of God. When a person is confronted by the preached word, the past becomes alive again in the context of faith.

This scholarly hermeneutic was advocated by neo-orthodox theologians (Barth, Brunner, F. Gogarten) and the Heideggerian existentialists of Bultmann's school. For Barth (ET 1928, 522-44) the Bible contains the word of God, but it becomes such only when listeners are confronted by the *viva vox*, preaching and teaching. Bultmann declared the message to be authoritative when it confronts an individual to condemn inauthentic existence and to elicit response— the acceptance of freedom and responsibility (Pannenberg, 153-62).

A less radical mode of interpretation views the text as authoritative when it describes situations parallel to our own. Since believers face many of the same problems as did their biblical counterparts, their elicited response may be a guideline for the modern age when properly translated from that cultural context. The rationale behind the biblical text is applied to the modern situation in a fashion appropriate to human need. Preaching should relive authentically the experience of the text in order to find the common spiritual bond between ancient and modern people. When the text addresses religious needs in similar situations, it speaks with authority.

Scholars sympathetic to artistic and literary dimensions perceive scriptural images, not in logical, ideational, or positivistic categories, but as poetic and symbolic images that inspire. Nonrational symbols communicate transcendent truth more effectively than propositions and evoke a full range of intellectual and emotive response: doctrine, liturgy, preaching, teaching, and art. Biblical authority lies in the power of its symbols to evoke a full religious response (F. Farrar 1886; L. S. Thornton 1950; G. Moran; H. Frei; L. Alonso-Schökel 1965, 91-105, 296-99, 376-85).

d. *Christocentric models.* A norm from part of the biblical text may provide the *norma normans* ("the norm that norms" which alone informs all other doctrine) to interpret the rest of the text, and Christians often appeal to Christ or to the proclamation of the gospel as such a norm. There are different ways to view Christ as the center of the process. The Christ-event, the death and resurrection of Jesus, might constitute the gospel and serve as the locus of authority (Luther's justification principle). Nineteenth-century scholars sought to rediscover the real teachings of the historical Jesus in order to build an authentic Christianity on this foundation. In response, twentieth-century Christians would view the Christ of faith, the living Lord of the church, as the source of authority.

Luther is singled out as the exemplar of this approach, for he described the Bible as the cradle wherein lay the Christ child, and his theological and exegetical point of departure was the expression "what drives Christ home." In the same tradition, Barth described Christ as the "immediate Word of God," while the Bible was a "derived" word of God, and tradition and the preached message (*viva vox*) were the word in a dependent sense (also H. Cunliffe-Jones 1948; J. Reid 1957; Dodd 1929).

E. Käsemann (1964, 63-107, 169-95) took this principle to its logical conclusion when he spoke of the "canon within the canon" of Romans, Galatians, and 1–2 Corinthians. These works contain the gospel in its purest form; divergent views in the remaining books are subordinate. Hence the "primitive Catholicism" of the later epistles remains inferior to the charismatic and egalitarian theology of Paul.

e. *Limitation.* Various theologians limit the authority of the Bible in order to grant other theological sources greater respect. Roman Catholic minimalists elevated the importance of tradition by declaring that God merely provided negative assistance to biblical authors to prevent error (Jahn) or that God merely approved the creation of the texts subsequent to their writing (Bonfrére, Sixtus, Haneberg). Liberal Protestants subordinated biblical authority to religious feeling as a source for theology (Schleiermacher, Herder, J. D. Michaelis, Griesbach); biblical authority lay only in its experiential dimension. Later nineteenth-century Protestants tempered biblical authority with German Idealism. Finally, twentieth-century theologians often emphasized that biblical authority must be balanced with philosophy, the humanities, social sciences (Social-scientific Criticism*§), and current human need in the theological process.

3. *Conclusion.* Modern critical historical consciousness has led theologians to view biblical authority in a broader context. The biblical text was created by a developmental process: oral tradition, development of the written text, Redaction*§, textual transmission, and canonization. Scripture was produced by an ongoing process of tradition-making and theologizing, and the process did not end with the creation of the canon.

Recognition of this dynamic process may lead to several new observations: (a) The relationship between Scripture and tradition is closer than has been admitted by Protestants and more fluid and dynamic than admitted by Roman Catholics. (b) Inspiration as a *charism* should be applied properly to the entire process of creating the text. (c) Inspiration, however, is not the cause for authority but a chief characteristic of an authoritative text; nor is inspiration limited to just canonical writings. (d) The gospel or the "rule of faith" or "the tradition" is the guiding theological and interpretative norm underlying the Scriptures, which in turn are the norm for later Christian traditions. (e) To declare Christ, the resurrection, or the gospel testimony as the ultimate authority is theologically ideal; but ultimately these notions are too abstract to be a *theologoumenon* to undergird any concrete discussion of biblical authority. (f) Finally, the canon has authority because it contains the spiritual experiences of the earliest communities of faith and has inspired generations of Christians past and present. The Scriptures contain the paradigms of the divine process still operative today (see Achtemeier 1980,114-47; Gnuse 1985, 102-24).

Bibliography: W. J. Abraham, *The Divine Inspiration of Holy Scripture* (1981). P. Achtemeier, *The Inspiration of Scripture: Problems and Proposals* (1980). R. S. Alley, *Revolt Against the Faithful: A Biblical Case for Inspiration as Encounter* (1970). L. Alonso-Schökel, *The Inspired Word: Scripture in the Light of Language and Literature* (1965). J. Barr, *The Bible in the Modern World* (1973); *The Scope and Authority of the Bible* (1980); *Holy Scripture: Canon, Authority, Criticism* (1983). K. Barth, *The Word of God and the Word of Man* (1924; ET 1928); *Church Dogmatics 1, 1-2* (1932; ET 1936). D. L. Bartlett, *The Shape of Scriptural Authority* (1983). J. Barton, *People of the Book? The Authority of the Bible in Christianity* (1988). D. M. Beegle, *The Inspiration of Scripture* (1963); *Scripture, Tradition, and Infallibility* (1973). P. Benoit, *Aspects of Biblical Inspiration* (1965). G. Berkouwer, *Holy Scripture* (1975). P. A. Bird, "The Authority of the Bible," *NIB* (1994) 1:33-64. J. Bright, *The Authority of the OT* (1967). E. Brunner, *Revelation and Reason: The Christian Doctrine of Faith and Knowledge* (1941; ET 1946). J. T. Burtchaell, *Catholic Theories of Biblical Inspiration Since 1810: A Review and Critique* (1969). R. Bryant, *The Bible's Authority Today* (1968). H. von Campenhausen, *The Formation of the Christian Bible* (1972). Y. Congar, *La Tradition et les traditiones* (1960). H. Cunliffe-Jones, *The Authority of the Biblical Revelation* (1948). S. Davis, *The Debate About the Bible: Inerrancy versus Infallibility* (1977). C. H. Dodd, *The Authority of the Bible* (1929). F. W. Farrar, *History of Interpretation* (Bampton Lectures, 1886). R. Gnuse, *The Authority of the Bible: Theories of Inspiration, Revelation, and the Canon of Scripture* (1985). F. Greenspahn (ed.), *Scripture in the Jewish and Christian Traditions: Authority, Interpretation, Relevance* (1982). C. F. Henry, *God, Revelation and Authority,* 2 (1976). A. G. Herbert, *The Authority of the OT* (1947). A. A. Hodge and B. B. Warfield, *Inspiration* (1881). R. Johnston, *Evangelicals at an Impasse: Biblical Authority in Practice* (1979). E. Käsemann, *Essays on NT Themes* (1964). D. Kelsey, *The Uses of Scripture in Recent Theology* (1975). O. Loretz, *The Truth of the Bible* (1964; ET 1968). J. McKenzie, "The Social Character of Inspiration," *CBQ 24* (1962) 115-24. D. K. McKim (ed.), *The Authoritative Word: Essays on the Nature of Scripture* (1983). J. Moltmann, *Theology of Hope: On the Ground and the Implications of a Christian Eschatology* (1964; ET 1967). J. H. Newman, *On the Inspiration of Scripture* (ed. J. D. Holmes and R. Murray, 1967). M. A. Noll, *The Princeton Theology 1812–1921: Scripture, Science, and Theological Method from A. Alexander to B. B. Warfield* (1983). J. C. O'Neill, *The Bible's Authority: A Portrait Gallery of Thinkers from Lessing to Bultmann* (1991). J. Orr, *Revelation and Inspiration* (1910). W. Pannenberg, *Revelation as History* (1961; ET 1968). C. Pinnock, *The Scripture Principle* (1984). K. Rahner, *Inspiration in the Bible* (1961, 1964²). K. Rahner and J. Ratzinger, *Revelation and Tradition* (1966). J. K. S. Reid, *The Authority of Scripture: A Study of the Reformation and Post-Reformation Understanding of the Bible* (1957). H. G. Reventlow, *The Authority of the Bible and the Rise of the Modern World* (1980; ET 1985). A. Richardson, *The Bible in the Age of Science* (1961). A. Richardson and W. Schweitzer (eds.), *Biblical Authority for Today* (1951). J. B. Rogers (ed.), *Biblical Authority* (1977). J. B. Rogers and D. K. McKim, *The Authority and Interpretation of the Bible* (1979). W. Sanday, *Inspiration* (Bampton Lectures, 1894²). J. Scullion, *The Theology of Inspiration* (1970). N. Snaith, *The Inspiration and Authority of* *the Bible* (1956). **P. Synave and P. Benoit,** *Prophecy and Inspiration* (1961). **L. S. Thornton,** *The Form of the Servant* (3 vols. 1950). **F. Turretin,** *The Doctrine of Scripture* (1847; ed. and tr. J. Beardslee, 1981). **B. Vawter,** *Biblical Inspiration* (1972). **B. B. Warfield,** *The Inspiration and Authority of the Bible* (1948). **G. E. Wright,** *The God Who Acts* (SBT 8, 1952). **R. Youngblood** (ed.), *Evangelicals and Inerrancy* (1984)

R. GNUSE

THEOLOGICAL APPROACHES

Canonical Criticism

A definition of this term and the approach to interpretation implied by it are complicated by a lack of scholarly consensus. Related terms include "canonical criticism" (Sanders 1984), "composition-critical approach" (*Kompositionsgeschichte*, R. Rendtorff 1983 [ET 1985]), "canon-contextual analysis" (G. Sheppard), or (more loosely) "a canonical approach" and "assessing the role of canon in understanding the Old Testament" (B. Childs). What all of these approaches share is an effort to describe how ancient traditions are to be interpreted when they form part of a "scripture" within a religion.

The term *canon* is equivocal, signifying either the "norm, standard, or ideal" or "list, catalogue, or fixed measure." It was first used by the church father ATHANASIUS as a synonym for the Bible around 350 C.E. Only in much later periods did Jews use the term to refer to the Hebrew Bible. In premodern introductions to Scripture, Christians traditionally treated the issues of text and canon before moving on to considerations of specific books of the Bible. In the modern period, this order was reversed because canonical issues seemed to belong to the latest stages of the Tradition History*§ of the Bible; therefore, they were considered less significant for modern historical interpretation of either the Bible or the ancient traditions contained in it.

Despite its late usage, the term canon has recently proved helpful, especially for certain Hebrew Bible scholars, as a way to call attention to a basic feature of Scripture often overlooked in modern historical-critical exegesis: the special semantic implications of a "scripture" within Judaism and Christianity. Historical criticism in the modern period usually sought to recover the original versions of biblical traditions. Even if a prebiblical tradition was once an oral unit of Prophecy‡†§, it would not be canonical in the sense of being Scripture, nor does the absence of claims of Inspiration*§ necessarily preclude a tradition from becoming a normative and revelatory part of Scripture. The logic of the scriptural context is not that of modern historical writing. Scripture is riddled with historical anachronisms, and the context often warrants an interpretation that must exceed, or even contravene, an original author's intent. While some conflicting traditions have been harmonized, others remain remarkably disharmonious-like those found in the juxtaposition of opposing or differing claims.

In sum, historical-critical inquiry into the nature of Scripture has led many scholars to the conclusion that a semantic transformation occurred whenever prebiblical traditions were incorporated into the larger canonical context of Scripture. The unity of the Bible lies neither in a common historical property (or "center") to these prebiblical traditions, nor in notions of development in the history of ancient religious ideas like those found in modern schemes of salvation history. Instead, the later editors of the Bible assigned diverse ancient traditions to particular larger contexts based on a variety of religious or nonreligious factors. This insight is not a theological judgment by biblical scholars but simply a historical claim about the nature of the form and function of a scripture within religion. Such comparative religionists as W. C. Smith have strongly supported this canonical approach within religions generally. Perhaps the best way to show the internal debates among advocates of a canonical approach is to consider the positions of its first two major architects—Sanders§ and Childs§—then to consider other subsequent developments.

1. *Canonical Process and Canonical Hermeneutics: James A. Sanders.* Sanders coined and popularized the term *canonical criticism* in his book *Torah and Canon* (1972). He emphasized that his proposal calls for a special stance on the Bible—that it is an integrative "extension of biblical criticism" rather than merely another technique for analyzing the Bible. In contrast to

Childs, Sanders considers as "canonical" any normative use of a tradition from the time of the Israelite prophets to contemporary Christian preaching; the canonization of the Hebrew Bible and the New Testament are only milestones in that larger canonical process.

In light of this long process of canonical interpretation leading to the formation of the Bible, Sanders has sought to find some continuity in what he calls "canonical hermeneutics." He has attempted to discern some constant factors that explain the difference between true and false prophecy in ancient Israel, and assuming that these factors constitute a theological norm for contemporary Christian preaching. While canonical Hermeneutics*§ necessarily change over time, true canonical hermeneutics must maintain interpretation in support of "monotheistic pluralism" and in opposition to various subtle types of polytheism. Scripture itself unevenly illustrates adherence to this principle. Still, the Hebrew Bible and especially the New Testament repeatedly show, for Sanders, how the same canonical tradition proved to be adaptable to new situations with quite different "true" implications for each generation of believers.

Sanders proposes that "comparative Midrash" should be the study of how authoritative traditions are interpreted according to canonical hermeneutics. In this way he focuses on "the shape in the hermeneutics of the biblical authors." For example, he argues that the different authors of Ezek 33:24 and Isa 51:2-3 referred to the same normative tradition with opposite conclusions. Nonetheless, both are correct because they each applied properly the same canonical hermeneutics to different social contexts. By locating the key to proper interpretation in the canonical hermeneutics employed by the various interpreters, Sanders can view the Bible as a relatively open collection of normative traditions. He is, thus, understandably less concerned than Childs, Rendtorff, or Sheppard with the final form of Hebrew Bible.

Nonetheless, Sanders has also offered some contextual descriptions of how books constitute whole, canonically significant collections in the Hebrew Bible. In this regard, Childs praises Sanders's theological assessment of the form and function of the Pentateuch (Pentateuchal Criticism‡§). Sanders assesses the effect of separating Deuteronomy from the rest of the Deuteronomistic History‡§ (Josh–2 Kgs). The resulting Mosaic collection of five books (Gen to Deut) became the crucial norm of the Torah for later Judaism. By this arrangement, the events of the conquest and the monarchy are qualitatively distinguished from the definitive locus of Mosaic revelation and are made subordinate to its expression of God's covenant with Israel— past, present, and future.

2. *The Canonical Context: Brevard S. Childs.* In *Biblical Theology in Crisis* (1970), Childs began to explore what he called "the canonical context," especially the relationship between the Hebrew Bible and the New Testament. He defined canon as "the rule that delineates the area in which the church hears the Word of God." Later, he introduced nomenclature of "the canonical shape" in a reexamination of Isaiah, the psalms, the crossing of the sea, and Daniel. In a programmatic article in 1972, "The Old Testament as Scripture of the Church," he set out his view of the interconnections between books in the Pentateuch. The same orientation appears in his commentary on Exodus (1974), in his introductions to the Old Testament (1979) and the New Testament (1984), and in his *Biblical Theology of the Old and New Testaments* (1992). Childs has come to reject Sanders's terminology of "canon(ical) criticism" for his own work because it implies either an extension of historical criticism or another method of conventional historical analysis. His "canonical approach" has been consistently aimed at a description of what he considers to be the significance of the canonical context for the interpretation of Scripture.

In contrast to Sanders, Childs established his academic reputation as a tradition-historian and form critic (Form Criticism*§) who resists identifying the term canon with every authoritative tradition in the prebiblical period or with the process of tradition history. Rejecting the possibility of detecting canonical hermeneutics in the process of the history of prebiblical traditions, Childs argues only that the later formation and canonization of Scripture reflected "a hermeneutical activity which continued to shape the material theologically in order to render it accessible to future generations of believers" (1985, 6). The resulting canonical context of Scripture subordinated the intent of earlier authors and editors to this larger purpose. Modern redaction critics usually focus on minor additions and miss the full effect of this resultant text, which now has its own quite autonomous context. Childs has spoken occasionally of the "canonical intent" to express just this distinction between the sense made explicit by the canonical context and historical reconstructions of editorial intents, or *Tendenzen*.

A distinctive feature of Childs's description of the canonical approach is what he calls the "shape" of a biblical section, book, or collection of books. He argues that this description should not be confused with a purely Literary*§, Rhetorical*§, or Structuralist*§ assessment, on the one hand, or as part of an exercise in Redaction Criticism*§, on the other hand. Instead, "shape" corresponds to a larger impression of the form and function of a text, preliminary to a close, philological interpretation of its full context and content. Thus, Childs states, "The canonical shaping serves not so much to establish a given meaning to a particular passage as to chart the boundaries within which the exegetical task is to be carried out" (1979, 83). This dimension may or may not reflect such specific editorial activity as "canon conscious redactions" (see below). It consists essentially of a description of how the form of Scripture lends itself to its theological function as Scripture within the believing community.

A Christian concern with the overarching form of biblical books as a key to their role as Scripture is certainly not a new one in the history of interpretation. In premodern periods, one frequently can find appeals to the "scope" of a text that helped to establish the *usus loquendi* or normative, literal sense in church interpretation. *Scope* included attention especially to how a text properly coheres within its context and within the aim of the Scripture as a whole. As is the case with Childs's shape, the signs of a text's scope often depended on appeals to the beginnings and endings of books, titles, and evidence of transitions that seemed to establish its essential purpose by marking out the boundaries, limits, and possibilities for the full interplay of biblical interpretation. The shape of a text points to its coherence as Scripture and to its relation to the subject matter of Scripture as a whole. Childs tends to highlight those elements in the shaping of a book that indicates elements of continuity.

Because he concentrates on these positive boundaries of a text, Childs shows less interest in the role of contextual ambiguity, extra-textual reference, undecidability, or the survival of systemic dissonance inherited from the tradition-historical process. One might also argue that what should be acknowledged as different and thoroughly modern about Childs's shape is that he takes up the old concern with scope, but frames it specifically in response to the atomization of Scripture by various modern historical-critical methods. While the polemical tone of his work may seem, at times, to devalue historical criticism entirely, Childs actually relies on the results of modern criticism to state with new precision how different prebiblical traditions conjoin in the shaping of biblical books within Scripture. In any case, at the heart of Childs's approach lies a way to claim Postmodern*§ continuity with the old Roman Catholic and Protestant search for the true literal sense of Christian Scripture.

Consequently, when Childs describes the shape of the final text of a biblical book, he is fully aware that he concentrates on a recognition of the specific literary boundary or textual arena in which proper theological interpretation takes place. For example, the historicized psalm titles link certain prayers to events in the life of David as described in 1–2 Samuel, so that the resulting presentation of both the public and the private life of David contributes to a biblical anthropology. Psalm 1 identifies the prayers as a commentary on the Torah, and the royal psalms (rendered as messianic in the context of the psalter) recommend the reading of these biblical prayers as sources of prophetic promise, as asserted elsewhere (2 Sam 23:1-2 and 1 Chr 25:1-8).

As another example, in Isaiah 1–39, Isaiah 1 provides an introduction to the entire book; the song in chapter 12 concludes the first section by looking to a time when God's "wrath will turn" to "comfort" (12:1, author's translation); and finally, the placement of the narrative in Isaiah 39 anticipates the very Babylonian exile presumed in Isa 40–66, when words of comfort are offered by the prophet to Israel. Conversely, Isa 40–66 announces "new things" (e.g., 42:9, etc.) of promise that have credibility on the basis of fulfillment of "former things" familiar in Isa 1–39.

In another instance of canonical shaping, the association of Solomon with Prov, Qoh, and Cant designates a corpus of biblical wisdom literature in distinction from the Torah and the Prophets. Although not all the traditions in these books are Wisdom literature in terms of ancient Near Eastern genre designations, they are now to be read sapiently within Scripture as a guide to knowledge and skills shared with the rest of the world. Furthermore, the ending of Qoheleth asserts a complementarity between the Torah of Moses and the wisdom of Solomon without entirely resolving how future readers would reconcile the differences between divinely given wisdom and Torah.

Childs has, likewise, sought to detect similar features in the New Testament. For example, the editorial addition "The Gospel According to Luke" reflects an alteration in how the original memoir is to be read as one of the Gospels. By separating Acts from Luke with the Gospel of John, the effect is made even more emphatic. Luke is to be read as a gospel alongside the other three even if it were not originally intended as such. The four Gospels, despite many glaring differences, are biblically interpreted together as witnesses to the one gospel of JESUS. So, too, the Pauline Epistles form a single collection, wedding so-called genuine Pauline letters written before the Gospels with later Pauline pastorals (Pastoral Letters[†§]) that reflect a later synthesis of gospel traditions.

What the canon of Scripture resists is any assumption of great interpretive significance based on a sharp distinction between either the historical and the biblical PAUL or the historical and the biblical Jesus. The testimonies of Scripture normatively and sufficiently express the historical significance of Paul and Jesus for faith within a believing community. Any attempt to make truth claims in the language of Christian faith based on prebiblical or purely historical inquiry risks setting aside the very logic that underlies the formation of both Scripture and the church. Because canon and community are dialectically related and formative of each other, the religious community finds, in Scripture, a mirror of its own identity and confession. Without the self-reflection illuminated by competent biblical interpretation, the specific dimensions of Christianity may become blurred or will be lost entirely.

3. *Attempts at Refinements and Collaboration.* Students of Childs have sought to advance the same perspective in a variety of ways. For example, Sheppard has proposed that one may identify certain "canon conscious redactions" that assert a context between books and traditions not originally intended to be read together. Increasingly, contributions to a canonical approach have pursued interdisciplinary areas outside conventional biblical studies, including the history of interpretation within church and synagogue, Literary Criticism*[§], comparative religions, and historical theology. Because these investigations must take seriously the postbiblical history of religion, a renewed concern has developed to recognize the hermeneutical differences between Jewish interpretation of Hebrew Scripture and the semantic differences in the Christian adaptation of the same as Hebrew Bible. At a minimum, a canonical approach redefines the role of biblical studies within the encyclopedic horizon of both religion in the university and theology in the seminary.

Among numerous related studies, only some representative ones can be mentioned here. Rendtorff's introduction to the Old Testament (1985) is a good example of a highly independent contribution that builds directly on canon contextual considerations, especially those of

Childs. Its major contribution in this respect lies in its close attention to detail and its argument for marked repetitions and transitions not pursued by Childs. Often, this evidence involves the recurrence of unusual phrases, formulae, or key word connections. Similarly, J. Blenkinsopp offers a fresh examination of the relationship between prophecy and Torah within the formation of Scripture (1977).

Because these assessments accept, depend on, and respond to modern historical criticism, they all stand in opposition to fundamentalism and its modern brand of right-wing historicism. Many approaches not labeled as canonical may well belong to this approach, broadly conceived. For example, R. Brown[§] acknowledges in similar ways that the context of Scripture has changed our perception of the literal sense, although he allows the Roman Catholic teaching magisterium to determine what of that literal sense belongs to the binding "canonical sense" of Scripture (1981). J. Neusner likewise has explored the nature of canonical authority in Judaism, concentrating particularly on the implications of the oral Torah for canonical Jewish interpretation (1983). The spontaneity and independence of these contributions suggest that they belong to a major theme in current debates regarding the nature of Scripture and the contours of Jewish and Christian interpretation.

Bibliography: J. Barr, *Holy Scripture: Canon, Authority, Criticism* (1983). **J. Barton,** *Reading the OT: Method in Biblical Study* (rev. ed. 1996) 77-103. **J. Blenkinsopp,** *Prophecy and Canon: A Contribution to the Study of Jewish Origins* (SJCA 3, 1977). **R. Brown,** *The Critical Meaning of the Bible* (1981). **B. S. Childs,** *Biblical Theology in Crisis* (1970); "The OT as Scripture of the Church," *CTM 43* (1972) 709-22; "The Sensus Literalis of Scripture: An Ancient and Modern Problem," *Beiträge zur Alttestamentlichen Theologie* (FS W. Zimmerli, ed. H. Donner et al., 1976) 80-95; *Introduction to the OT as Scripture* (1979); *The NT as Canon: An Introduction* (1984); *OT Theology in a Canonical Context* (1985); *Biblical Theology of the Old and New Testaments* (1992); *Isaiah.* (OTL, 2001). **J. Neusner,** *Midrash in Context* (1983). **R. Rendtorff,** *The OT: An Introduction* (1983; ET 1985). **J. A. Sanders,** *Torah and Canon* (1972); *Canon and Community: A Guide to Canonical Criticism* (GBS, 1984); *From Sacred Story to Sacred Text: Canon as Paradigm* (1987). **G. T. Sheppard,** "Canon Criticism: The Proposal of B. Childs and an Assessment for Evangelical Hermeneutics," *Studia biblica et theologica 4, 2* (1974) 3-17; *Wisdom as a Hermeneutical Construct* (BZAW 151, 1980); "Canonization: Hearing the Voice of the Same God Through Historically Dissimilar Traditions," *Int 36* (1982) 21-33; "Canon," *EncRel 3* (1987) 62-69.

G. T. Sheppard

THEOLOGICAL APPROACHES

Evangelical Biblical Interpretation

Evangelical has a broad range of meaning in the Christian world. However, in this context the term refers to the conservative Christian movement originating in the twentieth century that has rejected the higher critical conclusions concerning biblical texts and the radical skepticism inherited from the Enlightenment and has sought to retain the Reformation doctrines. Contrary to popular opinion, the movement is not monolithic; rather, it represents a wide diversity of traditions and religious groups, from high church to low church and from extreme conservatives to moderates.

The Evangelical movement emerged from the ferment of the conservative-liberal controversies of the nineteenth century. In Germany, that century saw the complete triumph of higher-critical concerns. First the Tübingen school of tendency criticism in the first half of the century and then the history-of-religions school (*Religionsgeschichtliche Schule*[*§]) at the end of the century cast more and more doubt on the veracity of the Bible. F. C. Baur[§] originated the Tübingen school when he rewrote the history of the early church along Hegelian lines, arguing that the Jewish Christianity of the early decades of the first century (the thesis) was opposed by the Hellenistic Jewish Christianity of the Pauline school in the middle decades (the antithesis) and was taken over by Hellenistic Christianity in the early part of the second century (the synthesis). One of Baur's students, D. F. Strauss[§], applied this model to the life of Jesus[*§], arguing that Jesus was turned into a mythical or supernatural figure by the early church. The history-of-religions school took a more Darwinian approach, arguing that all religions have their origins in their predecessors and that Christianity moved from a Jewish religion to a Jewish-Hellenistic and finally to a Hellenistic religion during the New Testament period. Many adherents (e.g., O. Pfleiderer[§], E. Hatch[§], W. Bousset[§], and R. Reitzenstein[§]) centered on Iranian and Hellenistic origins of Christianity.

These movements were opposed by a large number of conservative scholars. In Germany, T. von Zahn[§] wrote important works on New Testament introduction and the Canon[†§], and A. Schlatter[§] wrote on the Jewish (not Hellenistic) origins of Paul's[†§] thought and on New Testament Theology[†§]. In England, the "Cambridge trio" of J. B. Lightfoot[§], B. F. Westcott[§], and F. HORT championed a conservative approach to the New Testament while remaining proponents of critical methodology. In fact, Westcott is generally credited with introducing higher critical study of the Gospels into England, and Lightfoot's magisterial *Apostolic Fathers* stemmed the tide of Baur's theories in England.

In the United States, the liberal/conservative battle took place from 1870 to 1920. Until that time, the American church was predominantly conservative, but in the universities and seminaries a counter movement began to grow, mainly influenced by German higher criticism. When conservative professors retired they were often replaced by younger critical scholars, many of whom had been educated in Europe. In addition, such popular preachers as H. Beecher and L. Abbott combined a pietistic morality with critical views on the Bible, championing a new understanding of biblical Authority[*§] and its relation to theology. A good example of this approach would be the Evangelical Alliance, founded in 1846. J. McCosh, president of Princeton, used this forum to reconcile Scripture with Darwinism in 1873. For the next few decades, higher criticism increasingly dominated the alliance, which became the Federal Council of Churches in 1908.

Conservatives responded in diverse ways. Some, like the evangelist D. Moody, believed that the best approach was that of Gamaliel in Acts 5:38-39: "Keep away from these men and let them alone; because if this plan or this undertaking is of human origin, it will fail; but if it is of

God, you will not be able to overthrow them." Therefore, he centered upon revivalism and refused to take part in the debates. Others believed in apologetic response; e.g., B. B. Warfield[§] (who produced a succession of articles on biblical infallibility, later collected into *The Inspiration and Authority of the Bible* 1948). A series of Bible conferences from 1876 to 1910 stressed apologetics to answer the higher critics and biblical Prophecy[‡†§] to warn of the growing apostasy (2 Thess 2:3) seen in the liberal group. In 1895 the Niagara Conference developed a five-point program that became the basis of a movement: (1) the inerrancy of Scripture, (2) the virgin birth, (3) the deity of Jesus Christ, (4) a substitutionary theory of atonement, and (5) the physical resurrection and second coming of Jesus. Coalescence around these points led to the most famous work of this period, the twelve-volume *The Fundamentals* (1910-15), written by conservative scholars from a broad array of denominations to defend the five points as well as cardinal tenets like traditional views of authorship and date of biblical books, the attribution of the *Logia Jesu* to Jesus, and similar issues. This series of books led to the use of the term "fundamentalists" for those adhering to the principles advocated therein.

As higher criticism came to dominate an increasing number of universities and seminaries, fundamentalists began to found their own schools, with the Bible at the core of the educational experience. Thus began the Bible institute movement, whose goal was to develop church leaders and teachers rather than to train young people in a broad-based arts-centered education. Contemporary Christian education drew little theory from its secular counterpart but centered on pragmatics and theology. The purpose was not so much to retreat from the world as it was to return to the Bible-centered education of the Reformation period. Nevertheless, the rift between fundamentalists and others became greater and greater.

Two events made this rift complete. First, the so-called "monkey trial" of J. Scopes in 1925 heaped ridicule on fundamentalism. Scopes, charged with teaching evolution in a Dayton, Tennessee, public school in defiance of state law, was defended by the famous trial lawyer C. Darrow. W. J. Bryan, four-time candidate for the presidency, assisted the prosecution. Darrow publicly humiliated Bryan and belittled fundamentalist beliefs. Second, in 1929 the last bastion of conservative theology, Princeton, came under the control of the "modernists" (the term often used for higher critics). As a result, J. G. Machen[§] and R. Wilson resigned from Princeton and moved to Philadelphia, establishing Westminster Theological Seminary. The separation was absolute; there was no interaction between the two camps.

As a result, fundamentalism retreated into itself and refused to dialogue with the broader intellectual world. Moreover, for the next two decades its adherents split into a series of sectarian groups that failed even to interact with one another: Presbyterians and Anabaptists[§], dispensationalists and Reformed moved farther apart. The ensuing years saw numerous disputes over issues that had not previously divided the conservative movement—paedobaptism, predestination, and chiliasm or millenialism. Although conservatives came from virtually every Protestant tradition, until the 1930s there had been a remarkable unity in the movement. However, the various groups ceased to dialogue with each other once they lost their "common enemy." Differences began to take center stage. Denominations started to demand adherence on peripheral as well as cardinal issues, and denominational splits began to multiply.

A new theory of biblical interpretation also became dominant in the fundamentalist movement. C. Hodge[§] and Warfield had drawn on the philosophy of F. Bacon[§] and later T. Reid in developing their views on the authority and interpretation of the Bible. This philosophy, known from its association with Reid and other Scot thinkers as "Scottish common sense realism," held that objective knowledge could be derived through the senses; Hodge and Warfield, therefore, proposed that the Bible could be understood simply by reading it. Because many fundamentalists believed that critical tools were unnecessary, even dangerous, an inductive approach to Bible study resulted. A person would simply sit down with the Bible (preferably the KJV) and

222

study it, looking for key terms and themes. Biblical truth was thus accessible to the average person, and little special training was needed. Inductive study moved synthetically from the whole to the parts, searching for major themes. Theology was determined by prooftexting, or searching for key verses to anchor a doctrine; it was believed that one or two verses were sufficient to anchor a doctrine biblically. In this sense, one of the more influential books was R. A. Torrey's *What the Bible Teaches* (1898), which sought to prove doctrines "scientifically" (in 500 pages) by anchoring them to specific texts. Hermeneutics*§ was identified, not with critical study of the biblical texts, but with personal interaction with them.

Thus, the 1930s and early 1940s were characterized by withdrawal from the public arena and internalization within specific traditions. Not only did fundamentalists as a whole refuse to speak to the broad world of scholarship, those from divergent traditions—Reformed, Anabaptist, Arminian, dispensational, and Pentecostal—did not communicate with one another. However, while splits resulted for the most part in a proliferation of small, disenfranchised denominations, the movement itself did not taper off. Statistics show that fundamentalism actually grew in number during the 1930s and 1940s due to evangelistic fervor and a revivalist spirit.

In the early 1940s a new attitude emerged within some segments of fundamentalism and was quickly seen as a separate camp within the conservative movement; it began to be identified as "evangelicalism." In September 1941 the fundamentalists formed the American Council of Christian Churches and, in October of that same year, the National Association of Evangelicals was formed at Moody Bible Institute. Interestingly, the two groups held many of the same doctrinal beliefs, but they differed in attitudes toward outsiders. Seven characteristics distinguished evangelicalism: (1) a commitment to dialogue with the world of scholarship; (2) a rejection of radical separation (i.e., the refusal to interact with anyone not following the fundamentalist creed); (3) openness on non-cardinal issues, e.g., modes of baptism, Calvinism/Arminianism, eschatological differences; (4) cooperative evangelism, e.g., the involvement of mainline denomination pastors in Billy Graham crusades; (5) a more eclectic education, as seen in the formation of Fuller Seminary in 1947; (6) eclectic political allegiance, involving the refusal to demand a flag-waving conservatism; (7) social concern, seen in the emergence of missionary agencies, like World Vision, that center on relief and care for the poor.

Several vital organizations and publications appeared during this period, including the magazine *Christianity Today* (1945), which became a forum for a more open discussion of theological and social issues; the Tyndale Fellowship, founded at the Cambridge in 1944; and the Evangelical Theological Society, founded in the United States in 1949. The purpose of the latter two was to bring academic scholarship back into the mainstream of the evangelical world. Evangelical scholars began to interact with the broader world of scholarship, although this was not always easy. For instance, G. Ladd of Fuller Seminary was refused membership in the Gospels section of the Society of Biblical Literature§ in the early 1950s because of his conservative writings. Progress was slow; nevertheless, such formidable scholars as F. F. BRUCE (the only person in history named president of both New Testament and Old Testament international societies), R. Harrison, E. Ellis, and L. Morris led the way. By the 1970s a resurgent evangelical scholarship began to claim its place in the world of scholarship; I. Marshall, R. Longenecker, R. Martin, G. Wenham, and others were recognized in the broader fraternity of scholars. Still, a certain amount of disdain often greeted conservative scholars because they were suspected of fundamentalist and obscurantist positions by mainstream academics.

At the same time, debates on Hermeneutics*§ and the Authority*§ of Scripture began to cause divisions within evangelical churches. Many evangelical scholars had strong doubts about the doctrine of inerrancy, and forums like the International Council of Biblical Inerrancy on Scripture (1978) and on hermeneutics (1982) failed to resolve the issue. The Evangelical Theological Society debated higher-critical conclusions regarding Redaction Criticism*§ from

1976 to 1982, finally accepting the validity of a nuanced approach. Wide diversity became apparent on such issues as the role of women in the church, the unity of Isaiah, and Pauline authorship of the pastorals (Pastoral Letters[†§]). In short, evangelicalism had become a divided movement.

Still, the movement continued to grow, both in number and in academic prestige. In the 1980s Tyndale Fellowship sponsored a six-volume *Gospel Perspectives* series in which a number of evangelical Gospel scholars demonstrated the historical veracity of the Gospels. By the 1990s evangelicals were not only members of academic societies but also chaired major seminars within them. The new era of tolerance as well as the quality of the work produced by scholars like G. Fee, H. Williamson, D. Carson, and N. T. Wright has brought evangelical scholarship back into the mainstream as an equal partner.

Biblical interpretation among evangelicals centers on several issues. Foremost, of course, is the authority and centrality of Scripture for doctrinal formulation. Although debate over inerrancy (the belief that the Bible is without error in scientific or historical detail as well as in doctrinal matters) remains, there is universal agreement regarding infallibility (the belief that the Bible is the Word of God and completely authoritative and true on doctrinal issues). Evangelicals recognize not just the author of biblical books but also the Author behind those books; therefore, the Bible contains a timeless message, binding upon the church at all times. This is a key difference between conservative and nonconservative interpretation. For the latter, the Bible is a set of open-ended symbols to be interpreted on the basis of the current context. For the former, the current context must be challenged and, if necessary, changed by biblical truth. The Postmodern rejection of absolute truth is not shared by evangelicals, who believe that there is one source of final truth: the Bible.

This does not mean that evangelicals take a naïve approach to biblical interpretation. While some do employ an atomistic, prooftexting technique in Bible study, the majority reject simplistic methods for sophisticated approaches grounded in the world of scholarship. According to the predominant view, the text is not considered to be autonomous from the author; rather, it is seen from an intentionalist perspective. The author/text/reader dilemma is resolved by centering on the text. The author produces a text with a set of intended messages, and the reader studies that text in order to discover those intended messages. While readers cannot get back to the author, they can search for signs embedded in the text that guide them to the intended messages. The author, of course, is not present to guide the reader, and the preunderstanding of the reader (the product of church tradition and reading community) certainly has some controlling influence on the interpretation. But does this automatically generate the interpretation? Or can readers go beyond such forces to discover the intended meaning of a biblical text? Certainly polyvalence or multiple meanings attributed by different readers is a necessary result, but can one go behind these to discover the probable meaning of a text? Evangelicals believe not only that the probable meaning can be discovered but also that it must be discovered due to the very nature of the biblical text as the word of God. For example, 1 Pet 3:21 ("And baptism . . . now saves you ... as an appeal to God for a good conscience") is at the heart of the debate over baptism as a salvific force. While scholars are divided over the interpretation of this verse, evangelicals believe that it can be understood as originally intended. The predominant evangelical interpretation is that "good conscience" is a subjective genitive ("out of a good conscience") rather than an objective genitive ("for a good conscience"); and so baptism "saves," not in the sense of baptismal regeneration, but in the sense that it "appeals" to the God who has already saved the person.

Two major interpretive approaches have been suggested. The first is associated with E. Hirsch (1967), who argues for separating what the text meant (the single intended meaning that must be the goal of all interpretation) and what it means (the many possible significances of that single meaning in various contexts). The scholars who follow Hirsch believe that it is possible to get behind the latter in order to discover the former. As M. Silva says, "The moment we look at a text we contextualize it, but a self-awareness of that fact opens up the possibility of modifying our point of reference in the light of contradictory data" (1983, 148). Such scholars recognize the importance of the reader in the act of interpretation, but they believe that it is possible for readers to study and determine the original meaning of a text.

The second approach is A. Thiselton's "action theory," based on the work of J. Austin and J. Searle. Thiselton begins with the "transformative power" of the Bible to draw readers into its world of meaning and to transform their understanding. Biblical truth functions at both static (propositional truths) and dynamic (life-changing mechanisms) levels. The Bible is not just "a handbook of information and description"; it entails "a whole range of dynamic speech-acts" that are based on "the truth of certain states of affairs in God's relation to the world" (1980, 437).

The means by which this is accomplished is the classic grammatical-historical method supplemented by modern hermeneutical theory. First, we learn to work with our preunderstanding positively. Awareness of our own worldview and theological underpinnings keeps us from turning presupposition into prejudice. The best way to do this is to respect and learn from opposing theories about the meaning of the text, to allow these theories to challenge our understandings and drive us to a reexamination of the text from a new perspective. In one sense, we study the text from the vantage point of our own system, and in another sense we bracket our traditional understanding in an openness to new possibilities. The resulting tension forces us to be more honest with the text: e.g., when studying a difficult passage, like Rom 9–11, on sovereignty and justification, both Arminians (Arminius§) and Calvinists (Calvin§) need to open themselves to each other's interpretation and look at the text in a new way.

Exegetical methodology combines grammar, semantics, background, and biblical theology to ascertain those embedded clues to the original, intended meaning of the text. Grammar and semantics help readers to go behind their community-driven interpretation to consider the ancient meaning of the words. Here the recent school of discourse analysis is critical for seeing the message as a whole and not as an atomistic series of isolated parts. The larger context within which a pericope is encased becomes essential to its fuller meaning. In John 7:37-39, for example, there are several difficult aspects, including whether "the one who believes in me" in v. 38a belongs with v. 38 or v. 37 and whether "out of his innermost being" (author's translation) refers to the believer or to Christ. Grammatically, the answer to the first issue is that it belongs to v. 37 ("let the one who believes in me drink"); and due to the strong Christology of the context in chap. 7, it is more likely that Christ is the source of the Holy Spirit in vv. 38-39. Primarily, evangelicals are concerned to seek John's original meaning and not just one interesting possibility among many.

Background is another essential component guiding the reader back to a text-driven interpretation. Within the extensive debate over sociological analysis (Sociology and Hebrew Bible/New Testament Studies†‡§), evangelicals prefer social description (seeking the background behind the text itself) to sociological interpretation (speculating about the social dynamics that led to the production of the text). In other words, they seek to deepen understanding of the text rather than to use current sociological theory to revise our understanding of the history behind the text. Seeing the conquest of Canaan as a "peasant revolt" or the early church as a "millenarian sect" is viewed as reductionistic and revisionist. However, to study the ancient military and topographic details behind Joshua and Judges is seen as extremely helpful; and to look at the influence of sociological factors behind Paul's tent-making as a key to his mission strategy is regarded as an important contribution. The key is that the text guides the employment of the critical tools.

Biblical theology is also crucial to discovering the author's intention. Most biblical books are theological at the core, so evangelical interpretation looks at the developing theological threads that together weave the tapestry of the text. These threads are discovered by studying the developing text and seeing how the theological emphases emerge, context by context. The theology of a book is found, not just in the parts, but more in what the parts contribute to the whole. According to Thiselton's speech-act theory, one must consider the locutionary aspect (the theological message), the illocutionary force (how the text involves the reader in its message), and the perlocutionary purpose (what the text asks the reader to do with its message). All of this constitutes the biblical theology of a text.

Finally, there is systematic theology. Evangelicals for the most part accept K. STENDAHL's classic distinction between biblical theology as descriptive and systematic theology as normative. However, they rework the relation between the two, arguing for a direct movement from exegesis (the historical meaning of individual texts) to biblical theology (the theology of the early church derived from collating passages into the theological message of a book or an author) and systematic theology (the contextualization of biblical theology into church dogma for today). Mainly, evangelicals believe that the task is not finished until interpreters have discovered and applied God's truths derived from Scripture to develop a systematic theology for the modern church. Two principles guide this pursuit: (1) A systematic theology is possible as biblical passages are collated into "covering laws" for doctrinal statements; and (2) the theological task is mandatory for the church. In other words, it is not enough to determine the meaning of a passage; one must also determine what the passage contributes to the theology and life of the church.

Bibliography: D. A. Black and D. S. Dockery (eds.), *NT Criticism and Inter*pretation (1991). **G. Bray,** *Biblical Interpretation Past and Present* (1996); **D. A. Carson and J. D. Woodbridge** (eds.), *Scripture and Truth* (1983). **N. F. Furniss,** *The Fundamentalist Controversy, 1918-1931* (Yale Historical Publications, Miscellany 59, 1954). **N. Hatch and M. Noll** (eds.), *The Bible in America: Essays in Cultural History* (1982). **E. D. Hirsch,** *Validity in Interpretation* (1967). **W. C. Kaiser and M. Silva,** *An Introduction to Biblical Hermeneutics: The Search for Meaning* (1994). **W. W. Klein, C. I. Blomberg, and R. L. Hubbard,** *Introduction to Biblical Interpretation* (1993). **G. B. Marsden,** *Fundamentalism and American Culture: The Shaping of Twentieth-Century Evangelicalism, 1870-1925* (1980). **G. R. Osborne,** *The Hermeneutical Spiral: A Comprehensive Introduction to Biblical Interpretation* (1991); "Evangelical Interpretation of Scripture," *The Bible in the Churches: How Various Christians Interpret the Scriptures* (ed. K. Hagen, Marquette Studies in Theology 4, 1994). **E. D. Radmacher and R. Preus,** *Hermeneutics, Inerrancy, and the Bible* (1984). **J. Rogers and D. McKim,** *The Authority and Interpretation of the Bible: An Historical Approach* (1979). **M. Silva,** *Biblical Words and Their Meaning: An Introduction to Lexical Semantics* (1983). **A. C. Thiselton,** *The Two Horizons: NT Hermeneutics and Philosophical Description* (1980); *New Horizons in Hermeneutics* (1992). **D. F. Wells and J. D. Woodbridge,** *The Evangelicals: What They Believe, Who They Are, Where They Are Changing* (1975). **J. D. Woodbridge,** *Biblical Authority: A Critique of the Rogers-McKim Proposal* (1982).

G. R. OSBORNE

THEOLOGICAL APPROACHES

Hebrew Bible Innerbiblical Interpretation

Innerbiblical interpretation concerns how the authors of the Hebrew Bible and the New Testament cited and alluded to Hebrew Bible materials. The process of reuse, reinterpretation, and reapplication of previous texts from within the Hebrew Bible can be described most accurately as "innerbiblical exegesis" (M. Fishbane 1996; but see L. Eslinger 1992 and B. Sommers 1996). The end product of this exegetical tradition is a richly textured collection of documents incorporating residual literary traditions of the great ancient Near Eastern civilizations as well as the original literary traditions of ancient Israel.

Fishbane has undertaken the most thorough examination of innerbiblical exegesis (1979, 1985, 1989, 1996). Distinguishing between the textual tradition (*traditum*) and its transmission in a new interpretive context (*traditio*), he has established four basic categories in relation to the Hebrew Bible: scribal comments and corrections, also known as glosses (J. Weingreen 1957); legal exegesis; aggadic exegesis; and mantological exegesis (Fishbane 1985). Fishbane works from the assumption that the Torah (Pentateuch) was historically and literarily antecedent to the other portions of the Hebrew Bible Canon§.

1. *Glosses.* While no one doubts that complex oral traditions underlie the scribal heritage of the Hebrew Bible, the task of the biblical scholar is firmly rooted in the final form of the written text. This written witness is, however, the product of a lengthy process of transmission and redaction. Whether for the purposes of clarification, theological conformity, or legal uniformity, the *traditum* was revised and transmitted to new groups in new time by scribes (1 Chr 27:32), who inserted various taxonomic elements common to most anthological writings: superscriptions, colophons, titles, generic indicators, and closures. Glosses are most apparent in the poetic and wisdom traditions (Pss 3:1; 72:20; Prov 25:1; 31:1), but they also occur in other portions of the Hebrew Bible (Lev 6:2, 7; 7:37-38; Num 6:21; 1 Kgs 11:41; 1 Chr 9:1). Scribes annotated the text for purposes of clarification, using the particles *hû'* and *hî'* to mark the changes in place names (Gen 14:17; Josh 18:13; 1 Chr 11:13), and frequently contemporized anachronistic references (Gen 12:6; Josh 15:8-10; 1 Kgs 6:38; Esth 2:16; 3:7). Explanatory and parenthetical comments often intrude into the text, disturbing the flow of syntax (Isa 29:10; Ezek 3:12) and sometimes confusing what must originally have been quite clear to the original readers (Lev 19:19). Fishbane (1996) suggests that this intrusive form of annotation was employed when the scribes were faced with a fixed *traditum* (e.g., Deut 22:12; 2 Sam 7:10; 1 Kgs 5:22 [MT], where it appears that older terms were simply reworked with more contemporary language). As the textual traditions were developed and standardized, the scribes also undertook to "clarify" misleading orthographic features and variant grammatical forms (Weingreen 1957).

2. *Legal Exegesis.* The giving of the law at Mt. Sinai was—according to the final narrative— a part of the constitutive act of ancient Israel; along with the various teachings given in the wilderness between Sinai and the entrance into the land, it forms the core of the Hebrew Bible. The history of the development of the legal corpus is complex and suffers from a lack of source material. Critical reconstructions of the text suggest a millennium or more of composition and transmission, during which the ongoing interpretation of the *traditum* flourished. As one explores the texture of the legal traditions, it is possible to discern a variety of exegetical methods as well as patterns of legal reflection, interpretation, and transformation, which Fishbane classifies as legal exegesis. This process of legal reflection and transformation served to clarify ambiguities in the *traditum*, as is seen in the case of the "Hebrew slave" (Exod 21:2; Lev 25:39-46; Deut 15:12-17). In later times there was also a concern to expand the parameters of the law in the interest of comprehensiveness. This can be seen in the laws for the atonement of sins committed

in ignorance (Num 15:25-26; Lev 4:20*b*); the laws for the making of vows (Num 6:2; 30:3); the laws concerning accidental death (Num 35:16); and the laws for returning other people's livestock (Deut 22:1-2; Exod 23:4), where a variety of particles and conjunctions are employed to expand the parameters of legal application. Other frequent elements in legal exegesis are the harmonizing of contradictions (e.g., those found in the ordinances for seventh-year release: Neh 10:32; cf. Exod 23:11; Deut 15:1-2) and the unifying of legal traditions with the descriptions of the historical narratives (2 Sam 5:21; cf. Deut 7:25 and 1 Chr 14:12; 1 Kgs 6:7; cf. Deut 27:5-6). Finally, the reapplication of the law to a new situation often posed exegetical problems for the ancient interpreter that needed to be resolved (the law of the second Passover, 2 Chr 30:1-3, 15; cf. Num 9:1-14; the law on mixed marriages, Ezra 9:1-2; cf. Deut 7:1-6; 23:4-7).

3. *Aggadic Exegesis.* This third category is concerned with the reapplication of the *traditum* to facilitate theological and historical understanding. It is distinct from legal exegesis insofar as the sources employed represent the whole canon of the Hebrew Bible. The prophets (Prophecy and Prophets, Hebrew Bible‡§) are among the primary practitioners of *aggadic* exegesis, often reworking legal traditions for rhetorical purposes. Frequently the *traditio* employed by the prophetic writer is itself the end result of an *aggadic* reworking of an older *traditio*. This is the case with the holiness motif developed by the prophet Jeremiah (Jer 2:3; see also Exod 19:4-6; Lev 22:14-16; Deut 7:6; Ezra 9:1-2). In Isaiah, the prophet interprets the language of the fast in order to highlight the socially oriented character of true religion (Isa 58:1-2; cf. Lev 16:31; 23:24). In both these cases *aggadic* exegesis, while reflecting an expanded interpretive *traditio*, does not abrogate the legal *traditum*.

In other situations, there is a more conscious attempt at theological innovation. The punishment of children for the sins of parents (Exod 20:5) presented a theological dilemma to a later generation highlighted by the Deuteronomist's unambiguous rejection of the principle (Deut 7:9-10; 24:16). The resulting contradiction became the nexus for Ezekiel's *aggadic* discussion of sin and punishment (Ezek 18:2-4, 18-32), in which the legal principle is invoked, affirmed, and then abandoned in favor of a more "gracious" divine attitude toward sin.

Aggadic exegesis also occurs in the presentation of the heroes of old in later texts. The patriarchs are frequently appealed to in this light (Abraham in 2 Kgs 13:23; Neh 9:7; Ps 47:9; Isa 51:2; 63:16, Jer 33:26; Ezek 33:24; and Jacob in Ps 14:7; Isa 43:1, 22). Related, but with its own emphasis, is the *aggadic* development of the verbal traditions of ancient Israel's faithful (Deut 31:4-6; Josh 1; see also 1 Kgs 2:1-9, esp. 3-4).

4. *Mantological Exegesis.* The last of Fishbane's categories is *mantological* exegesis, by which he means the reformulation and reinterpretation of prophetic oracles so that they continually "make sense and project a conceivable future" (1996, 46). Whether the focus of the oracle was doom or blessing, the condition of expectation eventuated. However, when fulfillment was then deferred a reinterpretation of the prophetic *traditum* became necessary (see R. Carroll 1979), thus the scribes sometimes emended toponyms by using the demonstrative pronouns *hû'* and *hî'* for purposes of clarification or specification (Isa 9:13-14). Such specification was also used, with or without the deictic particles, in dreams and visions and in their interpretations (Gen 41:26-30; Dan 4:17-23; 5:25-27; Zech 4:2-6*a*, 10*b*-14). More problematic than such clarifications was the interpretation of oracles that were once clear but later seemed obscure (Isa 16:13-14; Jer 25:9-12; Ezek 29:17-20; cf. 2 Chr 36:19-21; Lev 26:34-35; Daniel 9—12). Daniel's reinterpretation of Jeremiah 25, for example, is particularly significant for employing an angelic mediator to clarify the apparent misunderstanding of the Jeremiah *traditum* (see esp. Dan 9:20-27).

The term Midrash*§, though usually applied to later normative Jewish writings, is also appropriate to the framers of the biblical traditions (2 Chr 13:22; 24:27; Ezra 7:10). The two Chronicles passages are particularly important because they use the noun *midrāš* in the same sense as that found in later rabbinic texts. The postexilic roots of midrash—the use of biblical phrases in later biblical works with meanings different from their original context—were identified by A. Robert (1934, 1944) and are scattered throughout the Hebrew Bible. Genesis (S. Sandmel 1961), Deuteronomy (G. Vermes 1961), Ezekiel (L. Zunz 1966; J. Halperin 1976; F. F. Bruce 1972), Psalms (B. Childs 1971; Bruce), and Chronicles (Zunz; Weingreen 1951-52; T. Willi 1972) have all been identified as books that reflect midrashic activity or, as appears to be the case in Chronicles, are midrashes.

The case for Chronicles as midrash found early support in the work of W. Barnes (1896). More recently, the term *midrash* has given way to "exegesis" (Willi 1972). In either case the focus is on the reworking of an authoritative text by secondary authors to produce changes in language, style, content, and ideology (H. Williamson 1982; S. Japhet 1977 [ET 1989]). This happens in two complementary ways. Working from an authoritative *Vorlage*, the chronicler transposed, sometimes literally and sometimes in a drastically altered form, the existing textual material, which he then juxtaposed with his own original material (Japhet 1989). His apparent principal sources were the former prophets, particularly Samuel-Kings (P. Vanutelli 1931-34; A. Bendavid 1972; S. McKenzie 1985). Evidence from Qumran (Dead Sea Scrolls§) suggests that the *Vorlage* may already have contained some of the chronicler's emendations (W. Lemke 1965). The possibility that 2 Kings 20 was reused in Isaiah 38 suggests that an even earlier practice of midrash-like activity on the part of the biblical authors (A. Konkel 1993; Williamson 1994) may have formed the precedent for the Chronicler's work.

Bibliograph: P. R. Ackroyd, "Some Interpretive Glosses in the Book of Haggai," *JJS* 7 (1956) 163-68; *Studies in the Religious Tradition of the OT* (1987). **G. Aichele and G. A. Phillips** (eds.), *Intertextuality and the Bible* (*Semeia* 69-70, 1995). **M. Amihai** et al. (eds.), *Narrative Research on the HB* (*Semeia* 46, 1989). **B. W. Anderson,** "Exodus Typology in Second Isaiah," *Israel's Prophetic Heritage: Essays in Honor of James Muilenburg* (ed., B. W. Anderson et al., 1962) 177-95. **G. W. Anderson** (ed.), *Tradition and Interpretation* (1979). **W. E. Barnes,** "The Midrashic Element in Chronicles," *Expositor* 5, 4 (1896) 426-39. **A. Bendavid,** *Parallels in the Bible* (1972). **F. F. Bruce,** "The Earliest OT Interpretation," *OTS* 17 (1972) 37-52. **A. M. Brunet,** *Le Chroniste et ses sources* (1953). **R. P. Carroll,** *When Prophecy Failed: Cognitive Dissonance in the Prophetic Traditions of the OT* (1979). **D. A. Carson and H. G. M. Williamson** (eds.), *It Is Written: Scripture Citing Scripture* (1988). **B. S. Childs,** "Psalm Titles and Midrashic Exegesis," *JSS* 16 (1971) 137-50. **J. Day,** "A Case of Inner-Scriptural Interpretation: The Dependence of Isaiah xxvi.13-xxvii.11 on Hosea xiii.4-xiv.10 (Eng. 9) and Its Relevance to Some Theories of the Redaction of the Isaiah Apocalypse," *JTS* 31 (1980) 109-19. **S. Draisma** (ed.), *Intertextuality in Biblical Writings: In Honour of Bas van Iersel* (1989). **L. Eslinger,** "Inner-biblical Exegesis and Inner-biblical Allusion: The Question of Category," *VT* 42 (1992) 47-58. **M. Fishbane,** "Numbers 5:11-31: A Study of Law and Scribal Practices in Israel and the Ancient Near East," *HUCA* 45 (1974) 25-45; *Text and Texture: Close Readings of Selected Biblical Texts* (1979); *Biblical Interpretation in Ancient Israel* (1985); *The Garments of the Torah: Essays in Biblical Hermeneutics* (1989); "Inner-Biblical Exegesis," *HB/OT: The History of its Interpretation* (ed., Magne Sæbø 1, 1, 1996) 33-48. **G. B. Gray,** "The Parallel Passages in 'Joel' and Their Bearing on the Question of Date," *Expositor* 8 (1893) 209-25. **J. Halperin,** "The Exegetical Character of Ezek. X.9-17," *VT* 26 (1976) 129-41. **M. Herr,** *Continuum in the Chain of Transmission* (1979). **P. R. House** (ed.), *Beyond Form Criticism: Essays in OT Literary Criticism* (1992). **C. Houtman,** "Ezra and the Law," *OTS* 21 (1981) 91-115. **S. Japhet,** *The Ideology of the Book of Chronicles and Its Place in Biblical Thought* (1977; ET BEATAJ 9, 1989); *I and II Chronicles* (OTL, 1993). **K. Koch,** *The Growth of the Biblical Tradition* (1969). **A. H. Konkel,** "The Sources of the Story of Hezekiah in the Book of Isaiah," *VT* 43

(1993) 462-82. **B. Lategan and W. Vorster** (eds.), *Text and Reality: Aspects of Reference in Biblical Texts* (SemeiaSt, 1985). **W. E. Lemke,** "The Synoptic Problem of the Chronicler's History," *HTR* 58 (1965) 349-63. **T. Longman,** *Literary Approaches to Biblical Interpretation* (Foundations of Contemporary Interpretation 3, 1987). **S. L. McKenzie,** *The Chronicler's Use of the Deuteronomistic History* (HSM 33, 1985). **A. Robert,** "Les attaches litteraires bibliques de Prov I-IX," *RB* 42 (1934) 42-68, 172-204, 374-84; *Le genre litteraire du Cantique des cantiques* (1944). **S. Sandmel,** "The Haggada Within Scripture," *JBL* 80 (1961) 105-22. **N. Sarna,** "Psalm 89: A Study in Inner Biblical Exegesis," Biblical and Other Studies (ed. A. Altmann, 1963) 29-46. **I. L. Seeligmann,** "Voraussetzungen der Midraschexegese," *Volume du congrès 1956* (VTSup 1, 1953) 150-81. **P. A. Smith,** *Rhetoric and Redaction in Trito-Isaiah* (VTSup 62, 1995). **B. D. Sommers,** "Exegesis, Allusion, and Intertextuality in the HB: A Response to L. Eslinger," *VT* 46 (1996) 479-89. **M. Sternberg,** *The Poetics of Biblical Narrative* (1985). **S. Talmon,** *Literary Studies in the HB* (1993). **B. Uffenheimer and H. G. Reventlow** (eds.), *Creative Biblical Exegesis: Christian and Jewish Hermeneutics Through the Centuries* (JSOTSup 59, 1988). **P. Vanutelli,** *Libri Synoptici Veteris Testamenti* (1931-34). **G. Vermes,** *Scripture and Tradition Within Judaism* (SPB 4, 1961). **J. Weingreen,** "The Rabbinic Approach to the Study of the OT," *BJRL* 24 (1951-52) 166-90; "Rabbinic-Type Glosses in the OT," *JSS* 2 (1957) 149-62; *From Bible to Mishna: The Continuity of Tradition* (1976). **T. Willi,** *Die Chronik als Auslegung* (FRLANT 106, 1972). **H. G. M. Williamson,** *I and II Chronicles* (NCB, 1982); *The Book Called Isaiah: Deutero-Isaiah's Role in Compilation and Redaction* (1994). **C. Winquist** (ed.), *Text and Textuality* (Semeia 40, 1987). **L. Zunz,** *Die gottesdienstlichen Vorträge der Juden* (1966).

C. S. McKenzie

THEOLOGICAL APPROACHES

New Testament Innerbiblical Interpretation

Throughout the New Testament, citations, allusions, themes, and types drawn from the Hebrew Bible surface repeatedly, indicating that the New Testament debt to the Hebrew Bible (particularly the Septuagint translation) was pervasive. This New Testament use of the Hebrew Bible has been a major area of interest in twentieth-century scholarship.

Numerous attempts have been made to understand the development and significance of New Testament innerbiblical interpretation. A primary impetus for twentieth-century scholarly investigation was the work of R. Harris (1916, 1920), who argued that the prevalence of Hebrew Bible citations and allusions in the New Testament can be accounted for by an early Christian indebtedness to testimony collections (cf. Fitzmyer 1974, 59-89). These alleged collections would have consisted of groupings of relevant testimony texts that witnessed to the fulfillment of Hebrew Bible prophecies (Prophecy and Prophets, Hebrew Bible[‡§]) in the ministry of Jesus[*§] and the church, used polemically by the early Christians in their contacts with Jews. While the existence of a specific unified collection of this sort remained hypothetical, C. H. Dodd[§] (1952) reinforced the key premise in Harris's work by arguing that New Testament writers relied on key Hebrew Bible passages for elucidation of their theological affirmations but that, rather than selecting isolated prooftexts, they focused on large blocks of prophetic materials (e.g., Isaiah, Jeremiah) and the psalms, which they referenced *en bloc* through isolated citations and allusions. Thus these large blocks of Hebrew Bible material, rather than simply the cited text, form the "substructure" of New Testament theology. B. Lindars (1961) took Dodd's proposal one step further, arguing that one could study the New Testament use of the Hebrew Bible for shifts in application and modification, in order to determine internal New Testament doctrinal development from early apologetic use of a particular text to a more nuanced theological use of that same text in a later New Testament period. The interest reflected in the trajectory from Harris to Lindars concerns the basic issue of how the New Testament writers utilized Hebrew Bible texts to develop and sustain theological arguments.

From early on, attention was also given to the mechanics of New Testament interpretation of the Hebrew Bible. For instance, questions of Canon[§] and Hermeneutics[*§] were addressed already in O. Michel's early work on Paul's[†§] use of the Hebrew Bible (1929). The interest in Paul's interpretative method was central from the beginning; numerous studies set out to analyze his midrashic process (Midrash[*§]), comparing it with both rabbinic and Second Temple Jewish writers (J. Bonsirven 1939; E. Ellis 1957), a process that was given further impulse after the discovery of the Qumran pesher texts (Dead Sea Scrolls[§]). These concerns have expanded into the study of Jewish hermeneutic practices in general, focusing on their relevance for understanding New Testament interpretation of Scripture (J. Doeve 1954; L. Goppelt 1939 [ET 1982]; R. Longenecker 1975; M. McNamara 1978; S. Sowers 1965; B. Chilton 1994; J. Barton 1986; R. Bauckham 1990), which has culminated in comparative studies of certain passages, contrasting New Testament and Jewish interpretations (C. Evans 1989; M. Callaway 1986). Scholarship has thus grown increasingly interested in learning what the cultural and social environment of early Christianity can contribute to understanding the New Testament use of the Hebrew Bible.

From this interest in the mechanics of interpretation, many issues have come to the fore. For instance, some scholars set about trying to uncover the text form of the Hebrew Bible used by early Christians (E. Freed 1965; K. Stendahl 1967). Others have made use of later Jewish lectionary cycles as a way of explaining the patterns and conjunctions of various Hebrew Bible references in the New Testament (A. Guilding 1960; M. Goulder 1974). Defining the term

"Midrash" has also taken on increasing importance (R. Le Deaut 1971; J. Neusner 1987; A. G. Wright 1967; G. Porten 1979), as has its application to particular New Testament texts (M. Gertner 1962; M. Miller 1971; J. Derrett 1977-95). In recent scholarship, the debate has centered on what constitutes a quotation/citation as opposed to an allusion (E. Porter 1997), as from the beginning scholars have categorized New Testament citations using a diverse—and often conflicting—set of criteria. There has been an increasing tendency to return to the direction of such scholars as Dodd and Lindars in attempting to understand the function and role Hebrew Bible citations perform in New Testament theological expression, providing some scholars with the basis for a coherent biblical theology (H. Hübner 1996). This takes into account that innerbiblical interpretation is more than a mechanical act; it is an argumentative strategy to persuade readers (C. Stanley 1997). Thus scholars differentiate between different types of uses: e.g., the messianic application in the Gospels (D. Juel 1988) as contrasted to the ecclesiological utilization in Paul (D. Koch 1986; R. Hays 1989). Moreover, scholars have increasingly recognized that one cannot speak generally about the use of the Hebrew Bible in the New Testament but must refer to the function and use of the Hebrew Bible in specific writers and texts, thus spawning myriad studies focusing on individual New Testament writings/writers (R. Gundry 1975; J. Marcus 1992; A. Suhl 1965; C. Evans and J. Sanders 1993; T. Holtz 1968; B. Schuchard 1992; F. M. Braun 1964; A. Hanson 1974, 1991; Koch; Hays; Stanley 1992; J. Fekkes 1994), specific SYNOPTIC narratives (W. Stegner 1989; D. Moo 1983), and the influence and interpretation of a particular Hebrew Bible text in its appropriation by a variety of New Testament writers (Hay; M. Hooker 1959; J. Gnilka 1961). The citation of Hebrew Bible texts has also been utilized in the investigation of the interrelationship of New Testament writings (S. New 1993).

The study of innerbiblical interpretation in the New Testament must inevitably begin with a treatment of both the diversity of uses and the basic problem of identifying when that use takes place, which has been a perennial problem. There are three basic categories of New Testament use of the Hebrew Bible: citations, allusions, and echoes. The simplest to identify is direct citation, when a writer explicitly intends to reference a specific Hebrew Bible text (see lists in G. Archer and G. Chirichigno 1983; Hübner 1997-; B. McLean 1992). The formula quotations—which include a short introductory citation formula, often followed by reference to the Hebrew Bible writer/"author"/text—are the most apparent examples of direct Hebrew Bible citation (Matt 1:23, 4:15-16; Mark 12:10-11*a*; Luke 20:42*b*-43; John 12:38-40, 19:24; Acts 2:16-21, 25-28; 8:32-33; Rom 9:25-29; Gal 4:27; Eph 4:8; Heb 2:6-8; 3:7-11; 10:5-7; Jas 4:6; 1 Pet 2:6-10; see Fitzmyer 1974, 3-58). Some direct citations of the Hebrew Bible simply appear without any introduction in places where there is little doubt that both writer and readers knew that a quotation from the Hebrew Bible was intended (Gal 3:6, 11-12; Heb 10:37-38; 13:6; 1 Pet 3:10-12). Moreover, the New Testament writers often include a chain of citations (Rom 3:10-18; 15:9-12; 2 Cor 6:16-18; 1 Pet 2:6-10) in which a variety of texts on a related theme are strung together, a phenomenon that initially led to the testimony book hypothesis. In addition, one finds both conflations of Hebrew Bible texts (in which two Hebrew Bible texts are combined into one reference; Matt 2:6; Mark 1:2-3; Acts 7:7) and numerous modifications in the Hebrew Bible citation in order to conform the text to the writer's argument (see Rom 1:17, where Paul drops the personal pronoun in order to obtain a dual meaning in Hab 2:4). In many of these instances it is evident that the New Testament writers were not concerned with uncovering the original intent of the Hebrew Bible writer. Rather, texts were often used for what they would contribute to christological and ecclesiological exegesis in the church, without regard for their larger context and meaning in the Hebrew Bible. At the same time, there are instances in which the larger context of the Hebrew Bible is apparently in view (the use of Lev 19 in Jas 2; see L. T. Johnson 1982). Overall, there is no hard and fast rule about the relationship of Hebrew Bible citation in the New Testament to its larger Hebrew Bible context; one must analyze each instance in turn.

Direct citations are by far the least common aspect of Hebrew Bible use in the New Testament. Most prominent are allusions to Hebrew Bible texts, which are made throughout the New Testament. It becomes particularly difficult to establish when these allusions were intended by an author, when they would have been understood by the readers (irrespective of authorial intent), and when they were unintentional, simply echoes of biblical language resulting from people so thoroughly immersed in the Hebrew Bible text and thought world that their own words were unconsciously shaped by and modeled on its patterns. The Bible of the early church, it must be remembered, was the Hebrew Bible (2 Tim 3:16), and first-century Christians were taught to mine the Scriptures for their theological and moral formation. Hence, the language of that formation is, from beginning to end, explicitly biblical. Consequently, it is difficult in many cases to separate allusion from echo and both of these from quotation (J. Paulien 1988; Porter). Is the allusion just a direct citation without introduction that the reader is expected to catch? Is the allusion subtler, belying the author's indebtedness to the Hebrew Bible for theological expression? Or is the writer even aware of alluding to the Hebrew Bible? These are difficult questions, and the fact that, at one time or another, a Hebrew Bible text has been postulated to underlie almost every verse in the New Testament demonstrates the far-reaching implications of this debate. It is clear, however, that there are many intentional allusions in the New Testament (for some possible allusions see Exod 3:14 in John 18:5-6; Isa 49:1 in Gal 1:15; Isa 45:23 [LXX] in Phil 2:10-11 and Rom 14:11; Job 13:16 [LXX] in Phil 1:19; Isa 40:6-8 in Jas 1:10-11; Gen 1:1-5 in John 1:1-5; Dan 9:27 in Mark 13:14; [cf. Hays]). Of course, many of the allusions that exist now are the end result of exegetical reflections and developments prior to the existence of the present text (see Phil 2:10-11, which is probably a Christian hymn fragment).

The New Testament evinces a variety of uses of the Hebrew Bible in its innerbiblical exegesis. There are straightforward citations often used as prophetic prooftexts (Matt 12:17-21), sometimes in a pesher-like mode, as one finds at Qumran (Acts 2:22-36; 15:13-18). Scripture is also used to bolster theological (Rom 4:6-8; Gal 3:10-14; Heb 10:15-17) and practical arguments (1 Cor 10:7; 2 Cor 6:16-18; 8:15; 9:9; Jas 2:8). Hebrews presents some fine examples of midrashic exegesis in which the exegetical reflection is still embedded in the sermon (Heb 3:7-4:13; 7:1-17). There is at least one explicit example of the use of allegorical interpretation, wherein a Hebrew Bible story is understood to contain a deeper, symbolic meaning corresponding to various components of a literal interpretation (Gal 4:21-31). The New Testament also has several instances of the ancient Jewish practice of rewriting the Bible, a convention in which the biblical story is retold with some modifications in light of the specific purposes of the writer (Acts 7; 13:16-22; Hebrews 11). Moreover, there are numerous examples of typological exegesis, in which typology is premised on the Hebrew Bible text, thus forming a paradigm or *exemplum* for either theological argument or moral exhortation. For instance, the exodus event provides a typology of the Corinthian community in 1 Cor 10:1-14; and Adam provides a type of Christ in Rom 5:12-21 (cf. 2 Cor 3:1-18 [S. Hafemann, 1995]; Hebrews 11 [P. Eisenbaum, 1997]; Jude 5-13). This common use of the Hebrew Bible as *paradeigma* reflects the strong emphasis placed on examples in Greco-Roman education and rhetoric. Also notable is the typological value of certain characters like Moses in Matthew (D. Allison 1993) and the figure of the Son of Man (Dan 7:13-14) throughout the Gospels. Furthermore, certain key events, themes, and institutions of the Hebrew Bible take on a typological or paradigmatic quality in the New Testament (creation, exodus/new exodus [Isaiah]; covenant/new covenant [Jeremiah]; priesthood, prophecy/prophets, kingly office, "anointed one"). Finally, one must consider one of the foundational uses of the Hebrew Bible by early Christian writers: the generation of New Testament narratives based on Hebrew Bible models (Stegner, Moessner, Aus, Daube, Derrett [cf. Dan 12:6-7 and Rev 10:5-7]). Here it becomes apparent that, when early

Christians told their stories, they were often consciously modeling them on the prior narratives of the Hebrew Bible.

Bibliography: D. C. Allison, *The New Moses: A Matthean Typology* (1993). G. L. Archer and G. C. Chirichigno, *OT Quotations in the NT: A Complete Survey* (1983). R. Aus, *Barabbas and Esther and Other Studies in the Judaic Illumination of Earliest Christianity* (SFSHJ 54, 1992); *Samuel, Saul, and Jesus: Three Early Palestinian Jewish Christian Gospel Haggadoth* (SFSHJ 105, 1994). J. Barton, *Oracles of God: Perceptions of Ancient Prophecy in Israel After the Exile* (1986). R. Bauckham, *Jude and the Relatives of Jesus in the Early Church* (1990). J. Bonsirven, *Exégèse Rabbinique et Exégèse Paulinienne* (Biblioteque de la theologie historique, 1939). F. M. Braun, *Jean le Théologien: Les Grandes Traditions D'Israel L'Accord des Écritures D'Aprés le Quatrieme Évangile* (Ebib, 1964). M. Callaway, *Sing, O Barren One: A Study in Comparative Midrash* (SBLDS 91, 1986). B. Chilton, *Targumic Approaches to the Gospels: Essays in the Mutual Definition of Judaism and Christianity* (1986); *Judaic Approaches to the Gospels* (USF International Studies in Formative Christianity and Judaism 2, 1994). C. H. Dodd, *According to the Scriptures: The Sub-Structure of New Testament Theology* (1952). D. Daube, "A Reform in Acts and Its Models," *Jews, Greeks, and Christians: Religious Cultures in Late Antiquity* (ed. R. Hamerton-Kelly and R. Scroggs, SJLA 21, 1976) 151-63. R. Le Deaut, "Apropos a Definition of Midrash," *Int* 25 (1971) 259-82. J. D. M. Derrett, *Studies in the NT* (1977-95). J. W. Doeve, *Jewish Hermeneutics in the Synoptic Gospels and Acts* (1954). P. M. Eisenbaum, *The Jewish Heroes of Christian History: Hebrews 11 in Literary Context* (SBLDS 156, 1997). E. E. Ellis, *Paul's Use of the OT* (1957); *The OT in Early Christianity* (1991). C. A. Evans, *To See and Not Perceive: Isaiah 6:9-10 in Early Jewish and Christian Interpretation* (JSOTSup 64, 1989). C. A. Evans and J. A. Sanders, *Luke and Scripture* (1993). C. A. Evans and J. A. Sanders (eds.), *Paul and the Scriptures of Israel* (JSNTSup 83, 1993); *The Gospels and the Scriptures of Israel* (JSNTSup 104, 1994); *Early Christian Interpretation of the Scriptures of Israel* (JSNTSup 148, 1997). J. Fekkes, *Isaiah and Prophetic Traditions in the Book of Revelation* (JSNTSup 93, 1994). J. A. Fitzmyer, "4QTestimonia and the NT," *Essays on the Semitic Background of the NT* (SBLSBS 5, 1974) 59-89; "The Use of Explicit OT Quotations in Qumran Literature and the NT," *Essays on the Semitic Background of the NT* (SBLSBS 5, 1974). 3-58. E. Freed, *HB Quotations in the Gospel of John* (NovTSup 11, 1965). M. Gertner, "Midrashim in the NT," *JSS* 7 (1962) 267-92. L. Goppelt, *Typos: The Typological Interpretation of the OT in the New* (1939; ET 1982). J. Gnilka, *Die Verstockung Israels: Isaias 6,9-10 in der Theologie der Synoptiker* (1961). M. D. Goulder, *Midrash and Lection in Matthew* (1974). A. Guilding, *The Fourth Gospel and Jewish Worship: A Study of the Relation of St. John's Gospel to the Ancient Jewish Lectionary System* (1960). R. H. Gundry, *The Use of the OT in St. Matthew's Gospel* (NovTSup 18, 1975). A. T. Hanson, *Studies in Paul's Technique and Theology* (1974); *The Prophetic Gospel: A Study of John and the OT* (1991). R. Harris and V. Burch, *Testimonies* (2 vols. 1916, 1920). S. J. Hafemann, *Paul, Moses, and the History of Israel: The Letter/Spirit Contrast and the Argument from Scripture in 2 Corinthians 3* (WUNT 81, 1995). D. M. Hay, *Glory at the Right Hand: Psalm 110 in Early Christianity* (SBLMS 18, 1973). R. B. Hays, *Echoes of Scripture in the Letters of Paul* (1989). T. Holtz, *Untersuchungen über die alttesta-mentlichen Zitate bei Lukas* (TUGAL 104, 1968). M. D. Hooker, *Jesus and the Servant: The Influence of the Servant Concept of deutero-Isaiah in the New Testament* (1959). H. Hübner, "NT Interpretation of the OT," *HB/OT 1, 1* (1996) 332-72; *Vetus Testamentum in Novo* (1997-). L. T. Johnson, "The Use of Leviticus 19 in the Letter of James," *JBL* 101 (1982) 391-401. D. H. Juel, *Messianic Exegesis: Christological Interpretation of the OT in Early Christianity* (1988). D.-A. Koch, *Die Schrift als Zeuge des Evangeliums: Untersuchungen zur Verwendung* *und zum Verstandnis der Schrift bei Paulus* (BHT 69, 1986). **B. Lindars,** *NT Apologetic: The Doctrinal Significance of the OT Quotations* (1961). **R. N. Longenecker**, *Biblical Exegesis in the Apostolic Period* (1975). **B. H. McLean,** *Citations and Allusions to Jewish Scripture in Early Christian and Jewish Writings Through 180 C.E.* (1992). **M. McNamara,** *The NT and the Palestinian Targum to the Pentateuch* (ArBib 27*a*, 1978). **J. Marcus,** *The Way of the Lord: Christological Exegesis of the OT in the Gospel of Mark* (1992). **O. Michel,** *Paulus und seine Bibel* (BFCT 2, 1929). **M. P. Miller,** "Targum, Midrash, and the Use of the OT in the NT," *JSJ* 2 (1971) 29-82. **D. P. Moessner,** *Lord of the Banquet: The Literary and Theological Significance of the Lukan Travel Narrative* (1989). **D. J. Moo,** *The OT in the Gospel Passion Narratives* (1983). **J. Neusner,** *What Is Midrash?* (GBS, 1987). **D. S. New,** *OT Quotations in the Synoptic Gospels and the Two-Document Hypothesis* (SBLSCS 37, 1993). **J. Paulien,** "Elusive Allusions: The Problematic Use of the OT in Revelations," *BR* 33 (1988) 37-53. **G. Porten**, "Midrash: Palestinian Jews and the HB in the Greco-Roman Period," *ANRW* II.19.2 (1979) 103-38. **S. E. Porter,** "The Use of the OT in the NT: A Brief Comment on Method and Terminology," *Early Christian Interpretation of the Scriptures of Israel* (ed. C. A. Evans et al., JSNTSup 148, 1997) 79-96. **B. G. Schuchard,** *Scripture Within Scripture: The Interrelationship of Form and Function in the Explicit OT Citations in the Gospel of John* (SBLDS 133, 1992). **S. G. Sowers,** *The Hermeneutics of Philo and Hebrews*: A Comparison of the Interpretation of the Old Testament in Philo Judaeus and the Epistle to the Hebrews (1965). **C. D. Stanley,** *Paul and the Language of Scripture: Citation Technique in the Pauline Epistles and Contemporary Literature* (SNTSMS 69, 1992); "The Rhetoric of Quotations: An Essay on Method," *Early Christian Interpretation of the Scriptures of Israel* (ed. C. A. Evans et al., JSNTSup 148, 1997) 44-58. **W. R. Stegner**, *Narrative Theology in Early Jewish Christianity* (1989). **K. Stendahl,** *The School of St. Matthew and Its Use of the OT* (1968). **A. Suhl**, *Die Funktion der alttestamentlichen Zitate und Anspielungen im Markusevangelium* (1965). **A. G. Wright,** *The Literary Genre Midrash* (1967).

T. C. PENNER

THEOLOGICAL APPROACHES

Inspiration of the Bible

Beginning in the nineteenth century, there has been considerable interest in the inspiration of the Bible. The discussion of that topic is closely linked to the authority of the bible and, hence, is extensively covered in that entry. There remains, however, to set the question into its earliest historical context.

J. Leipoldt (1961) has traced the early history of the idea of inspiration, illuminating in a remarkable way the dominant role it plays among the Greeks and its virtual absence among the Hebrews. In oriental religions, the gods are directly accountable for holy texts, either writing them or dictating them to scribes. In Egypt, Thot is both god of the scribes and scribe for the gods and, since 2000 B.C.E., many writings were attributed to him, the autograph being considered reliable.

Among the Hebrews, Yahweh commanded Moses to serve as scribe (Exod 34:27-28), although in the Elohist narrative it was God who wrote the Torah on the tablets and then gave them to Moses (Exod 24:12). Even more directly, the tablets are described as written by the "finger of God" (Exod 31:18; 32:16), similar to the portrayal of the code of Hammurabi as coming from Shamesh, the sun god. Later, such anthropomorphisms were rejected, and the angel of the Presence was seen as dictating (or writing down) the law to Moses (*Jub* 1:27; 2:1). Rabbinic belief in the preexistence of the law before creation assumes the existence of a heavenly original, and it was asserted that the history as well as the law existed in tablets written in heaven (*Jub* 23:32; 31:32; 32:28; *T. Levi* 5:4). In Ethiopic book of Enoch, after it is said that the angel Uriel did the writing (*1 En.* 33:3), this is changed to Enoch's doing the writing himself (*1 En.* 33:4).

Strictly speaking, inspiration emerged among the prophets of Israel (Prophecy and Prophets, Hebrew Bible‡§) when they seemed to lose their rationality and uttered syllables or words no one could understand. Yet this prophetic rapture did not carry revelation (1 Sam 10:10). Although the Spirit is described as descending upon a person to bring about a certain action and "the word of the LORD," the difference between prophet and God was always maintained, and the prophet always had the right of refusal to carry the message. The experience of Jonah is perhaps meant to illustrate that.

Among the Greeks, the idea of inspiration flourished, beginning at least as early as Euripides' *Bacchae*, in which the dramatist sought to fathom the mental attitude of a man who prophesied after the total deity had passed into his body or when he was captured and forced to serve his god. But inspiration as madness, described as a "special gift from heaven and the source of the chief blessing from heaven," was most fully developed by Plato in the *Phaedrus* and *Ion*. Previously, Democritus had written that "whatever a poet writes being driven by God and the holy spirit is certainly beautiful," and Hesiod conceived of divine inspiration when he wrote that the Muses of Mount Olympus "had breathed a Divine voice [or syllables?] into him" (*Theogony* 31). According to Plato, God takes away the minds of the poets and possesses them, and the priceless words are spoken in a state of unconsciousness. Yet Plato decried the invention of writing and described all writings as dangerous (*Phaedrus*) because what is written is no longer under the protection of the author, and written words are simply not adequate to express the truth. The highest truths must be communicated orally and "written in the soul," which is the only true form of writing.

The most detailed discussions of this topic came in connection with the oracles. Cicero observed that the SIBYLLINE books had a certain deliberate artistry that could hardly have come about in a state of ecstasy, but must have been constructed in a writer's workshop. The longest treatment this subject received was from Plutarch, who was struck by the fact that the high priestess of Delphi no longer spoke in verses. He rejected the suggestion that perhaps she no longer spoke for Apollo and proposed instead that god does not provide the words, but only inspires the author with the subject. "God gives her only the images and concepts and kindles in her soul a light that she may know the future; in that consists her dependence upon God."

Solid evidence of the belief that holy writings depend on holy inspiration for authority is first found in the Greek-speaking segment of Judaism. The concept of the writer's union with God appears in many sources here, but not, for some reason, in Aristeas§ (second cent. B.C.E.), where one might expect it. Although Aristeas firmly believed in the miraculous origin of the Greek translation of the Hebrew Bible, he did not avail himself of a theory of inspiration to account for it. In rabbinical circles, the theory of inspiration figures hardly at all, and one can be reasonably certain that it was virtually never discussed in the first century.

Certainly the New Testament writers had little interest in the issue. Yet Jesus*§ would appear to follow Hebrew Bible patterns when he referred to David's speaking (not writing?) "by the Holy Spirit" (Mark 12:36) and thus indicated that the source of what David said was beyond himself. Likewise, he urged his disciples not to worry about what they shall say when they are arrested, but to "say whatever is given you at that time, for it is not you who speak, but the Holy Spirit" (Mark 13:11). It is almost as if we were back in Plato's world. Paul[†§], on the other hand, made it very clear that Christians are not out of control when the Spirit possesses them, for "the spirits of the prophets are subject to the prophets" (1 Cor 14:32). In his dealing with the Hebrew Bible, Paul displayed a freedom in going beyond it, but also in viewing it as fully expressive, not only of God's purpose and will, but also of human individuality. In citing one prophet he wrote, "Then Isaiah is so bold as to say. . . . " (Rom 10:20).

In this respect, Paul was not followed. Later Christian sources stressed the lifelessness of man (Epiphanius 48; *Odes of Solomon* 6:1; Justin Martyr), all assuming that the human writer is passive and under the complete control of God. Second Tim 3:16 takes a mediating position, which uses the rare word *theopneustos* to distinguish secular writings from those that have their origin in God. No theory of inspiration is here in view, but the stress is laid on the usefulness of Scripture, which has its origin in God (E. Schweitzer 1968). The Scriptures are not called *hagios* here, as throughout the rest of the New Testament, but rather *hiera*; only the gospel and people are called "holy" (Rom 1:2). Second Peter 1:20-21 speaks of " moved by the Holy Spirit," and one has the clear impression that they had no choice. For the most part, people, not writings, were considered inspired (G. Lampe 1962).

In subsequent years all this changed, and many nonbiblical views came to dominate the discussions of inspiration. The authority of the Bible had, at one time, been assured by the way in which its message transformed lives, but—as ages of uncertainty came through the demise of Christianity as a state religion or dominant culture and as views of inspiration changed— attempts were made to impose a theory of inspiration on the Scriptures. It is ironic that often those who proclaimed a "high view of Scripture" actually went outside of Scripture to find a view of inspiration.

There is little evidence that theories of inspiration have made any difference in how the biblical text has been interpreted over the generations. Rather, it has been the conviction that God was the inspiring power behind the events described and that, at times, God inspired writers to preserve for posterity their witness to the faith in these Scriptures. Since the discussions of inspiration came not from within the Scriptures themselves but as an answer to outside detractors, they served only a modest apologetic purpose. The risk that such an approach takes is that it detracts from an inductive study of the Scriptures and distorts the original function and purpose of the Scriptures, which is to witness to the reality of a covenanting God.

Bibliography: W. J. Abraham, *The Divine Inspiration of Holy Scripture* (1981). **P. Achtemeier,** *The Inspiration of Scripture* (Biblical Perspectives on Current Issues, 1980). **L. Alonso-**

Schöckel, *The Inspired Word: Scripture in the Light of Language and Literature* (1965). **D. Beegle,** *The Inspiration of Scrip*ture (1963). **P. Benoit,** *Aspects of Biblical Inspiration* (1965). **J. T. Burtchaell,** *Catholic Theories of Biblical Inspiration Since 1810: A Review and Critique* (1969). **A. A. Hodge and B. B. Warfield,** *Inspiration* (1881). **G. W. H. Lampe,** "Inspiration and Revelation," *IDB* 2 (1962) 713-18. **J. Leipoldt,** "Die Frühgeschichte der göttlichen Eingebung," *Von den Mysterien zur Kirche: gesammelte Aufsätze* (1961) 116-49. **J. McKenzie,** "The Social Character of Inspiration," *CBQ* 24 (1962) 115-24. **J. H. Newman,** *On the Inspiration of Scripture* (ed. J. D. Holmes and R. Murray, 1967). **R. D. Preus,** *The Inspiration of Scripture: A Study of the Theology of the Seventeenth Century Lutheran Dogmaticians* (1955). **W. Sanday,** *Inspiration* (1896). **E. Schweitzer,** θϵ ʹοπνϵυστος" *TDNT* 6 (1968) 453-55. **J. Scullion,** *The Theology of Inspiration* (1970). **N. Snaith,** *The Inspiration and Authority of the Bible* (1956). **P. Synave and P. Benoit,** *Prophecy and Inspiration: A Commentary on the Summa theologica II-II, Questions 171-178* (1961). **K. R. Trembath,** *Evangelical Theories of Biblical Inspiration A Review and Proposal* (1987). **P. M. Van Bemmelen,** *Issues in Biblical Inspiration: Sanday and Warfield* (1987). **B. Vawter,** *Biblical Inspiration* (1972). **B. B. Warfield,** *The Inspiration and Authority of the Bible* (1948).

W. KLASSEN

THEOLOGICAL APPROACHES

Orthodox Biblical Interpretation

Orthodox biblical interpretation is grounded in the historical tradition of the Orthodox Church and in the various uses of the Old Testament (on the use of "Old Testament" instead of "Hebrew Bible," see the Publisher's Introduction) and the New Testament in worship, preaching, teaching, pastoral guidance, spirituality, and theology. Orthodox biblical interpreters normatively hold to an integral unity between, on the one hand, the Authority*§ of holy Scripture as the canonical record of divine revelation and, on the other hand, the hermeneutical function (Hermeneutics*§) of tradition for the actualization of the biblical witness in the concrete ministries of the church through the grace of the Holy Spirit. The Orthodox interpretive tradition has, from antiquity, produced a variety of methodologies and results, a variety framed by a broad doctrinal consensus and open to incorporating new elements on the basis of the church's faith and critical reason.

1. *The Heritage of the Church Fathers.* The most creative period of Orthodox biblical interpretation (from the second through the fifth cents.) embraces such figures as Justin Martyr§, Irenaeus§, Origen§, Athanasius§, Basil of Caesarea§, Gregory of Nazianzus§, Gregory of Nyssa§, Chrysostom§, and Cyril of Alexandria§, who were primarily biblical theologians and engaged the Scriptures directly according to contemporary exegetical methodologies. For the Orthodox, the works of these church fathers contain normative presuppositions, principles, and patterns of biblical interpretation that are closely bound up with the formation of the biblical CANON and that carry comparable authority to the biblical witness.

Among these normative elements are the following: (1) A christocentric approach to the Old Testament as prophetic testimony to Christ, the new covenant, the church, and the Christian life; (2) Christ as the new criterion of salvation fulfilling and replacing the Mosaic law; (3) the unity of the Old Testament and the New Testament as opposed to the depreciation or even rejection of the Old Testament by heretical groups; (4) the harmonious coherence and interdependence between the Scriptures and the church's developing evangelistic, liturgical, homiletical, catechetical, and creedal traditions; (5) the hermeneutical role of the church's doctrinal discernment expressed in particular creedal teachings (rule of faith) and significantly operative in the canonization of the church's Scriptures; (6) the creatively free and interrelated use of allegorical, typological, and grammatical exegesis accompanied by an emphasis on the spirit rather than the letter of Scripture; (7) holistic attention to the entire landscape of the larger biblical canon interpreted according to the central aim or unifying purpose (*skopos*) of particular books and passages; (8) the role of the living tradition as the decisive and final hermeneutical agent, especially in cases of widely disputed matters, expressed through ecumenical councils and reception by the whole church (e.g., the Nicene-Constantinopolitan Creed as doctrinal summary of biblical truth); (9) and the primacy and centrality of the Bible as the word of God to be celebrated, read, and obeyed by the church and by all believers.

The patristic exegetical tradition richly drew from all the themes of Scripture, such as election, covenant, Prophecy‡†§, law, incarnation, sacrifice, redemption, atonement, justification, sanctification, resurrection, new creation, and the coming kingdom. It developed a distinct transformative view of salvation as deliverance from the powers of sin, Satan, corruption, and death through union with Christ and the indwelling of the Spirit (that is, true participation in the divine grace and life), the basis of humanity's glorification (*theosis* or divinization). The primary aims of the church fathers were to advance the gospel of Christ and to serve the practical needs of the church. Their ideal was to achieve a synergistic harmony between the Old Testament and the New Testament, grace and free will, personal faith and good works, Scripture and tradition, and the church's doctrine and the gift of reason. Confronting internal and external controversies, patristic exegesis combined fidelity to divine revelation with significant openness to the intellectual legacy of antiquity, notably philology, philosophy, and ethics. From Judaism, the church fathers inherited a high view of Scripture; yet they developed an awareness of its human language, character, and limitations, thus passing down a dynamic rather than mechanistic view of Inspiration*§ and revelation. Historical realism and precision in doctrinal disputes, as well as wisdom in practical teaching and guidance, necessitated movement toward contextual grammatical exegesis (Athanasius, Basil, Chrysostom). The universality of Christian truth compelled engagement with contemporary intellectual currents, which produced erudite results. However, beyond formal methods and technical principles the church fathers never lost sight of the mystery of the living God behind the witness of Scripture and that authentic exegesis involved charismatic activity and a spiritual vision (*theoria*) in which the Holy Spirit actualized the transformative power of biblical truth in the interpreter and in the life of the church.

2. *The Traditionalist Period.* The legacy of the church fathers exercised tremendous impact on subsequent Orthodox tradition. Biblical authority remained formally supreme. As a treasure of divine revelation, Scripture became a holy artifact receiving enduring veneration in liturgy and piety. The meditative reading of the Bible, especially in monasticism and through its influence, continued as a pillar of spirituality; and theological works featured generous citations of biblical texts. For the faithful, the biblical witness was generally communicated through the ubiquitous use of Scripture in a flowering of liturgical services, hymnology, and iconography. Worship featured ample readings from the Old Testament and the New Testament. Numerous feasts celebrating biblical events and personages, especially the life and work of Christ, generated countless hymns and prayers rehearsing biblical accounts, images, teachings, and miracles. Sacred Art§ depicted the whole biblical story from creation to final judgment, imprinting the biblical drama on the ecclesial memory.

In terms of actual exegetical work, the long traditionalist period was marked by a paucity of material as a result of a structural shift from direct, concentrated engagement with the Scriptures to overwhelming dependence on the church fathers, a shift already evident in the christological controversies of the fifth and sixth centuries. Maximus the Confessor (sixth cent.) viewed the Bible as a lamp on the lampstand of the church and taught that an exegete should depend on the church fathers more than on one's very breath. Canon 19 of the Quinisext Council (691) formally enjoined church leaders and teachers to follow set teachings usually promoted through collections of patristic interpretations (*anthologia*). A few erudite interpreters who left behind whole commentaries, namely Oikoumenios (sixth cent.), Theophylaktos, and Zigabenos (eleventh–twelfth cents.), as well as Nikodemos the Haghiorite (seventeenth cent.), are largely dependent on patristic exegetical works, especially those of Chrysostom.

However, faithfulness to tradition and concern for doctrinal security did not, in principle, imply rigid control or total absence of creativity. In his *Amphilochia*, Photius the Great (ninth cent.), one of the foremost scholars of Byzantium, took up such questions as the Bible's linguistic idiom, errors in the transmission of manuscripts, and problems of translation from Hebrew to Greek as well as obscurities in Scripture with exemplary philological and interpretive skill. Symeon the New Theologian (tenth–eleventh cents.), in numerous works based on direct reading of Scripture and appeals to his own mystical experiences, stirred Byzantine institutionalism with a vibrant call to charismatic renewal, including adult baptism of the Holy Spirit according to Jesus'†§ dialogue with Nicodemus (John 3). Much later, Kosmas Aitolos (eighteenth cent.) led an evangelistic revival in northwestern Greece, preaching the gospel and exhorting the people to study the Scriptures in groups.

The Reformation and Western proselytism in Orthodox lands significantly sharpened traditionalist sensibilities. The local councils of Constantinople (1638) and Jerusalem (1672) condemned the Calvinistic teaching (Calvin[§]) of Patriarch Cyril Lukaris, who advocated the narrower Old Testament canon and the authority of the Bible over the church. In an isolated instance, Patriarch Jeremiah III of Constantinople formally prohibited the reading of the Bible by the faithful (1723). Under these circumstances, the church fathers—as holders of the unerring key to the Bible, the infallible authority of the church, and the notion of Scripture and tradition constituting two sources of revelation (echoing Roman Catholic theology)—became hallmarks of traditionalism. Moreover, the lack of education and printed material due to various historical circumstances, the popular concentration on the lives and miracles of saints, and a tendency toward formalism in worship all reinforced traditionalism, which in various ways obscured the prophetic witness and renewing power of God's written word in the church.

3. *The Modern Period.* The modern period (nineteenth–twenty-first cents.) has been marked by a creative, albeit tense, encounter between traditionalism and the new learning of liberal ideologies and critical methodologies derived from the West. The most vigorous interaction first occurred in Russia, where long contacts with Western traditions led to systematic theological studies on the basis of critical standards in numerous universities and academies. This course of affairs resulted in calls for and official efforts toward church renewal, but these were cut short by the Bolshevik Revolution (1917). In Greece, after political independence from four hundred years of Ottoman rule (1830) and the establishment of two universities in Athens (1837) and Thessalonike (1926), a significant tradition of theological scholarship, including biblical interpretation, was established, which has continuously matured until today. Similar developments took place in other Orthodox countries (e.g., Romania, Serbia, and Bulgaria); but political conditions and language barriers make it difficult to ascertain their contours.

In the Greek Orthodox Church, the traditional use and interpretation of the Bible have been qualified by three creative, if stressful, challenges. First, the translation of the Bible into modern Greek, although not in principle objectionable according to Orthodox theology, was associated with Protestant proselytism and provoked violent traditionalist reactions. Nevertheless, the translation in periodic new editions, accompanied by the required original and officially approved text, has endured with uneasy reception by the church. Second, the establishment of the Brotherhood of Life (1907), a biblically oriented and moderately controversial renewal movement, has exercised widespread impact on Greek society through organized evangelical preaching, the systematic publication of catechetical material for children and adults, the establishment of ongoing Bible study groups, and other educational activities directed at parents, students, scientists, educators, and other professionals. Its greatest luminary was P. Trembelas, whose remarkable and diverse scholarly output included full commentaries on the Gospels, Acts, and Pauline Epistles as well as publication of the New Testament with an interpretive paraphrase for the average believer. Third, the academic study of Scripture by specialists trained in critical standards—notably such older scholars as V. Vellas, P. Bratsiotis (1951), V. Ioannidis, and S. Agouridis (1976), as well as more recent scholars like D. Trakatellis, E. Oikonomou, J. Karavidopoulos (1986), J. Panagopoulos (1994), and P. Vasileiadis—has successfully established biblical scholarship as a field in its own right. Although its influence has seemed limited outside of professional circles, this tradition of scientific biblical studies has raised old and new hermeneutical questions in sharper terms.

Contemporary Orthodox hermeneutical discussion usually begins with G. Florovsky's (1960, 1972) concept of neopatristic synthesis. According to Florovsky, the neopatristic task of Orthodox theology must combine inseparable aspects of doctrinal integrity and creative theological vision rooted in the life of faith (i.e., recovering the mind of the church fathers rather than merely quoting them). While Florovsky did not pursue the hermeneutical question in its modern context at length, his proposal helped to anchor the use of historical and critical standards in both patristic and biblical fields. Thus all Orthodox biblical scholars have, in principle, affirmed the value of critical Literary*§ and historical methodologies according to international standards, and conduct a full range of scholarship within broad doctrinal parameters.

The burning issue concerns what is peculiarly Orthodox about Orthodox biblical studies. For Agouridis and others, the answer lies in the dynamic vision of the great church fathers working in the ecclesial context, which permits unhindered biblical research and a certain boldness in liberating the voice of Scripture toward the contemporary renewal of a patriarchal society and an institutionalized church. For J. Breck (1986), an American Orthodox biblical scholar, the distinctively Orthodox factor is the actualization of God's word in worship, where the Holy Spirit bridges the distance between biblical and modern thought. J. Romanides (1978), a Greek Orthodox dogmatic theologian, points to the model of the charismatic saint (one who lives the transfigured life in continuity with the apostles and the saints of all ages) as the unerring guide to biblical interpretation and its application in new circumstances. J. Panagopoulos (1991–97) formulates an ecclesial hermeneutic, combining christological, biblical, and patristic elements, according to which Scripture and church become one in worship, with Scripture witnessing to the soteriological mystery of Christ and the church becoming the living Bible of Christ.

These positions do not seem entirely adequate to the quest for a uniquely Orthodox approach to the Bible. Freedom of research for the liberation of Scripture's authentic witness is fundamental to international scholarship. Worship as actualization of biblical truth is important for all Christian traditions. The charismatic saint as unerring interpreter of biblical texts lacks wide support even in the patristic literature. An unqualified identity between Scripture and church has usually left little room to the Orthodox for constructive criticism of church life on the basis of Scripture's authority. The exposition of a specifically Orthodox approach to Scripture must be pursued in terms of a richer hermeneutical model that both differentiates and integrates the functions of historical exegesis, doctrinal interpretation, and spiritual appropriation of Scripture's transformative power. A holistic Orthodox hermeneutic will reflect the classic patristic interdependence between Scripture and tradition, granting particularly needed attention to Scripture's authority for the church. The ecumenical persuasiveness of Orthodox biblical interpretation will depend on the continued growth of biblical studies in the Orthodox Church and their essential evangelical impact on both the church's theology and its life.

Bibliography: S. Agouridis, *The Bible in the Greek Orthodox Church* (1976). **G. Barrois,** *Scripture Readings in Orthodox Worship* (1977). **P. Bratsiotis,** "The Authority of the Bible: An Orthodox Contribution," *Biblical Authority for Today* (ed. A. Richardson and W. Schweitzer, 1951) 17-29. **J. Breck,** *The Power of the Word in the Worshiping Church* (1986). **D. Burton-Christie,** *The Word in the Desert: Scripture and the Quest for Holiness in Early Christian Monasticism* (1993). **H. Chadwick,** "The Bible and the Greek Fathers," *The Church's Use of the Bible: Past and Present* (ed. D. E. Nineham, 1963) 25-39. **G. P. Fedotov,** "Orthodoxy and Historical Criticism," *The Church of God: An Anglo-Russian Symposium* (ed. E. L. Mascall, 1934) 91-104. **G. Florovsky,** "The Ethos of the Orthodox Church," *Orthodoxy: A Faith and Order Dialogue* (Faith and Order Paper 30, 1960) 36-51; *Bible, Church, Tradition: An Eastern Orthodox View* (1972). **R. M. Grant,** "The Appeal to the Early Fathers," *JTS* 11 (1960) 13-24. **T. Hopko,** "The Bible in the Orthodox Church," *SVTQ* 14 (1970) 66-99. **J. Karavidopoulos,** "Das Studium des Neuen Testaments in der griechisch-orthodoxen Kirche in Vergangenheit und Gegenwart," *BTZ* (1986) 2-10. **V. Kesich,** *The Gospel Image of Christ* (1992). **V. Kesich and T. Stylianopoulos,** "Biblical Studies in Orthodox Theology," *GOTR* 17 (1972) 51-85. **A. Louth,** *Discerning the Mystery: An Essay on the Nature of Theology* (1993). **J. Panagopoulos,** *He Hermeneia Peso Hagias Graphes sten Ekklesia ton Pateron* (2 vols. 1991–97); *Eisagoge sten Kaine Diatheke* (1994). **J. Pelikan,** *The Christian Tradition*, vol. 2, *The Spirit of Eastern Christendom* (1974); *Christianity and Classical Culture: The Metamorphosis of Natural*

Theology in the Christian Encounter with Hellenism (1993). **J. Romanides,** "Critical Examination of the Applications of Theology," *Proceedings of the Second Congress of Orthodox Theology* (ed. S. Agouridis, 1978) 413-41. **M. Santer,** "Scripture and the Councils," *Sobornost* 7 (1995) 99-111. **T. Stylianopoulos,** *The NT: An Orthodox Perspective*, vol. 1, *Scripture, Tradition, Hermeneutics* (1997). **P. Valliere,** "The Liberal Tradition in Russian Orthodox Tradition," *The Legacy of St. Vladimir: Byzantium, Russia, America* (ed. J. Breck, 1990) 93-106. **N. M. Vaporis,** *Translating the Scriptures into Modern Greek* (1994). **N. Zernov,** *The Russian Religious Renaissance of the Twentieth Century* (1963).

T. S. TYLIANOPOULOS

THEOLOGICAL APPROACHES

Biblical Theology to 1800

While it may be argued that, in the seventeenth century, J. Cocceius's§ *Summa doctrinae de foedere et testamento Dei* (1673) or even B. Spinoza's§ *Tractatus Theologico-Politicus* (1670) were types of biblical theology, the technical use of the term "biblical theology" to describe a new approach to biblical exegesis first entered general use at the end of the eighteenth century. Even then its essence was in some doubt. J. Thiess (1797, 185) commented: "One might well give up the idea of realizing a biblical theology even theoretically, given such different attempts which by their very nature contradict each other. Still the putting together of the true notions of religion which are scattered in the Bible is a worthwhile undertaking, especially for the instruction of the general populace and youth." This comment could describe biblical theology ever since for, unlike certain exegetical disciplines like Textual*§ or Pentateuchal Criticism‡§ (where the method tends to define the investigation), in biblical theology wide divergences in method and result are typical.

In essence, biblical theology was (and largely still is) an attempt to winnow out of the Bible what is important by the application of standards and techniques that are not necessarily part of the biblical tradition. Before the eighteenth century, exegesis was approached in this manner; however, in the eighteenth century this procedure became both self-conscious and systematic. In order to understand how this development came about as part of a revolution in theological thinking, it is necessary to be aware of how exegesis was affected by both changes in the intellectual climate and new developments in the theory and technique of scholarly work.

Unlike the nineteenth century, the eighteenth century was a period when social discourse ran ahead of social change. Although society as a whole appeared stable, those who moved in the world of ideas felt a growing unease over the separation of things that had been thought to go together. Thus religion and tradition were separated by the new scientific method's demand for proofs even in religion; elite and popular religion were separated by the problem of how to reconcile personal religion with established religion; religion and citizenship were separated by the question of how to belong to two spheres, each with a claim to ultimate authority; and religion and community were separated by the new emphasis on personal responsibility.

Yet, despite the upsets these new developments produced in the area of religion, the eighteenth century was characterized (especially in Germany) not so much by growing secularism as by attempts to formulate a religious position less vulnerable to the factors that made the older theologies obsolete. Whatever their opponents may have suggested, even such major critics of orthodoxy as Edelmann, J. Dippel, H. S. Reimarus§, G. Lessing§, K. F. Bahrdt, and J. B. Basedow aimed at reforming religion rather than destroying it; and some even appealed to the Authority of the Bible*§ for their programs. Inevitably, the Bible, considered to be the center of Protestant doctrine, was brought into the day-to-day debates, whether as the object of serious moral objection (thanks to Spinoza and the English Deists; Deism§), or as the answer to the dislocating effect of new ideas on the structure of society as a whole.

In the theory and technique of scholarly work, several developments were important. First, a new sense of history emerged as it gradually became clear that the people of past ages did not think and act in the same way as their modern successors. Just as historians began to trace the changes that had taken place in church doctrine so also biblical scholars became more aware of the historically conditioned nature of many passages in the Scriptures. It was also realized that different ways of thinking were to be found in the Bible and that an appreciation of these perspectives was necessary before one could begin interpretation, even if one did not wish to follow J. G. Herder's§ advice that the only way to understand Hebrew Poetry‡§ was to recite it to the rays of the rising sun. By the end of the century the importance of comparative material from other religions began to be felt. Furthermore, technical methods in exegesis were refined, especially in the areas of philology and textual studies. These developments were a source of self-conscious satisfaction among the learned, for in the last quarter of the eighteenth century many scholars agreed that theology had made great strides and that even more astonishing and certain results could be expected.

During the eighteenth century, the term "biblical theology" could be used either conventionally, to describe a division of theology as it existed, or exceptionally, to make a claim for a radically different departure in theology. In conventional use, biblical theology was generally employed with approval, for in Protestant circles, at least, there was a strong sense that all theology must be biblical. Biblical theology could also be used to distinguish exegesis from other theological undertakings like systematics or church history. It was generally assumed, at the outset of the century, that within Scripture there were no inconsistencies (*analogia fidei*) and that, therefore, the work of exegesis was to set out the unified system that was to be found there despite appearances to the contrary. It was from this standpoint that collections of biblical texts were made to prove various doctrines like the oneness of God, the nature of the Trinity, or the INSPIRATION of Scripture. Such important texts were known collectively as *dicta classica*. Perhaps the best-known collection was S. Schmidt's work *Collegium Biblicum* (1671, 1676[2]), whose influence can still be seen in C. von Ammon's[§] choice of texts for comment. In these collections, texts were arranged according to the traditional forms of Lutheran orthodox theology with little attention being paid to the circumstances of their origins.

In nonconventional use, biblical theology was employed to seize the high ground in controversy; for this purpose it could be invoked by people of very different outlooks. Two examples from much the same time illustrate how the term could be given different associations. In the middle of the eighteenth century, C. Döderlein (not to be confused with the more important J. Döderlein), writing from the Pietist tradition (1758; Pietism[§]), argued that the use of philosophy has always had a deleterious effect on the correct interpretation of the Bible. Although he began with Hillel[§], it is clear that his main targets were theologians who made use of the new philosophy of the Enlightenment, in particular S. Baumgarten[§]. In fact, Döderlein was echoing P. J. Spener's[§] use of the term biblical theology; the difference is that Spener's target was a moribund Lutheran orthodoxy while Döderlein's was the new impulses set loose by Baumgarten and others.

That biblical theology could almost simultaneously be used to support opposing positions is shown by A. Büsching, a student of Baumgarten's who had lost faith in his master's system. Büsching's inaugural dissertation (1756) appears to be an unremarkable, even pedestrian, work; but in two later editions (1757 [GT 1758]), he showed his rationalist leanings, thinly disguised as a series of questions appended to the texts he listed.

It tended to be the radicals who appealed to the Bible to justify their position. For example, although Bahrdt (1769-70) claimed to interpret the Bible, in reality he presented his own radical Enlightenment view of religion with very little attention to the evidence. J. Hofmann[§] (1770) provided one possible answer to Bahrdt's sort of radicalism and perhaps to Bahrdt himself. An able, if somewhat conservative, representative of orthodoxy, Hofmann criticized those who extol the Bible only to disparage theology and who proclaim the words of Scripture only to proscribe the meaning of Scripture from the church of Christ. For Hofmann, apart from popularizing it for the unlearned, there were two ways of treating theology: one that is drawn from the Bible alone and the other that includes the writings of theologians who have translated into their own words what Scripture teaches. The first, biblical theology, is better for winning the minds of learners; the second, for seeing the totality of religion at a single glance. Both are to be done together. Hofmann then went on to deplore the neglect by those who call themselves theologians of the study of Scripture.

In many disputes the difficulty lies, not with the clarity of the argument, but with the pertinency of the evidence. By the latter part of the eighteenth century, it was no longer possible to overlook the fact that, as well as being unsystematic, the Bible does not lend itself easily to systematization; there are simply too many passages that are inconsistent, irrelevant, or offensive. In theory, the arguments of Hofmann or even of Döderlein are most attractive, and similar arguments are still offered today. But apart from the philosophical difficulties involved, the fact is that the radicals were right about individual passages far too often to be ignored. The question was whether a new synthesis could be found that would allow for both the value of the Bible and honesty about moral convictions and exegetical insights.

Biblical theology emerged as a response to the factors discussed above; the ensuing disagreements among its four most prominent advocates (G. Zachariae, J. P. Gabler, Ammon, and G. Bauer) about its nature sprang from the particular factors each author was responding to. All four would have agreed that it was necessary to combine new methods of exegesis and the new awareness of biblical thought-worlds in the work of interpretation, while at the same time they had no doubt that the Bible's essential significance was to be defended. All four would have echoed in some way the general feeling that the Bible is best suited for the instruction of the unlearned (note the views of J. Theiss and of Hofmann, above); all would also have agreed that not everything in the Bible is suitable for this purpose. Their differences begin after this point.

Zachariae[§] belonged to an earlier generation for whom philosophy was much less problematical in matters of religion. The defense and explanation of revelation could be left in the hands of the philosophers. Biblical theology should distinguish between what was only of historical importance in the Bible and what was meant as a message to all people of all times; here the eighteenth-century emphasis on universality is apparent. In the wake of the new emphasis on system as part of science, Zachariae felt that some sort of order, albeit not the strict order of dogmatics, should be produced in a biblical theology; just the collection of random evidence was not enough.

Gabler[§] agreed to a great extent with Zachariae but introduced more strongly the distinction between religion and theology: Religion is the minimum knowledge necessary to live a Christian life, whereas theology is the preserve of the learned. The eighteenth-century worry about the danger to public order if common people did not have adequate beliefs is apparent here. For Gabler, the work of biblical theology was to seek out the universal truths embedded in the historical circumstances of Scripture; in effect, such a biblical theology was identical with religion and was to be distinguished from dogmatic theology, although it formed the basis of the latter. Gabler also emphasized that Israel's religion should be seen as a historical entity entitled to study in its own right.

Ammon refused to find any sort of intermediate doctrinal order in the Bible, arguing that the Easterners who wrote the Bible were more attracted to the products of fantasy than to the demonstrations of reason. However, he saw a virtue in the diversity within the Bible, for, whereas a systematic presentation of religion was the product of a single mind, in the Bible different people could find images appropriate to their own view of religion. In this respect, Ammon is almost in complete opposition to Gabler's emphasis on finding universal truths behind the diversity of Scripture. Rather than being a throwback to the older *collegium biblicum*, however, it is apparent that Ammon's work reflects another eighteenth-century concern: How does one reconcile the reality of private religion with the need for public statements, such as creeds? It was also Ammon's conviction that God's gradual revelation to humanity is reflected in the documents of the Bible.

Of all the early biblical theologians, G. Bauer[§] was the most prolific, writing various books around the theme of biblical theology. He came much closer than Ammon to Gabler's demand for a historical treatment of Israel's religion; but Gabler felt that although Bauer was methodologically more correct, Ammon was frequently the deeper commentator on individual passages. In fact, Bauer was already beginning to move into a type of biblical theology that is simply a history of Israel's religion focused on scholarship, without concern for the relevance of the Bible to current religion. Here, his area of concern was very different in emphasis from that of the other three writers.

The emergence of biblical theology in the eighteenth century, then, should be seen not as a simple linear development of a desire to separate biblical theology from the dominance of systematics but, rather, as the result of a parallelogram of forces, social, philosophical, religious, and scholarly. It had as much to do with the society of its writers as with the society of the Bible; as such, it was a curious amalgam destined by its very nature to be unstable. On the other hand, without some interplay with the world of its readers, the Bible would have become a dead letter, as irrelevant to society in general as the soon to be recovered Babylonian or Egyptian religion (Egyptology and Biblical Studies[§]).

Bibliography: C. F. von Ammon, *Entwurf einer reinen biblischen Theologie* (1792); *Entwurf einer Christologie des alten Testaments* (1794); *Biblische Theologie* (3 vols. 1801-22). **K. Bahrdt,** *Versuch eines biblischen Systems der Dogmatik* (2 vols. 1769-70). **G. L. Bauer,** *Theologie des alten Testaments* (1796); *Theologie des Neuen Testaments* (4 vols. 1800-1802); *Beylagen zur Theologie des alten Testaments* (1801); *Biblische Moral des Alten Testaments* (2 pts. 1804-5). **A. Büsching,** *Theologiae e solis Sacris Litteris concinnatae et ab omnibus rebus et verbis scholasticis purgatae* (1756, 1757; GT *Gedanken von der Beschaffenheit und dem Vorzug der biblisch-dogmatischen Theologie vor der scholastischen* 1758). **C. Döderlein,** *Feyerliche Rede von den hohen Vorzügen der biblischen Theologie vor der Scholastischen* (1758). **H. Frei,** *The Eclipse of Biblical Narrative: A Study in Eighteenth and Nineteenth-century Hermeneutics* (1974) 165-82. **J. P. Gabler,** "De justo discrimine theologiae biblicae et dogmaticae regundisque recte utriusque finibus," *Kleinere Theologische Schriften* (1831) 2:179-98. **J. Hofmann,** *Oratio de Theologiae biblicae praestantia* (1770). **G. Hornig,** *Die Anfange der historisch-kritischen Theologie: J. S. Semlers Schriftverständnis und seine Stellung zu Luther* (1961). **W. F. Hufnagel,** *Handbuch der biblischen Theologie* (2 vols. [vol. 2 incomplete], 1785, 1789). **H.-J. Kraus,** *Die Biblische Theologie: Ihre Geschichte und Problematik* (1970). **K. Leder,** *Universität Altdorf: Zur Theologie der Aufklärung in Franken. Die Theologische Fakultät in Altdorf, 1750-1809* (1965). **O. Merk,** *Biblische Theologie des Neuen Testaments in ihrer Anfangszeit: ihre methodischen Probleme bei Johann Philipp Gabler und Georg Lorenz Bauer und deren Nachwirkungen* (1972). **M. Saebø,** "J. P. Gablers Bedeutung für die Biblische Theologie," *ZAW* 99 (1987) 1-16. **J. Sandys-Wunsch,** "G. T. Zachariae's Contribution to Biblical Theology," *ZAW* 92 (1980) 1-23. **J. Sandys-Wunsch and L. Eldredge,** "J. P. Gabler and the Distinction Between Biblical and Dogmatic Theology: Translation, Commentary, and Discussion of His Originality," *SJT* 33 (1980) 133-58. **R. Smend,** "J. P. Gablers Begrundung der biblischen Theologie," *EvT* 22 (1962) 345-57. **J. O. Theiss,** *Einleitung in die neuere Geschichte der Religion, der Kirche, und der theoligischen Wissenchaft* (1797). **G. T. Zachariae,** *Biblische Theologie oder Untersuchung des biblischen Grundes der vornehmsten theologischen Lehren* (5 vols. 1771-85).

J. SANDYS-WUNSCH

THEOLOGICAL APPROACHES

Hebrew Bible Theology

Biblical theology emerged as an independent area of inquiry in the eighteenth century together with, and as a consequence of, historical study of the Bible (L. Baumgarten-Crusius 1828, 4). Historical-critical study also posed the principal problems confronting the discipline it helped to create. These problems were seen to center on determining what in the Bible was of abiding validity in view of its irreducibly historical character. J. P. Gabler's[§] solution was to join the "grammatical-historical" interpretation of Scripture to a theory of human reason's "development by stages" (C. Hartlich and W. Sachs 1952, 46). He made it the task of Hebrew Bible and biblical theology to extract from historically determined modes of expression the unchanging truth contained in them so that it could be delivered to dogmatics for contemporary elaboration (Hartlich-Sachs, 22-46; B. Ollenburger 1985).

One implication of Gabler's proposal is that the Hebrew Bible is lower than the New Testament on reason's developmental scale. G. Bauer[§] adopted this view already in 1796 when he published the first Hebrew Bible theology. In arguing that Hebrew Bible and New Testament theology must be distinguished from each other and carried out independently from dogmatics, and in his emphasis on religious ideas or concepts and their historical development from particular to universal, Bauer set the tone for the nineteenth-century discussion. The following briefly sketches the main lines of this discussion during and after the nineteenth century, especially as carried on in German Protestant circles (Ollenburger 1992).

1. *From Philosophy to History.* The first Hebrew Bible theologies of the nineteenth century, contained in the biblical theologies of C. Ammon[§], W. de Wette[§], and G. Kaiser, were set within a philosophical framework. For Ammon, the task of biblical theology was to provide a more adequate foundation for dogmatic theology through a critical study of the texts in order to free them from the "nimbus of illusory ideas" (1801). Thus, he cited the traditional proof texts of doctrinal loci and tested them against the criterion of rationality. That criterion, understood in a Kantian moral sense (I. Kant[§]), Ammon regarded as crucial because only what is judged rational can be carried over into dogmatics.

De Wette's approach was somewhat more historically oriented, but the method of his *Biblische Dogmatik* (1813[1]) is grounded in the Kantian anthropology of J. Fries (J. Rogerson 1984, 36-41). This anthropology provided de Wette a hermeneutical foundation (Hermeneutics[§]) for understanding the Hebrew Bible's religious ideas in their purity, distinguished from the mixed historical forms that clothe them (de Wette 1831). The first task of Hebrew Bible theology, then, is to identify the "fundamental idea on which everything depends" (1831, 38), which is "the moral idea, free of myth, of one God as a holy will" (1831, 63). This idea is expressed in Hebraism's "ideal universalism" and in its "symbolic particularism," which de Wette identified with the theocracy. He claimed that Israel was prone to misunderstand this particularism by reducing the universal character of God's rule to nationalism, thus preparing the way for Judaism. Unfortunately, this claim appeared in various forms in many subsequent Hebrew Bible theologies.

Kaiser provided a different kind of framework, subsuming the Hebrew Bible under "the universal history of religion" and, ultimately, under "the universal religion." The particularity of Hebrew Bible religion (Judaism) is to be understood only in relation to religion in general, and then, together with Christianity and all other particular religions, taken up into a genuine catholicism (1813, 12). By describing the "principal moments" of religion in a dialectical fashion and drawing random insights from philosophy, Kaiser pared from the Hebrew Bible the temporal ideas that must be left behind in the universal religion of humanity. In the process, he invented new categories for this task, such as geofetishology, anthropotheology, cosmocraty, demonophany, using this monstrous vocabulary (much as Ammon and de Wette used the vocabulary of philosophy and dogmatics to get beyond the Hebrew Bible's particularity) but producing, in his case, a vacant universalism.

Alongside and occasionally in response to those philosophically grounded presentations were others that sought to proceed in a purely historical manner. Baumgarten-Crusius made the first attempt in 1828, followed immediately by C. Gramberg[§]. However, they were overshadowed in both methodological clarity and influence by D. von Coelln[§], who modeled his presentation of Hebrew Bible theology on de Wette's but claimed that neither de Wette nor anyone else had fulfilled the strictly historical requirements of Hebrew Bible theology. From Coelln's work it is clear that what he really opposed was the use of philosophical categories. His understanding of Hebrew Bible theology's task—to differentiate the universal from the particular or the "inexact forms of representation" from the "pure concepts" hidden in them (1836, 1:11)—was otherwise hardly different from de Wette's. Following Bauer, Coelln argued that these judgments can and must be made by historical criticism, which follows the Hebrew Bible's religious ideas in their process of formation through the New Testament, where they are deepened and broadened to form the basis of a universal religion (1836, 1:4). Hebrew Bible theology was for him, as it was for de Wette and Baumgarten-Crusius, the first chapter of historical theology (R. Dentan 1963, 33) and one foundation of dogmatic theology.

The methodological tension between the philosophical and historical approaches was resolved in a higher unity—*aufgehoben*, as he put it—by W. Vatke[§], whose *Biblische Theologie* (1835) was the only part of a proposed six-part biblical theology he was permitted to publish (M. Brömse 1984). Hebrew Bible theology must be historical, Vatke argued, because it pursues the idea of Hebrew Bible religion, expressed in its various religious representations, through the "principal moments" of its historical development. But historical criticism by itself is subjective; it is not concerned with truth because it is not properly scientific (Vatke 1835, 156). It can only achieve scientific status and relative objectivity by being taken up into a philosophically grounded conceptual analysis. G. W. F. Hegel provided the tools for such an analysis, which is scientific because it comprehends the most universal horizon possible, history as a whole. Conceptual analysis will necessarily be historical because the concept of a religion is unfolded in a historical dialectic: The subjectivity of the concept and the objectivity of its manifestations are resolved in the idea of Israel's religion. Hegel's philosophy was thus Vatke's hermeneutical foundation for a theological understanding of the history of Hebrew Bible religion.

While Vatke's Hebrew Bible theology was grounded in a philosophical method, it was also the first to have a thoroughly historical character, thus exhibiting a remarkable harmony of method and form. The most notable of his historical observations was that the system of legislation in the Pentateuch (Pentateuchal Criticism[‡§]) came after and not before the prophets (Vatke 1835, 204). That observation had its effect in the later elevation of the prophets (Hebrew Bible Prophecy and Prophets[‡§]) to the pinnacle of Hebrew Bible religion (J. Blenkinsopp 1984, 8-9). Vatke also presaged later developments by emphasizing the need to understand Israel's religion from the perspective of its completed history. His philosophical language is as dense as Kaiser's is monstrous, but Vatke's methodological rigor and consistency remain unexcelled.

2. *From Salvation History to History of Religion.* Vatke's synthesis did not survive him—B. BAUER's equally Hegelian work (1838) took no account of historical criticism—but his historical organicism was taken up, apart from a Hegelian framework, by a series of conservative scholars oriented to salvation history (*Heilsgeschichte*): J. Steudel (1840), H. HÄVERNICK (1848), G. Oehler[§] (1845), J. von Hofmann[§], and H. Schultz[§] (1869). They were influenced to greater or lesser extents by a tradition of mystical Pietism[§] and speculative history rooted in Württemberg and Tübingen (L. Diestel 1869, 698-708) and absorbed by Hegel and by

F. Schelling as well (J. Toews 1980, 13-26). Salvation historians put particular emphasis on the facts (*Tatsachen*) of God's activity in Israel, which constitute its history as an organic whole. They further assumed that the history narrated in the Hebrew Bible corresponds more or less to an actual course of events within world history and should be the central subject matter of Hebrew Bible theology, and also that participation in the spirit of revelation is a condition for understanding this history (Oehler, 32-34; Schultz, 1:72). Steudel, Hävernick, and Oehler were unable, however, to display their historical emphases in the body of their Hebrew Bible theologies, which thus reflect a certain inconsistency between theory and execution.

This inconsistency was overcome by von Hofmann, particularly in his *Schriftbeweis*. He wrote no separate Hebrew Bible theology, but conceived biblical and historical theology to be engaged in testing systematic theology's exposition of what each (Protestant) Christian is absolutely certain: reconciliation with God through Jesus*[§] Christ. According to Hofmann, the trinitarian life of God unfolded first into the world's history and then into Israel's, giving each biblical fact and each text its necessary place within the organic sequence of salvation history. The power and consistency of Hofmann's thought is as awesome as his language is forbidding. In that, and other respects, he resembles Vatke.

The salvation historians were soon overshadowed by the historians of religion, particularly by J. Wellhausen[§], as is demonstrated in Schultz's career. In 1848, Schultz edited Hävernick's work, and the first edition of his own *Alttestamentliche Theologie* (1869) reflects the influence both of the salvation historians and of H. Ewald[§]. In the second edition (1878), however, he accepted Wellhausen's late dating of the law and, in subsequent editions, (through 1896) moved still further toward history of religion. The first to conceive Hebrew Bible theology purely as the history of Israel's religion was A. Kayser in 1886 (the third and following editions of his work, titled *Geschichte der Israelitischen Religion*, were written by K. Marti).

H. Gunkel[§] and the history-of-religion school (*Religionsgeschichtliche Schule*[*§]) brought the writing of Hebrew Bible theologies to a temporary halt, not because they were not theologians ("Biblical exegesis is theological exegesis"; Gunkel 1913, 24) but because they conceived theology to be concerned with religion as opposed to dogmatics. Religion, Gunkel declared, is fundamentally piety, to be discovered in the Hebrew Bible by penetrating to the inner life of its authors (1913, 25). Gunkel wanted to go behind the religious representations and concepts of the Hebrew Bible in order "to be present at the birth of its deepest thoughts" (1926-27, 533). B. Stade[§], a friend and follower of Wellhausen, wrote a Hebrew Bible theology as late as 1905, even though Gunkel and his circle had already made it an anachronism. Stade defined Hebrew Bible theology in a way reminiscent of G. Bauer: It has the task of tracing the origin and progressive development of those religious ideas that formed the content of Jewish faith and are "for that reason, the historical presupposition of Christianity" (1905, 2). He also wanted to distinguish those Hebrew Bible religious concepts whose development can be traced into Judaism but were not taken up by Jesus and his apostles. Consequently, "the New Testament is the best source for the theology of the Hebrew Bible" (Stade 1893, 93).

The stalemate to which Wellhausen and Gunkel helped bring Hebrew Bible theology eventually spawned a series of reflections on method from different points of view by Hebrew Bible scholars united only in their agreement that Hebrew Bible theology had to be conceived anew (J. Hayes and F. Prussner 1985, 151-66). J. Käberle (1906) repudiated the history-of-religion movement and suggested a return to salvation history, beginning from the New Testament and a concept of revelation adequate to Christian faith. W. Staerk[§] granted history of religion its due but called for systematic and philosophical reflection on the historical data from a phenomenological point of view, so that Hebrew Bible theology may "come to its fulfillment as a component of systematic theology, which it was from the beginning and which it must remain" (1923, 390). R. Kittel[§] complained that, in the contemporary academic climate of fascination with

Mesopotamian parallels (Pan-Babylonianism[§]), it was as if *extra babylonem nulla salus* (outside of Babylon there is no salvation; 1921, 96). History-of-religion research must be expanded into Hebrew Bible theology, he argued, by employing a philosophy of dogmatics of religion in order to penetrate to the Hebrew Bible's essence and truth. C. Steuernagel[§] (1925) proposed the systematic presentation of Hebrew Bible religion in categories drawn from its historical analysis, without borrowing either these categories or Hebrew Bible theology's methods from philosophy or dogmatics.

This methodological discussion concluded with a debate between O. Eissfeldt[§] (1926 [ET 1992]) and W. Eichrodt[§] (1929 [ET 1992]). Eissfeldt claimed that the history of Israelite and Jewish religion should be sharply distinguished from Hebrew Bible theology, since they employ two different approaches that correspond to different functions of the human spirit: active knowing and passive believing. History of religion is objective, although it depends on an "empathetic reliving" of its object (Eissfeld 1926, 20), and it makes no judgments about validity or truth. Hebrew Bible theology, on the other hand, cannot be a historical inquiry because it is concerned with what is timelessly true as determined by a particular confession. Eissfeldt assumed that historical-critical research could not penetrate to the "proper essence" of Hebrew Bible religion and was thus unable to answer the questions of faith assigned to Hebrew Bible theology. In Eichrodt's judgment, this view preserved the integrity of history of religion but compromised that of Hebrew Bible theology by moving it outside the framework of Hebrew Bible scholarship and of historical inquiry generally.

Eichrodt argued in response that historical investigation could reach the essence of Hebrew Bible religion, but he redefined the essence of the Hebrew Bible as that "deepest meaning of its religious thought world which historical investigation can discover" through an analysis that cuts across the various historical levels of the Hebrew Bible (1992, 33). He argued further that all historical research presupposes a subjective moment and that the interpreter's Christian confession provides the content of that moment in Hebrew Bible theology, which must be considered a legitimate part of historical scholarship.

3. *From Eichrodt to von Rad.* Eichrodt went beyond these arguments in his *Theology of the Hebrew Bible* (1933-39 [ET 1961-67]). In both his theological understanding of history and his threefold division of Hebrew Bible theology—God and the people, God and the world, God and the human—he drew heavily on his teacher, O. Procksch[§], whose own treatment was published posthumously in 1950. Eichrodt's decisive innovation was his proposal to center all of Hebrew Bible theology around the idea of covenant as the concept that "enshrines Israel's most fundamental conviction-namely, its sense of a unique relationship with God" (Eichrodt 1933-39, 17). While the term "covenant" appears infrequently or not at all in some parts of the Hebrew Bible (and has various meanings elsewhere), Eichrodt appealed to a "stock of spiritual values firmly established at the outset," which lies behind the Hebrew Bible's diversity and attends its "incessant growth" (1933-39, 32) and which is historically expressed through covenant. Criticisms of Eichrodt often fail to attend to the particular way in which he spoke of covenant and especially the importance he attached to Moses as the founder of Israel's religion; it was through Moses' direct and unmediated "intercourse with God" (1933-39, 293) that Israel was introduced to "a new understanding of the whole nature of God" (1933-39, 290) in the opening moment of its history. Thus the structure of Israel's religion was the product of the charismatic endowment of one personality—Moses the mediator—and to understand the forces at work at its beginning is to grasp its enduring essence—and the New Testament as its fulfillment (1933-39, 26). It is in these terms that Eichrodt understood the concept of covenant and for these reasons that he insisted on its historical origin with Moses.

The coherence Eichrodt achieved between the historical and the systematic components of Hebrew Bible theology marked his work as an advance over the earlier contemporary efforts by

E. König[§] (1923) and E. Sellin[§] (1933), and was not superseded by the later ones of L. Köhler[§] (ET 1957), E. Jacob (ET 1958), and T. Vriezen[§] (ET 1958). While Eichrodt finally broke through the methodological impasse in Hebrew Bible theology brought about by the history of religion school, his work may also be seen as the crowning achievement of history of religion in Hebrew Bible theology, especially when it is compared with E. Troeltsch's[§] comments in "The 'Dogmatics' of the Religionsgeschichtliche Schule" (1913).

After Eichrodt, the methodological debate addressed the question of what, if not covenant, constituted the center (*Mitte*) of Hebrew Bible theology (R. Smend 1970). G. von Rad[§] concluded that such a debate was beyond resolution, since there is no unifying center to the various theologies within the Hebrew Bible. He argued that both the history-of-religion approaches and the more recent systematic efforts had failed to identify and to carry out the theological task of Hebrew Bible theology, whose proper subject matter is neither the reconstructed history of Israelite religion nor the Hebrew Bible's thought-world but "Israel's own explicit assertions about Jahweh" (von Rad 1962, 105). These assertions were made primarily in the form of historical confessions, whose growth and development provided the key to both the growth of the Hexateuch (1966) and Hebrew Bible theology's method. Israel reshaped its historical confessions, its saving history, in a continuing "process of actualization" (1962, 119) that enabled each generation to understand itself as Israel, God's people. Hebrew Bible theology, according to von Rad, has the task of interpreting Israel's history as Israel presented it, not as critical scholars are able to reconstruct it, because in this confessed and narrated history is to be found "what Israel herself regarded as the proper subject-matter of her faith, namely, the revelation in word and deed of Jahweh in history" (114). From this, it followed for von Rad that the Tradition-historical[‡*§] method had the best fit with Hebrew Bible theology (1965, 321) and that "re-telling [*Nacherzählen*] remains the most legitimate form of theological discourse on the Hebrew Bible" (1962, 121).

In this way, von Rad gave the Hexateuch and the historical books central place in Hebrew Bible theology. The prophets required separate treatment because they proclaimed an interruption in the saving history (1962, vii), while the psalms and Wisdom literature were treated under the category of "Israel's answer." This arrangement of the presentation follows consistently from von Rad's premises. Since "Israel's faith is grounded in a theology of history" (1962, 106), the traditions that give foundational testimony to that faith are theologically prior to others that judge Israel's life in relation to its confession or that engage in reflection in relation to it or in independence from it. In thus demonstrating his own priorities, von Rad claimed merely to be following those of the Hebrew Bible.

Even though von Rad was heavily influenced by a line of Hebrew Bible theologians reaching from Hofmann to Procksch, his *Theology* marked a radical departure in the history of the discipline (R. Martin-Achard 1984, 14). By identifying Hebrew Bible theology's subject matter with the Hebrew Bible's historical confessions, he wanted to avoid either confusing salvation history with some objective history or resolving theological diversity by appealing to a putative center, a dogmatic scheme, or some underlying piety. At the same time, his sharp differentiation of the history of Israel (as reconstructed by scholars) from the history narrated in the Hebrew Bible and his refusal to identify a principle of unity (prior to the New Testament) were seen by critics to constitute major problems for Hebrew Bible theology. Consequently, his *Theology* prompted a vigorous reassessment of the method and task of Hebrew Bible theology (H. G. Reventlow 1985, 59-133).

4. *The Discussion After von Rad.* The methodological reassessment has not yet been concluded, and no new consensus has emerged. The problem of the relation between Hebrew Bible theology and history remains unresolved and is perhaps insoluble in the way it has often been cast (G. Michalson 1985). Efforts have been made to go beyond von Rad's distinction between

"narrated" and "objective" history by insisting on the priority of objective history (F. Hesse 1958; G. E. Wright 1970; R. de Vaux 1972), by uniting history and tradition (R. Rendtorff; Smend 1977, 49-68), by challenging the Enlightenment conception of history (C. Westermann 1985), or by concentrating on a philosophical hermeneutics that dissolves the problem (Reventlow 1979). H. Gese, on the other hand, attempted to expand von Rad's method by giving it an ontological grounding that identifies the history of tradition with revelation (Gese 1974, 11-30; 1977, 301-26). In a similarly idealistic vein, P. Hanson has taken Israel's confessional tradition to be a response to historical events understood in terms of a divinely guided dialectical expansion of reality (1978, 1986). In quite a different direction, J. Barr[§] (1976) and J. Collins (1979) suggest turning to the notion of story or "history-like" narrative (see H. Frei 1974); similarly, D. Patrick (1981) pursues a literary-dramatic approach centering on the identity of Yahweh. More recently, Collins (1990) has proposed a historically critical biblical theology that examines biblical assertions about God for their functional role in motivating behavior, while L. Perdue announces "the collapse of history"—the erosion of historical categories as dominant within Hebrew Bible theology—in light of both internal problems and the emergence of diverse questions, issues, and methods.

Meanwhile, proposals to resolve the second major problem presented by von Rad—that of Hebrew Bible theology's center or simply the organization of its material—have been equally diverse. Some scholars have suggested that Yahweh, or the concept of God, should serve as a center (G. Hasel 1974; J. McKenzie 1974, 23-28; R. Clements 1978, 23-24); but it is not clear that this solves or even addresses the problem. W. Zimmerli[§] went further by proposing the name Yahweh as Hebrew Bible theology's center but understanding "center" in a dynamic way that emphasizes God's freedom in revealing the divine self to Israel through act and word as witnessed in the Hebrew Bible (G. Coats 1985, 245). In this way, he could emphasize with von Rad the narrative character of Israel's confession and could, at the same time, accept the insight of Wellhausen and of Smend that "Yahweh the God of Israel" must be taken along with "Israel the people of Yahweh" (Zimmerli 1980, 445-47; Smend 1970; G. Fohrer 1972). Westermann reflects even more clearly the influence of von Rad in giving central place to the historical, verbal character of Hebrew Bible theology (1982), but he goes beyond von Rad by contrasting the "saving God" to the "blessing God" in the Hebrew Bible and locating the dimension of blessing within the comprehensive framework of creation. H. Schmid has carried this last point still further by proposing that it is creation, and not history or saving history, that constitutes the comprehensive horizon of Hebrew Bible theology.

H. Preuss's recent work returns to Eichrodt's more systematic conception of Hebrew Bible theology, which has to offer "an overview of the world of faith and witness of the Hebrew Bible" (1995, 1). Preuss argues that the center and fundamental structure of that faith is "YHWH's historical activity of electing Israel for communion with his world," which obligates Israel and the nations (1995, 25). O. Kaiser[§] pursues a similar course but claims that the Torah is the Hebrew Bible's center, while its theological unity lies in the "basic relation" of Yahweh to Israel and the "basic equation" of righteousness and life, which the first commandment brings together (1993, 350).

5. *New Departures.* Several scholars in North America, working in the wake of the biblical theology movement's collapse (B. Childs[§] 1970), have departed radically from Eichrodt and von Rad. E. Martens (1981) organizes Hebrew Bible theology around Yahweh's programmatic promises in Exod 5:22-6:8. S. Terrien (1978) brings together the variety of Hebrew Bible (and New Testament) materials under a number of dialectically related motifs governed by God's elusive presence, thereby integrating dimensions of Israelite faith left peripheral by Eichrodt and von Rad. W. Brueggemann has suggested reducing the dialectic to two poles: "God's omnipotence and God's pathos" (corresponding to "structure legitimation" and "the embrace of

pain"; Brueggemann 1986, 70; 1992). For P. Hanson the dialectic is between the visionary and the pragmatic dimensions of the community (1978, 1986), while for J. Sanders it is the dynamic of stability and adaptability in the canonical process (1976, 1984). Childs§, prescinding from bipolar dialectics, also ascribes central importance to the CANON; he differs from Sanders in his emphasis on the canonical (final) shape of the text as providing the proper context and object of theological inquiry (1985). R. Knierim, in his proposal for a systematic Hebrew Bible theology, claims that neither tradition-historical nor Canonica*§ approaches are adequate; rather than providing a solution, they raise acutely the problem of the Hebrew Bible's plural theologies. Knierim seeks to discern semantic priorities among the various theologies in the Hebrew Bible in order to correlate them systematically while preserving their individual character.

If Hebrew Bible theologians in the early and mid-nineteenth century worried about giving the discipline a properly historical character, some scholars at the end of the twentieth century are concerned with its theological character. For Childs this has meant joining the Hebrew Bible and New Testament of the Christian Bible, as canonical witness to Jesus Christ, in a biblical theology that converses freely and critically with dogmatic theology (1992; similarly, F. Watson 1997). Brueggemann intends his *Theology of the Hebrew Bible* to be both Christian and theological but not strictly confessional: A Christian reading of the Hebrew Bible respects the availability of its theology to other than Christian construals (1997, 199). R. Rendtorff (1993), recently appreciative of Childs's emphasis on the canon, has a particular concern for Christian conversation with Judaism, a concern that intensifies with O. Kaiser's invocation of Bultmann's reference to Israel's history as a disaster (Kaiser 1993, 86) and with A. Gunneweg's insistence on the New Testament as the criterion for Christian reception of the Hebrew Bible (Gunneweg 1993, 36; contrast M. Oeming 1987, 237). While, or because, Gunneweg reads the Hebrew Bible in this manner, he conducts his Hebrew Bible theology as a history of Israel's religion. For different reasons R. Albertz (1994-96), among others, argues that, in the current situation, the history of Israel's religion has greater merit for the discipline than does Hebrew Bible theology. The debate between Eissfeld and Eichrodt still lives.

6. *Conclusion.* The situation at the start of the twenty-first century is marked by great variety and also by debate about Hebrew Bible theology's appropriate aims, the way it should conceive its material, and the strategies it should employ—signs of ill health, perhaps, or possibly of vitality (Ollenburger 1995). Brueggemann, whose *Theology* adopts a courtroom metaphor, argues that the Hebrew Bible is disputatious, offering both testimony and counter-testimony (1997, 317). P. Trible's Feminist*§ proposal, which puts issues of gender and sex at the forefront, articulates a countertestimony to prevailing models and interests, as does I. Mosala's work from South Africa, which critically interrogates biblical texts and their interpreters. Jewish scholars have offered constructive proposals (for Tanakh theology, M. Goshen-Gottstein 1987), trenchant criticism of past and current practice, and substantive theological interpretation (J. Levenson 1993). Hebrew Bible theology, with its increasing diversity, has not evolved into the kind of stable, foundationalist discipline that Gabler envisioned. We may regard this as the secret of its life and of its several resurrections.

Bibliography: R. Albertz, *A History of Israelite Religion in the OT Period* (2 vols. 1994-96). **C. F. Ammon,** *Biblische Theologie* (3 vols. 1792, 1801-22). **J. Barr,** "Story and History in Biblical Theology," *JR* 56 (1976) 1-17. **B. Bauer,** *Die Religion des Alten Testamentes in der geschichtlichen Entwicklung ihrer Principien (Kritik der Geschichte der Offenbarung,* 1838). **G. L. Bauer,** *Theologie des alten Testaments, oder, Abriss der Religion Begriffe der Alten Hebraer* (1796). **L. F. O. Baumgarten-Crusius,** *Grundzüge der biblischen Theologie* (1828). **J. Blenkinsopp,** "OT Theology and the Jewish-Christian Connection," *JSOT* 28 (1984) 3-15. **M. Brömse,** "W. Vatkes philosophische Theologie im Streit der Polemik und Apologie,"

Vergessene Theologen des 19. und frühen 20. Jahrhunderts (ed. E. Herms and J. Ringleben, 1984) 129-45. **W. Brueggemann,** "The Costly Loss of Lament," *JSOT* 36 (1986) 57-71; *OT Theology: Essays on Structure, Theme, and Text* (ed. P. D. Miller, 1992); *Theology of the OT: Testimony, Dispute, Advocacy* (1997). **B. S. Childs,** *OT Theology in a Canonical Context* (1985); *Biblical Theology of the Old and New Testaments* (1992). **R. E. Clements,** *Old Testament Theology: A Fresh Approach* (1978). **G. W. Coats,** "Theology of the HB," *The HB and Its Modern Interpreters* (SBLBMI 1, ed. D. A. Knight and G. M. Tucker, 1985) 239-62. **J. J. Collins,** "The 'Historical Character' of the OT in Recent Biblical Theology," *CBQ* 41 (1979) 185-204; "Is a Critical Biblical Theology Possible?" *The HB and Its Interpreters* (Biblical and Judaic Studies 1, ed. W. H. Propp et al., 1990) 1-17. **D. G. C. von Cölln,** *Die biblische Theologie* (1836). **W. M. L. De Wette,** *Biblische Dogmatik: Alten und Neuen Testaments* (1813[1], 1831[3]); *Lehrbuch der christlichen Dogmatik in ihrer historischen Entwicklung dargestellt* (1831[3]). **R. C. Dentan,** *Preface to OT Theology* (1963). **L. Diestel,** *Geschichte des Alten Testamentes in der christlichen Kirche* (1869). **W. Eichrodt,** *Theology of the OT* (3 vols. 1933-39; ET 2 vols. 1961-67).; "Does OT Theology Still Have Independent Significance Within OT Scholarship?" *The Flowering of OT Theology* (ed. B. C. Ollenburger et al., 1992) 30-39. **O. Eissfeldt,** "The History of Israelite-Jewish Religion and OT Theology," *The Flowering of OT Theology* (ed. B. C. Ollenburger et al., 1992) 20-29. **G. Fohrer,** *Theologische Grundstrukturen des Alten Testaments* (1972). **H. W. Frei,** *The Eclipse of Biblical Narrative* (1974). **J. P. Gabler,** "An Oration on the Proper Distinction Between Biblical and Dogmatic Theology and the Specific Objectives of Each," *The Flowering of OT Theology* (ed. B. C. Ollenburger et al., 1992) 489-502. **H. Gese,** *Vom Sinai zum Zion: Alttestament* (BEvT 64, 1974); "Tradition and Biblical Theology," *Tradition and Theology in the OT* (ed. D. A. Knight, 1977) 301-26. **J. Goldingay,** *Theological Diversity and the Authority of the OT* (1987). **M. H. Goshen-Gottstein,** "Tanakh Theology: The Religion of the OT and the Place of Jewish Biblical Theology," *Ancient Israelite Religion* (ed. P. D. Miller et al., 1987) 617-44. **C. P. W. Gramberg,** *Kritische Geschichte der Relgionsideen des Alten Testaments* (2 vols. 1829-30). **H. Gunkel,** *Reden und Aufsätze* (1913); "The 'Historical Movement' in the Study of Religion," *ExpTim* 38 (1926-27) 532-36. **A. H. J. Gunneweg,** *Biblische Theologie des Alten Testaments: Eine Religionsgeschichte Israels in biblisch-theologischer Sicht* (1993); **P. D. Hanson,** *Dynamic Transcendence* (1978); *The People Called: The Growth of Community in the Bible* (1986). **C. Hartlich and W. Sachs,** *Der Ursprung des Mythosbegriffes in der modernen Bibelwissenschaft* (1952). **G. F. Hasel,** "The Problem of the Center in the OT Theology Debate," *ZAW* 86 (1974) 65-82; *OT Theology: Basic Issues in the Current Debate* (1991[4]). **H. A. C. Havernick,** *Vorlesungen über die Theologie des Alten Testaments* (1848). **J. H. Hayes and F. Prussner,** *OT Theology: Its History and Development* (1985). **F. Hesse,** "Die Erforschung der Geschichte Israels als theologische Aufgabe," *KD* 4 (1958) 1-19. **J. C. K. Hofmann,** *Der Schriftbeweis* (1852-55); *Interpreting the Bible* (1860; ET 1959). **E. Jacob,** *Theology of the OT* (ET 1958). **G. P. C. Kaiser,** *Die biblische Theologie* (1813-21). **O. Kaiser,** *Der Gott des Alten Testaments: Theologie des Alten Testaments,* vol. 1, *Grundlegung* (1993). **A. Kayser,** *Die Theologie des alten Testaments* (1886). **R. Kittel,** "Die Zukunft der alttestamentlichen Wissenschaft," *ZAW* 39 (1921) 84-99. **R. P. Knierim,** "The Task of OT Theology," *The Task of OT Theology: Substance, Method, and Cases* (1995) 1-20. **J. Köberle,** "Heilsgeschichtliche und religionsgeschichtliche Betrachtungsweise des Alten Testaments," *NKZ* 17 (1906) 200-222. **L. Köhler,** *Old Testament Theology* (ET 1957). **E. König,** *Theologie des Alten Testaments* (1923). **J. D. Levenson,** *Sinai and Zion: An Entry into the Jewish Bible* (1985); *Creation and the Persistence of Evil: The Jewish Drama of Divine Omnipotence* (1988); *The HB, the OT, and Historical Criticism* (1993). **J. L. McKenzie,** *A Theology of the OT* (Doubleday Image Book, 1974). **E. A. Martens,** *God's Design: A Focus on OT Theology* (1981). **K. Marti,** *Geschichte* *der Israelitischen Religion* (1897). **R. Martin-Achard,** *Permanence de l'Ancien Testament* (1984). **G. E. Michalson Jr.,** *Lessing's "Ugly Ditch" : A Study of Theology and History* (1985). **I. J. Mosala,** *Biblical Hermeneutics and Black Theology in South Africa* (1989). **G. F. Oehler,** *Prolegomena zur Theologie des Alten Testaments* (1845). **M. Oeming,** *Gesamtbiblische Theologien der Gegenwart* (1987[2]). **B. C. Ollenburger,** "Biblical Theology: Situating the Discipline," *Understanding the Word* (ed. J. T. Butler et al., 1985) 37-62; "From Timeless Ideas to the Essence of Religion: Method in OT Theology Before 1930," *The Flowering of OT Theology* (Sources for Biblical and Theological Study 1, ed. B. C. Ollenburger et al., 1992) 3-19; "OT Theology: A Discourse on Method," *Biblical Theology: Problems and Perspectives* (ed. S. J. Kraftchick et al., 1995) 81-103. **D. Patrick,** *The Rendering of God in the OT* (OBT 10, 1981). **L. G. Perdue,** *The Collapse of History: Reconstructing OT Theology* (OBT, 1994). **H. D. Preuss,** *OT Theology* (OTL, 2 vols. 1995-96). **O. Procksch,** *Theologie des Alten Testaments* (1950). **G. von Rad,** *OT Theology* (2 vols. 1962-65); *The Problem of the Hexateuch and Other Essays* (1966). **R. Rendtorff,** "Alttestamentliche Theologie und israelitisch-jüdische Religionsgeschichte," *Zwischenstation: FS fur K. Kupisch 60* (ed. H. Gollwitzer and J. H. E. Wolf, 1963) 208-22; *Canon and Theology: Overtures to an OT Theology* (OBT, 1993). **H. G. Reventlow,** "Basic Problems in OT Theology," *JSOT* 11 (1979) 2-22; *Problems of OT Theology in the Twentieth Century* (ET 1985). **J. W. Rogerson,** *OT Criticism in the Nineteenth Century* (1984). **J. A. Sanders,** "Adaptable for Life: The Nature and Function of Canon," *Magnalia Dei: The Mighty Acts of God* (ed. F. M. Cross et al., 1976) 531-60. *Canon and Community: A Guide to Canonical Criticism* (GBS, 1984). **H. H. Schmid,** "Creation, Righteousness, and Salvation: 'Creation Theology' as the Broad Horizon of Biblical Theology," *Creation in the OT* (IRT 6, ed. B. W. Anderson, 1984) 102-17. **H. Schultz,** *Alttestamentliche Theologie* (1869, 1878; ET 2 vols. 1892). **E. Sellin,** *Israelitisch-Judische Religionsgeschichte* (Alttestamentliche Theologie auf religionsgeschichtlicher Grundlage, 1933). **R. Smend,** *Die Mitte des Alten Testaments* (ThStud 101, 1970); "Tradition and History: A Complex Relation," *Tradition and Theology in the OT* (ed. D. A. Knight, 1977) 49-68. **B. Stade,** "Über die Aufgaben der biblischen Theologie des Alten Testaments," *ZTK* 3 (1893) 31-51; *Biblische Theologie des Alten Testaments* (Grundriss der theologische Wissenschaften, 1905). **W. Staerk,** "Religionsgeschichte und Religionsphilosophie in ihrer Bedeutung für die biblische Theologie des Alten Testaments," *ZTK* 21 (1923) 389-400. **J. C. F. Steudel,** *Vorlesungen über die Theologie des Alten Testaments* (1840). **C. Steuernagel,** "Alttestamentliche Theologie und alttestamentliche Religionsgeschichte," *Vom Alten Testament* (ed. K. Budde, 1925) 266-73. **S. Terrien,** *The Elusive Presence: Toward a New Biblical Theology* (Religious Perspectives 26, 1978). **J. E. Toews,** *Hegelianism: The Path Toward Dialectical Humanism* (1980). **P. Trible,** "Five Loaves and Two Fishes: Feminist Hermeneutics and Biblical Theology," *TextsS* 50 (1989) 279-95. **E. Troeltsch,** "The 'Dogmatics' of the Religionsgeschichtliche Schule," *AJT 17* (1913) 1-21. **W. Vatke,** *Die Biblische Theologie wissenschaftlich dargestellt* (1835). **R. de Vaux,** "Is It Possible to Write a 'Theology of the OT?' " *The Bible and the Ancient Near East* (1972) 49-62. **T. C. Vriezen,** *An Outline of OT Theology* (1958). **C. Westermann,** *Elements of OT Theology* (1982); "The OT's Understanding of History in Relation to that of the Enlightenment," *Understanding the Word* (ed. J. T. Butler et al., 1985) 207-19. **G. E. Wright,** "Historical Knowledge and Revelation," *Translating and Understanding the OT* (ed. H. T. Frank and W. L. Reed, 1970) 279-303. **W. Zimmerli,** *OT Theology in Outline* (1978); "Biblische Theologie: 1. Altes Testament," *TRE* (1980) 6:426-55.

B. C. Ollenburger

THEOLOGICAL APPROACHES

New Testament Theology

The roots of a critical understanding of New Testament theology are to be found in the Reformation principle of *sola scriptura*. In the attempt to free the Bible from the authority of the church, the Bible itself, having to stand on its own, became the subject of critical scrutiny. The work of R. Simon[§] illustrates the development of the critical process: Simon showed, especially through Textual Criticism*[§], that at many points the Bible is textually unreliable; e.g., the ending of Mark (16:9-20) and the story of the adulteress (John 7:53-8:11) are not supported by the earliest manuscripts. In both Lutheran and Reformed orthodoxy, however, the Bible came under a new form of church dominance in the compendia of biblical texts, referred to as biblical theologies, that were supposed to form the foundation of church dogma.

The crucial breakthrough to a theology of the New Testament as we know it came with the programmatic inaugural address of J. P. Gabler[§] on Mar. 30, 1787, in Altdorf, Bavaria, in which he called for a clear distinction between the tasks of biblical and dogmatic theology. For him, biblical theology had to be free from determination by dogmatic theology so that theologians had a sound biblical basis for the production of a dogmatic theology. The purpose of biblical theology is to mediate between the plain teachings of biblical religion and the subtle, sophisticated formulations of dogmatic theology. To enable biblical theology to accomplish its task effectively, Gabler further divided it into two distinct steps: "true" biblical theology, which presents biblical religion in a historical, systematic fashion, and "pure" biblical theology, which distinguishes between contingent features that are valid only in particular historical circumstances and truths that are valid for all times.

Gabler's program, further divided into Hebrew Bible and New Testament theology, has been praised for establishing biblical theology as a separate discipline. In the new discipline's subsequent history this independence was misconceived as meaning that Hebrew Bible and New Testament theology had no relationship to dogmatic theology. Consequently, Hebrew Bible and New Testament scholars took upon themselves the task of dogmatic theology as well, no longer distinguishing between what Gabler identified as the distinctive tasks of biblical and dogmatic theology.

It was left to F. C. Baur[§] to define what it means to provide a thoroughly historical interpretation of the New Testament. He showed that it is insufficient to clarify the historical circumstances of individual writings; what is needed is a clarification of the history by which the various writings are interconnected. He came to this understanding for the first time in his famous article "Die Christuspartei der korintischen Gemeinde, der Gegensatz des paulinischen und petrinischen Christentums in der ältesten Kirche, der Apostel Petrus in Rom" (1831, repr. 1963). In this study he recognized the interaction of three religious forms, the first two of which—natural religion and Judaism—continued to function after their absorption into the third—the developing Christian religion. In the course of his future work, he increasingly fixated on a schema of New Testament history characterized by the opposed tendencies of a Petrine-Jewish and a Pauline-pagan form of Christianity that moved toward a synthesis in the developing Roman Catholic Church. However, whatever objections may be raised against Baur's highly schematized understanding of the history of primitive Christianity, he must be credited with making it inescapably clear that no New Testament writing can be understood adequately unless it is interpreted in terms of its place in the development of primitive Christian history.

Baur's student D. F. Strauss[§] had a different understanding of history. In contrast to the opposition between a supernaturalist and a naturalist form of interpretation (the latter had one of its most eminent interpreters in H. S. Reimarus), Strauss proposed a mythological interpretation, drawing on the insights of the Mythology*§ school of J. G. Eichhorn§, Gabler, G. Bauer§, and W. de Wette§. In his famous *Das Leben Jesu* (1835), he played the supernaturalist and naturalist interpretations of the Gospels against each other to show that only a mythological interpretation could do them justice. In this interpretation he was inspired by the conviction that the New Testament expresses universal ideas, not of a single individual, but of primitive Christian communities over a longer period of time: "By New Testament myths nothing else is to be understood than the expression of primitive Christian ideas formulated in spontaneously poeticizing legends" (1835, 1:75). With regard to JESUS, Strauss wrote, on the one hand, that Jesus "held and expressed the conviction that he was the Messiah; this is an indisputable fact" (1835, 2:469; ET 1846, 2:6; 1972, 284), although Strauss developed the idea only gradually (1835, 2:469-75; ET 1846, 2:6-13; 1972, 284-88). On the other hand, he wrote, "The author is aware that the essence of the Christian faith is perfectly independent of his criticism. The supernatural birth of Christ, his miracles, his resurrection and ascension, remain eternal truths, whatever doubts may be cast on their reality as historical facts" (1835, 1:VII; ET 1846, 1:xi; 1972, lii).

Baur complained that, in his inquiry, Strauss had ignored historical factors, e.g., the interrelationships between the Synoptics (see Synoptic Problem‡§) and the history of their origins. Strauss did indeed ignore that aspect of New Testament history; but he drew attention to another equally, if not more important, aspect—namely, that history takes place, not at the level of literature, but in the reflections of ordinary believers from whom emerged the conceptions that subsequently became the subject matter of the New Testament writings. The impetus Strauss gave to the investigation of that aspect of history was taken up later in the century in the *Religionsgeschichtliche Schule**§ (RGS).

J. Weiss§ indicated the direction the RGS would take in his study of the kingdom of God in Jesus' preaching (1892 [ET 1971]). W. Bousset§, a fellow member of the RGS, replied critically to Weiss (1892), stating in his preface that, although he admired A. Ritschl's§ understanding of the kingdom of God as an ethical ideal, that concept of the divine kingdom had nothing in common with the similarly named concept in Jesus' teaching. Jesus' teaching was grounded in the Jewish apocalyptic idea of two world orders, the present evil age and the future age of the kingdom of God, which would be inaugurated by a cataclysmic event. Jesus could be understood only in terms of the Jewish apocalyptic thought-world in which he lived.

Weiss's conception was subsequently popularized by A. Schweitzer§ (1906 [ET 1910, 1913, repr. 1966]), who called an end to the liberal quest for the historical Jesus. This quest, according to Schweitzer, sought Jesus, "believing that when it had found Him it could bring Him straight into our time as a Teacher and Saviour. It loosed the bands by which He had been riveted for centuries to the stony rocks of ecclesiastical doctrine, and rejoiced to see life and movement coming into the figure once more, and the historical Jesus advancing, so it seemed, to meet it. But he does not stay; He passes by our time and returns to his own" (1966, 620; ET 1910, 397). All that remains that is relevant for the present is the Spirit, through whom we can still encounter Jesus. "He comes to us as One unknown, without a name, as of old, by the lakeside, He came to those men who knew Him not. He speaks to us the same word: 'follow me!' and sets us to the tasks which He has to fulfill for our time" (1966, 630; ET 1910, 401).

Schweitzer (1913) had brought the liberal quest for the historical Jesus to a close as a negation, not of its feasibility, but of Jesus' compatibility with nineteenth-century liberal thought. In Schweitzer's interpretation, Jesus was willing to take on himself the burden of the suffering that preceded the transition between the two apocalyptic ages after it became clear to him that suffering was demanded of him to fulfill, for the rest of humanity, the petition he had taught his followers, "Lead us not into temptation (travail)." Consequently, because Jesus provoked the Jewish authorities into executing him in order to usher in the kingdom of God, he could be understood only within the framework of Jewish Apocalypticism*§. Here Schweitzer did not

discuss the work of M. Kähler§ (1892 [ET 1964]), who brought the liberal quest for the historical Jesus to an end in a different, more radical way by showing that the "historical" Jesus was purely a product of the historians and had nothing to do with the Jesus who actually lived. The
Gospels do not provide the kind of information on which a life of Jesus could be reconstructed; they could more appropriately be understood in the category of sermon.

In response to Weiss's study, Bousset, evidently remaining in this regard within the bounds
of nineteenth-century liberalism, argued that, even though Jesus was a participant in first-
century Judaism, he could not be comprehended fully in terms of that thought-world. Another
reason, however, may have motivated Bousset's negative reaction. The conception of apocalypticism with which Weiss (1892) operated and, similarly, Schweitzer (1913), was relatively
mild. When Weiss was writing his book, Bousset and H. Gunkel§ (another member of the RGS)
were involved in more far-reaching investigations of Jewish apocalypticism, resulting in
Gunkel's (1895) and Bousset's (1895) works that inaugurated the RGS's new method of interpretation in which New Testament Christianity was understood as a development within the
framework of first-century Hellenistic religions. In both of these writings, the world of Jewish
apocalypticism was no longer considered alien to the New Testament but as the thought-world
out of which it emerged. The bizarre nature of the Jewish apocalypticism described by Gunkel
and Bousset may explain why Bousset was unwilling to accept Weiss's claim that Jesus is
understandable only within such a framework.

Other important works also reflect the method of the RGS. Bousset (1913 [ET 1970]) traced
the "history of the belief in Christ from the beginnings of Christianity to Irenaeus." W. WREDE
(1897 [ET 1973]) outlined the task for a so-called New Testament theology as the description
of the history of primitive Christianity as a developing religion, for which the New Testament
writings and all of primitive Christian literature are relevant up to the time of the apologists,
who mark a new turn in Christianity's development. Wrede (1901 [ET 1971]) also argued that
the motif of a messianic secret in Mark's thought determined the structure of the gospel, thus
anticipating what, in the middle of the twentieth century, became popularly known as Redaction
Criticism*§.

The influence of the RGS came to an end with the rise of dialectic theology, initiated by K.
Barth§ (1919 [ET 1933]). The change in atmosphere in theological thinking is clearly expressed
by R. Bultmann§, who can be considered as belonging to a second generation of the RGS, in
the introduction to the fifth edition of Bousset's *Kyrios Christos* (1913 [ET 1970]): "Today we
can ask whether [the intention of the RGS to present the religion of primitive Christianity and
to use the New Testament as a source for this] can do justice to the New Testament, and whether
we are not rather to turn back again to the old question about the theology of the New
Testament" (vi; ET, 9).

What sparked dialectic theology was the collapse of confidence in Western culture brought
about by WWI, ushering in a mood of existential anxiety and alienation that lasted into the middle of the twentieth century. Barth (1921 [ET 1933]) argued that in 1 Corinthians 15 Paul†§ was
not concerned with the "last things"—which are expected to happen apocalyptically at the end
of the present age and so effectively remain on the plane of history—but with the "end things,"
which occur whenever a person becomes aware of standing before the Almighty. Bultmann
accepted Barth's interpretation of what Paul tried to communicate in the chapter but maintained
that in expressing the meaning of the end, as understood by Barth, Paul used the apocalyptic
language of his own time. In that way Bultmann accepted simultaneously the fundamental
insights of both Barth's dialectical approach and those of the RGS. Through *Sachkritik*, a critique of an author's forms of expression on the basis of the intended subject matter, it was possible to distinguish between the subject matter and the means of its expression. Bultmann elaborated this method of interpretation with great care in his program of demythologizing (1941),

where he translated the meanings that were expressed in mythological language in the New Testament into existentialist language. Bultmann used the existential concepts developed by his colleague M. Heidegger to translate into contemporary language the meanings expressed in mythological language in the New Testament. This method of interpretation did not derive from the philosophy of Heidegger, nor did it peel off the mythological shell to get at the kernel of the intended meaning; but, as in the German *Entmythologisieren* (cf. the English "demythologize"), it delved into the meanings through mythological language and reformulated them in existentialist language.

Through the work of the philologist C. Lachmann (1935), C. Wilke[§] (1838), the philosopher C. Weisse[§] (1838), and H. Holtzmann[§] (1892), the problem of the relationship between the Synoptics found a solution that has become standard in New Testament scholarship: the so-called two source theory, according to which Mark was the oldest gospel, and, in an earlier version, one of the sources of the other two Synoptics. The remaining common material in Matthew and Luke, almost exclusively sayings, comes from a second shared source, referred to by the abbreviation Q for the German word for source, *Quelle*. In the same year as the appearance of Barth's *Der Römerbrief*, two works appeared that signaled a new approach to the study of the Synoptics that had significant implications for New Testament theology. K. Schmidt[§] (1919) argued that Mark reveals that the oldest Jesus tradition "was not a continuous report, but a multitude of individual anecdotes that have been arranged generally according to a material point of view" (1919, 317); and M. Dibelius[§] (1959[3] [ET 1965]) investigated the forms of the Synoptic tradition. These works were followed by Bultmann's study (1921, 1958[4] [ET 1968[2]]), in which he focused on the layers of development of the traditions in the Synoptics. Each of these works questioned the ability of New Testament scholars to reconstruct a life and the thought of the historical Jesus and highlighted the role of the church in the formulation of the Gospel materials.

Bultmann subsequently wrote a book in which he claimed to do no more than present a picture of Jesus as he was seen in the earliest layers of the tradition (1926 [ET 1934]). In a later work (1948-53 [ET 1951-55]) he presented Jesus' teaching as being only a presupposition for the theology of the New Testament (1948-53, 1; [ET 1951-55] 3) because the Christian faith emerged only with the early church's faith in Christ, which originated in the postresurrection appearances of Jesus. Bultmann carried out his program of existentialist interpretation of the New Testament with incomparable skill and consistency in this work, an achievement that remains without rival as a theological interpretation of the New Testament.

Bultmann's understanding that Jesus' teaching was only the presupposition for an New Testament theology, that the history of Jesus, except for the mere fact of his having existed, was of no significance for the development of the Christian faith, led to opposition among his own followers, initiated by an address by E. Käsemann[§] (1954 [ET 1982]) at the annual meeting of Bultmann's students, "die alte Marburger," in 1953. Schweitzer had brought the liberal quest of the historical Jesus to a conclusion with a Jesus who returned to his own time without relevance for the present, except when we discover his Spirit as the disciples did of old "by the lake-side." Liberal theology wanted to move back from Jesus the Hellenistic Savior, as presented especially by Paul, to Jesus the teacher of simple ethical truths. In dialectic theology and what followed in Bultmann's existentialist interpretation, it was precisely Jesus the Christ, the Lord, as presented in the writings of Paul and John, who was in the foreground. In the new quest of the historical Jesus, the movement was once more back to the historical Jesus, but now no longer by abandoning the Christ, as he was understood in the developing Christian church; to the contrary, there was an attempt to find the Christ of the church in the Jesus of history. Expressing what was at stake theologically, Käsemann (1964 [ET 1969]) assessed a decade of investigation of the relationship of the Christ of the church to the historical Jesus that produced works

by G. Bornkamm[§] (1956) and H. Conzelmann (1959), a collection of essays on the historical
Jesus by E. Fuchs[§] (1960 [ET 1964]), and another "alte Marburger" address, in this case by
H. Braun[§] (1957).

Käsemann especially took issue with Bultmann's assertion that only the fact of Jesus' existence was decisive for New Testament theology, which Bultmann reasserted in his Heidelberger
address (1960 [ET 1964]), in which he assessed with certain skepticism the so-called new quest
of the historical Jesus. Käsemann also took issue with Braun's claims that the only continuity
between Jesus and the early church was the constancy of the self-understanding and that there
was no historical continuity, especially not in the Christology, positions for which Bultmann
commended Braun in his address because he was the only one who carried out "the intention
of an existentialist interpretation most consistently" (1960, 21). Käsemann objected that, "with
the predicate 'Christian' [in such interpretations] we bring to expression an understanding of
existence of the world for which Jesus is merely the spark, and Christ the mythological cipher."
What was at stake in the quest launched by Käsemann's 1953 address (1954) was the grounding of the early church's proclamation in Jesus' teaching. According to Käsemann, anything
short of that would be a surrender to docetism.

Käsemann objected to Bultmann's program of interpretation on two more crucial points:
eschatology and the understanding of God's justice. A key feature of Bultmann's existentialist
interpretation was the dehistoricizing of eschatology, as Barth had already done (1921 [ET
1933]). Eschatology was to be understood in the sense of an encounter with God at every
moment, not as something that lay, apocalyptically, at the end of history. Käsemann found this
devaluation of history untrue to the New Testament and appealed to apocalypticism (which
Bultmann had taken to be the mere form of Paul's expression in 1 Corinthians 15) to reaffirm
the importance of history. By means of apocalyptic imagery, Paul expressed his understanding
that salvation does not merely concern the individual but also all of creation. This concern for
the world as God's creation was already present in Käsemann's return to a quest for the historical Jesus and is stated succinctly in his formulation that for Paul the body meant "this piece of
the world that I am," signifying the human being's intricate binding to the world. Käsemann
was unwilling to surrender the world as God's creation to godless powers and, in this sense, he
wrote that he learned theology from the Nazis—that is, he rejected the Nazi claim that theology belonged in the church; and the world, to the Nazis. In a similar way, he interpreted the justice of God in Paul, not as a limitation to the existential justification of the individual sinner,
but as an expression of God's concern for all of creation.

For his protests Käsemann received qualified support but also opposition from within the
school, including Conzelmann's polemic against his comment that apocalypticism was the
"mother of theology" (1965 [ET 1966]). Since these controversies in the Bultmann school, very
little of theological interest has happened in New Testament interpretation.

Anglo-Saxon, specifically British, New Testament interpretation has gone its own way, using
methods developed to counter deistic arguments (Deism[§]). This approach, summarized by
C. Leslie[§], reached its apogee with W. Paley[§] (1790, 1794). Paley defined the tasks of the interpreter as establishing the truth of the biblical evidence and basing interpretation on that evidence; i.e., the task of the interpreter is to evaluate and interpret the evidence, not to substitute
alternative information. From that point of view, the concern of German scholarship to uncover
what lies behind the biblical evidence, particularly as practiced by the RGS, becomes incomprehensible. This is nowhere clearer than in the work of J. Dunn, in which the term "evidence"
recurs (1985). In an earlier work (1980), Dunn musters an incredible amount of information
from the environment of the New Testament only to conclude: "We cannot claim that Jesus
believed himself to be the incarnate Son of God; but we can claim that the teaching to that effect
as it came to expression in the later first-century Christian thought was, in the light of the whole

Christ-event, an appropriate reflection on and elaboration of Jesus' own sense of sonship and eschatological mission" (1980, 254). This reminds one of M. Hooker's (1959) conclusion that the influence of Isaiah 53 as an interpretation of Jesus' suffering was relatively late and that, therefore, the idea of the suffering Messiah could have originated only from Jesus, not in terms of the concept of the Messiah, but of the Son of Man. "Jesus realized that the Son of Man himself must suffer with his people, since he alone was the perfectly righteous man" (1959, 162).

Similar claims for the reliability of the evidence characterize the work of W. Manson[§]: "The nerve of the argument is that when we examine the early Christian convictions . . . we find a singular unanimity. It is natural to infer that such close agreement between men as different as Peter and Paul is the result neither of accident nor design; that their claims for Jesus tally because they are founded on facts" (1956, 215-16). C. H. Dodd[§] may have provided the most precise formulation of this principle: "[A Christian philosophy of history] must in the end account for all the facts accessible to our observation, but it starts from the Christian valuation of a particular set of facts" (1938, 25). British interpretation has remained inductive throughout its history, which has the advantage of allowing the biblical material to speak for itself without the interpreter trying to control it through critical inquiry. In that regard, even where there was agreement between British and German scholars concerning the results of their research, they were still worlds apart in what it meant. For British scholars, the results confirmed their evidence; for German scholars, it was the results themselves on which one had to rely.

Over the past decades a large number of new methodologies have been developed, most of the time going begging for questions to which they might be able to provide the answers: Literary*[§] interpretation (A. Wilder, W. Beardslee, R. Funk, J. D. Crossan, D. Via, R. Tannehill, N. Peterson, S. Moore), the social background of the New Testament (G. Theissen, W. Meeks, A. Malherbe, J. Gager), linguistics/semantics (E. Güttgemanns, E. Nida, J. Louw, D. Hellholm), Structuralism/Semiotics*[§] (D. Patte, J. Delorme), rhetoric (H. Betz; W. Wüllner; G. Kennedy), to mention only a few. Significant other work concerning New Testament interpretation in this period was the expansion of what has traditionally been called introduction to the New Testament to a history of early Christian literature, as had been proposed by Wrede (1901), P. Vielhauer[§] (1975), and H. Koester (1982 [ET 1982]). Furthermore, E. P. Sanders (1977) corrected the mistaken understanding of works righteousness as a characteristic feature of rabbinic Judaism, an insight crucial for the interpretation of Paul.

Among significant New Testament theologies that have appeared since the late nineteenth century, apart from Bultmann's in 1948-53, the following are worth mentioning: H. Holtzmann (1896-97); A. Schlatter[§] (1909-10); P. Feine[§] (1910, 1951[8]); H. Weinel[§] (1911); M. Meinertz (1950); J. Bonsirven[§] (1951 [ET 1963]); H. Conzelmann (1967 [ET 1967]); K. Schelkle (1968-76 [ET 1971-78]); J. Jeremias[§] (1971 [ET 1971], the first volume of an uncompleted New Testament theology); W. Kümmel[§] (1969 [ET 1973]); E. Lohse (1974); L. Goppelt[§] (1975-76 [ET 1981-82]); H. Hübner (1990-95); P. Stuhlmacher (1992); A. Weiser[§] (1993); J. Gnilka (1994). Other significant works related to the issue of a New Testament theology are O. Cullmann's[§] works (1946 [ET 1964]; 1965 [ET 1967]) in which he posed, in opposition to Bultmann's dehistorisizing existentialist approach, an understanding of the New Testament as the culmination of the history of salvation. The above list reveals a remarkable absence of significant comprehensive works on New Testament theology in the almost three decades between Weinel (1911) and Bultmann (1948-53), whereas the four decades beginning with Bultmann saw thirteen major new works.

An important development in recent study is the inclusion of the input and circumstances of "marginals" (blacks, women, the poor) in the interpretive process, thereby expanding the hermeneutical horizon (although that frequently results in a corresponding tendency to include only in the horizon a limited number of these groups). The most promising of these may be the reappropriation of the Bible by Latin American Liberation Theology*§ at a popular level (from where the impetus came) as well as in scholarly circles. In Latin America, the distance between the New Testament and the contemporary situation, which was created by historical criticism, has been reversed by placing primary focus on the situation of the interpreter who addresses the biblical texts for answers. The immediacy of the situations of the interpreter and of the biblical text, which sometimes border on the naïve, nevertheless produces new hermeneutical insights. At the scholarly level, the implications of these insights are being investigated by scholars like C. Boff (ET 1987) and J. Croatto (1987) in order to establish sound principles through which they can be made more fruitful.

One marked feature of late twentieth and early twenty-first century study on New Testament methodology is diversity in both New Testament theology itself and within the study of New Testament theology as an object. Many scholars now recognize that there is no true New Testament theology but many theologies: Matthew, Mark, Luke, John, Paul, etc. Each New Testament writer is a theologian in his own right (Dunn, 1990). Further, the methodological pluralism of the contemporary exegetical scene has affected the study of New Testament theology, especially Postmodernism*§ and Poststructuralism*§ (Via, 2002). Only in retrospect will we know whether this methodological pluralism is a bane or a blessing.

Bibliography: W. Baird, *History of NT Research* (2 vols. 1992, 2002). K. Barth, *Der Römerbrief* (1919; ET 1933); *Die Auferstehung der Toten* (1921; ET 1933). F. C. Baur, "Die Christuspartei der korintischen Gemeinde, der Gegensatz des paulinischen und petrinischen Christentums in der ältesten Kirche, der Apostel Petrus in Rom," *TZT* (1831) 61-206 (repr. in K. Scholder [ed.], *F. C. Baur: Ausgewählte Werke in Einzelausgaben* 1 [1963] 1-146). H. Boers, *What is NT Theology? The Rise of Criticism and the Problem of a Theology of the NT* (1979). C. Boff, *Theology and Praxis: Epistemological Foundations* (ET 1987). J. Bonsirven, *Théologie du nouveau testament* (1951; ET 1963). G. Bornkamm, *Jesus von Nazareth* (1956). W. Bousset, *Jesu Predigt in ihrem Gegensatz zum Judentum* (1892); *Der Antichrist in der überlieferung des Judentums, des Neuen Testaments, und der alten Kirche* (1895); *Kyrios Christos* (1913; ET 1970). H. Braun, "Der Sinn der neutestamentlichen Christologie," *ZTK* 54 (1957) 341-77. R. Bultmann, *Die Geschichte der synoptischen Tradition* (1921, 1958[4]; ET 1968[2]); *Jesus* (1926; ET 1934); "Neues Testament und Mythologie," Offenbarung und *Heilsgeschehen* (1941) 27-69 (repr. in H. W. Bartsch, ed., *Kerygma und Mythos* 1951, 15-53; ET 1953, 1-44); *Theologie des Neuen Testaments* (2 vols. 1948-53; ET 2 vols. 1951-55; *Das Verhältnis der urchristlichen Christusbotschaft zum historischen Jesus* (1960; ET 1964). H. Conzelmann, "Jesus Christus," *RGG³* 3 (1959) 619-53; "Zur Analyse der Bekenntnisformel I. Kor. 15, 3-5," *EvT* 1, 2 (1965) 1-11 (ET, *Int 20* 1966, 15-25); *Grundriss der Theologie des Neuen Testaments* (1967; ET 1967). J. Croatto, *Biblical Hermeneutics: Toward a Theory of Reading as the Production of Meaning* (1987). O. Cullmann, *Christus und die Zeit: Die urchristliche Zeit- und Geschichtsauffassung* (1946; ET 1964); *Heil als Geschichte* (1965; ET 1967). M. Dibelius, *Die Formgeschichte des Evangeliums* (1959³; ET 1965). C. H. Dodd, *History and the Gospel* (1938). W. Doty, *Contemporary NT Interpretation* (1972). J. Dunn, *Christology in the Making* (1980); *The Evidence for Jesus* (1985); *Unity and Diversity in the New Testament: An Inquiry Into the Character of Earliest Christianity* (1990²). P. Feine, *Theologie des Neuen Testaments* (1910, 1951⁸). E. Fuchs, *Zur Frage nach dem historischen Jesus* (1960; ET of a selection in *Studies on the Historical Jesus* 1964). J. Gnilka, *Theologie des Neuen Testaments* (1994). L. Goppelt, *Theologie des Neuen Testaments* (2 vols. 1975-76; ET 1981-82). H. Gunkel, *Schöpfung und Chaos in Urzeit und Endzeit: Eine religionsgeschichtliche Untersuchung über Gen 1 und Ap Joh 12* (1895). H. J. Holtzmann, *Lehrbuch der historisch-kritischen Einleitung in das Neue Testament* (1892); *Lehrbuch der neutestamentlichen Theologie* (2 vols. 1896-97).

M. Hooker, *Jesus and the Servant: The Influence of the Servant Concept of Deutero-Isaiah in the NT* (1959). **H. Hübner,** *Biblische Theologie des Neuen Testaments* (3 vols. 1990-95). **J. Jeremias,** *Neutestamentliche Theologie* (1971; ET 1971, 1st vol. of an uncompleted NT theology). **M. Kähler,** *Der sogenannte historische Jesus und der geschichtliche biblische Christus* (1892; ET 1964). **E. Käsemann,** "Das Problem des historischen Jesus," *ZTK* 51 (1954) 125-53 (ET in *Essays on NT Themes* 1982, 15-47); *Das Verhältnis der urchristlichen Christusbotschaft zum historischen Jesus* (1960; ET 1964); "Sackgassen im Streit um den historischen Jesus," *Exegetische Versuche und Besinnungen* 2 (1964) 31-68 (ET *NT Questions of Today* 1969, 23-65). **H. Koester,** *Einführung in das Neue Testament* (1982; ET 1982). **W. Kümmel,** *Das Neue Testament: Geschichte der Erforschung seiner Probleme* (1958; ET 1972); *Die Theologie des Neuen Testaments nach seinen Hauptzeugen* (1969; ET 1973); *Das Neue Testament im 20. Jahrhundert* (1970). **C. Lachmann,** "De ordine narrationum in evangeliis synopticis," *TSK* 8 (1835). **E. Lohse,** *Grundriss der neutestamentlichen Theologie* (1974). **W. Manson,** "The Life of Jesus: Some Tendencies in Present-day Research," *The Background of the NT and Its Eschatology* (ed. W. D. Davies and D. Daube, 1956) 215-16. **M. Meinertz,** *Einleitung in das Neue Testament* (2 vols. 1950). **O. Merk,** *Biblische Theologie des Neuen Testaments in ihrer Anfangszeit* (1972). **R. Morgan,** "Introduction: The Nature of NT Theology," *The Nature of NT Theology* (1973) 1-67. **R. Morgan with J. Barton,** *Biblical Interpretation* (1988). **W. Paley,** *Horae Paulinae, or The Truth of the Scripture History of St. Paul Evinced* (1790); *A View of the Evidences of Christianity* (1794). **H. Räisänen,** *Beyond NT Theology: A Story and a Programme* (1990). **E. P. Sanders,** *Paul and Palestinian Judaism: A Comparison of Patterns of Religion* (1977). **K. Schelkle,** *Theologie des Neuen Testaments* (4 vols. 1968-76; ET 1971-78). **A. Schlatter,** *Die Theologie des Neuen Testaments und die Dogmatik* (2 vols. 1909-10). **K. Schmidt,** *Der Rahmen der Geschichte Jesu* (1919, repr. 1964). **A. Schweitzer,** *Geschichte der Leben-Jesu-Forschung* (1913, repr. 1966); *Von Reimarus zu Wrede* (1906; ET 1910). **D. F. Strauss,** *Das Leben Jesu* (1835; ET *The Life of Jesus Critically Examined,* tr. G. Elliot, 1846; new ed. 1972). **G. Strecker** (ed.), *Das Problem der Theologie des Neuen Testaments* (1975). **Stuhlmacher,** *Biblische Theologie des Neuen Testaments* (1992). **D. O. Via,** *What Is New Testament Theology?* (*GBS,* 2002). **P. Vielhauer,** *Geschichte der urchristlichen Literatur* (1975). **H. Weinel,** *Biblische Theologie des Neuen Testaments: Die Religion Jesu und des Urchristentums* (1911). **A. Weiser,** *Theologie des Neuen Testaments II: Die Theologie der Evangelien* (1993). **J. Weiss,** *Die Predigt Jesu vom Reiche Gottes* (1892; ET 1971). **C. H. Weisse,** *Die evangelische Geschichte, kritisch und philosophisch bearbeitet* (2 vols. 1838). **C. Wilke,** *Der Urevangelist oder exegetisch kritische Untersuchung über das Verwandschaftsverhältnis der drei ersten Evangelien* (1838). **W. Wrede,** *Über Aufgabe und Methode der sogenannten neutestamentlichen Theologie* (1897; ET 1973); *Das Messiasgeheimnis in den Evangelien: Zugleich ein Beitrag zum Verständnis des Markusevangeliums* (1901; ET 1971).

H. BOERS

THEOLOGICAL APPROACHES

Apocalypticism

Although a widely used word, "apocalypticism" remains without an equally widely agreed-upon definition. In biblical interpretation it can refer to (a) certain traditions of literary activity in ancient Judaism and Christianity; (b) the religious ideas and imagery that characterize this literature, chief among them judgment, the near end and/or transformation of the world, and a claim of access to secret knowledge about the world's destiny and/or structure; or (c) social movements that initiated and responded to the apocalyptic message. Some scholars have attempted to clarify terminology by avoiding the substantive use of "apocalyptic" and by distinguishing apocalypse (genre), apocalyptic eschatology, and apocalypticism (Hanson 1976). Attempts to restrict the word *apocalypticism* to a type of eschatology, to a symbolic universe, to historical movements, or to forms of communal behavior, however, have not yet succeeded; an understanding of apocalypticism as it has been used in scholarly literature requires looking at the interplay of literature, ideas, and movements.

Biblical interpretation has tended to place the flourishing of apocalyptic literature from the second century B.C.E. through the second century C.E. This period became the focus not only because it includes the two canonical (Canon of the Bible§) apocalypses (Daniel, c. 166 B.C.E.; Revelation, c. 90–96 C.E.), but also because it is crucial to the understanding of the career of JESUS and of the emergence of early Christianity. The range of apocalypticism is far wider, however. Hanson placed "the dawn of apocalyptic" between the exile in the sixth century and the later fifth century, locating it in ,a movement represented by Isaiah 24–27; 34–35; 56–66; Malachi; Zephaniah 9–14; and possibly Joel. Most other scholars see this material as proto-apocalyptic and begin discussion of apocalyptic literature in the third century B.C.E. with the *Book of the Watchers* (*1 Enoch* 1–36), perhaps the earliest example of the apocalypse genre.

1. *Judaism in Antiquity.* Scholarly attention to Jewish apocalypticism has generally waned with the literature resulting from the fall of the Temple in 70 C.E. (*4 Ezra, 2 Baruch, 3 Baruch, Apocalypse of Abraham*). It is certainly the case that Jewish apocalypticism underwent definitive changes after 135 C.E., but it cannot be said to have disappeared. Apocalyptic eschatology perdured in rabbinic literature. Not only traditions of ascent and revelation but also works belonging to the apocalypse genre reemerged in the literature of Jewish mysticism. There is also the problematic evidence of Jewish apocalyptic works reworked by Christians, the date and original extent of which are very difficult to determine. A Falasha work called the *Apocalypse of Gorgorios* has been dated as late as the fourteenth century.

2. *Early Christianity.* Scholars once assumed that the delay of the Parousia meant the disappearance or transformation of Christian apocalypticism. Montanism was frequently seen as a brief revival of Christian PROPHECY and apocalyptic fervor, but it is increasingly recognized that apocalypticism has remained a force throughout Christian history. Apocalypticism continued in antique Christianity under three guises: the continued production and use of apocalypses and related literature, the emergence of apocalyptic traditions of interpretation, and apocalyptic movements.

Montanism did indeed manifest the continuation of early Christian prophecy and apocalyptic expectation. The Donatists, at some points, also exhibited the traits of an apocalyptic movement. It is important, however, not to limit apocalypticism to movements that can be seen as sectarian. Early Christianity continued to produce and use apocalypses (e.g., *Shepherd of Hermas, Apocalypse of Pet*er) and to rework Jewish apocalypses, testaments, and oracles (e.g., *Sibylline Oracles, Testament of the Twelve Patriarchs*). Whereas once Gnosticism (Gnostic Iinterpretation§) was seen entirely in terms of realized eschatology and was thus treated as the opposite pole of apocalypticism, apocalyptic aspects of Gnosticism are now more widely recognized, and a number of Gnostic works are now recognized as apocalypses (2 *Apocalypse of James, Gospel of Mary, Hypostasis of Archons*).

Perhaps the broadest stream of continued apocalyptic activity was interpretive. Hippolytus's *Commentary on Daniel* is among the earliest surviving biblical commentaries. Not only Daniel and Revelation but also 1 and 2 Thessalonians, 1 John, the Synoptic[§] apocalypses (Matt 24:1–26:2; Mark 13; Luke 21:5-36), the *Sibyllines* and the oracle of Hystaspes, Virgil's *Eclogue*, and many biblical texts that later interpretation would not view as apocalyptic were grist for the mill of early Christian apocalyptic interpretation. Irenaeus[§] already exhibited the major foci of Christian interpretation: the theory that the world's destined age is six days of a thousand years each (the cosmic week), the conviction of the thousand-year reign of the saints as the seventh day (chiliasm or millennialism), and the speculation on the antichrist (*Adv. Haer.* 5.28-36). Hippolytus defers the reign of the saints to a date two hundred years in the future, and Irenaeus argues against speculation on the name of the antichrist. But in Lactantius's *Divine Institutes* 7 (between 304 and 314), these elements combine as they would frequently in later Christian interpretation to argue for the nearness of consummation.

3. *Apocalypticism in Medieval Christianity.* Medieval interpreters of apocalypses tended to interpret biblical apocalypses as symbols of the church on earth (Jerome's adaptation of Victorinus of Pattau's commentary on Revelation), literally by adapting Daniel and Revelation to contemporary circumstances (the mid-tenth century Adso of Montier-en-Der's *De ortu et tempore Antichristi* relating the antichrist's coming to the Frankish kingdoms), and in various mystical and spiritual writings (the twelfth cent. writers Hildegard of Bingen and Elisabeth of Schönau).

4. *Apocalypticism and Scholarly Biblical Criticism.* Apocalypticism and the production of apocalyptic literature has never entirely disappeared from Western Christianity, but the rise of historical criticism provided a turning point at which scholarly interpretation and apocalyptic expectation diverged radically. While as major a thinker as J. Edwards[§] continued to make apocalyptic predictions, the rationalist critique focused heavily on the problem of the fulfillment of prophecy and of the apocalyptic expectations of Jesus and his followers. In *A Discourse of the Grounds and Reasons of the Christian Religion* (1724) and *Scheme of Literal Prophecy Considered* (1727), A. Collins[§] showed his awareness of *vaticinium ex eventu* (prophecy of an event after the event's occurrence) and correctly placed the visions of Daniel in the reign of Antiochus IV Epiphanes. H. S. Reimarus[§] (*Wolfenbüttel Fragments* [pub. posthumously, 1774–78]) took over Collins's treatment of prophecy and the messianic expectations of Jesus and his disciples.

Thus apocalypticism entered the nineteenth-century scholarly world under the shadow of this critique and of the noncanonical status of much of the literature. Yet a few interpreters (F. Lücke, E. Reuss, A. Hilgenfeld) saw apocalypticism as the link between the two testaments, arising out of biblical prophecy, and sought to delineate its history. More widely influential was J. Wellhausen's[§] interpretation of apocalyptic writers as rigid borrowers and imitators who took over material from the prophets and from Persian religion in an unreflective and uncreative fashion. Wellhausen set the tone of scholarly attitudes toward apocalypticism. In some degree, this tendency to denigrate apocalypticism was part of the general desire of Christian scholars to view the Judaism of the Second Temple as having degenerated from the true Israelite religion of the prophets; Jesus' preaching was seen as a restoration of this true Israelite religion.

At the turn of the twentieth century, R. Charles[§] produced editions, translations, and descriptions of apocalyptic works that did not share Wellhausen's evaluation of this literature. Identifying the apocalyptic writers as heirs of the prophets and as the product of a branch of Phariseeism, he saw them as indigenous to Judaism and central to the interpretation of early Christianity. His work, though not without flaws, was tremendously influential, especially among English-speaking scholars.

Throughout the early part of the twentieth century, attention to apocalypticism was dominated by the questions of its origin and of its relation to Jesus and early Christianity. Both of these questions polarized most interpreters.

Scholars of the Hebrew Bible were most concerned with the question of the origin of apocalypticism. The English scholars H. Rowley[§] and D. Russell saw its origin in prophecy and gave it a positive evaluation, identifying its vision of history under God's direction as its characteristic and lasting contribution to theology. The tradition-historical studies (Tradition History*[§]) of H. Gunkel[§], S. Mowinckel[§], A. Bentzen[§], and the *Religionsgeschichtliche Schule**[§] in general made it possible to see apocalyptic use of mythic traditions, not as foreign influences, but as arising from sources deeply embedded in the life of Israel and of Judaism. German scholars continued to be heavily influenced by Wellhausen's view, in general distancing apocalypticism from prophecy and stressing foreign and, particularly, Persian influence.

The question of the relation of apocalypticism to early Christianity was equally disputed. In the early part of the twentieth century, English-speaking scholarship generally took for granted apocalypticism's significance for the New Testament. Although less widely accepted by German and French-speaking scholars, this case was put forward in its most acute form by A. Schweitzer[§], whose critique of nineteenth-century readings of Jesus identified Jesus' message as apocalyptic. His interpretation of Paul[†§] presented him as an "apocalyptic mystic." But in succeeding years, New Testament scholars tended to distance Jesus and early Christianity from apocalypticism. This tendency reached its peak with R. Bultmann[§] and those of his followers who sought to present both Jesus and Paul as demythologizing theologians.

By 1960, apocalypticism had begun to be an important and controversial concept for German theology and for New Testament interpretation. In this context, E. Käsemann[§] made his claim that "apocalyptic . . . is the mother of all Christian theology." Between 1959 and 1969 a number of attempts to describe the social setting of apocalypticism appeared. These interpretations tended to depict apocalypticism as the product of a persecuted and prophetic minority (O. Plöger, P. Vielhauer). The study and first publications of the Qumran finds (Dead Sea Scrolls[§]) gave new impetus to the study of apocalypticism, providing not only a wide variety of new texts but also unsettling ideas about the character of Jewish apocalyptic expectation and drawing attention to the relationship between expectation and exegesis (N. Dahl 1964; L. Hartmann 1966).

5. *Scholarship Since 1970.* In 1970, K. Koch published a history of the investigations of apocalypticism that also called for more disciplined historical and literary study (also J. Schmidt 1969). Originally titled *Ratlos vor die Apocalyptik*, his study was published in English in 1972 as *The Rediscovery of Apocalyptic*. As the English title suggests, Koch articulated the concerns of a turning tide in scholarship. Since then, a proliferation of scholarly study of apocalypses and apocalypticism have attempted both to free apocalypticism from the negative theological evaluations with which it had been burdened and to clarify the formal categories and the social and compositional context of apocalyptic literature.

P. Hanson (1962) traced the development of apocalyptic eschatology and the resurgence of mythic imagery in later prophetic literature. He proposed two apocalyptic movements in the period of the sixth to fifth centuries B.C.E. that responded to the oppression at the hands first of the Persians and then of the Zadokites by creating a "counteruniverse" in which God's justice could create a new cosmic order. He described the second century in terms of multiple offshoots of an original apocalyptic resistance to the Seleucids.

Most scholars since Hanson have accepted his description of the origins of apocalyptic eschatology. The question of origin has receded in favor of interest in describing the genre of apocalypses and the relation of apocalypticism in Judaism and early Christianity to similar phenomena in the wider Hellenistic world. Apocalypticism is seen, not as deriving from wisdom, but as sharing a scribal and learned context with wisdom; concern with "foreign influence" has been supplanted by the recognition of apocalypticism as a tradition that is both indigenous to Judaism and shares elements with similar developments in other Hellenistic cultures (J. Smith 1975).

With the description of the Enoch literature as the first true apocalypses, the third century B.C.E. has become the starting point for most study of Jewish apocalypticism. The dominance of cosmology over eschatology in the Enoch material has drawn attention to the cosmological interests of the apocalypses (M. Stone 1976, 1980; M. Himmelfarb 1983, 1988). *First Enoch's* connection with priestly and official circles has helped to move scholars from explaining the apocalypses as the product of oppression and persecution toward seeing their eschatological concerns as products of more varied crises (Stone 1976, 1980; J. Collins 1979, 1987; A. Y. Collins 1984, 1988). It is primarily the eschatological aspects of apocalypticism that engage scholars who use anthropological descriptions of millenarian sects to describe apocalypticism as the context of Jesus, Paul, and early Christianity (J. Gager 1975; A. Segal 1980, 1986; D. Flusser 1988; W. Meeks 1983, 1986).

The shift from genetic to generic description has been accompanied by more widespread collaboration and communication between Christian and Jewish scholars and among international scholars. The Society of Biblical Literature[§] Genres Group on apocalypses has articulated a definition of the genre and has studied apocalypses, not only in Judaism and early Christianity, but also in Greco-Roman, Persian, and Egyptian religions, as well as in Gnosticism (J. Collins 1979). The International Colloquium on Apocalypticism (Uppsala 1979) likewise addressed itself to apocalypticism in the ancient Mediterranean and in the Near East, focusing on questions of phenomenology, genre, and social setting (D. Hellholm 1983). The shifts described above and the definition of apocalypse as genre (articulated by the SBL Genres Group) have provided a basis for discussion, but consensus should not be overstated. The definition of the genre remains disputed, as do nearly all aspects of apocalypticism.

The question of the experiential aspect or compositional setting remains. There are explicit links between early Christian prophecy and at least those apocalypses that are not pseudonymous (Revelation, *Shepherd of Hermas, Passion of Perpetua and Felicity* 11:1–13:8). Throughout the literature, vision narratives show connections with shamanistic practice and visionary literature elsewhere. Yet the scholarly, or at least conventional, character of the material is also made clear, in particular in the use of pseudonymity (J. Collins 1979, 1987). An analogy might be made with the practice of keeping a dream journal, in which interpretive tradition and experience inform each other. While investigations of Qumran's apocalyptic exegesis continue (M. Horgan 1979), questions have been raised about the use of the Qumran texts to explain apocalypticism (*JNES* 49 1990, 101-94). A variety of cautions have been raised about the anthropological models of millennial movements to describe the movements that produced the Jewish and Christian apocalypses, Paul's mission, or the prophetic career of Jesus (J. Collins 1979, 1987; Meeks in Hellholm 1983). Especially in the case of Revelation, attention has been given to the political context (E. Schüssler Fiorenza 1985; A. Y. Collins 1984), including that of sexual politics in the communities of Revelation (A. Y. Collins 1988). At present the most urgent and fruitful area of investigation seems to be the investigation of literary and social functions not only of the apocalypse as a form but also of smaller apocalyptic forms and apocalyptic language (A. Y. Collins, Meeks, both in Hellholm).

The diverse and complex history of scholarly interpretation of apocalypticism in the nineteenth and twentieth centuries should not distract us from the recognition that apocalypticism has continued to be a viable mode of political discourse. Interpreters as diverse as H. Lindsey and A. Boesak find in it a medium to address their worlds.

Bibliography: P. J. Alexander, *The Byzantine Apocalyptic Tradition* (1985). **A. Boesak,** "Your Days Are Over: The Promises of God Confront the State," and "At the Apocalypse: The

South African Church Claims Its Hope," *Sojourners* 17:8 (1988) 19-20, 28-35. **W. Bousset,** *Die Offenbarung Johannis* (1906). **O. Capitani and J. Miethke,** *L'attesa della fine dei tempi nel Medioevo* (Annali dell'Instituto Storico Italo-Germanico in Trento 28, 1990). **A. Y. Collins,** *Crisis and Catharsis: The Power of the Apocalypse* (1984); "Early Christian Apocalypticism," *ANRW* II.25.6 (1988) 4665-711; *The Gospel and Women* (1988). **J. J. Collins** (ed.), *Apocalypse: The Morphology of a Genre* (*Semeia* 14, 1979); *The Apocalyptic Imagination: An Introduction to the Jewish Matrix of Christianity* (1987). **J. J. Collins** et al, (eds.), *The Encyclopedia of Apocalypticism* (3 vols. 1998). **N. A. Dahl,** "Eschatologie und Geschichte im Lichte der Qumran-texte," *Zeit und Geschichte: Dankesgabe an R. Bultmann zum 80. Geburtstag* (ed. E. Dinkler, 1964) 3-18 (ET in *The Crucified Messiah and Other Essays* 1974). **R. K. Emmerson and B. McGinn,** *The Apocalypse in the Middle Ages* (1992). **D. Flusser,** "Jewish and Christian Apocalyptic," *Judaism and the Origins of Christianity* (1988) 229-465. **J. Gager,** *Kingdom and Community: The Social World of Early Christianity* (Prentice-Hall Studies in Religion, 1975). **I. Gruenwald,** *Apocalyptic and Merkavah Mysticism* (AGJU 14, 1980); *From Apocalypticism to Gnosticism: Studies in Apocalypticism, Merkavah Mysticism, and Gnosticism* (BEATAJ 14, 1988). **P. D. Hanson,** "Apocalypticism," *IDBSup* (1976) 28-34; *The Dawn of Apocalyptic* (1975); "Prologomena to the Study of Jewish Apocalyptic," *Magnalia Dei: The Mighty Acts of God* (ed. F. M. Cross, W. Lemke, and P. D. Miller, 1976) 389-413. **L. Hartman,** *Prophecy Interpreted: The Formation of Some Jewish Apocalyptic Texts and of the Eschatological Discourse Mark 13 par.* (ConBNT 1, 1966). **D. L. Hellholm** (ed.), *Apocalypticism in the Mediterranean World and the Near East: Proceedings of the International Colloquium on Apocalypticism, Uppsala, August 12-17, 1979* (1983). **M. Himmelfarb,** *Tours of Hell: An Apocalyptic Form in Jewish and Christian Literature* (1983); Tours of Heaven," *Jewish Spirtuality,* vol. 1 (ed. A. Green, 1988) 145-65. **M. Horgan,** *Pesharim: Qumran Interpretations of Biblical Books* (CBQMS 8, 1979); *JNES* 49 (1990) 101-94. **E. Käsemann,** "Die Anfänge christlicher Theologie," *ZTK* 57 (1960) 162-85 (ET "The Beginning of Christian Theology," *JTC* 6, 1969) 17-46. **K. Koch,** *Ratlos vor die Apokalyptik (1970;* ET *The Rediscovery of Apocalyptic* 1972). **H. Lindsey,** *The Late Great Planet Earth* (1970). **B. McGinn,** *Apocalyptic Spirituality* (CWS, 1979); "Early Apocalypticism: The Ongoing Debate," *The Apocalypse in English Renaissance Thought and Literature: Patterns, Antecedents, and Repercussions* (1984) 2-39. **W. A. Meeks,** *The First Urban Christians* (1983); *The Moral World of the First Christians* (LEC 6, 1986). **F. J. Murphy,** "Introduction to Apocalyptic Literature" *NIB* (1996) 7:1-16. **E. A. Petroff,** Medieval Women's Visionary Literature (1986). **T. Pippin,** *Death and Desire: The Rhetoric of Gender in the Apocalypse of John* (Literary Currents in Biblical Interpretation, 1992). **O. Plöger,** *Theocracy and Eschatology* (ET 1968). **M. Reeves,** *Joachim of Fiore and the Prophetic Future* (1977). **J. M. Schmidt,** *Die jüdische Apokalyptik: Die Geschichte ihrer Erforschung von den Anfängen bis zu den Textfunden von Qumran* (1969). **A. F. Segal,** "Heavenly Ascent in Hellenistic Judaism, Early Christianity, and Their Environment," *ANRW* II.23.2 (1980) 1333-94; *Rebecca's Children: Judaism and Christianity in the Roman World* (1986). **J. Z. Smith,** "Wisdom and Apocalyptic," *Religious Syncretism of Antiquity* (ed. B. Pearson, 1975) 131-56. **M. Stone,** "Lists of Things Revealed in Apocalyptic Literature," *Magnalia Dei: The Mighty Acts of God* (ed. F. M. Cross, W. Lemke, and P. D. Miller, 1976) 414-52; *Scriptures, Sects and Visons: A Profile of Judaism to the Jewish Revolt* (1980). **P. Vielhauer,** "Apocalypses and Related Subjects: Introduction," *NT Apocrypha* 2 vols. (ed. E. Hennecke et al., 1964; ET 1965) 579-607.

M. R. D'ANGELO AND E. A. MATTER

SOCIAL SCIENCE METHODS

Social-Scientific Criticism

Social-scientific criticism, in its broadest sense, applies methods and theories to biblical texts in an attempt to reconstruct the social worlds behind these texts (e.g., ancient Israel) while simultaneously illuminating the lives of the people living in these worlds. The implementation of this method reflects a paradigm shift away from the questions asked by historical critics and biblical theologians, recognizing the limited ability of the older models to shed light on these ancient social worlds. New theories generated through the social sciences provide biblical scholars with models for understanding social and religious phenomena that are different from those found in the dynamics of modern life.

The models and approaches of social-scientific criticism include a variety of subdisciplines of the social sciences whose relevance for analyzing the Bible as a social document are still being tested. Most important among these subdisciplines are Sociology*§, which is interested in locating and analyzing patterns of social behavior that provide generalizations about social change; and anthropology and its subdisciplines, such as Archaeology*§ and structural anthropology, which are less concerned with generalizations, focusing instead on the comparative study of human behavior. The combined application of these methods allows the researcher to reconstruct various social dimensions of the biblical text.

Although social-scientific criticism is regarded by many scholars as a recent addition to the list of paradigms employed for interpreting the Bible, interest in analyzing the social processes that gave rise to the biblical texts has historical roots. Scholars in the Middle Ages (e.g., Rashi§, Samuel ben Meir§, J. Bekhor Shor§, and Hugh of St. Victor§) were interested in understanding the culture surrounding the text rather than in relying solely on the then popular allegorical method of interpretation (R. Wilson 1984, 2-3). Later, Renaissance scholars became interested in the Cross-Cultural*§ connections between ancient Israel and the rest of the ancient Near East. Representative of early anthropological studies that attempted to understand the social structure and religious customs of ancient Israel and that served as precursors for contemporary social-scientific criticism are those of W. R. Smith§ (1889) and J. Wellhausen§ (1897). These two scholars employed an evolutionary model to explain social phenomena in the Hebrew Bible, using a general comparative method that linked early Israel to the pre-Islamic bedouin Arabs as well as to elements of contemporary Arabic culture. By examining these elements alongside classical Arabic texts, Wellhausen and Smith believed that it was possible to reconstruct the religion and society of ancient Israel. Their anthropological approaches were accepted by later scholars like J. Pedersen§ (1920-34 [ET 1926-40]) and R. de Vaux§ (1958-60 [ET 1961]), whose studies of social life in ancient Israel followed, and whose works are also considered classics. However, the methods employed in these studies are now recognized as relying on comparative data whose relevance to the study of ancient Israel is questionable.

Pioneering studies in historical-critical methods provided examples of both the importance and the limits of other approaches in relationship to social-scientific criticism. For example, the Tradition-Historical research of M. Noth§ (1948) builds on comparative evidence from Greek amphictyonies, whose social organization centered around a common religious shrine maintained by members of the tribal confederation. H. Gunkel's§ form-critical studies (Form Criticism*§) explored the social location of the biblical text in order to understand the social processes that fostered its development from oral tradition to literary production. These studies (and the work of Wellhausen and Smith) understood ancient Israel to be a pastoral nomadic society. Yet this pastoral nomadic model, the basic assumption on which these earlier studies were grounded, is no longer tenable; it neglects to take into consideration the dynamic of change in social structures over time or from one social setting to another. Moreover, statements regarding behavioral patterns are descriptive (subjective) rather than analytic (objective).

By contrast, in *Ancient Judaism* (1952; originally published as journal articles, 1917-19) social scientist M. Weber[§] presented a sustained sociological analysis of the Hebrew Bible as evidence for his theories of capitalism, anticipating theories currently embraced by biblical scholars. His reconstruction of early Israel depicted a society dependent on two economic bases: seminomadic groups and settled agriculturalists. According to Weber, the bond between these groups was cemented by their common commitment to a covenant and to the authority of charismatic individuals who arose at particular junctures in history. This loosely organized mixed multitude evolved, over time, into a hierarchical structure that slowly eroded the freedom and the authority of the family unit, usurping power for itself. The onset of the monarchy, Weber argued, led to the stratification of society into the landowners and the landless. This economic distinction and the corruption and exploitation to which it gave rise were the focus of the prophets (Prophecy and Prophets, Hebrew Bible[‡§]), who opposed this system of injustice, drawing on the covenant tradition and on the social equality that existed before the monarchy. Thus Weber's reconstruction of ancient Israel explored the changing institutions of society and related these changes to both political and economic conditions. His theories of the history of ancient Israel were developed further by A. Lods[§] (1930) and A. Causse[§] (1934, 1937), who noted tensions between the indigenous Canaanites and the nomadic Israelites.

The 1960s and 1970s marked a watershed as increasing numbers of scholars applied the methods and theories of social-scientific criticism in reconstructing their histories of ancient Israel. Focusing on socioeconomic conditions, G. Mendenhall[§] (1973) rejected Noth's thesis of the amphictyonic social organization in ancient Israel because the biblical tradition does not support the theory that ancient Israel had a central shrine. Moreover, Noth's argument located the amphictyony in an urban setting, while Mendenhall argued that early Israel was a peasant-based tribal federation that revolted against its Canaanite overlords and bound itself together through a covenant tradition with God. Ultimately, Mendenhall's reconstruction moves from a socioeconomic perspective to one that emphasizes the ethical dimensions of this revolution at the expense of political forces.

Using an explicitly sociological model for analyzing biblical data, N. Gottwald[§] (independently of Mendenhall) focused on premonarchical Israel (1979). His writings refute the pastoral, nomadic societal model for early Israel and interpret the so-called conquest as a retribalization effort by a peasant population. Gottwald's theory relies on sociologist K. Marx, who argued that the roots of historical change lie in economic and social forces. Gottwald suggested that Israel emerged from a retribalization movement within the hierarchical Canaanite social structure. He then examined the process by which disaffected, disenfranchised peasants revolted against a hierarchical power structure and retribalized along egalitarian lines. (Note: The distinction between a peasant who controls the products of his or her labor and sells them in a free economy and a peasant whose labor and produce are subject to hierarchical political systems is crucial in this analysis.) Gottwald's study exemplifies the sociological perspective that connects socioeconomic processes and Ideological[*§] analysis for the purpose of reconstructing the social history of biblical periods.

Social-scientific studies that have provided a greater understanding of the social life of ancient Israel have focused on kinship and family, marriage, kingship, the queen mother, and sacred prostitution. Although earlier studies of these topics cannot be ignored, they are of limited usefulness, being based on comparative data of questionable relevance for interpreting ancient Israel. Nonetheless, scholarly investigation builds on comparative data whose relevance for understanding the biblical tradition is continually being tested. For example, Wilson (1980) applied anthropological and sociological methods to gather data on the social roles of Israel's

276

prophets. He referred to the entire spectrum of prophetic activity in ancient Israel by the general term "intermediary." Thus he employed terminology that he believed would not oversimplify the ancient or modern data on prophecy but would, instead, relate the individuals being analyzed to their cultural settings and not to the supernatural. Wilson distinguished between two types of intermediaries: central and peripheral. Central intermediaries seek to maintain the status quo of the society; peripheral intermediaries seek social change, since they tend to lack social status and function on the fringes of society. Wilson maintained that central and peripheral intermediaries are not opposites but lie along a continuum where movement is possible; a shift from one category of intermediary to the other usually indicates a shift in the nature of the intermediary's social role (1980, 27-28).

While Wilson's study of prophecy drew on comparative anthropological and sociological data, D. Petersen (1981) applied sociological role theory in order to understand the prophetic function. B. Long (1982) and T. Overholt (1989) represent biblical scholars who have turned to British structural anthropology (the study of social phenomena in terms of how the phenomena function within the larger social structure) and ethnographies (descriptions rather than analyses) of Native Americans for their studies of Israelite prophecy.

Thus the current theoretical scene is made up of diverse social-scientific paradigms. Concurrent with the rise of social-scientific criticism in the 1960s was the beginning of women's studies in North America, which resulted in scholarship that focused on gender issues in the Bible (Feminist Interpretation*§). Approaches from the social sciences provided biblical scholars with an avenue to explore the power and danger (due to their polyvalence of meanings) of biblical stories that inform contemporary attitudes about women's social roles. C. Meyers (1988) relied on comparative data to contextualize gender issues within the preindustrialized non-Western peasant society of the Hebrew Bible. Her research centered on the social analysis of early Israel developed by Gottwald but focused specifically on women's role in the central highlands in premonarchical Israel. She argued that equality between the sexes existed in Israel's formative years and that the institution of the monarchy and the development of hierarchical political structures saw the erosion of women's power and authority vis-à-vis those of men. The impact of hierarchical social control under the monarchy as the context for the limitation of women's roles (as well as those of men) has found corroboration in studies of the Deuteronomistic law code as an institutionalized means for change in family organization. These studies show that the power of the nuclear family was expanded at the expense of the power of the extended kinship group (C. Pressler 1993).

The social world of family and kinship in ancient Israel is a topic whose importance is recognized by theorists from diverse social-scientific perspectives. Comparative anthropological data has helped scholars to reconstruct the kinship basis of ancient Israelite social organization, making it possible to locate the interconnection between the family household, the clan, and the lineage, while recognizing that these terms may hold different meanings in different periods. For example, the *bê'âb* ("father's house") referred, in the postexilic period, to individuals able to trace their ancestry to those who took part in the Babylonian exile, while earlier in Israelite history the term referred to a co-residential unit composed of related individuals and servants. Precision in analyzing residential units cannot always be found in Hebrew terminology because the same Hebrew term is often used to delineate more than one of the groupings analyzed by social scientists.

The analysis of kinship organization in light of cross-cultural data provides the opportunity for the integration of social-scientific research paradigms. For example, the topics of family structure, gender, and political organization converge in N. Steinberg's analysis of Genesis (1993). Her work reveals the patrilineal basis for marriage and family in ancient Israel, with a preference for patrilineal endogamy as the genealogical skeleton of the family line of Terah through his son Abraham. Of related interest, N. Jay's (1992) sociological and anthropological investigation of sacrifice leads her to argue that the ancient Israelite emphasis on patrilineage required a ritualization process that shifted reproductive emphasis away from the mother, who biologically bore a son, to the father in whose patrilineage the son takes his place. The conclusions of Steinberg and Jay complement Wilson's earlier study (1977) of the anthropological significance of genealogies in social and political organization. Moreover, social anthropologist J. Goody's (1990) cross-cultural analysis of kinship and family frequently includes examples from the Hebrew Bible, illustrating that ancient Israel can be understood in light of preindustrialized non-Western patrilineally based societies.

Finally, of particular interest to scholars is the social world of Israelite religion. Social anthropologist M. Douglas (1966) studied dietary practices as a reflection of Israelite social organization. Her research revealed that the ancient Israelite distinction between clean and unclean symbolizes the biblical world's attempt to classify and organize the disorderly natural world around it. Douglas's interpretation of Israelite religion has been influential in the writings of biblical scholars, who now understand the meaning and function of the ritual laws of the Bible as expressions of Israelite social concerns. Just as Douglas's work has been embraced by biblical scholarship, so also the approach of structural anthropologist C. Lévi-Strauss has been employed by E. Leach (1969) to analyze the biblical narratives. Leach's work, comparing biblical narratives and mythological traditions (Mythology and Biblical Studies*§), serves to undermine the putative dichotomy between the biblical tradition and the so-called primitive narrative tradition emphasized by earlier theological approaches to the texts.

To realize the potential of social-scientific criticism, biblical scholarship must move toward integration of the results of social-scientific research paradigms. After this has been accomplished, there must be a synthesis of the findings of social-scientific criticism with the conclusions of historical-critical study and theology as well as those of archaeology (an enterprise presently under way). Finally, this synthesis must be accomplished with methodological sensitivity to the biblical material and proper use of appropriate comparative data.

Boer (2002) contains essays responding to, critiquing, and expand upon Gottwalds work. Douglas has expanded her anthropological analysis to Numbers (1993) and further refined her work on Leviticus (1999). Perdue (1997) contains recent studies of the Israelite family. Sparks (1996) discusses Israelite understandings of ethnicity. Van Seters (1999) has written a full length social science commentary on the Pentateuch. Recent collections of social science studies on the Hebrew Bible are in Chalcraft (1997) and Simkins and Cook (1999),

Bibliography: **Roland Boer,** *Tracking "The Tribes of Yahweh": On the Trail of a Classic* (JSOTSup 351, 2002). **R. P. Carroll,** *When Prophecy Failed: Cognitive Dissonance in the Prophetic Traditions of the OT* (1979). **C. E. Carter and C. L. Meyers** (eds.), *Community, Identity, and Ideology: Social-scientific Approaches to the HB* (Sources for Biblical and Theological Study 6, 1996). **A. Causse,** "Du Groupe ethnique a la communauté religieuse: Les Problèmes Sociologique du Judaisme," *RHPR* 14 (1934) 285-335; *Du Groupe ethnique a la communaut, religieuse: Les Problemes Sociologique de la religion d'Israel* (*Études d' histoire et de philosophie religieuses* 33, 1937). **D. J. Chalcraft,** *Social-Scientific Old Testament Criticism: A Sheffield Reader* (Biblical Seminar Series 47, Sheffield Rseaders series 12, 1997). **A. Deissmann,** *Light from the Ancient East* (1908; ET rev. ed. 1927). **M. Douglas,** *Purity and Danger: An Analysis of Concepts of Pollution and Taboo* (1966); *In the Wilderness: The Doctrine of Defilement in the Book of Numbers* (JSOTSup 158, 1993); *Leviticus as Literature* (1999). **H. Eilberg-Schwartz,** *The Savage in Judaism: An Anthropology of Israelite Religion and Ancient Judaism* (1990). **J. Flanagan**, *David's Social Drama: A Hologram of Israel's Early Iron Age* (JSOTSup 73, 1988). **J. Goody,** *The Oriental, the Ancient, and the Primitive: Systems* *of Marriage and the Family in the Pre-industrial Societies of Eurasia* (1990). **N. K. Gottwald,** *The Tribes of Yahweh: A Sociology of the Religion of Liberated Israel, 1250-1050 BCE* (1979). **N. Jay,** *Throughout Your Generations Forever: Sacrifice, Religion, and Paternity* (1992). **E. Leach,** "The Legitimation of Solomon," *Genesis as Myth and Other Essays* (1969). **N. P. Lemche,** *Ancient Israel: A New History of Israelite Society* (BibSem 5, 1988). **A. Lods,** *Israel, des origines au milieu du VIIIe siecle* (1930). **B. O. Long,** "The Social World of Ancient Israel," *Int* 37 (1982) 243-55. **D. B. Martin,** "Social-scientific Criticism," *To Each Its Own Meaning: An Introduction to Biblical Criticisms and Their Application* (ed. S. L. McKenzie and S. R. Haynes, 1993) 103-19. **G. Mendenhall,** *The Tenth Generation: The Origins of the Biblical Tradition* (1973). **C. Meyers,** *Discovering Eve: Ancient Israelite Women in Context* (1988). **M. Noth,** *A History of Pentateuchal Traditions* (1948; ET 1972). **T. W. Overholt,** *Channels of Prophecy: The Social Dynamics of Prophetic Activity* (1989). **J. Pedersen,** *Israel: Its Life and Culture* (1920-34; ET 1926-40). **L. G. Perdue,** ed., *Families in Ancient Israel* (Family, Religion, and Culture, 1997). **D. L. Petersen,** *The Roles of Israel's Prophets* (JSOTSup 17, 1981). **C. Pressler,** *The View of Women Found in the Deuteronomic Family Laws* (1993). **M. Daniel Carroll R.** *Rethinking Contexts, Rereading Texts: Contributions from the Social Sciences to Biblical Interpretation* (JSOTSup 299, 2000) **J. W. Rogerson,** *Anthropology and the OT* (1979). **R. A. Simkins and S. L. Cook,** *The Social World of the Hebrew Bible: Twenty-Five Years of the Social Sciences in the Academy* 87 (*Semeia,* 1999). **D. L. Smith,** *The Religion of the Landless: The Social Context of the Babylonian Exile* (1989). **W. R. Smith,** *The Religion of the Semites* (1889, 1894[2], repr. 1972). **K. L. Sparks,** *Ethnicity and Identity in Ancient Israel: Prolegomena to the Study of Ethnic Sentiments and Their Expression in the Hebrew Bible* (1996). **L. Stager,** "The Archaeology of the Family in Ancient Israel," *BASOR* 260 (l985) 1-35. **N. Steinberg,** *Kinship and Marriage in Genesis: A Household Economics Perspective* (1993). **J. Van Seters,** *The Pentateuch: A Social-Science Commentary* (Trajectories 1, 1999). **R. de Vaux,** *Ancient Israel: Social Institutions* (1958-60; ET 1961). **J. Wellhausen,** *Reste arabischem Heidentums* (1897). **R. R. Wilson,** *Genealogy and History in the Biblical World* (YNER 7, 1977); *Prophecy and Society in Ancient Israel* (1980); *Sociological Approaches to the OT* (GBS, 1984).

N. Steinberg

SOCIAL SCIENCE METHODS

Sociology and Hebrew Bible Studies

Although some social scientists define sociology as one among other Social-scientific*§ specialties, it will be used here as a cover term for the whole body of the social sciences as they are used in a systematic study of the structure and development of the totality of a given society. Sociological studies may be divided into three broad categories that may, at times, be intertwined: (1) social description, (2) social history, and (3) social theory.

Social description is essentially the explanation and elucidation of the institutions and customs of the biblical community. Its primary source is the biblical text, augmented and illuminated by archaeological evidence. Judicious but limited use is made of information derived from ancient, and occasionally modern, societies deemed comparable to the biblical community; but the biblical texts are the controlling factor. Social history may be understood in two ways. First, it takes into account the changes that took place in the long history of the biblical community. Social descriptions of one era may be vastly different from those of another period, since there is recognition that the life of the biblical community was dynamic, not static. Social historians as a rule, however, restrict themselves to a description of the changes (what happened) and bracket consideration of the reasons for those changes (why it happened). Second, social history may refer to attempts to pay more attention to factors often omitted or minimized in traditional histories, which tend to focus on politics, rulers, aristocrats, and the producers and transmitters of high culture. The social historian attempts to adduce evidence, often sparse in the preserved texts, that delineates as broad a picture as possible of the total life of the society. Family structures, the means of economic production, daily life of the mass of the population, etc. are used to provide a picture of the social unit as a whole and to describe the changes that took place in that unit. The emphasis remains, however, on the description of change and not on an explanation of the causes of change.

An increasing number of scholars contend that social description and social history as defined above are inadequate for the sociological task. Although these scholars use social description and social history, they maintain that sociological study must also attempt to account for social change. A primary feature of their program is the use of macrosocial theory. Macrotheory (which will be discussed more fully below) concentrates on the total life of a given society, often uses Cross-Cultural*§ models to illuminate data from that society and/or to fill in lacunae in the data, and relies on the generalizing conclusions of one or more recognized social theorists. The extent to which macro-theory may be appropriate for study of the Hebrew Bible is perhaps the most important, and as yet unresolved, issue to be confronted. Before addressing the contemporary state of the discussion, however, it is appropriate to give a brief overview of sociological interpretation prior to the middle of the twentieth century.

1. *Brief History of Sociological Study to the Mid-twentieth Century.* Occasional references that may be called social description are to be found in the Hebrew Bible itself and in scattered comments in Jewish and Christian interpreters in the succeeding centuries. Concentrated and more systematic sociological study of the Hebrew Bible, however, began in the mid-nineteenth century as a response to the finds of Near Eastern Archaeology*§ and the emergence of the social-scientific disciplines of cultural anthropology and sociological theory. (H. Hahn [1954] provides a convenient summary of the period 1850-1950: for anthropology, 44-82; sociology, 157-84; and archaeology, 185-225. A briefer but useful account is that of R. Wilson 1984, 1-25.)

The anthropologist who most influenced Hebrew Bible studies was E. Tylor, who assumed that a universal primitive mentality lay behind all cultural forms, including religion, and that these forms developed through a common evolutionary process. Since there was a common beginning and a common process, material from widely separated societies could be used in comparative studies. Hebrew Bible scholars, led by W. R. Smith[§], quickly began to use Tylor's method. Smith restricted his comparative studies primarily to early Arab societies, with occasional material from contemporary bedouin groups; but J. Frazer[§] expanded this approach by including, somewhat unsystematically, evidence for all societies, ancient and modern, that seemed to have some bearing on the beliefs and customs of the biblical community.

Cultural anthropologists following Tylor abandoned the broad comparative approach and insisted that anthropology should focus on the total life of one society. Comparative materials could be used only in a secondary illustrative manner. Most, although not all, biblical scholars responded to this change by withdrawing from overt use of anthropology for biblical study.

The most significant social theorist for Hebrew Bible studies was (and, in modified forms, continues to be) M. Weber[§]. Many of his specific conclusions, limited as they were by his dependence on the biblical scholarship of his day, are today abandoned or radically revised. However, two of his major points—that religion provided the uniting bond for the people called Israel (covenant), and that leadership of this covenant people originally resided in charismatic figures not located in an established political setting—continue to have considerable influence in biblical studies, albeit in a number of divergent forms.

Two of his general theses also remain of central importance in sociological study. First, he insisted that a macro-social theory must make use of ideal types, hypothetical constructs that may be used to compare and elucidate actual situations; and these ideal types, when expanded, may then provide a macro-social model. Second, he rejected the Marxist view, which saw religion arising solely from the material conditions of life. It is too much to maintain, as has often been said, that Weber gave religion the earlier role in shaping societal structures. It is more accurate to understand his position as affirming a dynamic interaction between the spiritual values of a society and the socio-cultural matrix in which those values are operative. Full attention must be given to each and not in isolation from the other. Each influenced and was influenced by the other.

A number of scholars in the 1920s and 1930s—both in larger works like the histories of A. Causse[§] and A. Lods[§] and in more limited, specialized studies—directly or indirectly used Weber's insights regarding the interaction of religion and society. A potentially promising, but ultimately abortive, foray into sociological study was made by the Chicago school, represented in Hebrew Bible studies especially by W. C. Graham and H. G. May (see also L. Wallis). Graham and May attempted to trace the development of religious concepts in the context of the changing social process. Their primary concern was not with Israelite society as such but with the aspects of that society that might contribute to a fuller understanding of the nature and the development of Israelite religion.

2. *Contemporary Sociological Study.* The "new" sociological study of the Hebrew Bible is, as was noted above, not altogether new. Attention to the importance of economics, social organization, and social Psychology*[§] appeared in the works of, e.g., A. Alt[§], M. Noth[§], W. F. Albright[§], J. Pedersen[§], and others who followed their leads. Further, form-critical studies (see Form Criticism*[§]) by their very nature were required, in theory at least, to take seriously the social setting. It is fair to say, however, that, for the most part, sociological observations were of an unsystematic nature and paid little if any attention to sociological theory as such.

While recognizing that there are threads of continuity in sociological study of the Hebrew Bible from the mid-nineteenth century to the present, two features may be deemed distinctive of the contemporary period: (a) a more systematic use of macro-theory and (b) more attention to the role of techno-economic factors in the study of society. Macrotheory, as mentioned earlier, concentrates on the total life of a society and may use crosscultural models to fill in lacunae in the data directly available from that society. To this extent it is akin to one of the definitions of social history discussed earlier. The new approach, however, makes more refined use of techno-economic data.

Archaeology, particularly as it has shifted from emphasis on description to explanation; physical anthropology; geography; climatology; demography; and other disciplines, techniques, and methods not ordinarily included in the social sciences are increasingly employed. Use of such information is, of course, not altogether new in sociological study; but it is now more pervasive and more refined. It seems evident that, as more data become available and as existing data are evaluated by more rigid macro-theoretical methods a more comprehensive social history of Israel, although certainly not a complete one, can be written. (For more detailed discussion of specific contemporary contributions to sociological study of the Hebrew Bible, see the excellent bibliographies in N. Gottwald 1983, 168-84; 1985, 1612-65; a good overview of a number of the most important works through 1983 in Wilson; and a succinct summary of the state of the field through 1985 in R. Culley.)

The following areas of Hebrew Bible study have received extensive attention from scholars using sociological methods.

a. Israel's origins and the formation of the state. The problem that has thus far been most broadly addressed is the question of Israel's origins and the formation of the state. It has long been a commonplace assumption of biblical study that Israel's origins are to be found in a nomadic or seminomadic society. This was true whether a conquest model or a settlement model for Israel's emergence in Canaan was adopted. This view also underlay Weber's starting point that early Israelite society is to be understood as a result of the inner tension between those Israelites who reflected the institutions and ideals of a desert society and those who were rooted in an agricultural society.

This prevailing, though not unanimous, view was directly challenged by G. Mendenhall[§] (1962), who proposed a more appropriate model, which, although recognizing the catalyst supplied by a small group of Yahweh worshipers, stressed the central role of disaffected Canaanite serfs. (Wallis had, much earlier, made a strikingly similar proposal.) Gottwald[§], although operating from an ideological perspective quite different from Mendenhall's, has developed the general thesis with massive sociological data. Techno-economic studies by Mendenhall, Gottwald, and many others have attempted to provide evidence for the model popularly called "peasant revolt," which has found favor with a number of Hebrew Bible historians and has found its way into many popular textbooks. On the other hand, it has also been sharply criticized as being a pure construct with no biblical evidence to support it.

It is too early to judge whether the seminomadic theory has been dealt a fatal, or even a serious, blow; however, two significant items for a broader contribution of sociological study of the Hebrew Bible emerge from the debate as it has been carried on thus far. First, it has highlighted the necessity of using techno-economic data available both in the biblical texts and in cogent cross-cultural models. Further research on such data may support or refute the theory, but such research is now seen to be mandatory. Second, and perhaps more important, although the use of a new sociological model may or may not provide new answers, it poses new questions that must be addressed to the biblical texts. That, in itself, is a not insignificant contribution.

b. The emergence of the monarchy. Closely related to and in part congruent with the issues of Israel's origins is analysis of the emergence of the monarchy. Two major issues have largely dominated sociological study of this question. The first is an attempt to give a social description of the structure of Israelite society in the period prior to the formation of the nation state; the second is to propose reasons for the social change from confederacy (tribal league) to monarchy. With respect to the former, most proposals have used the anthropological model of movement from family to extended family based on genuine kinship, to tribe (clan), to chiefdom, to state (geographical, though stereotypically related to kinship.) Some scholars, however, question whether the biblical evidence or cross-cultural anthropological data will permit so stylized a description. Further study is mandatory before a more precise description than the admittedly uneven and inconsistent picture given in Judges and in the early chapters of 1 Samuel can be affirmed with confidence.

The most attractive feature of the preceding model is that of chiefdom, which seems to provide the best explanation of the reign of Saul and of the early reign of David (J. Flanagan 1988). It is proposed that, even before Saul, larger or smaller geographical areas were under the sway of local chiefs, who had displaced familial units for purposes of military defense and regulation of trade. Thus the development of chieftaincy paved the way for the emergence of the state.

Most historians, accepting the biblical evidence at face value, assert that military and political pressure from the Philistines was the single factor that precipitated the rise of the nation state. Certain recent studies maintain that the picture is much more complicated. Although agreeing that the Philistines were a (if not the) critical factor, they insist that fuller recognition needs to be given to the economic collapse, especially of international trade, that characterized the late Bronze Age. It is not yet clear whether the data adduced are compelling. It may well be that the older view focusing on Philistine military pressure is more cogent; but, at the very least, the new sociological studies are valuable in posing new questions, if not necessarily providing new answers.

c. Prophecy. A third area that has received considerable sociological attention is Prophecy[‡†§]. Social theory, social psychology, and cross-cultural anthropological studies have been used to examine anew a wide variety of issues, the first dealing with the social location of prophecy and the prophets. While earlier scholars were primarily concerned with the relationship between the prophets and the cult, recent studies have extended this issue to include not only the cult, but also the establishment as a whole, distinguishing between prophets who worked within the establishment and those who were outside it. This is a useful perspective but should be tempered by the recognition that the same prophet could from time to time be cast now in one role, now in another.

Another aspect of social location is the attempt to refine and sharpen the social setting (*Sitz im Leben*) of prophetic oracles. The most promising result thus far is the awareness that the quest for the original setting, valuable as it was, is not adequate. One should consider not only the setting in which the genre arose (and not all genres may be related to a specific setting) but also the variety of settings in which specific oracles might be used. Further, attention should be given to the broader cultural environment within which prophetic oracles were pronounced or later circulated. The interlocking of a broad variety of matrices within society constitutes the most valuable vantage point for determining the interaction between oracle and hearer/reader.

Social function is closely related to social location. The older view of the prophets as isolated religious geniuses proclaiming beautiful spiritual and moral truths has largely been abandoned. The prophets were intimately involved in societal life, and recent sociological study has emphasized that this involvement took two opposing forms: social maintenance and social change. Prophets located within the establishment buttressed the legitimacy of that establishment while the outsiders condemned existing social conditions and called for radical change. This paradigm is useful but not exhaustive; some aspects of prophecy cannot be reduced to social concerns.

Sociological study has also addressed the question of prophetic authority and legitimacy, making use of cross-cultural anthropological studies. Although legitimacy and authority may derive from institutional structures, it is societal consensus about how a prophet should behave and acceptance of the general contours of his/her message that ultimately bestow legitimacy and authority.

Anthropological studies have been used to illuminate prophetic behavior in both its physiological and its psychological manifestations. The nature and social impact of ecstatic behavior and stereotypical speech patterns in a number of cultures have been evaluated by socio-psychological criteria. The extent to which such cross-cultural data may be useful in the study of biblical prophets is not yet clear, but a promising beginning has been made (Wilson 1984, 26-27, 67-80).

d. Apocalypticism. A number of studies have examined the sociological factors that contributed to the ebbing (cessation is too strong a word) of prophecy and the emergence of Apocalypticism*§. On the theoretical level, it is proposed that the seedbed of apocalypticism lies in an experience of group alienation and/or a sense of felt deprivation. Anthropological studies of current or recent messianic/millenarian movements have been used to explicate the social setting of apocalypticism in the biblical texts. Sociological studies have also attempted to contribute to the much-discussed issues of the date of apocalypticism's origin and of its literary and ideational sources.

P. Hanson (1985), drawing primarily on the so-called sociology of knowledge, has dated the dawn of apocalypticism in the early postexilic period, which he has depicted in terms of a polarity between realists and visionaries. The sociological contribution to delineating the sources of apocalypticism has, to this point, been minimal. It is increasingly clear that apocalypticism has no univocal source. Further sociological investigations may clarify the interactions among prophecy, royal cult, myth-wisdom, and Hellenistic sources that coalesced to form its shape and content.

e. Law and wisdom. Finally, cultural anthropologists outside the field of biblical studies have devoted considerable attention to biblical laws, especially those relating to purity and sacrifice (Douglas 1966), and responses by biblical scholars have been forthcoming. It is probable that new sociological studies will review the still-classic treatments of Alt and Noth on the origins of Israelite law. In the last decades of the twentieth century, there has also been considerable scholarly debate on the locus of Israelite wisdom, with clan ethic, royal court, or school being most prominently proposed. It seems likely that no single social setting provides a comprehensive explanation, but reinvestigation of the germane texts from a sociological perspective, as yet in a nascent form, may shed light on the issue. The few studies available thus far tend to indicate that our present wisdom texts, as distinguished from the origins of wisdom as such, come from a relatively well-to-do socio-economic group. Whether further study will confirm or negate this provisional conclusion remains moot.

3. *Problems and Prospects.* Sociological study of the Hebrew Bible has been criticized even by scholars who accept, in principle, its potential contribution. (A more fundamental criticism by some anthropologists who maintain that social science methods can legitimately be used only for living societies ["social scientists study living people not books"] is too sweeping and hardly represents a substantive position in the social sciences.) Criticisms vary in scope and intensity but fall into three major categories.

First, considerable caution must be exercised in choosing a particular macrotheory as a paradigm for assessing the data (e.g., adoption of a Marxist perspective will yield quite different results from the use of Weberian or one of the many neo-Weberian approaches). Biblical scholars engaged in the sociological enterprise need to be aware of the enormous diversity existing among social scientists and to keep abreast of developments in the social sciences. Pluralistic use of social theory is desirable, although it should not be diluted to an eclecticism that selects from here and there social theories and comparative examples that seem to elucidate a particular issue. Sociological rigor is mandatory.

Second, crosscultural materials may be useful in a supplementary manner but should not be used in an extensive and indiscriminate way when evidence in the biblical texts is sparse or lacking altogether. The biblical texts must remain the primary source. And third, there is the question of the centrality of sociological methods for interpretation. Does sociological study, as some of its practitioners seem to imply, provide a paradigmatic breakthrough, or is it a useful, but auxiliary, discipline for historical study as it was for Weber? It is probable that most Hebrew Bible scholars, at least for the foreseeable future, will adopt the latter option (Wilson 1984, 28-29).

What, then, are the prospects for the future of sociological study? Some of the problems already addressed in this article—e.g., early Israelite history, prophecy, and apocalypticism—will surely be expanded and refined. Two others—law and wisdom—seem ripe for detailed investigation. Two further areas of study may be suggested. The first is the sociology of litera-ture, not to be confused with the "new" Literary*§ criticism, whose relationship with sociolog-ical study remains problematical. Investigations in this area will not be simply an extension and refinement of the social setting in which biblical texts emerged, although this is legitimate and necessary. Sociology of literature, as defined here, while paying careful attention to the origi-nal setting and function of a text, focuses on the continuing sociological impact of the text in the ongoing life of the communities that preserved it. Ultimately such study will embrace the whole question of the origin and significance of Canon§. The second area is the complex issue of the sociological setting of early Christianity and its interaction with Judaism. Intense study of both canonical and noncanonical literature of that period has yielded fruitful results.

It might be expected that sociological study will issue in new textbooks that take much more seriously the sociological dimensions of the Hebrew Bible (Gottwald [1985, 1993] is already an example). Finally, as the results of sociological study become more pervasive, covering the whole of the biblical period, it may become possible to produce a genuine social history that will take due account of the total structure of the biblical community, the nature of the litera-ture it produced, and the social worlds underlying both its structure and its literature.

Boer (2002) contains essays responding to, critiquing, and further developing Gottwald's work. Douglas has extended her anthropological analysis of purity in the Hebrew Bible to Numbers (1993) and further developed it for Leviticus (1999). Sparks has investigated the con-cept of ethnicity in ancient Israel (1996). Van Seters has written a full scale commentary on the Pentateuch that incorporates a sociological approach. Recent collections of sociological studies of the Hebrew Bible include Daniel Carroll R. (2000) and Simkins and Cook (1999).

Bibliography: Roland Boer, *Tracking "The Tribes of Yahweh": On the Trail of a Classic* (JSOTSup 351, 2002). **C. E. Carter and C. L. Meyers** (eds.), *Community, Identity and Ideology: Social Science Approaches to the HB* (Sources for Biblical and Theological Study 6, 1996). **D. J. Chalcraft,** *Social-Scientific OT Criticism* (BibSem 47, 1997). **R. E. Clements** (ed.), *The World of Ancient Israel: Sociological, Anthropological, and Political Perspectives* (1989). **R. C. Culley,** "Exploring New Directions," *The HB and Its Modern Interpreters* (ed. D. A. Knight and G. M. Tucker, SBLBMI 1, 1985) 167-200. **M. Douglas,** *Purity and Danger: An Analysis of Concepts of Pollution and Taboo* (1966); *In the Wilderness: The Doctrine of Defilement in the Book of Numbers* (JSOTSup 158, 1993); *Leviticus as Literature* (1999). **J. W. Flanagan,** *David's Social Drama: A Hologram of Israel's Early Iron Age* (SWBA 35, 1988). **N. H. Gottwald,** "Sociological Method in Biblical Research and Contemporary Peace Studies," *ABQ* 2 (1983) 142-84. *The HB* (1985). *The HB in Its Social World and in Ours* (SemeiaSt, 1993). **H. F. Hahn,** *The OT in Modern Research* (1954; rev. ed. 1966). **P. D. Hanson,** "Apocalyptic Literature," *The HB and Its Modern Interpreters* (ed. D. A. Knight and G. M. Tucker, SBLBMI 1, 1985) 465-88. **B. Lang** (ed.), *Anthropological Approaches to the OT* (IRT 8, 1985). **N. P. Lemche,** *Early Israel: Anthropological and Historical Studies on the Israelite Society Before the Monarchy* (VTSup 37, 1985). **A. D. H. Mayes,** *The OT in Sociological Perspective* (1989). **G. E. Mendenhall,**

"The Hebrew Conquest of Palestine," *BA* 25 (1962) 66-87. **L. G. Perdue,** *Families in Ancient Israel* (The Family, Religion, and Culture Series, 1997). **M. Daniel Carroll R.** *Rethinking Contexts, Rereading Texts: Contributions from the Social Sciences to Biblical Interpretation* (JSOTSup 299, 2000). **J. W. Rogerson,** *Anthropology and the OT* (1978); "The Use of Sociology in OT Studies," *Congress Volume* (VTSup 36; 1985) 245-56; (ed.), *The Bible in Ethics: The Second Sheffield Colloquium* (1995). **W. Schottroff,** "Soziologie und Alten Testament," *VF* 19 (1974) 46-66. **R. A. Simkins and S. L. Cook,** *The Social World of the Hebrew Bible: Twenty-Five Years of the Social Sciences in the Academy 87* (*Semeia*, 1999). **K. L. Sparks,** *Ethnicity and Identity in Ancient Israel: Prolegomena to the Study of Ethnic Sentiments and Their Expression in the Hebrew Bible* (1996) **J. Van Seters,** *The Pentateuch: A Social-Science Commentary* (Trajectories 1, 1999). **R. R. Wilson,** *Sociological Approaches to the OT* (1984).

J. F. PRIEST

SOCIAL SCIENCE METHODS

Sociology and New Testament Studies

1. *Interest in Knowledge.* Sociologically oriented exegesis has two different interests in knowledge of the biblical text, one historical and the other hermeneutical (Hermeneutics*§). The historical interest consists in understanding through Social-scientific*§ (or, more specifically, sociological) categories the reality a text represented or constituted at the time of its origin. Theological, philological, psychological (Psychology and Biblical Studies*§), and other categories are not dismissed as improper but, rather, as insufficient. This insufficiency can be addressed by including the social world of the New Testament age in the interpretative process. One must ask what typical interpersonal behavior was like both in the Christian communities and in their larger environment. Who had regular social interaction with whom? Who commanded? Who obeyed? Who was economically dependent upon whom? Beyond this, one must investigate the causal and functional relationships in which these social actualities took place. For example, the relationship between early Christianity and slavery is not sufficiently grasped until one asks not only what the social position of slaves was in the primitive Christian communities, but also which external social influences appeared in this arrangement, and what influence this arrangement had on the greater social reality. The historical interest directing such questions can be focused on individual New Testament texts as well as on an array of these texts.

The hermeneutical interest in knowledge begins with the insight that communication requires that communicants share a common social world. Thus, knowledge of the social world of the New Testament is necessary for communication with New Testament texts but knowledge of the place of the interpreter in his or her social world is also vital. In its full sense, therefore, sociologically oriented exegesis requires mediation between diverse social worlds.

2. *Types.* Sociologically oriented exegesis is not a unitary method. A distinction can be made between socio-historical, sociological, and materialistic exegesis. Such a differentiation has some justification, but it is nonetheless problematic.

The relationship between socio-historical and sociological exegesis is often laid out as one between description and explanation (i.e., between the collection of historical material and the interpretation of that material with the help of sociological theory). It is reasonable to ascribe to social history the depiction of typical interpersonal behavior, and to sociology the interpretation of the broader social functions of this behavior. Thus, socio-historical exegesis can be seen as the necessary precondition for actual sociological exegesis. To be sure, this distinction is not absolute: No assembling of material is free of theory, and not every theory is applicable to all forms of material. Accordingly, it is impossible to engage in only one of the two endeavors to the exclusion of the other, though different emphases are permissible.

Materialistic exegesis fits the framework of a sociologically oriented exegesis in its stress on the significance of social actualities and processes for the origin as well as for the understanding of New Testament texts. Materialistic exegesis also shares the concern to uncover the societal and political relevance of the New Testament for our time. In what has become its classical form in the work of F. Belo (1975 [ET 1981]) and M. Clévénot (1976 [ET 1985]), materialistic exegesis, however, exhibits two peculiarities: It uses structural methods (Structuralism and Deconstruction*§) to interpret texts; it is based on a materialistic hermeneutic that makes use, above all, of K. Marx and L. Althusser; and it consciously asserts a fixed philosophical, psychological, political, and economic worldview as the interpretative horizon of the New Testament.

The often-raised objections to materialistic exegesis—that it has an inadequate historical orientation (structuralism), an insufficient capacity for self-correction, and an unfounded denial of the relative autonomy of the text in relation to the means of production (historical material-ism)—are too severe. While of some merit regarding the classical representatives of this approach, such objections are invalid for later attempts (e.g., that of C. Myers in 1988, to develop a polit-ical reading that stands between materialistic and sociological exegesis and attempts to draw on elements of modern Literary*[§] criticism).

Apart from Myers's socio-literary approach and related methods (S. Freyne 1988), two other methodologies cannot be brought under the tripartite schema of socio-historical, sociological, and materialistic exegesis. The first of these is the cultural-anthropological method—repre-sented above all by B. Malina and based on the work of M. Douglas—in which the social expe-rience (i.e., the evaluative interpretation of social conditions by the society at large) is the central focus. Of primary interest in this approach is how the interpretation expresses itself in the formation of symbols and in the communication of the respective societies. The second approach is the socio-rhetorical method, which employs a combination of elements from diverse disciplines (rhetoric, modern literary criticism, and the sociology of literature). According to V. Robbins, "A socio-rhetorical approach . . . analyzes the text as a strategic state-ment in a situation characterized by 'webs of significance' containing an intermingling of social, cultural, religious, and literary traditions and conventions in the Mediterranean world" (1984, 6).

3. *History of Research.* The history of sociologically oriented exegesis of the New Testament can be divided into two phases. The first extends from 1880 to 1930; the second, from 1970 to the present. Before 1880, New Testament exegesis showed scarcely any interest in the social realities of early Christianity and its environment.

a. 1880-1930. During this period a series of books and articles appeared (E. Hatch 1883; C. Heinrici 1887; A. von Harnack 1884, 1893[2], 1902; E. von Dobschütz 1902; E. Lohmeyer 1921, 1925; J. Jeremias 1923; R. Schumacher 1924; C. Cadoux 1925; F. Grant 1926; W. Bauer 1927) that were concerned with the social aspects of early Christianity (the forms of the community, the life of the community, its mission, its environment). The reconstruction of the life of the lower classes of imperial Rome by A. Deissmann[§] (1908, 1923[4]), based on papyri and inscrip-tions, became extremely well known. Deissmann's intention was to uncover the social back-ground of the New Testament. The rise of New Testament Form Criticism*[§] after 1919 (K. Schmidt 1919; M. Dibelius 1919; R. Bultmann 1921), with its search for the *Sitz im Leben* of New Testament genres, displayed a sociological interest in the wider sense. Such an interest was more specific in one movement of the so-called Chicago school, particularly in the works of S. J. Case[§] and S. Mathews[§] (who, from the standpoint of functionalism, interpreted early Christianity as an answer to the needs of society).

b. After 1970. After its practical disappearance for forty years (for a variety of reasons: dialectical theology, existential interpretation, redaction criticism, structuralism), the sociolog-ical approach to exegesis experienced a spectacular comeback in the seventies (also for various reasons: the crisis in historical-critical exegesis, a general interest in the social sciences in the sixties). This development led to a host of relevant investigations and to a confusing differenti-ation of approaches and methods (see below).

c. The relation of sociologically oriented exegesis and historical-critical exegesis. The soci-ological orientation is not a break with traditional historical criticism; it is, rather, (at least in many forms) a discharging of claims long-since made but still unfulfilled by historical criticism. Programmatic assertions relative to the history of New Testament times, the history of religions (*Religionsgeschichtliche Schule**[§]), form criticism, and even redaction criticism*[§] have long included references to the necessary consideration of the social dimension, e.g., social history, sociological determination of the *Sitz im Leben*, the connection between religious concepts and collective living conditions, and the connection between the evangelists' redaction and the situation of their communities. Such purposes were first realized in specifically social-scientific research and in some sociological investigations.

4. *Selected Approaches.*

a. Socio-historical approaches. M. Hengel's[§] (1968 [ET 1981]) approach can be understood as socio-historical research with a strong orientation toward historical criticism. In this treatment, the social circumstances of the succession to the historical Jesus*[§] were set off from the teacher-pupil relationship of the late rabbinate and from the succession of apocalyptic prophets (Apocalypticism*[§]; also Prophecy and Prophets, Hebrew Bible*[§]). The closest parallel to the calls of the disciples is, according to Hengel, "the call of the Hebrew Bible prophets through the God of Israel himself" (ET 1981, 98).

A. Malherbe (1977, 1983[2]) was as socio-historically oriented as Hengel. Malherbe stressed that "we should strive to know as much as possible about the actual social circumstances . . . before venturing theoretical descriptions or explanations of them" (1983[2], 20). In this work, based on lectures, he largely limited himself to the former: illuminating the relationship between Paul[†§] and the church in Thessalonica by a comparison of 1 Thess with texts from philosophical communities, especially from the Epicureans; investigating the social status of the early Christians and supporting a "new emerging consensus" (1983[2], 118 [cf. 31]), according to which this status is set clearly higher than in the earlier *communis opinio*; and discussing the issues of house-churches and hospitality in the early church.

P. Lampe offered a significant study in local social history (1987, 1989[2]). He made use of mainly literary but also epigraphic and archaeological sources in order to (among other things) reconstruct the distribution of Christians in Rome and the fractionalization of the Christian community. He pursued general as well as prosopographical information and characterized the relationship between both as the attempt "to color with concrete instances, generalizations which the sources themselves make" rather than to "project individual cases drawn from the sources onto a representative level—and by what method, even?" (1989[2], XI). Lampe came close to a sociology of knowledge when he went beyond the socio-historical explanation of the daily life of Christians in Roman cities to suggest "correlations between the situation and the expression of faith" (1989[2], 347; italics original), e.g., in the Shepherd of Hermas, in Marcion[§], in the Valentinians, etc. In doing so he protected himself against social history's monocausal explanations of theology: "Not static (e.g., super/substructure), but only more complex dynamic models will, in my estimation, help us further, if we want to uncover something of the mutual correlations between theology and social reality" (1989[2], 348; italics original). Lampe did not, however, present such models in his socio-historically oriented study.

Several studies in the 1990s focused on the question of egalitarian communities in early Christianity. Both A. Clarke (1993) and J. Chow (1992) tried to explain many of the problems Paul dealt with in 1 Corinthians by comparing the pattern of leadership in the Corinthian community to that of non-Christian Greco-Roman leadership. In their view, Paul struggled to replace secular hierarchical models of patronage and friendship that continued to shape the minds of the Corinthian community with truly Christian, egalitarian ones. This thesis has been countered by T. Schmeller (1995), whose comparison between Pauline communities and Greco-Roman associations offers a more nuanced view: Both kinds of groups show mixtures of hierarchical and egalitarian elements; what seems to be specific of Christian communities, however, is that solidarity forms part of their group-identity.

b. Specifically sociological approaches. Various exegetes have made use of M. Weber's[§] *verstehender Soziologie* (sociology of understanding objective meaning), in particular of his concept of charismatic authority and its routinization, in order to illuminate the structures of authority in the Jesus movement and in the early Christian communities. B. Holmberg (1978) showed how, in the early church, and especially with Paul, a process of institutionalization took place in which the purely charismatic relationship of authority between Jesus and his circle of disciples was gradually intermingled with rational and traditional elements. What is new in Holmberg's reconstruction is that this institutionalization is not understood as the inevitable fall from an original peak but as an intended and much longed-for manifestation of the authenticity of the charisma (1978, 166). With this move Holmberg seizes on the further inner-sociological development of the Weberian model. A charismatic movement not only calls the existing society into question but also is "in principle nothing less than the founding anew of society" (1978, 146). A primary institutionalization is already introduced by the charismatic leader (here the historical Jesus), then a secondary institutionalization is established by the administrative or leadership staff (here Paul in particular). In the early church the last development leads to such forms of authority as "the literal Jesus-tradition, the Christian moral teachings and code of behavior, the cult, and the all-powerful group of leaders" (1978, 201).

Probably the most influential contributions to the sociological exegesis of the New Testament stem from G. Theissen. Depending on the subject matter, Theissen combines Weber's charisma model with conflict or functionalistic theories. His best-known work, *Sociology of Early Palestinian Christianity* (1977, 1985[4] [ET 1978]), has been expanded via some essays in his collected volume, *Social Reality and the Early Christians* (1979, 1989[3] [ET 1992]). "The Jesus movement is...the renewal movement which Jesus called forth within Judaism in the Syro-Palestinian region from c. 30 to 70 C.E." (1985[4], 9). Its "inner structure was determined by the interaction of three roles: the wandering charismatics, their sympathizers in the local communities, and the revealer" (1985, 14). Jesus, the founder of the movement and its first wandering charismatic, remained after Easter as the transcendent revealer, its charismatic leader. The locally settled followers of the movement still did not form proper communities but, rather, as individual sympathizers and material supporters were the charismatically governed. In between the wandering charismatics and their sympathizers stood the disciples of Jesus in the narrower sense, who even before Easter constituted the charismatically qualified leadership staff of the movement and who after Easter (as wandering charismatics) became the actual bearers of the movement. Jesus' radical teachings of the renunciation of homeland, family, and possessions were meant only for the circle of wandering charismatics and were passed on by them. Their message of reconciliation was not drawn upon for the solution of the social crisis in Palestine, which was too sharply torn between class and political factions. While the Jesus movement was a failure there, it enjoyed great success in the Hellenistic cities. This transition brought with it, to be sure, a clear transformation: Local communities became the center of the movement, and the radical teachings, which could not be realized under sedentary conditions, were replaced by a socially conservative patriarchalism of love.

In addition to its expression in Weber's models, the sociology of knowledge has found repeated application in New Testament exegesis in the work of J. Elliott (1981). According to Elliott's analysis, it is an aim of 1 Peter to reconcile the community it addresses with their status as outsiders in society. They are encouraged to not give in to hostility and persecutions, which are to be understood as society's pressure to conform. To this end 1 Peter makes use of the image of the house: The house of the saints is cut off from the world, and as *oikos pneumatikos* (a spiritual house) the saints live in the *paroikia* (foreign parts). Precisely because they appear to the world as eccentrics, they prove themselves the elect. Thus a theological idea is used to legitimize a social reality. The image of the house is particularly good for this purpose because the community was, in fact, organized in house-churches; consequently, the social reality of being legitimized itself provides the image-material for theological reflection.

A broad palette of sociological lines and models was applied by both J. Gager (1975) and W. Meeks (1983). Gager's was concerned to apply tentatively to early Christianity sociological and anthropological models that are standard in the study of other religions in order to find new

insight on old issues: "the relationship between religion and social status, the enthusiastic character of the earliest Christian communities, their gradual transformation into a formidable religious and social institution, and the emergence of Christianity as the dominant religion of the
later Roman Empire" (1975, 2). Gager has gone farther than many other scholars. He investigates not only the social position of the early Christians and applies Weber's charisma model
to the structures of authority in the early church, as is usual, but also interprets early Christianity
as a millenarian movement. Further, he explains the Christian mission, active despite the delay
of the Parousia, through use of L. Festinger's theory of cognitive dissonance. Gager adheres to
the view that study of other religious movements (e.g., the Melanesian cargo cult) may fill in
much data otherwise lacking in the New Testament, as long as these movements belong to the
same sociological type as early Christianity.

More cautious but no less multifaceted is Meeks's study. He has presented a broad spectrum
of analyses of Pauline Christianity, from social history (e.g., city life and mobility in the
Roman Empire); to theoretical sociological approaches relating to status, the distribution of
power, etc.; to questions regarding the sociology of knowledge. Meeks has described himself
as a sociological eclectic and a moderate functionalist (1983, 6-7). His differentiated investigations regarding social status show that the Pauline communities offer a social cross section
of urban society from which only the highest and lowest levels are absent. The members of
these communities who most stand out are those with a higher inconsistency of status. Also of
high interest are the correlations between faith convictions and social situation, which Meeks
depicts without attempting to trace the one causally back to the other. Thus, for example, the
experience of social contradictions in the community corresponds to faith in the crucified
Messiah, who is then raised to the status of co-ruler with God: "They are weak in terms of
social power and status . . . yet they are exhilarated by experiences of power in their meetings"
(1983, 191).

c. Combinations of new exegetical approaches. While the interpreters presented up to this
point have remained more or less within the framework of historical criticism and sociology, S.
Freyne (1988) has included other new exegetical approaches in his work. In particular, he has
attempted to link sociological interest with literary criticism. Although, as the author confirms,
a sociological reading is interested in the "extra-textual referent," and literary criticism is, conversely, interested in the "intra-textual, fictional world" (1988, 7), Freyne sees a compatibility
nonetheless: "We cannot a priori exclude the possibility that some realistic features of the
narrative dimension of our texts may have a genuine contribution to make in recovering the
presumed actual world behind these texts" (1988, 12). Such realistic elements spring from the
concern of the author to persuade the reader via the probability of the presentation. Narrative
analysis of the text can, therefore, be helpful for a historical and sociological concern. Freyne
further sees a hermeneutical advantage in allowing the texts to speak first, instead of immediately analyzing them historically with specific interests. Consequently, he raises first of all the
narrative picture of Galilee in the individual Gospels (according to places, persons, and plot)
and tries, in a second step, to reconstruct Galilee as a social world (politically, ecologically, economically, culturally, religiously) and as the context of the Jesus movement. The resulting
analysis shows how Galilee, with its mix of traditional religious and progressive, barrier-break-
ing features became fertile ground for the Jesus movement.

d. Conclusion. In summary, one can recognize three trends in sociologically oriented exegesis of the New Testament: (1) The original excitement over the discovery of sociological models appears to have given way to a more critical stance. Socio-historical investigations again
enjoy great interest, with few theoretical handicaps. (2) The connection between social reality
and symbol-building, especially with regard to ideology (Ideological Criticism*§), is becoming
increasingly important. The "social world" is understood more and more as a "symbolic uni-

verse." (3) Combinations of the sociological with other novel approaches, especially with modern literary criticism, are gaining in importance.

More recent sociological investigations of the New Testament include: Burnett's reaction to and critique of the usual socio-exegetical emphasis on community and dyadic personality (2001), collections of essays using sociological approaches (Esler 2000; Pilch 2001; Stegemann, Malina, and Theissen 2002), analysis of first-century Palestinian social conditions (Hanson and Oakman 1998), full-length social-science commentaries (Malina and Pilch 2000, Malina and Rohrbaugh 2003[2]), reconstructions of ancient personalities (Malina and Neyrey 1996), revisions and updates of existing works (Malina 1981, 2001[3]), analysis of *basileia tou theou* ("kingdom of God," Malina, 1999), publication of sociologically oriented reference works (Pilch 1999), studies of the ancient family (Roh 2001), a comprehensive analysis of Pauline theology in light of Victor Turner's concept of liminality (Strecker 1999), and investigations into the symbolic world of early Christianity (Theissen 1999).

Bibliography: U. Bail (ed.), *Gott an den Rändern: Sozialgeschichtliche Perspektiven auf die Bibel* (1996). D. L. Balch (ed.), *Social History of the Matthean Community: Cross-disciplinary Approaches* (1991). W. Bauer, "Jesus der Galiläer," *Festschrift A. Jülicher* (1927) 16-34. F. Belo, *A Materialist Reading of the Gospel of Mark* (1975; ET 1981). K. Berger, "Wissenssoziologie und Exegese des Neuen Testaments," *Kairos* 19 (1977) 124-33. R. Bultmann, *The History of the Synoptic Tradition* (FRLANT 29, 1921, 1979[9]; ET 1963, 1968[2]). G. W. Burnett, *Paul and the Salvation of the Individual* (Biblical Interpretation 57, 2001). C. J. Cadoux, *The Early Church and the World: A History of the Christian Attitude to Pagan Society and the State Down to the Time of Constantius* (1925). S. J. Case, *The Evolution of Early Christianity: A Genetic Study of First-century Christianity in Relation to Its Religious Environment* (1914); *The Social Origins of Christianity* (1923); *The Social Triumph of the Ancient Church* (1934). J. K. Chow, *Patronage and Power: A Study of Social Networks in Corinth* (JSNTSup 75, 1992). A. D. Clarke, *Secular and Christian Leadership in Corinth: A Socio-historical and Exegetical Study of 1 Corinthians 1-6* (AGJU 19, 1993). M. Clévénot, *Materialist* Approaches to the Bible (1976; ET 1985). F. Crüsemann, "Grandfragen sozialgeschichtlicher Exegese," *EvErz* 35 (1983) 273-86. A. Deissmann, *Light from the Ancient East: The NT Illustrated by Recently Discovered Texts of the Graeco-Roman World* (1908, 1923[4]4; ET 1927). M. Dibelius, *From Tradition to Gospel* (1919; ET 1971). E. von Dobschütz, *Die urchristlichen Geimeinden: Sittengeschichtliche Bilder* (1902). M. N. Ebertz, *Das Charisma des Gekreuzigten: Zur Soziologie der Jesusbewegung* (WUNT 45, 1987). J. H. Elliott, *A Home for the Homeless: A Sociological Exegesis of 1 Peter: Its Situation and Strategy* (1981). P. F. Esler (ed.), *The Early Christian World* (2000). S. Freyne, *Galilee, Jesus, and the Gospels: Literary Approaches and Historical Investigations* (1988). A. Funk, *Status und Rollen in den Paulusbriefen: Eine inhaltsanalytische Untersuchung zur Religionssoziologie* (IThS 7, 1981). J. G. Gager, *Kingdom and Community: The Social World of Early Christianity* (1975). N. K. Gottwald (ed.), *The Bible and Liberation: Political and Social Hermeneutics* (1983); (ed.), "Social-scientific Criticism of the HB and Its Social World: The Israelite Monarchy," *Semeia* 37 (1986) 1-147. F. C. Grant, *The Economic Background of the Gospels* (1926). K. C. Hanson and D. E. Oakman. *Palestine in the Time of Jesus: Social Structures and Social Conflicts* (1998). A. von Harnack, *Lehre der zwölf Apostel nebst Untersuchungen zur ältesten Geschichte der Kirchenverfassung und des Kirchenrechts* (TU, 2, 1-2, 1884, 1893[2]); *Die Mission und Ausbreitung des Christentums in den ersten drei Jahrhunderten* (1902). D. J. Harrington, "Second Testament Exegesis and the Social Sciences: A Bibliography," *BTB* 18 (1988) 75-85. E. Hatch, *Die Gesellschaftsverfassung der christlichen Kirchen im Alterthum: Acht Vorlesungen* (1883). C. F. G. Heinrici, *Erklärung der Korinthierbriefe in 2 Bänden*, vol. 2, *Das zeite Sendschreiben des Apostels Paulus an die*

Korinthier (1887). **M. Hengel,** *The Charismatic Leader and His Followers* (BZNW 34, 1968; ET 1981); *Property and Riches in the Early Church: Aspects of a Social History of Early Christianity* (1973; ET 1974). **R. F. Hock,** *The Social Context of Paul's Ministry: Tentmaking, and Apostleship* (1980). **B. Holmberg,** *Paul and Power: The Structure of Authority in the Primitive Church as Reflected in the Pauline Epistles* (ConBNT 11, 1978); *Sociology and the NT: An Appraisal* (1990). **R. A. Horsley,** *Jesus and the Spiral of Violence: Popular Jewish Resistance in Roman Palestine* (1987); *Sociology and the Jesus Movement* (1989). **R. A. Horsley and J. S. Hanson,** *Bandits, Prophets, and Messiahs: Popular Movements in the Time of Jesus* (1985). **J. Jeremias,** *Jerusalem in the Time of Jesus: An Investigation into Economic and Social Conditions During the NT Period* (1923; ET 1969). **E. A. Judge,** "The Social Identity of the First Christians: A Question of Method in Religious History," *JRH* 11 (1980/81) 201-17; *Rank and Status in the World of the Caesars and St. Paul* (1982). **H. C. Kee,** *Community of the New Age: Studies in Mark's Gospel* (1977, 1983[2]); *Christian Origins in Sociological Perspective: Methods and Resources* (1980); *Knowing the Truth: A Sociological Approach to NT Interpretation* (1989). **H. G. Kippenberg,** *Religion und Klassenbildung im antiken Judäa: Eine religionssoziologische Studie zum Verhältnis von Tradition und gesellschaftlicher Entwicklung* (1978). **H.-J. Klauck,** *Hausgemeinde und Hauskirche im frühen Christentum* (SBS 103, 1981). **W. G. Kümmel,** "Das Urchristentum II: Arbeiten zu Spezialproblemen. b: Zur Sozialgeschichte und Soziologie der Urkirche," *TRu* 50 (1985) 327-63. **P. Lampe,** *Die stadtrömischen Christen in den ersten beiden Jahrhunderten: Untersuchungen zur Sozialgeschichte* (WUNT 2, 18, 1987, 1989[2]). **E. Lohmeyer,** *Soziale Fragen im Urchristentum* (Wissenschaft und Bildung 172, 1921); *Vom Begriff der religiösen Gemeinschaft: Eine problemgeschichtliche Untersuchung über die Grundlagen des Urchristentums* (1925). **A. Malherbe,** *Social Aspects of Early Christianity* (Rockwell Lectures, 1977, 1983[2]). **B. J. Malina,** *The NT World: Insights from Cultural Anthropology* (1981, 2001[3]); *Christian Origins and Cultural Anthropology: Practical Models for Biblical Interpretation* (1986). **B. J. Malina,** *The Social Gospel of Jesus: The Kingdom of God in Mediterranean Perspective* (Rauschenbusch Lectures, 1999). **B. J. Malina and Jerome H. Neyrey.** *Portraits of Paul: An Archaeology of Ancient Personality* (1996). **Bruce J. Malina and John J. Pilch,** *Social-science Commentary on the Book of Revelation* (2000). **B. J. Malina and R. L. Rohrbaugh,** *Social-science Commentary on the Synoptic Gospels* (2003[2]). **S. Mathews,** *The Social Teaching of Jesus: An Essay in Christian Sociology* (1897); *The Atonement and the Social Process* (1930). **W. A. Meeks** (ed.), *Zur Soziologie des Urchristentums: Ausgew"hlte Beitr"ge zum frühchristlichen Gemeinschaftsleben in seiner gesellschaftlichen Umwelt* (TB 62, 1979); "The Social Context of Pauline Theology," *Int* 36 (1982) 226-77; *The First Urban Christians: The Social World of the Apostle* Paul (1983). **H. Mödritzer,** *Stigma und Chrisma im Neuen Testament und seiner Umwelt: Zur Soziologie des Urchristentums* (NTOA 28, 1994). **C. Myers,** *Binding the Strong Man: A Political Reading of Mark's Story of Jesus* (1988). **C. Osiek,** "The Social Sciences and the Second Testament: Problems and Challenges," *BTB* 22 (1992) 88-95. **John J. Pilch** ed., *Social Scientific Models for Interpreting the Bible: Essays by the Context Group in Honor of Bruce J. Malina* (Biblical Interpretation 53, 2001). **John J. Pilch,** *The Cultural Dictionary of the Bible* (1999). **V. Robbins,** *Jesus the Teacher: A Socio-Rhetorical Interpretation of Mark* (1984). **Taeseong Roh,** *Die* familia dei *in den synoptischen Evangelien: eine redaktions- und sozialgeschichtliche Untersuchung zu einem urchristlichen Bildfeld* (NTOA 3, 2001). **R. L. Rohrbaugh,** "Methodological Considerations in the Debate over the Social Class of Early Christians," *JAAR* 52 (1984) 519-46; "'Social Location of Thought' as a Heuristic Construct in NT Study," *JSNT* 30 (1987) 103-19; (ed.) *The Social Sciences and NT Interpretation* (1996). **T. Schmeller,** *Brechungen: Urchristliche Wandercharimatiker im Prisma soziologisch orientieter Exegese* (SBS 136, 1989); "Soziologisch orientierte Exegese des Neuen Testaments," *BK* 44 (1989) 103-10;

"Sociological Exegesis of the NT," *TD* 37, 3 (1990) 231-34; *Hierarchie und Egalität: Eine sozialgeschichtliche Untersuchung paulinischer Gemeinden und griechisch-römischer Vereine* (SBS 162, 1995). **K. L. Schmidt,** *Der Rahmen der Geschichte Jesu: Literarkritische Untersuchungen zur ältesten Jesusüberlieferung* (1919). **L. Schottroff,** *Befreiungserfahrungen: Studien zur Sozialgeschichte des Neuen Testaments* (TB 82, 1990). **W. Schottroff and W. Stegemann** (ed.), *Der Gott der kleinen Leute: Sozialgeschichtliche Bibel Auslegungen* (2 vols. 1979²); *Traditionen der Befreiung: Sozialgeschichtliche Bibelauslegungen* (2 vols. 1980). **R. Schumacher,** *Die soziale Lage der Christen im apostolischen Zeitalter* (1924). **J. H. Schütz,** *Paul and the Anatomy of Apostolic Authority* (1975). **J. E. Stambaugh and D. L. Balch,** *The NT in Its Social Environment* (LEC 2, 1986). **E. and W. Stegemann,** *Urchristliche Sozialgeschichte: Die Anfange im Judentum und die Christusgemeinden in der mediterranen Welt* (1993). **W. Stegemann, B. J. Malina, and G. Theissen,** eds., *The Social Setting of Jesus and the Gospels* (2002). **W. Stenger,** "Sozialgeschichtliche Wende und historischer Jesus," *Kairos* 28 (1986) 11-22; *"Gebt dem Kaiser, was des Kaisers ist. . . . " : Eine sozialgeschichtliche Untersuchung zur Besteurerung Palästinas in neutestamentlicher Zeit* (BBB 68, 1988). **C. Strecker,** *Die liminale Theologie des Paulus: Zugänge zur paulinischen Theologie aus kulturanthropologischer Perspektive* (FRLANT 185, 1999). **G. Theissen,** *Sociology of Early Palestinian Christianity* (TEH 194, 1977, 1985⁴; ET 1978); *Social Reality and the Early Christians: Theology, Ethics, and the World of the NT* (WUNT 19, 1979, 1989³; ET 1992); "Vers une théorie de l'historie sociale du christianisme primitif," *ETR* 63 (1988) 199-225; "Die pragmatische Bedeutung der Geheimnismotive im Markusevangelium: Ein wissenssoziologischer Versuch," *Secrecy and Concealment: Studies in the History of Mediterranean and Near Eastern Religions* (ed. H. G. Kippenberg and G. G. Stroumsa, 1995) 225-45; *The Religion of the Earliest Churches: Creating a Symbolic World* (1999). **D. Tidball,** *An Introduction to the Sociology of the NT* (1983); *The Social Context of the NT: A Sociological Analysis* (1984). **E. Troeltsch,** *The Social Teaching of the Christian Churches* 1 (1912; ET 1931). **H.-J. Venetz,** "Der Beitrag der Soziologie zur Lektüre des Neuen Testaments: Ein Bericht," *Methoden der Evangelienexegese* (ed. J. Pfamatter, *ThBer* 13, 1985) 87-121.

T. SCHMELLER

CONTEXTUAL APPROACHES

Afrocentric Biblical Interpretation

Afrocentricity is the concept that Africa and persons of African descent must be understood as making significant contributions to world civilization as proactive subjects within history, rather than being regarded as mere passive objects in the course of history. Afrocentrism requires reconceptualizing Africa as a center of value and a source of pride without in any way demeaning other peoples and their historic contributions to human achievement. The term *Afrocentricity* (Asante 1987) refers to an approach that reappraises ancient biblical traditions, their exegetical history in the West, and their allied hermeneutical implications (Hermeneutics[§]). An impressive number of scholarly volumes appeared on this subject in the 1980s and 1990s, which attempted to clarify the ancient cultural (and biblical) views of race and ancient Africa. Together they represent efforts in "corrective historiography," which demonstrate clearly that a new stage in biblical interpretation has arrived.

It is no longer enough to limit the discussion to "Black theology" or even to "African theology." Instead, scholars must acknowledge that Africa, its people, nations, and cultures have made direct primary contributions to the development of many early biblical traditions and have played significant roles in biblical history. Rather than viewing ancient Africa negatively, or minimizing its presence in and contributions to biblical narratives and thought (as has been all too often the case in Western scholarly guilds) the continent obtains a more favorable appropriation by those who wish more accurately to interpret the Bible and to appreciate the inherent racial and ethnic diversity or multiculturalism of the salvation history the Bible depicts.

Throughout the world it has become standard for Christians to think of almost all of the biblical characters—from Noah, Abraham, Moses, the pharaohs, and even the Queen of Sheba, Mary and Joseph (the parents of Jesus*[§]), and virtually all New Testament personalities—as somehow typical Europeans. For example, most modern sacred Christian art portrays Mary, the mother of Jesus, as a European. Consequently, most people today believe that the mother of Jesus of Nazareth resembled the ordinary European of today. Such presumptions are only now being substantively challenged through Afrocentric modes of biblical interpretation, as studies devote more attention to ancient iconography and to the importance of Egyptian (Egyptology and Biblical Studies[§]) and Ethiopian civilizations in the shaping of the biblical world (M. Bernal 1987, 1991). Thus, today there is a critical need to examine not only how this distorted view emerged in Western history but also how the Bible treats Africa in general and black people in particular.

Three basic factors must be placed at the forefront of any discussion of this kind. First, the maps of the ancient biblical lands must be considered. Countries in Africa (Egypt, Cush, Put, and Punt) are mentioned again and again in the Bible. The Hebrew Bible alone refers to Ethiopia over forty times and Egypt over one hundred times. Many ancient biblical and extrabiblical sources mention Egypt and Ethiopia together, almost interchangeably. Scarcely are such ancient African locations portrayed fully in biblical maps produced in Europe and especially in the United States. Usually, Western biblical cartographers show as little as possible of the African continent, while by contrast they highlight areas to the north in Europe and Eurasia that are seldom, if ever, referred to in the Bible.

Second, the Bible provides extensive evidence that the earliest of its people must be located in Africa. The creation story (Gen 2:8-14) indicates that the first two rivers of Eden are closely associated with ancient Cush, whose Hebrew name the Greeks would later translate as "Aithiops" or Ethiopia (literally "burnt face people"). Genesis 2:11-12 connects the Pishon River with "Havilah," the direct descendent of Cush (Gen 10:7). The Gihon River, the second river in Eden (Gen 2:13), is described as surrounding the whole land of Cush. Biblical scholars usually date this composite Jahwist (J) tradition in the tenth century B.C.E., suggesting that these verses are an early reference to the African river system known today as the Blue and the White Nile rivers. (The name "Nile" derives from the Latin *nilus*, but the Genesis story predates the Latin language.) Clearly, wherever else Eden extended, a substantial portion was within the continent of Africa.

Third, the ancient land of Canaan was an extension of the African land mass and, in biblical times, African peoples frequently migrated from the continent proper through Canaan/Palestine to the East along the Fertile Crescent to the Tigris and Euphrates river valleys of ancient Mesopotamia. Thus, the term *Afro-Asiatic* is probably the most accurate way to identify the mixed stock of people who populated the ancient Near East. "Eurasians" and even Europeans (Greeks and Romans) begin to feature in later biblical narratives; but the fact remains that the earliest biblical people, by modern Western standards of racial types, would have to be classified as Blacks (meaning that they had African blood and some physical features similar to those of African Americans today).

The modern student of biblical history and interpretation has to keep in mind that the ancient authors of the Bible, together with the Greeks and the Romans, had no notion of color prejudice. As startling as it may seem to those schooled in modern European, South African, and North American modes of scriptural interpretation, the Bible actually reflects a world before color prejudice or racial discrimination (Snowden 1983). The authors/redactors of the Bible had a rather favorable attitude about black people and, as a result, the Bible often reflects the ancient greatness of African people and their civilizations. For example, Gen 10:8 identifies Nimrod, son of Cush, as "a mighty warrior;" Solomon marries the daughter of the pharaoh (1 Kgs 3:1, 7:8; 2 Chr 8:11); and the heroine of the Song of Songs is "black and beautiful" (Cant 1:5). Once one tackles the problem of how to define *Black*, it becomes quite easy to see that most of the early characters of the Bible would have to be classified as such, even though the biblical authors had no notion of race in the modern sense of the term.

Over a century of Bible study by leaders in the black church shows clearly that Blacks long ago rejected the latter-day, postbiblical view that they were the progeny of the accursed Ham (the curse is actually directed at Ham's son Canaan and is not racially motivated; see Gen 9:18-27). D. P. Seaton, a prominent leader in the African Methodist Episcopal Church, represents the thinking of Blacks who have identified a more wholesome interpretation of their role in biblical history. In a work written in 1895, Seaton displayed considerable knowledge about the Bible, the location of ancient religious sites, and the significance of many biblical characters, providing extensive descriptions of tombs, villages, and other ancient sites he visited during several field trips to Palestine. Regarding Ham and his descendants, Seaton observed: "Because these Hamites were an important people, attempts have been made to rob them of their proper place in the catalogue of the races. The Bible tells us plainly that the Phoenicians were descendants of Canaan, the son of Ham, and anyone who will take the time to read the Bible account of their lineage must concede the fact." What is particularly noteworthy about Seaton's study is his profound awareness of racism among the respected biblical scholars of his day.

In the last decades of the twentieth century, both in the United States and in Africa, there was a resurgence of what may now be called Afrocentric approaches to the Bible, (e.g., R. Bailey 1995; C. Copher 1993; C. H. Felder 1991; M. A. Oduyoye 1995; and A. Smith 1995). Caution, however, is advised, for students of the Bible must avoid the tendency of taking the sons of Noah—Shem, Ham, and Japheth—as representing three different races (Whites, Blacks, and Asians). The traditional approach of European missionaries and others was to designate Ham as the father of Blacks, who were allegedly cursed in Gen 9:18-27 (T. Peterson 1975); but it is absurd to claim that Noah and his wife could produce offspring that would constitute three distinct racial types. In fact, "Ham" does not mean "black" in Hebrew; it means "hot" or "heated." Moreover, there is no curse of Ham in this passage, for the text explicitly says, "Let Canaan be cursed" (Gen 9:25). Any discussion on the subject of Blacks in the Bible should be held suspect if its author tries to argue that Blacks constitute the "Hamitic" line only.

Black women and men are fully a part of the Bible's salvation history (Felder 1989, 1991). Moses was an Afro-Asiatic and, according to Num 12:1, he married a Cushite or Ethiopian woman. The Queen of Sheba, a black African (1 Kgs 10:1-13; 2 Chr 9:1-12; also see Gen 10:6-9), is called "the queen of the South" in Matt 12:42. The New Testament mentions another Black queen: Candace, queen of the Ethiopians, who ruled from her ancient Ethiopian capital at Meroe (Acts 8:26-40). For years, persons of African descent have taken heart upon reading the celebrated passage in Ps 68:31: "Let princes come out of Egypt and let Ethiopia hasten to stretch forth her hand to God!" (KJV). But today there is a much greater basis for Blacks to celebrate and otherwise take seriously their rich ancient heritage in the sacred Scriptures, for the real Black presence is by no means limited to isolated verses here and there.

Despite all the evidence indicating a manifest Black biblical presence, Eurocentric church officials and scholars in most of the prestigious academies and universities of Europe and the United States have tended to deny, or otherwise to overlook or minimize the fact that black people are in any significant way part of biblical history. This standard academic and popular Western tendency has had grave consequences for persons of African descent. Thus, modern biblical scholarship is just beginning to overcome centuries of tragic biases against Blacks and their biblical history, biases that continue to find expression in the view that Blacks are to be thought of as mere "hewers of wood and drawers of water" (Felder 1991, 132).

In the period between 367 C.E. (the date of Athanasius's canonical lists) and the Enlightenment, Europeans recast the Bible into a religious saga of European-type people. What makes this racialist tendentiousness so difficult to counteract is that such reinterpretations of ancient ethnographic realities are accepted as fact by many scholars in the Western academic community. These scholars teach and influence others throughout the world, thereby effectively recasting biblical history in terms and images that are distinctly favorable to Whites while literally displacing Blacks. The result has been that even Blacks portray biblical characters within their churches as totally unlike themselves. For biblical characters to be viewed in black images is still seen as a terrible thing by many Blacks around the world.

One need not hesitate to suppose that Mary looked like the other Palestinian women of Nazareth of her day. It is more historically accurate to portray her physiognomy as that of an ancient Afro-Asiatic, who probably looked like a typical modern Yemenite, Trinidadian, or African American. Several factors challenge the traditional Western perception of the Madonna and child: Matt 2:15, quoting from Hosea 11:1, reads "out of Egypt, I have called my son." The passage describes how Mary and Joseph fled to Egypt to hide the infant Jesus from King Herod. Imagine the divine family as white Europeans "hiding" in Africa! It is doubtful that they would remain unnoticed, for despite centuries of European scholarship that has diligently sought to portray Egypt as an extension of southern Europe, it has always been part of Africa.

Literally hundreds of shrines of the Black Madonna have existed in many parts of North Africa, Europe, and Russia. These are not weather-beaten misrepresentations of some original white Madonna; rather, they are uncanny reminders of the original ethnography of the people who inhabited ancient Palestine during Jesus' time and earlier. The "sweet little Jesus boy" of the Negro spiritual was, in point of fact, quite black. While that song intones "we didn't know it was you," it reminds most modern Christians that they still do not know what Jesus actually looked like.

The maps of biblical lands need to be reassessed in light of more recent studies that show the true attitudes about race in the ancient Greco-Roman ethos. At that time all of Africa was referred to as Ethiopia, while present-day Sudan was called Ethiopia proper. The greatness of the people from these areas was proverbial. Recall Ps 87:1-4, which asserts that not only were the Ethiopians among those who fully knew the God of ancient Israel but also that they may have been born in Israel ("This one was born there," Ps 87:4*b*)! Similarly, Isaiah 11:11 includes Blacks among the righteous remnant, whereas Isa 18:1-4 celebrates those from "the land of whirring wings . . . sending ambassadors by the Nile," a people "tall and smooth," "feared near and far."

Although Greeks and Romans are frequently mentioned in the Bible, Mary, Joseph, and Jesus were neither Greek nor Roman. So how did Jesus of Afro-Asiatic birth become whiter and whiter over the years? The answer is neither complicated nor profound; it is a simple matter of paint. Medieval and Renaissance artists skillfully employed the painter's brush, and gradually began to depict Jesus in images more familiar and favorable to persons of European descent. Thus, there developed a brand-new manger scene and an infant Jesus for all the world, not least the Third World, to adore. Jesus' parents also were reimaged, as ancient darker (and clearly more African) icons were discarded or destroyed in favor of more modern ones. These altered artistic representations still remain in many cathedrals of Europe and North and South America as well as in a great new basilica on Africa's Ivory Coast. Clearly, Africa has for too long stretched out its hand to biblical characters remolded as non-Black.

In Jer 13:23*a* the rhetorical question is raised, "Can Ethiopians change their skin?" In the sixth century B.C.E., Jeremiah knew that it was unnecessary for any Ethiopian to attempt to do so; that kind of thinking seems peculiar to our own modern age of pseudo-scientific theories of White supremacy and Negroid inferiority, a most "enlightened" by-product of what is known as the Western Enlightenment.

Many contemporary persons may think of a black Jesus as an oddity or as a scandalous distortion of reality. The claim may be tolerated as long as it is limited to the theological metaphors of black theologians like J. H. Cone or A. Boesak, but it is not taken seriously as ancient ethnography. Many Europeans and Euro-Americans insist that Jesus was Semitic and, as such, Middle Eastern. However, to call Jesus "Semitic" is not helpful inasmuch as this nineteenth-century term refers, not to a racial type, but to a family of languages including both Hebrew and Ethiopic. Moreover, about the same time the European academy coined the term Semitic, it also created the geographical designation "Middle East," an expression that would have made no sense to Herodotus, to Strabo, or even to Thucydides, much less to biblical personalities. The point of creating a so-called Middle East was to avoid talking about Africa. It was a sign of academic racism, which sought to de-Africanize the sacred story of the Bible along with the whole sweep of Western civilization.

Whether one considers the "Table of Nations" that appears in Gen 10 as a historical record, the fact remains that centuries before Jesus of Nazareth, those who compiled the list of the descendants of Noah appeared to have an ideological intent. They insisted that Canaan was a direct descendant of Ham—in fact, his son; the very one who is conveniently cursed in Genesis 9 in order to discredit his right to his own land. Furthermore, when the Greeks rose up to conquer the land of Canaan after the exile, they infused Greek culture into the subjugated peoples of their empire. Greek culture became the standard of acceptance in the Greco-Roman world, leading both those in power and those dominated to be as Greek as possible and to flee northward for cultural roots. In contrast, when Jesus' parents fled Herod's domain in order to protect Jesus, they followed the established trail to Africa—not to Europe! Bernal (1987, 1991) suggests that the ancient African centered model for the dawn of civilization was later co-opted by a "white/pure" European model. Certainly historians should take seriously that the models for the origins of culture changed simultaneously with the rise of racism and anti-Semitism.

Subsequent Western civilization took a different path from that of the holy family—namely, one leading straight to Europe— aided by artists paid by the church and its universities, who sought to please those in power as opposed to rendering ethnographically accurate biblical characters. Hollywood completed this revisionist imaging through movies like C. B. DeMille's *The Ten Commandments, The Robe, The Greatest Story Ever Told,* and *Ben Hur,* films in which Europeans magically populated the entire region of ancient Palestine, rendering its inhabitants White. The people of ancient Palestine have never been the same.

The essays in Wimbush (2000) and Bailey (2003) indicate the state of Afrocentric intepretation of the Bible at the start of the twenty-first century.

Bibliography: D. T. Adamo, *Africa and the Africans in the OT* (1998). **M. K. Asante,** *The Afrocentric Idea* (1987). **R. C. Bailey,** "They Are Nothing but Incestuous Bastards: The Polemical Use of Sex and Sexuality in Hebrew Canon Narratives," *Reading from This Place,* vol. 1 (ed. F. F. Segovia and M. A. Tolbert, 1995) 121-38; ed. *Yet With a Steady Beat: Contemporary U. S. Afrocentric Biblical Interpretation* (SemeiaSt 2003). **M. Bernal,** *Black Athena: The Afro-Asiatic Roots of Classical Civilization* (2 vols., 1987, 1991). **A. A. Boesak,** *Black Theology, Black Power* (1978). **C. B. Copher,** "3,000 Years of Biblical Interpretation with Reference to Black Peoples," *JITC 30, 2* (1986) 225-46; "The Black Presence in the OT," *Stony the Road We Trod: African American Biblical Interpretation* (ed. C. H. Felder, 1991) 146-64; *Black Biblical Studies: An Anthology of C. B. Copher: Biblical and Theological Issues on the Black Presence in the Bible* (1993). **C. H. Felder,** *Troubling Biblical Waters: Race, Class, and Family* (1989); (ed.), *Stony the Road We Trod: African American Biblical Interpretation* (1991). **N. F. Gier,** "The Color of Sin/The Color of Skin," *JRT* 48, 1 (1991) 42-52. **C. J. Martin,** "A Chamberlain's Journey and the Challenge of Interpretation for Liberation," *Semeia* 47 (1989) 105-35. **M. A. Oduyoye,** *The Sons of the Gods and the Daughters of Men: An Afro-Asiatic Interpretation of Genesis 1–11*, vol. 2 (1984); "Biblical Interpretation and the Social Location of the Interpreter: African Women's Reading of the Bible," *Reading from This Place,* vol. 1 (ed. F. F. Segovia and M. A. Tolbert, 1995) 2:33-51. **T. Peterson,** "The Myth of Ham among White Antebellum Southerners" (diss. Stanford University, 1975). **A. Smith,** "A Second Step in African Biblical Interpretation: A Generic Reading Analysis of Acts 8:26-40," *Reading from this Place,* vol. 1 (ed. F. F. Segovia and M. A. Tolbert, 1995) 213-28. **F. M. Snowden Jr.,** *Blacks in Antiquity* (1970); *Before Color Prejudice: The Ancient View of Blacks* (1983). **L. A. Thompson,** *Romans and Blacks* (1989). **J. Vercoitter, J. Leclant, F. M. Snowden Jr., and J. Desanges,** *The Image of the Black in Western Art,* vol. 1; *From the Pharaohs to the Fall of the Roman Empire* (1976). **V. L. Wimbush,** ed., *African Americans and the Bible: Sacred Texts and Social Textures* (2000).

C. H. FELDER

CONTEXTUAL APPROACHES

Asian Biblical Interpretation

Asia is a vast continent characterized by tremendous racial, cultural, and religious diversity. As a part of their religio-cultural heritage, Asians had a long history of encounter with sacred texts—Hindu, Buddhist, Confucianist, Daoist, and Islamic—before the advent of Christianity on Asian soil. While Christianity arrived in many parts of Asia much earlier, it was not until the nineteenth century, at the heels of European colonization, that Christianity began to create some impact in Asian societies. As a result, the Bible began to be translated into the vernacular of the Asian people, and, in the process, it was read and interpreted by Asians in their own socio-cultural contexts.

1. *Wissenschaft.* In biblical scholarship, the dawn of historical-critical methodology marked a significant paradigm shift in the interpretation of the Bible. Clearly, since the methodology's introduction a significant number of Asian biblical scholars (mostly trained in the West) have adopted this *wissenschaftlich* (purely academic) approach, as evidenced in the works of several early scholars. T. Ishibashi (Japan) published an introduction to the Hebrew Bible and a history of Israelite religion and culture in the 1920s. Z. Watanabe (Japan) was interested in the intersection between the historical-critical study of the Bible and its function as the canonical text (Canon of the Bible§) for the faith community, leading him to the publication of his trilogy entitled *The Doctrine of the Scriptures* (1949–63). K. Uchimura (Japan) approached the biblical texts from historical, grammatical, and philological perspectives but also sought to relate them to the context of the Bible as a whole and to the lives of readers. Joo-sam Yang (Korea) introduced historical-critical methodology to Korean scholars, arguing that in order to understand and interpret the Bible one needs to know the history of the Bible and its historical and literary contexts. His writings similarly reveal his acquaintance with the debate on Mosaic authorship of the Pentateuch (Pentateuchal Criticism‡§), although he sidestepped the issue by focusing on the "holy instruction" of the text.

This *wissenschaftlich* approach to the Bible has continued among Asian scholars. C.H. Kim (Korean American) has compared the structures of the available Christian letters of recommendation and the New Testament letters of commendation with familiar Hellenistic letters of recommendation (Kim 1972). T. Ishida (a significant figure in the study of the united monarchy in ancient Israel) investigates the issues of charismatic leadership and dynastic succession and, applying historical-critical analysis to the sources in Samuel and drawing on his knowledge of ancient Near Eastern literature, argues strongly that the Israelite monarchy was dynastic from the beginning (Ishida 1977). Citing Eli and Samuel as examples, he notes that hereditary leadership was already in place during the *sopet* regime. He further argues that the ideological conflict on the eve of the monarchy (1 Sam 8:7; 10:19; 12:12) was over monarchy versus theocracy, not over dynastic versus charismatic rule. Thus Ishida shows that A. Alt§ was wrong in suggesting that the Israelite monarchy was charismatic in its original conceptualization. The continued influence of the *wissenschaftlich* approach is seen in the volume of conference papers Ishida edited (1982).

The Indonesian scholar S. Widyapranawa wrote a strongly theological commentary on Isaiah (1990) that is another example of the *wissenschaftlich* approach because it is built on the results of the historical-critical method. In his comments on Isa 7:14-16, in reference to the *'almâ* as a sign Yahweh gives to Ahaz, Widyapranawa notes: "Now since a sign in the biblical sign should be concrete and actual, it is not clear who this young woman is. She would have to be someone familiar to both Ahaz and Isaiah" (41-42). C. L. Seow (Singapore) is perhaps the most prominent Asian biblical scholar. In his Harvard dissertation, "Ark Processions in the Politics of the Monarchy" (1984), he used the tools of comparative Semitics and historical criticism to show the connection of the ritual procession of the ark to the ancient Near Eastern myth of the divine warrior. His commentary on Ecclesiastes (1997) brings together the tools of historical criticism, socio-anthropological approaches, comparative Semitics, and text linguistics. Through his detailed analysis, Seow sees Qohelet as a sage who not only stood in the wisdom tradition, but "also made his own distinctive contributions, often in agreement with most of the tradition but at times in criticism of it" (1997, 69).

Not all Asian scholars have viewed the historical-critical method positively. For example, Jia Yu-ming (China) used the hermeneutical (Hermeneutics*§) methods of *scriptura ipsius interpres*, thematic interpretation, and emphasis on cultivating spirituality as the ultimate goal of biblical interpretation (1921).

2. *Cultural Hermeneutics*. Asian scholars have always interpreted the Bible in the context of their own cultures and native religious traditions. Some scholars speak in terms of contextualization, while others use Asian religious categories to understand the Christian tradition, especially JESUS. Scholars have begun to refer to their hermeneutical approaches as "cross-textual," "dialogical," or "dialogical imagination," through which the realities of Asian cultures are brought into conversation with those of the biblical tradition.

C.S. Song (Taiwan) raised concerns about the nature of history, especially what is termed "salvation history," and its relation to world history (1976). He sees history first as a story in which a historian has put into continuity things and events that seem disjoined. Second, history consists not only of chronological data but also of the meaning of life and death. This meaning often disrupts the continuity of history (e.g., through revolution). He goes on to note that biblical history derives its meaning from God's redemptive acts, or disruptions of historical continuity, which are comparable to revolutions, describing the exodus as God's revolution *par excellence* and maintaining that the most drastic revolutionary act of God's redemption took place in the person of Jesus Christ on the cross. From a contextual perspective, Song goes on to argue that there have been two disruptions in salvation history since WWII: The failure of Western missionaries to incorporate the masses of humanity in Asia into salvation history and China's resolute rejection of Christianity. He looks for a different meaning behind these disruptions, suggesting that Asian Christians should engage in theological reflection concerning a direct relationship of Asia to God's redemption that bypasses Western Christianity entirely. He argues that Israel's history under God is but a model of how God would deal redemptively with other nations.

Song's unceasing concern for the daily struggles and sufferings of Asians is revealed in his later works. In his 1990 book he poses the question of whether Jesus conceived of himself as a paschal lamb. Exegeting the Gospel account of the Last Supper and comparing it to the Passover narrative of Exodus 12–13, Song identifies a significant difference between the two accounts—namely, that God passed over the paschal lamb but remained with Jesus in his crucifixion. He suggests, therefore, that the event of the cross surpassed that of the Passover. Moreover, from a discussion of the various meanings of *hyper pollōn*, he contends that it should be understood as "in behalf of and representing all peoples." The conclusion Song draws from this study is that Jesus represents the crucified people and that he identifies with the struggles and sufferings of the Asian people.

The work of E. Singgih (Indonesia) also illustrates the importance of contextualization in Asian biblical scholarship. Singgih argues that, in order to take theological and exegetical contextualization seriously, attention must be given to the reinterpretation of the biblical context, systematic-dogmatic tradition, and modern context (1982, 70) by particularly drawing upon J. Banawiratma's dialogical comparison of Jawanese society and John's Gospel (1977).

V. Chakkarai (India), in his 1926 monograph on Christology, used the Hindu concept of *avatΑr* (incarnation) to understand Jesus, proposing that Jesus is the dynamic and permanent incarnation of God.

Wu Lei-ch'uan (China) attempted the union of Christian faith and Chinese culture by using Confucian categories in his interpretation of the Bible. He used the ancient Chinese concept of *Tien-tzu* (Son of Heaven) to understand Jesus as Christ (1936). Influenced by the understanding of the *Tien-tzu* as one who was at once the king who ruled the people, the prophet who taught them the heavenly will, and the priest who offered sacrifices on their behalf, Wu's conceptualization of Jesus is very political. For instance, he suggests that even as a twelve-year-old boy, Jesus had thoughts about serving as a political Christ when he said that he must be concerned about his Father's affairs (Luke 2:49), a statement Wu interpreted as foreshadowing both a political revolution to liberate the Jewish people from Rome and a social revolution to rebuild a moral society.

Asian scholars have begun to name their hermeneutical approaches. In a programmatic essay, Kwok Pui-Lan (Hong Kong) advocates a dialogical approach (1989). Using the term "dialogical imagination," she points out that "biblical interpretation in Asia . . . must create a two-way traffic between our own tradition and that of the Bible" (1989, 30) and that "it is dialogical, for it involves a constant conversation between different religious and cultural traditions" (1989, 31). She further notes that her hermeneutical model emphasizes plurality of meanings, multiplicity of narratives, and a multiaxial framework of analysis since such a model is rooted in the pluralism and diversity of Asia. She later insists that Asians "have to avoid superimposing a European framework on the development of Asian hermeneutics, which must remain rooted in its own specific cultural context" (1995, 39).

R. Sugirtharajah (Sri Lanka) uses a similar dialogical approach, which he defines as one that "acknowledges the validity of the varied and diverse religious experiences of all people and rules out any exclusive claim to truth by one religious tradition" (1990b, 13). Studying Paul's conversion experience (Acts 9:1-9; 22:3-16; 26:9-18; Gal 1:11-17), Sugirtharajah seeks to show that Jesus was not introducing a new tradition but rather reiterating a forgotten aspect of the availability of God's mercy and grace to all. Paul's experience on the Damascus highway, therefore, is to be seen as a transformation as he began to retrieve the neglected elements of his own tradition in light of Jesus' words and actions.

A. Lee (Hong Kong) uses "cross-textual hermeneutics" (1993a). Responding to events that led to the return of Hong Kong to China, Lee asked what roles and functions the church could play during the time of transition (1985). He compares the role of Nathan the prophet in the David-Bathsheba story with the role of the remonstrator in the Chinese tradition, especially Wei Cheng in the court of Emperor Tang Tai Tsung. In this role, Wei Cheng had to remind the emperor of his responsibilities, as a parent of his people, to show concern for them and work for their well-being. Nathan played a similar role when he called David to accountability for the murder of Uriah.

Lee's second work (1994) is a cross-textual analysis of the biblical creation narratives, especially Genesis 1–11, and the ancient Chinese creation myth Nu Kua, one of the oldest Chinese stories of the origin of humanity. A female creator, Nu Kua, fashions human beings from the yellow earth, expertly sculpting the rich and noble but dripping mud from a rope to form the poor and lowly. In another version she re-creates the universe damaged by chaotic forces, including its social harmony and cosmic order. Thus this myth reveals both "anthrogonic" and "sociogonic" concerns. Lee observes that, in the Chinese tradition, Nu Kua is seen both as a human being who is becoming divine and as a divine being who is becoming human. Such a concept, he notes, presents a theological challenge to the Christian monotheistic faith; moreover, biblical creation stories are often reduced to a doctrine of creation. He is concerned with the way in which Asian Christians can begin to incorporate the worldview of Asian traditions into their theological formulation.

3. *Liberation Perspectives.* Since the introduction of Liberation Theology*§, liberation perspectives have found a home among many Asian biblical scholars. Such perspectives have a

strong appeal for Asian scholars, first, because the socioeconomic situations in many parts of Asia are underdeveloped or developing. Many people live below the poverty level, the exploitation of the poor is an everyday reality, and many Asians live under oppressive governments. Second, since liberation theology is, by definition, contextual theology, it is a natural fit for those already engaged in contextual interpretation. In the 1970s Korea underwent a period of rapid economic and social change. Koreans also experienced political oppression and injustices under the military regime. Since no one was allowed to criticize the government, the people, especially the poor and laborers, were powerless to resist injustices. In this context, *minjung* theology emerged as a theological voice of Korean Christians in their struggle for democracy and human rights.

The sources of this theological voice are the Bible and the traditions and social biography of the *minjung* (the mass of the people). For example, N. D. Suh, a primary voice in the early conceptualization of *minjung* theology, argues that the total witness of the Bible may be clarified and understood in terms of two historical events—the exodus in the Hebrew Bible and Jesus' crucifixion and resurrection in the New Testament. They are paradigms of God's intervention in the political and socio-economic histories of the people (1981).

Two biblical scholars have made significant contributions to biblical interpretation from the perspective of *minjung* theology. B. M. Ahn, attempts a historical-critical study of the term *ochlos* and uses it to provide a biblical ground for *minjung* theology (1981). He suggests that the term *ochlos* in Mark's Gospel is indicative of a social class that has been marginalized and abandoned—namely, the sinners, the tax collectors, and the sick. They are the *minjung*, the alienated, dispossessed, and powerless. It is this group with whom Jesus sided and to whom he proclaimed the coming of God's kingdom.

C. Moon draws parallels between the social history of the Korean *minjung* and the Hebrews, using a rather Albrightian model (W. F. Albright[§]) of the exodus and the possession of the land of Canaan vis-à-vis a thirteenth-century exodus that took place during the reign of Rameses II (1985). Moon describes the Hebrews as *habiru*, as "rebels standing in defiance of the prevailing social or power structure," and adds, "the *habiru*, therefore, were part of the *minjung* of their time, driven by their *han* (grudge or resentment) to act against what they felt to be injustices imposed on them by those in power" (1985, 4). Clearly, Moon's understanding of the ancient Hebrews is influenced by and reconstructed from the experiences of the *minjung* in Korean history. In another chapter on the prophets (Prophecy and Prophets, Hebrew Bible[‡§]), he further suggests that the suffering and oppression in modern Korea are similar to that of ancient Israel during the eighth century B.C.E., particularly during the time of Amos and Micah (1985, 41-49). According to Moon, Micah's central concern was the suffering of "my people," who were oppressed and robbed of their property by the ruling class of Judah. As a commoner, Micah stood on the side of the oppressed and acted as their advocate, living and identifying with the *minjung*.

C. Abesamis (Philippines) declares unambiguously that his main exegetical instrument is "solidarity with the struggling poor of the Third World and viewing things through the eyes of the poor" and uses the concept of "reign-kingdom of God" in a number of his writings. He understands this concept as a new earth of justice and liberation without hunger and sorrow "where we finally attain to the full status of the sons and daughters of God" (1993, 67).

In an extensive study of the mission statements in Mark and Q (1987b), Abesamis shows that both accounts reveal that Jesus' mission centered around the proclamation of the reign-kingdom of God and justice and liberation for the poor and the oppressed. Clearly found in Q (Matt 11:2-6; Luke 7:18-23), the latter is implicitly present in Mark in such statements as "good news of God" (Mark 1:14-15).

In India, liberation theology found expression in the form of *Dalit* theology, beginning in the 1980s. The term *dalit* refers to oppressed peoples, especially the "untouchables," who belong at the bottom of the caste system. A. Nirmal locates the basis of *Dalit* theology in Deut 26:5-12 (1988). He suggests that, in this ancient Israelite creedal statement, concepts of being "few in number," of recognizing their "affliction," of achieving liberation through "terror," and of securing "a land flowing with milk and honey," are paradigmatic for *Dalit* theology. D. Carr argues that "Matthew provides the most comprehensive model for *Dalit* theology" (1994, 284). Understanding the "lost sheep of the House of Israel" as the "despised Galileans, the exploited poor, the physically handicapped who were deemed cursed, the hated tax gatherers and the stigmatized women sex workers," (1994, 239-40) Carr sees strong parallels between Matthew's depiction and the situation of the *Dalits*, who are "an oppressed, ostracized and stigmatized group" (1994, 244), and argues that Matthew affirms God's partiality toward them.

4. *Feminist Hermeneutics.* Scholars have rightly noted that feminism is an extension of liberation theology. While liberation theologians are most concerned with socioeconomic and political injustic, feminist theologians critically add the issue of gender inequality in their critical engagement. Kwok Pui-lan (Hong Kong) has presented ten theses as the foundation of her Feminist Interpretation*§ (1995), including critically examining the politics of biblical authority*§ and the historical-critical method; taking seriously the story of women of color, particularly their multiple oppression in terms of class, gender, and race; and condemning anti-Semitism and oppression and discrimination against any racial group. Her analysis of Jesus and the Syrophoenician woman (Matt 15:21-28; Mark 7:24-30) well illustrates her feminist concerns: "[this story] brings into sharp focus the complex issues of the relationship among different racial and ethnic groups, the interaction between men and women, cultural imperialism, and colonization" (Kwok 1995, 72). Investigating the intersection of anti-Judaism, sexism, and colonialism in the history of interpretation of this story, she offers sharp criticism of the use of the salvation-history model to interpret this story. Such a model stresses the unequal status of Jesus and the woman and, by interpreting the woman's remarks as signifying her faith and humility, portrays her as a paragon of Christian virtue. Moreover, the story has also been read as shifting the blessing of God's salvation from the Jews to the Gentiles, thus condoning anti-Judaism. Kwok further notes that, when the gospel was spread to Asia, the faith and humility of the Syrophoenician woman was used as a model for the "heathens" of Asia to emulate in order to support colonialism and imperialism.

Seeing women's struggles as a struggle for liberation, A. Gnanadason (India) calls for a reexamination of the issue of biblical authority and a reinterpretation of biblical texts from the perspective of women. She has suggested that, in the story of Jesus and the Samaritan woman (John 4:5-30), the source of empowerment in the narrative is embedded, not only in Jesus' dialogue with an outcast, but also in his transformation of the woman into a missionary to the Samaritans (1992). She also notes that the woman's leaving her water jar behind symbolizes her break from a "life of oppression and sinfulness so as to internalize the liberating power of the living water" (1992, 120).

5. *Postcolonial Interpretation.* Kwok's work "Woman, Dogs, and Crumbs" (1995, 71-83), is an example of the Postcolonial*§ interests that some Asian biblical scholars are beginning to exhibit. P. Chia (Malaysia) provides an alternative reading to Daniel 1 whereby representation, resistance, colonization, and neocolonialism are at work (1997). By studying the narrator's plot and the characterizations of Nebuchadnezzar, Daniel, and others, Chia argues that what lies behind the stories is postcolonialism as an ideology (Ideological Criticism*§). In articulating a representation of the colonized past and of the voices of the exile, the narrator reflects a colonized identity and a postcolonial ideology, mirrored through the characters in the stories. The renaming of Daniel and his friends in the Chaldean language is seen as an act of colonization by Nebuchadnezzar that is countered by Daniel's resistance to the royal food, an act of rejecting the king's claim of colonial power over life and death.

Using the context of postcolonial Hong Kong after its reversion to China, Lee attempts a rereading of Isaiah 56–66 (1997). He begins by describing the "highly hybridized" (culturally Chinese and pragmatically British, in economy and legal structures) sociocultural context of Hong Kong. Postcoloniality in such a context, Lee argues, must then be understood "in terms of the conscious effort to combat marginalization and to reaffirm the denied or allocated subjectivity of Hong Kong against British colonizer before and the Chinese sovereign power at present." These efforts will include reappropriating traditions, retrieving repressed histories, and negotiating a different "in-between" identity. Turning his attention to the context of Trito-Isaiah, Lee notes that the community in Babylon was made up primarily of a younger generation who had begun to create a sense of identity as a people from Palestine living in a foreign land. The returnees from exile, then, must have been quite different from those left behind in Palestine in terms of their lifestyles, cultural orientations, sociopolitical identities, and religious practices. Just as in the situation in Hong Kong, where there are different voices and models for constructing the future of the city, there were also dissenting movements and conflicting voices in the postexilic community of ancient Israel.

6. *Conclusion.* There is no one method of Asian biblical interpretation. Asian biblical scholars have generally utilized three broad categories of biblical exegesis: Western *wissenschaft,* interpretation from their own cultural perspective, and interpretation (relying upon postcolonial thought) in light of various forms of oppression and the colonial heritage. Scholarship in the first category continues and deepens the insights of traditional academic biblical study. Scholars using the final two categories not only supplement Western *wissenschaft,* but also creatively apply biblical texts to their own cultural setting, challenge Western political and economic policies toward Asia, and stimulate fresh reflection upon the Bible and its relationship to and use by the surrounding culture.

Bibliography: **C. H. Abesamis,** *Salvation, Historical and Total: Towards a Faith-life That Is Biblical, Historical, Indigenous* (The Integral Evangelism Series, 1978); *On Mark and the New World, the Good News: Letters from C. Abesamis* (1983); *Where Are We Going: Heaven or New World?* (Foundation Books, 1986); *The Mission of Jesus and Good News to the Poor: Biblico-pastoral Considerations for a Church in the Third World* (Nagliliyab 8, 1987a); "The Mission of Jesus and Good News to the Poor: Exegetico-Pastoral Considerations for a Church in the Third World," *AJT* 1 (1987*b*) 429-60; *A Third Look at Jesus: A Catechetical Guidebook* (1988); "Some Paradigms in Re-reading the Bible in a Third World Setting," *Mission Studies 7* (1990) 21-34; "The Contextual and Universal Dimensions of Christian Theology: A NT Perspective," *Bangalore Theological Forum* 24 (1992) 16-23; "A Third Look at Jesus and Salvation: A Bible Study on Mark 1:14-15," *Asian Christian Spirituality: Reclaiming Traditions* (ed. V. Fabella et al., 1992) 134-41; "Heart of the Matter: Re-discovering the Core-Message of the NT in the Third World," *Any Room for Christ in Asia?* (ed. L. Boff and V. Elizondo, 1993) 63-76. **B. M. Ahn,** "Jesus and the *Minjung* in the Gospel of Mark," Minjung *Theology: People as the Subjects of History* (ed. The Commission on Theological Concerns of the Christian Conference of Asia, 1981) 138-52; "The Body of Jesus-event Tradition," *EAJT 3* (1985) 293-310. **D. S. Amalorpavadass,** "The Bible in Self-renewal and Church-renewal for Service to Society," *Voices from the Margin: Interpreting the Bible in the Third World* (ed. R. S. Sugirtharajah, 1991) 316-29. **C. Amjad-Ali,** "The Equality of Women: Form or Substance (1 Cor 11:12-16)," ibid., 185-93. **K. Arayaprateep,** "The Covenant: An Effective Tool in Bible Study," *SEAJT 18* (1977) 21-31. An Asian Group Work, "An Asian Feminist Perspective: The Exodus Story (Exod 1:8-22, 2:1-10)," *Voices from the Margin* (ed. R. S. Sugirtharajah, 1995²) 255-66. **T. C. Bacani, Jr.,** *God's Own People in the Scriptures* (1965); *The Bible for the Filipinos* (1989). **J. B. Banawiratma,** *Jesus Sang Guru: Pertemuan Kejawendengan Injil (Jesus the Teacher)* (1977). **R. Budiman,**

"Contextual Witness and Exegesis," *Study Institute "Contextual Exegesis" di Ujung Pandang, 1980* (1981) 50-56. **N. C. Capulong,** "Land, Power, and People's Rights in the OT: From a Filipino Theological Perspective," *EAJT 2* (1984) 233-50. **D. Carr,** "A Biblical Basis for Dalit Theology," *Indigenous People, Dalits: Dalit Issues in Today's Theological Debate* (ISPCK Contextual Theological Education Series 5, ed. J. Massey, 1994) 231-49. **V. Chakkarai,** *Jesus the Avatar* (Indian Series, 1926). **P. M. Chang,** "Jeremiah's Hope in Action: An Exposition of Jer 32:1-15," *EAJT 2* (1984) 244-50. **S. H. Chao,** "Confucian Chinese and the Gospel: Methodological Considerations," *AJT 7* (1987) 17-40. **T. C. Chao,** "The Articulate Word and the Problem of Communications," *IRM 36* (1947) 482-89. **P. P. Chia,** "Intersubjectivity, Intertextuality, Interconnectivity: On Biblical Hermeneutics and Hegemony," *Jian Dao 5* (1996) 1-21; "On Naming the Subject: Postcolonial Reading of Daniel 1," *Jian Dao 7* (1997) 17-36. **A. P. Corleto, Jr.,** "Creation and Fall in Genesis 1–3 and Philippine Creation Myths," *Diwa 7* (1982–83) 1-17. **A. Gnanadason,** "Towards an Indian Feminist Theology," *We Dare to Dream: Doing Theology as Asian Women* (ed. V. Fabella and S. A. L. Park, 1989) 117-26; "Indian Women: New Voices, New Visions," *Third World Theologies in Dialogue: Essays in Memory of D. S. Amalorpavadass* (ed. J. R. Chandran, 1991) 143-51; "The Holy Spirit Liberates and Unites," *We Belong Together: Churches in Solidarity with Women* (ed. S. Cunningham, 1992) 116-21; "Dalit Women: The Dalit of the Dalit," *Indigenous People, Dalits: Dalit Issues in Today's Theological Debate* (ed. J. Massey, 1994) 168-76. **T. Ishida,** *The Royal Dynasties in Ancient Israel: A Study on the Formation and Development of Royal-dynastic Ideology* (BZAW 142, 1977); (ed.), *Studies in the Period of David and Solomon and Other Essays* (1982); "Adonijah the Son of Haggith and His Supporters: An Inquiry into Problems About History and Historiography," *The Future of Biblical Studies: The Hebrew Scriptures* (SemeiaSt, ed. R. E. Friedman and H. G. M. Williamson, 1987) 165-87; "The Role of Nathan the Prophet in the Episode of Solomon's Birth," *Near Eastern Studies: Dedicated to H.I.H. Prince Takahito Mikasa on the Occasion of His Seventy-fifth Birthday* (ed. M. Mori et al., 1991) 133-38; "The Succession Narrative and Esarhaddon's Apology: A Comparison," *Ah, Assyria . . . Studies in Assyrian History and Ancient Near Eastern Historiography Presented to H. Tadmor* (ed. M. Cogan and I. Eph'al, 1991) 166-73. **Y. M. Jia,** *Shen-dao-Shueh* [*The Way of God*] (1921). **P. Kalluveettil,** "The Marginalizing Dialectics of the Bible," *BiBh 11* (1985) 201-14. **M. Katoppo,** *Compassionate and Free: An Asian Woman's Theology* (Risk Book Series 6, 1979). **H. Kayama,** "The Cornelius Story in the Japanese Cultural Context," *Text and Experience: Towards a Cultural Exegesis of the Bible* (BiSe 35, ed. D. L. Smith-Christopher, 1995) 180-94. **C. H. Kim,** *Form and Structure of the Familiar Greek Letter of Recommendation* (1972); "Reading the Bible as Asian Americans," *NIB* (1994) 1:161-66. **E. K. Kim,** "Who Is Yahweh? Based on a Contextual Reading of Exod 3:14," *AJT3* (1989) 108-17. **H. Kinukawa,** "The Story of the Hemorrhaging Woman (Mark 5:25-34) Read from a Japanese Feminist Context," *BibInt 2* (1994) 283-93; *Women and Jesus in Mark: A Japanese Feminist Perspective* (The Bible and Liberation Series, 1994); "On John 7:53–8:11: A Well-Cherished but Much-Clouded Story," *Reading from This Place: Social Location and Biblical Interpretation in Global Perspective 2* (ed. F. F. Segovia and M. A. Tolbert, 1995) 82-96. **G. Koonthanam,** "Yahweh the Defender of the *Dalits*: A Reflection on Isaiah 3:12-15," *Jeev 22* (1992) 112-23. **P.-L. Kwok,** "God Weeps with Our Pain," *EAJT 2* (1984) 228-32; "Discovering the Bible in the Non-biblical World," *Semeia 47* (1989) 25-42; *Discovering the Bible in the Non-biblical World* (The Bible and Liberation Series, 1995); "Chinese Christians and Their Bible," *BibInt 4* (1996) 127-29. **S. Largunpai,** "The Book of Ecclesiastes and Thai Buddhism" *AJT 8* (1994) 155-62. **A. C. C. Lee,** "Doing Theology in Chinese Context: The David-Bathsheba Story and the Parable of Nathan," *EAJT 3* (1985) 243-57; "Returning to China: Biblical Interpretation in the Postcolonial Hong Kong," *BibInt 7* (1999) 156-73; "The 'Critique of Foundations' in the Hebrew Wisdom

Tradition," *AJT 4* (1990) 126-35; "Biblical Interpretation in Asian Perspective," *AJT 7* (1993a) 35-39; "Genesis 1 from the Perspective of a Chinese Creation Myth," *Understanding Poets and Prophets: Essays in Honour of G. W. Anderson* (JSOTSup 152, ed. A. G. Auld, 1993b) 186-98; "The Chinese Creation Myth of Nu Kua and the Biblical Narrative in Genesis 1–11," *BibInt 2* (1994) 312-24; "Death and the Perception of the Divine in Qohelet and Zhuang Zi," *Ching Feng 38* (1995) 69-81; "Exile and Return in the Perspective of 1997," *Reading from This Place: Social Location and Biblical Interpretation in Global Perspective*, vol. 2 (ed. F. F. Segovia and M. A. Tolbert, 1995) 97-108; "Feminist Critique of the Bible and Female Principle in Culture," *AJT 10* (1996) 240-52. **K. Y. Liem,** "Enacting the Acts of God: One Important Aspect of Life and Proclamation of Jesus and Paul," *SEAJT 14, 2* (1973) 21-33. **C. Lo,** "Chinese Biblical Interpretation in the Eyes of a Chinese Christian," *BibInt 4* (1996) 124-26. **T. Manikkam,** "Towards an Indian Hermeneutics of the Bible," *Jeev 12* (1982) 94-104. **A. Mariaselvam,** *The Song of Songs and Ancient Tamil Love Poems: Poetry and Symbolism* (AnBib 118, 1988). **N. Minz,** "A Theological Interpretation of the Tribal Reality," *RelSoc 34* (1987) 71-85. **C. H. S. Moon,** "An OT Understanding of *Minjung*," Minjung *Theology: People as the Subjects of History* (ed. The Commission on Theological Concerns of the Christian Conference of Asia, 1981) 119-35; *A Korean* Minjung *Theology: An OT Perspective* (1985). **J. G. Muthuraj,** "NT and Methodology: An Overview," *AJT 10* (1996) 253-77. **D. P. Niles,** "Examples of Contextualization in the OT," *SEAJT 21, 2* (1980) 19-33; "The Word of God and the People of Asia," *Understanding the Word: Essays in Honor of B. W. Anderson* (JSOTSup 37, ed. J. T. Butler et al., 1985) 281-313. **A. P. Nirmal,** "A Dialogue with Dalit Literature," *Towards a Dalit Theology* (ed. M. E. Prabhakar, 1988) 64-82. **C. Panackal,** "The Option of the Poor in the Letter of James," *BiBh 15* (1989) 141-53. **M. Pongudom,** "Creation of Man: Theological Reflections Based on Northern Thai Folktales," *EAJT 3* (1985) 222-27. **D. N. Premnath,** "The OT Against Its Cultural Background and Its Implications for Theological Education," *AJT 2* (1988) 98-105; "The Concepts of Rta and Maat: A Study in Comparison," *BibInt 2* (1994) 325-39. **R. J. Raja,** "The Gospels with an Indian Face," *Vid 55* (1991) 61-72, 121-41. **S. Rayan,** "Jesus and the Poor in the Fourth Gospel," *BiBh 4* (1978) 213-28. **G. Robinson,** "Jesus Christ, the Open Way and the Fellow-struggle: A Look into the Christologies in India," *AJT 3* (1989) 403-15. **K. K. Sacon and K. Matsunaga,** "Biblical Scholarship, Japanese," *ABD* 1:737-40. **S. J. Samartha,** *The Search for New Hermeneutic in Asian Christian Theology* (1987); *One Christ—Many Religions: Toward a Revised Christology* (1991); "Religion, Language, and Reality: Towards a Relational Hermeneutics," *BibInt 2* (1994) 340-62. **C. L. Seow,** *Myth, Drama, and the Politics of David's Dance* (HSM 44, 1989); *Ecclesiastes* (AB 18C, 1997). **E. G. Singgih,** *Dari Israel ke Asia: Masalah Hubungan di Antara Kontekstualisasi Teologia dengan Interpretasi Alkitabiah* [*From Israel to Asia: The Relationship Between Contextual Theology and Biblical Interpretation*] (1982); "Let Me Not Be Put to Shame: Towards an Indonesian Hermeneutics," *AJT 9* (1995) 71-85; "Contextualization and Inter-religious Relationship in Java: Past and Present," *AJT 11* (1997) 248-62. **G. M. Soares-Prabhu,** "Towards an Indian Interpretation of the Bible," *BiBh 6* (1980) 151-70; "The Historical-Critical Method: Reflections on Its Relevance for the Studies of the Gospels in India Today," *Theologizing in India* (ed. M. Amaladoss et al., 1981) 314-49; "The Kingdom of God: Jesus' Vision of a New Society," *Indian Church in the Struggle* (ed. D. S. Amalorpavadass, 1981) 579-608; "The Prophet as Theologian: Biblical Prophetism as a Paradigm for Doing Theology Today," *AJT 2* (1988) 3-11; "Interpreting the Bible in India Today," The Way Supp, 72 (1990) 70-80; "Class in the Bible: The Biblical Poor as a Social Class?" *Voices from the Margin: Interpreting the Bible in the Third World* (ed. R. S. Sugirtharajah, 1991) 147-71; "Jesus in Egypt: A Reflection on Matt 2:13-15, 19-21 in the Light of the OT," *EstBib 50* (1992) 225-49; "The Table Fellowship of Jesus: Its Significance for *Dalit* Christians in India Today," *Jeev 22* (1992) 140-59;. "Anti-Greed and Anti-Pride: Mark 10:17-27 and 10:35-45 in the Light of Tribal Values," *Jeev 24* (1994) 130-50; "Two Mission Commands: An Interpretation of Matt 28:16-20 in the Light of a Buddhist Text," *BibInt 2* (1994) 264-82; "The Bible as Magna Carta of Movements for Liberation and Human Rights," *The Bible as Cultural Heritage* (ed. W. Beuken et al., 1995) 85-96; "Laughing at Idols: The Dark Side of Biblical Monotheism (an Indian Reading of Isa 44:9-20)," *Reading from This Place: Social Location and Biblical Interpretation in Global Perspective*, vol. 2 (ed. F. F. Segovia and M. A. Tolbert, 1995) 109-31. **C. S. Song,** "From Israel to Asia: A Theological Leap," *Theology 79* (1976) 90-96; *Jesus, the Crucified People* (1990); *Jesus and the Reign of God* (1993); *Jesus in the Power of the Spirit* (1994). **R. S. Sugirtharajah,** " 'For You Always Have the Poor with You': An Example of Hermeneutics of Suspicion," *AJT 4* (1990a) 102-7; *Studies 7* (1990b) 9-20; "The Bible and Its Asian Readers," *BibInt 1* (1993) 54-66; "Inter-faith Hermeneutics: An Example and Some Implications," *Mission, the Text and the Texts: Some Examples of Biblical Interpretation in Asia* (1993); "Introduction and Some Thoughts on Asian Biblical Hermeneutics," *BibInt 2* (1994) 251-63; "From Orientalist to Post-colonial: Notes on Reading Practices," *AJT 10* (1996) 20-27; "Orientalism, Ethnonationalism, and Transnationalism: Shifting Identities and Biblical Interpretation," *Ethnicity and the Bible* (ed. M. Brett, 1996) 419-29; "Texts Are Always with You: Christians and Their Bibles," *Hindu-Christian Studies Bulletin 9* (1996) 8-13. **N. D. Suh,** "Historical References for a Theology of *Minjung*," Minjung *Theology: People as the Subjects of History* (ed. The Commission on Theological Concerns of the Christian Conference of Asia, 1981) 155-82. **M. T. Thangaraj,** *The Crucified Guru: An Experiment in Cross-cultural Christology* (1994). **I. Vempeny,** Krzna *and Christ: In the Light of Some of the Fundamental Concepts and Themes of the Bhagavad Gita and the NT* (1988). **S. W. Wahono,** *Gambaran-gambaran Kontekstuil Hubungan Yahweh dan Bangsa Israel di dalam Perjanjian Lama* [*Descriptions of the Contextual Relationship Between Yahweh and the Israelites in the OT*] (1979). **S.-K. Wan,** "Allegorical Interpretation East and West: A Methodological Enquiry into Comparative Hermeneutics," *Text and Experience: Towards a Cultural Exegesis of the Bible* (ed. D. L. Smith-Christopher, 1995) 154-79. **Z. Watanabe,** *The Doctrine of Scriptures* (1949–63). **S. H. Widyapranawa,** *The Lord Is Savior: Faith in National Crisis: A Commentary on the Book of Isaiah 1–39* (ITC, 1990). **A. Wire,** "Chinese Biblical Interpretation Since Mid-century," *BibInt 4* (1996) 101-23. **L.-C. Wu,** *Chi-du-chiao yu chung-kuo wun-hwa* [*Christianity and Chinese Culture*] (1936). **K. K. Yeo,** "Amos (4:4-5) and Confucius: The Will (Ming) of God (Tien)," *AJT 4* (1990) 472-88; "The Rhetorical Hermeneutic of 1 Corinthians 8 and Chinese Ancestor Worship," *BibInt 2* (1994) 294-311; "A Rhetorical Study of Acts 17:22-31: What Has Jerusalem to Do with Athens and Beijing?" *Jian Dao 1* (1994) 75-107; "The 'Yin-Yang' of God (Exod 3:14) and Humanity (Gen 1:26-27)," *ZRGG 46* (1994) 319-32; "Isa 5:2-7 and 27:2-6: Let's Hear the Whole Song of Rejection and Restoration," *Jian Dao 3* (1995) 77-94; *Rhetorical Interaction in 1 Corinthians 8 and 10: A Formal Analysis with Preliminary Suggestions for a Chinese Cross-cultural Hermeneutic* (1995); "A Confucian Reading of Romans 7:14-25: *Nomos* (Law) and *Li* (Propriety)," *Jian Dao 5* (1996) 127-41; "Christ-centered Multi-cultural Hermeneutics: The Examination of Gal 2:15-16, 3:1-20," *Jian Dao 7* (1997) 57-76; *What Has Jerusalem to Do with Beijing? Biblical Interpretation from a Chinese Perspective* (1998). **J. Y. H. Yieh,** "Cultural Reading of the Bible: Some Chinese Christian Cases," *Text and Experience: Towards a Cultural Exegesis of the Bible* (BiSe 35, ed. D. L. Smith-Christopher, 1995) 122-53. **A. M. Zabala,** "Advent Reflections on Col 1:15-20 in the Philippines Setting," *AJT 3* (1989) 315-29.

J. KUAN

CONTEXTUAL APPROACHES

Cross-Cultural Biblical Interpretation

The Christian Bible is, among other things, a cultural text. Its textual features document theological and doctrinal elements and embody the spiritual and political aspirations of a people whose way of life, customs, and manners are very different from those of contemporary readers. Thus, reading these texts can be a difficult endeavor. Cross-cultural biblical interpretation seeks to overcome the remoteness and strangeness of the texts by employing the reader's cultural resources and social experiences to make links across the cultural divides, thus illuminating the biblical narratives. This approach to interpretation invites readers to use their own indigenous texts and concepts to make hermeneutical sense of biblical texts and concepts imported across time and space. In opening up biblical narratives, cross-cultural Hermeneutics§, to use R. Schreiter's categories (1997, 29), draws on the three-dimensional aspects of a culture: ideational (worldviews, values, and rules), performantial (rituals and roles), and material (language, symbols, food, clothing, etc.). In other words, using indigenous beliefs and experiences, cross-cultural hermeneutics attempts to provide important analogies with ancient texts that readers from other cultures may not notice or be aware of. What, in effect, such readings have done is to make culture an important locus for hermeneutics.

The emergence of indigenous ways of reading the Bible by the peoples of the Third World has given the impression that cross-cultural hermeneutics is something recent and exotic, confined to cultures "out there" and absent from Western readings. Biblical interpretation, however, has always been culturally specific and has always been informed and colored by reigning cultural values, be they Western, Eastern, or Southern. Western scholars have not been free from such tendencies. For example, when H. S. Reimarus§ and D. F. Strauss§ extended the use of the critical methods developed in the linguistic and historical disciplines during the eighteenth century to investigation of biblical narratives, when R. Bultmann§ mobilized M. Heidegger's existential philosophy to interpret New Testament kerygma, or when current biblical scholars borrow critical methodologies and theories from contemporary Literary*§ or social science studies (Social-Scientific Criticism*§), they, too, are engaged in cross-cultural hermeneutics in the sense that they are trying to relate ancient texts to their own contexts by employing the Western cultural codes of their time. Such practices, however, tend to be treated as value free and to be subsumed under the rubric of scientific exegesis. Yet even a brief perusal of the history of hermeneutics will reveal that there has never been an interpretation that has been without reference to or dependence on the particular cultural codes, thought patterns, and social location of the interpreter.

Surveying the field of cross-cultural biblical interpretation, one can identify at least three modes of cross-cultural reading: conceptual correspondences, narratival enrichments, and performantial parallels.

1. *Conceptual Correspondences.* The first mode is to seek textual or conceptual parallels between biblical texts and the traditions of one's own culture. Such an effort, unlike historical criticism, looks beyond the Judaic or Greco-Roman context of the biblical narratives and seeks corresponding conceptual analogies in the readers' textual traditions. Indian Christian interpreters of an earlier generation were the pioneers in this mode. K. Banerjea demonstrated remarkable similarities between biblical and Vedic texts. He selected overlapping narrative segments that touched on the creation, the fall, and the flood from the great wealth of Vedic writings and juxtaposed them with passages from the Bible, emphasizing that the expectations of the Indian texts were fulfilled in Christianity. A. Appasamy borrowed key ideas from *bhakti*, the Hindu devotional tradition, to make sense of Johannine†§ spirituality. By conscripting concepts

like *moksa* (liberation), *antaryamin* (indweller), and *avatar* (incarnation) as a way of getting into the thought world of John, Appasamy invested these Hindu concepts with Christian meanings and also accentuated the role of Jesus*§. In China, Wu Lei-ch'uan was engaged in a similar exercise, attempting to integrate Confucian concepts with biblical ones. He utilized the fundamental Confucian concept of highest virtue, *jen*, as well as those of *Tien-tzu* (Son of Heaven) and *Sheng Tien-tzu* (Holy Son of God) to elucidate the Holy Spirit and the role of Jesus (J. Yieh 1995). The Japanese theologian K. Kitamori's (1965) employment of *tsura* to explain the pain of God; the South African artist A. Mbatha's (1986) use of *ubunto* to appropriate the story of Joseph as that, not of an individual, but of a community (1986); and G. West's (1993) recovery of the African notions of *indlovukazi* (first wife), *inthandokazi* (favorite wife), and *isancinza* (helper to the wife) as interpretative keys to explain the matrilineal presence and power and to determine the role of Leah, Rachel, Bilhah, and Zilpah also fall within this mode.

In this same mode, insights from popular culture are summoned to critically illuminate biblical texts. O. Hendricks (1994), an African American, calls for the use of such cultural expressions as blues, soul, and jazz to formulate a "guerrilla exegesis." Australian aboriginals' attempts to translate aboriginal dreaming stories in Christian terms, citing passages from both testaments to convey the essential moral message (A. Pattel-Gray 1995), and the reclamation of two pivotal Indian tribal values, anti-pride and anti-greed, that resonate with the Markan narrative (Mark 10:17-27, 35-45) as an alternative model for a world driven by greed and consumerism are further examples of the use of elements from popular culture (see G. Soares-Prabhu 1995).

2. *Narratival Enrichments*. The second mode of cross-cultural reading is to place some of the popular folktales (Folklore*§), legends, riddles, plays, proverbs, and poems that are part of the common heritage of a people alongside biblical materials, thus drawing out their hermeneutical implications. C. Song, the Taiwanese theologian who pioneered the method of creatively juxtaposing myths (Mythology and Biblical Studies*§), stories, and legends with biblical narratives, often goes beyond the written word to the symbolic meaning. In *The Tears of Lady Meng* (1982), Song blends a well-known Chinese folktale with the biblical theme of Jesus' death and resurrection. P. Lee (1989) juxtaposes the book of Ruth and a Yuan period Chinese drama, "The Injustice Done to Ton Ngo." Both stories are about a daughter-in-law and her devotion to her mother-in-law, and both emerge out of a patriarchal society. Although the two stories differ in plot, the ethical and metaphysical perspectives shine through. S. Rayan, in his essay "Wrestling in the Night" (1989), juxtaposes in an imaginative way three texts, two ancient—the Bhagavadgita and the book of Job—and one modern—the posthumous writings of a young girl, eponymously entitled the Poems of Gitanjali. These three works represent three religious traditions: Hindu, Jewish, and Islamic. In spite of the time span and the different religious orientations, the characters Arjuna, Job, and Gitanjali testify that sorrow and pain are universal. All three wrestle with death, pain, love, and God; and through sorrow and anguish each grows in faith and love. Africans too are engaged in retrieving their folk-tales. The "Parable of the Two Brothers," a popular story among the Sukuma people of Tanzania, has interesting parallels with the Lukan prodigal son. Both these stories have a father and two sons, and in both the younger son is received back into the family and rewarded. Although in their plots and in their thematic emphases they may differ, the additional insights that the Sukuma parable provides, such as values of community and unity, can enrich the biblical story.

3. *Performantial Parallels*. The third mode of cross-cultural reading is to utilize ritual and behavioral practices that are commonly available in a culture: The Johannine saying of Jesus, "Very truly, I tell you, unless you eat the flesh of the Son of Man and drink his blood, you have no life in you. Those who eat my flesh and drink my blood have eternal life, and I will raise them up on the last day; for my flesh is true food and my blood is true drink" (John 6:53-55),

may sound awkward and cannibalistic to those who are reared with Western Enlightenment values. But read analogically to Malawian witchcraft talk, as A. Musopole (1993) has done, the saying takes on a different meaning: "Anyone who feeds on Jesus takes into themselves the very life-force of Jesus to re-enforce their own lives" (1993, 352). Such a reading can be understood metaphorically as a eucharistic saying or literally as witchcraft talk.

The African concept of the trickster, though it differs from context to context, is also a helpful channel through which to appraise the behavior of some biblical characters who, viewed from a Western moral perspective, may seem unreliable and deceitful. From an African trickster point of view, such actions are recognized as performed by people who lack power and live in hopeless situations. Trickery is something men and women often turn to in situations where they have no other recourse. Abraham's deceptive statements to Pharaoh and Abimelech (Gen 12:10-20; 20:1-18), the explanation given by Hebrew midwives for their unwillingness to discharge Pharaoh's order to kill all male children born to Israelites (Exod 1:15-19), and Delilah's attempts to woo and overcome Samson (Judges 16) are examples of the trickster role played in the Bible by individuals who are otherwise powerless (N. Steinberg 1988).

In assessing cross-cultural hermeneutics, one finds both positive and negative features. Positively, cross-cultural hermeneutics has enabled Christian interpreters to gain credibility and cultivate deeper contact with their own people, who otherwise would have regarded Christians as foreigners in their own country. A variety of culture-informed interpretations has offered counter-readings to those of Western interpretations, with their ethnocentric and rationalistic prejudices, and helped to reverse the missionary condemnation of indigenous cultures. The mobilization of cultural insights has served as an acknowledgment that religious truths were present in indigenous cultures even before the arrival and introduction of Christianity. It has also strengthened the notion that indigenous people are not passive receivers; rather, they are architects of their own hermeneutics. Creatively intermixing and synthesizing biblical faith with indigenous religion has enabled, for instance, Mayan identity in Guatemala to survive.

Negatively, in pressing for comparable cultural elements, cross-cultural hermeneutics has tended to overemphasize the positive aspects of ancient cultures while overlooking their dehumanizing aspects. It is tempting to assume that indigenous people have access to privileged knowledge in unraveling the mysteries of ancient texts. However, to do so would be to reinscribe a hermeneutical hierarchy in which some have an unequal access and relation to texts. Cross-cultural hermeneutics became a celebratory event when indigenous people were assumed to lead a settled life and were thought of in terms of cultural wholes. But now, at a time when there is an intermixing of cultures both at popular and elitist levels and when local/global and vernacular/cosmopolitan divides are shrinking and people's lives are being rearranged by globalization, finding culture-specific analogues may be an increasingly difficult task. Alternatively, of course, the new multivision may throw up its own hitherto undiscovered parallels.

Bibliography: *Biblical Interpretation: A Journal of Contemporary Approaches* 2 (no. 3, 1993; special issue on Asian hermeneutics). **M. Brett** (ed.), *Ethnicity and the Bible* (BIS 19, 1996). **C. H. Felder,** *Stony the Road We Trod: African-American Biblical Interpretation* (1991). **J. Healey and D. Sybertz,** *Towards an African Narrative Theology* (Faith and Culture Series, 1996). **O. O. Hendricks,** "Guerrilla Exegesis: A Post Modern Proposal for Insurgent African American Biblical Interpretation," *JITC* 22, 1 (1994) 92-109. **K. Kitamori,** Theology of the Pain of God (1965). **P. K. H. Lee,** "Two Stories of Loyalty," *Ching Feng* 32:1 (1989) 24-40. **A. Mbatha,** *In the Heart of the Tiger: Art of South Africa* (1986). **A. C. Musopole,** "Witchcraft Terminology, the Bible, and African Christian Theology: An Exercise in Hermeneutics," *JITC* 23, 4 (1993) 347-54. **A. Pattel-Gray,** "Dreaming: An Aboriginal Interpretation of the Bible," *Text and Experience* (ed. D. Smith-Christopher, 1995) 247-59. **S. Rayan,** "Wrestling in the

Night," *The Future of Liberation Theology: Essays in Honor of G. Gutierrez* (ed. M. H. Ellis and O. Maduro, 1989) 450-69. **G. M. Soares-Prabhu,** "Anti-Greed and Anti-Pride: Mark 10.17-27 and 10.35-45 in the Light of Tribal Values," *Voices from the Margin: Interpreting the Bible in the Third World* (ed. R. S. Sugirtharajah, 1995) 117-37. **R. Schreiter,** *The New Catholicity: Theology Between the Global and the Local* (Faith and Series, 1997). **F. F. Segovia and M. A. Tolbert** (eds.), *Reading from this Place,* vol. 2 (1995). **D. Smith-Christopher** (ed.), *Text and Experience: Towards A Cultural Exegesis of the Bible* (BiSe 35, 1995). **C. S. Song,** *The Tears of Lady Meng: A Parable of People's Political Theology* (1982). **N. Steinberg,** "Israelite Tricksters: Their Analogues and Cross-Cultural Study," *Semeia 42* (1988) 1-13. **R. S. Sugirtharajah** (ed.), *Voices from the Margin: Interpreting the Bible in the Third World* (new ed., 1995). **G. O. West,** *Contextual Bible Study* (1993). **J. Y. H. Yieh,** "Cultural Reading of the Bible: Some Chinese Christian Cases," *Text and Experience* (ed. D. Smith-Christopher, 1995) 122-53.

R. S. SUGIRTHARAJAH

CONTEXTUAL APPROACHES

Euro-American Biblical Interpretation

The method of interpretation that arose in Europe during the Enlightenment, and established itself in the German, English, and French speaking worlds is known as historical criticism. Not a single methodology, historical criticism consists of a number of philological, literary, and historical approaches complementing and correcting each other. The goal of historical criticism is the discovery of the meaning which the text had for its first readers. The means by which the original sense is determined is reason, rather than ecclesiastical tradition (Lessing[§]). Thus historical criticism is shaped by the values of the Enlightenment and seeks to enable human emancipation and pluralism. Yet in its origins, historical criticism is founded upon two theological principles: first, the distinction between Scriptures and the Word of God (Semler[§] 1771-75); second, the difference between biblical and dogmatic theology (Gabler[§] 1787). The first is motivated by the desire to discover in the ancient texts elements which might contribute to the ethical improvement of humanity; yet, as a hermeneutical principle, it leads inevitably to the invalidation of the doctrine of the verbal inspiration of Scripture. The second principle aims at establishing biblical theology as an independent discipline based upon historical and philological methods, yet results in a distinction between exegesis and interpretation which may be taken to imply relativism. Despite its illuminating results, historical criticism has met with resistance from fundamentalists and traditionalists, who do not share its basic theological principles.

The practice of historical criticism depends upon resources which make possible comparison, contrast, and analysis in a systematic fashion. Consequently, the energies of Euro-American scholars have been devoted to the creation of tools deemed indispensable for historical-critical study of the Bible. Foremost among these is the critical text: for the Hebrew scriptures, the *Biblia Hebraica Stuttgartensia*; for the New Testament, the *Novum Testamentum Graece*. Also of great importance is the Greek translation of the Old Testament and Apocrypha called the *Septuagint* (a critical edition has been in preparation since 1931 and has been published in installments). An essential tool for the study of the gospels is the *Synopsis Quattuor Evangeliorum* (ed. K. Aland[§]), which presents parallel passages from the four gospels, supplemented by numerous citations from the church fathers. Lexica are crucial to an understanding of the language and thought of the biblical texts. Of special importance for the study of the New Testament is Walter Bauer's[§] *Greek-English Lexicon of the New Testament and Other Early Christian Literature* (revised and edited by F. Danker); abundant citations from Jewish, Greek, and early Christian literature illuminate the usage of New Testament writers and make possible the recovery of the rich, connotative meaning of words and phrases. A window into the language of ordinary life is provided by Moulton and Milligan, *Vocabulary of the Greek Testament* (1929) illustrated from the papyri, ostraca, and inscriptions. Basic orientation to the social, cultural, and religious environment is provided by collections of documents (e.g., Barrett 1989), and by historical introductions (e.g., Koester 1995).

Four types of criticism are deemed rudimentary to historical exegesis in the tradition of Euro-American scholarship: text criticism, source criticism, form criticism, and redaction criticism. The appropriate application of these methods to the text is determined by the nature of the material, not by rules inherent in the methods themselves. As historical disciplines, each type of criticism is subject to change and development, as more is learned about the principles of composition and the formation of tradition. Naturally, there are differences of interest and emphasis among practitioners that affect the outcome of exegesis.

Text criticism is the evaluation of the manuscripts of Scripture with the goal of reconstructing the original wording of the text. Text criticism is necessary because the autographs of the biblical writings have not been preserved. The existing manuscripts vary greatly in age and quality. The variant readings must be compared and evaluated in order to establish the earliest tradition and the best possible text. While the goal of text criticism can only be achieved approximately, it is a crucial step in determining the sense which the author intended. The first critical editions of the New Testament—that is, those which adduce different readings for individual passages—were prepared by J. A. Bengel[§] (1734) and J. J. Wettstein[§] (1751). Wettstein also supplied numerous parallels from Greek and Latin authors. Of great importance for the history of text criticism was the work of Constantin von Tischendorf[§] (1869-1874), who discovered Codex Sinaiticus at St. Catherine's monastery, and Codex Ephraemi, a palimpsest. In their superb critical edition (1881-82), Westcott and Hort distinguished four principal text-types on the basis of similarities between the manuscripts. The modern critical edition of the New Testament is based upon the work of Eberhard Nestle[§], continuously updated by subsequent editors (Erwin Nestle, Kurt Aland).

Source criticism is the attempt to identify and reconstruct the sources used in the composition of the canonical writings. The criteria employed are those of literary criticism in general: unusual vocabulary, stylistic peculiarities, conceptual variations, hiatus, etc. The results of source criticism remain hypothetical, yet are necessary to explain the textual phenomena. Source criticism holds the promise of providing access to earlier stages of biblical tradition. The principal achievement of source criticism of the Old Testament is the "Documentary Hypothesis" of pentateuchal origins, which identified four sources: Jahwist, Elohist, Priestly, Deuteronomist. Applied to the gospels, source criticism disclosed the "Synoptic Problem," namely that the first three gospels share a relationship, agreeing with one another in certain respects, but disagreeing in others. Early attempts at a solution to the Synoptic Problem (the original gospel theory, the oral tradition theory, the fragment hypothesis) proved unsuccessful, yet contained valuable insights. Careful investigation led to the recognition of literary dependance among the first three gospels, an insight embodied in the "Two-Source Hypothesis": that Mark is the earliest gospel and was used by Matthew and Luke as a source; and that Matthew and Luke used a second source consisting primarily of sayings, called the "Sayings-Source" or *Logienquelle* (abbreviated *Q*). Strong arguments may be offered in favor of both premises of the hypothesis (the sequence of the material, stylistic improvements, etc.), so that the majority of scholars hold to some form of this hypothesis. Attempts to clarify remaining aspects of the Synoptic Problem (i.e., the "minor agreements" between Matthew and Luke) have led to greater appreciation of the complexity of the compositional history of Mark. Advances in source criticism have isolated additional sources in the gospels: a pre-Markan passion narrative, collections of miracle stories, and further collections of sayings (e.g., the Sermon on the Mount). Applied to the Pauline epistles, source criticism has resulted in the recognition that several of the canonical texts are composite works. 2 Corinthians may consist of as many as five letter-fragments (10-13; 2:14-6:13, 7:2-4; 1:1-2:13, 7:5-16; 8; 9) and an anti-Pauline interpolation (6:14-7:1). Philippians is probably a collection of three letters. Strong arguments have been made for the composite character of 1 Corinthians, as well (Weiss). While source criticism is resisted by traditionalists and conservatives, it remains an indispensable tool of scholars who are determined to probe the origins of the biblical tradition.

Form criticism seeks to identify the oral traditions incorporated in the biblical texts and to trace these traditions to social situations in the life of the community. Form criticism is based upon the observation that the oral traditions of folk-cultures tend to assume fixed forms whose stylistic laws may be described. The pioneers of form criticism noted that certain biblical texts (i.e., Genesis, the gospels) make the impression of being works in which different kinds of material have been loosely combined, through the addition of a chronological and geographical framework. The successful pursuit of form criticism depends upon the ability to distinguish between the editorial activity of an author and the traditions which the author had at his disposal. The separation of tradition from redaction has as its object the reconstruction of the original form of the tradition, to which the editor has added an introduction, conclusion, characteristic words, motifs, etc. Once the unit of oral material has been identified, it may be classified by comparison with similar forms of oral tradition (e.g., prophetic sayings, parables, miracle stories, paraenesis, etc.). Form critics observe that the different forms of tradition originate in specific settings in the life of a community; thus form criticism culminates in sociological insights. Form criticism has illuminated the tradition of the legends of Genesis (Gunkel[§] 1910) and the origin and function of the Psalms (Gunkel 1933). The greatest contribution of from criticism has been to understanding the formation of the gospels: the Christian movement began not with the composition of a gospel, but with the proclamation of past and future things (kerygma and apocalypse), then proceeded to interpretation, teaching, exhortation, etc. (Herder[§] 1797). The primitive forms of the gospel tradition are derived from preaching and instruction: paradigmatic stories, novelle, legends, paraenesis (Dibelius[§] 1933[2]); apophthegmata, dominical sayings, miracle stories, etc. (Bultmann[§] 1931[2]). Form criticism has also been applied to the epistolary literature of the New Testament, disclosing confessional formulae, hymns, vice-catalogues, etc., and providing insights into the preaching and worship life of early Christian communities. A recent development in form criticism is the recognition that the forms of ancient rhetoric have shaped the composition and structure of biblical texts, esp. the epistles (H. D. Betz 1979).

Redaction criticism seeks to determine the perspectives according to which the authors of the biblical texts have selected and composed their materials. The goal of redaction criticism is the reconstruction of the author's theology. The presuppositions of redaction criticism are already implicit in source and form criticism; but redaction criticism focuses upon the meaning of the text in its final form. Redaction criticism conceives of the biblical authors not merely as collectors of traditional material, but as representatives of religious communities and exponents of their theologies. For the method of redaction criticism, it is essential to understand how and where the editorial activity of an author is to be discerned. Naturally, the beginning and end of a pericope are places where one frequently finds the editor at work providing a frame. Moreover, each author has a characteristic vocabulary which a concordance allows one to establish. A detailed outline of a passage is essential for recognizing how an author has arranged the materials and what compositional principles have been at work. Of great importance is recognition of the theological themes which the authors lift up. Obviously, synoptic comparison is crucial for redaction criticism of the gospels. While the task of redaction criticism embraces many biblical writings, the method has been applied with special success to the Synoptic Gospels, producing sharp portraits of the theologies of Luke (Conzelmann 1957), Mark (Marxsen 1959), and Matthew (Bornkamm, G. Barth, Held 1960). Redaction criticism has also been applied to the Pauline epistles, clarifying Paul's theological perspective through analysis of his redaction of traditional material, such as the "Christ-hymn" in Philippians 2:6-11 (Lohmeyer 1961[2]).

A recent development in Euro-American scholarship is the investigation of the history of concepts and motifs that appear in the biblical text. Interpreters recognize that biblical authors frequently appropriate concepts from the cultural environment in order to convery a theological message. Motif analysis has as its goal the elucidation of the meaning of a concept in its cultural context and the analysis of the use of that concept by a biblical author. The practice of motif analysis presents difficulties for beginning interpreters, because it presupposes broad knowledge of the cultural context. Nevertheless, guidance may be found in the lexica and theological dictionaries, and in commentaries which adduce parallels from Jewish (Strack-

Billerbeck§) and Hellenistic (Wettstein 1751-52, Berger and Colpe 1987) sources. By use of this method, light has been thrown upon the motif of "slavery" in Paul's theology (D. Martin 1990), for example.

A second recent development is the revival of history-of-religions comparison as a method of biblical scholarship. The efforts of the "history-of-religions school" in the 19th century focused on the question of the influence of ancient Near Eastern and Hellenistic religions upon early Christianity (Boussett§, Heitmüller§, Reitzenstein§). In its current reincarnation, the history-of-religions method aims at establishing analogies and differences between the biblical tradition and comparable traditions in the Jewish and Greco-Roman worlds. Its method is phenomenological as well as historical. Significant insight has been gained into Paul's relationship to the popular philosophers (Malherbe 1987, 1989) and the similarities and differences between early Christian communities and the Hellenistic mystery cults (Klauck 1986²).

Bibliography: K. Aland, ed. *Synopsis Quattuor Evangeliorum* (1985⁴) **C.K. Barrett, ed.,** *The New Testament Background: Selected Documents* (1989). **J. A. Bengel,** *H ΚΑΙΝΗ ΔΙΑΘΗΚΗ Novum Testamentum Graecum* (1734). **K. Berger and C. Colpe,** *Religionsgeschichtliches Textbuch zum Neuen Testament* (Texte zum Neuen Testament 1, 1987; ET ed. M. E. Boring, K. Berger, C. Colpe, *Hellenistic Commentary to the New Testament* [1995]). **H. D. Betz,** *Galatians* (Hermeneia, 1979). **W. Boussett,** *Jesu Predigt in ihrem Gegensatz zum Judentum* (1892); *Der Antichrist in der Überlieferung des Judentums, des neuen Testaments und der Alten Kirche* (1895, repr. 1983; ET *The Antichrist Legend: A Chapter in Christian and Jewish Folklore* [1896; repr. AARTTS 24, 1999]); *Die Offenbarung Johannis* (1896); *Der Apostel Paulus* (1898); *Die Religion des Judentums im neutestamentlichen Zeitalter* (1903; since the 3rd ed., *Die Religion des Judentums im späthellenistischen Zeitalter* [1926, 1986]); *Die jüdische Apokalyptik, ihre religionsgeschichtliche Herkunft und ihre Bedeutung für das Neue Testament* (1903); *Das Wesen der Religion dargestellt an ihrer Geschichte* (1903); Jesus (1904); *Was wissen wir von Jesus?* (1904); *Hauptprobleme der Gnosis* (1907); *Die Bedeutung Jesu für den Glauben* (1910); *Kyrios Christos: Geschichte des Christusglaubens* (1913; ET 1970); *Jüdisch-Christlicher Schulbetrieb in Alexandrien und Rom* (1915); *Religionsgeschichtliche Studien: Aufsätze zur Religionsgeschichte des hellenistischen Zeitalters* (NovTSup 50, ed A. F. Verheuele, 1979). **G. Bornkamm, G. Barth, H. J. Held,** *Überlieferung und Auslegung im Matthäusevangelium* (WMANT 1, 1960; ET *Tradition and Interpretation in Matthew* [NTL, 1963]). **R. K. Bultmann,** *Die Geschichte der synoptischen Tradition* (1931²; ET *The History of the Synoptic Tradition*, rev. ed. 1968). **H. Conzelmann,** *Die Mitte die Zeit* (BHT 17, 1957; ET, *The Theology of St. Luke* [1960]). **H. Conzelmann and A. Lindemann**, *Interpreting the New Testament* (Peabody, MA: Hendriksen, 1997). **M. Dibelius,** *Die Formgeschichte des Evangeliums* (1933², ET From Tradtion to Gospel [1971]). **K. Elliger and W. Rudolph,** eds. *Biblia Hebraica Stuttgartsenia,* (1997⁵). **J. P. Gabler**, "De justo discrimine theologiae biblicae et dogmaticae regundisque recte utriusque finibus," *Kleinere theologische Schriften* (1831) 179-98 (ET in J. Sandys-Wunsch and L. Eldridge, "Johann Philipp Gabler and the Distinction Between Biblical and Dogmatic Theology: Translation, Commentary, and Discussion of His Originality," *SJT* 33 [1980] 133-58). **K. Grobel**, "Biblical Criticism," *IDB* 1 (1962) 407-18. **J. H. H. Gunkel,** *Genesis* (1910³; ET 1997); *Das Märchen im Alten Testament* (1917; ET, *The Folktale in the Old Testament,* ET 1987); *Einleitung in die Psalmen* (1933; ET *An Introduction to the Psalms,* 1998). **W. Heitmüller,** *Im Namen Jesu: Eine sprach-und religionsgeschichtliche Untersuchungen zum Neuen Testament, speziell zur altchristlichen Taufe* (1903); *Taufe und Abendmahl bei Paulus: Darstellung und religionsgeschichtliche Beleuctung* (1903), *Taufe und Abendmahl im Urchristentum* (1911). **J. G. Herder,** *Von Gottes Sohn, der Welt Heiland: Nach Johannes Evangelium* (1797; ET selected portions in W. G. Kümmel, *The New Testament: The*

History of the Investigation of its Problems [1972] 79-83). **F. Hahn**, *The Old Testament in Modern Research* (Philadelphia: Fortress Press, 1966) **J. Hayes and C. Holladay**, *Biblical Exegesis: A Beginner's Handbook* (Atlanta: John Knox, 1982). **H.-J. Klauck,** *Herrenmahl und hellenisticher Kult: Eine religionsgeschichtliche Untersuchung zum ersten Korintherbrief* (NTAbh 15, 1986²). **H. Koester,** *Introduction to the New Testament* (2 vols., 1995²). **E. Krentz,** *The Historical-Critical Method* (Philadelphia: Fortress Press, 1975). **W. G. Kümmel,** *The New Testament: The History of the Investigation of its Problems* (1972) **G. E. Lessing,** "Bibliolatrie," *Gesammelte Werke* (10 vols, ed. P. Rilla, 1957) 8.482-89; "The Education of the Human Race," in *Lessing's Theological Writings: Selections in Translation with an Introductory Essay* (H. Chadwick, ed; 1957) 82-98; "On the Origin of Revealed Religion," in *Lessing's Theological Writings: Selections in Translation with an Introductory Essay* (H. Chadwick, ed; 1957) 104-106. **E. Lohmyer**, *Kyrios Jesus: Eine Untersuchung zur Phil. 2, 5-11.* (1961²) **D. Lührmann,** *An Itinerary for New Testament Study* (Phialdelphia: Trinity Press International, 1995). **A. J. Malherbe,** *Paul and the Thessalonians: The Philosophic Tradition of Pastoral Care* (1987); *Paul and the Popular Philosophers* (1989). **D. B. Martin,** *Slavery as Salvation: The Metaphor of Slavery in Pauline Christianity* (1990). **W. Marxsen,** *Der Evangelist Markus: Studien zur Redaktionsgeschichte des Evangeliums* (FRLANT n.s. 49, 1959²; ET *Mark the Evangelist: Studies on the Redaction History of the Gospel* [1969]). **J. H. Moulton and G. Milligan,** *TheVocaublary of the Greek Testament, Illustrated from the Papyri and Other Non-literary Sources* (1929, repr. 1997). **E. McKnight,** *What Is Form Criticism?* (1969); **E. Nestle and K. Aland,** eds. *Novum Testamentum Graece* (1993²⁷); **N. Perrin,** *What Is Redaction Criticism?* (1969) **R. Reitzenstein,** *Poimandres: Studien zur griechisch-ägyptischen und frühchristlicher Literatur* (1904); *Hellenistische Wundererzählungen* (1906); *Die hellenistischen Mysterienreligionen: Nach ihren Grundgedanken und Wirkungen* (1927³, repr. 1966; ET *Hellenistic Mystery-Religions: Their Basic Ideas and Significance* (1910; ET PTMS 15, 1978); *Die Göttin Psyche in der hellenistischen und frühchristlichen Literatur* (1917); *Das mandäische Buch des Herrn der Grösse, und die Evangelienüberlieferung* (1919); *Das iranische Erlösungsmysterium: Religionsgeschichtliche Untersuchungen* (1921); (with H. H. Schaeder), *Studien zum antiken Synkretismus aus Iran und Griechenland*, Teil 1, *Griechische Lehren* (1926); *Die Vorgeschichte der Christlichen Taufe* (1929). **D. J. S. Semler,** *D. Joh. Salomo Semlers Abhandlung von freier Untersuchung des Canon* (4 vols., 1771-75; ET, selected portions, W. G. Kümmel, *The New Testament: A History of the Investigation of Its Problems* [trans. S. M. Gilmour and H. C. Kee; 1972] 63-69). **H. L. Strack and P. Billerbeck, eds.,** *Kommentar zum Neuen Testament aus Talmud und Midrasch* (4 vols. in 5, 1954-61). **G. Strecker**, *History of New Testament Literature* (1997) **G. Strecker and U. Schnelle,** *Einführung in die neutestamentliche Exegese* (1993) **C. von Tischendorf,** *Novum Testamentum Graece* (3 vols., 1869-84). **B. F. Westcott and F. J. A. Hort,** *The New Testament in the Original Greek* (2 vols., 1881-82). **J. J. Wettstein** *Η ΚΑΙΝΗ ΔΙΑΘΗΚΗ Novum Testamentum Graecum* (2 vols., 1751-52; 1 vol. repr. 1962). **U. Wilckens,** "Über die Bedeutung historischer Kritik in der modernen Bibelexegese," *Was heisst Auslegung des Heiligen Schrift?* (1966.

L. L. Welborn

CONTEXTUAL APPROACHES

Hispanic American Biblical Interpretation

An explicit and self-conscious focus on biblical interpretation on the part of Hispanic Americans or Latinos, from the standpoint of their status as an ethnic minority group within the country, accompanies the emergence of Hispanic American theology on the United States theological scene at the end of the 1980s and the beginning of the 1990s. With the rise of theological reflection on the reality and experience of Hispanic Americans comes a corresponding interest in biblical HERMENEUTICS, in the interpretation of the Bible from the point of view of and with regard to such a reality and experience. Two different sequential developments can be readily identified within this newly constituted reading tradition of the Bible.

At first, such a turn to the Bible was profoundly theological in nature. The early voices in the movement, given their primary training in theological studies (broadly conceived, ranging from constructive theology, to social ethics, to church historiography, to pastoral theology), turned to the biblical texts for reflection, inspiration, and argumentation in the elaboration of their respective theological constructions. In this initial phase of the movement the hermeneutical element remained, by and large, subordinate to the primary theological aims of the discussion. In time this use of the Bible became a much more self-conscious critical activity and, hence, profoundly hermeneutical in character. Subsequent voices whose primary training was in biblical studies began to examine the use of the Bible on the part of their theological colleagues and to turn to the biblical texts in the light of both contemporary biblical criticism and the aims of the movement as a whole. In this second phase of the movement, the theological element remained, for the most part, secondary to the prevailing hermeneutical aims of the discussion.

Such a concern with biblical interpretation among Hispanic American theologians and critics in the late 1980s and early 1990s should be seen as neither unique nor fortuitous but, rather, as yet another sign of the times. Indeed, the emergence of this concern can be readily accounted for by a variety of developments, all ultimately interrelated and interdependent, in the social fabric of the country, the world of the academy at large, the field of theology in general, and the discipline of biblical studies in particular.

At the broadest level of American society, the social upheavals of the 1960s and 1970s set the stage through the various movements of emancipation unleashed in the country, among which both the Mexican American and the Puerto Rican communities—the long-standing Hispanic American communities in the country—featured prominently. Such movements clamored for an end to cultural prejudice, social discrimination, economic injustice, and political marginalization. In the process, the larger society became highly conflicted, or (to put it differently) long-standing conflicts were brought to the fore more sharply than ever before. As a result Hispanic Americans began to analyze, critically as well as assertively, their history in the country, their present fragile condition in society, and their dreams and visions for the future. Such was the beginning of the long process of conscientization, of self-understanding and self-reflection, on the part of the group as a minority.

From the viewpoint of the academy, such social turmoil led to drastic changes in the conception of knowledge throughout the 1970s and 1980s. Across the disciplinary spectrum, in the human sciences as well as in the social sciences, the object of study was no longer regarded as universal and unidimensional and its analysis as objective and disinterested. On the contrary, analysis was now perceived as profoundly contextual and perspectival, while the object of study was approached as local and multidimensional. The pursuit of knowledge had thus become highly conflicted as well, as the various constitutive factors of human identity—including race and ethnicity—began to be seen not only as sharply diversifying the object of study, but also as directly affecting the process of analysis. From such a theoretical point of view, issues of representation, power, and ideology became foremost in every discipline. As a result, the study of Hispanic Americans—in terms both of the group as a whole and the different segments within the group—became a valid exercise in its own right, whether in terms of history and literature or culture and society. What had begun as a social movement eventually turned into an intellectual movement as well, lending ever greater maturity and sophistication to the ongoing process of conscientization on the part of the group.

With regard to the field of theology, the study of Christianity as a religion, such social upheavals and academic transformations were clearly reflected in the swift processes of decentralization and globalization at work in the theological world as the traditional Western hold on theological reflection became increasingly fractured throughout the 1970s and 1980s. From a global point of view, theological construction was now actively pursued in all corners of the world, beginning with Latin America and then rapidly spreading to the continents of Africa and Asia. From the viewpoint of the United States, a similar process ensued as theological construction was increasingly undertaken by ethnic and racial minority groups, commencing with African American theology (Afrocentric Interpretation*§) and ultimately witnessing the emergence of such other theologies as Hispanic American theology, Native American theology, and Asian*§ American theology. As with every other discipline, theological studies also became highly conflicted, forced to take into consideration the local and multidimensional character of their object of study as well as the contextual and perspectival nature of the process of analysis. Inevitably, given their increasing numbers in the field, what had already become a social and intellectual movement was now also turning into a theological movement for Hispanic Americans.

Within the field of theology, all of the different areas of study could not help being directly affected by such developments, and biblical criticism was no exception. The signs were clear. To begin with, the long-established critical paradigm in the discipline—historical criticism— was severely challenged, eventually being displaced by a number of other critical paradigms and thus yielding a situation of pronounced methodological and theoretical diversity. In the process, increasing importance was placed on the role of readers and on the reading process (Reader-response Criticism*§) in the task of interpretation, ultimately leading to a view of all interpretation as both contextual and perspectival. Consequently, close attention to the social location and the Ideological*§ stance of readers became imperative. The result was pronounced sociocultural diversity. The traditional conception of the discipline as a rigorously scientific exercise involving an empiricist worldview as well as universal and disinterested readers yielded to a radically different view of biblical interpretation as highly conflicted, both at the level of the text and the level of the reader. Quite naturally, the emerging theological movement among Hispanic Americans spawned a corresponding concern for biblical hermeneutics as Hispanic American theologians and critics sought to examine, from the viewpoint of their self-understanding and self-reflection as a minority group, their interpretation and use of the biblical texts. In the end, the process of conscientization had come to embrace the world of biblical criticism as well, giving rise to a new and self-conscious reading tradition of the Bible.

In this turn toward the Bible and biblical criticism, the two different developments within the movement noted above—the theological and the hermeneutical—can be distinguished in terms of their positions on five fundamental issues of interpretation: (1) perceived affinity with the text, (2) proposed locus of Liberation*§ in the text, (3) point of entry into the text, (4) validity in interpretation, and (5) perceived agenda of liberation in the text.

The initial, primarily theological, approach shows a clear commitment to the hermeneutics of liberation in the interpretation and use of the Bible. For these early voices, the biblical texts constituted an effective weapon in the struggle against prejudice, discrimination, injustice, and marginalization as well as a faithful ally in the struggle for liberation. All concerned adopted variations of a basic model of liberation hermeneutics involving both a formal analogy between the past and the present, between the relationship of the Bible and the relationship of the group to their respective sociohistorical and sociocultural contexts, and a basic correspondence between Hispanic Americans today and the people of God in the Bible. These variations were the result of different positions adopted with regard to the five key issues of interpretation listed above.

This first phase in the interpretation and use of the Bible by Hispanic Americans may be summarized as follows: (1) With respect to perceived affinity with ancient texts on the part of present-day readers who come from a very different sociocultural and sociohistorical context, the Bible was looked upon as neither distant nor strange; and the biblical texts were seen as easily accessible to Hispanic Americans. The life and struggle of the biblical people of God were seen as anticipating the life and struggle of Hispanic Americans today, making it possible for the latter to identify with the Bible and its message of liberation.

(2) In terms of the proposed locus of liberation within the text, two major positions emerged: the concept of a canon within the Canon*§, on the basis of which the rest of the Bible was to be judged, and the notion of a unified and consistent text. Either way, the Bible was looked upon as conveying a message of liberation—a God not at all removed or foreign, but rather a God who was on the side of Hispanic Americans.

(3) Regarding the point of entry into the text, marginalization and oppression were seen as the key to the liberating message of the Bible, although oppression and marginalization were defined in different ways and thus resulted in different constructions of the God of liberation. At a fundamental level, however, it was the similar experience of oppression and marginalization that allowed Hispanic Americans to identify with the biblical people of God.

(4) In terms of validity in interpretation or correct and incorrect readings, despite different emphases there was a general call for a resistant biblical reading from the experience of oppression and marginalization aligned against reading strategies associated with power and privilege. (5) With respect to the perceived agenda for liberation in the text, a common utopian and subversive vision of liberation prevailed. This vision, which encompassed different views of the new order, questioned the present world order while advancing an alternative.

The subsequent predominantly hermeneutical approach reveals a continued commitment to a hermeneutics of liberation in the interpretation and use of the Bible. Alongside such a commitment, however, these later voices begin to offer a much more guarded picture of the Bible as an effective weapon and faithful ally in the struggle against oppression and for liberation.

This second phase in the interpretation and use of the Bible on the part of Hispanic Americans may be depicted as follows: (1) In terms of perceived affinity with the text, the consensus on correspondence between the people of God and Hispanic Americans gives way to a more guarded approach to the question of distance and kinship. The Bible emerges as a more distant and strange text, a text whose accessibility to Hispanic Americans becomes problematic. The reasons for such a move in favor of distancing differ: a view that the concept of a chosen people of God has xenophobic connotations and ramifications; the ever-present danger of enslaving the ancient text; a view of the text as a culturally and historically removed other.

(2) Regarding the proposed locus of liberation within the text, while the consensus on the Bible as a liberating text perdures, this message is now perceived as more ambiguous. The Bible begins to be seen as a source of both liberation and oppression. Thus, in effect, the God of the Bible emerges as a God who may actually work against the liberation of Hispanic Americans, while the message of liberation can fall victim to the captivity of present-day readers or can be understood in different ways by different readers.

(3) With respect to the point of entry into the text, the consensus of marginalization and oppression as key to the liberating message of the Bible still holds, with oppression and marginalization again being defined in different ways. However, the process of identification with the people of God on the part of Hispanic Americans is depicted as more difficult given such factors as the oppressive tactics of the people of God in the Bible, the differences among Hispanic Americans, and the problem of pointing to any one experience in particular as the key to the liberating message of the Bible.

(4) Regarding the question of validity in interpretation, the consensual call for a reading of resistance also continues, a reading similarly characterized as biblical and distinguished from reading strategies associated with power and privilege. At the same time, such a reading becomes more complex insofar as it must remain attuned to the different voices present in the text, be made subject to constant self-revision, or deny the possibility of any one reading as the correct reading.

(5) In terms of the perceived agenda of liberation, the consensus regarding a highly utopian and subversive vision of liberation prevails. At the same time, such a vision becomes more subtle: It is now a vision that must choose among competing biblical ideologies and (where one biblical ideology must prevail in place of another) a vision that calls for theological and hermeneutical dialogue, or a vision that emphasizes both the multiplicity of readers and visions and their mutual engagement.

As an explicit and self-conscious reading tradition of the Bible, Hispanic American hermeneutics has witnessed rapid development during its brief life span, from its initial moorings in the discourse of countermodernity (given its option for the classic patterns of the hermeneutics of liberation) to its recent engagement with the discourses of postmodernity (Postmodern Biblical Interpretation*§) as reflected in its growing concern with issues of representation, power, and ideology in interpretation. In this, it has followed the course of Hispanic American theology, becoming ever more diverse and sophisticated in the process. As additional voices continue to join its ranks, participate in its discussions, and seek to shape its discourse, such sophistication and diversity are bound to grow at an even more rapid pace, making of Hispanic American biblical interpretation an increasingly vibrant, complex, and powerful reading tradition of the Bible.

Pedraja's Hispanic Christology (1999) includes a discussion of biblical Christology from a Hispanic perspective. One sign of the maturity of Hispanic biblical interpretation is the recent dialog between Hispanic and African American theologians that includes a discussion of the role of the Bible (Pinn and Valentin 2001). Isasi-Díaz, T. Matovina, and N. M. Torres-Vidal (2002) relate specific biblical passages to specific themes in Hispanic ministry: baptism and the call to ministry, the power of the resurrection, etc.

Bibliography: A. J. Bañuelas, "U.S. Hispanic Theology," *Missiology* (April 1992) 275-300. **V. Elizondo,** *Galilean Journey: The Mexican American Promise* (1983). **E. C. Fernández,** "'Reading the Bible in Spanish': U.S. Catholic Hispanic Theologians' Contribution to Systematic Theology," *Apuntes* 14 (1994) 86-90. **F. García-Treto,** "The Lesson of the Gibeonites: A Proposal for Dialogic Attention as a Strategy for Reading the Bible," *Hispanic/Latino Theology: Challenge and Promise* (ed. A. M. Isasi-Díaz and F. F. Segovia, 1996) 73-85; "Crossing the Line: Three Scenes of Divine-Human Engagement in the HB," *Teaching the Bible: Discourses and Politics of Biblical Pedagogy* (ed. F. F. Segovia and M. A. Tolbert, 1998). **J. L. González,** *Mañana: Christian Theology from a Hispanic Perspective* (1990). "Reading from My Bicultural Place: Acts 6:1-7," *Reading from This Place, vol. 1, Social Location and Biblical Interpretation in the United States* (ed. F. F. Segovia and M. A. Tolbert, 1995) 139-48; "Metamodern Aliens in Postmodern Jerusalem," *Hispanic/Latino*

Theology: Challenge and Promise (ed. A. M. Isasi-Díaz and F. F. Segovia, 1996) 340-50; *Santa Biblia: The Bible Through Hispanic Eyes* (1996). **A. M. Isasi-Díaz**, "La Palabra de Dios en nosotras: The Word of God in Us," *Searching the Scriptures*, vol. 1, *A Feminist Introduction* (ed. E. Schüssler Fiorenza, 1993) 86-100; " 'By the Rivers of Babylon': Exile as a Way of Life," *Reading from This Place*, vol. 1, *Social Location and Biblical Interpretation in the United States* (ed. F. F. Segovia and M. A. Tolbert, 1995) 149-63. **A. M. Isasi-Díaz, T. Matovina, N. M. Torres-Vidal** (eds.), *Camino a Emaús: Compartiendo el ministerio de Jesús* (2002). **P. Jiménez** (ed.), *Lumbrera a nuestro camino* (1994); "In Search of a Hispanic Model of Biblical Interpretation," *JH/LT* 3 (1995) 44-64. **L. G. Pedraja,** *Jesus is My Uncle: Christology from a Hispanic Perspective* (1999) 87-99. **A. B. Pinn and B. Valentin,** *The Ties that Bind: African-American and Hispani- American/Latino/a Theology in Dialogue* (2001). **H. J. Recinos,** *Hear the Cry! A Latino Pastor Challenges the Church* (1989). **J. D. Rodríguez,** "De 'apuntes' a 'esbozo': diez años de reflexión," *Apuntes* 10 (1990) 75-83. **C. G. Romero,** *Hispanic Devotional Piety: Tracing the Biblical Roots* (Faith and Culture Series, 1991); "Tradition and Symbol as Biblical Keys for a U.S. Hispanic Theology," *Hispanic Theology in the United States* (ed. A. F. Deck, 1992) 41-61; "Amos 5:21-24: Religion, Politics, and the Latino Experience," *JH/LT* 4 (1997) 21-41. **J. P. Ruiz,** "Beginning to Read the Bible in Spanish: An Initial Assessment," *JH/LT* 1 (1994) 28-50; "Contexts in Conversation: First World and Third World Readings of Job," *JH/LT* 2 (1995) 5-29; "Four Faces of Theology: Four Johannine Conversations," *Teaching the Bible: Discourses and Politics of Biblical Pedagogy* (ed. F. F. Segovia and M. A. Tolbert, 1998). **F. F. Segovia,** "A New Manifest Destiny: The Emerging Theological Voice of Hispanic Americans," *RelSRev* 17, 2 (April, 1991) 102-9; "Hispanic American Theology and the Bible: Effective Weapon and Faithful Ally," *We Are a People! Initiative in Hispanic American Theology* (ed. R. S. Goizueta, 1992) 21-50; "Reading the Bible as Hispanic Americans," *NIB* (1994) 1:167-73; "Toward a Hermeneutics of the Diaspora: A Hermeneutics of Otherness and Engagement," *Reading from This Place*, vol. 1, *Social Location and Biblical Interpretation in the United States* (ed. F. F. Segovia and M. A. Tolbert, 1995) 57-74; "Toward Intercultural Criticism: A Reading Strategy from the Diaspora," *Reading from This Place*, vol. 2, *Social Location and Biblical Interpretation in Global Perspective* (ed. F. F. Segovia and M. A. Tolbert, 1995) 303-30.

F. F. SEGOVIA

CONTEXTUAL APPROACHES

Biblical Interpretation and the Holocaust

Whatever position one takes in the ongoing debate over the uniqueness of the Holocaust—defined here as the systematic attempt to exterminate European Jewry in the 1930s and early 1940s—there can be little doubt that it is an event of major consequence for the twentieth century. Nonetheless, although there have been innumerable volumes published on the implications of the Holocaust for historical, philosophical, ethical, and theological studies, there is a dearth of works that specifically consider either the theoretical or practical effects of the event on biblical interpretation. This is not to deny that since the 1940s there have been people reading the Bible differently because of the Holocaust; rather, it is to recognize that human situatedness in a post-Holocaust milieu has only begun to penetrate significantly into either academic or religious publications concerned with biblical interpretation (T. Linafelt 1994, 2000).

1. *Jewish Interpretation.* The place where one is most likely to find reference to the Bible in relation to the Holocaust is in Jewish theological responses to the event. While not primarily concerned with the effects of the Holocaust on how one reads the Bible, these works will typically mine the Bible for paradigms to explain the event and its significance for Jewish religious thought. One such biblical paradigm, used mainly by Orthodox thinkers, is the notion that the Holocaust is a punishment for the sins of the Jewish people (J. Teitelbaum 1959-61). While biblically rooted, this model has been understandably rejected by most Jews (both Orthodox and otherwise) as well as by non-Jews (esp. I. Greenberg 1977, 23). One can identify four other biblical models that have been employed in an attempt to explain the Holocaust (S. Katz 1990, 749): (a) the binding of Isaac by Abraham, (b) the notion of a "Suffering Servant" from Isaiah, (c) the "hiding" of the face of God found in a number of psalms, and (d) the story of Job. Although all of these examples no doubt offer some comfort to survivors and their families and address certain aspects of the Holocaust, each ultimately fails to comprehend or explain it.

Another line of thinking holds that one should not read the Bible in hopes of explaining the Holocaust; rather, one should allow the event to impinge on the way one reads the Bible. An early example of this approach is R. Rubenstein's (1966) rejection of texts that depict God's working in history in favor of priestly texts concerning ethical and ritual matters. The most explicit (albeit brief) theoretical statement of this position is E. Fackenheim's *The Jewish Bible After the Holocaust* (1990; see Linafelt 1994). Fackenheim argues that the Holocaust represents such a rupture in history that one cannot today read the Bible in the same way that it was read before the event. Although A. Neher's earlier book, *The Exile of the Word* (1980), made a similar point with an exploration of the incommensurability of biblical patterns of silence with the silence of God at Auschwitz, Fackenheim more directly engages the discipline of biblical studies.

Two writers who have done sustained interpretive work from this theoretical orientation are E. Wiesel and D. Blumenthal. Although the Bible tends to pervade all of Wiesel's work, his three volumes of collected "biblical portraits" (1976-91) offer the best entry into his agonistic relationship with the Bible. The portraits in these volumes are primarily composed of Wiesel's retelling of biblical stories and their midrashic complements. Still, the Holocaust continues to erupt into these retellings, thereby problematizing the tradition and forcing us to read the stories differently. Thus Job becomes "Our Contemporary," and the story of Cain and Abel becomes "The First Genocide" (Wiesel 1976). Blumenthal, in the central section of his book *Facing the Abusing God* (1993), demonstrates a post-Holocaust hermeneutic (Hermeneutics*§) in the exegesis of four psalms. He provides a verse-by-verse commentary in four different voices (reminiscent of the Talmud or the rabbinic Bible): a philological commentary ("Words"), comments from the Hasidic tradition ("Sparks"), an emotional-spiritual commentary ("Affections"), and a counter-reading of the texts in light of the experience of abuse or the Holocaust ("Con-verses"). On each page the four voices surround the biblical text, not only vying for space and for the reader's attention but actively contradicting each other, thereby creating an interpretive approach that mirrors the fragmentary nature of post-Holocaust thought.

2. *Christian Interpretation.* Among Christian writers, the most significant interface between the Holocaust and biblical studies has resulted as a side effect of the renewed emphasis on Jewish-Christian relations. For many Christian thinkers, the Holocaust demands a rethinking of latent anti-Judaism in traditional Christian theology as well as in the New Testament (e.g., P. van Buren 1980-88; P. von der Osten-Sacken 1986). Thus New Testament scholarship in the 1980s and 1990s tends to emphasize the Jewishness of JESUS in the Gospels (e.g., J. H. Charlesworth 1988; P. Fredriksen 1988; P. Meier 1991) and God's continuing faithfulness to Israel in the thought of Paul[†§] (e.g., L. Gaston 1987; J. D. G. Dunn 1990; N. Lohfink 1991). Although these writers do not typically mention the Holocaust, it is no doubt a driving force behind the trend to underscore Jesus' ethnicity (C. Williamson 1993, 48-106). However, they stress that a serious reconsideration of anti-Jewish tendencies in Christian thought would be necessary whether or not the Holocaust had taken place; the event has simply moved these issues to center stage. Still, the question of how Christians might read the Bible differently in light of the specific event of the Holocaust has scarcely been raised.

One way in which a more serious engagement between the Holocaust and Christian biblical interpretation might take place is by pursuing the hermeneutical implications of the widespread Jewish appropriation of the crucifixion image in works of art. Paintings such as M. Chagall's *White Crucifixion* and *The Martyr* and M. Hoffman's *Six Million and One,* as well as sculptures such as G. Segal's *The Holocaust* in San Francisco's Lincoln Park, illustrate a trend in post-Holocaust Jewish art wherein the traditional Christian symbol of crucifixion is transformed into a Jewish symbol of suffering and persecution (Z. Amishai-Maisel 1982; C. Quehl-Engel 1994). What might it mean to reread the passion narratives of the New Testament through the hermeneutical lens of this artistic image? This is just one example of how a Christian post-Holocaust hermeneutic might be manifested. (A move in this direction may be seen in J. Marcus 1997.)

The 1990s witnessed increased public interest of Americans in the Holocaust, evidenced by massive turnouts at the United States Holocaust Memorial Museum in Washington, D.C., and the reception of S. Spielberg's movie *Schindler's List.* If this interest continues, it may in fact seep into biblical scholarship and result in a more profound engagement between biblical and Holocaust studies.

Bibliography: Z. **Amishai-Maisels,** "The Jewish Jesus," *Journal of Jewish Art* 9 (1982) 85-104. D. R. **Blumenthal,** *Facing the Abusing God: A Theology of Protest* (1993). J. H. **Charlesworth,** *Jesus Within Judaism* (1988). J. D. G. **Dunn,** *Jesus, Paul, and the Law* (1990). E. **Fackenheim,** *The Jewish Bible After the Holocaust: A Re-reading* (1990). P. **Fredriksen,** *From Jesus to Christ* (1988). L. **Gaston,** *Paul and the Torah* (1987). I. **Greenberg,** "Cloud of Smoke, Pillar of Fire: Judaism, Christianity, and Modernity after the Holocaust," *Auschwitz: Beginning of a New Era?* (ed. E. Fleischner, 1977) 7-55. S. T. **Katz,** "Jewish Philosophical and Theological Responses to the Holocaust," *Encyclopdeia of the Holocaust* (4 vols. ed. I. Gutman, 1990) 2:748-51. T. **Linafelt,** *review of E. Fackenheim's The Jewish Bible After the Holocaust in Koinonia 6, 2* (1994) 114-18; "Mad Midrash and the Negative Dialectics of Post-Holocaust Biblical Interpretation," *Bibel und Midrasch* (ed. G. Bodendorfer and M. Millard, FAT 22, 1998) 263-74; (ed.) *Strange Fire: Reading the Bible After the Holocaust* (2000). N. **Lohfink,** *The Covenant Never Revoked: Biblical Reflections on Christian-Jewish Dialogue*

(1991). **J. Marcus,** *Jesus and the Holocaust* (1997). **J. P. Meier,** *A Marginal Jew: Rethinking the Historical Jesus* (ABRL, 1991). **A. Neher,** *The Exile of the Word: From the Silence of the Bible to the Silence of Auschwitz* (1981). **C. Quehl-Engel,** "Jewish Interpretative Art on Christian Anti-Judaism and the Holocaust: A Visual Hermeneutic for Christian Theology," *The Holocaust: Progress and Prognosis, 1934-94* (1994) 591-604. **R. L. Rubenstein,** *After Auschwitz: Radical Theology and Contemporary Judaism* (1966). **J. Teitelbaum,** *Va'Yoel Moshe* (3 vols. 1959-61). In Hebrew. **P. M. van Buren,** *A Theology of the Jewish Christian Reality* (3 pts. 1980-88). **P. von der Osten-Sacken,** *Christian-Jewish Dialogue: Theological Foundations* (1986). **E. Wiesel,** *Messengers of God: Biblical Portraits and Legends* (1976); *Five Biblical Portraits* (1981); *Sages and Dreamers: Biblical, Talmudic, and Hasidic Portraits and Legends* (1991). **C. M. Williamson,** *A Guest in the House of Israel: Post-Holocaust Church Theology* (1993).

T. LINAFELT

CONTEXTUAL APPROACHES

Mujerista Biblical Interpretation

The actual way Latinas use the Bible provides the starting point for *mujerista* biblical interpretation. *Mujerista* (from *mujer*, meaning "woman") interpretation expresses the struggle of Latina women for liberation. Several key elements enter into *mujerista* considerations of biblical texts.

First, Latino Christianity has been heavily influenced by the Spanish Roman Catholicism of the sixteenth century, which had limited biblical content. African (Afrocentric Interpretation*§) and Amerindian religious understandings and practices, added later, have also contributed to present-day Latino Christianity. Catholicism's current attention to the Bible and the centrality of Scripture in Protestant churches, especially in the evangelical and charismatic traditions (including Pentecostal churches), also influence an increasing number of Latino Christians. These factors, plus the widespread use of the Bible in the dominant American (United States) culture, are taken into account in *mujerista* biblical Hermeneutics*§.

Second, although Latinas' everyday use of the Bible is the starting point of *mujerista* hermeneutics, it must be recognized that a great number of Latinas do not consult the Bible in their daily lives. Scripture is difficult to use appropriately because of the complexity of the biblical writings, the variety of messages in them (some contradictory), and the substantial difference between the Bible's social-historical contexts and that of contemporary Latinas.

Third, the critical lens of *mujerista* theology is Liberation*§, which, for Latinas, is a matter of physical and cultural survival. Indeed, in *mujerista* hermeneutics the Bible is accepted as divine revelation and as authoritative (Authority of the Bible*§) only insofar as it contributes to Latinas' liberation endeavors.

Using Latinas' liberation as the critical lens establishes the primary systematic criterion for use of the Bible: the needs of those engaging Scripture. To understand this, one has to realize that the majority of Latinas know the Bible mostly from hearing it read in their churches, through a kind of oral tradition rather than through the reading and studying of texts. Latinas listen to and employ biblical stories in their discussions and struggles, not so much because they believe Scripture is the Word of God that tells them what to do or not to do, but because it aids them in understanding what is happening and in gaining courage for their efforts. The Bible stories taken up by Latinas are those that involve characters they can understand, characters who have also struggled for survival. Thus, the appropriation of stories from a book Latinas know as important and authoritative often is a highly creative process in which central elements of the stories can be changed while peripheral ones are highlighted. It is not that the integrity of the text is unimportant for Latinas; it is, rather, that the need to survive takes precedence.

Being linked to the people of biblical stories helps Latina communities understand that their struggle is an ancient one. The stories appropriated by Latinas put them in contact with their forebears and teach them that they must never grow weary of contesting oppression; for although they may not be able to change oppressive situations, they can provide inspiration for others and can contribute to the favorable conditions others need to become involved in the struggle for liberation. For all oppressed persons, such a struggle involves becoming subjects of their own history. This requires that women and men become strong moral agents capable of making choices, of acting, of challenging, and of creating meaning even in the midst of oppression. Latinas are aware of the dangers presented by the use of the Bible as an authority when they have little or nothing to say about the way it is interpreted. Accepting as legitimate an interpretation of the Bible that is not their own—that is not determined by Latinas—can result in others controlling their lives.

A nonbiblical Christianity has been a good vehicle for the inclusion of Amerindian and African beliefs and practices in Latino Christianity, an inclusion that is at the heart of popular religiosity. It is questionable whether this will continue if Latinas do not have a say in how to interpret and apply the Bible. Many Latinas who use the Bible do so under the tutelage of priests and pastors who control its interpretation and utilization in Latino churches. Exclusion from the process of interpretation is not conducive to the development of Latinas' moral agency. Moreover, the majority of Latinas who regularly use the Bible seem to do so in a predominantly individualistic and pietistic way. Although such appropriation is questionable insofar as the development and enhancement of moral agency is concerned, for Latinas it may be an appropriate starting place if they reject interpretation that limits the use of Scripture to personal consolation and salvation.

In *mujerista* biblical hermeneutics the Bible is intrinsic to a process of conscientization—a process of critical reflection on action that leads to an awareness of oppression. In this process, the Bible should be used to learn how to learn; to involve the people in an "unending process of acquiring new pieces of information that multiply the previous store of information" (J. Segundo 1976, 97-124). The Bible is a treasury of such information: stories of valiant women, of women who found ways to survive in the midst of the worst oppression, of communities of resistance. These stories help to make obvious problems that may have existed for a long time but that Latinas have failed to recognize. Such appropriation of the biblical repository does not apply what the Bible says directly to the situation at hand; rather, it makes using the Bible an important element in the development of moral agency. Thus, in *mujerista* biblical interpretation Scripture plays an important role as Latinas reflect on who they are as Christians and on what attitudes, dispositions, goals, values, norms, and decisions they value as they struggle to survive and to liberate themselves.

Bibliography: **J. Gonzalez,** *Mañana: Christian Theology from a Hispanic Perspective* (1990) 9-87. **A. M. Isasi-Díaz,** "La Palabra de Dios en Nosotros: The Word of God in Us," *Searching the Scriptures* (2 vols. ed. E. Schüssler Fiorenza, 1993) 1:86-97. **J. L. Segundo,** *The Liberation of Theology* (1976) 97-124. **E. Schüssler Fiorenza,** "Towards a Feminist Biblical Hermeneutics: Biblical Interpretation and Liberation Theology," *The Use of Scriptures in Moral Theology* (ed. C. E. Curran and R. A. McCormick, Readings in Moral Theology 4, 1984) 354-82.

A. M. Isasi-Díaz

Womanist Biblical Interpretation

1. *Historical Overview. a. The Black theology movement.* Womanist biblical interpretation arises from the groundbreaking and creative development in African American theological thought (Afrocentric Biblical Interpretation*§) called womanist theology. Womanist theology emerged out of the watershed Black theology movement of the 1960s and 1970s that ratified emphatically what theologians acceded theoretically—the ideologically and culturally conditioned roots and character of all theology—thus exploding the myth of a presumed rational objectivity and critiquing the Eurocentric Ideological*§ and racial hegemony that has historically permeated traditional theology. Affirming the thesis that theology in the Christian tradition refers to the critical investigation of a person's or a community's belief in the divine and that the ultimate values of a religion should (and will) be viewed and interpreted from a people's own experience and social location, pioneering theologians J. Cone, J. Grant, J. Roberts, G. Wilmore, and other African American Christian theologians in major divinity schools and seminaries throughout the United States for the first time attempted to construct systematic theologies from the Black perspective. Thus the African American experience, with its legacy of struggle arising from slavery, oppression, resistance, and survival in the New World—in sum, the lived experience of black peoples, including the Black church and Black culture—is necessarily a starting point for doing theology (Cone 1969; J. Evans 1987; Grant 1989; D. Hopkins 1993; C. Lincoln 1990).

b. Womanist theology. Like Black male theologians, womanist theologians disavow the still-pervasive mythological tenet of Christian theology and biblical interpretation as disciplinarily, ideologically, and culturally disinterested (i.e., devoid of methodologically and practically "interested" or advocacy presuppositions and agendas; R. Bultmann [1948-53; ET 1952-55] 289-96). Like other Liberation*§ theology movements, Black male, womanist, and Feminist*§ theologies make explicit their starting point for doing theology (E. Schüssler Fiorenza 1993, 1-21; R. Sugirtharajah 1991, 1-70).

Womanist theology begins with the experience of black women as its point of departure. Like feminist theologians, womanist theologians critique the hegemony of male-articulated understandings of the Christian faith and authenticate the significance of the gospel as read within the context of women's experience, validating (in particular) black women's experience as the primary source and context for understanding the nature of God and God's Word to humanity (Grant 1989, ix). Womanist theologians also affirm the struggle against the evils of androcentrism and patriarchy that foster gender subordination and oppression. Similarly, like Black male theologians, womanist theologians critique the pervasiveness of White supremacy in traditional religion that fosters the evil of racial domination and oppression. But womanist theologians recognize the dynamics and politics of gender, race, and class as interlocking systems in an overarching structure of domination in their lives (F. Steady c. 1981, 7-42); as such, the phenomenology of womanist theological analysis (and biblical interpretation) is multidimensional, inclusive of multiple anthropological referents in both genesis and scope.

Womanist theology privileges African American women's historic and contemporary experiences, voices, and perspectives purposefully, self-consciously, and practically as both a starting point and as a resource for doing theology. The theological expressions "womanist," "womanist theology," and "womanist biblical interpretation" arise from A. Walker's definition of the term:

Womanist 1. From womanish. (Opp. of 'girlish,' i.e., frivolous, irresponsible, not serious.) A black feminist of color. From the black folk expression of mothers to female
children, 'You acting womanish,' i.e., like a woman. Usually referring to outrageous,
audacious, courageous or willful behavior. Wanting to know more and in greater depth
than is considered 'good' for one. Interested in grown-up doings. Acting grown up. Being
grown up. Interchangeable with another black folk expression: 'You trying to be grown.'
Responsible. In charge. Serious (1983 xi).

Walker's culturally coded womanist concept provides significant clues for work undertaken by
womanist theologians, with direct implications for the work of womanist biblical interpreters,
in at least three ways.

First, Walker's womanist concept suggests that a womanist is a black feminist who is self-
identified and constructively assertive—able to interpret reality and define her objectives in
order to secure the well-being of herself and others (recalling heroines like H. Tubman), accent-
ing the quality of life and survival interests of black women (D. Williams 1993, 20-21). As a
theology that is a critical and constructive reflection on the Christian faith, womanist theology
validates black women's intellectual and generative knowledge base and their functions as creators, models, and purveyors of wide-ranging and transformative theological discourses and
praxes, subjugated knowledge, and emancipatory traditions that effect revolutionary and liberating personal, communal, ecclesial, and sociopolitical change for women and men alike (a
womanist is a universalist by temperament; Walker, xi-xii).

Second, whereas traditional Eurocentric masculinist and feminist theological worldviews and
discourses and the early writings of Black male liberation theologians have historically fostered
black women's invisibility and subordination, womanist theology renders Black women's experiences decisively visible and their contributions in the formation, assessment, and critique of
religious and theological meaning inestimable in the academic study of religion.

Third, Walker's allusion to the rich and historic tradition of the transmission of "mother wit"
(Wisdom) between mother and daughter in the definition comprises one of many cultural codes
pointing to the primacy and crystallization of such values as mutuality, relationality, kinship and
friendship networks, and familial and communal empowerment in women-centered activities
and formed traditions in the African American community. Whereas some feminist theorizing
more normatively privileges an individualistic worldview and various degrees of female separation in the face of inequality (D. King 1988, 58; P. Couture 1996, 94-104), the effectiveness
and resiliency of women-centered networks of resistance and care and the well-being of black
women, men, families, and communities comprise a recurrent motif in womanist theological
discourses (K. Cannon 1995, 47-56; C. J. Sanders 1995, 84-94; Williams 1993, xiv).

2. *The Project and Tasks of Womanist Biblical Interpretation. a. The Bible in womanist biblical
interpretation.* Womanist biblical interpretation is premised on at least three assumptions about the
centrality and function of the Bible in the African American community. First, the Bible remains,
for a significant number of African American women and men, the primary (though not exclusive)
conduit of the community's understanding of God's being and actions—i.e. the church's
book—and a plumb line for the life and practice of the Christian community (Evans 1987, 33).

For black women, God's revelation, as witnessed in the Bible and read and heard within the
context of their experience, constitutes a primary source for their understanding of God—this,
in spite of the fact that for several centuries black slave women were prohibited from reading
the Bible. As Hebrew Bible scholar R. Weems so cogently observes: "For African-American
(Protestant) women the Bible has been the only book passed down from her ancestors, and it
has been presented to her as the medium for experiencing and knowing the will of the Christian
God" (1991, 63; Grant 1993, 279).

Unwilling to jettison the Bible—in spite of its uses and abuses against African Americans by proslavery jurists, apologists, and others in the dominant European culture of seventeenth-, eighteenth-, and nineteenth-century America to provide the *argumentum* and *invidium par excellence* (a definite and supreme appeal to prejudices) in support of chattel slavery—womanist biblical interpreters and generations of African Americans have found, in many of its traditions, stories, and themes, affirmation of enduring ancestral traditions; the valuation of communal solidarity motifs and biblical mandates enjoining love, mercy, and justice; and the critical paradigms that informed their quest for freedom and inspired hope (cf. God's deliverance of Israel from Egypt, Exod 1:1-15; and the description of Jesus in his earthly ministry as vested with power to deliver women and men from the death-dealing effects of individual and structural sin and oppression to a new life of redemptive and communal wholeness, Luke 4:16-20; 8:40-48; Williams 1993, 148-52). Similarly, stories of female and male personalities in the Hebrew Bible and in the Christian Scriptures, inclusive of black Africans in the ancient Near East and in the Greco-Roman world (e.g., the Queen of Sheba in 1 Kgs 10:1-10, 13; Ebed-Melech in Jer 38:7-13; and the Ethiopian eunuch in Acts 8:26-40; Afrocentric Interpretation*§) inspire unyielding perseverance, strength in weakness, hope in the face of despair, the possibilities of a radically transformed and renewed life in the face of a multiplicity of death-dealing forces.

The previously cited biblical motifs and others hold special interest for African Americans continually assailed by the racial Moloch that sought to circumscribe the integrity of their lives and the promise of their potential on the American landscape. In short, black people have developed an experiential sympathy with much of the Bible, for they have found within its stories ancient symbols of their own predicament and of their own struggle for liberation (C. Felder 1989, 6).

Second, if womanist biblical interpreters have corroborated that the Bible has functioned as a historic, life-giving, and empowering resource for both African Americans and the larger human community because they find their story in the biblical story, they also acknowledge the problematics of the Bible as a pervasively androcentric, patriarchal text. As such, womanist biblical scholars impart a HERMENEUTIC of suspicion to the interpretative task (see Schüssler Fiorenza 1984), recognizing, for example, that recovering the religious beliefs, experiences, and history of women in the Hebrew Bible and the Christian Scriptures is methodologically problematic, as much because the Scriptures were written and mediated by males and male-dominated institutions and interests as because the larger interests of the biblical writers often display a dialectic of concealment, redacted traditional interests encased in artistically and rhetorically nuanced figures and symbols. Thus, biblical traditions necessarily require critical analysis to assess their meanings within their own socio-historical and ideological context, and critical discernment regarding their possible use and relevance in emancipatory struggles.

Third, womanist biblical interpreters have consistently heralded the need to identify and demystify the reality and effects of multiple, interlocking ideologies and systems of hegemony and domination inscribed within the biblical traditions and stories and within traditional male and female (including feminist) Eurocentric critical exegetical theories and practices.

b. Tasks of womanist interpreters. The multiple tasks of womanist biblical interpreters in the production of womanist religious scholarship are informed as much by their training in the standard and traditionalist methodologies and practices of biblical criticism in the academic guild as they are by the discourses, values, sociopolitical and religious experiences, and cosmological worldview of African American culture. While the tasks of womanist biblical interpreters are richly diverse and eclectically wide-ranging, four tasks are briefly noted here.

First, womanist interpreters expand on earlier works and on the appropriate recovery, analysis, and reconstruction of the texts and of their worlds as well as on the history of the Hebrew

Bible and the New Testament, including an analysis of their symbolic universes, rhetorical character, and the luminous depths and ideological complexities of their sacred histories. The reconstruction of the historic faith traditions embedded within both the Hebrew Bible and the New Testament must necessarily include a recovery of the history of women within the biblical traditions, including a recognition of the methodological complexities attending such reconstructions (B. Brooten c. 1985).

Biblical scholar R. Weems has shown that the recovery and excavation of women's history can yield unsettling historical conundrums about the complexities of women's experience of, e.g., the social constructions of violence and gender, including the role of religious language in reinforcing domination (1989). It can likewise provide a blueprint for the possibilities of enhanced emancipatory practices and commitments (1988). Weems aptly demonstrates that, even when the hermeneutic aim is the recovery of women's history and agency in biblical texts, the interpreter must always have in view the persons for whom the text is interpreted. That is, given a range of possible audiences, womanist consciousness notably has in view the multiple ways in which the interpretive strategy "arouses, manipulates, and harnesses African American women's deepest yearnings (1991, 59)."

Second, in addition to recovering women's history in the Judeo-Christian tradition, womanist biblical interpreters seek to reclaim the neglected histories and stories of the presence and function of Black peoples within divergent biblical traditions, including an assessment of the significance for the respective biblical writer of the African Blacks as active participants in the salvation dramas of ancient Israel (see Gen 16:1-15; 21:8-21; 1 Kgs 10:1-10; Jer 38:7; 39:16) and in the early Christian movement (see Matt 12:42; Luke 11:31; Acts 8:26-40; for a detailed explanation of the significance of ethnographic identity for a biblical writer, see C. Martin 1989; Afrocentric Interpretation*[§]). In a related task, womanist biblical interpretation includes, within its purview, the need for critical exploration of the origin and evolution of religiously sanctioned and mythological ideas about "blacker" and "blackness" in the history of ideas in both Christian and Western social thought. Topics for analysis include the historic antecedents and expressions of "Blacks" and "blackness" in Greco-Roman thought, within the writings and ideas of patristic theologians (the early church fathers and mothers), and within medieval Christendom (Martin 1989; see also the important work of R. Hood 1994).

Third, while attending to such issues as gender, subjectivity in interpretation, the construction of power in social relation, and the possibilities of liberatory intellectual, social, and ecclesial transformations arising from critical exegetical practices in collaboration with white North American and European feminist interpreters, womanist biblical interpreters must nevertheless continue to challenge the persistent and still normative narrowness of vision of feminist theologians and biblical interpreters on the subject of race. The still negligible attention given to issues of ethnicity and race in feminist theological discourses and practices ignores the reality of race and ethnicity as legitimate sites of dialogic exchange and contestation in biblical interpretation and diminishes the significance of the power and the effects of the simultaneity of gender, race, and class variants in their assessment of biblical meaning. Womanist biblical interpreters and theorists who have examined the politics of ethnicity, class, equality, and difference in the Hagar and Sarah traditions in the Hebrew Bible (Gen 16:1-15; 21:1-21) and the consequential historical and political effects of traditionalist interpretations of these texts on generations of black and white women (Gal 4:21-31), have demonstrated that the "technologies of race" must be taken as seriously as gender in biblical interpretation. For the most extensive and erudite analysis of the Hagar and Sarah story in this regard, see D. Williams (1993) and Weems's useful explanation of the implication of these biblical traditions for contemporary women (1988).

A fourth task of womanist biblical interpretation is the retrieval and documentary analysis of the effective history of the Hebrew Bible and the Christian Scriptures in Western culture in general, and on peoples of African descent in Black diasporic communities in particular. The socio-historical and political effects of exegetical readings and practices on generations of African Americans, for example, continues to be documented by womanist scholars (for a "metalanguage of race" in feminist theory, see E. Higginbotham 1995). Ethicist K. Cannon (1985) contrasts the effects of the oppressive use of the Bible by proslavery apologists with the liberation hermeneutic upheld by women and men in the Black churches during the antebellum period of American history. Similarly, in her story of the origin and function of the household codes, Martin contrasts the glaring contradictions in the strategic use of the domestic codes to provide philosophical legitimation for the subordination of women (through the use of a literalist hermeneutics) with the abandonment of the literalist hermeneutic strategy to advance the argument for the abolition of chattel slavery by nineteenth-century abolitionists (Martin 1991, 206-31).

There are at least four recent studies relevant to womanist and African American interpretations of the Bible. V. L. Wimbush (2000) has edited a collection of articles dealing with African Americans, the Bible, politics, art, literature, etc. B.K. Blount has reinterpreted New Testament ethics in light of the African American slave experience and African American spirituals (2001). B. R. Braxton interprets Galatians in light of the African American experience using reader response criticism (Literary Theory*§) and includes womanist perspectives (2002). Wimbush has written a short history of African American interaction with the Bible (2003).

Bibliography: B.K. Blount, *Then the Whisper Put on Flesh: New Testament Ethics in an African American Context* (2001) **B. R. Braxton,** *No Longer Slaves: Galatians and African American Experience* (2002). **B. J. Brooten,** "Early Christian Women in the Cultural Context: Issues of Method in Historical Reconstruction," *Feminist Perspectives on Biblical Scholarship* (SBLBSNA 10, ed. A. Y. Collins, 1985). **K. D. Brown,** "God Is as Christ Does: Toward a Womanist Theology," *JRT* 46 (1989) 7-16. **R. Bultmann,** *The Theology of the NT* (1948-53; ET 1952-55). **K. Cannon,** "The Emergence of Black Feminist Consciousness," *Feminist Interpretation of the Bible* (ed. L. Russell, 1985) 30-40; *Black Womanist Ethics* (American Academy of Religion, Academic Series 60, 1988); *Katie's Canon: Womanism and the Soul of the Black Community* (1995) 47-56. **P. H. Collins,** *Black Feminist Thought: Knowledge, Consciousness, and the Politics of Empowerment* (1990). **J. H. Cone,** *Black Theology and Black Power* (1969). **J. H. Cone and G. S. Wilmore,** *Black Theology: A Documentary History* (1979, 1993²). **P. D. Couture,** *Blessed Are the Poor? Women's Poverty, Family Policy, and Practical Theology* (1991); "Weaving the Web: Pastoral Care in an Individualistic Society," *Through the Eyes of Women: Insights for Pastoral Care* (ed. J. S. Moessner, 1996). **T. M. Eugene,** "Moral Values and Black Womanists," *JRT* 14 (1988) 23-34. **J. H. Evans,** *Black Theology: A Critical Assessment and Annotated Bibliography* (1987); *We Have Been Believers: An African-American Systematic Theology* (1992). **C. H. Felder,** *Troubling Biblical Waters: Race, Class, and Family* (1989); (ed.) *Stony the Road We Trod: African American Biblical Interpretation* (1991). **E. Schüssler Fiorenza,** *Bread Not Stone: The Challenges of Feminist Biblical Interpretation* (1984) 1-22; *Searching the Scriptures: A Feminist Introduction* (1993). **J. Grant,** *White Woman's Christ and Black Woman's Jesus: Feminist Christology and Womanist Response* (1989); "Womanist Theology: Black Women's Experience as a Source for Doing Theology, with Special Reference to Christology," *Black Theology: A Documentary History* (ed. J. H. Cone and G. S. Wilmore, 1993) 2:273-89; *Perspectives on Womanist Theology* (1995). **D. L. Hayes,** *Hagar's Daughters: Womanist Ways of Being in the World* (1995). **C. M. Haywood,** *Prophesying Daughters: Nineteenth-century Black Women Preachers, Religious Conviction, and Resistance* (1998). **E. B. Higginbotham,** "African American Women's History and the Metalanguage of Race," *We Specialize in the Wholly Impossible: A Reader in Black Women's*

History (ed. D. C. Hine, W. King, and L. Reedy, 1995) 3-24. **R. E. Hood**, *Begrimed and Black: Christian Traditions on Blacks and Blackness* (1994). **D. N. Hopkins**, *Black Theology USA and South Africa: Political and Cultural Liberation* (1988); *Shoes That Fit Our Feet: Sources for a Constructive Black Theology* (1993). **D. K. King,** "Multiple Jeopardy, Multiple Consciousness: The Context of a Black Feminist Ideology," *Signs: Journal of Women in Culture and Society* 14 (1988) 42-72. **C. E. Lincoln,** *The Black Church in the African American Experience* (1990). **C. J. Martin,** "A Chamberlain's Journey and the Challenge of Interpretation for Liberation [Acts 8:26-40]," *Semeia* 47 (1989) 105-35; "The Haustafeln (Household Codes) in African American Biblical Interpretation: 'Free Slaves' and 'Subordinate Women,' " *Stony the Road We Trod: African American Biblical Interpretation* (ed. C. H. Felder, 1991) 206-31. **D. Patte**, *Ethics and Biblical Interpretation: A Reevaluation* (1995). **J. D. Roberts,** *Black Theology Today* (1983); *The Prophethood of Black Believers: An African American Political Theology for Ministry* (1994). **C. J. Sanders,** *Empowerment Ethics for Liberated People: A Path to African American Social Transformation* (1995); *Living the Intersection: Womanism and Afro-centrism in Theology* (1995). **F. C. Steady,** *The Black Woman Cross-culturally* (1981). **R. S. Sugirtharajah,** *Interpreting the Bible in the Third World* (1991). **E. M. Townes,** *Womanist Justice, Womanist Hope* (1993). **A. Walker**, *In Search of Our Mother's Gardens: Womanist Prose* (1983); *In a Blaze of Glory: Womanist Spirituality as Social Witness* (1995). **R. J. Weems,** *Just a Sister Away* (1988); "Gomer: Victim of Violence or Victim of Metaphor?" *Semeia* 47 (1989) 87-104; "Reading Her Way Through the Struggle: African American Women and the Bible," *Stony the Road We Trod: African American Biblical Interpretation* (ed. C. H. Felder, 1991) 57-77. **D. S. Williams,** "Womanist Theology: Black Woman's Voices," *Christianity and Crisis* 47 (1987) 66-70; *Sisters in the Wilderness: The Challenge of Womanist God-talk* (1993). **V. L. Wimbush,** *African Americans and the Bible: Sacred Texts and Social Textures* (2000); *The Bible and African Americans: A Brief History* (Facets 2003).

C. J. MARTIN

LIBERATION OR IDEOLOGICAL APPROACHES

Cultural Studies

1. *Definition of Cultural Studies and Its Role in Biblical Studies.* "Cultural studies" resists a rigid definition, but its proponents usually see it as a practice of both cultural critique and cultural intervention (b. hooks 1990, 124-25). As a practice of cultural critique it posits conjunctural (i.e., historically specific) analyses of all parts of culture to expose their operations of power in the production of identity and in the maintenance of hegemony. As a practice of intervention within culture, it participates in culture in several ways: through the democratization of culture, the creation of collectives to link scholars across disciplines and to connect intellectuals to grassroots organizations, and the production of more liberative forms of pedagogy.

In biblical studies, cultural studies likewise has a dual role. On the one hand, as a form of cultural critique it assesses the contributing role of contextualization (or social location) for biblical reading strategies, interpretation practices, and evaluation standards (F. Segovia 1995*a*, 370-378). On the other hand, it reclaims the residual or lost voices refracted through biblical texts (E. Schüssler Fiorenza 1984, 15), opens up spaces for so-called marginalized readings of these texts (J. P. Ruiz 1995, 73-84; O. Hendricks 1994, 92-109), creates collectives or coalitions to offset insidious neutralizing practices of interpretation validity (Bible and Culture Collective 1995, 15-19), and decries pedagogical theories that support unilateral lines of authority (G. West 1993, 131-46). Cultural studies as an exegetical method utilizes the dual roles of critique and intervention. As a cultural critique it assesses the contributing role of contextualization (or social location) for biblical reading strategies, interpretation practices, and evaluation standards (Segovia 1995a, 370-378). It also reclaims the lost voices of biblical texts (Schüssler Fiorenza 1984, 15), promotes so-called marginalized readings of these texts (J. P. Ruiz 1995, 73-84; O. Hendricks 1994, 92-109), creates collectives or coalitions to offset insidious practices that negate the validity of other interpretations (Bible and Culture Collective 1995, 15-19), and decries hierarchical or autocratic pedagogy (G. West 1993, 131-46).

2. *Development of the Cultural Studies Paradigm.* Cultural studies' democratization of culture places it within the broad parameters of Postmodernism*§, yet its intellectual roots lie deep in several theoretical fields: the mass market (commodification) theory of the Frankfurt school, the hegemony theory of A. Gramsci (1891-1937; specifically, on dominant groups' continuous use of civic formation to win the consent of resisting, dominated groups), L. Althusser's (1918-90) view of ideology as a dynamic complex of structural constraints (or systems of representation), M. Foucault's (1926-84) view of knowledge discourses as power, and pragmatism's pedagogical theory.

F. Segovia has given a persuasive history of the influence of the cultural studies paradigm in biblical studies (1995*a*, 2-7). Arguing that biblical criticism has evolved in three stages, he avers that the initial dominance of historical criticism (biblical criticism's first stage, which began in the mid-nineteenth cent.) gave way between the mid-1970s and the mid-1990s to two other types of biblical criticism—namely, biblical Literary Criticism*§ and biblical sociocultural criticism (stage two). Later in the 1990s (stage three), these approaches merged interests to set off an explosion of methodologies or "a situation of radical plurality"—that is, the emergence of the cultural studies paradigm in biblical studies (Segovia 1995a, 4-15, esp. 4).

3. *Distinctions Within Cultural Studies.* At least two significant formulations of cultural studies have emerged: the first, British; the second (typically known as "cultural criticism"), North American. In its British form, cultural studies began with the British sociologists (Sociology and Hebrew Bible/New Testament Studies*§) of culture: R. Williams, R. Hoggart, and E. Thompson. Later it confronted the French "linguistic turn" under S. Hall's influence; and, in

the most recent decades, it has taken an interest in a variety of subaltern studies (à la Gramsci). In this formulation, proponents of cultural studies produced the Centre for Contemporary Cultural Studies (now known as the Department of Cultural Studies), cross-fertilized with FEM-INIST work in the British Women's Studies Group, and published works in several important journals (e.g., *Screen and Culture, Media, Language*) for the investigation of power relations in a variety of literary and nonliterary discursive practices.

In its North American form, C. West and b. hooks are representative. Writing apart and together, they demonstrate several emphases: the democratization of culture, the decolonization of representations, the critical retrieval of subjugated voices, and the construction of provisional forms of liberative pedagogy.

Both formulations have influenced biblical studies. For example, I. Mosala (influenced by S. Hall), exploits cultural studies to expose the biblical authors' possible collusion with hegemony. K. Cannon's critique of slavery's use of the so-called Hamite hypothesis (1995, 119-28) owes much to C. West's ruminations on Gramsci. And S. Reid's challenge to the African American scholar or preacher to read the biblical texts with the African American community (1994-95, 476-87) evokes b. hooks and C. West's charge to black intellectuals to remain connected to grassroots communities (b. hooks 1990, 130; West 1989, 231).

4. *Cultural Studies' Relation to Other Methods of Biblical Interpretation*. With Marxist theory, cultural studies shares an interest in ideology but not in the fashion of classical Marxists, who defined ideology as false consciousness (i.e., a narrow set of ideas or beliefs naturalized to promote dominant class interests). Cultural studies' proponents most often prefer to view ideology as a wide range of competing values of which many are neither economically based nor institutionally grounded.

Because of its multidisciplinary history and its keen interest in relations of power, cultural studies bears striking parallels to many vibrant approaches under the banner of Postmodernism*[§]. With poststructuralist theory (Structuralism and Deconstruction*[§]), it shares concerns about the state and production of knowledge and the complex notion of identity. With feminist studies, it enjoys a rich cross-fertilization. Both approaches have origins in radical politics; both also use collectives, resist passive absorption models of learning, and embrace the interface between theory and the ethnographic documentation of experiences (S. Franklin, C. Lury, and J. Stacey 1991, 1-19). Segovia's history of biblical studies reveals the influence of historical criticism, Literary*[§] criticism, and sociocultural criticism on the cultural studies paradigm. Furthermore, both the critical and the interventionist interests of cultural studies are found in a number of current critical approaches to the Bible. Exploiting the cultural critique dimension, biblical Ideological Criticism*[§] questions the use of the exodus-conquest narratives as sources of Liberation*[§] because these texts support the annihilation of Canaanite people and because the texts have been used against Native Americans in support of manifest destiny (R. Liburd 1994, 79). Likewise, feminist biblical criticism has exposed both the patriarchal character of the biblical texts and the androcentric interests of biblical studies (Schüssler Fiorenza 1984, 5). Taking on the interventionist dimension of cultural studies, ideological criticism advocates an ethics of accountability (T. Pippin 1996, 51-78). Feminist biblical criticism and the biblical criticism of other marginalized groups have sought to rewrite the histories of ancient biblical cultures and to recover the residual voices of the biblical texts (Schüssler Fiorenza 1984, 15; R. Bailey 1995, 25-36).

5. *Examples of a Cultural Studies Approach to the Bible*. Among the several examples of a cultural studies approach to biblical studies, three are particularly illustrative: the *Postmodern Bible* (1995), the two volumes of *Reading from This Place* (1994, 1995), and B. Blount's *Cultural Interpretation* (1995). Like other proponents of cultural studies, the authors of the *Postmodern Bible* worked collaboratively (in the Bible and Culture Collective) to offset the pol-

itics of exclusion. In the cultural studies tradition of criticism, they proffer solid critiques of contemporary biblical practices of interpretation, particularly on the questions of suppressed meaning, the formation of identities, and the use of the Bible to "ratify the status quo" (1995, 4). *Reading from This Place* encourages multiple interpretations (thus a democratization of culture) through its exposure of strategies of reading the Bible with a wide variety of scholars within and beyond North America. In addition, its authors intervene in culture in proffering liberative yet provisional forms of pedagogy to teach the Bible. In *Cultural Interpretation,* Blount's goal is to reorient biblical interpretation through the genuine interchange of so-called peripheral and centrist interpretations. Moreover, his broadening of culture to include several biblical approaches becomes evident in his examination of several interpretive strategies (e.g., R. Bultmann's existentialist hermeneutics; the *campesinos'* biblical hermeneutics in *The Gospel in Solentiname* 1976-82; the North American slaves' biblical hermeneutical strategy in the Black spiritual; and the Black preacher's biblical hermeneutics in sermons), even as he exposes the limitations of each. All of these examples of cultural studies prove the heuristic value and prominence of this recent paradigm in biblical studies.

6. *Summary.* In sum, with its dual goals of culture critique and culture intervention, cultural studies is a vital part of the academic landscape, the postmodernist focus on difference, and the current practices of biblical studies. Under the cultural studies paradigm, moreover, biblical studies moves outside the walls of a strict discipline to examine all discursive practices critically and, potentially, to create more liberative relations of power in society.

Bibliography: V. Anderson, *Beyond Ontological Blackness: An Essay on African American Religious and Cultural Criticism* (1995). R. C. Bailey, "'Is That Any Name for a Nice Hebrew Boy?': The De-Africanization of an Israelite Hero," *The Recovery of the Black Presence: An Interdisciplinary Exploration* (ed. R. C. Bailey and J. Grant, 1995) 25-36. The Bible and Culture Collective, *The Postmodern Bible* (1995). **B. K. Blount,** *Cultural Interpretation: Reorienting NT Criticism* (1995). **K. Cannon,** "Slave Ideology and Biblical Interpretation," *The Recovery of the Black Presence* (1995) 119-28. **D. N. Fewell,** "Reading the Bible Ideologically: Feminist Criticism," *To Each Its Own Meaning* (ed. S. Haynes and S. McKenzie, 1993) 237-51. **S. Franklin, C. Lury, and J. Stacey** (eds.), *Off-Centre: Feminism and Culture Studies* (1991). **H. Giroux, D. Shumway, P. Smith, and J. Sosnoski,** "The Need for Cultural Studies: Resisting Intellectuals and Oppositional Public Spheres," *Dalhousie Review* (1984) 472-86. **S. Hall,** "Cultural Studies and Its Theoretical Legacies," *Cultural Studies* (ed. L. Grossberg, C. Nelson, and P. A. Treichler, 1992) 277-94. **O. Hendricks,** "Guerila Exegesis: A Post-Modern Proposal for Insurgent African American Biblical Interpretation," *JITC 22* (1994) 92-109. **b. hooks,** *Yearning: Race, Gender, and Cultural Politics* (1990); "Representing Whiteness in the Black Imagination," *Cultural Studies* (1992) 338-46. **V. Leitch,** *Cultural Criticism, Literary Theory, Poststructuralism* (1992). **R. Liburd,** "'Like . . . a House Upon the Sand': African American Biblical Hermeneutics in Perspective," *JITC 22* (1994) 71-91. **I. Mosala,** *Biblical Hermeneutics and Black Theology in South Africa* (1989). **C. Nelson,** P. A. Treichler, and L. Grossberg, "An Introduction," *Cultural Studies* (1992) 1-22. **T. Pippin,** "Ideology, Ideological Criticism, and the Bible," *Currents in Research: Biblical Studies 4* (1996) 51-78. **S. B. Reid,** "Endangered Reading: The African-American Scholar Between Text and People," *Cross Currents* (1994-95) 476-87. **J.P. Ruiz,** "New Ways of Reading the Bible in the Cultural Settings of the Third World," *The Bible as Cultural Heritage* (Concilium 1995, 1, ed. W. Beuken and S. Freyne, 1995) 73-84. **F. Segovia,** "Cultural Studies and Contemporary Biblical Criticism: Ideological Criticism as a Mode of Discourse," *Reading from This Place,* vol. 2 (ed. F. Segovia and M. A. Tolbert, 1995a) 1-17; "The Significance of Social Location in Reading John's Story," *Int 49* (1995b) 370-78. **E. Schüssler Fiorenza,** *Bread Not Stone: The*

Challenge of Feminist Biblical Interpretation (1984). **M. A. Tolbert,** "Reading for Liberation," *Reading from This Place,* vol 2 (1995) 263-76. **C. West,** *The American Evasion of Philosophy: A Genealogy of Pragmatism* (1989); "The New Cultural Politics of Difference," *Out There: Marginalization and Contemporary Cultures* (ed. R. Ferguson, 1990) 19-36; "The Postmodern Crisis of the Black Intellectuals," *Cultural Studies* (1992) 689-705. **G. West,** "No Integrity Without Contextuality: The Presence of Particularity in Biblical Hermeneutics and Pedagogy," *Scriptura 11* (1993) 131-46.

A. Smith

LIBERATION OR IDEOLOGICAL APPROACHES

Ideological Criticism

When discussing ideological criticism, one must be clear about the definition of ideology. Although the term has acquired the pejorative connotation of "false consciousness," in contemporary theory it usually refers to a complex system of ideas, values, and perceptions held by a particular group that provides a framework for the group's members to understand their place in the social order. Ideology constructs a reality for people, making the bewildering and often brutal world intelligible and tolerable. Ideology motivates people to behave in specific ways and to accept their social position as natural, inevitable, and necessary.

Ideologies should not be identified with "reality," however. While they help to foster and sustain a distinctive worldview that structures and informs people's lives, ideologies also disguise or explain away features of society that may be unjust. For example, some ideologies help to explain why certain people in a society are accorded economic privileges. Other ideologies provide a rationalization for why a particular gender or race is allowed to perform specified actions while others cannot. In these and other ways, ideologies "resolve" inequalities, struggles, and contradictions that individuals or groups may experience in their everyday lives (Eagleton 1991.)

Ideological criticism investigates (1) the production of the text by a particular author in a specific, ideologically charged historical context, (2) the reproduction of ideology in the text itself, and (3) the consumption of the text by readers in different social locations who are themselves motivated and constrained by distinct ideologies. In its broadest sense, ideological criticism examines ideology at work in three variables of biblical interpretation: the author, the text, and the reader.

Investigations of gender or racial ideologies in the biblical text and in its interpretation can be understood as ideological criticism. In biblical circles, however, such studies are usually classified as Feminist*§ criticism or African/Asian/Hispanic American Hermeneutics*§, respectively. Influenced by Marxist or materialist theories, early proponents of ideological criticism more narrowly defined networks of economic class relations involved in the production of the biblical text. These critics investigated ways in which ideology "explained" unequal distribution of wealth, prestige, and control over the means of production (land, natural resources, etc.) in a given population. They analyzed ways in which the dominant class generated ideologies in order to reproduce and legitimate specified class relations. As some of the first to take seriously the material and economic conditions under which the biblical text was constructed, the works of N. K. Gottwald (1979, 1985, 1993) have been foundational for developing ideological criticism as a biblical method of interpretation. Social class and access to material resources cannot, however, be studied in isolation. Because socioeconomic relations and opportunities have often been determined by one's gender or race, ideological critics have begun to make use of these categories in order to calculate their impact on class relations (G. Yee 1995, 152-167; R. Carroll 1994; D. Jobling 1991; articles by I. Mosala and R. Weems in Jobling and T. Pippin 1992, 25-34.)

Ideological criticism, more narrowly defined, uses Literary*§-critical methods within a historical and social-scientific frame (Social-Scientific Criticism*§) in a comprehensive strategy for reading the biblical text. Ideological critics have a twofold task in their investigation: an extrinsic and an intrinsic analysis. Extrinsic analysis uses the historical and social sciences to help reconstruct or unmask the material and ideological conditions under which the text was produced. The primary focus of an extrinsic analysis is the mode of production dominant in the society that produced the text—i.e., the social relations (family, status, class, gender, etc.) and forces (e.g., technology, politics, law, education) that interconnect in a society's material production. In ancient Israel, for example, three dominant modes of production can be identified. The tribal period was characterized by a familial mode of production that valued kin group connections and had no outside agencies that taxed their resources. The monarchical and colonial periods had a tributary mode of production in which various social classes paid tribute or taxes to the state or to foreign powers, with the lower classes carrying the heaviest burden. Finally, Judaism under Roman hegemony operated under a slave mode of production. The ideological critic examines the social structures, relations, groups, and interests that profited under a particular mode of production and those that were deprived under it.

An extrinsic analysis of a biblical text is particularly concerned with the category of power. It tries to determine the types of social, political, and economic structures wielding power when the text was written; and it clarifies the kinds of power these structures exhibit—formal or informal, legal, cultic, or religious. Extrinsic analysis investigates power groups according to gender, class, race, religion, region, etc., to see if any patterns of power emerge. It determines the control these groups exert over the means of production and sources of power; and it explores the antagonisms, clashes, and contradictions that exist wherever power operates.

Since ideologies themselves are forms of power that influence and direct social groups, an extrinsic analysis searches for the ways in which groups produce and manipulate ideology to legitimate or exert their place in society—that is, it examines whose interests are being served by ideologies. Further, extrinsic analysis identifies and locates a society's disempowered voices or interests and determines how these break down according to gender, race, and class. It tries to reconstruct alternative ideologies that may have resisted the dominant ones.

Just as each text has been written by a particular author, so also an extrinsic analysis scrutinizes the author's position in society and access to power, exploring the circumstances under which the author produced the text. It investigates the author's own ideology, comparing it with the ideologies of the time and noting the author's complicity with or challenge to the dominant ideology.

In an intrinsic analysis, the ideological critic takes up literary critical methods to examine how the text assimilates or "encodes" socioeconomic conditions to reproduce a particular ideology in its rhetoric. Feminist literary criticism, Narrative Criticism*[§], and Structuralism and Deconstruction*[§] are some of the literary methods that have been useful for the method's intrinsic analysis. The ideological critic assumes that the text symbolically resolves real social contradictions by inventing and adopting "solutions" for them. For example, the *Malleus Malleficarum*, a medieval treatise by two Roman Catholic priests, explained a wide range of personal and social disorders—such as male sexual impotency and lust, harvest failures, miscarriages, and plagues—as the demonic acts of witches. Scapegoating of witches led to the widespread persecution and slaughter of lower-class women in particular during the Middle Ages. During the nineteenth century, however, tracts like Godey's *Lady's Book* flourished, which promoted what came to be called the "cult of true womanhood." Women were not regarded as evil or demonic, but, rather, as morally superior to men. Ruling the household as queen, women were mothers and keepers of hearth and home. They provided a refuge of peace and tranquility for their husbands, who struggled in the brutal jungle of the outside world. Nevertheless, women were still economically dependent on and respectfully submissive to their husbands and confined to the home. The ideology of the "cult of true womanhood," moreover, was primarily a middle to upper-class phenomenon. White slaveholders did not apply this ideology to black women, nor did Boston Brahmins to their Irish immigrant maids.

Of course, with these examples or any other, different texts exist that present opposing dominant ideologies and offer their own solutions to social problems and conflicts. An intrinsic analysis, then, tries to discover the precise relationship of the specific text's ideology to the ideology(s) surrounding and affecting its production.

To determine a text's ideology, an intrinsic analysis takes special note of the "absences" in the text. In the words of Marxist literary critic P. Macherey, "In order to say anything, there are other things which must not be said" (1978, 85). In arguing for what it regards as the "truth," the text cannot indicate matters that will deny that truth. By focusing on the text's gaps and absences, one can unmask the dominant ideologies and recover the voices of the silenced—perhaps women, the conquered, the foreign, and the poor. In attempting to resolve contradictory opinions and articulate the "truth," the text must conceal and repress these voices. An intrinsic analysis attempts to retrieve them.

Intrinsic analysis also entails a close reading of the text's rhetoric, the literary ways in which a text attempts to convince its readers to embrace a certain ideology. Because it is a means of persuasion, rhetoric is thus a form of power; it unites groups, moves them to action, reinforces attitudes and beliefs, and universalizes local standards and principles. The text reproduces ideology in a style pitched to a specific audience. It appropriates literary genres and devices (e.g., sermons, refrains, exhortations) that will particularly appeal to and persuade this audience. The text manipulates literary features, such as irony, plot, characterization, and point of view, to convey a certain ideology. This ideology is revealed in who speaks, who sees, and who acts in a text, and especially in who does not.

Extrinsic and intrinsic analysis can be viewed as a Janus-like operation, given the intricate relationship between ideology's production in a particular place and time and reproduction in a particular text. Used as a means of interpreting the biblical text, ideological criticism begins first with a preliminary intrinsic analysis, taking note of any ideological gaps, inconsistencies, and dissonant voices. It then works backward, so to speak, to determine the social location of production hinted at in the text. An extrinsic analysis then determines the nature of the material-ideological disputes the text's ideology tries to resolve. Finally, a more complete intrinsic analysis determines how the text encodes and reworks the ideological conditions of its production.

Because ideological criticism investigates both text and context inclusively, it helps to shed light on the economic, political, and historical circumstances of the text's production, which are often overlooked by literary-critical methods. Because it grapples with the text as an ideological reproduction of a specific sociohistorical context, ideological criticism uncovers a textual politics often overlooked by historical and social-scientific methods. Lacking a literary theory that investigates the workings of textual ideology, historical and social-scientific methods often naively regard the text as a "mirror" of the past or dismiss the text as useless for sociohistorical reconstruction. Ideological criticism, however, presumes that the text itself is a sociohistorical artifact.

For example, ideological criticism reveals that the text of Isa 40–55 is "a weapon of struggle to preserve the sociocultural identity and political future of a former Judahite ruling elite faced with dissolution in Babylonian society" two generations after it lost its power base in Judah (Gottwald in Jobling and Pippin 1992, 43). In Judges 17–20 the Deuteronomist (Deuteronomistic History*§) deliberately portrays the Levites in a negative way to promote the centralization of worship under Josiah's reform policies (Yee 1995). Several postexilic texts incorporate two pervasive myths—that of the empty land and of the Canaanite pollution of the land—to legitimate the resettlement claims of the Second Temple community (Carroll in Jobling and Pippin 1992, 79-93).

Ideological criticism is one of the more recent methods to be used by biblical scholars, and its impact on biblical interpretation remains to be seen. Its interdisciplinary utilization of historical, social-scientific, and literary methods makes ideological criticism a more inclusive method, offering exciting possibilities for biblical studies. Because of its focus on the biblical text as a site of struggle for competing ideologies during its production in antiquity, ideological criticism can help the exegete to become more aware of how the biblical text is currently being used to support opposing groups. Such an analysis can enable the exegete to become conscious of personal ideological blind spots and constraints to produce a more ethically responsible reading.

Bibliography: R. P. Carroll, "The Myth of the Empty Land," *Semeia* 59 (1992) 79-93; "On Representation in the Bible: An *Ideologiekritik* Approach," *JNSL* 20 (1994) 1-15; "An Infinity of Traces: On Making an Inventory of Our Ideological Holdings. An Introduction to Ideologiekritik in Biblical Studies," *JNSL* 21 (1995) 25-43. **D. J. A. Clines,** *Interested Parties: The Ideology of Writers and Readers of the HB* (1995). **T. Eagleton,** *Ideology: An Introduction* (1991). **N. K. Gottwald,** *The Tribes of Yahweh: A Sociology of the Religion of Liberated Israel, 1250-1050 BCE* (1979); *The HB: A Socio-Literary Introduction* (1985); "Social Class and Ideology in Isaiah 40-50: An Eagletonian Reading," *Semeia* 59 (1992) 43-57; *The HB in Its Social World and in Ours* (1993). **D. Jobling,** "Feminism and 'Mode of Production' in Ancient Israel: Search for a Method," *The Bible and the Politics of Exegesis* (ed. D. Jobling, P. Day, and G. T. Sheppard, 1991) 239-51; "Deconstruction and the Political Analysis of Biblical Texts: A Jamesonian Reading of Psalm 72," *Semeia* 59 (1992) 95-127. **D. Jobling and T. Pippin** (eds.), *Ideological Criticism of Biblical Texts* (*Semeia* 59, 1992). **P. Macherey,** *A Theory of Literary Production* (tr. Geoffrey Wall, 1978). **I. J. Mosala,** *Biblical Hermeneutics and Black Theology in South Africa* (1989); "The Implications of the Text of Esther for American Women's Struggle for Liberation in South Africa," *Semeia* 59 (1992) 129-37. **R. Weems,** "The Hebrew Women Are Not Like the Egyptian Women: The Ideology of Race, Gender and Sexual Reproduction of Exodus 1," *Semeia* 59 (1992) 25-34. **G. A. Yee,** "Ideological Criticism: Judges 17-21 and the Dismembered Body," *Judges and Method: New Approaches in Biblical Studies* (ed. G. A. Yee, 1995) 146-70.

G. A. YEE

LIBERATION OR IDEOLOGICAL APPROACHES

Liberation Theologies

1. *Historical Development.* The type of biblical interpretation to be described here developed in Latin America in the course of the 1960s and was received and further developed in other parts of the Third World. Within this method of interpretation, one can distinguish two levels: the popular liberation movements and the more theologically oriented liberation theologies.

On the popular level there are scarcely any historical precedents in Latin America. The reading of the Bible was prohibited to the Roman Catholic people for centuries and was propagated only by individual figures (like M. da Concieção) since the 1920s. In most cases, the people knew the Bible only from song texts (a method of evangelization used by the Jesuits) and from the worship service (F. Rolim 1988; J. Konings 1984). An illustrative example of the traditional popular understanding of the Bible is the interpretation of Christ. Against the background of the reality of their own lives, the people see him as either the suffering, defeated, powerless one, with whom they can identify, or the heavenly ruler who is depicted with the insignia of the colonial rulers and who legitimates their rule. In the first case, Christ's resurrection plays almost no role; in the second, his saving death is scarcely present (J. Araújo 1984; R. Azzi 1985[2]; G. Casalis 1984; D. Irrarazaval 1986; S. Trinidad 1984).

Conversely, the contemporary Latin American liberation theology and its particular form of exegesis have their precursors. The most frequently named is B. de Las Casas , whom E. Dussel goes so far as to designate "the greatest theologian of the sixteenth century" (1985, 72). In contrast to most theologians of his time, Las Casas argued less philosophically and juridically than biblically. For example, he condemned the dispersion, enslavement, and forced christianization of the Indians, noting that God had given the Law neither to Abraham (as an individual) nor to the oppressed in Egypt, but only to Israel after the exodus because a free people was the necessary precondition for the giving of the Law (Las Casas 1957/58, 2:197). In the extermination of the Indians by the Spanish, Christ is crucified again, "not once, but thousands of times" (1957/58, 2:511).

Similar applications of biblical texts are found in the writings of modern liberation theologians; nevertheless, it is hardly correct when Las Casas's awareness, which is astonishingly critical for its time, is traced back to his biblical orientation (contra J. Pagalday 1988, 49; G. Gutiérrez 1985[2], 57-58). His contemporary, for instance, V. de Quiroga (1538-65, bishop of Michoacán, Mexico), supported his defense of the Indians more with philosophical texts and church doctrine than with biblical texts (J. Moreira 1985, 47). Brazilian clerics took part in the revolutions of 1817 and 1824 primarily because they were influenced by the Enlightenment ideas of French philosophers (Azzi 1985[2], 29). A. Vieira (mid-seventeenth cent.) on the other hand, justified the enslavement of blacks biblically (Col 3:22-24; Eph 6:5-9; 1 Pet 2:18-21; Luke 12:37), while G. Leite condemned this practice philosophically (E. Hoornaert 1982, 36, 54-55, 78-79; 1985, 67).

These examples show that a biblical orientation was neither necessary nor a sufficient condition for nonimperialistic theological thought. Nevertheless, there is a line of emancipatory biblical interpretation that can only be alluded to here with a few names (for individual treatments see the collective works of Faculdade 1985[2]; P. Richard 1985): A. de Montesinos (sixteenth century: defense of the Indians with, e.g., Luke 3:4; Ezekiel 34); P. de Córdoba (sixteenth century: the oppression of the Indians surpasses that of the Israelites in Egypt); M. Lacunza y Diaz (eighteenth century: resort to Daniel and the Apocalypse); J. Morelos y Pavón (eighteenth century: the liberation of Israel from oppression in Egypt and Babylon as an inspiration for the struggle for liberation in Mexico); and A. Pallais (ninteenth-twentieth centuries: exodus motif of central significance).

The process through which a strong theological trend emerged from these individual voices who superseded the "theology of development," and within which the popular understanding of the Bible was radically transformed, still has not been completely studied (Azzi 1985[2]; C. Boff 1986[3], 83-84; Dussell 1985, 1985[2]; 1988, 364-76; A. Garcia Rubio 1983[3], 33-75; C. Mesters 1987[4]; C. Pinto da Silva 1988; R. Poblette 1979; S. Silva Gotay 1985[2]). One can distinguish between political-economic and ecclesial-theological factors, which stand in reciprocal relationship with each other. To the first group belong the increasing oppression and pauperization in Latin America, the interpretation of these processes through the theory of dependence, and, further, the success of the Marxist revolution in Cuba. The ecclesial-theological factors (the influence of Vatican II and of theological developments in the First World) are in part independent of these political and economic ones, but they are also in part the answer to the altered social realities (the radicalization of the engagement of laity in the Acción Católica, meetings of theologians, and church documents like those from Medellin and Puebla).

It is true that liberation theology was, from the beginning, biblically oriented (J. Konings 1984, 85). Nonetheless, the interest in the Bible and its emancipatory interpretation are certainly secondary to the participation of Christians in the revolutionary process and to the adoption of modern sociological categories (Sociology and New Testament/Hebrew Bible Studies*[§]) in theology. A particular exegesis had doubtlessly strengthened and fertilized the development of liberation theology, but this exegesis itself was a consequence. In the new social and theological context, the Bible had something new and interesting to say.

2. *Popular Exegesis in Latin America: Forms, Texts, Themes.* In Latin America, groups of Christians who read the Bible together are formed out of a variety of motives. There may be liturgical causes (e.g., a preparation for Christmas, a campaign for fraternity), external events that concern the community (e.g., expulsions of peasants from their land), or simply the desire for more community. In addition, Bible courses are being offered more frequently (e.g., in Brazil by the Centro de Estudos Biblicos [CEBI], whose central figure is Mesters; see W. Schürger 1995). Exegetically trained facilitators from such organizations visit the grassroots communities and motivate them to come to grips with the texts on their own, while offering exegetical assistance with restraint. Furthermore, the reading of the Bible plays a significant role at the interregional meetings of agricultural workers, unions, and the like that are organized by the church (Mesters1988; A. Steiner 1985; J. Swetnam 1984).

On this level, biblical interpretations are mainly oral. If they are documented in writing (instructions to and results of Bible meetings), it is only in duplicated pages and pamphlets of the simplest kind that never go beyond the boundaries of the respective parish or diocese. Nevertheless, pertinent publications are also available in foreign countries. The best known is E. Cardenal's *Das Evangelium der Bauern von Solentiname* (1981 [ET *The Gospel in Solentiname* 1976]); others include the anonymous publications "Parables of Today," "Amostras da hermeneûtica dos pobres," "A luta pela Reforma Agrária e a Bíblia" (further: E. Bambamarca 1983[3]; M de Barros Souza 1983, 1983; M. Garcia Gutierrez 1983; R. McAfee Brown 1988; Mesters [1983b]; A. Reiser and P. Schoenborn 1981; Rolim 1988; C. Rowland and M. Corner 1989; T. Schmeller 1994).

In such documents, one discovers a preference for the Hebrew Bible over the New Testament. This emphasis may in part be due to the more concrete images of the Hebrew Bible, but it derives primarily from the possibility for the people of Latin America to identify with Israel. In Israel's history there is a recognizable "project of God" (Mesters 1984[5]) that has not yet been completed but that includes the similarly perceived Latin American reality today. It can be seen in Israel's exodus and conquest as God frees the people from oppression in Egypt, desiring equality for them rather than hierarchy, productive autonomy instead of exploitation, etc.

In the following age of the biblical story, the project is often darkened, especially through the monarchy, but the prophets continue to point to it. The project is completely realized through JESUS, who, as a poor man, announced the reign of God to the poor and fights for it against oppression and exploitation. His message of brotherhood and sisterhood and solidarity with the marginalized of society is confirmed through the resurrection. It is set forth in the practice of the first churches, which presents a clear picture of the project according to the Acts of the Apostles (e.g., in the community's holding of goods in common).

Besides these indicated themes, the psalms play a great role, especially those that reflect the experience of the exile. Jer 22:16 is often quoted in order to bring out the priority of liberating practice over any religious talk. The Wisdom books find approval on account of their proximity to Latin American folk wisdom. From Maccabees and Ezra-Nehemiah one gains inspiration for the revolutionary situation today and for the reconstruction that needs to follow the revolution (C. Boff 1986³, 46-47).

In the New Testament, besides Jesus' work in general and the Sermon on the Mount[†§] in particular, his Parables[†§] are of primary importance because of their rural local color and their simplicity. Also often referred to is Mary, the mother of Jesus, who becomes a figure of identification for the oppressed, and her Magnificat, which is understood literally as a basic text of revolution. While the letters of Paul[†§] play hardly any role, the Apocalypse of John is very important: "The Apocalypse is a writing that shows that God is in the struggle. That there will be no liberation without much suffering beforehand. The Apocalypse explains emphatically that we must be steadfast to the end. What counts is the certainty of the victory. . . . Whether it is the Roman Empire of that age, whether it is the authoritarian state today, the Apocalypse shows the state to be a wild animal. . . . The peasant can struggle from now on because he knows that this new heaven and this new earth are our hope" (Barros Souza1983b, 86-87).

3. *The Exegesis of Liberation Theology in Latin America: Forms, Texts, Themes.* Although biblical impulses were important for liberation theology from the beginning, liberation theology went a long time without developing its own academic exegesis. Either it fell back on the exegetical tradition of Europe or North America or it dealt with biblical texts only in the framework of systematic theology. Only in the last decades of the twentieth century has exegesis from the standpoint of liberation theology attained greater significance. The *Estudos Biblicos*, which previously were only an appendix to the *Revista Ecclesiastica Brasileira*, have been published independently since 1984 (e.g., "The Bible as the Remembrance of the Poor," 1 [1984]; "The Way of Liberation," 2 [1984]; "Reading the Bible from the Real Conditions of Life," 7 [1985]). Moreover, J. Comblin is publishing a commentary series (*Epistola aos Filipenses* 1985) over the whole Bible for which seventy volumes are planned, and since 1988 the *Revista de Interpretação Bíblica Latino-Americana* has appeared in both Spanish and Portuguese editions. What was true of popular exegesis is also, though less starkly, true for the more strictly academic exegesis of liberation theology: The Hebrew Bible has rather more significance than the New Testament. At the same time, however, there is an attempt to consider each text and each theme in the framework of the whole Bible. Two great theme-complexes are central: (a) the biblical witness to liberation in the history of the people of God and (b) the biblical obligation to carry out liberation today.

a. The biblical witness to liberation. This witness is treated, on the one hand, in studies based directly on biblical terminology and conceptions of "liberation" and "oppression" (e.g., T. Hanks 1983; R. Ortega 1978; E. Tamez 1982). On the other hand, it appears in investigations of all sorts of texts and themes from the standpoint of liberation. In this context, liberation can be understood in a variety of ways. Thus one differentiates between (1) "political, economic, social, and cultural liberation"; (2) "anthropological, historical, and communitarian self-discovery of humanity"; and (3) "salvation in a theological sense," all of which represent "different levels of a comprehensive historical process and which mutually condition one another" (H. Goldstein 1977, 67-68). Liberation theology does not, therefore, reduce liberation to the political and economic plane (as is frequently charged), but neither does liberation theology reduce liberation to a spiritual and otherworldly plane (with which liberation theology charges traditional theology). This more comprehensive understanding is based theologically on the denial of the separation of the order of creation from the order of salvation, of nature from the supernatural, of history from salvation history. There is only the one process of liberation, in which different aspects may be relevant depending on the situation. For Latin America today liberation is, above all, a liberation from hunger, injustice, and oppression.

The Hebrew Bible theme referred to most frequently is the exodus of Israel out of Egypt. Just as God led the chosen people in concrete historical reality, as God freed them from oppression and made them God's people, so God also does today with the marginalized masses in Latin America. The exodus event is one of the many embodiments of the kingdom of God in the Hebrew Bible (G. Pixley 1983[2]) that all have in common an overthrow of "social breaches"—i.e., an end of marginalization and the disintegration of certain groups through "reconciliations" (covenant and covenant renewals; Konings 1975).

In the New Testament, the Synoptic[†§] Gospels and, in particular, the praxis of Jesus are of special interest. The historical Jesus is especially referred to (J. Segundo 1985; J. Sobrino 1978[2]), although little attention is given to the reconstruction of his life. Most scholars, in fact, do not make a primary distinction between the historical Jesus and the kerygmatic Christ (C. Bussmann 1980, 67-68). Luke 4:18-19 serves as the summation of Jesus' work and for liberation theology is one of the key texts of the New Testament. The kingdom of God announced by Jesus is not given a unitary explanation but can be described in relatively general terms as a utopian expression of a last, universal sense that represents a comprehensive revolution in the structures of the world (L. Boff 1974, 1979), as a liberation of the poor from material and social oppression (Sobrino 1979), or even more concretely as a classless society without private property (J. Miranda 1982). The political implications of the work and message of Jesus present themselves in a corresponding variety but are always emphasized. They are either the indirect result of his particularly religious appearance (e.g., Croatto, Exodus 1981; S. Galilea 1984), or they are seen as direct political activity after the manner of the Zealots (Pixley 1983[2]). These implications are to be grasped in the conflicts Jesus provokes—conflicts that can be determined to be primarily confrontations with the Jewish religious authorities (theologians, Temple aristocrats), with the apparatus of the Roman state (slave society, Roman totalitarianism), or more generally with the privileged rich. Even more often one finds the interpretation that Jesus' critique of the traditional legitimation of exploitation and oppression through religious ideology led to a political conflict (Pixley 1983[2]; I. Ellacuría 1984; Croatto, Exodus 1981; Political Dimension 1984; also, A. McGovern 1983). The execution of Jesus is, in any case, no mere misunderstanding or blunder; rather, it is the reaction of persons in power to his direct or indirect subversive activity. Seen in this light, Jesus' death seals his life but can still be interpreted as a failure that includes him with all those who have suffered unjustly (Bussmann 1980, 136). Thus, the inclusive side of the death of Jesus is stressed more than the exclusive (Sobrino 1986, 296). The resurrection of Jesus only makes the liberation he has brought complete because it guarantees a good end to the process already begun (L. Boff 1979). It is not simply the "good news" for all people; rather, as the resurrection of the crucified one, it represents first of all hope for all persons crucified in history (Sobrino 1986, 296).

Other New Testament texts are clearly of less interest to liberation theologians than the Synoptic Gospels. The Pauline doctrine of justification is understood not only in individual and existential terms but also in political and economic terms: Sin is also (or above all) social injustice and exploitation; the law causes alienation from reality and leads to dependence and an absence of freedom; justification is a process that allows the new person to come into existence, liberating from egoism and participation in oppressive structures to love and comportment in solidarity (Croatto, Exodus 1981; Miranda 1974; E. Barreto Cesar 1983). The Gospel of John is also sometimes read in terms of liberation theology (Miranda 1977; see S. Phillips 1978 for the use of Scripture by Segundo).

The way in which liberation theologians attempt to answer the pressing question of a specifically Christian bearing as opposed to revolutionary violence on the basis of the New Testament is also revealing. Here there are essentially three positions, with the third being by far the most widely represented: (1) Jesus' practice of spilling his own blood rather than the blood of others is obligatory for Christians today and must define the particular style of a Christian liberation struggle (Ortega 1978, 73-74). (2) Jesus himself defended and approved the use of violence (his words on swords, cleansing of the Temple) and is a model for Christians even for a violent revolutionary engagement on behalf of the poor (Miranda 1982). (3) Jesus' practice and message were, to be sure, nonviolent, but this attitude was tactically conditioned (Pixley 1983[2]), prophetic-charismatic (Galilea 1984), or only one biblical paradigm among many (J. Míguez Bonino 1975) and is therefore not normative for today; it is the situation in Latin America, not the commandment or the model of Jesus, that urges a policy of nonviolence.

b. The biblical obligation to act for liberation today. This obligation is, according to liberation theology, particularly recognizable in the prophets of the Hebrew Bible. Such texts as Isa 42:5-7; Hos 4:1-2; 6:6; Mic 3:9-12; and, in particular, the oft-cited text of Jer 22:13-16, define true knowledge of God as acts of justice and intervention on behalf of the oppressed (see McGovern 1983, 464; G. Gorgulho 1978, 293-94). Furthermore, the salvific future promised by the prophets (as in Zech 8:7-17) is tied to acts that free the poor, the orphans, and the widows (Gorgulho 1978, 294). Just as Jesus understood himself only in connection with the kingdom of God, so also can Christians understand themselves only in connection to Jesus. The Christian must therefore follow his service to the kingdom of God, which means engaging oneself for love and justice. Only this orthopraxy, which today in Latin America is especially important on a political-economic plane, allows Jesus to be understood (Sobrino 1978[2]). The kingdom of God has a present and a future aspect: It is given concrete realization in each actual act of liberation (each experience of liberation is resurrection); however, it cannot be identified with any of these acts of liberation but, rather, always remains in the future and only makes possible the construction of imperfectly and provisionally better societies through the promise that this engagement is not senseless (L. Boff 1974; Míguez Bonino 1975; A. Fragoso 1971). An unbroken continuity between human society and the kingdom of God is only rarely postulated (e.g., by Miranda 1982).

Concerning the determination of the justice brought by Jesus and to be realized by Christians, liberation theology bases its claims with particular alacrity on the Gospel of Matthew and its concept of "righteousness" (*dikaiosynē*; so Matt 5:10, 20; 6:33; Gorgulho 1978). The most widely cited New Testament text in liberation theology (next to Luke 4:18-19; see above) is Matt 25:31-46, the depiction of the last judgment, focused on orthopraxy as opposed to orthodoxy. The decisive acts of mercy it portrays must today in Latin America be understood politically and collectively (G. Gutiérrez 1992[10], 189).

4. Methodology and Hermeneutics. The exegesis of Latin American liberation theology applies about the same range of methods as does the exegesis of the First World. Next to a continuation of historical criticism, structuralist (Croatto; Structuralism and Deconstruction*[§]), psychological (Alves; Psychology and Biblical Studies*[§]), feminist (Tamez; Feminist Interpretation*[§]), anthropological (Segundo), and, above all, sociological approaches (Anderson, Barros Souza, Gorgulho, Richard, M. Schwantes; Sociology Hebrew Bible/New Testament*[§]) can be recognized. What constitutes the peculiarity of liberation-theological exegesis, however, is its close connection with the reading of the Bible among the people of Latin America.

a. Popular exegesis. A basic methodological feature of Bible study groups in Latin America is to proceed, not from the text, but from one's own life. Because those taking part are not fundamentally concerned with interpretation of the Bible as such but with their own lives, questions from real life must first be formulated before they can be answered from the Bible. The first part of such a study, therefore, consists of a discussion of the actual situation, particularly with regard to the socioeconomic sphere, since the most urgent problems lie here. To this end, one can present either a significant story (Mesters, 1983*b*; E. Bambamarca 1983[3]; Anonymous 1985), or show a picture (Anonymous, Parables), which can then draw the participants into a conversation leading to the expression of their problem. As a second step, a biblical text is chosen and described, allowing the given situation to be seen in light of the will of God. In some circumstances the planning of concrete measures results as a third step (so, e.g., by the eleventh national meeting of the grassroots congregations of Mexico; Garcia Gutierrez 1983). This schema is spread widely as "Seeing-Judging-Acting."

For the connection between life situation and the text of the Bible there are two fundamental models. The first is older and appears to arise primarily where exegetical assistance is lacking: Persons, actions, and events in the Bible and today are more or less clearly identified. Thus the story of Jesus can be told anew with a leader of *campesinos* as the protagonist; instead of the magi, a bishop, a professor, and a physician visit the newborn; instead of fleeing into Egypt, the family flees into the slums of a large city; in the place of baptism and anointing appears the free acceptance of the problems of the *campesinos* (Bambamarca 1983[3], 166-71, 182-83; further examples in Reiser-Schoenborn 1981, 165, 176, 293-98). The second basic model avoids direct identification and attempts to differentiate biblical from contemporary situations through a catalogue of questions that are applied to both sides. The so-called "Readings over Four Sides" (Anderson-Gorgulho 1987[2]) investigate the economic side (Who produces? Who consumes? How is labor divided, etc.?), the political side (Who exercises power? How?), the social side (Which groups are there? What is family life like?), and the ideological side (What do people think of life? Of religion? Of society?). The "twenty-point method" examines contemporary reality and the text of the Bible respectively according to names, titles, groups, places, vocations, conflicts, economic connections, etc.

The fundamental Hermeneutic*[§] is established on the basis of the "co-naturality" (i.e., natural affinity; Mesters 1980, 564) between the people of the Bible and the people of Latin America. The oppressive situation and the liberation process begun in the name of God are in both cases the same; therefore, the people look into the Bible, not as through a window, excited to see what is taking place on the other side, but as into a mirror that reflects one's own life (F. Betto 1988, 126). A "contemporaneity exists between the historical memory of the oppressed of biblical times and the practical memory of the poor in Latin America" (Schwantes 1986, 386). Because the Bible was written by the poor, it can only be legitimately interpreted by poor people (Richard 1987[4], 25).

The dealing of the people of Latin America with the Bible can be characterized in terms of these categories: immediate, free, subjective, and emancipatory (Schmeller 1987, 158-62; Gorgulho 1988; C. Gudorf 1987). The people understand themselves as the immediate addressees of the Bible even when the necessity of translation is strongly recognized. They feel themselves free to appropriate some texts literally and some figuratively. One group of farmers at a Bible convention set forth the hermeneutic principle: "We must not understand the text of Scripture literally (1) if it does not correspond to our reality, and (2) if the force of older texts has been set aside through the command of love given by Jesus" (cited by Mesters 1980, 564). The subjective approach shows itself in the already indicated lack of interest in an understanding of text as text or as a testimony of the past without present consequence. The text serves exclusively to understand one's own life better. "The Bible is the catalogue of the world, which the Christian receives from the Creator, in order to be able to understand the sense of the exhibitions of life . . . An exhibition without a catalogue confuses the visitors. A catalogue without an exhibition is absolute nonsense" (Mesters 1984[2], 162). Finally, both the selection and the exegesis of the biblical text are determined by a strong emancipatory interest. Reading in the framework of a political-economic liberation process allows one to discover systematic features in the Bible and thus strengthens the engagement of Christians in this process.

b. *Academic exegesis.* As stated above, the academic pursuit of liberation theology is not fundamentally different in its exegetical interests and pronouncements from the reading of the Bible among the people. What it contributes is a hermeneutical foundation for this popular style of reading and the provision of exegetical means and knowledge that are not specifically Latin American, but that can work there in a stimulating and corrective fashion.

Concerning the hermeneutical act of Bible reading, according to C. Boff, two models are practiced: "the correspondence of terms" and "the correspondence of relations" (1986[3], 237, 241; similarly Konings 1980; Rowland and Corner 1989, 54, 78). The first model corresponds to the described identifiable exegesis among the common people. Here, such equations are set up as "the power of the Romans" = "imperialism"; "the power of the Sadducees" = "dependent bourgeoisie"; "the political comportment of Jesus" = "participation of Christians in the revolutionary process" (1986[3], 239), without taking into account the changed contemporary context. According to Boff, only the second model is hermeneutically responsible because it does not simply copy biblical pronouncements and solutions but sees them in their historical context and attempts to come to corresponding but not necessarily identical solutions today. Therefore, it is not enough to say merely "the political engagement of Jesus" = "the political engagement of Christians" but, rather, "the political engagement of Jesus"/"the historical social context at that time"="the political engagement of Christians"/"the current social context." If the same communication is intended, the alteration of the context necessitates an alteration in the pronouncement (Konings 1980).

Croatto (1989) takes a different path to similar results. Following Ricoeur he designs a Semiotic*[§] hermeneutic. The central term here is "excess of meaning" (*Sinnüberschuss*). As with any text, the meaning of the biblical text is not determined by the conditions of its historical formation. The text leaves its original context behind with its original meaning (decontextualization) and realizes an aspect of "excess of meaning" whenever it is introduced into a new context by a reader who then "rereads" it ("recontextualization"). This process of a "creation of meaning" (*Sinnschöpfung*) is found in the Bible; however, one must be careful to read the text within its same "semantic axes" (Croatto 1989, 55) because not every "creation of meaning" is legitimate.

The problem broached here—that of a criterion of truth for biblical interpretation—is answered with a reference to praxis. Where the biblical interpretation of the community supports the process of liberation on its various levels (but particularly in its socioeconomic and political aspects), the interpretation is true and legitimate. A certain risk cannot be excluded in the exegesis, however, because one cannot know whether a particular exegesis was justified before one sees the results (Barreto Cesar 1983, 396; Gudorf, 16).

5. *Biblical Exegesis in Liberation Theologies and Grassroots Movements Outside of Latin America.* Finally, during the last thirty years of the twentieth century, a similar form of biblical interpretation developed outside of Latin America in other oppressive situations. In form, preferred texts and themes, methodology, and hermeneutics, one can clearly observe analogies on the popular as well as the academic plane. These cannot be dealt with in detail here, however (for a selection of representative contributions, see R. Sugirtharajah 1991). These movements go back, in part, to the influence of Latin American liberation theology, but have their own roots in the history and situation of each land concerned. The most important appearances are the

minjung theology in Korea (J. Lee 1988; A. Mu 1981; K. Raiser 1988; of particular interest is Míguez Bonino 1988), the Black or AFROCENTRIC theology in the United States (C. Felder 1989; C. Gilkes 1989; V. Wimbush 1989), and the liberation theology and liberation movement among Blacks in South Africa (C. Banana 1979; C. Breytenbach 1989; B. Goba 1986; O. de Villiers 1987; I. Mosala 1986; W. Vorster 1984). Of further relevance is the document that appeared in July, 1989, "The Road to Damascus: Kairos and Conversion," to which thousands of Christians from South Africa, Namibia, South Korea, the Philippines, El Salvador, Nicaragua, and Guatemala put their signatures.

Bibliography: L. **Alonso Schökel,** "Exégesis y hermenéutica en Brasil," *Bib* 68 (1987) 404-7. L. R. **Alves,** "Páscoa, a travessia da esperança," *EstBib* 8 (1987²) 41-9. A. F. **Anderson and G. Gorgulho,** "A leitura sociológica da Bíblia," *EstBíb* 2 (1987²) 6-10. **Anonymous,** *Parables of Today,* n.d.; *A luta pela Reforma Agrária e a Bíblia* (1985); "Amostras da hermenêutica dos pobres," *Por trás da palavra* 8, 46 (1988) 16-28. A. **Antoniazzi,** *ABC da Bíblia* (1981); *La Palabra de Dios en la vida del pueblo: Manual de pastoral Bíblica* (1987).J. D. **de Araújo,** "Images of Jesus in the Culture of the Brazilian People," *Faces of Jesus: Latin American Christologies* (ed. J. Míguez Bonino, 1984) 30-38. R. **Avila,** *Biblia y liberación: Lectura de la Biblia desde América Latina* (Iglesia liberadora 6, 1976). R. **Azzi,** "A teologia no Brasil: Considerações históricas," *História da teologia na América Latina* (ed. Faculdade de teologia N. Senhora da Assunção, 1985²) 21-43. E. P. **de Bambamarca,** *Vamos caminando: Machen wir uns auf den Weg-Glaube, Gefangenschaft, und Befreiung in den peruanischen Anden* (1983³). C. **Banana,** "The Biblical Basis for Liberation Struggles," *IRM* 68 (1979) 417-23. E. E. **Barreto Cesar,** "Faith Operating in History: NT Hermeneutics in a Revolutionary Context" (diss., Emory University, 1983); *A fé como ação na história: Hermenêutica do Novo Testamento no contexto da América Latina* (Libertação e teologia, 1987). M. **de Barros Souza,** *A Bíblia e a luta pela terra* (Da base para a base 11, 1983*a*); "La lectura de la Bíblia en las comunidades cristianas populares," *Christus* 48, 567-68 (1983*b*) 50-53. F. **Betto,** "A Leitura da Bíblia em Nicaragua," *RCB* 31 (1988) 126-34. B. **Blount,** "Beyond the Boundaries: Cultural Perspective and the Interpretation of the NT" (diss., Emory University, 1992). C. **Boff,** *Theologie und Praxis: Die erkenntnistheoretischen Grundlagen der Theologie der Befreiung* (Gesellschaft und Theologie. Systematische Beiträge, 1986³). L. **Boff,** "Rettung in Jesus Christus und Befreiungsprozess," *Concilium* 10 (1974) 419-26; "Christ's Liberation versus Oppression: An Attempt at Theological Construction from the Standpoint of Latin America," *Frontiers of Theology in Latin America* (ed. R. Gibellini, 1979) 100-132; *Jesus Christus, der Befreier* (1986). C. **Bravo,** *Jesús hombre en conflicto* (Teología actual 1, 1986). C. **Breytenbach,** "Urchristliches zum heutigen Christsein-Reflexionen zur Rolle der Bibelwissenschaft im Schatten der Apartheid," *Freiburger Akademiearbeiten 1979-1989* (ed. D. Bader, 1989) 493-512. C. **Bussmann,** *Befreiung durch Jesus? Die Christologie der lateinamerikanischen Befreiungstheologie* (1980). J. L. **Caravias,** *El Dios de Jesús* (Iglesia viva, 1986); *Dios es bueno* (Biblia y pueblo 3, 1990). E. **Cardenal** (ed.), *The Gospel in Solentiname* (4 vols. 1976). G. **Casalis,** "Jesus-Neither Abject Lord Nor Heavenly Monarch," *Faces of Jesus: Latin American Christologies* (ed. J. Míguez Bonino, 1984) 72-76. G. **Collet** (ed.), *Der Christus der Armen: Das Christuszeugnis der lateinamerickanischen Befreiungstheologen* (1988). J. **Comblin,** "Critérios para um Comentario da Bíblia," *REB* 42, 166 (1982) 307-30; *Epístola aos Filipenses* (Comentario Bíblico NT, 1985); *Introdução geral ao Comentario Bíblico: Leitura da Bíblia na perspectiva dos pobres* (1985); *A novidade de Jesus* (8 vols. 1985/86). J. S. **Croatto,** "Befreiung und Freiheit: Biblische Hermeneutik für die 'Theologie der Befreiung,'" *Lateinamerika: Gesellschaft, Kirche, Theologie,* vol. 2, *Der Steit um die Theologie der Befreiung* (ed. H. J. Prien, 1981) 40-59; *Exodus: A Hermeneutics of Freedom* (1981); *Hermenéutica bíblica: Para una* *teoría de la lectura como producción de sentido* (1984); "Hermenêutica e lingüística: A hermenêutica bíblica à luz da semiótica e frente aos métodos histórico-críticos," *EstTeo* 24, 3 (1984) 214-24; "The Political Dimension of Christ the Liberator," *Faces of Jesus: Latin American Christologies* (ed. J. Míguez Bonino, 1984) 102-22; *Die Bibel gehört den Armen: Perspektiven einer befreiungstheologischen Hermeneutik (Ökuminische Existenz heute* 5, 1989). **F. Crüsemann**, "Anstösse: Befreiungstheologische Hermeneutik und die Exegese in Deutschland," *EvT* 50 (1990) 535-45. **E. Dussel**, *Herrschaft und Befreiung: Ansatz, Stationen, und Themen einer lateinamerikanischen Theologie der Befreiung* (1985); "Hipóteses para uma história da teologia na América Latina (1492-1980)," *História da teologia na Am,rica Latina* (ed. Faculdade de teologia N. Senhora da Assunçãao, 1985²) 165-96; *Geschichte der Kirche in Lateinamerika* (1988). **H. Echegaray**, *La práctica de Jesús* (1989³). **I. Ellacuría**, "The Political Nature of Jesus' Mission," *Faces of Jesus: Latin American Christologies* (ed. J. Míguez Bonino, 1984) 79-92; "Historicidad de la salvación cristiana," *Mysterium liberationis: Conceptos fundamentales de la teologia de la liberación I* (ed. I. Ellacuría and J. Sobrino, 1990) 323-72. **I. Ellacuría and J. Sobrino** (eds.), *Mysterium liberationis: Conceptos fundamentales de la teologia de la liberación* (2 vols. 1990). **Faculdade de teologia da igreja evangélica de confissão luterana no Brasil** (ed.), *Proclamar libertação: Auxílios homiléticos XIV* (1988). **Faculdade de teologia N. Senhora da Assunção** (ed.), *História da teologia na América Latina* (Teologia em diálogo, 1985²). **C. H. Felder**, *Troubling Biblical Waters: Race, Class, and Family* (1989). **A. Fragoso**, *Evangelium und soziale Revolution: Ein Kapitel lateinamerikanischer Theologie* (1971). **S. Galilea**, "Jesus' Attitude Toward Politics: Some Working Hypotheses," *Faces of Jesus: Latin American Christologies* (ed. J. Míguez Bonino, 1984) 93-101. **M. Garcia Gutierrez**, "La Biblia en la liberacíon del pueblo," *Christus* 48, 571 (1983) 29-33. **A. Garcia Rubio,** *Teologia da liberação: Política ou profetismo? Visão panorâmica e crítica da teologia política latino-americana* (Fé e realidade 3, 1983²). **E. S. Gerstenberger**, "Lectura Bíblica y realidad," *RevistB* 46, 13-14 (1984) 103-15. **R. Gibellini** (ed.), *Frontiers of Theology in Latin America* (1979). **C. T. Gilkes**, " 'Mother to the Motherless, Father to the Fatherless': Power, Gender, and Community in an Afrocentric Biblical Tradition," *Semeia* 47 (1989) 57-85. **B. Goba**, "The Use of Scripture in the Kairos Document: A Biblical Ethical Perspective," *JTSA* 56 (1986) 61-65. **J. Goldingay**, "The Hermeneutics of Liberation Theology," *HBT* 4, 2 (1982) 133-61; *HBT* 5, 1 (1983) 133-61. **H. Goldstein**, "Skizze einer biblischen Begründung der Theologie der Befreiung: Zur spezifisch lateinamerikanischen Hermeneutik," *Befreiende Theologie: Der Beitrag Lateinamerkas zur Theologie der Gegenwart* (ed. K. Rahner et al., 1977) 62-76, 161-63; *'Selig ihr Armen': Theologie der Befreiung in Lateinamerika . . . un in Europa?* (1989). **J. I. Gonzáles Faus,** *Jesúús y los ricos de su tiempo* (Série teología actual 2, 1987). **G. S. Gorgulho**, "Leitura da Bíblia e compromisso com a justiça," *REB* 38 (1978) 291-99; "Apostolado Bíblico no Brasil," *RCB* 31 (1988) 113-25; "Hermenéutica bíblica," *Mysterium liberationis: Conceptos fundamentales de la teologia de la liberación* (ed. I. Ellacuría and J. Sobrino, 1990) 169-200. **G. S. Gorgulho and A. F. Anderson,** *No tengáis miedo: Actualidad del Apocalipsis* (1981). **N. K. Gottwald** (ed.), *The Bible and Liberation: Political and Social Hermeneutics* (1983). **C. E. Gudorf**, "Liberation Theology's Use of Scripture: A Response to First World Critics," *Int* 41 (1987) 5-18. **G. Gutiérrez**, "A busca dos pobres de Jesus Christo," *História da teologia na América Latina* (ed. Faculdade de teologia N. Senhora da Assunção, 1985²) 45-61; *Theologie der Befreiung* (Systematische Beitrage 11, 1992¹⁰). **T. D. Hanks**, *God So Loved the Third World: The Biblical Vocabulary of Oppression* (1983). **E. Hoornaert**, *Kirchengeschichte Brasiliens aus der Sicht der Unterdrückten: 1550-1800* (1982). **D. Irrarazaval**, "Le Christ souffrant, seigneur des maltraités," *Jésus et la libération en Amérique Latine* (ed. J. van Nieuwenhove, 1986) 125-48. **J. A. Kirk**, *Liberation Theology: An Evangelical View from the Third World* (New Foundation Theological Library, 1979).

J. Konings, "A revelação Bíblica em face das rupturas sociais," *PerTeol* 7 (1975) 189-206; "Hermenêutica Bíblica e Teologia da libertação: Uma contribuição para discussão," *REB* 40 (1980) 5-10; "A leitura da Bíblia na perspectiva da libertação," *PerTeol* 15 (1983) 261-70; "Umgang mit der Bibel und Polarisierung in der brasilianischen Gesellschaft und Kirche," *NZM* 40 (1984) 81-91. **B. de Las Casas,** *Obras escogidas* (5 vols. Biblioteca de Autores Españoles 95.96.105.106.110, 1957/58). **J. Y. Lee,** "Minjung Theology: A Critical Introduction," *An Emerging Theology in World Perspective: Commentary on Korean Minjung Theology* (ed. J. Y. Lee, 1988) 3-29. **N. Lohfink,** *Options for the Poor: The Basic Principle of Liberation Theology in the Light of the Bible* (1987). **E. Lohse,** "Das Evangelium für die Armen," *ZNW* 72 (1981) 51-64. **R. McAfee Brown**, *Die Bibel neu gelesen: Anstösse aus der Dritten Welt* (1988); (ed.), "Kairos Central America: A Challenge to the Churches of the World," *Kairos: Three Prophetic Challenges to the Church* (1990) 71-107. **A. F. McGovern,** "The Bible in Latin American Liberation Theology," *The Bible and Liberation: Political and Social Hermeneutics* (ed. N. K. Gottwald, 1983²) 461-72. **C. Mesters,** *A prática libertadora de Jesus* (Suplemento do boletim "por trás da Palavra," n.d.); "Das Verständnis der Schrift in einigen brasilianischen Basisgemeinden," Concilium 6 (1980) 561-66; "The Use of the Bible in Christian Communities of the Common People," *The Challenge of Basic Christian Communities: Papers from the International Ecumenical Congress of Theology, Feb. 20-Mar. 2, 1980* (ed. S. Torres and J. Eagleson, 1981²) 197-210; *Carta aos Romanos* (1983a); *Vom Leben zur Bibel-von der Bibel zum Leben: Ein Bibelkurs aus Brasilien für uns* (2 vols. 1983b); *Flor sem defesa: Uma explicação da Bíblia a partir do povo* (1984²); *Um Projeto de Deus: A presença de Deus no meio do povo oprimido* (1984⁵); "Como se faz teologia Bíblica hoje no Brasil," *Estudos Bíblicos* 1 (1987⁴) 7-19; *Balanç‡o de 20 anos: A Bíblia lido pelo povo na atual renovação da igreja católica no Brasil, 1964-1984* (A Palavra na vida 7), 1988. **J. Míguez Bonino,** *Revolutionary Theology Comes of Age* (1975); (ed.) *Faces of Jesus: Latin American Christologies* (1984); "A Latin American Looks at Minjung Theology," *An Emerging Theology in World Perspective: Commentary on Korean Minjung Theology* (ed. J. Y. Lee, 1988) 157-68. **J. P. Miranda,** *Marx and the Bible: A Critique of the Philosophy of Oppression* (1974); *Being and the Messiah: The Message of St. John* (1977); *Communism in the Bible* (1982). **J. A. G. Moreira,** "El pensamiento teológico de D. Vasco de Quiroga," *Raíces de la teología latinoamericana: Nuevos materiales para la historia de la teología* (ed. P. Richard, 1985) 37-47. **I. J. Mosala,** "The Use of the Bible in Black Theology," *The Unquestionable Right to Be Free: Black Theology from South Africa* (ed. I. J. Mosala, 1986) 175-99. **A. B. Mu,** "Jesus and the Minjung in the Gospel of Mark," *Minjung Theology: People as the Subjects of History* (ed. K. Y. Bock, 1981) 136-51. **A. Müller and B. Kern,** "Die Armen entdecken die Bibel: Grundzüge der Bibellektüre in den lateinamerikanischen Basisgemeinden," *Wort und Leben: 500 Jahre Evangelisierung Lateinamerikas: Umkehr und Neubesinnung* (Berichte-Dokumente-Kommentare 37, 1988) 43-52. **R. Ortega**, *Liberando la Teología de la Liberación: Aporte Bíblico a la Teología de la Liberacíon* (CTP 3, 1978). **J. R. J. Pagalday,** " Bartolomeu des las Casas e o seu conceito de Evangelização," *História da evangelização na América Latina* (ed. Faculdade de teologia N. Senhora da Assunção, 1988) 42-54. **S. Phillips,** "The Use of Scripture in Liberation Theologies: An Examination of Juan Luis Segundo, James H. Cone, and Jurgen Moltmann" (diss., Southern Baptist Theological Seminary, 1978). **C. A. Pinto da Silva,** "Bíblia: A leitura que o povo faz," *RCB* 31 (1988) 135-50. **G. V. Pixley,** "Biblical Embodiments of God's Kingdom: A Study Guide for the Rebel Church" *The Bible and Liberation: Political and Social Hermeneutics* (ed. N. K. Gottwald, 1983²) 108-18; "God's Kingdom in First-century Palestine: The Strategy of Jesus," *The Bible and Liberation: Political and Social Hermeneutics* (ed. N. K. Gottwald, 1983²) 378-93; "The Poor Evangelize Biblical Scholarship," *ABQ* 2 (1983) 157-67. **R. Poblette**, "From Medellín to Puebla," *Churches and Politics in Latin America* (ed.

D. H. Levine, 1979) 41-54. **K. Raiser,** "A New Reading of the Bible? Ecumenical Perspectives from Latin America and Asia," *Creative Biblical Exegesis: Christian and Jewish Hermeneutics Through the Centuries* (ed. B. Uffenheimer and H. G. Reventlow, JSOTSup 59, 1988) 103-13. **A. Reiser and P. G. Schoenborn** (eds.), *Basisgemeinden und Befreiung: Lesebuch zur Theologie und christlichen Praxis in Lateinamerika* (1981). **P. Richard** (ed.), *Raíces de la teología latinoamericana: Nuevos materiales para la historia de la teología* (1985); "Bíblia: Memoria Historica dos Pobres," *EstBib* 1 (1987[4]) 20-30. **F. C. Rolim,** "A Bíblia nas comunidades ecclesiais de base," *RCB* 31 (1988) 165-79. **C. G. Romero,** "A Hermeneutic of Appropriation: A Case Study of Method in the Prophet Jeremiah and Latin American Liberation Theology" (diss., Princeton Theological Seminary, 1982; microfilm 1986). **C. Rowland,** "Theology of Liberation and Its Gift to Exegesis," *NBf* 66, 778 (1985) 157-72. **C. Rowland and M. Corner**, *Liberating Exegesis: The Challenge of Liberation Theology to Biblical Studies* (1989). **J. Saravia,** "A palavra de Deus no coração dos pobres," *El pueblo hace camino 1, 2* (1988) 15-19; *El camino de las paá bolas* (La buena noticia a los pobres, 1990). **T. Schmeller,** "Zugänge zum Neuen Testament in lateinamerikanischen Basisgemeinden," *MTZ* 38 (1987) 153-75; "Gottesreich und Menschenwerk: Ein Blick in Gleichnisse Jesu," *WiWei* 54 (1992) 81-95; *Das Recht der Anderen: Befreiungstheologische Lektüre des Neuen Testaments in Lateinamerika* (NTAbhNF 27, 1994). **W. Schürger,** *Theologie auf dem Weg der Befreiung-Geschichte und Methode des Zentrums für Bibelstudien in Brasilien* (EMMÖ 24, 1995). **M. Schwantes,** "Die Bibel als Buch der Befreiung," *EvK* 19 (1986) 383-87. **J. L. Segundo,** *Liberation of Theology* (1976); *The Historical Jesus of the Synoptics* (Jesus of Nazareth Yesterday and Today 2, 1985). **S. Silva Gotay,** "Origem e desenvolvimento do pensamento cristão revolucionário a partir da radicalização da doutrina social cristã nas décadas de 1960 e 1970," *História da teologia na América Latina* (ed. Faculdade de teologia N. Senhora da Assunção, 1985[2]) 139-64. **J. Sobrino,** *Christology at the Crossroads: A Latin American Approach* (1978[2]); "Das Verhaltnis Jesu zu den Armen und Deklassierten: Bedeutung für die Fundamentalmoral," *Concilium* 15 (1979) 629-34; "Le ressuscité est le crucifié: Lecture de la résurrection de Jésus à partir des crucifiés du monde," *Jésus et la libération en Amérique Latine* (Jésus et Jésus-Christ 26, ed. J. van Nieuwenhove, 1986) 291-307; "Centralidad del Reino de Dios en la teología de la liberación," *Mysterium liberationis: Conceptos fundamentales de la teologia de la liberación* I (ed. I. Ellacuría and J. Sobrino, 1990) 467-510. **A. Steiner,** "Zusammen mit dem Volk die Bibel lesen: Volksnahe Literatur zur Bibel in Brasilien," *BK* 40 (1985) 26-29. **R. S. Sugirtharajah** (ed.), *Voices from the Margin: Interpreting the Bible in the Third World* (1991). **J. Swetnam,** "Brazilian Catholics and the Bible," *TBT* 22 (1984) 376-80. **E. Tamez,** *Bible of the Oppressed* (1982). **S. Trinidad,** "Christology, Conquista, Colonization," *Faces of Jesus: Latin American Christologies* (ed. J. Míguez Bonino, 1984) 49-65. **N. Vélez,** "A leitura Bíblica nas Comunidades Ecclesiais da Base," *Revista de Interpretação Bíblica Latino-Americana* 1 (1988) 26-43. **P. G. R. de Villiers** (ed.) *Liberation Theology and the Bible* (1987). **W. Vogels,** "Biblical Theology for the 'Haves' and the 'Have-Nots,'" *ScEs* 39 (1987) 193-210. **W. S. Vorster,** "Apartheid und das Lesen der Bibel," *Wenn wir wie Brüder beieinander wohnten. . . .* (ed. J. W. DeGruchy and C. Villa-Vicenio, 1984) 117-36. **J. E. Weir,** "The Bible and Marx: A Discussion of the Hermeneutics of Liberation Theology," *SJT* 35 (1982) 337-50. **V. L. Wimbush,** "Historical/Cultural Criticism as Liberation: A Proposal for an African American Biblical Hermeneutic," *Semeia* 47 (1989) 43-55.

T. SCHMELLER

LIBERATION OR IDEOLOGICAL APPROACHES

Postcolonial Biblical Interpretations

1. *Introduction.* Postcolonial literary theory is an umbrella term that covers a multitude of literary practices and concerns of diverse races, empires, colonies, geographical centers, times, and genres. One of its defining characteristics is that it emphasizes the pervasiveness of imperialism and relates imperial expansion, impact, and response to certain literary practices and practitioners. To that end, postcolonial theories situate almost all reading and writing of the past three to four hundred years within the parameters of imperial and colonial currents of dominance and resistance, challenging all readers and writers to examine their practices for imperial and colonial currents of domination and suppression.

In literary practice the term postcolonial is used to "cover all the culture affected by imperial process from the moment of colonization to the present day" (B. Ashcroft et al. 1989, 20). This extended meaning recognizes that not all countries have achieved liberation and that various forms of colonialism exist (e.g., military, Ideological*[§], economical, and ecological). The extension of its meaning in a largely postindependence era comes with the shocking realization of continuing domination by the former colonizers and dependence of previously colonized nations. But as H. Bhabha underscores, the "post" in postcolonial gestures to the beyond and embodies an energy that transforms "the present into an expanded and ex-centric site of experience and empowerment" (1994, 4). In short, postcolonial discourse involves both critique and construction.

2. *Postcolonial Biblical Readers.* The categories of colonizer and colonized can be subdivided into some of the following reading and writing communities: colonizers, settler colonizers, indigenous or natives of settler colonies, oppositional decolonizers, and immigrants who live in former colonizing centers. Many of these groups can be identified with particular geographical areas consistent with the history of imperialism. A strict dividing line between their literary practices is often impossible, given that colonialism is largely about cultural contact and exchange; yet one can outline some of their methods of biblical interpretation.

3. *The Colonizers' Reading Practices.* Colonizers are historically described as imperial readers from Britain, France, Portugal, Germany, or from any former colonizing country. Their use of literature, especially the Bible, as a colonizing instrument entails imposing foreign literary canons on the colonized; interpreting all foreign places and cultures through the colonizers' texts; and denigrating the colonized peoples and their lands through texts that serve to uplift the colonizer.

First, a foreign literary canon, including the Bible, is transported by the colonizer from its specific cultural context and is marketed to the colonized as a universal standard for all cultures. A postcolonial biblical reader asks: How has the Bible been transported to nonbiblical worlds, and how has it been applied to other cultures? When white Western biblical readers maintain a hierarchical and exclusive place for biblical texts and other Western classics above the texts of the colonized, or when they resist developing multicultural readings of the Bible, then they participate in colonialism. Furthermore, when schools either ignore or teach the religions of the colonized in such a way as to undermine these dominated cultures, they serve as instruments of oppression.

Second, colonizers interpret foreign lands and claim authority over them through both biblical and Western texts. These texts' ideology inspired their colonial readers and validated their action as just; e.g., the reading of "the Great Commission" led many readers to regard the colonizing projects of their country as synonymous with the biblical text. Thus missionary D. Livingstone could "beg" his people to move to Africa and spread Christianity.

Third, colonial biblical interpretation involves readers of various backgrounds. Livingstone, for example, was a missionary, a doctor, a geographer, an explorer, an ethnographer, a natural scientist, and a writer of travel narratives. Many other readers never traveled abroad, but they were ardent supporters who read and perpetuated the constructions of traveling colonial agents. Fourth, colonial interpretations of the Bible were often the result of exegetical methods or interpretations hewn from imperial contexts and serving the interest of these empires. One can cite archaeological (Archaeology and The Hebrew Bible/New Testament*[§]) and anthropological paradigms of reading that often bolstered the colonizers' claims of racial superiority by claiming to understand the colonized peoples better than they understood themselves. F. Segovia (1995) exposed the colonizing ideology of historical-critical methods. Assuming that all readers were neutral and objective, this approach insisted on one univocal and universal interpretation of the Bible. Variant interpretations from readers of different social backgrounds were labeled eisegesis. Segovia suggests that the explosion of other methods of interpretation that consider the author, the text, and the reader should be seen within the global struggles of decolonization and liberation.

4. *Settler Colonizers' Reading Practices.* Settler colonies include white readers from Canada, the United States, Australia, South Africa, and New Zealand who assumed power over the natives of the land and turned the land into their permanent homes. The earliest white settler colonizers of the United States and South Africa claimed that they were the chosen race, that the native lands were their promised lands, and that the native populations were Canaanites who could either be enslaved or be annihilated. The Exodus text was used to claim these lands and to dispossess the natives. G. Tinker (1995, 175) holds that "nineteenth-century German imperialism, along with the prominence of German exegetical research continuing into the twentieth century, gave rise to conquest exegesis that has influenced most if not all Euro-American scholarship." The theoretical reading of such scholars, as A. Schweitzer[§], who were active colonial agents was widely accepted in biblical interpretation. Not surprisingly, the voice of biblical scholars of former imperial centers and settler colonies remained largely silent during the perpetration of international crimes of colonialism and holocaust.

Because settler colonies are also thoroughly multicultural contexts, it is notable that late twentieth century methods of biblical readings, which move away from colonizing ideologies, came to be, and still are, championed in North America rather than in European biblical schools. The North American context consists of Native Americans, settler colonists, descendants of African slaves, Hispanics (Hispanic American Interpretation*[§]), Holocaust*[§] survivors, Asian*[§] Americans, political refugees, professional workers who immigrate, and many others who constantly make problematic power relations proposed in methods of reading and writing. It is this diversity that creates a context in which methods of reading for liberation are more acceptable than in former colonizing centers.

5. *Indigenous Reading Practices.* Native populations living under the rule of settler colonizers do not have the option of political independence. These populations include the Native Americans of North America, the Aborigines in Australia, and the Maori in New Zealand. Since most native populations are still recovering from severe colonization, their voices are just beginning to be heard; yet their nativist and hybrid interpretations of resistance and collaboration were there in every stage of their colonization. The history of their various biblical interpretations still needs to be researched, documented, and analyzed.

R. Warrior (1991, 291), who reads the stories of Israel's wilderness wanderings through Canaanite eyes, notes Yahweh's command to annihilate the indigenous population. That "Canaanites have status only as the people Yahweh removes from the land in order to bring the chosen people in" is a characterization that expounds values authorizing imperialism. Further, since the Canaanites are annihilated for having worshiped different gods, interreligious praxis is equated to betrayal in the Joshua narrative. In short, the narrative not only provides for imperialism but also fails to provide for a multicultural reading of the Bible.

6. *Decolonizing Reading Practices.* Decolonizing readers are oppositional postcolonial readers from Africa, Asia, and Latin America who were colonized but fought and regained their political independence by assuming biblical interpretations of resistance, collaboration, nativism, nationalism, and hybridity. Decolonizing biblical readers of these diverse backgrounds have influenced one another not only at individual levels but also as a deliberate strategy of networking (M. Oduyoye 1993; R. Sugirtharajah 1991).

Latin American postcolonial biblical interpretations were perhaps the earliest to make their mark in biblical studies. Unlike Africans and Asians, Latin Americans were subjected to an earlier colonialism that established Christianity as the dominant religion and the languages of the colonizers as the means of communication; yet they fully employed the masters' tools to pull down the masters' houses. Latin Americans apply biblical texts and Western theories of Marxism to articulate interpretations of Liberation*§. First, their biblical interpretations resist dwelling on the ancient context of the text as the normative reference for the "correct" interpretation of the Bible. Latin Americans claim a better understanding of the meaning of biblical texts because of their experiences of poverty and the struggle they share with the exploited masses of JESUS' times. Their biblical interpretations critique oppressive neocolonial and local structures that continue to exploit them. Further, their readings challenge mainstream biblical interpreters to examine who benefits from their interpretations.

Most Asian and African biblical readers, on the other hand, were subjected to modern imperial and colonial currents that elevated Western cultures, claimed racial superiority, and discounted native cultures, races, and languages. Many, indeed, were christianized and learned to use the languages of their colonizers. Their religions and languages, however, remained a contending force in their contexts and became unavoidable factors in their postcolonial biblical interpretations.

Examples of these readings include the following: (a) The role of Egypt (Egyptology and Biblical Studies§), Ethiopia (Ethiopian Biblical Interpretation§), and Asian nations regarding the birth of the Christian church is emphasized (Oduyoye 1993; Sugirtharajah 1993); (b) Biblical stories are read in the context of other local religious texts or cultures. African culture is compared with those described in the Hebrew Bible; Jesus is compared with other sages and religious leaders. Inculturation and contextualization tended to preserve the superiority of Christian faith, but the colonized peoples insisted on the validity of their own cultures (E. Martey 1993, 65-70). The current scene reflects the bold refusal to designate any superiority to biblical religious claims (P. Kwok 1995; Sugirtharajah 1993); (c) Decolonizing readers embark on hybrid biblical interpretations from the early days of colonial contact. Many Asian and African intellectuals read biblical stories and legends with their own folktales (Folklore*§), myths (Mythology and Biblical Studies*§), and songs. Hybrid postcolonial biblical discourse resists the colonizing use of the Bible and seeks liberation by reading the Bible with, and not above, other world cultures; (d) Decolonizing postcolonial biblical readings include the interpretations of subalterns, or the base communities of the poor. This is evident with Asian and African readers as nonacademic readers are included in academic anthologies (West and Dube 1996); (e) Like Latin American readers, African and Asian readers emphasize their own socioeconomic contexts as they interpret the Bible rather than dwelling on the ancient origins of biblical texts. To this end their methods are largely theological; (f) Oppositional decolonizing biblical readers also question the ideology of biblical texts by asking: How are gender representations used in imperial and colonizing texts of the Bible? Why have the Bible and its readers functioned compatibly with the colonizing powers of their countries? Does the Bible encourage expansion into other nations? Does it authorize Christians to assume power over other cultures and lands? If so, how can we arrest the colonizing perspectives of the Bible and its readers? (M. Dube Shomanah 1997); (g) Decolonizing readers engage in a comparative or synoptic reading of secular Western classics with biblical texts. These largely ideological readings interrogate the representations of different cultures, people, and their lands in the Bible and in other Western canons to examine how these constructions legitimate the colonizers' assumption of power over foreign nations.

7. *Migrant Reading Practices.* Migrant reading practices include readings of African Americans, Hispanic Americans, Jewish Holocaust survivors, Asian Americans, refugees, migrant workers, and many other Two-Thirds World peoples who live in Western countries. Biblical readings of migrants differ, reflecting the different types of colonial oppression undergone, different stages of resistance, different methods, and different group interests. African Americans experienced colonization that severed them from their lands, cultures, and languages. To rely on the languages and cultures of their colonizers, therefore, is not optional in their struggles for liberation. For example, D. Walker (Walker and H. Garnet 1829) argued for the abolition of slavery by rereading the stories in Genesis and Exodus and in the ancient texts of Rome and Greece. Walker appealed to the biblical attestation that, as a slave in Egypt, Joseph was given a leadership role (Gen 41:37-45), that the house of Jacob was given the best land in Egypt and leadership (Gen 47:1-6), and that enslaved Israelites owned property (Exod 12:31-32, 37-39). Walker's strategy of using the masters' tools against them helped illustrate how the institution of chattel slavery could not be supported by their canon.

O. Hendricks (1995) delivered one of the boldest postcolonial biblical readings ever to be published in a Western scholarly journal. The title, "Guerilla Exegesis," alludes to the struggles and strategies of the colonized against the colonizer. It suggests a context where the colonizer is still very much in power but where the colonized peoples refuse to give up the struggle for liberation, instead adopting a persistent undercover strategy of resistance that allows them to hit and run. His essay exemplifies the abrogation of the masters' language, or the use of "english," not English (Ashcroft et al.). This postcolonial strategy is used by many former victims of colonialism who are now stuck with learning, writing, and reading in the languages of the colonizer. Countering centuries of colonizing art that depicted Jesus, Mary, and all biblical characters as blue-eyed blonds, Bibles produced by and for African Americans feature Black biblical characters. This attempt to recuperate Black presence in the Bible is one of the major steps toward its decolonization.

Biblical interpretations by Hispanic Americans also reflect an engagement with the imperialist currents of the past and present that have alienated them from their countries and cultures. Segovia, who describes himself as "a subject of a number of layers of colonialism" (1995, 3), presents a reading strategy of intercultural criticism framed within the global colonial and postcolonial struggles for power. Although it is a method informed by a bicultural experience of having "no home, no voice, and no face . . . following the dynamics of colonial discourse and practice," it "embraces biculturalism as its very home, voice, and face . . . following in the dynamics of decolonization and liberation" (Segovia 1996, 212). In short, intercultural criticism is a diaspora reading strategy born in the struggle with continuing colonial domination that continues to read texts for decolonization and liberation.

J. González's book (1996) is also an exposition of a Hispanic diaspora reading strategy from a Protestant perspective. A. Isasi-Díaz's works expound on *Mujerista**§, or Hispanic American women's reading strategies.

Many Jewish readers of the New Testament are among the immigrants who have entered the academic and church schools of the West. They challenge Christians to acknowledge that Jesus was a Jew and that biblical texts are Jewish texts. This reclaiming of Jewish heritage in biblical interpretation is a postcolonial response to the claims of racial superiority that characterized white Christian colonizing powers and that contributed to the Holocaust.

364

8. *Problems with Postcolonial Interpretations in Biblical Studies.* Turning to biblical studies (and to other sacred canons), there is a lack of comprehensive research on colonial biblical interpretations based on the study of travel narratives, letters, missionary reports, newspapers, novels, etc. The *Semeia* issue on *Postcolonialism and Scriptural Reading* (ed. L. Donaldson) should go a long way toward introducing a number of postcolonial methods of biblical interpretation. Similarly, the *Semeia* issue on *Women's Interpretations of the Bible in the Third World* (ed. K. Sakenfeld and S. Ringe) will also provide postcolonial feminist readings (Feminist Interpretation*§) of the Bible.

The biblical readings of the formerly colonized groups, however, are quite vibrant. African, South African, Asian, Indian, Latin American, Hispanic American, African American, Asian American, Native American, Pacific, or Two-Thirds World readers are actively generating biblical readings that take account of their experiences of colonial domination and seek liberating international relations. Nevertheless, problems still persist. Given the domination of Europeans and Americans in biblical studies, the interpretations of the formerly colonized have by and large occupied a peripheral place. These new interpretations are not always regarded as serious rigorous methods of biblical reading, nor have they been classified as systematic readings that demand engagement. For example, anthologies of biblical reading methods, written mostly by younger generations dedicated to liberation, remain surprisingly silent about postcolonial methods of biblical reading.

To a degree, the apathetic response of metropolitan scholars to most postcolonial biblical readings is methodologically related to the traditional separation of biblical studies from theology and church history. Many biblical scholars would rather regard postcolonial readings of Two-Thirds World masses as theological and belonging to church history, not biblical studies. Moreover, the silence of mainstream biblical studies toward postcolonial interpretations reflects the continuing dominance of the so-called developed over the underdeveloped, the First World over the Two-Thirds World masses.

What if mainstream academic and church biblical practitioners allowed themselves to view their interpretative practices under the categories of colonial and postcolonial literary practices? This would greatly enhance the mission of the academy and the church. Readers might assume ethical responsibility for international relations of the past and the present, since interpreters would begin to place themselves within the dynamics of colonizing and decolonizing communities. Readers might examine their biblical expositions to see if they build, maintain, or dismantle imperialism, seeking interpretations that promote international relations of liberating interdependence.

Recent postcolonial biblical studies include general overviews (Segovia 2000, Sugirtharajah 2002), the Bible in Australia (Boer 2001), a postcolonial approaches to John (Dube and Staley 2002, Kim 2001), postcolonialism and feminism (Dube Shomanah 2000), and postcolonialism and biblical hermeneutics in Asia (Sugirtharajah 1998).

Bibliography: I. **Amadiume,** *Male Daughters, Female Husbands: Gender and Sex in an African Society* (1987). G. **Anzaldua,** *Borderlands/La Frontera* (1987). B. **Ashcroft, G. Griffiths, and H. Tiffin,** *The Empire Writes Back: Theory and Practice in Post-colonial Literatures* (1989); (eds.), *The Post-colonial Studies Reader* (1995). A. **Bammer,** *Displacements: Cultural Identities in Question* (1994). C. **Banana,** "The Case for a New Bible," *"Rewriting the Bible": The Real Issues* (ed. I. Mukonyora, 1993) 17-32. H. K. **Bhabha,** *The Location of Culture* (1994). R. **Boer,** *Last Stop Before Antarctica: The Bible and Postcolonialism in Australia* (Bible and Postcolonialism 6, 2001) R. **Chow,** *Writing Diaspora: Tactics of Intervention in Contemporary Cultural Studies* (1993); K. **Dickson,** *Uncompleted Mission: Christianity and Exclusivism* (1991). L. E. **Donaldson,** *Decolonizing Feminisims:*

Race, Gender, and Empire-building (1992). **M. W. Dube** (ed.), *Other Ways of Reading: African women and the Bible* (2001). **M. W. Dube and Jeffrey L. Staley** (eds.), *John and Postcolonialism: Travel, Space and Power* (Bible and Postcolonialism 7, 2002). **M. W. Dube Shomanah**, "Towards a Post-colonial Feminist Interpretation of the Bible" (diss., Vanderbilt University, 1997). **M. W. Dube Shomanah**, *Postcolonial Feminist Interpretation of the Bible* (2000). **V. Fabella and S. A. Lee Park**, *We Dare to Dream: Doing Theology as Asian Women* (1989). **V. Fabella and M. Oduyoye** (eds.), *With Passion and Compassion: Third Worlds Women Doing Theology* (1990). **F. Fanon**, *Black Skins, White Masks* (1967). **C. Felder** (ed.), *Stony the Road We Trod: African American Biblical Interpretation* (1991). **J. L. Gonzàlez,** *Santa Biblia: The Bible Through Hispanic Eyes* (1996). **B. Harlow,** *Resistance Literature* (1987). **O. O. Hendricks,** "Guerilla Exegesis: Struggle as a Scholarly Vocation," *Semeia* 72 (1995) 73-90. **A. M. Isasi-Díaz,** *En la Lucha: In the Struggle. A Hispanic Women's Liberation Theology* (1993). **J. K. Kim,** "Woman and Nation: An Intercontextual Reading of the Gospel of John" (diss., Vanderbilt University 2001). **K. P. Lan,** *Discovering the Bible in the Non-Biblical World* (1995). **V. Lenero,** *The Gospel of L. Gavilan* (1979). **E. Martey,** *African Theology: Inculturation and Liberation* (1993). **R. Maunier,** *The Sociology of Colonies: An Introduction to the Study of Race Contact* 1 (1948). **C. T. Mohanty,** "Under Western Eyes: Feminist Scholarships and Colonial Discourses," *Third World Women and the Politics of Feminism* (ed. T. Mohanty et al., 1991) 51-80. **I. Mosala,** *Biblical Hermeneutics and Black Theology in South Africa* (1989). **V. Y. Mudimbe,** *The Invention of Africa: Gnosis, Philosophy, and the Order of Knowledge* (1988); *The Idea of Africa* (1994). **M. A. Oduyoye,** *Hearing and Knowing: Theological Reflections on Christianity in Africa (1993)*. **M. A. Oduyoye and M. R. A. Kanyoro** (eds.), *The Will to Arise: Women, Tradition, and the Church in Africa* (1992). **D. Quint**, *Epic and Empire: Politics and Generic Form from Virgil to Milton* (1993). **E. Said,** *Orientalism* (1978); *Culture and Imperialism* (1993). **A. J. Saldarini,** *Matthew's Christian-Jewish Community* (1994). **F. F. Segovia and M. A. Tolbert** (eds.), *Reading from This Place*, vol. 1, *Social Location and Biblical Interpretation in the United States* (1995); vol. 2, *Social Location and Biblical Interpretation in Global Perspective* (1995). **F. F. Segovia** (ed.), *What Is John: Readers and Readings of the Fourth Gospel* (1996); *Decolonizing Biblical Studies: A View from the Margins* (2000). **R. S. Sugirtharajah** (ed.), *Voices from the Margin: Interpreting the Bible in the Third World* (1991); (ed.), *Asian Faces of Jesus* (1993); *Asian Biblical Hermeneutics and Postcolonialism: Contesting the Interpretations* (Bible and Liberation, 1998); *Postcolonial Criticism and Biblical Interpretation* (2002). **R. S. Sugirtharajah and C. Hargreaves** (eds.), *Readings in Indian Christian Theology* (1993, 1995³). **T. Swanson,** "To Prepare a Place: Johannine Christianity and the Collapse of Ethnic Territory," *JAAR* 62 (1994) 241-63. **E. Tamez,** *Bible of the Oppressed* (1982). **M. Taussig,** *Shamanism, Colonialism, and the Wild Man: A Study in Terror and Healing* (1986). **N. wa Thiongo,** *Decolonising the Mind: The Politics of Language in African Literature* (1986); *Moving the Centre: The Struggle for Cultural Freedoms* (1993). **C. Tiffin and A. Lawson** (eds.), *De-scribing Empire: Post-colonialism and Textuality* (1994). **G. Tinker,** "Reading the Bible as Native-Americans," *NIB* (1995) 1:174-80. **D. Walker and H. H. Garnet,** *Walker's Appeal and Garnet's Address to the Slaves of the United States of America* (1994). **R. Warrior,** "Canaanites, Cowboys, and Indians: Deliverance, Conquest, and Liberation Theology Today," *Voices from the Margin: Interpreting the Bible in the Third World* (ed. R. S. Sugirtharajah, 1991) 287-95. **G. West and M. W. Dube** (eds.), *'Reading With': An Exploration of the Interface Between Critical and Ordinary Readings of the Bible, Semeia* 73 (1996). **G. Vermes,** *The Religion of Jesus the Jew* (1993). **P. Williams and L. Chrisman** (eds.), *Colonial Discourse and Post-colonial: A Reader* (1994).

M. W. DUBE SHOMANAH

GENDER-BASED APPROACHES

Gay/Lesbian Interpretation

The phrase "gay/lesbian biblical interpretation" can be understood in both a narrow and a broad sense. A narrow use of the phrase would refer to biblical interpretation carried out by individuals identified as lesbian or gay. More broadly, the phrase might refer to a mode of biblical interpretation that deals with issues thought to be of special interest to lesbians, gay men, bisexuals, and the transgender community irrespective of the sexual identity or sexual practices of the individual interpreter. Such issues could include, not only the specific topic of same-sex sexual relations, but also questions about the wider framework of social assumptions and practices within which same-sex sexual relations are given certain meanings. By way of comparison, some scholars working in the humanities and the human sciences use the phrase "lesbian and gay studies" to refer to an academic interrogation of the process whereby sexual meanings (e.g., the assumption of heterosexuality as a norm and homosexuality as a deviation) are produced and reproduced in culture and society. In a similar manner, a gay/lesbian biblical interpretation in the broad sense might focus on sexual meanings in relation to both the production and the reception of the biblical text, but in a manner that makes problematic certain normative assumptions about heterosexuality and homosexuality.

Several developments within society in general and the realm of biblical interpretation in particular make it possible today to raise the question of a gay/lesbian biblical interpretation. By the late 1960s, the impact of the sexual revolution, feminism, and lesbian and gay political movements began to be felt in churches and synagogues. Lesbians, gay men, and their supporters increasingly called for a gay-affirmative transformation of Jewish and Christian attitudes toward sexuality, sometimes using emergent Liberation Theologies*§ as models for articulating such a call. As a result, scholars and religious leaders began to reexamine both the traditional religious condemnations of same-sex sexual relations and the biblical texts usually cited to justify those condemnations. At the same time, an increasing interest among biblical scholars in the social world of the biblical texts opened the door for new questions about the social and cultural organization of gender and sexuality in the ancient world. Finally, a growing interest in interdisciplinary biblical interpretation has taken place simultaneously with the appearance of lesbian and gay studies across the humanities and the human sciences, allowing for the possibility that lesbian and gay studies will come to have an influence on biblical scholarship similar to the influence of Literary Theory*§, cultural anthropology, and Sociology*§.

Several trends in biblical interpretation have emerged as a result of these factors. First, a number of studies have tried to argue that supposed biblical condemnations of same-sex sexual contact have been overstated or misunderstood altogether. Levitical condemnations of sex between men, for example, are reinterpreted by some readers as condemnations of the cultic prostitution that was long thought to have been practiced among Israel's neighbors. Similarly, Pauline statements are reinterpreted by some readers as condemnations of the cross-generational sexual activity that was practiced among Greeks and Romans or as condemnations of same-sex sexual activity between heterosexual persons. A number of relationships between biblical characters of the same sex (such as Jonathan and David, Ruth and Naomi, and Jesus and the beloved disciple) have also been reinterpreted as having some sort of erotic dimension.

Flaws in at least some of these interpretations have become increasingly apparent, however. For example, the appeal to ancient cultic prostitution as the real object of biblical condemnation has become less convincing as scholars have increasingly come to question the widespread existence of such cultic practices. The appeal to Greco-Roman pederasty as an explanation for Pauline statements cannot adequately account for Paul's†§ apparent condemnation of female homoeroticism (Rom 1:26), since most of our evidence for ancient cross-generational sexual activity concerns males rather than females. To suggest that Paul intended to condemn heterosexuals who participate in homosexual activity but not homosexuals themselves is to import into Paul's world a distinction between "heterosexuals" and "homosexuals" that does not cohere with the ancient evidence. Perhaps most important, studies that argue that the biblical texts do not themselves condemn same-sex sexual activity frequently avoid the crucial question of whether the biblical texts, shaped as they are by the assumptions of another time and place, can really provide an adequate foundation for contemporary sexual ethics.

On the other hand, through their attempts to question the assumption that the Bible clearly condemns same-sex eroticism, scholars have demonstrated both the relative scarcity of such condemnations and the difficulties involved in understanding some of the texts in question. For example, two texts that have often been cited as condemnations of homosexuality, the story of Sodom in Genesis 19 and the story of the Levite and his concubine in Judges 19, are now widely interpreted as focusing on rape, violence, inhospitality, and divine retribution, even when it is acknowledged that the threat of some form of same-sex contact also plays a role in these stories. The process whereby the story of Sodom in particular came to be read as primarily a story about the evils of same-sex eroticism has been shown to be extremely complex (M. Jordan 1997).

Moreover, while the argument that the biblical texts do not oppose same-sex sexual contact has not been entirely convincing to most interpreters, attempts to make the argument have led to an increasing interest in the social and cultural assumptions that structure biblical attitudes toward homoeroticism. Thus, a second trend in biblical interpretation accepts elements of the traditional view that certain biblical texts look negatively upon same-sex sexual relations; but it insists upon the need to understand that negative assessment in the context of ancient sexual and gender codes. Feminist*§ research into the gender notions and gender-related social structures presupposed by the biblical texts has been an important influence in this regard. Biblical condemnations of same-sex sexual contact are now widely interpreted in terms of their relation to a sharp and hierarchical differentiation between culturally defined male and female gender roles.

So, for example, sex between men may have been viewed with horror by the authors of the Levitical codes (Lev 18:22; 20:13) in part because such activity was thought to involve the symbolic emasculation of one of the male partners. This emasculation was no doubt considered shameful in a society structured by rigid gender categories and hierarchy. Insofar as sexual contact between men was thought to blur the symbolic boundaries between men and women, the inclusion of a condemnation of male homoeroticism in the priestly sections of Leviticus also fits in well with a general tendency of that portion of biblical literature to emphasize the categories and distinctions according to which the world was thought to be ordered. A concern about both procreation and the potentially defiling nature of bodily emissions may underlie the Levitical condemnations of male same-sex sexual contact, while the emphasis on procreation in the Hebrew Bible may help to account for the complete absence therein of any reference to female homoeroticism. Since male seed seems to have been considered the crucial substance for conception in the ancient world, sexual activities that did not involve male ejaculation may have been less troubling to some observers than those sexual activities that did.

Paul, on the other hand, like some of his Jewish contemporaries (e.g., Philo§, Pseudo-Phocylides), does apparently condemn both male and female same-sex sexual contact. At least in Paul's case, however, such condemnation does not seem to have resulted from a concern about procreation and may have resulted instead from assumptions about proper gender roles. Indeed, Brooten's recent work on female homoeroticism (1996) suggests that such sexual contact may have been troubling for Paul not only because of its blurring of gender boundaries but also because of the perception that, by assuming a man's sexual role, a woman was usurping a man's social position or, at least, rebelling against a woman's subordinate social position. While such an interpretation is not accepted by all of Paul's readers, it does seem both to confirm that biblical norms about sexuality are related in complex but significant ways to ancient gender beliefs and to question any simplistic assumptions about the relevance or applicability of such norms to contemporary disputes over sexual ethics.

While a great deal of light has been shed on biblical attitudes toward sexual practice, much less work has been done on the production of readings of biblical texts from explicitly lesbian, gay, bisexual, or transgender reading locations. This is somewhat surprising given, on the one hand, the greatly increased emphasis among biblical scholars on reading strategies, Reader-response*§, and social location and, on the other hand, the growing influence of lesbian and gay studies and "queer theory" in the humanities and the human sciences. The relative scarcity of such readings of biblical texts may be due in part to professional and ecclesial factors that discourage biblical scholars from self-identifying as lesbian, gay, or bisexual or from working on gay-related projects. Most of the available examples of such readings tend to be theologically oriented (see, e.g., G. Comstock 1993) and give only minimal attention to the important work being done outside the fields of religious and theological studies. However specifically gay/lesbian readings of biblical texts have now appeared in Goss and West (2000) and Stone (2001). Nissinen catalogs in detail homoerotic behavior in the ancient world (1998). It seems likely that lesbian and gay readings of a whole range of biblical and related texts will constitute the next significant development in gay/lesbian biblical interpretation.

Bibliography: D. **Boyarin,** "Are There Any Jews in the History of Sexuality?" *Journal of the History of Sexuality* 5 (1995) 333-55. **R. L. Brawley** (ed.), *Biblical Ethics and Homosexuality* (1996). **B. J. Brooten,** *Love Between Women: Early Christian Responses to Female Homoeroticism* (Chicago Series on Sexuality, History, and Society, 1996). **G. D. Comstock,** *Gay Theology Without Apology* (1993). **L. W. Countryman,** *Dirt, Greed and Sex: Sexual Ethics in the New Testament and Their Implications for Today* (1988). **D. Good,** "Reading Strategies for Biblical Passages on Same-Sex Relations," *Theology and Sexuality* 7 (September 1997) 70-82. **R. E. Goss and M. West** (eds.), *Take Back the Word: A Queer Reading of the Bible* (2000). **M. D. Jordan,** *The Invention of Sodomy in Christian Theology* (Chicago Series on Sexuality, History, and Society, 1997). **D. B. Martin,** "Heterosexism and the Interpretation of Romans 1:18-32," *BibInt* 3(1995) 332-55. **M. Nissinen,** *Homoeroticism in The Biblical World: A Historical Perspective* (1998). **S. M. Olyan,** "'And with a Male You Shall Not Lie the Lying Down of a Woman': On the Meaning and Significance of Lev 18:22 and 20:13," *Journal of the History of Sexuality* 5(1994) 179-206. **R. Scroggs,** *The NT and Homosexuality: Contextual Background for Contemporary Debate* (1983). **K. Stone,** "The Hermeneutics of Abomination: On Gay Men, Canaanites, and Biblical Interpretation," *BTB* 27, 2 (1997) 36-41; *Sex, Honor and Power in the Deuteronomistic History* (JSOTSup 234, 1996); *Queer Commentary and the Hebrew Bible* (JSOTSup 334, 2001).

K. STONE

GENDER-BASED APPROACHES

Feminist Interpretation

Feminist biblical interpretation involves readings and critiques of the Bible informed by feminist theory and criticism, which are the conceptual means and analytic tools developed to envision and implement the goals of feminism, a movement committed to women's self-determination and to fashioning humane alternatives to prevailing male-dominated political and social structures. Assisting such social change is the reassessment of male-centered knowledge; the transformation of such knowledge to include women; and, where necessary, the generation of new knowledge.

Feminist biblical interpretation is as diverse as the theories and analytic tools it uses to study the Bible. Adding to its complexity and depth are the many stances from which feminist interpretation proceeds, for the Bible is read from differing theological positions, religious perspectives, and ideological interests (for examples see E. Schüssler Fiorenza 1993 and A. Brenner and C. Fontaine 1997). Feminists differ in assessing how religions contribute to women's oppression and empowerment. For example, Jewish and Christian feminists stand in tension with their traditions, neither completely dismissing nor completely endorsing the Bible and their communities' use of it, but subjecting it to criticism and reformulation. Other feminists subject to criticism the cultural impact of the Bible on women of specific cultures (A. Bach 1990, 1997; J. C. Exum 1993, 1996). For many feminists in developing nations, cultural critique and theological reformulation are simultaneous goals of Liberation*§ theology and Postcolonial Interpretation*§ (P. L. Kwok 1995; M. Oduyoye 1992).

Amid the diversity stands a core feminist conviction: Women are, "by nature," neither inferior to nor derivative of men; and men, "by nature," do not embody a normative humanity to which women are subordinated. Rather, women's humanity, with its attendant rights and responsibilities, including the authority to interpret sacred texts, must be acknowledged and respected by civil and religious communities. Feminist biblical interpretation presupposes women's authority to interpret Scripture, an authority systematically denied to women from early Christianity until recently. The duration of women's absence from the production of knowledge should not be eclipsed by the current acceptance and substantial development of feminist interpretation since the 1960s.

Focusing primarily on feminist interpretation of the Christian Bible and predominantly on Christian feminist work in the United States, this article discusses: (1) women's efforts to gain authority to interpret the Bible; (2) issues in feminist Hermeneutics*§; and (3) feminist biblical studies.

1. *Gaining Authority to Interpret the Bible. a. Historical overview.* Feminist biblical interpretation took root in the seventeenth century in Europe and in the United States and can be assigned to women's struggle not only to preach and teach the Bible but also to rid the world of slavery. The women involved did not use the word "feminist" to describe themselves; that term gained widespread use only in the 1960s. But because they resisted the patriarchal assumption that women, by nature, are subordinate to men and hence must defer to men's judgments, they may be regarded as feminist precursors. (For the development of feminist consciousness, see G. Lerner 1993; D. Riley 1988.)

i. Seventeenth and eighteenth centuries. Under the impact of the Protestant Reformation and its insistence that individual believers can interpret Scripture for themselves, several Protestant and sectarian Christian women of the seventeenth and eighteenth centuries claimed the authority to preach and to teach (e.g., E. Davis and Mrs. Attaway 1630s; A. Hutchinson 1591-1643; S. Wesley 1670-1742; for others see R. Tucker and W. Leifeld 1987, 171-244). These women justified their authority to interpret as being faithful to God's call for them to proclaim the truth of Scripture as they discerned it. For this stance many endured persecution and some suffered torture and death. For example, M. Dyer (seventeenth century), angered by the Puritans' excommunication of A. Hutchinson, spoke out on her behalf and was excommunicated and banished from this group. Nevertheless, Dyer returned to Boston to follow her call to preach and was executed by the Puritans in 1660. Shortly thereafter, M. F. Fox's *Women's Speaking Justified* (1667) became a primary resource for the numerous biblical passages from Genesis to Revelation to which seventeenth-century women appealed for vindication. In addition, the Great Awakening of the eighteenth century, with its emphasis on individual conversion and salvation, opened doors for women to become active members in religious communities as they voted, led prayers, offered testimonies, and preached.

ii. Nineteenth century. The defense of women's preaching as faithfulness to God's call continued in the works of P. Palmer (1859), C. Booth (1860), and A. Smith (1893). Early in the nineteenth century, on the basis of their equality with men in both civil and spiritual life, women began to contest men's interpretation of certain biblical texts as justifying women's subordination. M. Stewart (1830s) was the first woman in the United States to advance issues of social justice and gender equality before an audience of both men and women (see K. Baker-Fletcher in L. Russell and J. S. Clarkson 1996, 316). S. Grimk's *Letters on the Equality of the Sexes* (1838) is a signal text that anticipated arguments on equality later advanced by feminist biblical scholars.

A. Brown Blackwell, the first woman ordained in any Christian denomination, composed a thorough exegesis of 1 Cor 14:34-35 and 1 Tim 2:11-12 as the culminating project of her theological program at Oberlin. Although Oberlin refused to matriculate her in the theological course of study, the school published her essay (1849). She argued that the texts in question applied solely to the historical context in which they were written and were not intended to silence women in the church for all times. F. Willard (1888), founder of the Women's Christian Temperance Union—the largest nineteenth-century women's organization—also defended women's equality, making women's suffrage more palatable by creatively linking it with prohibition. Willard argued that the home, the sacred responsibility of women, could only be protected from moral depravity by combining the vote of men and women to defeat the liquor industry (S. Lindley 1996, 104).

At the close of the century E. C. Stanton[§], in her increasingly well-known *The Woman's Bible* (1898), emphasized the control men exercised over the Bible and its interpretation. She produced *The Woman's Bible* to provoke women into examining Scripture for themselves and to illustrate how interpreters employed this text to subjugate women. Two others who championed the rights of women and slaves in the United States based on their understanding of the Christian Bible are S. Truth[§] and A. Cooper[§]. Truth, considered one of the founders of Black feminism, relied on intuition and on her personal relationship with God as she interpreted biblical texts. She argued that Jesus came into the world by the power of God and a woman; therefore, women have been and will be called to leadership roles in both the religious and the secular worlds. Cooper, who earned a PhD from the Sorbonne in 1925, promoted Truth's views on women, drawing on the historical Jesus as the model for social justice and equality among the sexes, races, and classes.

Women and men began not only to question the status of women but also to examine the nature and gender of God. One who emphasized the androgynous nature of God and established a new Christian movement was M. Baker Eddy. Basing her theology on Jesus' healing miracles, Eddy established the Church of Christ, Scientist in 1884, a church devoted to healing through the power of prayer and meditation without the use of traditional medicine. This movement quickly spread throughout the United States, helped along by her book *Science and Health*

(1875, 1883²), which stressed that all reality is spiritual; sin, disease, and death are illusions that can be healed through mental discipline alone (Lindley 1996, 268-70). Christian Science opened doors for many women as they became leaders, healers, and missionaries, earning economic liberation. The addition of the Mother God in conjunction with a woman founder provided strong role models for women. Ironically, Eddy supported traditional gender roles and expelled potential women rivals from the movement, filling the executive offices with men.

iii. Twentieth century. Near the beginning of the century, K. Bushnell published a book of Bible studies (1905) that schooled women in textual and historical criticism of the Bible. Bushnell argued that the churches' resistance to women's equality and freedom in Christ was a fundamental scandal because it undermined central theological claims about soteriology. Like *The Woman's Bible*, however, her work was largely forgotten.

In Germany, H. Jahnow§ expanded her role in teaching women the Bible to include working with H. Gunkel§, the pioneer of Hebrew Bible Form Criticism*§. Jahnow's seminal study on Israelite laments (1923) remains relevant to Hebrew Bible studies. This and other works earned her the respect of the academy and an honorary doctorate in 1926, the highest degree then available for women in Germany. Until her death in the concentration camp at Theresienstadt, Jahnow was an outspoken proponent of women's rights and appealed to the academy and to the world to take women's scholarship seriously.

With the winning of suffrage in the United States in 1919, active political campaigning by women on a national scale ceased. Little has been written about women's preaching and teaching from the 1920s onward. Women were trained as professional biblical scholars in small numbers; most found teaching positions at women's colleges (D. Bass 1982). Meanwhile, efforts in the church to expand women's responsibilities and leadership roles in denominations and polities continued with slow, incremental success (G. Harkness 1972). Beginning in the late 1950s, theological schools and seminaries began to admit women in increasing numbers; the pace of admissions accelerated during the mid-1970s and early 1980s, a development that can be linked to the women's liberation movement which began in the late 1960s.

M. Crook, a professor of biblical studies at Smith College, wrote the first book by a female professional biblical scholar in support of feminist concerns (1964). She concluded that religion "is man-formulated, man-approved, and man-directed." Shortly thereafter, K. Stendahl (1966) published the first book by a male professional biblical scholar on the issues of women's changing roles and biblical Authority*§. These two books and M. Daly's *The Church and the Second Sex* (1968), with its explicit reliance on feminist theory (S. de Beauvoir 1952 [ET 1989]), placed core feminist issues on the scholarly theological table. These issues include the historical and theological issue of women in patriarchal religions, the hermeneutical dimension of biblical authority, and the role of feminist theory as a theoretical resource for religious studies.

Feminist biblical studies emerged as an academic discipline in the 1980s. Again, historical reviews and assessments are few. However, it is clear that schools and departments responded (sometimes reluctantly) to women students' pressure for the hiring of feminist scholars as well as the (sometimes begrudging) acknowledgment of the quality of feminist scholarship and interpretation.

b. Exegetical arguments for women's authority to interpret the Bible. Traditional Christian exegesis maintained that women are subordinate to and derivative of men in the order of creation and that a woman's purpose is fulfilled in her relationship to her husband, unless she is called to the religious life. This understanding arose from reading the second creation story (Gen 2:4*b*–3:24) and Paul's†§ affirmation of men's headship over women (1 Cor 11:2-9). "Eve's curse" (Gen 3:16) was also invoked to legitimate men's rule over women in the fallen world, and 1 Tim 2:11-14 furthered the connection between Eve's actions and men's hegemony: "Let a woman learn in silence with full submission. I permit no woman to teach or to have authority over a man; she is to keep silent. For Adam was formed first, then Eve; and Adam was not deceived, but the woman was deceived and became a transgressor." Women's speaking or teaching was also prohibited on the basis of 1 Cor 14:34-35. Finally, texts that enjoined women to obey their husbands (Eph 5:22-24; Col 3:18-19; 1 Pet 3:1-6) were taken to mean that women's authority must be surrendered to their husbands and so to men in general.

Women proposed various interpretative strategies to respond to these readings. One was to reinterpret the passages adduced. A second was to adduce countertexts that legitimated women's exercise of authority. A third was to demonstrate inconsistencies and biases in men's translation, thereby differentiating what Scripture said from what men said.

i. Reinterpreting key passages. Against the argument from the order of creation it was asserted that the Bible is not a divine revelation of the natural order but a collection of ancient myths about the creation of the cosmos and humanity's place within it. To continue to treat the accounts of the origins of humanity uncritically in light of later knowledge is foolish (Stanton 1898; Bushnell 1905; R. R. Ruether 1979). Instead, the myths need to be critically interpreted (V. R. Mollenkott 1977). Moreover, some argued, the creation of woman from Adam's rib is a patriarchal inversion and subversion of women's power to give birth (Daly 1966 and Ruether 1979).

Women also countered that "Adam," even in the second creation story, was not a male human being, but a sexually undifferentiated human being (Grimk 1838; P. Trible 1978). The subsequent creation of Adam and Eve did not render Eve subordinate or secondary (Grimk 1838; Willard 1888; Bushnell 1905; Trible 1978), nor did calling her "helper" (Trible 1978).

Finally, in terms of Christian theology, even if woman was subordinated in the fall, the salvific activity of JESUS restored men and women in the Christian community to their original relationship of equality before God (L. Russell 1976); to argue otherwise is to argue that Jesus' saving work was limited in scope (Bushnell 1905; L. Scanzoni 1974; N. Hardesty 1974; P. Gundry 1987).

In order to counter the explicit prohibitions of women's speaking, women interpreters contextualized Paul's remarks to the particular situation at Corinth. Because Paul accepted women praying and prophesying in Corinth, his prohibitions cannot be absolute. Some interpreters accounted for this inconsistency by alleging that 14:31-32 is an interpolation or that it is an instance of Paul's citing his adversaries (Bushnell 1905). A similar strategy was applied to 1 Tim 2:15's prohibition of women teaching.

ii. Appealing to countertexts. Interpreters argued that the second creation story's account of the woman's creation is countered with the first (Gen 1:26-27), in which the human being is described as both "male and female" and created in the image of God. In opposition to the use of 1 Cor 11:8-9 as establishing the priority of the second creation account, women adduced 1 Cor 11:11-12 ("Though woman cannot do without man, neither can man do without woman in the Lord; woman may come from man, but man is born of woman"; author's translation) as implying mutuality. Similarly, women countered the scriptural demand that wives obey their husbands (Eph 5:22; Col 3:18) with the passage that reminded men of their responsibilities to, or mutuality with, their wives (Eph 5:23; Col 3:19). Against 1 Cor 11:3-9, which grants headship to man, women presented Gal 3:28: "There are no more distinctions between Jew and Greek, slave and free, male and female, but all of you are one in Christ Jesus" (author's translation).

Finally, women produced texts that approve of women's speaking; e.g., John 20:21, in which Jesus sends Mary to announce his resurrection to the absent male disciples, and Matt 28:5-11, in which an angel as well as Jesus sends the women to carry news of the resurrection to the male disciples. Also, warrant is drawn from Peter's first speech after Pentecost (Acts 2:14-36), in which he cites the promises made in Joel 2:28-29: "I will pour out my spirit on all mankind.

Their sons and daughters shall prophesy . . . even on my slaves, men and women, in those days I will pour out my spirit" (author's translation). Women also appealed to the women in the Hebrew Bible who maintained positions of leadership and authority: e.g., Miriam, a prophet; Deborah, a prophet and judge; and Huldah, a prophet who authorized a newly discovered text as Scripture (see A. O. Bellis 1994; L. Bronner 1994).

iii. Demonstrating biases in men's translation. Grimk (1838) enumerated possible alternative translations and noted that an all-male clergy had a vested interest in women's subordination. Willard (1888) adduced numerous examples of biased translations, among them the issue of Phoebe as *diakonos* ("deacon" or "deaconess") or as *prostatis* ("elder" or "president"). She suggested that male clergy tended to play down Phoebe's leadership by calling her deaconess rather than deacon, a title suggesting significant church leadership. About a decade later Bushnell analyzed the problem as "sex bias," rooted simply in privileged control of the text: "Supposing women only had translated the Bible, from age to age, is there a likelihood that men would have rested content with the outcome? Therefore, our brothers have no good reason to complain if, while conceding that men had done the best they could alone, we assert that they did not do the best that could have been done" (1905, 372). In addition, M. Royden (1924) and L. Starr (1926) demonstrated the existence of "sex bias" in men's translations of biblical passages concerning women's leadership positions.

iv. Conclusion. By the 1970s the cumulative effect of these interpretive strategies made evident that direct appeal to the Bible's stance on women's subordination was little more than proof-texting justified on grounds other than simply that "the Bible said so." Further, the distinction between the Bible as "man's word" and as "God's Word" indicated that gender, as well as historical context, is a factor in contextualization and interpretation.

2. *Feminist Biblical Hermeneutics.* Feminist biblical hermeneutics explicates feminists' self-understanding in relation to biblical interpretation. Since much contemporary hermeneutical theory asserts that consciousness and text are mutually constituted through the process of interpretation, a key problem for feminist interpretation is whether feminists can find anything of value or (to put it theologically) anything revelatory in the Bible once its patriarchal and androcentric character is confronted. (C. Osiek 1985 offers a useful typology of feminist positions on this point.) A second key problem concerns the scope of feminist hermeneutics. Because no text comes unmediated, feminists cannot focus on the Bible as if it were a free-floating object but must contend with traditions of interpretation and their historical effects.

a. Evaluating the patriarchal Bible as Scripture. Even when translated without the distortions of sex bias, the Bible remains at least a product of the ancient patriarchal culture in which it originated and of the patriarchal cultures that transmitted it. A fundamental question is whether the Bible is anything more than an oppressive, patriarchal text; if it is not, feminist interest calls for its summary rejection. Among feminists who have rejected the Bible as an authority are Stanton (1895), M. J. Gage (1900), Daly (1966), and D. Hampson (1990).

For other feminists, awareness that women claim the Bible as a significant religious authority and source of empowerment cautions against dismissing it as simply and solely patriarchal. Women's testimony to the power of the Bible cannot be attributed simply to false consciousness; doing so gives too much power to patriarchal tradition and insufficiently respects women's subjectivity. Respecting the dual effect of the Bible as friend and enemy (M. A. Tolbert 1983) requires a critical approach to the text.

To use terms proposed by Osiek (1984), "loyalists" affirm the essential validity and goodness of the biblical tradition as the Word of God; when correctly interpreted, the Bible affirms women's full humanity (L. Scanzoni and N. Hardesty 1984; P. Gundry 1987; V. Mollenkott 1977; A. Mickelsen 1986). "Revisionists" distinguish the contingent patriarchal dimension of biblical texts from the enduring theological values expressed therein (P. Trible 1978, 1984).

"Liberationists" affirm God's concern for justice and liberation from oppression, locating that affirmation in biblical authority (Ruether 1979; Russell 1976) or in the community working for liberation (E. Schüssler Fiorenza 1984).

b. Dealing with tradition. Feminists bring a variety of concerns to their reading of the Bible. Historically, its teachings about women's status and relationships with men have been of great concern, but other issues have demanded attention as well.

i. Discovering women in the Bible. As women affirmed the intrinsic value of their experience in opposition to its androcentric marginalization, they sought themselves "in" the text as historical figures and as literary images. Rather than ponder David and Saul, women wondered about Michal and Bathsheba; rather than ask if Paul silenced women, they inquired after Chloe, Junia, Syntyche, and Euodia (F. Gillman 1992). Women asked why Sarah dismissed Hagar; why Martha is not praised; and why, if women learned about the resurrection first, they are excluded from ordination.

Contrary to male-dominated readings, feminists noted imagery from women's experience with pregnancy, mothering, and nurture; domestic work; and marriage as metaphors for the relationship between the deity and humanity. God's wisdom is personified as a woman in Proverbs, and women's delight in sexuality is affirmed by the Song of Songs.

ii. Inclusive language. Having discovered women in every layer of biblical tradition, from female judges to women missionaries, and having found female imagery for God and the kingdom of God, feminists insisted that liturgies and translations acknowledge women's presence and cease to render them invisible by exclusive use of androcentric language (N. Morton 1985; A. M. Bennett 1989) and by excluding texts about women from the lectionary (M. Procter-Smith 1990). Feminists also described the pain of invisibility and the fragmentation that comes with reading themselves into male-defined language (Morton 1985; Bennett 1989). They proposed that female imagery of God, like "Bakerwoman God," "Mother God," and "Sophia," be used in prayers, hymns, liturgy, and theology (B. Bowe 1992; M. Winter 1990).

iii. The maleness of Jesus. As feminists clarified the value of female identity and self, they wrestled with the significance of Jesus' maleness. C. Christ (1987) argued that women needed to envision the divine as female, and Ruether asked, "Can a male saviour save women?" (1979). The response to the statue Christa, which depicts a crucified woman, has shown how charged is the issue of Jesus' maleness, on the one hand, and women's suffering under men's domination, on the other. Christian feminists also examined Jesus' relationship to women as a warrant for changing gender roles in contemporary churches.

iv. Sexual violence. Feminists worked to free women's sexuality from men's control and from its association with sin, forged in the portrayal of Eve's transgression. Acutely conscious, for example, that rapists and batterers would assert that the women provoked or asked for the violence, women angrily read Adam's blaming Eve as his refusing responsibility. Feminists grieved over the concubine raped and dismembered (Judg 19) and for the sacrifice of Jephthah's daughter (Judg 11:34-40), and they pondered why women's bodies are repeatedly violated in biblical texts (see Gal 4:21-31; Rev 2:18-29, 17:15-18; also D. Fewell and D. Gunn 1993).

Feminists working in rape crisis centers and shelters for battered women listened to Christian women explain their shame at failing to endure suffering that would rescue their husbands and tell how teachings about obedience to husbands and fathers (Eph 5:21-23; Col 3:18-19; 1 Pet 3:1-6) left them with no sense of a right to reject sexual abuse and with intense guilt over their anger and sinfulness (S. Thistlethwaite 1985). Feminists wrestle with reinterpreting such texts and search for biblical perspectives that can assist women to heal from the trauma of sexual abuse.

c. Social location and biblical hermeneutics. Feminist theory affirms differences among women and complicates its analysis of women's experience by wrestling with elements of particularity.

Women's social location; the community and heritage from which a given feminist emerges and finds support; and issues of race, class, sexual preference, and gender become subject to hermeneutical reflection. Thus feminist biblical hermeneutics from a white, Western, middle-class perspective might focus on gender oppression and issues of subordination to men but not wrestle with other forms of oppression like poverty and racism. Feminist biblical hermeneutics has become aware of the need to pay greater attention to articulating the role of factors of social location in its self-understanding so that its self-description does not marginalize important members of its constituency. Attending to social location honors the diversity of women's experience and enriches the store of reading strategies for and insights into biblical texts. For example, R. N. Brock (1993) draws on the Japanese American tradition of honoring mature insight to formulate a hermeneutics of wisdom for understanding women's relationship to the CANON. This relationship is ambiguous and paradoxical because the Bible serves as a source for both freedom and oppression. A hermeneutics of wisdom takes seriously the need to incorporate Asian cultural experience and history into the reading of texts, the need to reject innocence as a biblical virtue, since it often reinforces victimization, and the need to retain the multilayered dimensions of those interpreting the Bible (Brock 1993, 64-5). *Mujerista**§ biblical scholars approach the Bible with the lens of liberation (see Schüssler Fiorenza [1993] for this and other feminist/womanist biblical approaches).

An outgrowth of feminist biblical hermeneutics is Womanist Interpretation*§ (from a term coined by A. Walker 1983, *xi-xii*). According to K. Baker Fletcher, "contemporary womanists challenge interlocking systems of oppression: racism, classism, homophobia, and ecological abuses" (in Russell and Clarkson 1996, 316). J. Grant (1989) emphasizes the survival strategies involved in womanist thought, while D. Williams (1993) declares womanists to be those who name their own experience. Womanists believe that mainline feminism has failed to acknowledge the complexities women of color face as members of at least two socially oppressed groups. For example, Williams argues that black women broaden the scope of patriarchy and consider white women to be participants in both patriarchy and black women's oppression. Even though both groups of women are exploited, there are different levels of exploitation; thus the unique experience of slavery and/or racism affects a womanist interpretation of biblical texts. Also, white feminism often silences the voices of women of color (including those in biblical texts) providing the need for womanist interpretations of the Bible. R. Weems (1991) proposes an investigation into all silenced voices in the text. This principle opens a doorway for analyzing women's complicity in women's oppression, class oppression, and ethnographic composition.

d. The scope of feminist biblical hermeneutics. Schüssler Fiorenza differentiates feminist biblical hermeneutics into a fourfold model of interrelated aspects. The need for a complex model arises from the many uses to which the Bible is put and from the conviction that women must become fully responsible for interpretation.

Because women have been excluded from the production of knowledge, feminists assume that the knowledge they inherit serves male-dominated interests and cannot be accepted as "critical" or "objective" knowledge. Critical analysis calls for a hermeneutics of suspicion toward tradition and traditional interpretations of biblical texts and for unmasking patriarchal assumptions that render women invisible, marginal, or incidental to the text or issue under discussion. The next interpretative task is to engage in a hermeneutics of remembrance that reconstructs women's historical agency in foundational Christian tradition. This requires critical methods for interpreting inclusive language and for considering canonical and extracanonical sources. The aim of this (re)interpretation is both to contest the patriarchal view of Christian origins as transmitted solely by men by constructing an alternative historical account and to empower women by restoring to them a past. Because the Bible is used as a source for theology, ethics, and policy formation, feminists also engage in a hermeneutics of proclamation that relates the reconstructed traditions to contemporary community life. Last, a hermeneutics of imagination is called for in recognition that not all knowledge is cognitive, by which contemporary women express empowering traditions in ritual, prayer, and creative means such as hymns, banners, and art.

Schüssler Fiorenza's model indicates the necessary breadth of feminist biblical hermeneutics and suggests a means for integrating critical biblical studies with other theological disciplines.

3. *Feminist Biblical Studies.* Feminist biblical studies developed rapidly over the 1980s and 1990s and has become increasingly sophisticated in its recasting of critical biblical studies and in its methods. Resistance to feminist biblical studies is rooted partly in the continuing sexism of academic institutions and theological education and partly in the centrality the notion of objectivity has had in critical biblical studies. Mainstream biblical scholarship has prided itself on its objectivity in the study of the Bible and has grounded that objectivity in methodology. Since feminist theory and criticism are invested in social change and the transformation of knowledge, their validity as critical disciplines is suspect. Feminist biblical scholars have argued strenuously that the vaunted ideal of objectivity masks male-dominated investments in interpreting the Bible as a patriarchal text. Feminist historical criticism and LITERARY criticism demonstrate the ideological investment of male-dominated biblical scholarship by contesting key assumptions regarding methods and by offering alternative historical reconstructions and literary analyses.

a. Feminist historical criticism. This form of criticism reconstructs biblical history as women's history by investigating the historical experience of women in biblical times and the role of women in shaping tradition.

i. Feminist historical criticism of the New Testament. The New Testament provides ample evidence of women's agency in early Christianity. There are many texts that name women or in which women act. This may seem to be an obvious point, but traditional historical criticism pays little attention to their presence. Even a cursory listing of women whom Paul commends demonstrates that women contributed to the spread of early Christianity. Phoebe, "a deacon of the church at Cenchreae" and a "benefactor of many" (Rom 16:1-2); Mary, "who has worked very hard" (Rom 16:6); Junia, "prominent among the apostles" (Rom 16:7); Chloe, a leader (1 Cor 1:11); Mary (Rom 16:6); Tryphaena and Tryphosa (Rom 16:12); and Euodia and Syntyche (Phil 4:2-3) are all lauded for their leadership on behalf of the church.

Given such textual evidence from Paul's letters and adding to it evidence from the narratives in the Gospels and Acts (and the many extracanonical traditions with reports about female Christian disciples), the decision to leave women's history unexplored reveals the selectivity with which "objective" historical criticism proceeds. Schüssler Fiorenza argues that historical reconstruction cannot evade selectivity because paradigms and frameworks govern historical reasoning. Her intent is not to establish feminist historical criticism as more objective than androcentric historical criticism but to demonstrate that every criticism and reconstruction serves interests. Such demonstration offers the possibility of regrounding the critical element of biblical studies in public discourse through evaluation of theological warrants, hermeneutical and historical paradigms, and political concerns.

ii. Examples of feminist historical reconstruction of Christian origins. Feminist interpreters have examined Jesus' relationships with women in order to counter the sexism they experience and to provide a higher authority than Paul, whose proscriptions were adduced against women's teaching with authority. Many concluded that Jesus liberated women from their secondary and degraded status in Judaism by treating them as equals and by ignoring ritual purity concerns (C. Parvey 1974; L. Swidler 1971; E. Tetlow 1980). Yet the reconstruction suggesting that emergent Christianity liberated women from an oppressive Judaism was seriously flawed by anti-Semitic depictions of the Judaism of Jesus' time (J. Plaskow 1990; Schüssler Fiorenza 1993; K. von Kellenbach 1994). Critical response to this reconstruction has generated more complete historical knowledge of Jewish, Christian, and pagan women in antiquity and alternative models for understanding the appeal of early Christianity to women.

Through epigraphical and archaeological means, B. Brooten (1982, 1985) has established that Jewish women exercised leadership and patronage in synagogues. R. Kraemer (1988, 1992) has assembled primary sources for the study of women and religion in antiquity and offered a Social-Scientific*§ account of the relative appeal of religions to women in ancient times, while L. Schottroff (1995) has investigated the social and material history of women. Schüssler Fiorenza (1983) has offered a theological reconstruction of Christian origins as a renewal movement within Judaism that proffered men and women "a discipleship of equals," a nonpatriarchal vision imperfectly embodied and ultimately suppressed by the second century. By means of rhetorical criticism, A. Wire (1990) has reconstructed the theology of the women prophets at Corinth whom Paul opposed. A. J. Levine (1994) has demonstrated that feminists require a clearer understanding of early Christianity and Judaism. Misconceptions have led many Christian feminists to declare Jesus a feminist based on the belief that he overrode the "oppressive purity laws" of the day. Levine argues that it is unclear that the purity laws were in effect or were being followed during the first century. Moreover, if they were followed, it is uncertain that these laws were deemed oppressive by those practicing them.

iii. Women and the Hebrew Bible. Several issues have dominated feminist historical studies of the Hebrew Bible: e.g., the contributions of women in the various historical layers (patriarchal times through postexilic Israel); the status of women in ancient Israelite society and cult; and the problems related to sexuality that led many women to explore fertility cults, goddess worship, and intermarriage with the indigenous population.

In the 1970s and early 1980s the study of the status of women in the Hebrew Bible, especially in the patriarchal narratives and law codes, frequently served to demonstrate the feminist claim that the Bible's patriarchal society was oppressive to women. The stories of violence against women (Genesis 34; Judges 11; 19; 1 Kings 13; 2 Kings 9) displayed men's disregard for women's humanity. The patriarchal narratives showed that the tradition regarded women as significant solely because they produce sons for the patriarch. Study of the teachings about women in the ancient cult, which underscored their exclusion from key cultic practices such as the priesthood, were often preparatory for the study of the New Testament's interpretation of religious leadership.

Since the mid 1980s, some critical works have emerged that contest the portrait of the Hebrew Bible as oppressively patriarchal. C. Meyers (1988) has used social-scientific models of preindustrial agrarian societies and Hebrew Bible texts to argue that women in premonarchical Israel were regarded with respect and had, if not leadership authority, significant power in their families because of their economic contributions to the household. A. Brenner (1985) has argued for a necessary distinction between the literary representation of women in the text and the social roles women may have actually played. P. Bird (1997) has recognized the need to recast the categories for studying women's religious experience, since categories cast in terms of leadership or cultic practice rendered women invisible (see P. Day [1989] for a reconceptualization of the gender roles in the Hebrew Bible).

b. Feminist literary criticism. Feminist literary criticism challenges the claim to objectivity in critical biblical studies. Those espousing objectivity assume that the reader of the text neither distorts nor informs it; the text is understood to surrender information in response to disciplined critical analysis. Feminist literary critics question the neutral role of the reader in even the most preliminary reading of the text and offer critical tools for studying the construction of meaning. Two major trends have developed: Narrative Criticism*§ and Reader-response Criticism*§. Narrative criticism examines the construction, representation, characterization, and image of women in the text to uncover how rhetoric may function ideologically. Feminist interest in the construction of meaning and in reader response has been complemented by trends in post-structuralist literary theory.

M. Bal (1988) has drawn on Semiotics*§ and Structuralism*§ to apply a feminist narratolog-ical approach to the book of Judges. She notes an ideological and political coherence that is reflected in the manner women are treated in the text. Traditional interpretations of Judges are gender biased; they center around the judges themselves, focusing on political and military sit-uations (the realm of men) instead of on the private sphere (the realm of women). Bal consid-ers such interpretations to be examples of a political coherence that "functions as closure; it allows critics to escape the painful experience of awareness of the deep-seated relationship between social institutions and violence against women" (1988, 237). This political coherence, she argues, has allowed many interpreters to insist that Judges 17–21, chapters containing sto-ries of extreme violence toward hundreds of women, are an appendix to the book. Bal disagrees and provides a "counter coherence" that concentrates on the marginalized, who live predomi-nantly in the private sphere where, in Judges, women are murdered (Jephthah's daughter, Samson's first wife, the Lévite's concubine), whereas men are murdered by women in the pub-lic sphere (Sisera, Abimelech, and Samson).

T. Pippin (1992) applies rhetorical and gender criticism to the book of Revelation as she examines the literary portrayals of the four feminine figures in this apocalypse (apocalypti-cism). Apocalyptic literature, she argues, serves a cathartic function by helping the reader to expunge unwanted feelings. In Revelation, women become the victims and scapegoats for male catharsis as men throw all of the evils and problems of the world onto the bodies of women. For example, two desires are acting simultaneously in the text: the desire for wealth and power, rep-resented in the bodies of the whore of Babylon and the prophet called Jezebel; and the desire for God's world, represented in the bodies of the woman clothed in the sun and the bride of Christ. These desires generate an ambiguous and dualistic portrayal of women and their bodies. In order to choose good over bad it is necessary to annihilate the "bad" women; therefore, both the whore and Jezebel are violently destroyed. In contrast, the "good" women are controlled (the bride) or sent away for safe keeping (the woman clothed in the sun). Pippin concludes that the apocalypse is not a safe place for women.

R. Weems (1995) explores the sexual and sexist metaphors employed by Hosea, Jeremiah, and Ezekiel to ascertain their capacity to condone sexist human power. She is motivated by such questions as why the prophets chose to humiliate women and their bodies to demonstrate God's love for the people and why there is such a fascination with naked, mangled female bodies. Weems builds on gender and on literary, sociological, and ideological criticism to explore these sexual metaphors.

Bal, Pippin, and Weems exemplify three of the feminist literary approaches that biblical scholars apply to biblical texts. Other feminist literary critics choose to focus on the images of women in the texts; however, there are limitations to such an approach. First, looking for images of good women promotes selectivity. For example, regarding the Gospel of Mark, argu-ments that women exemplify true discipleship systematically overlook the evil woman Herodias. Selective focus on the goodness of women, which is valuable in countering alienation and misogyny or sexist dismissal of women, can itself contribute to the stereotype that women are, by nature, more moral and more religious than men. Second, the images (especially of bad women but even of good women) were produced by men and should be subjected to cri-tique. For example, E. Fuchs's (1985) study of the characterization of women as deceptive excellently demonstrates how narrative treatment of women can confirm (e.g., by not giving their motives) the patriarchal ideology about women being deceitful. Similarly, the image of Wisdom in Proverbs is problematic. Both Lady Wisdom (good) and Lady Folly (bad) call out in the city for the young men. From all outward appearances both women are the same, serving only to confuse young men and reinforcing the belief that women are not to be trusted. Because of misleading images in the Gospel of Luke, T. Seim (1994), J. Schaberg (1987), and B. Reid (1996) have all leveled significant challenges to reading Luke as a book that empowers women.

A new trend in literary criticism and reader-response criticism is cultural criticism (Cultural Studies*§). Bach (1997) and Exum (1996) apply this critical method to issues of gender as they compare biblical texts with their representations in art and film. Both argue that readers are often influenced by these cultural representations of biblical women and bring these pre- (and sometimes mis-) conceptions to their readings of biblical texts.

J. Fetterly (1978) argues that the very process of reading androcentric literature causes women to define themselves in terms opposed to their identity as women. Biblical texts systematically mislead women by asking them to identify with the hero rather than with the heroine. Women read a narrative about Samson, for example, and identify with Samson, not Delilah; or they read about and identify with David, not Bathsheba. Fetterly's analysis clarifies how it is possible to ignore the female characters in the Bible and proposes that feminists intentionally read against the grain, distancing themselves from the male point of view by focusing on marginalized voices. This tack permits rereading biblical narratives not only by observing the marginalizing of female characters but also by reconstructing the voice of the silenced or marginalized reader. Bach (1997) does this with Michal and Abigail.

Feminists insist that reading is interested rather than neutral. This insistence leads to readings grounded in and exploratory of the variety of social locations from which women read. Analyses of and from social locations do not dispense with gender as a category, but chart or theorize its interactions with other factors in women's experience (e.g., class or status; race, ethnicity, or culture; geopolitical concerns; and sexual preference).

4. *Future Directions.* In its first two decades, feminist biblical interpretation succeeded in establishing the importance of feminist theory and criticism. This accomplishment required contesting traditional gender roles, especially the assumption that women are not authoritative interpreters of the Bible. In the future, other dimensions of gender will need to be studied, with an emphasis on the interrelation of gender, religion, and sexuality.

Because of the effort to draw attention to women's absence from biblical interpretation, feminists have stressed women's experience and readings. As greater numbers of women have taken up biblical studies, tensions among women have revealed fundamental questions: How is the diversity of feminist standpoints to be negotiated? Must feminist theory have a "dream of a common language" and, if so, how would consent to that dream be secured? What is the relationship between feminist cultural criticism and feminist theological hermeneutics? What is the relationship between academic feminist scholars and feminists outside of academia? All of these questions and more will be food for thought in years to come.

Feminist analysis of exegetical methodology and the Bible itself continue apace. J. Jobling (2002) provides a major overview of the theoretical issues. L. Schottroff, S. Schroer, and M.T. Wacker (1995 [ET 1998]) sketch the history of feminist exegesis from a continental European perspective and outline feminist reconstructions of the histories of ancient Israel and early Christianity. Detailed feminist commentaries and discussions on individual biblical books are available in the *Feminist Companion to the Bible* (A. Brenner 1998-2001) and the *Feminist Companion to the New Testament and Early Christian Writings* (A. Levine 2001-2002). Kwok Pui-lan (2000), M. Dube (2001), and M. Dube Shomanah (2000) address feminist biblical interpretation from a non-Western perspective and include postcolonial analyses and indigenous perspectives.

Bibliography: A. Bach, *Ad Feminam* (*USQR* 43, 1989); (ed.), *The Pleasure of Her Text: Feminist Readings of Biblical and Historical Texts* (1990); *Women, Seduction, and Betrayal in*

Biblical Narrative (1997). **K. Baker-Fletcher,** *A Singing Something: Womanist Reflections on Anna Julia Cooper* (1994). **M. Bal,** *Murder and Difference: Gender, Genre, and Scholarship on Sisera's Death* (ISBL, 1988). **D. C. Bass,** "Women's Studies and Biblical Studies: An Historical Perspective," *JSOT* 22 (1982) 6-12. **A. M. Bennett,** *From Woman-Pain to Woman-Vision: Writings in Feminist Theology* (ed. M. E. Hunt, 1989). **P. Bird,** *Missing Persons and Mistaken Identities: Women and Gender in Ancient Israel* (OBT, 1997). **M. Booth,** *Female Ministry: Or, Woman's Right to Preach the Gospel* (1860, 1975). **A. O. Bellis,** *Helpmates, Harlots, Heroes: Women's Stories in the HB* (1994). **S. de Beauvoir,** *The Second Sex* (1952; ET 1989). **B. Bowe** (ed.), *Silent Voices, Sacred Lives: Women's Readings for the Liturgical Year* (1992). **A. Brenner,** *The Israelite Woman: Social Role and Literary Type in Biblical Narrative* (1985); (ed.), *The Feminist Companion to the HB* (10 vols., 1993-96). **A. Brenner and C. Fontaine** (eds.), *A Feminist Companion to Reading the Bible: Approaches, Methods, and Stategies* (Feminist Companion to the Bible 1-11, 1997). **A. Brenner** (ed.), *Feminist Companion to the Bible* (vols. 2 and 6 with Carol R. Fontaine 1998-). **R. N. Brock,** "Dusting the Floor: A Hermeneutics of Wisdom," *Searching the Scriptures: A Feminist Commentary* (ed. E. Schüssler Fiorenza, 1993) 1:64-75. **L. L. Bronner,** *From Eve to Esther: Rabbinic Reconstructions of Biblical Women* (1994). **B. J. Brooten,** "'Junia . . . Outstanding Among the Apostles' (Rom 16:7)," *Women Priests: A Catholic Commentary on the Vatican Declaration* (ed. L. Swidler and A. Swidler, 1977) 141-44; *Women Leaders in the Ancient Synagogue* (BJS 36, 1982); "Early Christian Women and Their Cultural Context: Issues of Method in Historical Reconstruction," *Feminist Perspectives on Biblical Scholarship* (ed. A. Y. Collins, BSNA 10, 1985) 65-91; *Love Between Women: Early Christian Responses to Female Homoeroticism* (Chicago Series on Sexuality, History, and Society, 1996). **A. L. Brown,** "Exegesis of I Corinthians XIV, 34, 35 and I Timothy II, 11, 12," *Oberlin Quarterly* (1849). **K. C. Bushnell,** *God's Word to Women: One Hundred Bible Studies on Women's Place in the Divine Economy* (1905; repr., ed. R. B. Munson, 1976). **K. G. Cannon,** "The Emergence of Black Feminist Consciousness," *Feminist Interpretation of the Bible* (ed. L. M. Russell, 1985); *Black Womanist Ethics* (1988); *Katie's Canon: Womanism and the Soul of the Black Community* (1995). **E. A. Castelli,** "Les Belles Infidèles/Fidelity or Feminism? The Meanings of Feminist Biblical Translation," *JFSR* 6 (1990) 25-39. **C. Christ,** *The Laughter of Aphrodite: Reflections on a Journey to the Goddess* (1987). **A. Y. Collins,** (ed.), *Feminist Perspectives on Biblical Scholarship* (BSNA 10, 1985). **K. E. Corley,** *Private Women, Public Meals: Social Conflict in the Synoptic Tradition* (1993). **M. B. Crook,** *Women and Religion* (1964). **M. Daly,** *The Church and the Second Sex* (1966). **M. R. D'Angelo,** "Women Partners in the NT," *JFSR* 6 (1990) 65-86. **P. L. Day** (ed.), *Gender and Difference in Ancient Israel* (1989). **V. B. Demarest,** *God, Woman, and Ministry* (1978). **P. Demers,** *Women as Interpreters of the Bible* (1992). **S. E. Dowd,** "H. B. Montgomery's Centenary Translation of the NT: Characteristics and Influences," *PRSt* 19 (1992) 133-50. **M. W. Dube,** ed., *Other Ways of Reading: African Women and the Bible* (2001). **M. W Dube Shomanah,** *Postcolonial Feminist Interpretation of the Bible* (2000). **J. C. Exum,** *Fragmented Women: Feminist (Sub)versions of Biblical Narratives* (1993); *Plotted, Shot, and Painted: Cultural Representations of Biblical Women* (JSOTSup 125; Gender, Culture, Theory 3, 1996). **M. A. Farley,** "Feminist Consciousness and the Interpretation of Scripture," *Feminist Interpretation of the Bible* (ed. L. M. Russell, 1985). **J. Fetterley,** *The Resisting Reader: A Feminist Approach to American Fiction* (1978). **D. N. Fewell and D. M. Gunn,** *Gender, Power, and Promise: The Subject of the Bible's First Story* (1993). **M. A. F. Fox,** *Women's Speaking Justified* (1667). **E. Fuchs,** "Who Is Hiding the Truth? Deceptive Women and Biblical Androcentrism," *Feminist Perspectives on Biblical Scholarship* (ed. A. Y. Collins, BSNA 10, 1985) 137-44. **M. J. Gage,** *Woman, Church, State* (1900, 1972). **F. M. Gillman,** *Women Who Knew Paul* (Zacchaeus Studies NT, 1992). **J. Grant,** *White Woman's Christ and Black Women's Jesus: Feminist*

Christology and Womanist Response (1989); (ed.), *Perspectives on Womanist Theology* (1995).
S. M. Grimké, *Letters on the Equality of the Sexes* (1838). **P. Gundry,** *Neither Slave nor Free:*
Helping Women Answer the Call to Church Leadership (1987). **D. D. Hampson,** *Theology and*
Feminism (Signposts in Theology, 1990). **G. E. Harkness,** *Women in Church and Society: A*
Historical and Theological Inquiry (1972). **S. Heine,** *Frauen der frühen Christenheit* (1987; tr.
J. Bowden, ET *Women and Early Christianity: A Reappraisal* 1988). **T. Ilan,** *Jewish Women in*
Greco-Roman Palestine: An Inquiry into Image and Status (TSAJ 44, 1995). **A. M. Isasi-Díaz**
and Y. Tarango, *Hispanic Women Prophetic Voice in the Church: Toward a Hispanic Women's*
Liberation Theology (1988). **H. Jahnow,** *Das Hebraische Leichenlied im Rahmen der*
Völkerdichtung (BZAW 36, 1923). **J. Jobling,** *Feminist Biblical Interpretation in Theological*
Context: Restless Readings. (Ashgate New Critical Thinking in Theology & Biblical Studies
2002). **R. Kraemer,** *Maenads, Martyrs, Matrons, Monastics: A Source-book on Women's*
Religions in the Greco-Roman World (1988); *Her Share of the Blessings: Women's Religions*
Among Pagans, Jews, and Christians in the Greco-Roman World (1992). **C. C. Kroeger and**
J. K. Beck, *Women, Abuse, and the Bible: How Scripture Can Be Used to Hurt or to Heal*
(1996). **R. C. Kroeger and C. C. Kroeger,** *I Suffer Not a Woman to Speak: Rethinking 1 Tim*
2:11-15 in Light of Ancient Evidence (1992). **P. Kwok,** "Racism and Ethnocentrism in Feminist
Biblical Interpretation," *Searching the Scriptures: A Feminist Introduction* (ed. E. Schüssler
Fiorenza, 1993) 1:101-166; *Discovering the Bible in the Non-Biblical World* (Bible and
Liberation Series, 1995).; *Introducing Asian Feminist Theology* (2000). **A. L. Laffey,** *An*
Introduction to the OT: A Feminist Perspective (1988). **G. Lerna,** *The Creation of Feminist*
Consciousness from the Middle Ages to 1870 (Women and History 2, 1993). **A. J. Levine** (ed.),
"Women Like This": New Perspectives on Jewish Women in the Greco-Roman World (Early
Judaism and Its Literature 1, 1991); "Second Temple Judaism, Jesus, and Women," *BibInt* 2
(1994) 8-33; (ed.), *Feminist Companion to the New Testament and Early Christian Writings*
(2001-2002). **S. H. Lindley,** *"You Have Stept Out of Your Place": A History of Women and*
Religion in America (1996). **C. L. Meyers,** *Discovering Eve: Ancient Israelite Women in*
Context (1988). **A. Mickelsen** (ed.), *Women, Authority, and the Bible* (1986). **V. R. Mollenkott,**
Women, Men, and the Bible (1988). **E. Moltmann-Wendel,** *The Women Around Jesus:*
Reflections on Authentic Personhood (1982). **L. A. Moody** (ed.), *Women Encounter God:*
Theology Across the Boundaries of Difference (1996). **N. Morton,** *The Journey Is Home*
(1985). **W. Munro,** "Women Disciples in Mark?" *CBQ* 44 (1982) 225-41. **C. A. Newsom and**
S. H. Ringe (eds.), *The Women's Bible Commentary* (1992, 1998²). **J. Nunnally-Fox,**
Foremothers: Women of the Bible (1981). **M. A. Oduyoye and M. R. A. Kanyoro** (eds.), *The*
Will to Arise: Women, Tradition, and the Church in Africa (1992). **C. Osiek,** *Beyond Anger: On*
Being a Feminist in the Church (1984); "The Feminist and the Bible: Hermeneutical
Alternatives" *Feminist Perspectives on Biblical Scholarship* (ed. A. Y. Collins, BSNA 10,
1985); "Reading the Bible as Women," *NIB* (1994) 1:181-87. **P. Palmer,** *Promise of the Father, or*
a Neglected Speciality of the Last Days (1859, 1981). **C. Parvey,** "The Theology and Leadership
of Women in the NT," *Religion and Sexism* (ed. R. R. Ruether, 1974) 117-49. **M. D. Pellauer,**
Toward a Tradition of Feminist Theology: The Religious Social Thought of E. C. Stanton,
S. B. Anthony, and A. H. Shaw (Chicago Studies in the History of American Religion 15, 1991).
M. Peskowitz, *Spinning Fantasies: Rabbis, Gender, and History* (Contraversions 9, 1997).
T. Pippin, *Death and Desire: The Rhetoric of Gender in the Apocalypse of John* (1992).
J. Plaskow, *Standing Again at Sinai: Judaism from a Feminist Perspective* (1990); "Anti-
Judaism in Feminist Christian Interpretation," *Searching the Scriptures: A Feminist Commentary*
(ed. E. Schüssler Fiorenza, 1993) 117-29. **M. Procter-Smith,** *In Her Own Rite: Constructing*
Feminist Liturgical Tradition (1990). **B. E. Reid,** *Choosing the Better Part? Women in the*
Gospel of Luke (1996). **I. Richter Reimer,** *Women in the Acts of the Apostles: A Feminist*

Liberation Perspective (1995). **D. Riley,** *Am I That Name? Feminism and the Category of "Women" in History* (Language, Discourse, Society, 1988). **S. H. Ringe,** "A Gentile Woman's Story," *Feminist Interpretation of the Bible* (ed. L. M. Russell, 1985). **R. R. Ruether and E. McLaughlin** (eds.), *Women of Spirit: Female Leadership in the Jewish and Christian Traditions (1979).* **A. M. Royden,** *The Church and Woman* (The Living Church, 1924). **L. M. Russell** (ed.), *The Liberating Word: A Guide to Non-Sexist Interpretation of the Bible* (1976); (ed.), *Feminist Interpretation of the Bible* (1985). **L. M. Russell and J. S. Clarkson,** *Dictionary of Feminist Theologies* (1996). **L. D. Scanzoni and N. A. Hardesty,** *All We're Meant to Be: Biblical Feminism for Today* (1974; rev. ed., 1992[3]). **A. J. Schmidt,** *Veiled and Silenced: How Culture Shaped Sexist Theology* (1989). **J. Schaberg,** *The Illegitimacy of Jesus: A Feminist Theological Interpretation of the Infancy Narratives* (1987). **S. M. Schneiders,** *Women and the Word: The Gender of God in the NT and the Spirituality of Women* (Madeleva Lecture in Spirituality, 1986). **L. Schottroff,** *Let the Oppressed Go Free: Feminist Perspectives on the NT* (1993); *Lydia's Impatient Sisters: A Feminist Social History of Early Christianity* (1995). **L. Schottroff, S. Schroer, and M. T. Wacker,** *Feministische Exegese: Forschungserträge zur Bibel aus der Perspektive von Frauen* (1995; ET 1998). **E. Schüssler Fiorenza,** *In Memory of Her: A Feminist Theological Reconstruction of Christian Origins* (1983); *Bread Not Stone: The Challenge of Feminist Biblical Interpretation* (1984); *But She Said: Feminist Practices of Biblical Interpretation* (1992); (ed.), *Searching the Scriptures: A Feminist Commentary* (2 vols. 1993-94). **T. K. Seim,** *The Double Message: Patterns of Gender in Luke-Acts* (Studies of the NT and Its World, 1994). **M. J. Selvidge,** *Notorious Voices: Feminist Biblical Interpretation, 1550-1920* (1996). **A. Smith,** *An Autobiography: The Story of the Lord's Dealings with Mrs. A. Smith, the Colored Evangelist* (1893, 1988). **E. Stagg and F. Stagg,** *Woman in the World of Jesus* (1978). **L. A. Starr,** *The Bible Status of Women* (1926). **E. C. Stanton,** *The Woman's Bible* (2 vols. 1895-98). **K. Stendahl,** *The Bible and the Role of Women: A Case Study in Hermeneutics* (FBBS 15, 1966). **C. de Swarte Gifford,** "American Women and the Bible: The Nature of Woman as a Hermeneutical Issue," *Feminist Perspectives on Biblical Scholarship* (ed. A. Y. Collins, BSNA 10, 1985) 11-33. **L. J. Swidler,** "Jesus Was a Feminist," *SEAJT* 13 (1971) 102-10; *Biblical Affirmations of Woman* (1979). **E. M. Tetlow,** *Women and Ministry in the NT* (1980). **S. B. Thistlethwaite,** "Every Two Minutes: Battered Women and Feminist Interpretation" *Feminist Interpretation of the Bible* (ed. L. M. Russell, 1985). **M. A. Tolbert** (ed.), *The Bible and Feminist Hermeneutics* (*Semeia* 28, 1983). **E. M. Townes** (ed.), *Embracing the Spirit: Womanist Perspectives on Hope, Salvation, and Transformation* (1997). **P. Trible,** *God and the Rhetoric of Sexuality* (OBT, 1978); *Texts of Terror: Literary-Feminist Readings of Biblical Narratives* (OBT, 1984). **R. A. Tucker and W. L. Liefeld,** *Daughters of the Church: Women and Ministry from NT Times to the Present* (1987). **K. von Kellenbach,** *Anti-Judaism in Feminist Religious Writings* (AAR Cultural Criticism Series 1, 1994). **A. Walker,** *In Search of Our Mothers' Gardens: Womanist Prose* (1983). **R. J. Weems,** *Just a Sister Away: A Womanist Vision of Women's Relationships in the Bible* (1988); "Reading Her Way Through the Struggle: African American Women and the Bible," *Stony the Road We Trod* (ed. C. H. Felder, 1991) 57-77; *Battered Love: Marriage, Sex, and Violence in the Hebrew Prophets* (OBT, 1995). **J. R. Wegner,** *Chattel or Person: The Status of Women in the Mishnah* (1988). **F. E. Willard,** *Woman in the Pulpit* (1888). **D. S. Williams,** *Sisters in the Wilderness: The Challenges of Womanist God Talk* (1993). **M. T. Winter,** *WomanWord: A Feminist Lectionary and Psalter* (Women of the NT, 1990). **A. C. Wire,** *The Corinthian Women Prophets: A Reconstruction Through Paul's Rhetoric* (1990).

V. C. PHILLIPS

QUEST OF THE HISTORICAL JESUS

Quest of the Historical Jesus

1. *Eighteenth to Twentieth Centuries.* Since A. Schweitzer's[§] survey on this topic (1906), the beginning of the quest has customarily been dated with the posthumous publication of the writings of H. S. Reimarus[§] in the late eighteenth century and has relentlessly been related to methodological concerns.

The posthumous publication in the 1870s of excerpts from Reimarus's private manuscripts initiated the scholarly quest for the historical Jesus, even though some of his ideas were borrowed from earlier English Deists (Deism[§]). He argued that there was a basic discontinuity between Jesus' message and that proclaimed by his disciples after the crucifixion: that Jesus saw himself simply as the announcer of an imminent earthly Jewish kingdom, while the disciples created a new religion centering on the person of Jesus and containing concepts such as the deity, atoning death, and resurrection of Jesus, and the Trinity and sacraments. This transformation of Jesus' message was, according to Reimarus, a deliberate creation by the disciples, who were disillusioned at his death but unwilling to return to the drudgery of their former lives. After two centuries, debate still continues: What was the nature of the kingdom Jesus proclaimed? What was his vision of his own role?

Some questions about the four Gospels—their nature and interrelationships—were clarified during the nineteenth century. Scholars concluded that the Fourth Gospel was late and of less evidential value for the historical Jesus than are the Synoptics (D. F. Strauss 1840[4]; Synoptic Problem[†§]); that the Synoptics were interdependent ("somebody copied"); that Mark was the earliest of the three and was a source for Matthew and Luke (J. Weisse 1838; C. Wilke 1838); that the later two Gospels also used a common written source or sources (Weisse) subsequently called Q; and that Matthew and Luke had also each used independent oral or written traditions. While conservative German scholars contested these conclusions and British scholars played them down (F. Farrar 1874), the conclusions gradually gained wide acceptance. Perhaps equally or more significant was the change in attitude toward the supernatural element in the Gospels. Certainly the eighteenth-century English Deists had rejected this element, but they remained outside the mainstream of Christian scholarship. Yet by the end of the nineteenth century, dominant figures, especially in Germany, wrote lives of Jesus desupernaturalizing the gospel tradition. Even in England, where the supernatural was not explicitly denied and where the substantial historicity of the Gospels was still defended, writers began to place greater stress on the teachings of Jesus than on the supernatural elements in the tradition. Whenever scholars stressed the supernatural element it automatically helped to establish the uniqueness of Jesus. When that dimension was rejected or played down, uniqueness could be affirmed only by an appeal to his unique teachings or attitude. Furthermore, in traditional Christian thought, the "work of Christ" had an objective effect on the devil or evil (*Christus Victor*), on God (*Cur Deus Homo*), on human beings ("the transformation of humanity"), or in all three areas. But in the new developments, attention focused primarily or even exclusively on "the transformation of humanity" no matter what specific terminology was used. Even where the Gospels had been accepted as completely reliable historical documents there had been room for differences in the reconstruction of Jesus' career. But the questions now being raised about the reliability of the Gospels as sources opened the way for far more variations in the handling of these materials.

New techniques, new materials, and new perspectives on the quest emerged in the twentieth century. The earlier source criticism was supplemented by Form Criticism*[§], which sought to classify the Gospel materials according to stereotyped "forms" that had emerged in oral transmission (e.g., apothegms, wisdom sayings, parables, etc.) in order to identify the earliest version of an incident and the "life situation" that led to its being remembered and reshaped. Later, attention shifted from the isolated units of tradition back to the evangelists in Redaction Criticism*§; the attempt to determine the special interests and theologies of the writers, now viewed, not as mere compilers, but as deliberate theologians. It was hoped that these combined techniques would make it possible to trace the tradition backward to, or at least toward, the historical Jesus.

Also, new materials emerged during the nineteenth and twentieth centuries, materials that serve the quest at least indirectly. While the Hebrew Bible Apocrypha had always been known, other intertestamental literature was discovered, especially documents of Jewish apocalyptic (R. Charles 1913; Pseudepigrapha†§). There had been earlier attempts to interpret Jesus' career by using rabbinic literature produced from the second century C.E. onward (e.g., J. Lightfoot 1658-78), but now new attention was given to this field with critical editions and modern translations of rabbinic documents. This resulted in the massive compilation by Strack and P. Billerbeck§ (*Kommentar zum Neuen Testament aus Talmud und Midrasch* 1922-61), which needs to be used with care but is an invaluable collection. The discovery of the Dead Sea Scrolls§ in the 1940s provided background data on a branch of dissident Judaism, while the Nag Hammadi documents provided items that may reflect the Jesus tradition at least partly independent of the canonical Gospels, especially the Coptic Gospel of Thomas.

W. Wrede's§ argument (1901) that the Markan "Messiah secret" was a creation of the early community's interpretation of a nonmessianic Jesus received sharp criticism, but it forced scholars to consider the possibility of a transformation of the Jesus tradition by the post-resurrection community. Such skepticism was further developed by the more radical form critics, for whom the Gospels were primarily deposits of the postresurrection faith through which the authentic Jesus could be glimpsed only uncertainly. H. Riesenfeld (1957) challenged this radical historical skepticism, arguing that a controlled process transmitted the early church tradition about Jesus. Rabbinic literature displays an intense concern for this chain of transmission of rabbinic sayings; since the New Testament contains references to "receiving" and "handing on" a tradition, it reflects the same concern and terminology used by the rabbis (see B. Gerhardson, who worked out this thesis in detail in 1961). Nevertheless, questions remain: Did the rabbinic control system exist prior to 70 C.E.? Were the various Christian communities of the first century structured so that such a control system was possible? Do the contrasts between John and the Synoptics allow the assumption of such an organized control of oral tradition? However, this hypothesis is a reminder that oral tradition is not necessarily free-flowing gossip.

Debate continues concerning the degree of confidence to be placed in the gospel tradition. A central theological issue emerged, though not always expressed explicitly: Is the validity of the Christian faith dependent on the factual character of certain events recorded in the Gospels? If so, which events, and how is their authenticity to be established? If not, then is it the message of Jesus or some attitude attributed to him that has salvific meaning for those who respond? Those who have adopted largely or completely this second stance have followed various paths in their reconstructions of the historical Jesus. A. von Harnack's§ book (1901) is regarded as typical of the liberal "Lives of Jesus," with its stress on Jesus as the teacher about God the loving Father, the infinite value of the human soul, and the higher righteousness of the love commandment. A greater stress on social reform, in which Jesus' language about the kingdom is filled with content from the Hebrew Bible prophets, is found in the social gospel movement of the late nineteenth and early twentieth centuries.

The rediscovery of Jewish apocalyptic (Apocalypticism*§) led to stress on the eschatological element in the teaching attributed to Jesus, especially in the writings of J. Weis§ (1892) and Schweitzer (1901). Since this "consistent eschatology" emphasis understood Jesus to have (mistakenly) announced the imminent end of history and the world, this view was sharply contested by some as incompatible with Jesus' knowledge. But this eschatological emphasis has continued to be influential in differing ways. C. H. Dodd[§] turned "consistent eschatology" into "realized eschatology" with his insistence that the words of Jesus were meant in a different sense; i.e., the kingdom was present in his ministry. On the other hand, the Bultmann[§] school accepted the literal meaning of the eschatological words but then "appropriated" the message in terms of existentialism (R. Bultmann 1926, 1934). Many sought to solve the eschatology problem by urging that Jesus spoke of the kingdom not only as present in his ministry but also in a future, final fulfillment. It must be noted that Bultmann, always the skeptical historian, almost cut the link between the Jesus of history and the Christ of faith (only the "that" of the historical Jesus is decisive, not the "what"). But his students (e.g., G. Bornkamm[§]; 1960) pulled back from this position. A somewhat different rejection of Bultmann's skepticism and existentialism appeared in E. Stauffer's argument (1960), perhaps overconfident, that a reevaluation of Jewish and Hellenistic sources could indirectly substantiate the historicity of events recorded in the Gospels, e.g., the star of the magi.

With the undermining of confidence in the substantial accuracy of materials even in Mark and Q, efforts began to establish criteria of authenticity. Among these was "multiple attestation"—the presence of a given motif in more than one literary form (e.g., parable, controversy story). Also, it was claimed that Aramaisms were evidence of an early stage in the tradition; that personal names tended to be added in the later versions; and that the beginnings and endings of pericopes were more apt to have been modified by the evangelists than the central core. It was hoped that the researcher, by recognizing these tendencies, could work back from later to earlier versions of narratives. Then the Bultmann school advanced the "dissimilarity principle" as a master criterion. This principle meant that material in the tradition "dissimilar" to first-century Judaism and the developing faith of the early church was, in all likelihood, correctly attributable to Jesus himself. Obviously this ruthless approach to the tradition eliminated some material from Jesus since he must on occasion have reflected elements from Judaism, and surely some elements in the church's developing faith must have come from him. So the "coherence principle" was added to the "dissimilarity principle"; that is, once a minimum has been established by the dissimilarity test, the researcher is justified in adding to that minimum certain items that "cohere" with the established minimum (see N. Perrin 1976; and for critiques M. Hooker 1971a, 1971b and D. Mealand 1978). Probably no criterion yet proposed or to be proposed will ever establish complete historical certainty. The decision of each historian is the result of a multitude of factors, some objective, some subjective and even unconscious.

In the late twentieth century the situation was confused and once again in transition. Widely accepted dating of New Testament documents was challenged (e.g., see J. Robinson 1976), and some scholars placed the Fourth Gospel among the early Christian documents, thus reestablishing its historical value for the quest. It has been questioned whether the alleged "tendencies" in the development of the synoptic materials can be objectively established (E. P. Sanders 1963), and this, in turn, created skepticism about the identification of early and late versions of an incident. While a minority of scholars never accepted the priority of Mark or the existence of Q, the work of W. Farmer and his followers has forced a wide reopening of such questions and the reconstructions based on them. The conventional wisdom of Christian scholars about the relation of Jesus to traditional Jewish piety and the "sinners" has been called into question (e.g., Sanders 1985). In some circles of New Testament scholarship, attention has shifted from historical issues to the question of the meaning of language in itself and not as a means of access to some other historical reality (e.g., in Structuralism*[§]; D. Patte 1976).

2. *Alternative Perspectives.* A number of distinctive perspectives have emerged either to challenge or to enrich the dominant thrust of research on the historical Jesus. Some are more

concerned with the meaning of Jesus for contemporary life than with the reconstruction of his career in the first century.

The Christ Myth perspective was first developed academically by B. Bauer[§]. He began with an interest in Strauss's theory that the Fourth Gospel was predominantly mythological (Mythology and Biblical Studies*[§]) but, over the years, came to the conclusion that the entire gospel tradition was a personification of the myths of the Greco-Roman world (i.e., the community created its own founder out of these myths 1877). Late in the nineteenth century, a Dutch school of critics reached a parallel conclusion. The Christ Myth theory achieved its greatest development in the writings of A. Drews[§] and was popularized in English by the writings of such scholars as W. B. Smith. These views were sharply attacked in studies on the historicity of Jesus by M. Goguel[§] and S. J. Case[§].

For a time, some popular Marxist apologetic against Christianity adopted the Christ Myth theory, although this would not have been the view of Marx or Engels. Perhaps the first serious study on Jesus by Marxists was that of K. Kautsky (1908), who reduced Christianity to an expression of social and economic concerns and regarded religious interests as a form of self-expression. His work was also influenced by the Christ Myth theories of Bauer and his successors. European dialogue between Christians and Marxists has led some Marxists to recognize the reality of the historical Jesus and the positive significance of Christianity. M. Machovec (1976), though an atheist, writes about Jesus "with endless passion and enthusiasm" and recognizes Christianity's contribution to the resolution of genuine spiritual problems. (See also the less positive work of V. Gardavsky 1973.)

During the twentieth century, Jewish scholarship made many contributions to research into the career of Jesus. J. Klausner (1922), abreast of current New Testament scholarship, provided the first full-scale study. His extensive knowledge of first-century Judaism and related literature provided him with insights into Jesus' life. While rejecting Christian claims for Jesus and the supernatural element in the Gospels, he sought to reclaim Jesus as part of the great Jewish heritage. In his view, however, the ethic of Jesus was a heroic ethic for the elite, but quite impossible—and even destructive—for a normal society (see also D. Flusser 1969 and G. Vermes 1983). Furthermore, Jewish scholars have produced detailed studies of particular aspects of Jesus' career (P. Winter 1974). While rejecting specifically Christian claims for Jesus, Jewish scholars are often less skeptical about the reliability of the gospel tradition than some Christian scholars.

The Quran of Islam (Quranic and Islamic Interpretation[§]) assigns a significant place to Jesus, who is often called "Son of Mary" (esp. Sura 5). There are references to his virgin birth, his miracles, his function as a prophet and apostle of God, and to his being taken up to heaven by God for a role at the end of history (Sura 4). The crucifixion story is alluded to, but the passage is widely understood to mean that another person replaced Jesus on the cross. Modern Islamic scholars have little interest in the contemporary quest, but they have provided discussions on the doctrine of the Trinity (viewed as tritheism), the question of Jesus' death, and the concepts of atonement and redemption. (For a survey of Islamic thought, see W. Bijlefeld 1982 and articles by the Muslim scholars A. Merad 1968 and M. Ayoub 1980.)

The "conservative perspective" is an imprecise name for scholars who accept, in principle, the techniques of modern historiography but who challenge many of the assumptions, methods, and conclusions of the dominant academic tradition. Generally speaking they affirm that (a) the factual character of certain events recorded in the Gospels is essential for Christian faith, (b) the Gospels provide substantially reliable material about the historical Jesus, and (c) the supernatural element in the Gospels (e.g., the virgin birth and the bodily resurrection of Jesus) is a decisive part of the Christian faith. A 1966 volume edited by C. Henry includes essays from sixteen basically conservative scholars from the United States, Great Britain, Sweden, and Germany dealing with various aspects of the quest. It is, however, difficult to find full-scale lives of Jesus by these or other scholars of similar persuasion, although they have made valuable contributions to scholarship in commentaries and other specialized studies. In general works on the New Testament both B. Metzger[§] and F. F. Bruce[§] have included sections summarizing the career of Jesus as they understand the Gospel record (see also, I. Marshall 1977).

The Liberation Theologies*[§] out of Black theology (Afrocentric Interpretation*[§]), Latin American, and Feminist*[§] theology have one thing in common. From their various perceptions of oppression and discrimination they turn to the biblical tradition, including the Jesus tradition, seeking to discover and highlight those elements that stress God's concern for the oppressed. The quest as an academic pursuit is not a major concern for them, except insofar as its results serve their primary concern. Thus, Black theology is powerfully moved by the escape from slavery in the exodus and the journey to the Promised Land. Although there is very little evidence that Jesus attacked slavery as an institution, his stress on the equality of persons before God and his concern for the poor and the outcasts reinforces this theology. (See the relevant sections on Jesus in J. Roberts 1976 and J. Cone 1970.)

Liberation theologies arose out of the attempt of Christian thinkers to utilize the biblical tradition for the liberation of Latin American societies from the oppression and poverty that have engulfed a great majority of the population. Theologians in these countries are concerned with the meaning of Christ for them in their situation. They recognize that the situation in first-century Palestine was different from that in Latin American nations, where, according to their analysis, the issue is not so much underdevelopment as dependency on the industrialized world, especially the United States. Their extensive discussions of Christology refer, not to issues debated at Nicea or Chalcedon, but rather to the "practice" of Jesus in opposition to the dominant religious and political structures of his day. (C. Bussman 1985; H. Echegaray 1983; and J. Segundo 1985.)

Feminist theology is in a position different from that of Black or liberation theology. The latter two appeal directly to major biblical motifs, whereas the situation of feminist theologians is complicated by the Bible's general acceptance of patriarchal structures in which women were subordinate. This acceptance is also explicit in some New Testament passages. Feminists can appeal to the biblical protest against oppression, but in the Bible there is little if any recognition that women are among the oppressed. Fortunately there are elements in the Jesus tradition and elsewhere that assume a more equal status for women. Feminists can and do appeal to those items as well as arguing from the general proclamation of God's concern for the oppressed. E. Schüssler Fiorenza has sought "to employ a critical feminist hermeneutics in order to explore the theoretical frameworks of various discourses about Jesus the Christ." (Also C. Newsom and S. Ringe 1992.)

3. *The Current Scene.* The last decades of the twentieth century and the beginning of the twenty-first have witnessed a renewal of attempts to revive the search for a historical Jesus, a development now frequently referred to as the "Third Quest." Among them is J. Meier's work *A Marginal Jew: Rethinking the Historical Jesus*, a "consensus" reconstruction (3 vols. 1991, 1994, 2001). Even though a somewhat greater importance is attached to the Johannine[†§] material, Meier's historical Jesus is, in the end, derived primarily from the Synoptics, again keeping him well within conventional procedures of source selection. All the Gospels are interpreted primarily against the background of biblical and intertestamental Jewish materials, while less attention is given to contemporary Greco-Roman and Hellenistic materials. "Consensus" applies also to Meier's methodology. He has incorporated standard form- and source-critical methods for determining a text's authenticity and from those seasoned disciplines has systematically assembled and articulated his own uniquely defined list of criteria for judging a text's historical viability (1991, 167-84). Finally, with respect to methodology, Meier focuses on the

individual units of the early tradition, with less attention given to the narrative framework within which they have been placed. The results in the first volume are, then, a carefully documented life of Jesus, one that is systematically reasoned and even includes a full chapter exploring a probable chronological framework (Chronology, New Testament[§]) into which all this might be placed. The second volume follows with an extensive section on Jesus and John the Baptist and a reconstruction of Jesus' kingdom message defined in modified Jewish eschatological terms, and concludes with a detailed discussion of miracles, which for Meier are linked closely to Jesus' kingdom pronouncements. In his third volume, Meier analyzes Jesus' relationships with his disciples and other assorted followers and with his "competitors"—the Sadducees, Pharisees, Essenes, Samaritans, and others.

J. D. Crossan, arguably the most distinguished scholar within the widely publicized "Jesus Seminar" (see below), has produced a radically different portrait of Jesus (1991, 1994). The Gospel materials that Crossan declares "historical" often coincide with those used by earlier critics (see his inventory of the authentic sayings listed in xiii-xxvi), but his understanding of those texts is based consistently on a sociopolitical reading of the Gospel texts, one that in effect "de-eschatologizes" Jesus' historic proclamation. In Crossan's view, Jesus did not envision an eschatological upheaval like that embraced and anticipated in Jewish eschatological texts (cf. Meier, above); rather, as a "Mediterranean Jewish peasant," Jesus called for the emergence of a radically egalitarian society that would undo the prevailing inequalities sustained by Judaism's strict purity laws and by contemporary Greco-Roman hierarchical, patriarchal, social, and political structures (1991, xii). While many will question Crossan's dramatic departure from the more "traditional" eschatological and apocalyptic portraits of Jesus (e.g., cf. Meier 1991), his very carefully detailed study marks a hermeneutical reversal within historical Jesus studies that is no less revolutionary than Schweitzer's rejection of nineteenth-century social, political, and ethical versions of Jesus.

Much more popularly written are M. Borg's noneschatological reconstructions of the historical Jesus (1987, 1994). Borg, also associated with the Jesus Seminar, insists that any portrait depicting Jesus as a prophet of the imminent end time would necessarily render Jesus' eschatological affirmation a mistake and, by extension, unimportant or irrelevant both historically and theologically. Borg understands the historical Jesus as a Spirit-filled sage or prophet whose sayings and parables clashed radically with the conventional wisdom of the day and who announced, in ancient prophetic (not apocalyptic) style, an imminent, God-ordained upheaval. Jesus' mission within this situation was to institute a "revitalization movement," replacing the "politics of holiness" (represented in Pharisaic and temple piety) with a "politics of compassion," now graciously offered to those who traditionally had been neglected within the structures of conventional wisdom (outcasts, sinners, poor, women). Hence the future would be marked, not by history's apocalyptic end, but by God's new presence, transforming existing historical, political, social, and religious structures of the time.

In one way or another, Meier, Crossan, and Borg's views are all a part of a continuing and highly controversial search for a historical, "pre-Easter" Jesus. This task implies a larger question of the theological meaning derived from any viable encounter with that historical Jesus. L. T. Johnson, raising that question in his critique of the Jesus Seminar (1996), contends that the "real" Jesus is not derived simply by reconstructing the historical pieces of pre-Easter Jesus tradition in the New Testament, whether within or outside the New Testament Gospels. The Jesus of Christian faith was first and always proclaimed within a framework of ultimacy that did not emerge simply from such historical units, however carefully reasoned and assembled, but from the total story that emerged out of resurrection faith. Even if the historical units of that resurrection could be historically reconstructed, they could not of themselves yield the Christian theological affirmation that Jesus is Lord; that this resurrected Christ has been taken up into the very being of God. Certainly this issue cannot easily or quickly be resolved in this particular context, yet it does seem worth noting that any continuing discussion of the "real" Jesus, on whatever historical terms, must address the important relationship between the historical quest and its meaning for New Testament faith.

Perhaps the most challenging development of the late twentieth century in the search for the historical Jesus began in 1985 with the organization of the so-called Jesus Seminar under the leadership of R. Funk. Planned as a long-term, ongoing, collective research project, it has met biennially annually and has encouraged other New Testament scholars with standard research credentials to apply for membership as fellows. The initial phase, now largely completed, centered on the question: What did Jesus really say? A second phase asked: What did Jesus really do? The seminar first gathered and analyzed some 1,500 versions of 500 sayings attributed to Jesus from the traditional four Gospels and other sources from the first three hundred years of Christian history. The seminar also developed a new translation of these materials, called the Scholars Version, which attempted to avoid overly traditional and familiar language. The fellows then discussed the various forms in which these collected sayings occurred, indicating their judgments on historicity and nonhistoricity by voting with colored beads—red, pink, gray, or black. Red or black indicated firm votes for or against authenticity, while pink or gray expressed more hesitant judgments. The colors were converted into numbers (red=3; pink=2; gray=1; black=0), which were converted into decimals, added, then divided by the number of votes cast. Then the individual sayings were printed in the color indicated by the collective vote.

This led to the publication in 1993 of *The Five Gospels: The Search for the Authentic Words of Jesus*. After introductory material describing the whys and hows of the project, the four Gospels are quoted in full in the order Mark, Matthew, Luke, John, along with Thomas; obviously using the Scholars Version. The sayings of Jesus are printed in the color indicated by the collective vote of the fellows participating. Also, each saying or group of sayings is followed by a summary of the discussion that led to the vote on color, which is helpful in revealing the mind and thinking of the seminar fellows.

The image of Jesus that emerges has generated controversy. The Jesus of the seminar did not make or imply messianic claims, nor did he anticipate a divine culmination to history. *The Five Gospels* states that 82 percent of the words ascribed to Jesus in the Gospels were not actually spoken by him. Here, it is possible only to suggest areas of the debate that will continue. Does the Coptic *Gospel of Thomas* deserve to be ranked with the four traditional Gospels? It is known in its full form only through the fourth-century Nag Hammadi manuscript (although three fragments dated c. 200 C.E. appeared in the Oxyrhynchus materials). Although the seminar recognizes that the present text of Thomas is liberally gnosticized (Gnostic Interpretation[§]), it suggests that the original version—without these gnostic motifs—probably originated about the same time as the Q document (about 50-60 C.E.). How big a leap is this? (But see J. Kloppenborg 1990 and S. Patterson 1993 for studies that may explain the seminar's decision.) Again, Paul clearly took for granted a messianic Jesus, and his message anticipated a divine denouement to human history. Presumably he never saw or heard the historical Jesus, but he was in touch with various early Christian groups in the 30 to 60 C.E. period. Is there any evidence that he and they differed on these assumptions? Another point may be easily clarified by the fellows of the seminar. It reports that some two hundred accredited scholars participated in their program, but only seventy-four are listed by name and academic pedigree in *The Five Gospels*. Do the statistics resulting in the color-coding represent the votes of two hundred scholars, just those listed, or some combination?

A similar procedure was followed to ascertain the actual deeds of Jesus (Funk, et al 1998) with similar controversial results. They concluded that Jesus performed no miracles, was crucified as a public nuisance, and did not rise from the dead. Questions about the Jesus Seminar's methodology, similar to the questions above, have also been raised about their evaluation of Jesus' actual historical actions and ministry.

4. *Concluding Comment.* It is unlikely that the foreseeable future will bring consensus on the historical Jesus. The careful reader will recognize that even the most magisterial reconstruction of Jesus' career is built on the basis of incomplete and perhaps conflicting evidence. Each decision is made plausible by the magister's skill, but each decision still has alternative possibilities.

The Third Quest for the historical Jesus shows no signs of abating; the flood of publications continues. Whereas Crossan and other members of the Jesus Seminar have constructed a fundamentally noneschatological Jesus, D. Allison (1998) and B. Ehrman (1999) reconstruct Jesus' life and ministry as that of a Jewish apocalyptic prophet. Several scholars are trying to delineate the usefulness of the Johannine tradition for studying and reconstructing the historical Jesus (R. Fortna and T. Thatcher 2001). The members of the Jesus Seminar continue their work (R. Funk, et al 2000; R. Hoover 2002). "Traditional" reconstructions of Jesus, from a self-confessed faith perspective, include L. E. Keck (2000) and N. T. Wright (1992-2003). Perhaps the most radical reconstruction of the historical Jesus, apart from outright denial of Jesus' existence, is G. Lüdemann (2000). Some scholars are now making a concerted effort to correlate historical Jesus research with Palestinian archaeology (Reed 2000, Crossan and Reed 2001). Essay collections and published conference proceedings indicate debated methodological issues, new approaches, and continued research into established lines of inquiry (J. H. Charlesworth and W. P. Weaver 2000; U. H. J. Körtner 2002 [notable for its interaction with Bultmann's *Jesus*]; M. Labahn and A. Schmidt 2001; J. Schröter and R. Brucker 2002; A. Merz 2003). Detailed methodological discussions include B. Chilton and C. A. Evans (1999) and G. Theissen and D. Winter (1997). G. Thiessen and A. Merz (1998) give a comprehensive introductory overview of historical Jesus study. One recent remarkable development, in light of scholarly trends after Schweizer's demolition of the First Quest's psychologizing tendencies, is psychologically reconstructing Jesus' personality in light of modern psychological theory and current knowledge of ancient personality characteristics (Capps 2000; Miller 1997; van Aarde 2001). Van Voorst discusses ancient nonbiblical evidence about Jesus (2000).

There is perhaps only one conclusion that all Jesus researchers reach consensus on: This is an exciting time to do historical Jesus research.

Bibliography:

For surveys and bibliographies see R. Brown (1977, 1994), Grant, Kissinger, Pals, Schweitzer, Thompson, and Witherington (1990, 1994, 1995).

D. Allison, *Jesus of Nazareth: Millenarian Prophet* (1998). **Anselm,** *Why God Became Man* (1868). **Augustine,** *Harmony of the Gospels* (vol. 6 of NPNF, 1956). **M. Ayoub,** "The Death of Jesus, Reality or Delusion," *Muslim World* 70 (1980) 91-121. **B. Bauer,** *Christus und die Caesaren* (2 vols. 1877). **W. A. Bijlefeld,** "Some Muslim Contributions to the Christological Discussion," *Christological Perspectives: Essays in Honor of H. K. McArthur* (ed. R. E. Berkey and S. A. Edwards, 1982) 200-215. **M. J. Borg,** *Jesus, a New Vision: Spirit, Culture, and the Life of Discipleship* (1987); *Jesus in Contemporary Scholarship* (1994); *Meeting Jesus Again for the First Time* (1994). **G. Bornkamm,** *Jesus of Nazareth* (1960). **C. Brown,** *Jesus in European Protestant Thought, 1785-1860* (Studies in Historical Theology 1, 1985). **R. E. Brown,** *The Birth of the Messiah* (2 vols. 1977). *The Death of the Messiah* (ABRL, 2 vols. 1994). **F. F. Bruce,** *NT History* (1971) 163-204. **R. Bultmann,** *History of the Synoptic Tradition* (1921; ET 1963); *Jesus and the Word* (1926; ET 1934). **C. Bussman,** *Who Do You Say? Jesus Christ in Latin American Theology* (1985). **J. Calvin,** *Commentary on a Harmony of the*

Evangelists (1956-57). **D. Capps,** *Jesus: A Psychological Biography* (2000). **S. J. Case,** *Historicity of Jesus* (1912). **M. Casey,** *From Jewish Prophet to Gentile God* (1991). **R. H. Charles,** *The Apocrypha and Pseudepigrapha of the OT in English* (2 vols. 1913). **J. H. Charlesworth and W. P. Weaver,** *Jesus Two Thousand Years Later* (Faith and Scholarship Colloquies, 2000). **B. Chilton and C. A. Evans,** *Authenticating the Activities of Jesus* (NTTS 28.2, 1999). **A. Y. Collins,** *Feminist Perspectives on Biblical Scholarship* (BSNA, 1985). **J. H. Cone,** *A Black Theology of Liberation* (C. E. Lincoln Series in Black Religion, 1970) 197-227. **J. D. Crossan,** *The Historical Jesus: The Life of a Mediterranean Jewish Peasant* (1991); *Jesus: A Revolutionary Biography* (1994). **J. D. Crossan and J. L. Reed,** *Excavating Jesus: Beneath the Stones, Behind the Texts* (2001). **C. H. Dodd,** *The Parables of the Kingdom* (1935, rev. ed. 1961). **A. Drews,** *Die Christus Mythe* (1909-11). **H. Echegaray,** *The Practice of Jesus* (1983). **B. D. Ehrman,** *Jesus: Apocalyptic Prophet of the New Millennium* (1999). **W. R. Farmer,** *The Synoptic Problem: A Critical Analysis* (1964). **F. W. Farrar,** *The Life of Christ* (2 vols. 1874). **D. Flusser,** *Jesus* (ET 1969). **R. Fortna and T. Thatcher** (eds.), *Jesus in Johannine Tradition* (2001). **R. W. Funk and R. W. Hoover** (eds.), *The Five Gospels: The Search for the Authentic Words of Jesus* (1993); *Jesus as Precursor* (rev. ed. 1993). **Robert W. Funk,** et al, eds., *The Acts of Jesus: The Search for the Authentic Deeds of Jesus* (1998). **R. W. Funk,** et al., *The Once and Future Jesus/The Jesus Seminar* (2000). **R. W. Hoover** (ed.), *Profiles of Jesus* (2002). **V. Gardavsky,** *God Is Not Yet Dead* (1913). **B. Gerhardson,** *Memory and Manuscript: Oral Tradition and Written Transmission in Rabbinic Judaism and Early Christianity* (ASNU 22, 1961). **M. Goguel,** *Jesus the Nazarene: Myth or History?* (1933). **R. M. Grant,** *The Earliest Lives of Jesus* (1961). **A. von Harnack,** *What Is Christianity?* (1901). **A. F. Harvey,** *Jesus and the Constraints of History* (1980, Bampton Lectures, 1982). **C. F. H. Henry** (ed.), *Jesus of Nazareth, Saviour and Lord* (Contemporary Evangelical Thought, 1966). **J. H. Hill,** *The Earliest Life of Christ* (1910[2]). **M. Hooker,** "Christology and Methodology," *NTS* 17 (1971*a*) 480-87; "On Using the Wrong Tool," *Theology* 75 (1971*b*) 570-81. **Irenaeus,** *Against the Heresies* (ACW 55, 1992). **J. Jeremias,** *The Parables of Jesus* (1947, rev. ed. 1963). **L. T. Johnson,** *The Real Jesus: The Misguided Quest for the Historical* (1996). **K. Kautsky,** *Foundations of Christianity: A Study in Christian Origins* (1908; ET 1925). **L. E. Keck.** *Who is Jesus? History in Perfect Tense* (Studies on personalities of the New Testament, 2000). **W. S. Kissinger,** *The Lives of Jesus: A History and Bibliography* (GRLH 452, 1985). **J. Klausner,** *Jesus of Nazareth: His Life, Times, and Teaching* (1926). **J. S. Kloppenborg** et al., *The Formation of Q: Trajectories in Ancient Wisdom Collections* (SAC, 1987); *Q-Thomas Reader: The Gospel Before the Gospels* (1990). **U. H. J. Körtner.** *Jesus im 21. Jahrhundert : Bultmanns Jesusbuch und die heutige Jesusforschung* (2002). **M. Labahn and A. Schmidt** (eds.), *Jesus, Mark and Q: The Teaching of Jesus and Its Earliest Records* (JSNTSup 214, 2001). **J. Lightfoot,** *Horae Hebraicae et Talmudicae* (4 vols. 1658-78; ET 1979). **G. Lüdemann,** *Jesus After 2000 Years: What He Really Said and Did* (with contributions by Frank Schleritt and Martina Janssen, 2000; ET 2000). **H. K. McArthur,** *The Quest Through the Centuries: The Search for the Historical Jesus* (1966). **M. Machovac,** *A Marxist Looks at Jesus* (1976). **I. H. Marshall,** *I Believe in the Historical Jesus* (1977). **D. L. Mealand,** "The Dissimilarity Test," *SJT* 31 (1978) 41-50. **J. P. Meier,** *A Marginal Jew,* vol. 1, *Rethinking the Historical Jesus* (ABRL, 1991), vol. 2, *Mentor, Message, Miracle* (ABRL, 1994). **A. Merad,** "Le Christ Selon le Coran" *Revue de l'occident Musulman et da la mediterraneé* 5 (1968) 79-94. **A. Merz,** ed., *Jesus als historische Gestalt: Beiträge zur Jesusforschung : Zum 60. Geburtstag von Gerd Theissen* (FRLANT 202, 2003). **B. Metzger,** *The NT: Its Background, Growth and Content* (2003[3]) 89-194. **B. F. Meyer,** *The Aims of Jesus* (1979). **J. W. Miller,** *Jesus At Thirty: A Psychological And Historical Portrait* (1997). **C. A. Newsom and S. H. Ringe,** *The Women's Bible Commentary* (1992, exp. ed. 1998). **Origen,** *Commentary on John* (vol 9. *ANF,* 1912-27). **D. L. Pals,** *The Victorian "Lives"* *of Jesus* (1982). **D. Patte,** *What Is Structural Exegesis?* (GBS, 1976). **S. J. Patterson,** *The Gospel of Thomas and Jesus* (FF Reference Series, 1993). **N. Perrin,** *Rediscovering the Teaching of Jesus* (1976). **C. Peters,** *Das "Diatessaron" Tatians* (1939). **M. A. Powell,** *Jesus as a Figure in History: How Modern Historians View the Man from Galilee* (1998). **J. L. Reed,** *Archaeology and the Galilean Jesus: A Re-Examination of the Evidence* (2000). **H. S. Reimarus,** *Fragments* (ed. C. H. Talbert, 1970). **H. Riesenfeld,** *The Gospel Tradition and Its Beginnings: A Study in the Limits of "Formgeschichte"* (1957). **J. D. Roberts,** *A Black Political Theology* (1976) 117-38. **J. A. T. Robinson,** *Redating the NT* (1976). **J. M. Robinson** (ed.), *The Nag Hammadi Library* (1977, 1988²). **E. P. Sanders,** *The Tendencies of the Synoptic Tradition* (SNTMS 9, 1963); *Jesus and Judaism* (1985); *The Historical Figure of Jesus* (1993). **J. Schröter and R. Brucker** (eds.), *Der historische Jesus: Tendenzen und Perspektiven der gegenwärtigen Forschungen* (BZNW 114, 2002). **E. Schüssler Fiorenza,** *In Memory of Her* (1983) 105-59; *Jesus: Miriam's Child, Sophia's Prophet* (1994). **A. Schweitzer,** *The Quest of the Historical Jesus: A Critical Study of Its Progress from Reimarus to Wrede* (1906; ET 2001). **J. L. Segundo,** *The Historical Jesus of the Synoptics* (1985). **B. Smalley,** *The Study of the Bible in the Middle Ages* (1941, 1983³). **M. Smith,** *Jesus the Magician* (1976). **W. B. Smith,** *Ecce Deus: Studies of Primitive Christianity* (1913). **E. Stauffer,** *Jesus and His Story* (1960). **D. F. Strauss,** *Das Leben Jesu* (2 vol. 1840⁴; ET P. Hodgson, *The Life of Jesus* [1972-73]). **G. Theissen,** *The Gospels in Context: Social and Political History in the Synoptic Tradition* (1991). **G. Theissen and A. Merz** , *The Historical Jesus: A Comprehensive Guide* (1996; ET 1998). **G. Theissen and D. Winter,** *The Quest for the Plausible Jesus: The Question of Criteria* (1997; ET 2002) **W. M. Thompson,** *The Jesus Debate: A Survey and Synthesis* (1985). **A. van Aarde,** *Fatherless in Galilee: Jesus as Child of God* (2001). **R. E. Van Voorst,** *Jesus Outside the New Testament: An Introduction to the Ancient Evidence* (2000). **G. Vermes,** *Jesus the Jew: A Historian's Reading of the Gospel* (1983²). **J. Weiss,** *Jesus' Proclamation of the Kingdom* (1892; ET 1971). **J. H. Weisse,** *Die evangelische Geschichte kritisch und philosophisch bearbeitet* (1838). **C. G. Wilke,** *Der Urevangelist* (1838). **P. Winter,** *On the Trial of Jesus* (SJ, Forschungen zur Wissenschaft des Judentums, rev. ed. 1974²). **B. Witherington,** *The Christology of Jesus* (1990); *Jesus the Sage: The Pilgrimage of Wisdom* (1994); *The Jesus Quest* (1995). **W. Wrede,** *The Messianic Secret* (1901; ET 1971). **N. T. Wright,** *Who Was Jesus?* (1992); *Christian Origins and the Question of God* (3 vols. 1992-2003)

H. K. McArthur and R. F. Berkey

PSYCHOLOGICAL APPROACHES

Psychoanalytic Interpretation

S. Freud[§] once acknowledged that most of his discoveries about the unconscious mind had been anticipated by the poets of the past. Thus it should not be surprising that Psychology*[§] has been used in an effort to explain the origins, character, and effects of literature.

What makes a reading of a literary work "psychoanalytic"? To call a reading "psychoanalytic" or "Freudian" immediately introduces ambiguity because such an expression can refer to the use either of Freudian themes or of Freudian methods—that is, an interpretation of a literary work can be called "Freudian" or "psychoanalytic" with respect either to the substance of the text (what it reads) or to the interpretive procedures and techniques a reader uses (how it reads). Generally speaking, there are three points at which psychoanalysis can enter the study of a literary work: (1) examining the mind of the author, (2) examining the minds of the author's characters, or (3) examining the minds of the readers. There is a long tradition of Freudian criticism that examines the text for buried motives and hidden neurotic conflicts that generated the writer's art: In writing Hamlet, for example, it is claimed that Shakespeare was working through the death of his son (E. Jones 1949), or that, in writing *The Gambler,* Dostoevski was drawing on the prohibitions placed upon masturbation in his childhood (S. Freud 1928b). Because the hazards of examining an author's mind are inversely proportional to the amount of material available on the writer's life and private thoughts, it is never completely safe to guess at the psychoanalytic significance of a work of art, even that of a candid living author. For some major writers (like Chaucer, Shakespeare, and the biblical writers) we have only the most minimal sense (and often, none at all) of what their private lives may have been. Thus this form of psychoanalytic Literary*[§] criticism is generally viewed as speculative.

Most of Freud's own ventures into literature involved the analyses of literary characters. His initial remarks on the Oedipus complex were literary, involving both Hamlet and Oedipus. Hamlet, according to Freud, is "the hysteric" who delays action because he is paralyzed by guilt over Claudius's enactment of his own unconscious desires (1916-17, 335). A stream of essays by other analysts followed, mostly on other figures in fiction. They wrote what might be described as case studies of literature, works dealing with characters they categorized as neurotic. Most of these analysts emphasized Freudian themes like the Oedipus complex, anality, schizoid tendencies, latent or expressed homosexuality, guilt, etc. and the roles they played in literary characterizations.

Psychoanalytic fictional character analysis has not fallen into as deep a disrepute as concentration on the writer, in great part because fictional characters are viewed as representatives of life and as such can be understood only if we assume that they are "telling a truth." This assumption allows readers to find unconscious motivations, albeit in literary characters. For example, Abraham's actions and language reveal a great deal about him despite the fact that all we will ever know is contained in the 1,534 verses of Genesis.

On the other hand, literary characters are both more and less than human. This presents a problem. While one aspect of narrative characterization is to provide a mimetic function (to represent human action and motivation), another aspect is primarily textual (to reveal information to a reader or to conceal it). This situation has no precise parallel in life (although it can be argued that people often resemble literary characters in the masks they present to the world). As a result, examining a narrative character is not risk free either. For instance, contradictions in Abraham's character may result from the psychic complexities the biblical writer imagined or from the fact that Abraham is an agent in a literary narrative that has a highly developed system of conventions. His traits may be more a function of the requirements of the story line than of his personality.

Since authors may not provide much material for the theorists and since characters are not people, many scholars have shifted their focus from the interpretation of meanings embedded within a text to the processes of writing and reading. Rather than attempting to determine objective meanings hidden within a text (meanings a reader needs to extricate), these scholars concentrate on the subjective experience of the reader (interactions between reader/text/author) and the values and premises with which a reader approaches interpretation of a text (Reader-response Criticism*§). As within psychoanalysis, their foci are problems of indeterminacy, uncertainty, perspective, Hermeneutics*§, and subjective (and communal) assumptions and agreements.

Until the twentieth century, reading the Bible was thought to be a rather straightforward procedure. The goal was to respond "properly" by trying to understand the text and grasp the meaning. This changed once literary theory in general and psychoanalytic literary theory in particular gained acceptance within biblical studies.

Of course, psychoanalytic literary theory is no more a conceptually unified critical position among biblical scholars than among other literary theorists. The term is associated with those who examine the writer (D. Halperin 1993), the biblical characters (D. Clines 1990; Y. Feldman 1994; I. Rashkow 1993; D. Zeligs 1988), or the reader (Clines et al.). Further, the approaches are neither monolithic nor mutually exclusive. But biblical exegetes who use psychoanalytic literary theory seem to agree that meaning does not inhere completely and exclusively in the text and that the "effects" of reading Scripture, psychological and otherwise, are essential to its meaning. Ultimately, this type of literary criticism yields a way of looking at biblical narratives and readers that reorganizes both their interrelationships and the distinctions between them. As a result, recognizing the relationship of a reader to a text leads to a more profound awareness that no one biblical interpretation is intrinsically "true." The meaning of biblical narratives does not wait to be uncovered but evolves, actualized by readers (and interpreters).

The primary objection to psychoanalytic literary theory by biblical scholars and others seems to be among feminists (Feminist Interpretation*§), who critique the Freudian idea of penis envy. (For a number of different perspectives on the current state of the debate between feminists and various kinds of psychoanalysis see E. Wright 1992.) M. Torok (1964), for example, argues that a common phallic phase does not characterize the infantile development of both sexes; therefore, penis envy is not based on biological fact but is a misconception. Similarly, many feminist theorists read J. Lacan (who shifted from Freud's biological penis to the phallus as signifier) as more productive for feminist thinking. In addition, a number of French feminists have reevaluated the experience of the female body. In general, a major question for dissenting scholars is how to read various texts of psychoanalyses—simply "take the best and leave the rest" or "argue back" (J. Still and M. Worton 1993).

Clines has observed that "what has happened . . . in the last three decades can be represented . . . as a shift in focus that has moved from author to text to reader" (1990, 9-10); and E. McKnight notes that readers "use the Bible today . . . in terms of their values, attitudes, and responses" (1988, 14-15). Thus, whether wittingly or otherwise, more biblical scholars seem to be using some form of psychoanalytic literary theory in their reading, dissenters notwithstanding.

Recent psychoanalytic analyses of biblical texts include Jungian approaches (Brown 1998, Edinger 1999), an analysis of Genesis 1-11 (D. Dumas 2001), a study of Jesus' parables and capitalism (Kassel 2001), a collection of studies using varied psychoanalytic perspectives and methodologies (including Kleinian theory and the Oedipus complex; Kessler and Vandermeersch 2001), and an evaluation of Jesus' self-understanding in light of his fatherlessness (van Aarde 2001). Rollins (1999) and Kille (2001) provide introductory overviews of psychological interpretation of the Bible.

Bibliography: S. Brown, *Text and Psyche: Experiencing Scripture Today* (1998). **D. J. A. Clines,** *What Does Eve Do to Help? And Other Readerly Questions to the OT* (JSOTSup 94, 1990). D. Dumas, *La bible et ses fantômes* (Psychologie, 2001). **M. Eigen,** "The Fire That Never Goes Out," *Psychoanalytic Review* 79 (1992) 271-87. **E. F. Edinger,** *Archetype of the Apocalypse: A Jungian Study of the Book of Revelation* (ed. G. R. Elder, 1999). **Y. S. Feldman,** "And Rebecca Loved Jacob: But Freud Did Not," *Freud and Forbidden Knowledge* (1994) 7-25. **S. Freud,** *The Standard Works of S. Freud,* vol. 9, *Creative Writers and Day-Dreaming* (ed. and tr. J. Strachey, 1908e) 143-56; vols. 15 and 16, *Introductory Lectures on Psycho-Analysis* (ed. and tr. J. Strachey, 1916-17) 15:15-239, 16:243-463; vol. 21, *Dostoevsky and Patricide* (ed. and tr. J. Strachey, 1928b) 177-94. **S. R. Garrett,** "The 'Weaker Sex' in the Testament of Job," *JBL* 112 (1993) 55-70. **H. Haas,** *How to Psychoanalyze the Bible* (1939). **D. Halperin,** *Seeking Ezekiel: Text and Psychology* (1993). **U. Haselstein,** "Poets and Prophets: The Hebrew and the Hellene in Freud's Cultural Theory," *German Life and Letters* 45 (1992) 50-65. **N. Holland,** *Five Readers Reading* (1975). **E. Jones,** *Hamlet and Oedipus* (1949). **M. Kassel,** *Das Evangelium-eine Talenteschmiede?: tiefenpsychologische Revision eines verinnerlichten christlichen Kapitalismus* (Forum Theologie und Psychologie 1, 2001). **R. Kessler and P. Vandermeersch** (eds.), *God, Biblical Stories and Psychoanalytic Understanding* (2001). **D. A. Kille,** *Psychological Biblical Criticism* (GBS, 2001). **E. V. McKnight,** *Postmodern Use of the Bible: The Emergence of Reader-oriented Criticism* (1988). **S. D. Moore,** " 'Mirror, Mirror . . .': A Psychoanalytic Approach to Textual Determinacy Within Biblical Readings. Lacanian Reflections on E. S. Malbon's 'Text and Context: Interpreting the Disciples in Mark,' " *Semeia* 62 (1993) 165-83. **M. Ostow,** "S. and J. Freud and the Philippson Bible," *International Review of Psychoanalysis* 16 (1989) 483-92. **P. R. Raabe,** "Deliberate Ambiguity in the Psalter," *JBL* 110 (1991) 213-27. **I. N. Rashkow,** *The Phallacy of Genesis: A Feminist-Psychoanalytic Approach* (1993); *Taboo or Not Taboo: Sexuality and Family in the Hebrew Bible* (2000). W. G. Rollins, *Soul and Psyche: The Bible in Psychological Perspective* (1999). **J. R. Sauve,** "Joshua: A Story of Individuation," *Journal of Religion and Health* 31 (Winter 1992) 265-71. **J. Still and M. Worton** (eds.), *Textuality and Sexuality: Reading Theories and Practices* (1993). **W. R. Tate,** *Reading Mark from the Outside: Eco and Iser Leave Their Mark* (1995). **M. Torok,** " 'L'envie du Pénis' Sous la Femme," *La Sexualit' é Féminine: Nouvelle Recherche Psychanalyse* (1964). A. van Aarde, *Fatherless in Galilee: Jesus as Child of God* (2001). **R. E. Watts,** "Biblical Agape as a Model of Social Interest," *Individual Psychology: Journal of Adlerian Theory, Research, and Practice* 48 (1992) 35-40. **F. Wittels,** "Psychoanalysis and History: The Nibelungs and the Bible," *Psychoanalytic Quarterly* 15 (1946) 88-103. **W. Wolff,** *Changing Concepts of the Bible: A Psychological Analysis of Its Words, Symbols, Beliefs* (1951). **E. Wright** (ed.), *Feminism and Psychoanalysis: A Critical Dictionary* (1992). **D. F. Zeligs,** *Psychoanalysis and the Bible: A Study in Depth of Seven Leaders* (1988).

I. N. RASHKOW

PSYCHOLOGICAL APPROACHES

Psychology and Biblical Studies

The history of the application of psychological inquiry and insight to the Bible and to biblical studies unfolds in four phases: (1) the early church to 1700, (2) 1700 to 1915, (3) 1900 to 1970, and (4) 1970 to the present.

1. *The Early Church to 1700: The Study of the Psyche as a Branch of Biblical Anthropology and Christian Apologetics.* Franz Delitzsch[§] opened the second edition of his classic study *A System of Biblical Psychology* (1861 [ET 1867]) with the statement "Biblical Psychology is no science of yesterday. It is one of the oldest sciences of the church." He was correct in observing that the nature and destiny of the human psyche (soul), as delineated in scriptural tradition, constitute a continuing area of theological inquiry within Christian theology from the early church to the nineteenth century, even though it was not labeled as *psichologia* until 1530 (P. Melanchthon), and was informed as much, if not more, by the Greek philosophical schools than by the Bible up to the time of the Reformation.

Before the Reformation, the study of the psyche was marked by a twofold interest: (a) the need to elaborate a doctrine of the origin, life, purpose, and destiny of the self as a construct of soul (*psychE*), spirit (*pneuma*), and body (*soma*) expressive of the Christian revelation set forth in Scripture and elaborated in tradition; and (b) the need to relate this doctrine to the prevailing Platonic, Aristotelian, and Stoic "psychologies."

With the advent of the Protestant Reformation in the sixteenth century, subscription to the authority of Greek philosophy waned in favor of the Authority*[§] of Scripture, as evidenced in *Manuductio ad veram psychologiam e sacris literis* (*Guide to a True Psychology from Sacred Scriptures*), the 1619 treatise of C. Bartholinus, teacher of medicine and theology at the University of Copenhagen, which anticipated the biblical psychologies of the eighteenth and nineteenth centuries.

2. *1700 to 1915: Biblical Psychology as a Critical Theological Discipline.* The eighteenth century marks the beginning of a new era of scriptural interpretation that expanded the general work of biblical studies to include historical-critical (Euro-American Biblical Interpretation*) concerns. Contemporary with the new "scientific" approach to the Bible was the burgeoning acceptance of psychology as a bona fide field of study. The combination of these two elements resulted in four major works on biblical psychology: M. Roos, *Fundamenta psychologiae ex sacra Scriptura sic collecta* (1769); J. Beck[§], *Outlines of Biblical Psychology* (1843 [ET 1877]); J. Haussmann, *Die biblische Lehre vom Menschen als Grundlage wahrer Menschenkenntnis* (1848), which subsumed psychology under the broader category of biblical anthropology; and the landmark work of Franz Delitzsch, *A System of Biblical Psychology* (1861[2] [ET 1869]), a work that warrants special elaboration.

The table of contents in Delitzsch's work provides a paradigm of topics typical of biblical or Christian psychologies of the period: (a) the question of the preexistence of the soul; (b) creation and the trichotomous constitution of persons as a unity of spirit, soul, and body; (c) the fall and the emergence of sin, shame, and conscience; (d) the "natural condition" of the "I" (ego) as characterized by freedom, reason, spirit, the "seven powers of the soul," sleeping, waking, dreaming, health, and sickness; (e) the regeneration of the self and the phenomena of conscious and unconscious processes of grace, new life in the spirit, ecstacy, and *theopneustia* (the state of divine inspiration); (f) death; and (g) resurrection, as opposed to the extrabiblical doctrine of metempsychosis.

Four features of Delitzsch's approach merit special attention for their relevance to issues and terms that characterize subsequent work on psychology and biblical studies. (1) He insisted on "biblical psychology" as an "independent science" discrete from (though closely related to) biblical theology and dogmatics. (2) He differentiated "general psychology" from "biblical psychology," the former proceeding analytically from "psychical phenomena" to their causes, and the latter proceeding synthetically from the "psychology" in the biblical text to its application to the human condition. (3) He risked the use of "newly-coined words and daring ideas" that, surprisingly, proved to be harbingers of twentieth-century issues and terminology—e.g., his references to dreams, archetypes (*Urbild*), the "I" (ego), and to conscious and unconscious (*bewusste, unbewusste*) dimensions of experience. (4) With an eye to his profession as theologian, scholar, and clergy, he defended the inclusion of psychology within the ranks of critical biblical research as a God-given capacity "granted to the human soul . . . of raising itself above itself by self-investigation."

One of the last of the biblical psychologies prior to the emergence of depth psychology is M. Fletcher's *The Psychology of the NT* (1912). Fletcher cited the need to update the earlier work of Beck and Delitzsch, noting that "psychology [as well as historical criticism] is a science 'still in the making.'" Turning to the research of W. James (1902), J. Leuba (1912), and E. Starbuck (1914[4]), he praised the "new modern scientific psychology" for having "furnished the biblical student with a new instrument," first, to "analyze . . . the scriptural terms which describe the mental and moral nature of man"; second, to identify "the psychological conceptions of the NT writers"; and third, to enumerate, describe, classify, and if possible explain "all conscious states and processes" and to "seek to determine the conditions . . . under which they arise."

3. *1900 to 1970: Depth Psychological Approaches to the Bible*. The development of depth psychology in the first half of the twentieth century (S. Freud, C. Jung), with its exploration of the "unconscious," gave birth to a rich spectrum of psychological theories and methods that have been applied to biblical studies first by psychologists, therapists, clinically trained pastors, and theologians; and second, beginning around 1970, by biblical scholars. (The countervailing appearance of behaviorism, with its empiricist aversion to acknowledging an "inner life," made little impact on biblical Hermeneutics*[§], with the exception of works like R. Bufford's *The Human Reflex: Behavioral Psychology in Biblical Perspective* 1982.)

a. S. Freud. Freud's last work, *Moses and Monotheism* (1938), was the only work he dedicated exclusively to a biblical topic, although he had planned it as part of a vast undertaking that would apply psychological theory to the entire Bible. His influence on biblical hermeneutics, however, stems only in part from this work, which was a Psychoanalytic*[§] study of the hidden (i.e., repressed) meanings behind the religious symbols, stories, and rituals that originated with the exodus.

Of equal, if not greater, significance for later applications to biblical studies is Freud's general theory of unconscious factors operative in human behavior and expression (e.g., obsessive-compulsive behavior, paranoia, infantile wish-fulfillment, repression, projection, neurosis, psychosis, super-ego-oriented behavior informed by the conformity principle vs. ego-oriented behavior informed by the reality principle) and the psychological insight it might provide into biblical narratives, personalities, theological concepts, religious phenomena, stories, symbols, and rituals. Freud's hermeneutical goal was to enable humanity to achieve psychic health as exemplified for him in the figure of Michelangelo's *Moses*, which, for Freud, "becomes the bodily expression of the highest psychic achievement that is possible for a human being, the overpowering of one's own passions in favor of and in fulfillment of a destiny to which one has committed oneself."

From the 1920s to the present, beginning with the correspondence of Swiss theologian O. Pfister with Freud, an array of pastoral counselors, analysts, Literary*[§] critics, and theologians have turned to Freudian theory and method for psychological insight into biblical personalities, narratives, rituals, doctrine, and religious phenomena (F. Dolto and G. Sévérin 1979;

C. Healer 1972; T. Reik 1960; R. Rubenstein 1972; D. Zeligs 1974; cf. bibliographic essays in M. Sales 1979 and A. Vergote 1979).

b. C. Jung. The Bible plays a comprehensive role in JUNG's life and thought. The twenty volumes of his *Collected Works* contain allusions to dozens of biblical figures and to all but thirteen of the canonical writings (Canon of the Bible§). In addition, his writings demonstrate broad familiarity with the Hebrew Bible and New Testament Apocrypha§, second-century Gnostic§ literature, and critical biblical methods.

Although Jung nowhere sets forth a systematic psychological hermeneutic, he does demonstrate the presuppositions and approach of such a hermeneutic in "Answer to Job" (1952), his sole essay on a biblical text, in which he proposes that the biblical text is, among other things, an "utterance of the psyche." That is to say, the text is to be seen not only as part of a historical or literary process (as biblical criticism has pointed out) but also as part of a psychic process in which unconscious as well as conscious factors are at work. The function of such a text as the voice of the unconscious is to complement or correct the one-sidedness of conscious life either for the individual reader or for the entire culture. The mode in which these "truths anchored deep in the psyche" are expressed is the language of symbol and archetypal image like those found not only in Scripture but also in dreams, myths, fairy tales, MUSIC, ART, and literature from around the world.

The hermeneutical task for a psychological approach to the text involves a two stage process: (1) an objective recognition of the unconscious as well as the conscious origin, nature, and function of the language and symbolism of the text, and (2) a method of bringing the "complementary" message of the text to consciousness, which, for Jung, involves the twofold work of "amplification" and "active imagination." Amplification is the process of identifying, exploring, and "amplifying" the meanings the text evokes in hearers, past or present. Within the context of the church or synagogue this hermeneutical process is seen at work in sermons, Bible study groups, pastoral counseling, and private Bible meditation. Active imagination is the process of "translating" the text into a new medium, much in the same way traditional religious communities have sought to "ex-press" the text in painting, sculpture, stained glass windows, liturgy, poetry, drama, or song. The goal of a psychological hermeneutic is not to displace but to complement the work of historical-literary criticism by going beyond the literal-historical content of the text to focus on the value the text actually or potentially evokes in the conscious or unconscious life of individual readers or communities and to examine the significance of these values for human development.

From the mid-twentieth century to the present, a succession of Jungian-trained analysts, theologians, and counselors (S. Brown 1998; E. Drewermann 1984; E. Edinger 1986, 1999, and 2000; E. Howes and S. Moon 1973; M. Kelsey 1968; D. A. Kille 2001; Y. Kluger and N. Kluger-Nash 1999; F. Kunkel 1947 [ET 1988]; J. Sanford 1970, 1985; and H. Westman 1961) have amply demonstrated the application of a Jungian hermeneutic to a variety of biblical texts. Similarly H. Childs (2000) and W. Wink (2002) have applied Jungian insights to the study of the historical Jesus

c. Post-Freudian and post-Jungian developments. On the basis of the pioneering work of Freud and Jung, combined with subsequent analytical and clinical approaches developed by such figures as A. Boisen, V. Frankl, K. Horney, C. Rogers, K. Menninger, and H. Sullivan, a body of literature has emerged relating psychology to the Bible in a variety of ways: (i) the psychological analysis of biblical phenomena, e.g., demon possession (S. McCasland 1951), miracles (E. Micklem 1922), Prophecy[‡†§], audition, ecstacy, vision, Inspiration*[§] (G. Joyce 1910; J. Kaplan 1908; W. Klein 1956; J. Pilch 2002; J. Povah 1925; and van Aarde 2001), conscience (J. Rozell 1974), atonement (D. Browning 1966), and revelation (R. Frayn 1940); (ii) psychological studies of key biblical figures, e.g., Jesus*[§] (G. Berguer 1923; D. Capps 2000;

G. Hall 1917; J. Miller 1997; cf. A. Schweitzer 1913 [ET 1938]), Paul[†§] (J. Bishop 1975; D. Cox 1959; Healer; Pfister 1920; Rubenstein), Abraham, Jacob, Joseph, Saul, David, Solomon (Zeligs, Sanford), Satan (R. Kluger 1967), Judas (A. Nicole 1924), and the Holy Spirit (L. Dewar 1960); (iii) analysis of biblical symbols (e.g., E. Goodenough 1953-68; Diel; P. Henry 1979); (iv) research on parapsychological phenomena reported in the Bible (L. Heron 1974; J. Pilch 2002); (v) the psychology of biblical interpretation (C. Johnson 1983); (vi) biblical approaches to pastoral counseling (e.g., D. Capps 1981; W. Oates 1950); (vii) psychological analyses of biblical literature (J. Bruns 1959; Doloto and Sévérin; Drewermann; I. Gerber 1951; H. Harsch 1977; J. Henderson and M. Oakes 1963; R. Leslie 1965; Reik; P. Riceour 1980; Y. Spiegel 1972; E. Wellisch 1954; Westman; W. Wolff 1951); and (viii) the formation of the early Christian community (W. Meissner 2000).

4. *1970 to the Present: Psychological Criticism as a Discipline within Biblical Studies.* In his 1968 Festschrift article in honor of E. Goodenough[§], "The Psychological Study of the Bible," F. Grant[§] broke ranks with a long-standing suspicion of psychology among twentieth-century biblical scholars and issued a call for "a new kind of Biblical criticism," one that would heed Goodenough's suggestions concerning "the value and importance, even the necessity, of the psychological interpretation of the Bible." The "earlier disciplines are all necessary and impor-tant," Grant insisted, but "beyond the historical and exegetical interpretation of the Bible lies the whole new field of depth psychology and psychoanalysis."

Grant was not the first biblical scholar to consider the possibility of and need for applying the insights of psychology to biblical texts. W. Bousset[§], H. Cadbury[§], A. Deissmann[§], H. Gunkel[§], V. Taylor[§] (1959), and W. Sanday[§] can all be cited in varying degrees to similar effect. Bousset, for example, suggested that the source of the New Testament concept of preexistence is ulti-mately to be found, not only in history-of-religions processes (*Religionsgeschichtliche Schule*[*§]), but also "in the unconscious, in the uncontrollable depth of the overall psyche of the human community." Taylor, in his 1959 classic, *The Person of Christ in New Testament Teaching*, included a seldom-noted chapter on Christology and psychology in which he directed attention to Freud's and Jung's research into the nature of the unconscious. More recently, the writings of K. Berger (2003), S. Brown (1995), M. Buss (1980), A. Y. Collins (1984), D. Halperin (1993), D. Kille (1995, 2001), D. Miller (1995), J. Miller (1983), R. Moore (1978), M. W. Newheart (2001), I. Rashkow (2000), W. Rollins (1983, 1985, 1999), R. Scroggs (1977, 1982), G. Theissen (1987), M. A. Tolbert (1978), M. Willett-Newheart (1995), W. Wink (1978), and W. Wuellner and R. Leslie (1984) represent attempts by biblical scholars (as opposed to psychologists or psychoanalysts) to apply psychological insight to biblical interpretation.

Theissen's *Psychological Aspects of Pauline Theology* (1987) merits special elaboration as a landmark volume in this tradition by virtue of its being the first "methodically disciplined" attempt by a biblical scholar to integrate and apply the insights of three major psychological schools (learning theory, psychodynamic theory, and cognitive psychology) to the exegesis of five sets of Pauline texts. Learning theory examines the new images in the symbolic world of early Christianity that lead to new experience and behavior; psychodynamic theory focuses on the unconscious archetypes awakened by the Christian kerygma (Jung) or the unconscious conflicts it helps bring to light (Freud); and cognitive psychology is concerned with the cogni-tive restructuring of reality occasioned by the Christ event.

Theissen identifies his agenda as "psychological exegesis" (or, alternatively, "a hermeneuti-cally oriented psychology of religion"). He sees the goal of psychological exegesis coterminous with that of historical-critical exegesis—namely, "to make texts intelligible on the basis of their context in life." The special objective of psychological exegesis is to clarify the "psychic factors and aspects" involved, focusing specifically on the "new patterns of experience and behavior that appeared with ancient Christianity" as evidenced and expressed in the New Testament text.

402

Theissen concludes with the following apologia for the extended application of psychology to biblical studies: "We do not yet grasp what historical forces brought forth and determined early Christianity. . . . But beside and within this external history there is an inner history of humanity. . . . This internal history is no less important than the external. . . . Anyone who thinks that this religion can be illumined historically and factually without psychological reflection is just as much in error as one who pretends that everything about this religion can be said in this fashion."

5. *Summary.* The contribution of psychology and psychological criticism to biblical studies lies in two areas: (a) in the research undertaken from the early church through the twenty-first century in the biblical understanding of the human psyche, its origin, nature, purpose, and destiny and the religious and moral implications of such an understanding and (b) in the new research undertaken in the twentieth and twenty-first centuries in response to depth psychology and its developments, leading to the development of a psychologically informed exegetical and hermeneutic theory and method still in the making that can cast new light from a psychological perspective on the nature and relationship of the biblical text and its interpreters in the context of a broader humanity characterized by unconscious as well as conscious factors.

Bibliography: K. **Berger,** *Historische Psychologie des Neuen Testaments* (1991; ET tr. C. Muenchow, 2003). G. **Berguer,** *Some Aspects of the Life of Jesus: From the Psychological and Psycho-analytic Point of View* (1923). J. G. **Bishop,** "Psychological Insights in St. Paul's Mysticism," *Theology* 78 (1975) 318-24. W. **Bousset,** *Kyrios Christos: A History of the Belief in Christ from the Beginnings of Christianity to Irenaeus* (1970). S. **Brown,** "The Myth of Sophia," *Jung and the Interpretation of the Bible* (ed. D. L. Miller, 1995) 92-101; *Text and Psyche: Experiencing Scripture Today* (1998). D. S. **Browning,** *Atonement and Psychotherapy* (1966). J. E. **Bruns,** "Depth Psychology and the Fall: Jungian Interpretation of Genesis 3," *CBQ* 21 (1959) 78-82. R. K. **Bufford,** *The Human Reflex: Behavioral Psychology in Biblical Perspective* (1982). M. **Buss,** "The Social Psychology of Prophecy," *Prophecy: Essays Presented to G. Fohrer on His Sixty-fifth Birthday* (ed. J. Emerton, 1980) 1-11. D. **Capps,** *Biblical Approaches to Pastoral Counseling* (1981); *Jesus: A Psychological Biography* (2000). H. **Childs,** *The Myth of the Historical Jesus and the Evolution of Consciousness* (2000). A. Y. **Collins,** *Crisis and Catharsis: The Power of the Apocalypse* (1984). D. **Cox,** *Jung and St. Paul: A Study of the Doctrine of Justification by Faith and Its Relation to the Conception of Individuation* (1959). F. **Delitzsch,** *A System of Biblical Psychology* (1867). L. **Dewar,** *The Holy Spirit and Modern Thought: An Inquiry into the Historical, Theological, and Psychological Aspects of the Christian Doctrine of the Holy Spirit* (1960). F. **Dolto and** G. **Séverin,** *The Jesus of Psychoanalysis: A Freudian Interpretation of the Gospel* (1979). E. **Drewermann,** *Tiefenpsychologie und Exegese* (1984). E. **Edinger,** *The Bible and the Psyche: Individuation Symbolism in the OT* (1986); *Archetype of the Apocalypse: A Jungian Study of the Book of Revelation* (1999); *Ego and Self: The Old Testament Prophets from Isaiah to Malachi* (2000). M. S. **Fletcher,** *The Psychology of the NT* (1912[2]). R. S. **Frayn,** *Revelation and the Unconscious* (1940). S. **Freud,** *Moses and Monotheism* (1939). J. G. **Gager,** "Some Notes on Paul's Conversion," *NTS* 27 (1981) 697-703. I. J. **Gerber,** *The Psychology of the Suffering Mind* (1951). E. R. **Goodenough,** *Jewish Symbols in the Greco-Roman Period* 4 (1953-68). F. C. **Grant,** "Psychological Study of the Bible," *Religions in Antiquity: Essays in Memory of E. R. Goodenough* (ed. J. Neusner, 1969) 107-24. G. S. **Hall,** *Jesus, the Christ, in the Light of Psychology* (2 vols. 1917). J. **Halperin,** *Seeking Ezekiel: Text and Psychology* (1993). H. **Hark,** *Der Traum als Gottes vergessene Sprache: Symbolpsychologische Deutung biblischer und heutiger Träume* (1982). H. **Harsch,** "Psychologische Interpretation biblischer Texte," *Una Sancta* (1977) 39-45. C. T. **Healer,** *Freud and St. Paul* (1972). J. L. **Henderson**

and M. Oakes, *The Wisdom of the Serpent: The Myths of Death, Rebirth, and Resurrection* (1963). P. Henry, "Water, Bread, Wine: Patterns in Religion," *New Directions in NT Study* (1979) 203-24. L. Heron, *ESP in the Bible* (1974). E. B. Howes and S. Moon, *Man the Choicemaker* (1973). W. James, *The Varieties of Religious Experience: A Study in Human Nature* (Gifford Lectures 1901-2, 1902). C. B. Johnson, *The Psychology of Biblical Interpretation* (1983); *Journal of Psychology and Theology* (1973-). G. C. Joyce, *The Inspiration of Prophecy: An Essay in the Psychology of Revelation* (1910). C. G. Jung, "Answer to Job," *Collected Works* 11 (1952). J. H. Kaplan, *Psychology of Prophecy: A Study of the Prophetic Mind as Manifested by the Ancient Hebrew Prophets* (1908). M. Kassel, *Biblische Urbilder: Tiefenpsychologische Auslegung nach C. G. Jung* (1982). M. Kelsey, *Dreams: The Dark Speech of the Spirit* (1968). R. Kessler and P. Vandermeersch (eds.), *God, Biblical Studies and Psychoanalytic Understanding* (2001). D. A. Kille, "Jacob: A Study in Individuation," *Jung and the Interpretation of the Bible* (ed. D. L. Miller, 1995) 40-54, 117-21; *Psychological Biblical Criticism* (GBS, 2001). W. C. Klein, *The Psychological Pattern of OT Prophecy* (1956). R. S. Kluger, *Satan in the OT* (1967). Y. Kluger, *A Psychological Interpretation of Ruth: In the Light of Mythology, Legend and Kabbalah, with a companion essay by N. Kluger-Nash, Standing in the Sandals of Naomi, A Psychological Interpretation of Ruth* (1999). F. Kunkel, *Creation Continues: A Psychological Interpretation of the First Gospel* (1947; ET 1988). F. H. Lapointé "Origin and Evolution of the Term Psychology," *American Psychologist* 25 (1970) 640-46. R. Leslie, *Jesus and Logotherapy: The Ministry of Jesus as Interpreted Through the Psychotherapy of V. Frankl* (1965). J. H. Leuba, *A Psychological Study of Religion, Its Origin, Function, and Future* (1912). S. V. McCasland, *By the Finger of God: Demon Possessions and Exorcism in Early Christianity in Light of Modern Views of Mental Illness* (1951). D. McGann, *Journeying Within Transcendence: A Jungian Perspective on the Gospel of John* (1988). W. W. Meissner, *The Cultic Origins of Christianity: The Dynamics of Religious Development* (2000). E. R. Micklem, *Miracles and the New Psychology: A Study in the Healing Miracles of the NT* (1922). D. L. Miller (ed.), *Jung and the Interpretation of the Bible* (1995). J. Miller, "Psychoanalytic Approaches to Biblical Religion," *Journal of Religion and Health* 22 (1983) 19-29. J. W. Miller, *Jesus At Thirty: A Psychological And Historical Portrait* (1997). R. L. Moore, "Pauline Theology and the Return of the Repressed," *Zygon* 13 (1978) 158-68. M. W. Newheart, *Word and Soul: A Psychological, Literary, and Cultural Reading of the Fourth Gospel* (2001). A. Nicole, *Judas the Betrayer: A Psychological Study of Judas Iscariot* (1924). W. E. Oates, "The Diagnostic Use of the Bible: What a Man Sees in the Bible Is a Projection of His Inner Self," *Pastoral Psychology* 1, 9 (December 1950) 43-46. O. Pfister, "Die Entwicklung des Apostels Paulus: Eine religions-geschichtliche und psychologische Skizze," *Imago* 6 (1920) 243-90. J. J. Pilch, "Altered States of Consciosness in the Synoptics" *The Social Setting of Jesus and the Gospels* (ed. by Wolfgang Stegemann, Bruce J. Malina, Gerd Theissen, 2002) 103-17. J. W. Povah, *The New Psychology and the Hebrew Prophets* (1925). I. N. Rashkow, *Taboo or not Taboo: Sexuality and Family in the Hebrew Bible.* (2000). T. Reik, *Mystery on the Mountain: The Drama of the Sinai Revelation* (1959); *The Creation of Woman: A Psychoanalytic Inquiry into the Myth of Eve* (1960). P. Ricoeur, *Essays on Biblical Interpretation* (ed. L. Mudge, 1980). W. G. Rollins, *Jung and the Bible* (1983); "Jung on Scripture and Hermeneutics: Retrospect and Prospect," *Essays on Jung and the Study of Religion* (ed. L. H. Martin and J. Gross, 1985) 81-94; *Soul and Psyche: The Bible in Psychological Perspective* (1999). J. V. Rozell, "Implications of the NT Concept of Conscience," *Biblical and Psychological Perspectives for Christian Counselors* (ed. R. Bower, 1974) 151-209. R. Rubenstein, *My Brother Paul* (1972). M. Sales, S. J., "Possibilités et limites d'une lecture psychoanalytique de la Bible," *NRTh* 101 (1979) 699-723. J. Sanford, *The Kingdom Within: A Study of the Inner Meaning of Jesus' Sayings* (1970);

King Saul, the Tragic Hero: A Study in Individuation (1985). **A. Schweitzer,** *The Psychiatric Study of Jesus: Exposition and Criticism* (1913; ET 1948). **R. Scroggs,** *Paul for a New Day* (1977); "Psychology as a Tool to Interpret the Text: Emerging Trends in Biblical Thought," *ChrCent* 99 (1982) 335-38. **Y. Spiegel,** *Psychoanalytische Interpretationen biblischer Texte (1972); Doppeldeutlich: Tiefendimensionen biblischer Texte* (1978). **E. D. Starbuck,** *The Psychology of Religion: An Empirical Study of the Growth of Religious Consciousness* (1914[4]). **V. Taylor,** "Christology and Psychology," *The Person of Christ in NT Teaching* (1959). **G. Theissen,** *Psychological Aspects of Pauline Theology* (1987). **M. A. Tolbert,** *Perspectives on the Parables: An Approach to Multiple Interpretations* (1978). **A. van Aarde,** *Fatherless in Galilee: Jesus as Child of God* (2001). **H. Vande Kemp,** "Origin and Evolution of the Term 'Psychology': Addenda," *The American Psychologist* 35 (1980) 774; *Psychology and Theology in Western Thought, 1672-1965: A Historical and Annotated Bibliography* (1984). **A. Vergote,** "Psychoanalyse et interprétation biblique," *DBSup* 9 (1979) 252-60. **E. Wellisch,** *Isaac and Oedipus: A Study in Biblical Psychology of the Sacrifice of Isaac, the Akedah* (1954). **H. Westman,** *The Springs of Creativity: The Bible and the Creative Process of the Psyche* (1961). **M. Willett-Newheart,** "Johannine Symbolism," *Jung and the Interpretation of the Bible* (1995) 71-91. **W. Wink,** "On Wrestling with God: Using Psychological Insights in Biblical Study," *RelLife* 47 (1978) 136-47. **W. Wink,** *The Human Being: Jesus and the Enigma of the Son of the Man* (2002). **C. Wise,** *Psychiatry and the Bible* (1956). **W. Wolff,** *Changing Concepts of the Bible: A Psychological Analysis of Its Words, Symbols, and Beliefs* (1951).**W. H. Wuellner and R. C. Leslie,** *The Surprising Gospel: Intriguing Psychological Insights from the NT* (1984). **D. Zeligs,** *Psychoanalysis and the Bible: A Study in Depth of Seven Leaders* (1974).

W. G. ROLLINS